INSURANCE AND THE LAW OF OBLIGATIONS

Insurance and the Law of Obligations

ROB MERKIN AND JENNY STEELE

OXFORD
UNIVERSITY PRESS

OXFORD
UNIVERSITY PRESS

Great Clarendon Street, Oxford, OX2 6DP,
United Kingdom

Oxford University Press is a department of the University of Oxford.
It furthers the University's objective of excellence in research, scholarship,
and education by publishing worldwide. Oxford is a registered trade mark of
Oxford University Press in the UK and in certain other countries

First Edition published in 2013

Published in the United States of America by Oxford University Press
198 Madison Avenue, New York, NY 10016, United States of America

British Library Cataloguing in Publication Data
Data available

Library of Congress Control Number: 2013937232

ISBN 978–0–19–964574–9

Foreword

We are all bound by the laws of obligations one way or another. They are the un-noted attendants to our everyday activities such as buying a new washing-machine, driving the car to work, operating a bank account or cultivating a hedge as boundary to the garden. Law students will, after a moment's thought, point out how these activities involve the laws of contract, tort, trusts, land law and, even, criminal law. At the same time, perhaps without us realising it, insurance has now become central to life in the Western world. We take out life insurance, motor insurance, household insurance (which, like motor insurance, includes liability insurance), insurance against the cost of repairing goods (like the washing machine), travel insurance, personal accident insurance and payment protection insurance. In the business world, insurance against loss or liability can be found for any activity engaged in under the sun.

Yet the two legal worlds, that of the laws of obligations and that of the law of insurance, have always remained strangely apart. Thus, the received view of the law was that matters concerning insurance cover should be ignored when considering who the claimant is or his right to substantial damages or whether the defendant was being funded by an insurer. The fact that the claimant was actually a subrogated insurer and the defence was being maintained by the defendant's liability insurer have traditionally been treated as the unacknowledged elephants in the court room.

And the academic study of the laws of obligations and of insurance have maintained this curious divide. Insurance law is, traditionally, seen as something esoteric, an "add-on" to the general study of the laws of obligations and a subject that might be examined as an optional extra after the basics of the laws of obligations have been mastered.

This book is a trail-blazer because it challenges all these traditional attitudes and approaches. It demonstrates that insurance is central to the laws of obligations and how it has moulded the development of the common law of contract and tort in particular. So the authors ask such fundamental issues as how insurance has influenced the development of the law of tort, quite apart from the vexed questions raised by mesothelioma and asbestosis cases; how it has influenced the development of contractual obligations, particularly in business areas such as development and construction and oil and gas where, often, there are multi-parties all having insurance of various forms. The authors ask the pertinent question: is our attitude to the interpretation of commercial contracts and to tortious liability actually influenced by the knowledge of where and how the parties are covered by insurance; and if it is, is it not time this was acknowledged frankly?

The authors also analyse how the presence of insurance has fundamentally effected the evolution of both the practice and the substance of litigation. It is easy to forget that in many commercial cases it is an insurer who sues (in the name of the claimant) by right of subrogation and the defendant's case is actually being conducted by its liability insurer because the law has always insisted that be disregarded. The authors ask whether it is time that we recognise the central position that insurance takes in the way legal disputes are decided.

In one single volume the authors enable the reader to understand the philosophical basis of the law of insurance, the key practical aspects of insurance and re-insurance and, through a broad based analysis of different topics, where and how insurance and the law of insurance is now an intrinsic part of our laws of obligations. This book should be read by all scholars and practitioners who are concerned with the laws of obligations, insurance or both. It will shake them out of their insularity, make them question some of their pre-conceptions and provide much material for new debate and argument.

It might even make the judges have a rethink and some might say "about time too"!

Sir Richard Aikens
Lord Justice of Appeal

Preface

Ask any practising lawyer to describe the role of insurance in her or his professional activities, and the almost inevitable response will be: 'Pervasive'. The lawyer must have liability insurance just to participate in the profession, and it is important to monitor potential third-party claims so that they can be notified to insurers and so that information can be gathered for renewal negotiations. Everyday conveyancing requires the purchaser to be protected by insurance against the risk of destruction between contract and conveyance, and if funding is to be obtained from a mortgagee then there will be a demand for insurance protection over the secured property given that it is likely to be the borrower's major asset. Establishing a family trust entails obtaining professional indemnity insurance for the trustees, and setting up a company—whether family or multinational—entails obtaining directors' and officers' liability insurance for present and future incumbents. A personal injury victim will almost inevitably be seeking to recover any award of damages from the liability insurers of the tortfeasor, and it may be necessary to make immediate contact with those insurers to make sure that they are aware of the proceedings as well as ascertaining from the victim whether he or she has insurance funding for the litigation. Other victims seeking to recover damages for property or financial losses will be advised that it may only be worth pursuing a defendant who is insured, and in many such cases the victim will have first-party insurers who will pay losses and then seek to recoup their outlay by subrogation proceedings. Moving to the world of commercial transactions—sales, construction, licensing and the rest—contract negotiations inevitably involve agreement between the parties on the allocation of risks, who is to bear them, and who is to insure against them. The lawyer, in the same way as any other person tendering for work, may well have to satisfy the other party that there is adequate liability insurance in place to cover risk of loss.

All of these matters are about risk. If a party faces the risk of injury or loss, insurance will be taken out by way of protection. If a party is at risk of inflicting harm, insurance will be obtained to fund any award of damages. If the parties are entering a contractual relationship, they will determine where risks lie. The desire either to shift risk, or to protect against it where it cannot be shifted, is shared by most. The law of obligations, embracing both contract and tort, has to be seen in this context.

If it is the case that litigation is conducted or funded by insurers, damages are generally paid by insurers, and the very incidence of liability is underpinned by insurance, why is it also the case that the relevance of insurance is ignored, and indeed often denied, in analyses of the law of obligations? Academic orthodoxy, to begin with a focus on tort law, has the starting point that tort liability (or non-liability) is dictated by personal responsibility, and that the duty and standard of care, and indeed causation, in any one case have to be determined by principle and not by wider distributive notions. If that is right for tort, then it follows that contract liability should be determined in the same way. Insurance, therefore, is a personal decision and is the mechanism for enforcement and the spreading of loss throughout society rather than the driver of liability. The fortuitous presence or absence of insurance therefore tells us nothing about how legal principle should be developed.

This book argues that the orthodox approach should be reappraised. We suggest that an entirely different vision is possible if the starting point is relational. All contracts to a greater or lesser extent encompass risk allocation, and such allocation, varying with the degree of the contract's complexity, rests upon explicit insuring duties or implicit understandings as to how insurance is to be arranged. Of course risk allocation is not perfect, and the unforeseen is inevitable, but the agreed or assumed incidence of insurance may inform the court in ascertaining the objective intentions of the parties. Moving from there to tort, we then suggest that tort liabilities are relational to a far greater extent than has been recognized. Professional negligence claims, actions against suppliers or contractors and employment injuries all spring from contracts. Actions against neighbours, local authorities, medical practitioners and road users are, to a lesser and less obvious extent, also relational. It is only rarely that a novel situation, calling for the application of principle or legal policy in the absence of a familiar or agreed risk allocation, arises. Our analysis of insurance thus extends from the accepted distributional role to the equally significant but under-analysed relational role.

It may be appreciated that our analysis differs in one fundamental respect from much of what has gone before, and that is that we regard legal principle not as an overarching imposition of personal responsibility but, in many relationships, as a default mechanism. If the parties can agree which of them should bear a risk, and they act accordingly, then as long as there are no public policy considerations and no harm is inflicted on third parties there is no reason for high principle to intervene and to reverse their arrangements (particularly where it thereby allows a particular party, often an insurer, to subvert those arrangements). Other, social mechanisms with an influence on the allocation of risks are also sometimes in play. If particular activities raise familiar hazards (such as employing or driving), insurance may, as a matter of public policy, be demanded by the state. In the case of driving, the form of that insurance has been closely defined. We are of the view that the academic focus on the exceptional rather than the mundane distorts the portrayal of the significance of insurance in and to the law of obligations. That point has been made before in relation to the mass of cases which never reach court and are dealt with instead through routine settlement processes heavily influenced by insurance and insurers. Here we extend the point, in relation to the shaping of litigation and of legal doctrine.

The most fundamental objection to the doctrinal relevance of insurance perhaps stems from a fear that the ability of a person to insure, rather than legal principle and notions of personal responsibility, will thereby come to determine whether that person owes or is owed a duty or enhanced standard of care. We suggest that this objection has no part to play where the incidence of established risks has been agreed or understood: if the legal system regularly trumps those arrangements or understandings, the response will be that both potential claimants and potential defendants will have to insure, thereby unnecessarily increasing the cost of their activities. Our suggestion is, therefore, that once risks have been ascertained (by agreement or by law), the allocation arrangements (backed by insurance) adopted to deal with them should be honoured and not disregarded. Looking at that allocation explains a lot about the outcome of contract and tort cases. But to bring insurance out from the shadows may assist understanding of legal principles in a range of other ways, also. Certainly, it should assist in understanding the way that claims are framed—yet the framing of claims has been promoted within formalist approaches as an expression of the pure bipartite (or bipolar) relationship between two parties. It will also draw more attention to the boundaries of acceptable risk-shifting and loss-spreading, and therefore to different aspects of the idea of 'responsibility', such as wrongdoing which goes beyond mere negligence, or breaches of duty which constitute personal rather than vicarious liability. The implications of these factors for the very shape of the law have been underemphasized, because the habitual insurance of more routine risks and shortcomings (including vicariously) has also been neglected.

This book focuses on risk allocation, and also upon the role of insurance in spreading loss from the risks as allocated. It is not a treatise on insurance law, but rather a discussion of why insurance matters to obligations lawyers and why disregarding insurance removes our understanding of a key element in how the law actually works, and how its principles are developed and deployed. As we were writing, developments in the law seemed to us to sustain our view. In particular, the prolonged development of mesothelioma litigation, the dispute as to whether expert witnesses should have immunity from suit, and the enhanced focus on the operation of compulsory motor insurance, all gave us the opportunity to extend our analysis to matters of current concern. At the end of the day, we also hope that our analysis will help to equip obligations lawyers to make their own distinct contribution to the study of insurance as an important social institution.

We owe thanks to a number of individuals and organizations. Jenny owes a large debt of thanks to the Leverhulme Trust, whose funding through a Major Research Fellowship on 'Liability, Insurance, and Society' has secured the necessary research leave in which to develop the ideas in this book, and to York Law School for its support. We have had the help of a large number of colleagues in getting the book to completion. In the closing stages, Charlie Bishop gave us invaluable assistance in the preparation of the manuscript. Before that, various of the chapters were read in draft form and we benefited immeasurably from comments received from an almost embarrassing number of people. Though none should be held responsible for emerging arguments, many thanks are due to Kit Barker, Jill Poole, Paula Giliker, Bob Lee, James Goudkamp, Matt Dyson, Malcolm Clarke, Andrew Tettenborn, Paul Mitchell, Jamie Lee, Phillip Morgan, TT Arvind, and Carol Forrest, for their help and generosity in this respect. Meixian Song provided valuable research assistance on the history of workers' compensation. We would also like to thank the team at Oxford University Press, particularly Natasha Flemming and Emma Brady, for keeping this project on track so professionally at a very busy time. And, finally, we would like to thank our families. Jenny is grateful as ever to Adrian, Joe, and Theo for sharing valuable time with another book, and Rob is similarly grateful to Barbara for her accustomed forbearance.

Contents

Table of Cases

Table of Statutes

Table of Statutory Instruments

Table of EU Legislation

Table of International Agreements

List of Abbreviations

ABI	Association of British Insurers
AIDA	International Association of Insurance Law
AIG	American International Group, Inc
APIL	Association of Personal Injury Lawyers
ART	Alternative Risk Transfer
ATE	After the Event
BIA	British Insurers Association
BTE	Before the Event
CFA	Conditional Fee Agreement
CJEU	Court of Justice of the European Union
CLC	International Convention on Civil Liability for Oil Pollution Damage 1992
COBS	Conduct of Business Sourcebook
CP	Consultation Paper
CPR	Civil Procedure Rules
CRU	Compensation Recovery Unit (of the DWP)
D&O	Directors and Officers
DWP	Department for Work and Pensions
ECGD	Export Credit and Guarantee Department
EIB	Employers Insurance Bureau
EIL	Environmental Impact/Impairment Liability
EL	Employers' Liability
EQC	Earthquake Commission
ERISA	Employee Retirement Income Security Act 1974
FCA	Financial Conduct Authority
FOS	Financial Ombudsman Scheme
FSA	Financial Services Authority
FSCS	Financial Services Compensation Scheme
FSMA 2000	Financial Services and Markets Act 2000
GFC	Global Financial Crisis
GIBKR	General Insurance Broker
GISC	General Insurance Standards Council
HRA	Human Rights Act 1998
IBRC	Insurance Brokers Registration Council
ICOBS	Insurance Conduct of Business Sourcebook
INSPRU	Prudential Sourcebook for Insurers
IOB	Insurance Ombudsman Bureau
IUA	Insurance Underwriting Association
JCT	Joint Contracts Tribunal
LC	Law Commission
LCCD	Law Commission Consultation Document
LCCP	Law Commission Consultation Paper
LCIP	Law Commission Issue Paper
LEI	Legal Expenses Insurance
LMX	London Market Excess

MASS	Motor Accident Solicitors Society
MIB	Motor Insurers' Bureau
MII	Mortgagees' Interest Insurance
MMI	Municipal Mutual Insurance
OFT	Office of Fair Trading
ORSA	Own Risk and Solvency Assessment
P&I	Protection and Indemnity
PL	Public Liability
PPI	Payment Protection Insurance
PRA	Prudential Regulatory Authority
PRIN	Principles for Business
QOCS	Qualified One-way Costs Shifting
RDC	Running-Down Clause
RTA	Road Traffic Act
SPE	Special Purpose Entity
SRP	Supervisory Review Process
SSA	Social Sciences Association
SUP	Supervision
TNA	The National Archives
URDG	Uniform Rules on Demand Guarantee

PART 1

ESSENTIALS

1

Introduction: Insurance in the Law of Obligations

1.1 Our Aim

The aim of this book is to examine the part played by insurance in the law of obligations. The present chapter introduces and summarizes our argument and outlines the nature of the exploration to follow. For this introductory purpose, referencing in the chapter is kept deliberately light; readers will find discussion of relevant sources in the course of the argument as it unfolds.

We argue that insurance operates not at the periphery, but at the core of the law of obligations, in both practical and conceptual terms. Insurance, moreover, performs a number of different roles, and its influence is not to be reduced to the single contribution often attributed to it, namely, 'loss-spreading'. Insurance is not only a feature of public and social responses to risk, but also a core institution of the market and a key feature of market relationships. Indeed, public responses to risk often utilize the potential of insurance markets, which are themselves based upon contractual relationships. We therefore aim to familiarize readers with some little-understood, but centrally important, aspects of the law of obligations in action, and to provide the resources needed to appreciate the terrain afresh. At the same time, we reflect on the implications of our study for existing frameworks of analysis, and ask how incorporation of insurance at the core may affect those frameworks.

Surprisingly, given the range and significance of the issues to be unravelled here, the picture from which we start is one of relative neglect, and even, in some contexts, outright denial, of the conceptual significance of insurance for private law. We suggest that the way in which study of obligations is currently framed has, at least incidentally, had the effect of banishing insurance to the periphery. To some degree, this reflects a distinction between practice and theory which deserves close scrutiny.[1] But more particularly, we call attention below to the 'two-party' frame of analysis favoured by some important conceptual accounts, and which doubtless owes some of its appeal to the fact that it reflects a perspective which is, to one extent or another, more generally shared. Related to this is a near-universal emphasis among accounts of private law on liability principles, to the exclusion not only of recoverability or enforcement, but also of further questions of indemnity and contribution where insurance typically operates.[2] The need to bring these questions into equal focus is explored in 1.3.

[1] This point is made in relation to insurance in the law of contract by J Lowry and P Rawlings, 'Insurers, Claims and the Boundaries of Good Faith' (2005) 68 *Modern Law Review* 82.

[2] Arguably an exception is the law of restitution or unjust enrichment, much of which is concerned with recovering funds. The relationship between this branch of obligations law, and insurance, is difficult and particularly under-developed despite some close points of contact: see the discussion in 1.2 and 1.4.

Sometimes, however, the ousting of insurance is not merely incidental. Rather, a narrow frame of analysis has on occasion been adopted expressly in order to exclude insurance, among all factors, from discussion.[3] In particular, the exclusion of insurance from accounts of the law of tort has become received wisdom. We suggest that this singular treatment reflects a perception that insurance is a factor extrinsic to the law of obligations, incompatible with responsibility, and yet at the same time so potent that it threatens to replace tort principles with a loss-spreading logic which will reduce the law of tort to an empty shell. That in itself probably reflects the lasting effect of the historic role of insurance, for example in the development of strict liability regimes for workmen's compensation;[4] and this in turn helps to explain adherence to a particular account of what insurance is.[5] Our own perspective is different in a number of ways. We consider insurance to be part of a much broader set of phenomena relating to risk (in other words, it is not uniquely potent); we regard it as an inherent feature of private law and private arrangements and even as raising paradigmatic private law issues (it is not an extrinsic and unmanageable 'factor'); we do not associate it uniquely with a loss-spreading logic, and in any case do not regard its loss-spreading functions as free from issues associated with the law of obligations; and we consider it to be both unnecessary and undesirable to exclude it from the conceptual frame. Our exploration therefore also raises the questions of why existing accounts have neglected such a significant phenomenon; whether resistance to the conceptual relevance of insurance in private law can be coherently maintained; and what the sometimes deliberate blindness to insurance suggests both about working models of private lawyers, and about the way in which the current frame of analysis might be expanded.

The next section of this chapter introduces in outline the nature of insurance and the important ideas of risk allocation, risk-pooling, and loss-spreading which are used throughout. The following section, 1.3, introduces some of the conceptual hurdles in the path of our analysis, and indicates how we will deal with these hurdles. In order to position our account in relation to existing approaches, we then briefly outline our approach to aspects of the law of obligations, in 1.4. Section 1.5 outlines the structure of the book, and its contents as a whole.

Chapter 2 more directly addresses the nature of insurance itself, the boundaries of this complex phenomenon, and the ways in which insurance has been studied and conceptualized, drawing on a range of disciplines but with a view to highlighting points of significance for obligations law. In that chapter, addressing the nature and boundaries of the phenomenon of insurance, we question more reductionist approaches which associate or even define insurance in terms of largely extra-legal qualities such as actuarial expertise and governance of risks. We acknowledge a further, and still developing, set of associations related to insurance, particularly compatible with its contractual roots, and pertinent even in many of those areas where insurance does indeed operate to advance social policy and public purpose.

[3] We discuss and illustrate this in Chapters 8 and 9.

[4] Explored in Chapter 9.

[5] Elaborated in Chapter 2.

1.2 Insurance and Risk

1.2.1 Insurance

We will spend some time over the next two chapters identifying core elements of 'insurance', and of insurance relationships. Here, we merely identify some important features of the discussion to come. Insurance exists in both market and social forms, and in the latter case the rise of insurance is associated closely with the rise of the welfare state. Although there are plainly differences between these two forms, both are nonetheless legitimately seen as aspects of 'insurance'. It is overly restrictive to define insurance solely in terms of the kind of compensation payable and manner of risk-pooling employed—particularly as commercial insurance itself pools risks in a variety of ways, explored in Chapter 6. We suggest in Chapter 2 that approaches to insurance can be grouped around two 'poles' of analysis, which draw out different key features as typical, or even definitive, of the phenomenon of insurance. One, the 'actuarial' approach, has dominated sociological and indeed many legal understandings of insurance. This model highlights the collectivizing nature of insurance and its role in abstracting from individual instances to classes, on the basis of probabilities. The other has been prevalent in economic studies of insurance but is also compatible with regulatory definitions of insurance business. This defines insurance largely in terms of relationships in which risk is transferred from one party to another. We argue that this second approach, emphasizing the insurance relationship, deserves wider attention. Where market forms of insurance are concerned, even where the state too is engaged in some way, the well-known distributive effects of insurance are themselves achieved through a series of risk transfers. The risk-shifting activity of private parties constitutes the insurance market and neither its contribution to the development of the law of obligations, nor the potential contribution of obligations scholarship in advancing its understanding in relation to insurance, has been fully recognized.[6]

1.2.2 Risk allocation, risk transfer, and loss-spreading

Risk allocation, risk transfer, and loss-spreading are ideas used throughout this book, and we should offer some guidance here as to their meaning. Risk is *allocated* to a party when that party has the responsibility to deal with it, typically because they have an insuring obligation, a duty to indemnify the other against losses or claims, or the burden of a liability. Thus risk may be allocated by contract, by statute (directly by an obligation to insure, or indirectly by an obligation to make financial provision against specific contingencies such as pollution clean-up costs), or by the courts. Parties may themselves *transfer* risks by paying a premium or by otherwise contracting to shift it (or part of it), or by arguing that at least part of the loss or liability is attributable to other tortfeasors or indemnifiers. Losses are *spread* in a range of ways. They may be

[6] Subrogation is discussed in Chapter 5; contribution (with a focus on insurers) in Chapter 6; contractual duties in Chapter 7; tort duties in Chapter 8; illegality principles in Chapter 11; and civil litigation as a whole, in Chapter 13.

pooled or further transferred, or covered by new premiums or reinsurance; but firms and limited liability are themselves legitimately seen as means of spreading losses, as is social insurance. This final stage is arguably no more the hallmark of insurance than the second, particularly given the variety of mechanisms available to the 'insurer' to spread loss, for example over time; and given the significance of diversification of risk, and reinsurance.[7]

It is worth noting at this point that resistance to the significance of insurance for the law of obligations takes a number of guises, but one of its chief sources is its apparent reduction of personal responsibility to questions of channelling risk. Thus, our discussion of tort and (to a lesser extent) contract duties in terms of allocation of risks is likely to be met with particular resistance. In Chapters 7 and 8, we will therefore spend some time demonstrating the compatibility of private law duties with risk allocation rationales,[8] not least because this will help to highlight the significance of cases where the law does not permit the shifting or spreading of risks.

1.3 Challenges

We have already introduced some likely sources of resistance to our enterprise. In Chapter 2, we expand on the idea that a narrow representation of the nature of insurance has contributed to misunderstanding of its role. In this section, we say a little more about some other existing obstacles to the sort of analysis engaged in here, and how the discussion in later chapters will seek to change the frame of analysis.

1.3.1 Liability versus recoverability

The neglect of questions of enforcement or recoverability is perhaps the biggest factor in concealing the prevalence of insurance, and underlines the existence of a division between the conceptualization of private law, and its operation in practice, referred to above. Questions of recoverability are inherent to the behaviour of litigants, and to the shaping of litigation. Most commercial contracts contain a choice of law and arbitration or jurisdiction clauses, recognizing in advance that disputes are all but inevitable and that enforcement of obligations is essential. Such mechanisms are, however, treated as largely irrelevant by legal theory and indeed by much legal education. The concern of participants in the legal system with outcomes of litigation (not merely the generation of principles) has hidden implications, for the very shape of contracting behaviour, for tort law and its remedies, and for the way in which disputes are argued and—we suggest—decided. It is arguable that some of the most significant tort cases of recent decades have involved attempts to evade contractual or social allocations of risk in which the established insurance position was highly relevant. In response, tort reasoning has been adapted to reflect the importance of risk structures. The same issues may now be said to arise in relation to the law of unjust enrichment. Its broad conceptual framework leaves no obvious space for party risk arrangements to operate;

[7] These ideas are discussed in Chapters 2 and 6.

[8] Chapters 7 (Contract) and 8 (Tort).

but scholars, and the courts, have recognized the need to respond to risk issues both in cases where a contract has been discharged, and in cases where no contract has been entered into.[9] In later chapters we provide evidence of the practical inclinations of the courts in relation to risk arrangements; and of the degree to which courts are aware of the broad, general shape of insurance arrangements. But we would add that we are not seeking to replace principled reasoning with something more uniquely focused on recovery (whether this is thought of as compensation thinking, or reform thinking). Recognizing the presence of these factors changes the location of conceptual questions about responsibility, for example. It does not expunge them.[10]

1.3.2 Legal principle versus law in action

One particularly glaring example of the departure of law in theory from law in action is that the presence of insurers in the process of a legal claim—even the identity of one or more of the parties as an insurer rather than the nominal party—is treated as irrelevant in theoretical terms.[11] It is a curious feature of much legal theory that it requires certain core elements of reality to be suppressed.[12] Lawyers have a particular affinity, through their training, with the selection of 'relevant' and 'irrelevant' factors and are adept at this. We argue, however, that the presence of insurers in litigation is not a conceptually irrelevant factor. The reasons are fully developed and illustrated in Chapters 5, 7, 8, and 11, and are sketched in 1.4 and 1.5.

More broadly, where the 'gap' between law in action and law in the books is concerned, insurance is highly relevant. For example, insurance provides the funding for the bringing and defending of much litigation, as well as the source for recovery in many instances and in particular in virtually all personal injury cases.[13] Not surprisingly, it has featured strongly in socio-legal accounts.[14] Insurance, in this context, has

[9] Recognizing the parallel with the development of tort and particularly emphasizing the significance of risk allocation, see J Beatson, 'Restitution and Contract: Non-Cumul?' (2000) 1 *Theoretical Inquiries in Law* 83, 112 ('the position should be the same as that gradually emerging... in tort'). By contrast H Dagan, 'Restitutionary Damages for Breach of Contract: An Exercise in Private Law Theory' (2000) 1 *Theoretical Inquiries in Law* 115 compares a number of rationales other than risk allocation. P Davies, 'Risk in Unjust Enrichment' (2012) 20 RLR 57, argues that treatment of risk in unjust enrichment remains undeveloped, with a focus on 'risk-takers' (undertaking work without the benefit of a contractual risk structure). See also G Virgo, 'Demolishing the Pyramid—the Presence of Basis and Risk-Taking in the Law of Unjust Enrichment', in A Robertson and T Hang Wu, *The Goals of Private Law* (Oxford: Hart Publishing, 2009); A Goymour, 'Cobbling Together Claims' (2009) 68 CLJ 37 (why did risk issues affect an action in proprietary estoppel but not unjust enrichment on the same facts?).

[10] Chapter 11 (Illegality).

[11] In Chapter 5 we show that this was not the original rationale of the anonymity of the insurer in a subrogated claim, but that this anonymity is reinforced by existing theoretical accounts.

[12] See Kirby J, *Imbree v McNeilly* [2008] HCA 40, para 112, declaring that it was time to dispel a 'fiction' brought on by omitting consideration of insurance.

[13] Chapters 13 and 9.

[14] The key influence is HL Ross, *Settled Out of Court: the Social Process of Insurance Claims Adjustment* (New Brunswick NJ: Aldine Transaction Press, 1970, 2nd edn, 1980). Socio-legal accounts of insurance *per se* are less widely known, perhaps principally among insurance lawyers, eg S Kimball, *Insurance and Public Policy: A Study in the Legal Implementation of Social and Economic Public Policy* (Madison WI: University of Wisconsin Press, 1960). T Baker, 'Insurance in Socio-Legal Research' (2010) *U of Penn, Institute for Law and Econ Research, Paper No 10-07* discusses the potency of insurance in socio-legal studies.

been particularly associated with 'bureaucracy' (seen as the antithesis of judicial decision-making), and with the mass handling of claims.

In our view, the role of insurers in the processing of claims is significant and ought to be taken into account when addressing both the role of insurance, and the nature of liability. The association of these studies with reform agendas has meant that their significance has not been warmly embraced by the majority of doctrinal scholars. But equally, such studies may be thought about in terms of different lessons in changed times, including the commonalities between private and public handling of claims,[15] and the potential for market forms of 'governance'.[16] Such issues have only grown in importance in recent years, and we suggest that to appreciate the potential of private law, and particularly the law of contract, to contribute to social purposes will require attention to the operation of the law in context.

1.3.3 Policy, deep pockets, and the 'fortuity' argument

One key factor behind the exclusion of insurance from theoretical accounts of private law is a commonly encountered assumption that 'insurance' is to be associated with policy factors and particularly with 'deep-pockets' thinking. We are eager to move beyond this particular assumption and the debates that follow from it. Associated with the idea that insurance is essentially a 'policy' factor inclined to be used in order to attach liability to deep pockets is the suggestion that whether a tort defendant is insured is a purely private matter between the insurer and the assured. That bilateral insurance relationship is insulated from other bilateral relationships which give rise to the claim for a remedy. Two false obstacles, we suggest, are thus introduced. First is the idea that taking note of insurance necessarily means urging that liability follows insurance in order to secure compensation from deep pockets in an individual case. This is not the case. Insurance arrangements are so ubiquitous, and their general pattern often so well understood, that courts may very well perceive the claim as a means of evading the limitations of those arrangements. Taking note of insurance is commonly associated with the refusal of liability and rejection of duty, as we explain in Chapter 8, and not solely in instances where the claimant is thought to be insured (or, indeed, an insurer). The second false obstacle is the idea that the existence of insurance cover is purely fortuitous from the point of view of other parties.[17] We argue that consideration of party arrangements and relationships will, rightly in many cases, include consideration of insurance arrangements, whether those arrangements are privately negotiated,

[15] A point elaborated in a particular form by I MacNeil, 'Bureaucracy and Contracts of Adhesion' (1984) 22 Osgoode Hall LJ 5.

[16] For discussion based on case studies of public authority decisions in relation to roads, see S Halliday, 'The Regulation of Compliance with Public Law' (2013) *Public Law* 312–24.

[17] In *Davie v New Merton Board Mills* [1959] AC 604, at 627, and despite the long history of liability between employer and employee discussed in Chapter 9, Viscount Simonds described the existence of liability insurance on the part of an employer as fortuitous. This statement, as well as his comments in the unfortunate case of *Lister v Romford Ice and Cold Storage* [1956] AC 555, are often relied on as stating an 'orthodox' view that insurance is irrelevant to tort doctrine. In Chapter 5, we explain precisely why Viscount Simonds' approach in *Romford Ice* was misguided and should not, in any case, be relied on as evidence of the irrelevance of insurance. The case is powerful evidence to the contrary.

common practice, or legislatively mandated. In all of these circumstances, insurance arrangements are far from fortuitous so far as other parties are concerned. Just as insurance of D is not entirely fortuitous for C, so also the existence of C is hardly a surprise to D's insurer. The influence of bilateral arrangements on other parties, and the existence of a wider set of relationships, is brought into play.

1.3.4 Two-party models

This brings us to a particularly important element of our enquiry. The 'bipolar' or 'bipartite' model, which has been offered as definitive of private law,[18] is a particular barrier to understanding the nature of the role played by insurance. We consider insurance to be intrinsically and intimately related to many private arrangements, and from this point of view it inevitably raises the problem for two-party models that a third party (at least) is involved, and that this involvement is not purely a private matter. Not only do we argue that adoption of a narrow bipartite frame is likely to miss the manner in which the courts approach tort and contract duties; we also suggest that this narrow frame of reference systematically excludes the dimension of loss-spreading from view. Again, we are not suggesting that loss-spreading provides the answer to the puzzles of contract or tort liability. The point is, rather, that loss-spreading operates through party arrangements and does not operate without restriction; nor does it negate responsibility. We should open our eyes to the extent to which parties seek to place and spread losses using the resources of the law of obligations, and the nature of the restrictions applying to their ability to do so. These will not be discovered without reference to insurance arrangements and insurance law.

Our general point here is that the limitations of insurance, and the role of the law in defining and applying such limitations, are as instructive as its operation. All of this is suppressed by adopting an exclusive focus on two parties. The two-party model operates as a restrictive frame or perspective. It relegates issues of wider party relationships, including much activity which is vital to the operation and shape of the law of obligations, to the edges of the frame. To look at these aspects of the law is not to shift perspective from obligations to something beyond its boundaries; it is, rather, to broaden our perspective to include other parts of the same structure.

1.3.5 Loss-spreading, market, and state

As we see in the next chapter, insurance markets in many respects do not fit the common model of actuarialism and bounded risk pools assumed to characterize them. Losses are spread far and wide, across classes of business and national boundaries, by reinsurance

[18] Most influentially by E Weinrib, *The Idea of Private Law* (Cambridge MA: Harvard University Press, 1995), 1–2: 'The most striking feature of private law is that it directly connects two particular parties through the phenomenon of liability. Both procedure and doctrine express this connection.... In singling out these two parties and bringing them together in this way, private law looks... to a bipolar relationship of liability'. Many of the following chapters deal with doctrinal questions in light of the presence of multiple parties including insurers. The 'procedural' role of insurers in litigation is discussed particularly (though not uniquely) in Chapter 13.

and by capital market devices such as securitization. As the inadequacy of the model has been increasingly recognized, so it has had implications for the way insurance has been conceptualized outside legal scholarship. Obligations scholarship has yet to catch up with this trend, for the most part, even though it underlines the market character of insurance.

As we will see in Chapter 6, the insurance market spreads losses more widely than the state itself, but it does not do this without significant investment of legal resources. Market relationships and techniques of market regulation are engaged in loss-spreading. This is one of the reasons why 'loss-spreading' is not the answer to the puzzles of the law of obligations, but part of those puzzles. We illustrate that loss-spreading beyond mutual risk pools is definitively not to be associated solely with the guiding hand of government, and that a turn to the state is not the logical consequence of taking loss-spreading seriously. In fact, that is a hugely over-simplified assumption. Even where the spreading of losses is most strongly desired at a political level, states make use of the market in devising—or simply employing—means of spreading losses.[19]

1.4 Obligations

1.4.1 Contract

Broadly contractual relationships lie at the core of this book. Our approach to contract adopts a form of contextualism which we consider appropriate to analysis of the law of the market. Insurance contracts, in any case, have a long history and have helped to shape the law itself. So for example when addressing subrogation (the theme of Chapter 5), we emphasize the nature of insurance contracts as shaping the equitable response which has largely formed the insurer's remedies. Although we emphasize contractual relationships and in many instances underline the importance of party risk allocation, we do not suggest that the role of the courts is merely to give effect to the 'will' of the parties. Indeed, we suggest that in general terms the courts have responsibility for regulating insurance activities through the law of obligations, including the law of contract. For example, we suggest that the courts may interpret contractual duties in such a way as to control the exercise of subrogation rights—a possibility which is made less apparent, and perhaps even adversely affected, by redefinition of long-standing principles in terms of general principles of unjust enrichment.

Generally speaking, we consider that insurance is under-emphasized in existing accounts of the law of contract, relative to its practical and—we suggest—conceptual significance. While the relevance of insurance to contract has on occasion been directly denied,[20] it is more often under-emphasized (sometimes with unfortunate effects for understanding of the operating issues). One suggestion is that this follows from a more general rejection of the risk-allocation model of contracting.[21] Risk allocation, as we

[19] Discussed in Chapter 6 (loss-spreading) and Chapter 9 (compulsory insurance).

[20] Jane Stapleton, for example, extends her rejection of insurance as an operating factor in relation to tort duties to contractual duties, in a brief discussion referred to in Chapter 7: J Stapleton, 'Tort, Insurance and Ideology' (1995) 58 MLR 820.

[21] Chapter 7, 7.1 discusses the misplaced prediction that the significance of party risk allocation would decline and contract be absorbed by tort.

have already explained, is at the core of our analysis. We do not suggest that risk allocation is a complete or sufficient model of contracting. But on the most influential accounts of 'relational' contracting, risk allocation nevertheless anchors one part of the continuum of contractual relationships.[22] We would underline that the role of party risk allocation remains highly significant in contracting activity; and that its affinity with insurance is sufficient on its own to justify greater attention to insurance. In other words, insurance can be seen as paradigmatic of some important forms of contracting activity; and this sheds light both on the nature of insurance, and on the nature of contract. In Chapter 2, we explain why this does not imply an acontextual analysis.

The centrality of insurance to contract can be underlined in a range of ways. Hugh Collins, for example, uses the word 'insurance' to refer to the principles of the law of contract themselves, offering the means by which party expectations may be secured. These principles retain their significance in setting the essential element of trust and security on which contracting may be said to be based.[23] Similarly, economists of the stature of Kenneth Arrow and Joseph Stiglitz have recognized the centrality of risk and insurance to economic relations as a whole, to the extent that—as Tom Baker has identified—'insurance' is not perceived as confined to the products of insurers, but as provided 'any time that one party's actions have consequences for the risk of loss borne by another'.[24] By way of example, guarantees and indemnities between the parties commonly form a part of the pattern of contracting. Plainly, this is far broader than the idea of distribution within a common risk pool, and brings insurance to the centre of contracting.

Equally significant is that the element of futurity in contracting has been seen as definitive, so that contract may be defined as 'relations among people in the course of projecting exchange into the future'.[25] For MacNeil, the *nature* of the way in which contracting parties deal with the future is an essential marker of the nature of their relationship—a range of attitudes to future risk is associated with different forms of contracting, from the most 'transactional' (discrete exchanges in which definition of risk bearing is definitive) to the most 'relational' (in which the 'paper deal' is least definitive).[26] The issues here are significant both for the understanding of insurance, and we suggest for the understanding of contracting, and we defer fuller discussion to Chapter 2.

1.4.2 Tort

Various dimensions of our approach to tort, and of the influence of insurance in relation to tort, are outlined in 1.5, where we set out the structure of the book. However, a general feature of our account of tort may be underlined at this point. Parties, and indeed legislatures, regard negligently caused harm in particular as a pertinent risk for

[22] I MacNeil, 'The Many Futures of Contract' (1974) 47 S Cal L Rev 691.

[23] H Collins, *Regulating Contracts* (Oxford: Oxford University Press, 1999), 4.

[24] Tom Baker, 'On The Genealogy of Moral Hazard' (1996) 75 Texas Law Rev 237, 272. Baker quotes J Stiglitz, 'Risk, Incentives and Insurance: the Pure Theory of Moral Hazard' (1983) 8 *Geneva Papers on Risk and Insurance* 4: 'almost all economic relations are affected by risk, and by the problems of insurance and incentives to which this gives rise'.

[25] I MacNeil, 'Values in Contract: Internal and External' (1983) Nw U Law Rev 340, 341.

[26] How else can the use of non-binding 'comfort letters' for example, by the parent of a subsidiary contracting party confirming that its subsidiary will be kept in funds, otherwise be explained?

allocation and spreading, and such risks are often the subject of *ex ante* allocation accordingly. In light of this, the attempt to distinguish tort completely, both from contract and from social insurance, is misguided. Though negligence law will include reparation for some losses which result from weightier wrongs than mere carelessness, insurance in such instances may not respond. Insurance both shows the intimate link between negligence, and risk allocation and loss-spreading, and sets limits to recoverability. Those limits are themselves based in responsibility and set the boundary of legitimate loss-spreading. This raises issues which have seldom been recognized, let alone addressed.[27] Insurance, it may be argued, influences the very shape of the law of tort, which in some important respects defies explanation by 'internal' factors such as responsibility or rights. Insurance, in other words, is related to the dominance of negligence in the law of tort. The reach of insurance is not unlimited, and attention to its limits is as informative as attention to its core operation.

1.4.3 Unjust enrichment

We would make two general points about the relationship between unjust enrichment and insurance. The first relates to the involvement of insurers in creating the very subject matter from which some principles now categorized in terms of 'unjust enrichment' have been excavated. The loss-shifting arguments of insurers have been prominent in giving rise, over a long history, to principles of subrogation, contribution, and reimbursement, in particular. It is perhaps curious that the particular contribution of insurance in these principles is not identified and analysed, since insurance cases have been in the vanguard of development of commercial law.

The second point is that where restitutionary liabilities are concerned, insurance can be expected to play little direct part. This is for two reasons. First, many of the situations in which unjust enrichment claims may be brought rest upon some sort of deliberate or illegal conduct on the part of the assured, and that is not covered by insurance policies: these matters are addressed in Chapter 11. For the same reason, insurance policies will rarely respond to liability for breach of equitable obligations. Second, the general principle of indemnity insurance is that it responds to a loss. Insofar as the assured is seeking to recover for a benefit stripped away by principles of unjust enrichment, there is no possibility of recovery: as was said by Lord Phillips in *Moore Stephens v Stone & Rolls Ltd*,[28] 'If a person starts with nothing and never legitimately acquires anything he cannot realistically be said to have suffered any loss'.[29] Caution is required: the categorization of a remedy as restitutionary rather than compensatory may, therefore, have a negative impact on the capacity of the liable party to recover under an insurance policy.

This final point raises an analogy with the relationship between contract and tort, which has taken many years to clarify (and even now creates disagreement).[30] If contractual relations deal with risk, will unjust enrichment principles—which are formulated without express reference to risk—be allowed to develop so as to negate

[27] Discussed, in particular, in Chapters 11 and 12.
[28] [2008] EWCA Civ 644; [2008] 3 WLR 1146. [29] At para 5. [30] Chapter 8.

the risk allocations that are the product of party arrangements, whether those are broadly or narrowly read and interpreted, or to protect parties who have not secured the benefit of a contractual allocation of risks? Discussion of such issues is, as already noted, at a relatively early stage when compared with the 'painfully emerging' position in the law of tort,[31] and raises the question of how far the general principles of unjust enrichment are to be read as qualified by risk issues; and how far parties' own allocation of risks, where it exists,[32] guides the results. So far as there are boundary disputes between different branches of the law of obligations (as is the case, for example, in relation to subrogation),[33] it may be asked how far it is beneficial (or prudent) to subject existing legal principles to analysis in terms of 'unjust enrichment'. Reconceptualization will not necessarily bring the desired clarity and simplicity. Key principles may be displaced to the margins, or designated as exceptional, because they fail to fit the essential elements of the model. We suggest that the relationship between risk allocation and unjust enrichment is one which will need future attention.

1.5 Structure

The book is divided into three Parts. Part 1 includes introductory material. After the present chapter, Chapter 2 deals with the diverse character of insurance and its significant features so far as obligations law is concerned. It particularly develops the nature of the relationship between contract, and insurance in its market form. Chapter 3 explores core features of insurance contracts and the evolution of today's insurance market. Chapter 4 turns from contract to public law, underlining the relatively specific nature of statutory regulation of insurance in the UK, and significant recent changes.

Part 2 takes forward the themes identified in this introduction through analysis of the detailed operation of insurance in relation to private law. Chapter 5 is concerned with the important and enigmatic issue of subrogation. We argue that subrogation is an unseen force in shaping the law of obligations and that its importance is not always appreciated. We suggest that control of subrogation is essential and that the courts have developed an awareness of this which focuses on party risk arrangements. Chapter 6 deals with the ways in which insurance spreads losses, and gives evidence for our argument that loss-spreading through insurance does not resemble the favoured picture of closed risk pools in which risks may be adequately priced and distributed.

In Chapter 7, we evidence the significance of insurance as a form of risk allocation in commercial arrangements, and illustrate that the courts are often sensitive to the need to protect party arrangements. It is significant that these are often multi-party arrangements, and that claims for indemnification on the part of insurers while superficially giving substance to expanded relationships, for example by identifying reliance through a contractual chain, may well undermine contractual allocations. In these

[31] Beatson, n 9.

[32] Particular questions here surround the continuing effect of party risk allocations where contracts have been discharged: Beatson, n 9.

[33] Chapter 5.

situations, 'insurance' (in the sense of contracting with an insurer) is part of a continuum of ways in which parties may deal with risks. The search for party intentions is not confined to the intentions of insurer and assured—as, indeed, an insurer is frequently arguing that another party should be seen as a primary indemnifier.

In Chapters 8 and 9, we turn our attention from contract to tort. Chapter 8 focuses particularly on the role of insurance arrangements, of one sort or another, in the determination of tort duties. We begin with cases where tort operates within, or close to, a contractual 'matrix' in which the allocation of risks—and with it, inevitably, insurance—is in issue for the reasons explored above. We show that if decisions in relation to tort are guided purely by dominant responsibility-based accounts, applied without compromise or qualification, they will not improve on a contractual analysis, and the supplementing of contract with independent tort reasoning will not fulfil the promise it has been thought to offer. But we also venture beyond the confines of recognized contractual 'matrices'.[34] With an emphasis on the nature and structure of tort duties, we show that many claims seeking to expand the boundaries of tort have been influenced by the limits of contractual arrangements, and not solely where contract principles are unduly 'inflexible'. The inflexibility of doctrines such as privity is only one cause of such claims, which may also arise in an attempt to circumvent agreed allocations of risk. This is only a part of our discussion of the role of insurance in relation to tort. It is, however, a significant step in our analysis because it is opposed to the majority of established accounts.

Chapters 7 and 8 therefore take insurance and risk allocation to the core both of contract and of tort, with a focus on duties. However, we readily concede that where tort is concerned, the cases explored in Chapter 8, though conceptually significant, are not representative of the mass of tort claims. Chapter 9, dealing with compulsory insurance, focuses directly on the most familiar and 'conventional' of tort claims, namely road traffic accidents and employee injuries.

Part 3 is concerned with application. We consider a range of discrete issues, applying the lessons of the previous chapters. Chapter 10 is concerned with vicarious liability. Here we expand our argument that obligations law is not best addressed through an inflexible two-party frame. Vicarious liability is secondary liability which was defined in the nineteenth century through concepts which were initially related to risk allocation and became, inevitably, associated with loss-spreading. Understood in this way, vicarious liability also illustrates the limits of loss-spreading, and the intimate association between insurance and negligence, which has been a theme throughout.

These issues around the limits of loss-spreading are further emphasized in Chapter 11, which is concerned with *ex turpi causa* or illegality. The limits to loss-spreading are largely unexplored by tort lawyers, but they represent the operation of responsibility principles in a manner which shows the potential for recovery and liability to unravel. Addressing these issues in relation to fault going beyond mere negligence sheds light on the relative significance of responsibility and compensation in tort law, and on the nature of the relationship between tort and crime.

[34] The term 'contractual matrix' is explained in Chapter 8.

The remaining chapters deal with issues of particular current significance and take forward our argument. Chapter 12 shows how a number of threads from the book are brought together in the legal response to mesothelioma claims. We indicate the vital role played by insurance. Finally, the critical issue of insurance in litigation funding is explored in Chapter 13. There is no clearer illustration of the centrality of insurance than the manner in which civil litigation depends upon the insurance market. As we observed earlier, the available mechanisms for supporting litigation have a significant influence on its shape, and inevitably on the substantive law which emerges. The chapter emphasizes one of the points with which we started: it is hazardous for conceptual accounts of the law to omit the formative influences upon it, and particularly unfortunate for this to be done as a matter of choice.

2

Characterizing Insurance

2.1 Introduction: Actuarial or Relational?

In Chapter 1, we introduced the multiple roles of insurance in relation to the law of obligations. Insurance itself is a complex practice and institution, and its importance to law, economy, and society is hard to define with precision. Here we introduce some of the complexity of the character of insurance in order to improve understanding of the relationship between insurance and the law of obligations and, most importantly, to help move the debate to fresh ground. As part of this process, at the end of this section we offer a few words to distinguish our objectives from those of Kenneth Abraham in his important recent article, 'Four Conceptions of Insurance'.[1] We suggest that addressing the complex character of insurance in turn illuminates the potential importance of obligations scholarship in relation to the study of insurance, if obligations scholars should accept the challenge. In the next chapter, we explore the nature of insurance contracts more directly, in light of the argument here.

A particularly influential way of understanding insurance has focused on the characteristic techniques that it deploys, and their social implications.[2] This approach may be encapsulated as producing an 'actuarial' model or, as Baker and Simon express it, an actuarial 'vision' of insurance.[3] A model of insurance with these characteristics has appealed to scholars from a range of disciplines including sociology and economic and social history.[4] The actuarial model clearly has significant purchase among obligations scholars. For tort scholars in particular, the actuarial model is related to the historical relationship of insurance with legal innovations which spread the burdens of some of the most frequently encountered accidents; and with the rise of the welfare state through the notion of 'social insurance'. Insurance 'technology' in this model is related to the calculation of probability across large numbers of instances, producing regularity where, at an individual level, there is relative uncertainty. This, in turn, is associated both

[1] K Abraham, 'Four Conceptions of Insurance' (2013) 161 U Penn Law Rev 653.

[2] Note the influential work, in a Foucauldian tradition, of F Ewald. See, particularly F Ewald, 'Insurance and Risk', in G Burchell, C Gordon, and P Miller, *The Foucault Effect: Studies in Governmentality* (Chicago: University of Chicago Press, 1991:), focusing on insurance 'technologies', but also institutions, forms, and 'imaginaries'; T Baker and J Simon, *Embracing Risk: The Changing Culture of Insurance and Responsibility* (Chicago: University of Chicago Press, 2002), 'Introduction' (substituting 'visions' for Ewald's 'imaginaries').

[3] Baker and Simon, n 2, define the 'actuarial vision' of insurance as involving premiums paid in advance, guaranteed indemnity in the event of an insured loss, and risk-based premiums based on the best available information concerning expected losses (9–10). See also the influential argument of J Simon: 'The Ideological Effects of Actuarial Practices' (1988) 22 *Law and Society Review* 771–800.

[4] G Clark, G Anderson, C Thomann, and J-M von der Schulenburg (eds), *The Appeal of Insurance* (Toronto: Toronto University Press, 2010): 'neither the financial clout of the industry nor its ubiquity conveys the full measure of its social and political influence. The insurance industry has in fact become a primary agent of discipline and control over public and private behaviours...' (from the dust jacket).

with a degree of 'solidarity' or 'mutuality',[5] which is enabled by, or the product of, the emergence of 'risk' as a calculable alternative to 'uncertainty'.[6] The core contribution of insurance to this view has been loss-spreading: the ability to spread the risks of misfortune—and therefore its costs—across many shoulders, so that losses do not fall on a few; and the building of both security and solidarity. It will be seen that insurance so understood operates on 'populations' in order to translate uncertainty into more or less calculable,[7] distributable risk; and that it has an aggregating, generalizing nature.

These distributive, collectivizing features are not confined to market forms of insurance, and have been regarded as significant for scholars of public law and of the state. As Lowi argued in 1990, the 'welfare state', or 'the insurance state, or whatever it might be or become', had operated in the previous 40 years 'to democratize the burden of bad outcomes by removing most of the blame and indemnifying as many of the victims as possible'. But this, he argued, 'works precisely because the welfare state, functioning as it does through the reality and the conceptualization of insurance, works best at the level of the largest possible universe'.[8] This representation of insurance, incorporating aggregation, generalization, calculability across multiple instances, dilution of blame and individual responsibility, and a clear potential link with state or other collective action,[9] forms part of the 'actuarial model'.

The actuarial model by its nature views insurance at a macro level. Baker and Simon have contrasted the 'actuarial' model with models premised on 'embracing' risk,[10] which are underscored by a greater emphasis on individual responsibility for risk.[11] Ericson and Doyle, for their part, have supplemented the idea of 'spreading' risk with exploration of the way that insurance business may in different contexts act to 'embrace', 'absorb', or 'pre-empt' risks.[12] The contrast we draw in this chapter is rather

[5] 'Solidarity' is Ewald's term. As to 'mutuality' see M Dawson, *The Principles of Insurance Legislation* (New York: The Humboldt Library, 1895), cited by Baker and Simon, n 2, 3, arguing that insurance might succeed in building collective mutuality where religion had failed.

[6] There was insurance—particularly marine insurance—before the rise of probability science, but the latter put insurance on a scientific basis and arguably enabled it to spread, particularly to social policy: I Hacking, *The Emergence of Probability* (Cambridge: Cambridge University Press, 1975; 2nd ed, 2006); T Baker, 'On The Genealogy of Moral Hazard' (1996) 75 *Texas Law Review* 237, referring to the discovery of regularity in mortality tables and the growth of life insurance.

[7] On the distinction between uncertainty and risk see Ewald, n 2 (strictly confining 'risk' to the calculable); F Knight, *Risk, Uncertainty and Profit* (Boston MA: Houghton Mifflin, 1921) (emphasizing different types of predictability—some real, some empirically grounded—and the possibility of managing uncertainty); and on probability and risk, I Hacking, *The Taming of Chance* (Cambridge: Cambridge University Press, 1990); PL Bernstein, *Against the Gods: The Remarkable Story of Risk* (New York: John Wiley, 1996).

[8] TJ Lowi, 'Risks and Rights in the History of American Governments' (1990) 119 *Daedalus* 17, 40. Lowi argued that the insurance state operated less successfully at the regulatory level.

[9] In Chapter 9, we will see that in key areas the UK approach has included state adoption of the capacity of the insurance market. But this operates, of course, against the background of a developed system of social insurance.

[10] Baker and Simon, n 2.

[11] Noteworthy in this respect is 'post-welfare' use of insurance. For a UK example, see the proposal by the present Government to require the elderly to meet the first £75,000 of residential care costs but to pay for it by the use of insurance products which it is anticipated will be developed by the market: <http://www.guardian.co.uk/social-care-network/2013/feb/12/reasons-fearful-cap-social-care-costs>.

[12] R Ericson and A Doyle, *Uncertain Business: Risk, Insurance, and the Limits of Knowledge* (Toronto: Toronto University Press, 2004): 'absorbing' risks is explored in relation to earthquake insurance; 'pre-empting' risk is associated with terrorism insurance.

different, though compatible with elements of all of these phenomena, and is aimed specifically at locating insurance in obligations scholarship. For this purpose, we would emphasize that insurance is not only a distributive mechanism, but also a ubiquitous feature of market transactions and relations. We suggest that there is an existing model or vision of insurance, underlining its market role, which may be described as 'relational'.[13] The relational model or 'vision' of insurance leads to adoption of a rather different set of emphases from those associated with the actuarial model. We look at the relational model—focusing on the insurance relationship—and some of the supplementary arguments it brings, in 2.2. Here, we should say a few words about our choice of the word 'relational', what it implies, and what it should not be taken to imply.

The key feature of a 'relational' model is that it focuses on relationships between parties. In this instance, it considers insurance in terms of the party relations of which it is an inherent part. The relationship in issue in a given case may be between insurer and assured; but as we have already begun to explain in Chapter 1, further relationships may also enter the frame. These include relationships with other insurers or potential indemnifiers; with reinsurers; or with other contracting parties or potential tort claimants. Private law as a whole is concerned with the relationships between parties, and we contend that despite the complexity introduced by insurance and indemnity, the relational model has direct affinities with the structure of private law. We use the term in order to emphasize these affinities. However, ours is not a bipartite, nor a formal relational model. The significance of these points may be illustrated through application to tort duties: we argue that the relational character of such duties is relevant to an assessment of the part that might be played by risk-allocation concerns, and thus by insurance, in defining them.[14] The generality of these issues across private law is the reason why we have not preferred the alternative term 'transactional'. The label 'transactional' might have been too closely associated solely with contractual, rather than other relationships; and might have been taken to imply a certain style of contract, namely discrete transactions in the nature of arm's-length arrangements between parties.

Admittedly, the word 'relational', particularly in contract scholarship, itself may carry more specific connotations than we have in mind. Just as we do not have in mind a formal type of bipartite relationality, neither do we mean to imply, for example, that insurance relationships are necessarily long-term and cooperative, or that they necessarily contain features other than the transfer of risk, which are typically associated with a debated 'category' of relational contracts.[15] Far from it. However, our use of the term 'relational' has the intention of focusing not only on issues of risk transfer but also

[13] 'Relationality' in insurance is emphasized by T Baker, n 6, and is a widely used term in economic analysis.

[14] Chapter 8.

[15] The key works are those of Ian Macneil, particularly 'The Many Futures of Contract' (1974) 47 *S Cal L Rev* 691, discussed in Chapter 1. Note the denial of a *specific category* of 'relational' contracts—focused on the absence of a sharp means of distinguishing them from other contracts—on the part of M Eisenberg, 'Relational Contracts', in J Beatson and D Friedmann, *Good Faith and Fault in Contract Law* (Oxford: Clarendon Press, 2002). We do not maintain the existence of a discrete category of relational contracts.

of multi-party relations which are introduced in 2.2, and were discussed in Chapter 1. We would add that such analysis is inevitably sensitive to the context of the parties' relationship. The increasingly rich diversity of 'relational' scholarship, and the recognized need to study economic and contractual relationships in terms of their context, therefore provide us with an added incentive to use of the term.[16] We suggest that risk-allocation arrangements—like any other aspect of party relations—should be considered in the light of their context. That context may include a broader web of relations than is sometimes thought relevant to private law, and among the most significant features of that web is the involvement of insurance and insuring obligations and relationships. In many instances, the relevant context of insurance relationships is a complex, commercial one, in which purposive allocation of risks is key. But equally, the presence of consumers or vulnerable third parties may itself make a decisive difference to the way in which private law will approach insurance issues.[17]

In the chapters that follow, we emphasize that purchase of insurance, and bargaining around both duties to insure and the location of risk more generally, underpin and help to facilitate commercial relationships of every sort. 'Insurance' in a relational view is to be understood as primarily an arrangement through which the incidence of risk is identified and, where appropriate, allocated. Seen in this light, insurance is a key factor in party relations as they are addressed by private law, particularly through the law of contract and related sources of obligation and remedy, as well as the macro-level state regulation which is an emanation of the actuarial model. In later chapters, we indicate ways in which its presence could be better reflected in legal reasoning affecting the former, if the suspicion that insurance is necessarily connected solely to wider concerns *extrinsic* to the parties could be set aside. Insurance in the relational model is not so different from other devices for reducing uncertainty and transferring and locating risk (further discussed in the paragraphs that follow). It is ironic perhaps that insurance is often singled out by scholars of private law for exclusion among such concerns. Its identification with 'policy' is associated with the hold of the actuarial model and its collectivizing, social implications.

Insurance conceptualized in this second way has played an important role in economic theory,[18] but other disciplines have more recently developed their understanding of 'insurance' in a manner which recognizes some of the insights provided by this perspective.[19] Most particularly, this approach is needed when it becomes plain that actuarial techniques, while an important part of the overall picture, say little about the relational role of insurance.[20] From the point of view of obligations scholars, the opportunity offered by this vision of insurance is that it is fundamentally concerned

[16] Examples of growing interdisciplinary interest in 'relationality' are V Zelizer, 'How I Became a Relational Economic Sociologist and What Does that Mean?' (2012) 40 *Politics and Society* 145; and J Nedelsky, *Law's Relations: A Relational Theory of Self, Autonomy, and Law* (Oxford: Oxford University Press, 2011).

[17] An example is the analysis of subrogation in Chapter 5, including the possibility of subrogated actions against employees.

[18] See further the discussion in 2.2.

[19] See further 2.4.

[20] We indeed point out in Chapter 4 that the actuarial model was the sole concern of public law until 2000, when relational issues for the first time fell under the statutory spotlight.

with party relationships, and brings insurance into the core of obligations law. At the same time, we suggest that it does not necessarily lead to an assumption that 'freedom of contract' offers the key interpretive approach. Lawyers will be inclined to differ in their view of the relationship between insurance and private law, depending on which of these models most influences their understanding of insurance. In our view, they provide complementary elements of a proper understanding of insurance, and of its role in private law.

Simply articulating these two possibilities does not of course exhaust all the issues. Rather, they may be thought of as two 'poles of attraction' in thinking about insurance from the point of view of the law of obligations. The first represents insurance as fundamentally extrinsic to the law of obligations, and both actually and potentially transformative of the effects of the law of obligations in action. It probably has particular purchase among tort lawyers, partly because insurance has been linked to far-reaching historic reforms of the law of tort,[21] and (equally) to the critique of some of those reforms—and extensions to other fields, such as products liability—from a 'law and economics' perspective.[22] The major role of insurance in underpinning tort's monetary remedies has also proved hard to assimilate to existing theoretical structures; and this has been a recurring problem in debates about the proper focus of attention for tort scholars: should tort be seen in terms of delivery of compensation, continuous with other possible 'solutions'; or should it be seen in terms either of personal responsibility, or corrective justice, or of rights and duties, consistent with its nature as private law?[23] The second approach represents insurance as a core part of the relations between private actors and emphasizes that insurance is an established fixture in the law of obligations, and a ubiquitous concern of parties entering relationships of various types. If anything, in this view, it is the inherent significance of insurance to obligations law, the focus of the present volume, which needs to be more securely recognized; and the element of insurance in party arrangements deserves to be more fully scrutinized. On the other hand, this approach does not emphasize in quite the same way the *distinctiveness* of insurance; and 'insurance' in the core senses discussed in Chapter 3 (identified for the purposes of regulation) shades into other means of protecting from or shifting risk. Since contract and tort duties may themselves be interpreted as achieving the same thing, insurance contracts are inclined to become paradigmatic of contracts generally to the extent that relationships are approached in this way.

In the remainder of this chapter, different aspects of these two poles of attraction are identified. The first aspect considered (in 2.2) is broadly definitional: what features have been identified as constituting the essence of insurance and the insurance relationship,

[21] Particularly in the enactment of workmen's compensation statutes: K Abraham, *The Liability Century: Insurance and Tort Law from the Progressive Era to 9/11* (Cambridge MA: Harvard University Press, 2008), ch 2, 'The Original Tort Reform'. In relation to the UK, see the sources in Chapter 9 of the present volume.

[22] This is particularly evident in the history of products liability in the US, where the idea that tort should be aimed at optimizing loss-spreading was met by economic analysis on the part of such scholars as Epstein and Priest. The counter-arguments were themselves still couched in terms of insurance. Resistance to their accounts, in turn, has been influential in the denial that insurance is relevant at all to tort reasoning. For our attempt to get beyond the current received wisdom in this respect, see particularly Chapters 8 and 9.

[23] Discussed in Chapter 1.

and how does this relate to the distinction made above? In Chapter 3, we will see that legal definitions of insurance have been adopted for a range of purposes and that definitions have in each case been adapted to the purpose concerned. Here, our intention is different and more general—to identify in outline the features of insurance which might influence the kind of relationship which exists between insurance and private law, with reference to the essence of insurance.

The second aspect to be considered (in 2.3) relates to personal responsibility. The issues here surround factors which operate to qualify the popular image or 'vision' of insurance as diluting personal responsibility. In truth, insurance has had a long-standing relationship with, and influence upon, responsibility notions. The boundaries of insurance, for example, are policed by notions of fraud and 'moral hazard'. It has been argued that these aspects of insurance are growing in importance as part of the general trend toward re-emphasis upon individual responsibility notions.[24] The subsequent financial crisis and fiscal austerity have intensified this trend; though they also raise significant questions about the inequitable focus ideas of 'moral hazard', and its resurgent rhetorical dimension.[25] All of that aside, individual responsibility, reflected in a poor claims record, is enhanced by premium rating or, more seriously, the complete loss of insurance coverage essential to the carrying on of the relevant activity.

The third aspect to be considered (in 2.4) relates to the continuing element of uncertainty in insurance. It has been increasingly recognized among social theorists that whatever the theoretical and historical connections between insurance and a 'specialized' notion of risk, insurance business continues to operate in the presence of considerable uncertainty;[26] and that actuarial value and spreading within homogeneous risk pools do not fully represent the nature of insurance business. Social theory may be converging somewhat with more economic visions of insurance, through a focus on insurance business, and through renewed attention to earlier work on insurance contracts[27] and to uncertainty in a market context.[28] Insurance operates to shift and spread risks which are not susceptible to calculation with any degree of accuracy, somewhat in defiance of the actuarial model; and to do this, techniques beyond the pooling of risk are needed. This may ultimately undermine the sense that insurance delivers security. On the other hand, it also suggests that insurance can be

[24] Baker and Simon, n 2.

[25] Note the comments of Joseph Stiglitz about the focus of 'moral hazard' arguments on ordinary house buyers exposed to risk through excessive borrowing, and not on the irresponsibility of those involved in creating the risk-transfer devices which led to the collapse: J Stiglitz, *Freefall: Free Markets and the Sinking of the Global Economy* (Harmondsworth: Penguin, 2010), at 16–17 (moral hazard concerns 'shunted aside' in the failed banking sector). This is all the more notable given Stiglitz's role in generalizing 'moral hazard' as a conceptual tool and particularly in the relational model of insurance: Baker, n 6.

[26] A key work in this respect is Ericson and Doyle, n 12.

[27] Particularly C Heimer, *Reactive Risk and Rational Action: Managing Moral Hazard in Insurance Contracts* (Berkeley CA: University of California Press, 1985).

[28] P O'Malley, 'Uncertain Subjects: Risks, Liberalism and Contract' (2000) *Economy and Society* 460. O'Malley draws on the distinction between risk and uncertainty in a business context identified by Frank Knight, n 7, and suggests that the law of contract is a means of governing uncertainty. In his view, 'governmentality' theory, because of its focus on risk, has overlooked uncertainty. The link between uncertainty and contract, and the contrast with 'risk' (the core feature of actuarial models), provides a fruitful avenue for obligations scholarship which has so far not been taken up.

deployed to cover a wider range of risks than is sometimes supposed, and that its limits are not so easily reached as some have assumed, applying the actuarial model.[29] But at the same time, these developments further intensify the sense in which insurance is part and parcel of the issues typically raised by party transactions, rather than a distinctly 'scientific' solution to them. A new question arises; namely, to what extent is insurance not the solution to the problems of control of risk as it may appear according to the actuarial model, but potentially part of the problem itself?[30]

How, then, does our approach differ from that adopted by Kenneth Abraham in his recent contribution to debate about the nature of insurance and insurance law?[31] We would identify key differences as the generality of our approach to the phenomenon of insurance; the wider range of legal questions which we seek to address; and the flexibility of our understanding of a 'contractual' analysis. Abraham's article is focused above all on conceptions of insurance which bear directly on interpretation of insurance contracts. He argues that two fundamental questions recur in insurance law and scholarship. These are, first, to what extent should the language of an insurance policy affect its terms? And, second, what is the proper influence of 'public law' values on the scope of private insurance coverage? Similar questions, sometimes with substantial variation to suit the UK focus of our work, will be found addressed in various chapters of this book.[32] They are however primarily concerned with interpretation of insurance contracts, and do not exhaust the themes of our analysis, as already outlined. Abraham argues that four rival conceptions of insurance compete to provide answers to these two fundamental recurring questions. Of these four, he argues, only one—the 'contract conception'—is literally true. The others—the 'public utility-regulated industry conception';[33] the 'product conception';[34] and the 'governance conception'[35]—though significant are not only partial, but also metaphorical, defining insurance *in terms of something else*.[36] For Abraham therefore, insurance is, inherently, a contractual arrangement between parties. In turn, the contract conception is inherently related to ideals of freedom of contract.

Our analysis is more complex in at least two distinct ways. First, we suggest that the 'actuarial' model of insurance sketched here is not metaphorical in the sense attached to the three 'conceptions' of insurance, beyond the contractual model, outlined by Abraham. Rather, the actuarial model approaches the question of what is important about, and definitive of, insurance largely in terms of the distinctive techniques developed and applied by insurance in all its guises, and the social and legal implications of these.

[29] In particular, by some 'risk society' theorists, who predict the emergence of uninsurable risks hastening the demise of risk society. Catastrophe risk insurance is discussed in Chapter 6.

[30] Two pertinent questions can be identified. First, does insurance activity contribute to 'systemic risk'? This is discussed further in 2.4. Secondly, do insurers operate to subvert attempted risk arrangements? On this point see Chapter 5.

[31] Abraham, n 1, 653.

[32] Particularly Chapter 3 (Insurance Contracts) and Chapter 12 (The Asbestos Litigation).

[33] Explaining insurance as a private cartelized commodity so vital that it has to be regulated in the public interest.

[34] Treating insurance as a financial product rather than a contract for the provision of services, requiring the application of rules relevant to the former, ie, validity rather than meaning.

[35] Whereby insurance is regarded as a surrogate for government in controlling behaviour and preventing misfortune, so that policies should be construed accordingly.

[36] Abraham, n 1, 657.

We have already begun to outline the nature of these distinctive techniques in this section. Key, for example, is the use and development of concepts of 'risk' rather than uncertainty. The actuarial approach, understood in this way, has a long intellectual pedigree both outside and inside legal scholarship. It does not define insurance in terms of something else, though it does focus on characteristics other than the relationship of two contracting parties. It draws attention, as we have said, to the distinctive aggregating and distributive implications of insurance, across its private and social forms. The 'governance conception' reviewed by Abraham typically forms one aspect of this actuarial vision of the distinctive importance of insurance. It is not surprising that 'governance' models are only partial, since the contribution of insurance to governance is only one—albeit significant—implication of actuarial accounts. Second, and equally significant for our starting point, is that we would not interpret a 'contractual conception' so narrowly as to equate it with the dictates of freedom of contract or literal interpretation. Rather, to interpret insurance in terms of a relational model incorporates, in our view, many potential responses to the parties' relationship, not least because it typically expands the frame of reference to incorporate a number of different parties; and the resources of private law in responding to these relationships are not confined to contractual interpretation in a narrow form.

These differences reflect to some degree our different starting points. We began the previous chapter by pointing out that in this book we set out to explore the contribution of insurance to the shape of the law of obligations. That is a broader undertaking than answering the recurrent interpretive puzzles with which Abraham's article is concerned. But interestingly, the differences may also reflect some jurisdictional variation, both in the detailed approach to insurance contracts, and in the more general approach to various aspects of private law.

As far as insurance contracts are concerned, a number of cautions as to the relevance of US literature to the UK position may be issued, relating to questions which emerge later in the present work. First, insurance contracts are regarded in many US jurisdictions as 'consumerist', even when they cover commercial risks and indeed reinsurance, so that the interpretive doctrines of 'reasonable expectations of the assured' and *contra proferentem* figure in many decisions. This is not the case in the UK. Second, the regulation of insurers is at State rather than Federal level, so there is a less cohesive approach than that found in the UK. Third, the use of standard forms is not as widespread in the UK as Abraham asserts is the case in the US. This use may be the consequence of the requirement in many States of approval of policy terms as a condition of authorization to carry on business. That requirement does not exist in the UK. There is plenty of competition between the suppliers of consumer policies, and many commercial contracts are the result of individual negotiation using professional brokers. Fourth, the US immunity of insurance from antitrust law is not replicated in the UK other than in respect of co-insurance of the same risk. Finally, English law does not recognize a generalized concept of 'bad faith', under which US courts control the conduct of insurers on principles akin to administrative law and may award punitive damages for failure to settle.

In relation to obligations more generally, other differences also operate. In particular, there may be less readiness among English scholars to see questions of tort as other than 'relational', and as standing in marked distinction to contractual conceptions.[37] At the same time, the more flexible approach to the idea of a 'contractual' conception of insurance found in the present work reflects the current, contextual approach to interpretation of commercial contracts generally in the English courts. Beyond this, our approach considers party relations in terms of a web of legal rights and duties operating in particular contexts, and suggests that insurance fundamentally affects these party relationships. When we emphasize the relational, rather than broadly actuarial or narrowly transactional, interpretation of insurance, we imply this greater flexibility in interpretation of relationships which are, nevertheless, recognizably contractual.

2.2 In Search of the Nature of Insurance

It may not be possible to identify a single definition of insurance that is good for all purposes. In Chapter 3, we explore some definitions of insurance which operate in the law for particular purposes, identifying features which have been thought definitive of insurance, for the purpose of its regulation and for the attraction of particular legal doctrines, notably the concept of utmost good faith. To some extent, these concern themselves with placing the boundaries of 'insurance', at least for those specified purposes. Boundaries have been important to the law in relation to insurance. For example, English law has long sought to mark a boundary between legitimate speculation and insurance on one hand, and potentially harmful gambling on the other, through the notion of 'insurable interest'.[38] Some 'mutual' solutions—which operate to spread risks within a pool—have been found undesirable in policy terms because they are relatively susceptible to failure or to limited indemnity: the market devices used to diversify insurance have enhanced the reliability of commercial insurers, yet removed it from the simplest actuarial model.[39] In any event, the positions taken up by the law for particular regulatory purposes will themselves contribute to an understanding of the nature of insurance and its social role.

Our intention here is more general. We have suggested that for obligations scholars, a critical point is that if we were to seek the *essence* or true nature of insurance, there would be two poles of attraction in the rival potential answers. Complementary though they may be, important features of insurance congregate around these poles. We have introduced the actuarial and relational models in 2.1. These may be identified on one hand with the calculated spreading of risks, and particularly the distribution of losses within a risk pool (lessening the burden of misfortune on any individual by sharing its cost); and on the other hand with risk transfer, generally within a contractual framework.

Undoubtedly there are disciplinary influences over the way that the core nature of insurance is identified; and we deal with this in due course. Leaving this aside, to some

[37] See the transition from contract to tort questions in Chapters 7 and 8.

[38] Discussed in Chapters 3 and 5, as well as in 2.4.

[39] Chapter 9, 9.4, refers to attempts to enhance the security of compensation in the last years of the UK's Workmen's Compensation Acts.

extent the difference is one of the perspective from which the phenomenon is approached, yet rather different aspects of the phenomenon are identified as a consequence. The first perspective, emphasizing risk-spreading, looks at the matter from the point of view of what insurance might achieve across a group, what techniques have made this possible, and what both the spreading of losses, and the applicable techniques, mean for society. The second perspective focuses on the subject or purpose of individual arrangements and relationships, by which 'insurance' is provided. Taking this perspective into account, it is plain that there is considerable variety in the potential roles that loss-spreading might play. The spreading of losses may be a goal (the purpose of a set of arrangements, for example where shipowners pool their risks, or governments mandate motor insurance); it may be a technique (or technology), through which insurers are able to operate profitably while accepting risks; or it may simply be the consequence of insurance business. Loss-spreading as a *consequence* however need not reflect intentions directly, and its pattern may be uncertain. For example, there is the potential for more extensive loss-spreading than a simple actuarial model would envisage where insurers seek diversification and further indemnification through reinsurance or the use of the capital markets. The extent of these loss-spreading devices, and attendant legal issues, are reviewed in Chapter 6. In this guise, the shifting of risks is capable of spreading risks more widely than any single insurer could achieve; but the result is a pattern of risk-bearing which frequently precludes the identification of individual risks and losses. We will see in Chapter 6 that risk-spreading in this broader sense, and pooling of risk in the sense referring to a common risk pool, frequently diverge: scale, but also diversification, are key to covering risks.

This second approach appears to look at insurance through a narrower focus than the first, prioritizing the objectives of an insured party and its insurers. It is important to add that the allocation of risks between contracting parties is a key focus for this model. Just as the first approach has numerous implications for social relations, the second approach has its own deeper implications, related in particular to the impact of insurance as a feature of markets. From this view, the defining feature of insurance lies in reduction of uncertainty for the assured—and, we would add, for those doing business, or otherwise entering relationships with the assured[40]—by transferring a defined risk to another party, in return for a premium. The nature of insurance is thus to accomplish the transfer of 'risks'. 'Risk', in insurance terms, has a positive connotation, because it is what insurers seek: it is a positive feature of an insurance market that it is joined by 'new risks', for example. This second definition emphasizes the economic character of insurance and its role in market activity and in the economic planning of individuals and households.

Interestingly, general *definitions* of 'insurance' would appear to focus primarily on the risk *transfer* element of insurance which is so significant to the second encapsulation above—its role in enabling a party to pass a risk elsewhere. In other words, these

[40] Important to the discussion in Chapters 7 and 8.

definitions focus on what is involved in 'insuring' or in 'providing' (or purchasing) insurance. So, for example, Oxford Dictionaries (online) define insurance as:

> an arrangement by which a company or the state undertakes to provide a guarantee of compensation for specified loss, damage, illness, or death in return for payment of a specified premium.

Insurance here is an arrangement, by which a guarantee of compensation is secured; but it explicitly encompasses contributory forms of state insurance. Business Dictionary.com defines 'insurance' as follows:

> Risk-transfer mechanism that ensures full or partial financial compensation for the loss or damage caused by event(s) beyond the control of the insured party. Under an insurance contract, a party (the insurer) indemnifies the other party (the insured) against a specified amount of loss, occurring from specified eventualities within a specified period, provided a fee called premium is paid. In general insurance, compensation is normally proportionate to the loss incurred, whereas in life insurance usually a fixed sum is paid.

This approaches insurance in terms of a business arrangement, in which it is identified as a 'risk-transfer mechanism'. Insurers, too, may define 'insurance' in essentially transactional terms. According to Lloyd's Glossary, for example, which adopts a definition akin to that of regulatory law,[41] 'insurance' is:

> A contract whereby an insurer promises to pay the insured a sum of money or some other benefit upon the happening of one or more uncertain events in exchange for the payment of a premium. There must be uncertainty as to whether the relevant event(s) may happen at all or, if they will occur (eg death) as to their timing.

This identifies insurance with indemnity, rather than risk-pooling. On this approach, risk-pooling may be thought of as an important—and influential—aspect of how this is done, rather than as definitive.

Not surprisingly, some academic treatments of insurance contain compatible definitions. Thoyts describes the risk-transfer approach as the traditional one, and argues that it disguises the pooling of risk inherent to insurance business.[42] His point is that it is a mistake to think that an 'individual' contract is being entered into: rather, the cost of insuring is affected by others within the pool. This is an appropriate point, of interest in part because it qualifies the transactional model by reference to actuarialism, demonstrating that disciplinary perspectives on what is the 'received' model may vary considerably. Approaching the matter with the resources of obligations scholarship, one could also select other features of the insurance contract as relevant to understanding insurance as relational. In particular, it could equally be argued that the narrowly transactional focus of the above definitions is misleading because of the prevalence of long-term insurance relationships, and the adoption by insurer and

[41] Discussed further in Chapter 3.

[42] R Thoyts, *Insurance Theory and Practice* (London: Routledge, 2010), Chapter 1, 'Insurance as a Risk Transfer Mechanism'.

assured of responsibilities beyond the transfer of risk. In other words, it is possible that not all insurance contracts fall squarely at the 'transactional' end of the relational spectrum.[43]

Peter Zweifel and Roland Eisen, in their *Insurance Economics*,[44] provide a sophisticated economic analysis. They suggest that the phenomenon of insurance is essentially an emanation of business practice and recognize that the essence of a practice is hard to define. They propose that a guiding definition at the broadest level is that insurance is 'a means or procedure that *reduces uncertainty* with respect to the future'.[45] Plainly, if this is the meaning of insurance, then it is not tied to the distinctive features at the core of the actuarial model, though those techniques provide important 'technology' for achieving this goal.[46] They cite more confined definitions from the existing economic literature, for example:

> Insurance is the exchange of an uncertain loss of unknown magnitude for a small and known loss;[47]

and

> Insurance is the exchange of money now for money payable contingent on the occurrence of certain events.[48]

What is striking about all of these definitions—from the economics literature and the most generalist sources—is that they emphasize the nature and purpose of the insurance *relationship*, contract, or transaction, and in some instances make a link with the reduction of uncertainty. It is a short step to the conclusion that the contract of insurance, with an insurer, is not the only means of securing 'insurance'. We have already mentioned the argument that all contracts allocate risks, as do tort duties;[49] and the implication that the insurance contract offers a paradigm of this aspect of party relationships. But there are other implications too. As Neil Doherty has put it, an insurance policy may simply be perceived as a form of financial instrument, and 'the function of insurance' (which he, in common with the definitions above, identifies as being 'to transfer risk from one person to another'), can be achieved with other financial instruments in the capital markets.[50] These may have very different implications from the 'technologies' associated with the actuarial model. Where then does the nature of insurance business lie, and how should obligations scholars respond to this mixed picture?

[43] Compare M Clarke, *Policies and Perceptions of Insurance Law in the Twenty-First Century* (Oxford: Oxford University Press, 2005), 172–3, identifying insurance relationships in terms of a series of short-term contracts rather than as long-term contracts in the sense adopted by 'relational' contract theory. We would point out that in some contexts, risk transfer does not represent the only relationship between insurer and assured; and that non-renewal may have more significant effects than a 'discrete contracts' model suggests.

[44] (New York: Springer, 2012).

[45] Zweifel and Eisen, n 44, 2–3. See further the discussion in 2.4.

[46] A point amplified in the following discussion.

[47] Zweifel and Eisen, n 44, 3, translated from K Hax, *Grundlagen des Verscherungswesens* (Wiesbaden: T Gabler, 1964).

[48] K Arrow, *Aspects of the Theory of Risk-Bearing* (Helsinki: Yrjö Jahnssonin Säätiö, 1965).

[49] Chapter 1; and Baker, n 6.

[50] Introduction, in Zweifel and Eisen, n 44.

Insurers, as we have implied, deploy a range of techniques for managing the risks which they contract to bear. Actuarial pricing is only one of these; and risks certainly do not remain in a single homogenous pool.[51] For this reason, insurers may depart from actuarial pricing in either direction and for a number of reasons. They may consider it necessary to write business below the actuarial price for a period, allowing other income to provide for payments to cover insured losses: investment income is a key feature of insurance business and its derivation is the subject of intense public law scrutiny. But they may also demand returns far higher than the actuarial level, in order to reflect the inherent uncertainty still associated with large or concentrated losses. War, terrorism, and natural catastrophes are all in some sense predictable, but the scale of their devastation is not. Diversification; investment; time; and the capacity to use reinsurance capacity and financial markets to meet losses *ex post* are all additional techniques available to insurers, beyond the form of pooling or spreading inherent in actuarial pricing.

Zweifel and Eisen list (non-exhaustively) a number of aspects of 'insurance technology' within an insurance company, which may be compared with the actuarial model of the impacts of insurance. In a sense, they offer an economics-focused alternative. 'Insurance technology' on their account is diverse. It includes channels of distribution (for example the integration of writing or dispersal through use of brokers);[52] the composition of the risk portfolio; the management of risks associated with moral hazard; management of risks emanating from financial markets including loss of value of assets; management of reserves and capital investment; purchase of reinsurance and coinsurance; statistical analysis and forecasting; and issues relating to claims settlement and drafting of contractual terms. This armoury is quite diverse, and consistent with the idea that negotiation, transfer, and dispersal of risks, in addition to spreading across the like-risk pool, are core to insurance in practice. 'Risk-spreading' is not the end of the matter. An important addition to this preliminary list is 'Alternative Risk Transfer' technology, enabling insurance of 'catastrophic' risks.[53]

Whatever the core definition of insurance, insurance companies do indeed spread losses—but they are spread far more broadly than the image of the risk pool would suggest. Loss-spreading operates through numerous instances of risk transfer, and other sources of capital and income are sought to balance these risks. Exposure to loss is also managed through the relationship with the assured. Because of the contractual nature of risk transfer at all levels, understanding contract law and its regulatory potential (and limits) should be a key element in the study of insurance. Equally, because risk-shifting underpins contractual activity and forms the background also to many tort actions, obligations scholars have much to learn from attention to insurance relationships and arrangements.

[51] This will be explored in Chapter 6.

[52] In Chapter 3, 3.3 we review the way that insurance contracts are written and the implications for interpretation.

[53] Legal implications are discussed in Chapter 6.

2.3 Insurance and Responsibility

One of the sticking points for obligations scholars in accepting insurance as a proper subject for their attention is its apparent conflict with ideas of responsibility. A characteristic feature of the actuarial model of insurance, and a source of much concern, appears to be that it dilutes ideas of personal responsibility.[54] By definition (on the actuarial model), it acts upon aggregates and perceives events in terms of risks, which are dependent on some degree of empirical regularity. Superficially at least this seems to undercut the notion of fault. Indeed, it may be argued that planned insurance responses encapsulate *social* or collective responsibility—providing security for the most at risk. In the context of tort law, 'insurance' solutions and 'tort' solutions have been perceived as opposites, partly for this reason. So, for example, it has been argued that tort cannot be 'about' insurance, because tort is based on personal responsibility, and insurance has a different and inconsistent basis.[55]

It should be apparent from what has been said above that insurance does not negate the idea of responsibility, though it may succeed in changing or displacing its meaning in the context of private law.[56] One argument is that insurance enhances ideas of responsibility, even of individual responsibility, in certain respects.[57] Perhaps obviously, there is the idea of prudentialism in the form of a responsibility to insure. This may represent a responsibility to insure oneself (to avoid becoming a burden on others), including a responsibility to one's dependants to provide for them. But responsibility may also take the form of discharging an obligation to provide insurance funds to compensate others, or to cover a risk which would otherwise fall elsewhere. In this latter case, there is a responsibility or obligation to bear the cost of insurance.

The connections between insurance and responsibility are deeper than this, however. The responsible behaviour of assured parties is of evident importance to insurers, and the subject of much industry attention. Insurance has its own legacy in respect of moral ideas, closely linked to responsibility. Its technologies have always raised questions about how responsibility might be retained; and this has increasingly emerged as a core theme with the rise of neo-liberalism, and into the era of financial crisis.

Insurance has, since its origins, faced the idea that its existence is somehow contrary to good morals or public policy, or creative of immorality. Though tort lawyers have sometimes thought this particular to liability insurance, we suggest in Chapter 3 that there are grounds for doubting this. The idea of 'moral hazard', now encountered routinely in the discourse of economics, began its life in the language of insurance

[54] Lowi, n 8; Ewald, n 2.

[55] J Stapleton, 'Tort, Insurance and Ideology' (1995) 58 MLR 820. Stapleton extends the same reasoning to contract, as we see in Chapter 7.

[56] The relationship with criminal or other public law is more complex. The fact that a motorist or employer is required to insure does not dilute public law responses to dangerous driving or the provision of an unsafe working environment. However, the obligation to insure itself creates a new potential criminal liability. For the complications in a road traffic context: R Merkin and J Steele, 'Policing the Tort-Crime Boundary with the MIB', in M Dyson (ed), *Unravelling Tort and Crime* (forthcoming, 2014).

[57] T Baker, 'Risk, Insurance, and the Social Construction of Responsibility', in Baker and Simon, n 2, examines a number of forms of responsibility associated with insurance.

companies struggling to assert the morality of their business, partly by distinguishing it from immoral activities such as gambling,[58] and partly by emphasizing that insurance cover is conditional on good character. In 'moral hazard', insurers have given to the world an expression which now captures much about residual personal responsibility in the context of a world where many risks are distributed; and which is routinely used to analyse transactions and relationships of all kinds. Exclusions from the benefits of insurance cover may be either more, or less, demanding of individual responsibility than the law of tort.[59]

Where insurance most often appears to deviate from the law of tort is in its treatment of negligent behaviour, or lack of care. This is one of the key areas where scholars have formed entrenched positions against the relevance of insurance to tort law. While often mandating precautions, insurance does not typically draw the line against the transfer of risk at the point of carelessness. Indeed, the risk of carelessness is one of the key insurable risks. The compatibility between negligence and insurance is, we think, fundamentally important, not least because the developed law of tort does not, in our view, create general responsibility for harm caused by a lack of care either. Rather, 'negligence duties' identify those circumstances in which the risks created by negligence lie with one party rather than another. Tort duties are best seen as relational; and in this respect, their interaction with insurance relationships and with duties to insure is frequent and significant. It is partly for this reason, which also challenges the stark division between tort and contract duties in many instances, that we do not think it appropriate to condemn insurance factors of all kinds to the realms of (extrinsic) 'policy factors'. Insurance is part of the relational fabric of the law of obligations. As we saw in Chapter 1, its presence tends towards complexity generated from the nature of those relations, not towards simple answers based on overarching reasoning.

2.4 Uncertainty and Speculation

In the shifting pattern of insurance research, a feature of particular importance to the law of obligations stands out. This is recognition of the continued role of 'uncertainty', as a supplement to the calculation of risk inherent to the actuarial model. As the focus has shifted to what insurers do, and to the operation of insurance business, it has become increasingly recognized that insurance does not operate solely where risks are

[58] Baker, n 6. Baker identifies Kenneth Arrow's work on health insurance in the 1960s as the catalyst for generalization of the notion of moral hazard into legal and political debate, and into analysis of all transactions (267–9): K Arrow, 'Uncertainty and the Welfare Economics of Medical Care' (1963) 53 Am Econ L Rev 941. Notice however Knight's contention (n 7) that 'moral hazard' (the businessman's influence over the risks he runs) militated against 'external' insurance of typical 'business' risks. His conclusion was that the same techniques could be applied within the undertaking itself. Business risks raising moral hazard and precluding external insurance therefore encouraged growth (consolidation) in corporations, in his view. See further n 63. Arrow's conclusion in favour of state-provided health insurance underlines the complementary nature of actuarial and relational ideas of insurance.

[59] Chapters 10 and 11 take this further. Many distributive schemes incorporate restrictions which scrutinize the responsibility of the claimant. A non-contributory example is criminal injuries compensation which in the UK is limited to 'the blameless victim'—and blame need not be causative of the injury for which compensation is denied. On this point, note the discussion by D Miers, 'Criminal Injuries Compensation: the New Regime' (2001) JPIL 371.

satisfactorily calculable.[60] The distinction between insurable 'risk' and uninsurable 'uncertainty'—a distinction key to the actuarial model—is therefore in question.[61] While insurance emerged before the science of probability,[62] the new perspective emphasizes that the science of probability only explains a part of modern insurance business, too. Insurance also operates where risks are only very imperfectly calculable; and greater significance has begun to be attached to this insight. It is also true, however, that insurers may omit cover for risks that are eminently insurable, for example if the offer of insurance turns on overly broad categorization, or if insurers themselves become risk averse. Behaviour, not purely risk science, holds the key to insurer action in relation to the action of other risk-bearers. This should be no surprise, because it has long been recognized that all business risks are imperfectly calculable, and predictable only on an empirical basis.[63] To one extent or another, insurers may insure where little empirical basis can be established: the catalogue of novel or bespoke risks written by insurers is impressive.[64] In exchange, insurers engage further levels of indemnity and loss distribution, as well as seeking other mechanisms for meeting losses,[65] with evident effects (as we have pointed out) on the cherished idea that insurance consists in the pooling of risks between like risk-bearers.[66]

There is a sense in which this is a liberating insight, since it indicates that large risks do not necessarily and in themselves threaten to break the boundaries of society's capacity to spread or absorb them. In this expanded vision, the role of reinsurers, and their relationship to capital markets, is key in addressing the present role of insurance in society. A focus on the *business* of insurance has therefore been implicated in questioning the predictions of 'risk society' theorists that newer risks operate beyond the boundaries of insurance. These theories may be thought to work with unduly static

[60] Ericson and Doyle, n 12. Also C Heimer, 'Insurers as Moral Actors', in R Ericson and A Doyle, *Risk and Morality* (Toronto: Toronto University Press, 2003).

[61] T Baker, 'The Shifting Terrain of Risk and Uncertainty on the Liability Insurance Field', U Penn, ILE Research Paper No 10-32, Feb 2011, opens with a quotation from Ericson and Doyle (n 12), and suggests that 'The conceptual link between insurance and risk—with risk understood here as the calculable subset within a larger set of uncertainties' may be a concept so ingrained that it has become an impediment to understanding.

[62] Probability became established in relation to mortality tables for use in life assurance. For a history, see G Clark, *Betting on Lives: the Culture of Life Insurance in England 1695–1775* (Manchester: Manchester University Press, 1999). See also n 6.

[63] Knight, *Risk, Uncertainty and Profit*, n 7, ch VIII, espec 232. Knight identified different means of making uncertainty manageable despite this feature: these included consolidation (the grouping of risks); specialization (leading to concentration of risks, and thus consolidation); and diffusion ('the minute divisibility of ownership and ease of transfer of shares') (Knight, n 7, 254). Even those uncertainties least susceptible to empirical calculation could be better managed through any of these techniques; they were deployed by insurers but also by corporations, particularly where moral hazard rendered external insurance inapplicable (Knight, n 7, ch VII). Knight particularly mentioned the willingness of Lloyd's underwriters to cover risks that could not permit of calculation in any true sense, and identified the informed working of intuition as a means of dealing with such contingencies.

[64] A Google search on unusual insurance policies is entertaining. Quite how an insurer will rate the risk of alien abduction (or even impregnation) or the value of a celebrity's physical attributes is a matter for speculation even amongst those in the market.

[65] Particularly necessary in relation to natural catastrophes and perhaps terrorism risk. See for example H Kunreuther and E Michel-Kerjan, *At War with the Weather: Managing Large-Scale Risks in a New Era of Catatrophes* (Cambridge MA: MIT Press, rev edn, 2011), and further discussion in Chapter 6.

[66] See for example J Stapleton, n 55; and the discussion in Chapters 6 and 8.

ideas of insurance derived from the core elements of the actuarial model.[67] On the other hand, there is a further implication, which is that the spreading of risks is not necessarily planned or securely regulated either by law, or by the limits of scientific method. Risk *dispersal* is a feature of the fuller picture once reinsurance is encompassed; but there is also the capacity for inadvertent concentration of risks, raising the very issues which implicated financial instruments in the present economic crisis.[68] The immediate impact of insurance is, in other words, primarily to shift risks, including some which could arguably be designated 'uncertainties', and it is through a series of risk-shifting transactions and instruments that losses, finally, are spread. This has implications for what 'risk-spreading' is and how it operates. The implications may be either positive (the capacity to deal with uncertain risks and with change is increased), or negative (there may be unforeseen consequences of shifting risk, and insurance may ultimately become implicated in the 'systemic' risks associated with financial instruments). There are ongoing debates about the degree to which insurance—a key institution of security—now poses 'systemic' risks.[69]

In this move to recognize both relationality and business uncertainty, the contractual elements of insurance are of evident importance. As we have seen, this has not been entirely neglected by social theorists.[70] This in our view constitutes a little-explored, and much more positive challenge to obligations scholars than the distributive ideal implicit in actuarialism. The general point here is that insurance is not necessarily to be identified solely with the accepted 'actuarial' model, which has generally seemed an external force so far as the law of obligations is concerned, whether positively or negatively received. The essence of insurance may be found in risk-shifting and contractual activity, as much as in loss-spreading. Insurance, like other risk-shifting and loss-spreading techniques, operates to support productive exchange; but more than this, a focus on insurance business shows that it too is to some extent speculative and uncertain.

As we have seen, attempts were made many years ago to draw a distinction between insurance and gambling, in regulatory terms and to some extent in terms of the

[67] Ericson and Doyle, n 12, 17: almost anything can be made insurable—'All that it takes is two parties'. This is a clear reference to the contractual basis of insurance, operating *in distinction to* its actuarial basis, and emanating from the social theoretical literature on insurance. Equally, they propose that Mary Douglas and her followers neglect the willingness of insurers to insure in conditions of uncertainty.

[68] Ericson and Doyle, n 12, 38–39, on 'correlation risk' in relation to terrorism.

[69] The Geneva Association (The International Association for the Study of Insurance Economics, staffed from within the insurance and reinsurance industry) has published various papers suggesting that insurance companies do not pose the same risks as banks; that AIG was not brought down by its insurance business; and that insurers should be differently regulated. For example the Geneva Association, *Systemic Risk in Insurance: An Analysis of Insurance and Financial Stability* (March 2010), available at <http://www.genevaassociation.org/portals/0/Geneva_Association_Systemic_risk_in_Insurance_Report_March2010.pdf>, accessed 21 April 2013. Hallmarks of systemic risk identified for the purposes of international financial services regulation are size, interconnectedness, substitutability, and timing. Evidence that size, leverage, and diversification across insurance lines all *add to* a destabilizing effect in insurance consolidation, while geographic diversification contributes to stability, is presented in G Weiss and J Muhlnickel, 'Consolidation and Systemic Risk in the International Insurance Industry' (4 October 2012, SSRN), available at <http://papers.ssrn.com/sol3/papers.cfm?abstract_id=2135041>, accessed 21 April 2013.

[70] Heimer, n 27, O'Malley, n 28.

rhetoric of insurers themselves.[71] Today, developments have reopened this boundary in new ways, and the debate has begun to draw afresh on a long-standing distinction between useful and legitimate 'hedging'—using futures trading to reduce the risks associated with production—and more troublesome speculation or gambling, which may be destabilizing rather than productive of security.[72] In particular, the boundary between insurance and new financial instruments, and the potential for divergence between short-term gain and long-term financial security, has taken on a new significance in response to the financial crisis, itself precipitated by systemic risks produced by risk-transfer instruments. The spectacular collapse and rescue of the major and highly capitalized US insurance group, American International Group, Inc (AIG), illustrates the degree to which 'insurance' companies may operate beyond the bounds of what is actuarially secure. AIG was rescued by the US government in 2008.[73] While AIG's collapse was not precipitated by what might be called its traditional insurance business, the novel risk instruments which brought it down have themselves been conceptualized as a very complex—and dangerous—form of 'insurance' in the risk-transfer sense.[74] Insurance and financial markets are converging,[75] and the common ground between different institutions and techniques of risk management are a key contemporary concern.[76]

2.5 Conclusions

Insurance is an institution of the market which is directed at profit as much as security; and like obligations law, it necessarily has a close association with market relations. The actuarial model of insurance has had considerable purchase in making insurance appear to be extrinsic to, even incompatible with, the law of obligations. But an alternative relational model of insurance is advancing, and developments in sociological research mean that this is no longer the preserve of economic analysis. This model brings insurance to the core of obligations. Insurance, and related issues of risk transfer, indemnity, reinsurance, and so on, pose challenges not of simplicity

[71] See V Zelizer, *Morals and Markets: The Development of Life Insurance in the United States* (New York: Columbia University Press, 1979), on early US life assurance.

[72] An influential early analysis is E Patterson, 'Gambling and Speculation on Produce Exchanges' (1931) 40 Yale LJ 843.

[73] For identification of credit default swap business as the culprit, and close analysis of the regulatory gap associated with such business, see WK Sjostrom, 'The AIG Bailout' (2009) 66 Wash and Lee L Rev 943.

[74] Stiglitz discusses credit default swaps as a kind of 'insurance' offered by AIG, and without any basic restraint similar to 'insurable interest' which would prevent perverse incentives or prevent a collapse into pure gambling: J Stiglitz, *Freefall: Free Markets and the Sinking of the Global Economy* (Harmondsworth: Penguin, 2010), 169–74. Stiglitz adds that 'Consenting adults should be allowed to gamble... But they should not be allowed to gamble at the expense of the rest of us—and that's what happens when the gambling occurs inside the financial institutions, especially within the too-big-to-fail institutions' (174). This rests of course on a broad, relational concept of insurance.

[75] J Cummins and M Weiss, 'Convergence of Insurance and Financial Markets: Hybrid and Securitized Risk-Transfer Solutions' (2009) 76 *Journal of Risk and Insurance* 493–545.

[76] Discussed even before the financial crisis in TL Hazen, 'Disparate Regulatory Regimes for Parallel Activities: Securities Regulation, Derivatives Regulation, Gambling, and Insurance' (2005) 24 Ann Rev Banking and Fin Law 375; L Stout, 'Insurance or Gambling? Derivatives Trading in a World of Risk and Uncertainty' (1996) 14 Brookings L Rev 38. These sources relate to the US regulatory regime. The UK regime is discussed in Chapter 4.

(the translation of all questions into questions of loss-spreading) but of complexity. Actuarialism and aggregation are not the answer to all questions of responsibility for risk. But neither are they the last word on the nature of insurance, nor definitive of its relationship to obligations law. In assessing the role of law in its response to insurance relationships, the ambitions captured by the actuarial model—relating to aggregation, risk-spreading, and enhanced security—nevertheless always retain their significance to one degree or another.[77] It is against this background that we explore the role of insurance in the law of obligations in the chapters that follow.

[77] An example of this complexity is addressed in Chapter 12, exploring the role of insurance in the development of asbestos liabilities.

3

Insurance Contracts and Insurance Market

3.1 Introduction

In the previous chapter, we identified a relational model of insurance which does not, like the received actuarial model, imagine insurance to be a factor extrinsic to party relationships. Related to this was a renewed interdisciplinary interest in insurance as a business and a market, rather than as an abstract set of technologies. In the present chapter, we begin our exploration of substantive law in light of these insights. With a focus on the position in England and Wales, we introduce the particular nature of insurance contracts and the role of the courts in relation to their interpretation; and outline the ways in which the insurance market itself has developed to meet evolving risks. The exploration in the final sections of the chapter prepares the ground for our later analysis of interaction between different branches of the law of obligations, outlining some of the ways that insurance contracts have interfaced with the law of tort, and exploring some essential features of liability insurance.

3.1.1 First- and Third-Party Insurance

Crucial to the following discussion is the distinction between first- and third-party insurance. First-party insurance protects against loss of or damage to the assured's own person and real or intangible property or financial interests. Third-party insurance covers the risk that the assured may face financial or other liability to another. Third-party insurance is therefore distinctive in that the risks it covers are themselves created by law. It can equally be argued that in creating a liability, the law itself allocates a risk, shifting it from the claimant, on whom the risk otherwise falls as a consequence of the defendant's conduct, on to the defendant.[1] The law, in setting the level of liability, also plays a decisive role in defining (quantifying) the loss to be insured.[2]

Both forms of insurance are commonly contained within the same policy, albeit in different sections. A fully comprehensive motor policy will cover (first-party) injury to the driver and damage to the vehicle and (third-party liability) to any person who is injured or whose property is damaged by the assured's tortious driving. A business may obtain (first-party) cover for its property, for loss of business in the event of physical damage, and for any liability incurred by the business in respect of injury inflicted upon

[1] This is the theme of Chapter 8. More generally, see T Baker, 'On the Genealogy of Moral Hazard' (1996) 75 *Texas Law Review* 237, concluding that it is a mistake to equate liability backed by insurance with redistribution, in contrast to no liability. Where there is no liability, it may equally be said that potential claimants are 'insuring' potential defendants and the result is equally distributive (291).

[2] The intervention of insurers may in turn have a significant impact on the costs incurred and damages awarded: C Heimer, 'Insurers as Moral Actors', in R Ericson and A Doyle (eds), *Risk and Morality* (Toronto: Toronto University Press, 2003).

the person or property of others, be they employees (employers' liability insurance), innocent bystanders (public liability insurance), or purchasers or users of the business's goods (product liability).

There are two significant statutory differences in the treatment of first- and third-party insurance. First, there are no compulsory first-party policies in English law but, as Chapter 9 illustrates, there are numerous examples whereby persons are required to insure against liabilities arising out of particular activities. Secondly, in the event of the assured's insolvency, the proceeds of a first-party policy which belong to the assured[3] fall to be distributed as unsecured assets in whatever insolvency regime is applicable to the assured.[4] By contrast, in the case of a liability policy, proceeds are payable directly to any third party who has established and quantified the assured's liability, in accordance with the Third Parties (Rights against Insurers) Act 1930 (to be replaced from a date yet to be determined by the Third Parties (Rights against Insurers) Act 2010). Compulsory insurance and third-party claims are discussed, respectively, in Chapters 9 and 13.

3.2 When is a Contract One of Insurance?

We explored the general character of insurance in Chapter 2. Looking at the issue in terms of the insurance contract, the assured pays some form of premium to the insurers in return for which the insurers agree to make payment to the assured on the occurrence of an event which is uncertain either by reason that it may or may not happen (non-life) or by reason of when it will happen (life). Nevertheless, nowhere in legislation or judicial decisions is there an exhaustive definition of these concepts. That is because there is no single purpose for a definition, but rather a variety of purposes for which different definitions may be appropriate. The common law applies discrete rules to insurance contracts based upon the nature of information asymmetry and risk inherent in such transactions, statute dictates basic requirements for and relating to certain insurance contracts, and there is a comprehensive regulatory structure applicable to insurance business generally, explored in Chapter 4. The needs of each of these categories vary: the reason for asking the question whether a contract attracts a duty of 'utmost good faith'[5] is quite different from the reason for asking whether a contract forms part of a business which should attract prudential supervision. Closely related to insurance contracts are, for example, guarantees,[6] wagers,[7] risk-transfer devices,[8] and arrangements with brokers.[9] The line between these and insurance is not fixed and actually shifts, depending upon why the distinction is relevant. For example, guarantees and performance bonds are not contracts of insurance under any accepted definition of

[3] Proceeds may be mortgaged, or there may be co-assureds who are entitled to payment out of the proceeds in priority to the insolvent assured.

[4] Subject to a limited exception for life insurance in respect of married couples and their offspring: Married Women's Property Act 1884, s 11.

[5] A distinctive feature of insurance contracts, discussed in 3.3.

[6] *The Zuhal K and The Selin* [1987] 1 Lloyd's Rep 151.

[7] *Newbury v Reliance International Insurance* [1994] 1 Lloyd's Rep 83.

[8] *GMA v Storebrand* [1995] LRLR 333.

[9] *Pryke v Gibbs Hartley Cooper Ltd* [1991] 1 Lloyd's Rep 602.

insurance because the ultimate risk is not borne by the guarantor who will have a right of recourse against the debtor, but the business of issuing such securities is insurance business for regulatory purposes. That is because regulation of these instruments shares the same concern as regulation of insurance, namely the need to preserve the solvency of the contractual indemnifier, and therefore to provide security to the contracting party. Regulation, in this sense, is protective.

The common law also distinguishes between insurance and other contracts when categorizing terms, in the respects discussed below. However, parties are, subject to those principles dictated by public policy,[10] free to contract out of the consequences, and they frequently do so. There is little in the way of substantive legislation which distinguishes insurance from other arrangements. The Marine Insurance Act 1906 (explored in the next section) lays down a set of mandatory rules and default rules which apply to marine insurance contracts, but ever since the prohibition of wagering policies by the Marine Insurance Act 1745, re-enacted in the 1906 Act, attempts to disguise wagers as insurance have largely disappeared and the jurisdictional battle over the application of the legislation has shifted to the question whether the risk insured is marine or non-marine.[11] The Life Assurance Act 1774 requires insurable interest for life insurances, and we explore some aspects of its continuing influence in Chapter 5. The Third Parties (Rights against Insurers) Acts 1930 and 2010 allow the victim of an insolvent assured to bring proceedings against insurers where there is a contract of insurance in place. The Road Traffic Act 1988 demands insurance against liability for injuries caused by or arising out of the use of motor vehicles in public places, but the need for a definition is averted because the statutory requirements can be fulfilled by the alternative means of a deposit or security equivalent to insurance. The remaining pieces of legislation which impose compulsory insurance requirements do not seek to provide a definition of what is required.[12] There are also mentions of insurance in other legislation. For example, the Unfair Contract Terms Act 1977 excludes from its ambit contracts of insurance, and both the Rome I Regulation 2009 on applicable law[13] and the Brussels Judgments Regulation 2001[14] set out specific rules for insurance contracts, but the authorities on these matters do not proffer a general definition.

3.2.1 Classes of Insurance

The definition of 'insurance' matters most immediately in the context of regulation. As will be discussed in Chapter 4, until 2000 statutory regulation focused on solvency rather than substantive rights. The earliest legislation was based on the regulation of

[10] For example insurable interest (3.3).

[11] The distinction is clarified in *Mercantile Mutual Insurance (Australia) Ltd v Gibbs* [2003] HCA 39; [2003] 5 LRC 419. The distinction is crucial in Australia, as there are entirely separate regimes for the two forms of insurance: R Merkin, 'Australia: Still a Nation of Chalmers?' (2011) 30 UQLJ 189.

[12] Discussed in Chapter 9.

[13] Art 7.

[14] Arts 9–15. Due to be replaced in 2015 without substantive change by the European Parliament and Council Regulation 1215/2012/EU.

'insurance business carried on under policies of insurance', and the cases on the scope of the legislation turned not on the substantive question of whether the insurance activity was being conducted but rather on whether the activity manifested itself in 'policies'.[15] That wording was in due course replaced by what remains the modern formulation, attracting the regulatory structure to a person who is 'carrying out or effecting contracts'[16] of one or more of the eighteen specified classes of non-life (general) insurance and the nine specified classes of life and related (long-term) insurance. The division of business into classes is a result of the historical development of the regulation of the solvency of insurers, which began in 1870 with life business and was gradually extended to different classes of general business as their social and economic importance became apparent. We trace the development in Chapter 4, but here it suffices to identify the various classes so that risks covered by insurance can be easily appreciated.

(1) Accident: benefits payable on personal injury.

(2) Sickness: benefits payable on sickness or infirmity.

(3) Land vehicles: loss of or damage to vehicles used on land.

(4) Railway rolling stock: loss of or damage to railway rolling stock.

(5) Aircraft: loss of or damage to the machinery, tackle, furniture, or equipment of aircraft.

(6) Ships: loss of or damage to vessels used on the sea or on inland water, or upon the machinery, tackle, furniture, or equipment of vessels.

(7) Goods in transit: loss of or damage to all goods in transit, irrespective of the form of transport.

(8) Fire and natural forces: loss of or damage to property (other than property within classes (3)–(7)) due to fire, explosion, storm, natural forces other than storm, nuclear energy, or land subsidence.

(9) Damage to property: loss of or damage to property (other than property within classes (3)–(7)) due to hail or frost or any other event other than those identified in class (8).

(10) Motor vehicle liability: third-party liability arising out of or in connection with the use of motor vehicles on land.

(11) Aircraft liability: third-party liability arising out of or in connection with the use of aircraft.

(12) Liability of ships: third-party liability arising out of or in connection with the use of vessels on the sea or on inland water.

(13) General liability: third-party liability not covered by classes (10)–(12).

[15] *Hampton v Toxteth Co-operative Society* [1915] 1 Ch 721. *Hall D'Ath v British Provident Association* (1932) 48 TLR 240.

[16] The meaning of this phrase has proved elusive, and has been held to include the writing of risks and the paying of claims: *Re AA Mutual Insurance Co Ltd* [2004] EWHC 2430 (Ch); [2004] All ER (D) 34 (Dec); *Re Whiteley Insurance Consultants* [2008] EWHC 1782 (Ch); [2009] Lloyd's Rep IR 212.

(14) Credit: risks of loss arising from the insolvency of debtors or failure of debtors to pay their debts.

(15) Suretyship: loss arising from their having to perform contracts of guarantee[17] or having to honour bonds entered into by them.

(16) Miscellaneous financial loss: loss by way of business interruption, unforeseen expense, or other risks which are not of a kind such that contracts of insurance against them fall within any other class.[18]

(17) Legal expenses: loss attributable to incurring legal expenses, including litigation costs.

(18) Assistance: benefits, whether in cash or kind, for persons who get into difficulties while travelling or otherwise.

The nine classes of long-term business are:

(1) Life and annuity.
(2) Marriage and birth.
(3) Linked long term: annuities linked to income from property.
(4) Permanent health: benefits against incapacity from injury or sickness for a period of not less than five years.
(5) Tontines.[19]
(6) Capital redemption contracts.
(7) Pension fund management.
(8) Collective insurance.[20]
(9) Social insurance.[21]

3.2.2 Legal definitions of insurance

Various judicial definitions of insurance have been attempted.[22] These identify the basic elements in terms compatible with the 'relational' or 'risk-transfer' model outlined in Chapter 2, namely, a contractual right of recovery on the occurrence of an uncertain event which is adverse to the assured in return for payment of a premium.[23]

[17] As noted above, such contracts are not 'insurance' for any other purpose: *Trade Indemnity Co v Workington Dock and Harbour Board* [1937] AC 1; [1936] 1 All ER 454. However, such contracts are an established part of the business of insurers and thus have been brought within the regulatory structure.

[18] This general safety-net class has been held to include mechanical breakdown cover: *Digital Satellite Warranty Ltd* [2013] UKSC 7; [2013] 1 WLR 605.

[19] A form of mutual insurance under which the sums are payable to the last surviving member.

[20] A form of mutual life insurance confined to France.

[21] Relevant in those EU jurisdictions where private insurance companies are given responsibility for managing state social insurance schemes.

[22] M Clarke, *The Law of Insurance Contracts* (London: Informa, 6th edn, 2009), ch 1, 'Definition or Description?'

[23] *Prudential Insurance v Inland Revenue Commissioners* [1904] 2 KB 658; *Callaghan v Dominion Insurance Co* [1997] 2 Lloyd's Rep 541; *Republic of Iran Shipping Lines v Steamship Mutual Underwriting Association (Bermuda) Ltd* [2010] EWHC 2661 (Comm); [2011] 1 Lloyd's Rep 195.

A fruitful exercise is to consider the guidelines issued by the Financial Services Authority (FSA), the functions of which were transferred to the Financial Conduct Authority and the Prudential Regulatory Authority in 2013.[24] These are neither binding nor exhaustive, but show the approach of the FSA and now its replacement regulators in distinguishing between insurance and the various other forms of arrangement which may be found. Relevant considerations are the following but, as may be seen by our annotations, they do not always reflect either judicial decisions or market practice. Equally, it will be seen that the nature of the guidelines is consistent with the absence of any 'bright line' definition: a range of features exists, and these indicate whether the arrangement is more, or less, likely to be considered 'insurance'.

(1) '*Whether the provider has an absolute discretion as to whether any benefit is provided on the occurrence of the uncertain event. If so, there is unlikely to be a contract of insurance even though the discretion has never been exercised to deny a benefit.*' Such discretions may be found in the rules of professional bodies[25] and, most importantly, Protection & Indemnity (P&I) Clubs providing mutual liability insurance for shipowners, but the latter has been held to be insurance for the purposes of the 1930 (2010) Act.[26]

(2) '*Whether the provider has assumed the risk of loss by agreeing to provide a benefit or service, such assumption being an indication of insurance.*' Although insurance typically involves payment of a sum by the insurers, it suffices if the benefit is money's worth, for example repairs to damaged property[27] or the provision of a replacement, and the supply of services (for example roadside recovery[28]).

(3) '*Whether the contract is one under which the amount and timing of the payments made by the recipient make it reasonable to conclude that there is a genuine pre-payment for services to be rendered in response to a future contingency. If so, the contract is unlikely to be one of insurance.*'

(4) '*Contracts under which the provider undertakes to provide periodic maintenance of goods or facilities, whether or not any uncertain or adverse event (in the form of, for example, a breakdown or failure) has occurred, are unlikely to be contracts of insurance.*' The need for an uncertain event in times of occurrence (property, liability) or timing (life) is crucial to insurance. It was held in *Fuji Finance Ltd v Aetna Insurance Co Ltd*[29] that a contract which provides a number of triggers of payment, only one of which is the death of the life assured, is a life policy.

(5) '*Contracts under which, in consideration for an initial payment, the provider stands ready to provide services on the occurrence of a future contingency, on condition*

[24] Chapter 4.

[25] *Medical Defence Union v Department of Trade* [1979] 2 WLR 686.

[26] *Re Allobrogia Steamship Corporation* [1979] 1 Lloyd's Rep 190.

[27] *Re Sentinel Securities Ltd* [1966] 1 WLR 316; *Re Cavalier Insurance Co Ltd* [1989] 2 Lloyd's Rep 430; *Digital Satellite Warranty Cover Ltd v Financial Services Authority* [2013] UKSC 7; [2013] 1 WLR 605.

[28] However, this form of insurance has been exempted from regulation under the Financial Services and Markets Act 2000 (Regulated Activities) Order 2001, Art 12 where the provider does not carry on any other form of insurance business.

[29] [1997] Ch 173; [1996] 3 WLR 871.

that the services actually provided are paid for by the recipient at a commercial rate, are unlikely to be regarded as insurance.'

(6) '*The consideration paid by the recipient need not be in the form of a distinct premium.*' The consideration provided for most insurance policies is a single premium which purchases cover for an agreed period. Three modifications may be noted: mutual associations may demand additional premium during the policy year if losses exceed the insurance funds; insurance may be simply one element of a contract, eg membership of a society providing a variety of benefits; and some policies do not involve payment of any premium at all, the most obvious example being an After the Event (ATE) litigation policy which we describe in Chapter 13.

(7) '*If the provider assumes more than one obligation under a contract, some of which are insurance and some are not, then if the provider undertakes an identifiable and distinct obligation, that is, in substance an insurance obligation, the FSA is likely to find that by undertaking that obligation the provider has effected a contract of insurance even though that obligation is not substantial in comparison with the other obligations in the contract or in comparison with the rest of the provider's business.*' This substantiality test was doubted at first instance in *Digital Satellite Warranty Cover Ltd v Financial Services Authority*,[30] in favour of the view that a contract which contains different elements is to be regarded as composite so that parts of it may fall into different classes.

(8) '*A contract is more likely to be regarded as of insurance if the amount payable by the recipient under the contract is calculated by reference to either or both of the probability of occurrence or likely severity of the uncertain event.*'

(9) '*A contract is less likely to be regarded as of insurance if it requires the provider to assume a speculative risk (i.e. a risk carrying the possibility of either profit or loss) rather than a pure risk (i.e. a risk of loss only).*' This is the classic definition of a wager. The key element of insurance is risk transfer, a point indicated but (interestingly) not specified by this criterion. Thus an intermediary who writes risks as agent for insurers, and who pays claims on behalf of insurers, cannot be said to be entering into contracts of insurance because he does not undertake any liability.[31]

(10) '*A contract is more likely to be regarded as of insurance if it is described as such and contains terms that are consistent with that classification, eg the duty of utmost good faith.*' It was held in *HIH Casualty and General Insurance v Chase Manhattan Bank*[32] that a contract does not lose its identity as one of insurance simply because the rules of law which characterize insurance—in particular, the duty of utmost good faith—have been excluded.

(11) '*A contract does not cease to be one of insurance simply because the terms included are not usual insurance terms.*'

This rather imprecise picture forms the background to the regulation of insurance contracts via common law, in which contracts of insurance are subject to some distinctive principles.

[30] [2011] EWHC 122 (Ch); [2011] All ER (D) 01 (Feb).
[31] *Card Protection Plan v European Commission* Case C-240/99.
[32] [2003] UKHL 6; [2003] 2 Lloyd's Rep 61.

3.3 Principles of Insurance Contract Law: an Introduction

Insurance is simply one class of contract, albeit a specialized one. Insurance contracts have a distinctive history.[33] They were perhaps the first in England—by the Lloyd's SG Policy which was, after several decades of trial and error, perfected[34] by 1779 and which dominated the London and indeed international markets until it was abandoned in 1992—to achieve a standard form.[35] It should be emphasized from the outset that the process by which such contracts are written has implications for the way in which they may be interpreted.[36] What follows is an outline of the distinctive principles of insurance law. The aim is to offer the reader some orientation to prepare for the discussion of more complex and multi-party issues raised in later chapters, while also going some way to locate the potential contribution of insurance contracts to the study of contracting more generally.

3.3.1 The anatomy of an insurance contract

Insured risks vary from the relatively simple (for example a householder's policy) to the inordinately complex (for example an energy policy or a reinsurance treaty), but they have various common features, although not necessarily expressed in the same terms and not necessarily in the following order. The key provision is the insuring clause, which defines the subject matter of the policy. If it is a first-party insurance, the property or life will be identified. If it is a liability cover, the policy will define the activities protected: public liability policies may be general, but professional indemnity policies will restrict cover to liability arising out of the activities of the professional activities of the assured so that there is a need to distinguish between professional activities from, eg, business development[37] or recreational activities.[38] A part of the insuring clause will be the maximum sum insured (whether per claim or by way of annual aggregate for all claims) and the amount of any per claim'deductible'.[39] Large commercial policies are written in layers of cover, so that there will be a 'tower' consisting of the amount of the assured's deductible then a primary layer of cover up to a given financial limit, followed by one or more excess layers which are triggered when the loss exceeds the limits of the lower layer(s).

The insuring clause may be general, covering 'all risks', which is typical for goods in transit policies and other insurances on commercial property. Other types of cover will

[33] An excellent summary of the history of doctrine is given in M Lobban, *The Oxford History of the Laws of England* (Oxford: Oxford University Press, 2010), vol xii, 1-64.

[34] If that is the correct term for a document which over the next 200 years was subjected to a torrent of judicial abuse, including being described as drafted by a sadist with a sense of humour. A flavour may be found in *Arnould's Law of Marine Insurance and Average* (London: Sweet & Maxwell, 18th edn, 2013), para 2.22.

[35] Different readings of standardization, and their applicability to insurance, are discussed in the following paragraphs.

[36] Discussed in the following paragraphs. Note also Chapter 12 relating to asbestos liability in particular.

[37] *Sutherland Professional Funding Ltd v Bakewells* [2011] EWHC 2658 (Comm).

[38] *Caple v Sewell* [2001] EWCA Civ 1848; [2001] All ER (D) 466 (Nov). Contrast *Lane v Dive Two Pty Ltd* [2012] NSWSC 104.

[39] The first part of the loss borne by the assured, in consumer policies referred to as the assured's 'excess'.

list the insured perils. Whether the policy is all risks or confined to specific perils, there will be a number of excluded perils. The incidence of the burden of proof depends upon the nature of the policy. In all cases the assured must prove that a loss has occurred. Where the policy is against all risks, the assured does not have to show that any particular peril was the proximate cause of the loss, and instead the insurer bears the burden of proving that an exclusion was the proximate cause. By contrast, if the policy is against specific risks, the assured must show that his loss was proximately caused by a listed peril, and the insurers may then seek to demonstrate that an exclusion was also operative. The governing default principle is common law causation, a test which is in principle much the same as the 'but for' test applicable in tort.[40] However, insurance law has developed its response to causative questions independently of the law of tort. In practice, a first difference is that insurance law responds in an all-or-nothing fashion to the possibility of two (or more) concurrent causes of a loss,[41] whereas tort law recognizes apportionment—through contribution—where there are two or more tortfeasors, and tort liability is otherwise not averted by the presence of a second, non-tortious cause. A second significant difference stems from the fact that parties to insurance contracts are free to, and regularly do, vary the rules of causation by express term.[42]

Thereafter the policy will list the obligations of the parties, or, more accurately, the assured. These obligations will be expressed as conditions or warranties,[43] and will include the payment of the premium, a duty to take reasonable care, other obligations relating to the subject matter (such as security devices and inspections) and the procedures to be followed for the making of claims. Finally, the policy will contain dispute resolution provisions, including choice of law and choice of forum or arbitration.[44]

3.3.2 The placement process

Domestic and small business policies are written by single insurers. Large commercial risks may, however, be regarded as too large for a single insurer to accept, and here use is made of the subscription market whereby a number of insurers can agree to participate. Until 2009, the London subscription market operated a formation process

[40] *Orient-Express Hotels Ltd v Assicurazioni General SA* [2010] EWHC 1186 (Comm); [2010] All ER (D) 282 (May); *Employers' Liability Insurance 'Trigger' Litigation: BAI (Run Off) Ltd v Durham* [2012] UKSC 14; [2012] 1 WLR 867.

[41] If the loss is the result of the concurrent operation of an insured peril and a specifically excluded peril, the exclusion takes priority (*Wayne Tank and Pump Co Ltd v Employers Liability Assurance Corporation Ltd* [1974] QB 57; [1973] 3 WLR 483) whereas if an insured peril and an uninsured peril work together, there is no relevant exclusion and there is coverage (*Global Maritime Systems Inc v Syarkat Takaful Malaysia Berhad, The Cendor Mopu* [2011] UKSC 5; [2011] 1 Lloyd's Rep 560).

[42] Thus a policy may require loss to be caused solely and exclusively by an insured peril, so that any form of external contribution removes coverage. An example is *Southampton Leisure Holdings plc v Avon Insurance plc* [2004] All ER (D) 310 (Feb). There is complex and inconsistent authority on the question whether words such as 'arising from' or 'resulting from' modify the causation test: there is a review of the authorities in *British Waterways v Royal & Sun Alliance Insurance plc* [2012] EWHC 460 (Comm); [2012] Lloyd's Rep IR 562.

[43] The special meaning of these terms in insurance law is outlined in later paragraphs.

[44] Or sometimes all of them, creating a conflict which the courts generally resolve in favour of arbitration: *Sulamerica CIA Nacional De Seguros SA v Enesa Engenharia SA* [2012] EWCA Civ 638; [2013] 1 WLR 102.

which consisted of the presentation by the broker of a 'slip': a brief document summarizing the cover sought and taking effect in law as an offer. The slip would then be presented in succession to a series of underwriters, each subscribing to a percentage of the risk (a 'line') by signing and stamping ('scratching') the slip and thereby accepting the offer in the slip. Very often, an individual underwriter would amend the slip, by means of a 'subjectivity' affecting the terms of that underwriter's participation. A policy would be issued thereafter. All of this posed two problems: very often policy wording would not be issued, so that exactly what had been agreed was unclear (an intriguing feature of contracts whose very purpose is supposedly to determine who bears a risk); and where such wording did appear it might be inconsistent with the slip, giving rise to a series of difficult cases on rectification.[45] The slip was replaced in 2009 by a procedure under which the terms of the contract in full are presented to each underwriter in a standard framework form which identifies the broad headings to be included in the wording, the 'Market Reform Contract', for scratching. As before, subjectivities are added in the placement process, and each subscription creates a separate contract for the agreed line, with liability being several and not joint and several so that no one underwriter is liable beyond its own percentage subscription. The final version of a Market Reform Contract after presentation to the market is often one littered with handwritten amendments.

3.3.3 Drafting and standard forms

In the UK, consumer and small business policies are normally in forms devised by individual insurers for their own purposes and there is little room for negotiation. Similar phrases often appear, but they are based on both common experience and judicial interpretations and may vary widely in their terms and coverage.

As far as commercial risks are concerned, these are for the most part placed through brokers. Each firm of brokers has developed its own wordings for particular risks, and there may be significant differences between those wordings. Further, the underwriting process described above will generally result in changes being made on a case-by-case basis. The Lloyd's Market Association is itself constantly working on the drafting of clauses on particular matters, taking into account market changes and developing case law, and its efforts take the form of recommendations to both Lloyd's Syndicates and insurance companies. The International Underwriting Association[46] performs a similar task, and its primary achievement over 130 years has been the development of recommended standard wordings for marine policies, the 'Institute Clauses'. Both providers and—through their agents (brokers)—users, are represented in negotiations for recommended wordings, and the outcome is generally regarded as a fair compromise between the parties' conflicting interests and with the capability of reducing the costs of negotiation in any one case. If the correct balance is not achieved, the wordings

[45] *HIH Casualty and General Insurance v New Hampshire Insurance* [2001] EWCA Civ 735; [2001] 2 Lloyd's Rep 161.

[46] Before 1999 under the separate guises of the London Insurance and Reinsurance Market Association and the Institute of London Underwriters.

are disregarded: this may be seen from the fate of the International Hull Clauses 2003, which are rarely used because they are regarded as too favourable to insurers as regards restrictions on cover and as regards the claims obligations imposed upon policyholders: broker pressure has ensured that the market generally adheres to the more benign earlier versions of the Hull Clauses as promulgated in 1982 and 1996.

It would be wrong, therefore, to classify insurance policies as 'standard form' even though their content is heavily influenced by market organizations. That point aside, there is a prohibition in both UK and EU competition law on agreements between insurers fixing the terms on which cover is to be provided.[47] It is certainly more accurate to regard consumer policies as 'contracts of adhesion' in that they are normally presented on a 'take it or leave it' basis, but there is intense competition between insurers on terms and not just on premium rates.

The most common class of insurance disputes involves construction and the meaning of words.[48] Some of the factors pointed out in the previous discussion contribute to the likelihood that insurance contracts will be prone to such disputes: in large commercial risks the wording is generally prepared by brokers and submitted to underwriters for discussion, but those negotiating the actual placements are rarely legally qualified; shorthand expression is often used; market understandings of particular words may be assumed, but may differ from the law; there is a tendency to cut and paste from previous wordings, which can give rise to inconsistency or 'black holes'; and some policies appear to be drafted on the basis that the draftsman was paid by the word, the result of lengthy negotiation of particular points, with the wording reflecting exceptions to exceptions to exceptions. External lawyers are used by insurers to review wordings in general, but only rarely is legal advice taken when a particular risk is being written. Somewhere in the policy will be a list of defined terms as used in the rest of the document, but such definitions can on occasion be a distinct hindrance, as when the same word is used for two different purposes but the definition is suitable for only one of them.[49] So while there is limited standardization, it forms part of a mixed picture. That is the background to the interpretation of insurance contracts in the UK.

There is much US scholarship on contracting and on insurance contracts. Some work classifies certain insurance policies as 'contracts of adhesion'.[50] Indeed, it was through studies of life insurance contracts that the term 'contract of adhesion' was imported into common law scholarship,[51] and they have been referred to as the

[47] As far as the UK is concerned, the matter is governed by the general provisions of the Competition Act 1998. TFEU Art 101 prohibits restrictive agreements, but exemption is given to certain co-insurance arrangements, risk pools, and risk information exchanges by the Insurance Block Exemption, Council Regulation 267/2010/EC.

[48] This is reflected in the reported cases and also in the practical experience of the authors.

[49] For example, the word 'claim' in a liability policy can equally refer to the claim by the third party against the assured and the claim by the assured against the insurers, to which quite different considerations will apply.

[50] F Kessler, 'Contracts of Adhesion—Some Thoughts About Freedom of Contract' (1943) 43 Col L Rev 629. Some detailed qualifying features of such contracts were identified by T Rakoff, 'Contracts of Adhesion: An Essay in Reconstruction' (1983) 96 Harv Law Rev 1173. These include absence of negotiation of terms and the role of the 'adherent' as simply paying money in relation to the contract.

[51] Kessler, n 50, attributed the term to E Patterson, 'The Delivery of a Life Insurance Policy' (1919–1920) 33 Harv L Rev 198, though it is clear that Patterson drew it from French law.

'archetype' of such contracts.[52] In US scholarship, 'contracts of adhesion' are regarded with suspicion, interpretation of such contracts is recognized to raise issues of consumer protection, and they are thought to amount almost to 'private legislation',[53] so scrutiny is intense. The very idea of a 'contract of adhesion' implies a power imbalance. Kessler, who popularized the term, thought of them as a reflection of the rise of large corporations and decline in Western freedom.[54] It is also observed by some in the United States that insurance contracts are standardized. The two ideas have been run together and even addressed as the same phenomenon,[55] not surprisingly because contracts of adhesion are distinguished partly by their standard terms.[56]

All of this is to be regarded with some caution when addressing the position in the UK. It might be thought to pay insufficient weight to the varied nature of insurance contracts, some of which may be the result of inequality of bargaining but many of which are not,[57] and it also overlooks the evolution of wordings through trial and error and market experience. The role of the courts may in some cases be to protect the weaker party[58] and in others to choose between two equally plausible constructions of a complex commercial document.[59]

There indeed appears to be a marked difference between the approach of the English and US courts in the interpretation of insurance contracts.[60] It has been noted that US courts regard insurers as 'part of an industry which is affected by the public interest', so that insurers take on wider responsibilities than those who are parties to 'purely private contracts'.[61] There is little sign that English courts see insurance contracts as other than 'private', though this is not to deny that commercial contracts themselves are also recognized as giving rise in some circumstances to notions of relational fairness, trust,

[52] M Clarke, *Policies and Perceptions of Insurance Law in the Twenty-First Century* (Oxford: Oxford University Press, 2005), 138.

[53] Clarke, n 52.

[54] Priest suggests a belief on Kessler's part that a point of law of no greater significance than the 'postal rule' encapsulated the decline of Western democracy: G Priest, 'The Invention of Enterprise Liability' (1985) 14 J Leg Stud 461; G Priest, 'Contracts Then and Now: An Appreciation of Friedrich Kessler' (1995) 104 Yale Law J 2145.

[55] Clarke, n 52, draws on the very critical account of D Slawson, 'Standard Form Contracts and Democratic Control of Lawmaking Power' (1971) 84 Harv Law Rev 529.

[56] Given risk-reducing obligations and advice associated with insurance in many instances, there is an argument for extending Macneil's idea of 'bureaucratic goods', and approaching insurance as a 'bureaucratic service': I Macneil, 'Bureaucracy and Contracts of Adhesion' (1984) 22 Osgoode Hall LJ 5.

[57] The market strength of brokers is a vital countervailing power which theory disregards.

[58] Although in practice the weaker party to an insurance contract will have the protection of the Financial Ombudsman Service and will not need to seek recourse to the courts.

[59] The difference is between regulation via commercial expectation and regulation in line with public purpose. The two are not strongly differentiated by, eg, H Collins, *Regulating Contracts* (Oxford: Oxford University Press, 1999), ch 1, which is preoccupied with contrasting contextualism (which could mean either of these) with formalism.

[60] The great difference between the US and English context is illustrated by comparing the discussion here with J Stempel, 'The Insurance Policy as Statute' (2009–10) 41 McGeorge Law Rev 203. See also J Lowry and P Rawlings, 'Insurers, Claims and the Boundaries of Good Faith' (1995) 68 MLR 82, and R Hasson, 'The Special Nature of the Insurance Contract: A Comparison of the American and English Law of Insurance' (1984) 47 MLR 505.

[61] Lowry and Rawlings, n 60, 90–91, quoting *Continental Life & Accident Co v Songer* 603 P.2d 921 (Ariz. 1979).

and cooperation.[62] While it might very well be argued that there are differences in the way that English and US courts approach their role in relation to contracts in general,[63] there is also a specific difference in that the US courts have adopted a 'consumerist' approach to insurance policies which is based on the 'reasonable expectations of the assured', an approach eschewed in the UK.[64] It is our view that where public purpose is evident, and particularly where it is expressed in legislation, a perception of that purpose may tangibly influence the decision-making of the courts. Equally, the absence of such clear purpose has a similar, negative effect.[65] In the UK, the most tangible public purpose directly affecting insurance contracts has been in relation to liability insurance. In the United States, evident public purpose is much broader, and the drafting of standard contracts is itself a quasi-public process in some instances: standardization here may actually have a protective objective[66] and, through the interpretive efforts of the courts, a protective effect.

3.3.4 The law relating to insurance contracts

3.3.4.1 Sources of the law

Insurance is largely governed by common law, with—at least until recently—minor statutory intervention. The Marine Insurance Act 1906, along with the other legislative achievements of Parliamentary draftsman Sir Mackenzie Chalmers,[67] is a codifying measure which did not seek to modify or predict the law but rather embodied the principles laid down by the courts in the preceding 150 years, plus some old marine legislation, and in this sense it does not alter the dominance of the law developed by the courts. Many of the applicable concepts are unique to the marine market, although some are shared with non-marine law, but in practice much of the Act has been abandoned by the market, in the form of standard Institute Clauses for hull, cargo, war risks, and other perils. The only parts of the legislation that are mandatory are those founded on eighteenth- and nineteenth-century legislation and on the formalities of the contract (ss 22–24)[68] and demanding insurable interest

[62] We return to these issues below.

[63] It is hard to imagine an English lawyer confidently arguing, with George Priest, that 'Contracts is a course addressing the regulation of private transactions in which our courts, as self-conscious social engineers, are evaluated in terms of their ability to define rules that optimally assign risks and informational burdens in order to broadly enhance societal welfare': 'Contracts Then and Now', n 54 2145.

[64] The most recent rejection of the US principle is in *AstraZeneca Insurance Company Ltd v XL Insurance (Bermuda) Ltd* [2013] EWHC 349 (Comm); [2013] All ER (D) 08 (Mar).

[65] There are close parallels with bank regulation, as discussed by A Hudson, 'The Synthesis of Public and Private in Finance Law', in K Barker and D Jensen (eds), *Private Law: Key Encounters with Public Law* (Cambridge: Cambridge University Press, 2013). The author identifies a challenge to the rigidity of the public-private divide and particularly explores how 'regulations created and imposed by public bodies can fruitfully come to mould private law principles and rules as they apply to financial transactions'. Also J Beatson, 'Public Law Influences in Contract Law', in J Beatson and D Friedmann, *Good Faith and Fault in Contract Law* (Oxford: Clarendon Press, 1995).

[66] This is not unusual. For example, standard forms used in conveyancing operate to provide some protection to buyers and sellers by setting common professional standards.

[67] Including the Sale of Goods Act 1893, the Bills of Exchange Act 1882, and the Partnership Act 1890.

[68] Adopted to prevent the evasion of stamp duty on policy documents, but now largely redundant. LCIP 9 and LCCD 3 make proposals for their repeal.

(ss 4–15). There are no statutory mandatory rules for first-party non-life policies, other than the insurable interest requirement under the Life Assurance Act 1774, discussed in subsequent paragraphs. Such legislation as there is regulates the terms of motor and employers' liability insurance, matters discussed in Chapter 9.

In what follows we discuss the key points at which insurance law departs from ordinary contractual principles. It should be emphasized that the common law as developed in the eighteenth century in the marine market, and subsequently extended to non-marine policies, was designed for commerce. Consumer policies, which appeared in the second half of the twentieth century, were simply subjected to the same rules, often described as draconian in that the defences open to insurers are commonly unconnected to the circumstances of any claim that the assured may have and may well operate irrespective of any prejudice to the insurers. In more recent years, the courts have intervened to enhance the fairness of the operation of 'good faith', for example, with interpretation of commercial contracts leading the way.

At the beginning of 2006 the English and Scottish Law Commissions launched a comprehensive review of insurance law, a process which is due to be completed at the end of 2013. The Law Commissions had, by the end of 2012, published nine Issues Papers (LCIPs)[69] and three Consultation Documents (LCCDs),[70] the first of which resulted in legislation, the Consumer Insurance (Representations and Disclosure) Act 2012. Reference will be made to these documents at various points, and they are an excellent source of authority for the propositions discussed in the following paragraphs.

3.3.4.2 *Insurable interest and indemnity*

Insurance policies must be supported by insurable interest, in that the assured must be interested in the subject matter in order to insure it. Various attempts have been made to define insurable interest, although the modern formulation recognizes that interest exists if the assured stands to benefit from the preservation of the subject matter or to suffer loss if it is destroyed. In the past the formulation was more exacting, requiring a legal or equitable interest in the subject matter, though this could, by definition, not operate in the same way in relation to life insurance and the test there was that of pecuniary interest.[71] The test has been diluted in a variety of contexts, inevitable given that the complex commercial relationships which today exist could not have been contemplated in the eighteenth century when the requirement was formulated. It was

[69] The LCIPs are: 1 Misrepresentation and Non-Disclosure (2006); 2 Warranties (2006); 3 Intermediaries and Pre-Contract Information (2007); 4 Insurable Interest (2008); 5 Micro-Businesses (2009); 6 Damages for Late Payment (2010); 7 Insured's Post-Contractual Duty of Good Faith (2010); 8 Broker's Liability for Premiums (2010); 9 Requirements for a Formal Marine Policy (2010).

[70] The LCCDs are: 1 Misrepresentation, Non-Disclosure, and Breach of Warranty (2007); 2 Post-Contract Duties (2011); Business Insured's Duty of Disclosure and Warranties.

[71] Differing approaches are taken in *Lucena v Craufurd* (1802) 2 Bos & PNR 269, codification in the Marine Insurance Act 1906, s 5, and refinement by the Court of Appeal in *Feasey v Sun Life Assurance Corporation of Canada* [2003] EWCA Civ 885; [2003] Lloyd's Rep IR 637. There is a review of the latter case and other developments in J Birds, 'Insurable Interest—Orthodox and Unorthodox Approaches' (2006) JBL 224. There is a broader discussion of the appropriate principles in J Lowry and P Rawlings, 'Re-thinking Insurable Interest', with Commentary by Sir Jonathan Mance and Adrian Hamilton, QC, in S Worthington (ed), *Commercial Law and Commercial Practice* (Oxford: Hart, 2003).

recognized at an early stage that a bailee had the right to insure the subject matter in his possession to its full value even though his own interest was limited to his liability for its loss or destruction,[72] and in more recent years the courts have recognized 'pervasive' insurable interest which confers upon a subcontractor an interest in the entire construction project, thereby treating him as an insured party under a works policy and granting immunity from subrogation proceedings.[73] The various life investment products now on offer, particularly those involving discretionary trusts for family members, have at best sidestepped, and at worst ignored, insurable interest rules, but nevertheless they have regulatory approval. The rules as to the timing of insurable interest and the consequences of its absence differ between classes of insurance, but have a number of common objectives: the prevention of wagering; removal of the incentive to destroy (or, in life cases, murder) the subject of the policy; and preservation of the integrity of insurance as a commercial transaction.

The validity of wagers at common law led to the passing of the Marine Insurance Act 1745, re-enacted in the Marine Insurance Act 1906, and that measure now requires the assured to possess insurable interest when the policy is taken out (to prevent gambling) and also at the date of the loss (reinforcing the status of insurance as a contract which indemnifies for actual loss).[74] The position of non-marine property policies is less clear: there is one case which indicates that insurable interest is a common law requirement,[75] but the more generally accepted view is that the rules are a combination of the statutory prohibition on wagering in the Gaming Act 1845, s 18, requiring interest at the outset, and the indemnity principle, requiring proof of interest on loss. The repeal of the 1845 Act, s 18 by the Gambling Act 2005 has given rise to the possibility that non-marine policies no longer require interest on inception. Life policies are governed by a discrete regime, in the Life Assurance Act 1774; a measure prompted in part by the somewhat unsavoury practice of betting on the lives of famous people based upon newspaper reports of their health, and that measure has been construed—consistently with the principle that life policies are not contracts of indemnity[76]—as requiring interest only on inception but not on death.[77]

The law in relation to this important and distinctive concept is at best confusing and at worst illogical and unprincipled. Non-marine insurable interest has been abandoned in both Australia and New Zealand, seemingly without ill-effects.[78] However, the English and Scottish Law Commissions have confirmed the need for insurable interest and have recommended retention but with a broader definition based on the risk of

[72] *Waters v Monarch Fire & Life Assurance Co* (1856) 5 El & Bl 870.

[73] Chapter 7 examines the use of insurance in the construction industry and the significance of subrogation immunity to contractual allocations of risk.

[74] The indemnity principle can be modified by the use of a valued policy, under which the assured recovers an agreed sum in the event of the occurrence of an insured peril rather than a sum based upon the assured's actual loss. Valued policies remove disputes as to actual value and are used for many marine policies and for non-marine policies on unique items incapable of simple valuation, such as works of art.

[75] *Sadler's Co v Badcock* (1743) 2 Atk 554.

[76] Discussed in Chapter 5.

[77] *Dalby v India & London Life Assurance Society* (1854) 15 CB 364.

[78] Respectively the Insurance Contracts Act 1984 (Cth), ss 16–17, and the Insurance Law Reform Act 1985 (NZ), s 7.

prejudice following loss, and also with the removal of some of the surrounding iniquities and uncertainties, for example the existing rule that life policies without interest are not just void but also illegal.[79]

3.3.4.3 Utmost good faith

Insurance contracts attract a duty of utmost good faith, codified in the Marine Insurance Act 1906, ss 17–20 and manifested most significantly in a pre-contractual duty of disclosure imposed upon the assured.[80] This contrasts with the usual common law principle that silence does not constitute misrepresentation. However, the way that the law imposes the duty of good faith primarily upon the assured enhances, rather than dilutes, the capacity of insurance contracts to resemble 'contracts of adhesion', and in this sense its practical impact is typically quite contrary to the continuing duties of good faith which have been urged—and to some degree now belatedly accepted even in English law—in relation to contracts generally.[81] This is because 'utmost good faith' has its origins in information asymmetry and thus essentially moral hazard ideas focused on the assured. The law has its origins in *Carter v Boehm*,[82] in which Lord Mansfield confirmed that the asymmetry of information between assured and insurers required the assured to disclose to the insurers facts of which the insurers were unaware and which were material to the risk to be run. The allegation in the case itself—that the Governor of the fort at Sumatra had failed to disclose French aggression—was rejected because the fact was found to be known to the insurers and thus not within the duty,

[79] LCIP 4 and LCCD 2. The Law Commissions were influenced by the consideration that the insurance market was largely unaffected by the 2007 global financial crisis (GFC), in that the rules of insurable interest played some part in the exercise of prudence in underwriting. Those insurers who were affected by the GFC (notably AIG in the US) were brought down not by underwriting but by investing in the purchase of sub-prime debts. Note, however, discussion of the boundaries between 'insurance' and other arrangements in Chapter 2, and in preceding paragraphs. The—mostly favourable—responses to the Law Commission's proposals were published on its website in February 2013.

[80] The Marine Insurance Act 1906, s 17 is in general terms and extends to pre- and post-contractual duties imposed on both the assured and the insurers. However, ss 18–20, which amplify the principle, refer only to the assured's pre-contractual duty. The courts have yet to develop clear principles as to the assured's post-contractual duty and the insurers' pre- and post-contractual duties. There is further discussion in *Colinvaux's Law of Insurance* (London: Sweet & Maxwell, 9th edn, 2009), ch 6. The Law Commissions have confined their discussion to post-contractual matters, namely, fraudulent claims by assureds and late payment by insurers, although these would generally not be classified as 'good faith' issues.

[81] For acceptance of good faith in relation to English commercial contracts, see the comments of Rix LJ in *Socimer v Standard Bank London Ltd* [2008] EWCA Civ 116; [2008] 1 Lloyd's Rep 558 (a requirement of 'good faith and rationality'); and more recently Leggatt J in *Yam Seng Pte Ltd v International Trade Corporation Ltd* [2013] EWHC 111 (QB); [2013] All ER (D) 227 (Feb) (here associating continuing duties of good faith with long-term and 'relational' contracts, rather than those at the 'executory' end of the scale). However, the Court of Appeal in the subsequent case of *Mid-Essex Hospital Services NHS Trust v Compass Group UK and Ireland Ltd* [2013] EWCA Civ 200 sounded a cautionary note. The case required the Court to interpret a contractual duty of good faith; and this meant only that conduct must not be commercially unacceptable. The duty of good faith could not lead to a result which contradicted express terms of the contract.

[82] (1766) 3 Burr 1905. Lord Mansfield was clearly expressing a general contractual principle, but the utmost good faith principle was subsequently restricted to insurance. It may now be resurfacing in a more general form, from the combination of a series of other developments, most particularly in the consumer field, as pulled together by Leggatt J in *Yam Seng* (n 81).

but the reasoning itself has dominated the common law of insurance for the succeeding 250 years.

Reform proposals in the UK go back over half a century, but in recent years—and pending legislative reform—the courts have taken the lead in mitigating the rigours of the law as extended from geographically remote marine risks in the eighteenth century (where risk to underwriters might be thought particularly great), through other forms of policy and ultimately to consumer policies in the second half of the twentieth century. Much of the sting of the duty of utmost good faith was removed in a series of commercial cases starting with *Pan Atlantic Insurance Co v Pine Top Insurance Co*,[83] which superimposed upon the objective test of materiality—framed in terms of what would be relevant to a prudent underwriter—a subjective test by which the underwriter who accepted the risk is required to prove that, but for the silence or falsity on the part of the assured he would have acted differently in terms of acceptance of the risk, the premium charged, or the terms imposed. In a parallel development, the duty of disclosure is recognized as having been modified by the questions expressly asked of the assured, so that limited questions implicitly waive information outside their ambit[84] and answers which alert the insurers to further potential information are sufficient unless the insurers choose to follow up with more questions.[85] These are both extended examples of the waiver principle.

Developments in the courts aside, the duty of disclosure has diminished in significance in recent years. Policies on goods and cargoes, as well as reinsurance treaties and fleets of vehicles, are frequently written on a declaration basis, so that the underwriters agree up front that they will accept without further inquiry, and on a premium based on a percentage of the value of the subject matter, any risk falling within the substantive, temporal and aggregate, or individual financial limits of the cover. Such contracts normally operate automatically, so that as soon as the policyholder accepts a risk it is automatically fixed to the open cover or treaty.[86] There is clearly no room for a duty of disclosure in respect of individual risks, given that the underwriters have agreed that they will be accepted in any event. Further, contracts which are designed to transfer risk may be described as insurance but with all substantive elements of insurance law stripped out, so that full disclosure is replaced either with a right to say nothing[87] or with disclosure being confined to a limited group of individuals within the assured's organization.[88] As regards consumers, since 1977[89] insurers themselves have agreed to abandon reliance on non-disclosure and misrepresentation as against an honest

[83] [1994] 3 All ER 581; [1994] 3 WLR 677.

[84] Thus a question as to convictions in the previous five years would waive disclosure of earlier offences.

[85] *WISE Underwriting Agency v Grupo Nacional Provincial SA* [2004] EWCA Civ 962; [2004] 2 Lloyd's Rep 483.

[86] See, for the operation of such contracts: *Glencore International AG v Ryan, The Beursgracht* [2001] EWCA Civ 2051; [2002] 1 Lloyd's Rep 574; *Hanwha Non-Life Insurance Co Ltd v Alba Pte Ltd* [2011] SGHC 271; [2012] Lloyd's Rep IR 505. The distinction here is between a contract *of* insurance (a contract under which insurance is actually provided) and a contract *for* insurance (a framework arrangement which facilitates the insurance of future risks).

[87] *HIH Casualty and General Insurance v Chase Manhattan* Bank [2001] EWCA Civ 1250; [2001] 2 Lloyd's Rep 483.

[88] Typically the arrangement for credit policies obtained by banks.

[89] Chapter 4.

assured, and that practice has been overtaken by the Consumer Insurance (Disclosure and Representations) Act 2012, implementing the Law Commissions' proposals on the matter,[90] under which the duty of disclosure is abolished in consumer cases and the insurers' right to avoid for misrepresentation is confined to cases of fraud or cases where the assured has not acted reasonably in answering questions and the insurers would not have accepted the risk at all had the truth been told.

3.3.4.4 Policy terms

The distinction drawn by the common law, as partly codified by the Sale of Goods Act 1979, s 11, between the various types of contract terms which impose obligations upon the parties—conditions (important terms), warranties (ancillary terms), and innominate terms (whose significance depends upon the effect of breach on the contract)[91]—has no application to insurance. In an insurance policy, conditions are of secondary importance to warranties. Both are important devices in fixing the level of protection acquired by the assured. As discussed in the final sections of this chapter, interpretation of such terms may also affect third parties, particularly in relation to liability insurance.

Policy conditions regulate the duties of the assured and—as noted above—relate to matters such as payment of the premium, conduct towards the insured subject matter, and the making of claims. Such conditions are generally regarded as innominate, so that breach will rarely amount to an automatic repudiation by the assured and instead has to be assessed by reference to the effect on the future operation of the policy. In the overwhelming majority of cases[92] there will be no right to terminate for breach,[93] and instead the insurers will be confined to damages for any loss which can be shown to have been occasioned by breach. In practice, loss may be hard to prove.[94] It is the practice of many insurers to protect themselves by the device of deeming the condition to be a condition precedent to liability: breach of such a condition automatically discharges the insurers from any liability for the claim to which the condition relates, whether or not the breach has any causal connection to the loss and whether or not the insurers have suffered prejudice. Such terms are regularly described by the courts as draconian, and have to some extent been sidestepped by rulings that the insurer has not

[90] LCIPs 1, 2, and 3, and LCCD 1 and 2.

[91] *Chitty on Contracts* (London: Sweet & Maxwell, 31st edn, 2012), ch 12.

[92] Fraudulent claims clauses are exceptional in this regard: *Axa Insurance Co v Gottlieb* [2005] EWCA Civ 112; [2005] Lloyd's Rep IR 369, holding that if any part of a claim is fraudulent then all benefit under the policy is forfeited. LCIP 7 and LCCD 2 recommended no change in the law. Contrast the position where a claim in tort is partly fraudulent: it was held by the Supreme Court in *Fairclough Homes Ltd v Summers* [2012] UKSC 36; [2012] 1 WLR 2004 that there is no power to strike out the entire claim and that the claimant is entitled to damages for the non-fraudulent part, although it is almost certain that an award of indemnity costs against the claimant will see him leaving court worse off than when he entered it.

[93] For example, *Figre Ltd v Mander* [1999] Lloyd's Rep IR 193 (time is not of the essence for the payment of premium).

[94] *Milton Keynes Borough Council v Nulty* [2011] EWHC 2847 (TCC); [2011] All ER (D) 194 (Nov), affirmed on other grounds; *Hamilton v Hamilton* [2013] EWCA Civ 13; [2013] All ER (D) 201 (Jan), where damages (assessed, admittedly for no particular reason, at 15 per cent of the claim) for loss of opportunity to defend were awarded to a liability insurer which was not given timely notification of a potential claim against the assured.

done enough to convert the clause into a condition precedent, by narrow construction and by findings of an absence of breach.[95] This, therefore, is an instance of regulation of the parties' relationship through interpretation.

Insurance warranties were in their origin a means of describing the risk to be run by the insurers. The assured would thus be called upon to warrant that a vessel would be sailing in convoy or that it was in a seaworthy state at the commencement of the voyage. Early marine warranties were extended to other forms of policy and indeed taken beyond their initial function of risk definition to extend to matters such as timely payment of premium or the installation of burglar alarms. Where a term is found to be a warranty, it operates as an unconditional promise either of a state of affairs or of the assured's future conduct following the inception of the policy. Breach, whether trivial or significant, and whether or not connected to the loss, automatically brings the insurer's future potential liability under the policy to an end and anything done thereafter by the assured to correct matters cannot reinstate the coverage in the absence of consent on the part of the insurers or at least an estoppel against them.[96] Warranties were originally used to overcome the common law causation rule—which persisted until the beginning of the twentieth century—that the last event in a chain was the proximate cause of the loss. If, therefore, the insurers wished to be certain that they could exclude liability in specified circumstances, the use of the warranty meant that they would have an absolute defence even though the last (proximate) cause was an insured peril.[97] However, warranties are falling into disuse. The most recent cargo clauses (2009) make no reference to warranties and the most recent hull clauses (2003) use the term only in respect of double insurance. Although there have been numerous and conflicting authorities on warranties, the courts have in recent years proved to be hostile to them, and have adopted a *contra proferentem* approach to their interpretation, both in deciding whether a warranty has been created in the first place and, if so, in respect of the obligations laid down by it.[98]

The Law Commissions have struggled with the correct approach to policy terms; they have considered and rejected suggestions for reform along the lines adopted in Australia and New Zealand under which breaches of policy terms can be relied upon only if causative of the loss.[99] Instead, they have recommended that pre-contractual statements of fact should not constitute warranties[100] and should be treated as representations and thus subject to misrepresentation principles, a recommendation implemented in respect of consumer policies by the Consumer Insurance (Disclosure and Representations) Act 2012. They have also suggested that the breach of a policy term

[95] *Friends Provident Life and Pensions Ltd v Sirius International Insurance Corporation Ltd* [2005] EWCA Civ 601; [2005] 2 Lloyd's Rep 517.

[96] Marine Insurance Act 1906, ss 33–35.

[97] This was the explanation proffered by Lord Mance in *The Cendor Mopu* [2011] UKSC 5; [2011] 1 Lloyd's Rep 560.

[98] Recent examples include *Pratt v Aigaion Insurance Co SA, The Resolute* [2008] EWCA Civ 1314; [2009] 1 Lloyd's Rep 225, and *A C Ward & Sons Ltd v Catlin (Five) Ltd* [2009] EWCA Civ 1098; [2010] Lloyd's Rep IR 301.

[99] Insurance Contracts Act 1984 (Cth), s 54; Insurance Law Reform Act 1977 (NZ), ss 9 and 11.

[100] Achieved by use of the 'basis' clause in the proposal form, deeming every statement—material or otherwise—to be the basis of the contract.

should give a remedy only where the breach was subsisting at the date of the loss, thereby reversing the common law rule that a breach of warranty has the automatic and irremediable effect of terminating cover.

3.3.5 Summary

This section has introduced the nature of insurance contracts and the way that they are drafted, as well as some key aspects of the courts' approach to the insurance relationship. The response of the courts has not been notably oriented to protection of insured parties other than in certain particular respects; nor do the decisions of the courts strongly reflect a sense that insurance is a business with a public purpose, in the sense recognized in US insurance law. This, we have suggested, partly reflects the absence of strong public involvement in the regulation of insurance contracts and particularly of their terms. Even given this generally 'private' (or relational) set of concerns, however, the potential effectiveness of the courts should not be overlooked. We introduce some such avenues in the remaining sections of this chapter relating to tort, and continue the themes in the following chapters.

3.4 The Development of Risks and the Market for Insurance

3.4.1 Significance of the inquiry

In this section, we begin our broader enquiry into the relationship between insurance markets and legal duties. We suggest that the growth of insurance in the past five centuries has been, and remains, a response to the demand for protection against emerging risks, and that it is possible to match the growth of new forms of insurance to almost every significant industrial and commercial development. As new risks faced those engaged in commercial activities and, later, consumers, insurers were adept at developing new products offering appropriate insurance protection. The same is true of liability risks. It is impossible to divorce the allocation of risk by common law and statute from the rise of insurance, and much insurance has been a response to the changing legal landscape. Here we begin to illustrate how neglect of insurance leads to a restricted vision of the development of the law and of its practical operation. In relation to the operation of the law of tort in particular, Kenneth Abraham has referred to liability and insurance as a 'bipolar star', forming a common gravitational field.[101] Baker and Seigelman have recently suggested that 'little or nothing in Tort law makes sense except in the light of liability insurance'.[102] Neither of these assertions depends on liability insurance running ahead of tort. Liability insurance, we suggest, is related to liability in the same way that insurance in general is related to the emergence of recognized risks.

[101] K Abraham, *The Liability Century: Insurance and Tort Law from the Progressive Era to 9/11* (Cambridge MA: Harvard University Press, 2008).

[102] T Baker and P Siegelman, 'The Law and Economics of Liability Insurance: A Theoretical and Empirical Review', 1, available at <http://papers.ssrn.com/sol3/papers.cfm?abstract_id=1783793> citing T Dobhanzy, 'Nothing in Science Makes Sense Except in the Light of Evolution' (1973) 35 *American Biology Teacher* 125.

3.4.2 Early marine policies[103]

The earliest policies in England were almost certainly on maritime risks, and, although the origin of marine insurance has been attributed to various early civilizations, it probably owes most to the Lombards whose activities in this regard spread to England by the fifteenth century. Policies were written by individuals for individuals, often introduced by third-party intermediaries (later becoming known as 'brokers') and were negotiated in informal meeting places in London, at least until 1570 with the formation of the Royal Exchange as a meeting place. In 1576 the Chamber of Assurances was established as a central registry of marine policies within the Royal Exchange. The earliest surviving English policy is dated 1547 and the first recorded litigation gave rise to a judgment in 1588.[104] A special court for hearing hull claims was established by Parliament in 1601,[105] although it rapidly became a victim of the struggle for jurisdiction between the superior courts.[106]

The business of marine underwriting grew throughout the seventeenth century. Much of it was conducted in coffee houses, with underwriters unregulated and frequently unable to meet large or mass claims.[107] The first serious control of the insurance industry was by the Bubble Act 1720, a measure prompted by the formation of large numbers of companies seeking to emulate the success of the South Sea Company. Many of these speculations were at best unsound and at worst fraudulent. The Act prohibited the formation of new companies, and the only legal persons permitted to write marine insurance policies were two chartered bodies, Royal Exchange Assurance and London Assurance. In fact they wrote very little such business, and the excess demand was picked up by individual merchant underwriters whose activities were expressly preserved by the Bubble Act and who had by this time made Edward Lloyd's coffee house the focus of their activities, based upon Lloyd's evolution as the centre for the exchange of intelligence on ships and ship casualties. Although Lloyd's as an establishment dates from 1688, marine insurance was not transacted on the premises until shortly before the passing of the Bubble Act.[108] By the end of the eighteenth century, boosted by the need for marine cover from the almost continuous state of war with France and surviving a crackdown by the Marine Insurance Act 1743[109] on the use of marine policies to wager on the safety of ships,

[103] Leading works on the history of insurance include: J Park, *A System of the Law of Marine Insurances* (London: Saunders and Benning, 8th edn, 1842 (ed F Hildyard)); C Wright and CE Fayle, *A History of Lloyd's* (London: Macmillan, 1928); D Gibb, *Lloyd's of London: A Study of Individualism* (London: Macmillan, 1957); B Supple, *The Royal Exchange Assurance* (Cambridge: Cambridge University Press, 1970); G Clayton, *British Insurance* (London: Elek Books, 1971); HE Raynes, *A History of British Insurance* (London: Pitman, 3rd edn, 1983); O Westall (ed), *The Historian and the Business of Insurance* (Manchester: Manchester University Press, 1984).

[104] Park, n 103, lxxxiv–lxxv.

[105] 43 Eliz c 12.

[106] See, eg, *Came v Moy* (1658) 2 Sid 121, where it was held that a judgment did not preclude a further action in the courts of Equity.

[107] Notably following the loss of 92 merchant vessels in the Battle of Lagos in 1693.

[108] And shortly after the death of Lloyd himself, in 1713.

[109] Still in force, but now as the Marine Insurance Act 1906, ss 4–6, covered in 3.3.

Lloyd's had established itself as the dominant marine underwriting centre, with the famous standard form Lloyd's SG Policy. By the time that Lloyd's had reconstituted itself as a society in 1811 the only serious competition to it came from shipowners themselves, who formed societies—of doubtful legality under the Bubble Act—providing loss of hull cover on a mutual (non-profit-making) basis.

The repeal of the Bubble Act in 1824 led to the formation of numerous companies, facilitated by the successful struggle for limited liability for shareholders by the Joint Stock Companies Acts 1844 and 1856. While Lloyd's and insurance companies competed for marine business in the period immediately following the repeal of the Bubble Act, they were less willing to respond to the rapidly growing demand for a new form of cover, that of liability to third parties. The most important insured peril covered by the Lloyd's SG Policy was 'perils of the seas', but it became clear following the decision in *De Vaux v Salvador*[110] in 1836 that liability to another shipowner for damage caused by a collision was not within that formulation. Other liabilities were soon afterwards established, including those under: the Fatal Accidents Act 1846, allowing damages to be awarded to dependants of deceased persons, including crew members; the Harbours, Docks and Piers Clauses Act 1847, for collisions with fixed installations; and *The Westernhope*[111] in 1870, which removed the possibility of contractual protection for a shipowner where a cargo was lost by reason of deviation. Lloyd's and insurance companies were less than wholehearted in their response, and although collision liability cover was added to existing policies it extended to only three-fourths of any possible liability. Ship owners accordingly reverted to their pre-Bubble Act practice of forming mutual societies—the P&I Clubs—for protection against third-party claims. The Clubs competed with insurance companies and Lloyd's in the provision of cover for liability insurance, and in particular took up the missing one-fourth of cover for collision liabilities. Subsequently, the activities of Clubs were extended to war risks, to compete with Lloyd's and companies.

This, then, is the background to the present structure of the marine insurance market. Marine insurance business is now carried on by insurance companies and by underwriters at Lloyd's. Liability cover and war risks insurance is also written by those organizations, but in practice shipowners secure those forms of cover from their membership of P&I Clubs. Standard hull and machinery policies confine collision liability cover to three-fourths, with P&I Clubs picking up the remaining one-fourth, although the commercial market these days offers four-fourths cover.[112] The International Group of P&I Clubs, consisting of the leading thirteen Clubs, now provides insurance for 90 per cent of the world's fleet. It can be seen that not just the content of policies but, indeed, the very structure of the market, were in part driven by developments in the

[110] (1836) 4 A & E 420. [111] Unreported.

[112] The International Hull Clauses 2003 offer three-fourths collision liability cover, but extend the cover to four-fourths on payment of an additional premium. The 2003 Clauses are not in widespread use, mainly because they restrict cover for mechanical breakdown and latent damage, and contain fierce rules on fraudulent claims, but insurers remain prepared to extend coverage in this way even under earlier versions of the Clauses (adopted in 1983 and modified in 1996) which unamended are restricted to three-fourths cover.

law, which both created liabilities, and either restricted or permitted the extension of insurance business.

3.4.3 Other forms of insurance

Life insurance has a pedigree every bit as impressive as marine insurance. The idea of the provision of death and funeral benefits by mutual societies was known to the Greeks and the Romans more than two thousand years ago. It would seem that from the end of the sixteenth century onwards this form of cover was in use in England by the precursors of guilds and friendly societies. Many life policies were related to marine cover, and insured against the risk of capture by pirates. Other policies were nakedly a form of wagering on the lives of the famous, as we explore in Chapter 5.

Fire insurance developed later than marine and life insurance, and its existence in England can be pinpointed to the immediate aftermath of the Great Fire of London in 1666. Within forty years six fire offices had been established and almost from the outset disputes reached the courts.[113] The Bubble Act of 1720 ought in theory to have prevented the emergence of any new insurance companies, but the untested device of the Deed of Settlement was pressed into use to circumvent the measure and the Fire Insurance Duty Act 1782 finally recognized the legality of fire insurance companies.

The insurance market at the turn of the nineteenth century was, thus, limited to marine, life, and fire cover. But the rapid industrialization which was to follow gave rise to a series of new risks and new liabilities. The demand for protection against these risks was met by an array of specialist and quaintly named insurance companies formed for the purpose[114] rather than by Lloyd's, which did not stray beyond marine insurance until the end of the nineteenth century. One of the first challenges was the growth of rail transport, first witnessed by the opening of the Stockton to Darlington railway in 1825. The dangers of rail became manifest at the opening of the Liverpool and Manchester Railway in September 1830, when William Huskisson, President of the Board of Trade, was run over and killed by Stephenson's *Rocket*.[115] The frequency of railway accidents[116] led to the formation in 1848 of the first personal accident insurance company providing benefits to those injured on the railways, and others of the same type rapidly followed.[117] The 1840s and '50s also saw the formation of specialist insurers to provide cover against hailstone damage, injury to livestock, financial loss caused by fraudulent employees, smashed plate glass, and loss arising from the explosion of steam boilers. By the 1880s burglary insurance had emerged. A buoyant and innovative first-party insurance market was, by responding to emerging risks, firmly established in the second half of the nineteenth century.

[113] *Lynch v Dalzell* (1729) 3 Bro PC 497; *Sadler's Co v Badcock* (1743) 2 Atk 554.

[114] The history of those companies is given in the archive maintained by Aviva and archivist Anna Stone: <http://www.aviva.com/about-us/heritage/>, accessed 21 April 2013.

[115] S Garfield, *The Last Journey of William Huskisson* (London: Faber & Faber, 2002).

[116] <http://www.york.ac.uk/inst/irs/irshome/papers/rlyacc.htm>, accessed 21 April 2013.

[117] *Theobald v Railway Passengers Assurance* (1854) 10 Ex 45, further discussed in Chapter 5.

3.4.4 Interface with the law of tort

How did this developing insurance market of the mid-nineteenth century interface with tort? Abraham has warned against anachronistic exercises in appraisal of earlier cases which overlook the absence of liability insurance.[118] But it might also be said that tort itself was relatively undeveloped by this period. A snapshot of the law of tort in the 1840s would show recognition of liability, for example on common carriers, rail companies, carriage drivers, and occupiers, but at this stage the law was devoid of tidy principle and hampered by technical and procedural limitations.[119] The problems were most obvious in personal injury cases. Death negligently inflicted could not at common law give rise to any claim because the action died with the victim. Acceptance of the decision in *Priestley v Fowler*[120] all but denied a claim by a workman against his employer, on the grounds that the risk of any injury inflicted by the fault of a co-worker was one to be borne by the victim so that the employer was not answerable for it other than in those rare cases when the employer was personally at fault. Claims for financial loss and for property damage, although recognized, were rare. It followed that if there was to be compensation, and particularly for personal injury, it would in most cases have to be provided by insurance paid for by the victim himself. This was far-fetched in the case of workers, though mutual schemes did operate to cover some losses; but much less so in the case of wealthier rail passengers.

From the middle of the nineteenth century, there was a significant, albeit gradual, change in approach. The Fatal Accidents Act 1846 reversed the rule that a claim died with the claimant. The aberration that was *Priestley v Fowler* was partially corrected by the Employers' Liability Act 1880, conferring upon a workman the right to recover compensation if injured by reason of any defect in machinery or plant, or by reason of the negligence of a co-worker or independent contractor.[121] Strict liability for damage to neighbouring land, albeit on a limited basis, was recognized in principle by *Rylands v Fletcher*.[122] As already seen, the liabilities of shipowners were extended by common law and statute, and the fact that the victim was protected by insurance did not confer immunity on the third party responsible for the loss because the insurers, having paid an indemnity, were entitled to exercise subrogation rights against him.[123] With the onus switching from the victim to the wrongdoer the focus of insurance also shifted from the victim to the wrongdoer. Ship owners' P&I Clubs were formed to protect against claims. By the late 1850s the first policies on liability for injury caused by steam boilers were emerging.[124] On the passing of the 1880 Act a number of insurance

[118] Abraham, n 101, 17–19.

[119] WR Cornish and G de N Clarke, *Law and Society in England 1750–1950* (London: Sweet & Maxwell, 1989), p 486 ff.

[120] (1837) 3 M & W 1.

[121] Further discussed in Chapter 9.

[122] (1868) LR 3 HL 330.

[123] Chapter 5.

[124] C Parsons, 'From Accident to Liability—A Brief History of Liability Insurance' (2002) 17 *Journal of Insurance Research and Practice* 23. The Steam Boiler Assurance Company was formed in 1858 and the Midland Steam Boiler Inspection and Assurance Company was formed in 1862: Aviva online archive: <http://www.aviva.com/about-us/heritage/history-of-insurance/>, accessed 21 April 2013.

companies were immediately established to provide cover to employers who for the first time faced a significant risk of incurring liability towards their workers,[125] and the process continued when an alternative and more widespread right to compensation was granted by the Workmen's Compensation Act 1897. Such was the recognized prevalence of insurance that the 1897 Act even conferred upon an injured workman a prioritized claim against the insurance proceeds in the event of the employer's insolvency. Three years earlier the first motor vehicle appeared on the UK's roads:[126] despite stringent safety measures, the first fatality occurred in August 1896, and the first motor policy followed in November 1896. The Workmen's Compensation Act 1906 extended liability to disease, and also for the first time gave an injured employee a direct claim against insurers in the event of the employer's insolvency, and liability policies were adjusted to match the new statutory liability. Other forms of liability insurance were slower to develop, but it would seem that the first public liability policies began to appear at the end of the nineteenth century, growing out of liability policies written on specific risks.[127] Product liability insurance was first seen early in the twentieth century, in relation to known contamination of food products, and became more generalized after the recognition of the concept of product liability by the narrow rule in *Donoghue v Stevenson*.[128] The latter part of the nineteenth century also saw the introduction of professional indemnity insurance for doctors and druggists, the first liability policy for architects was written in 1922, and other professions followed.[129] This form of cover is now required by the rules or codes of practice promulgated by professional societies.

The matching of insurance to actual or perceived tort liabilities has continued to the present day. Environmental Impairment Liability (EIL) insurance was developed to grant protection against legislative strict liability for clean-up costs both in the UK and abroad, it having been found that ordinary public liability policies were inappropriate as they responded only to sudden and accidental losses rather than gradual seepage and they were of no assistance where clean-up was ordered by the state as no liability in damages was involved.[130] Companies were first permitted by the Companies Act 1989 to purchase insurance against liabilities faced by their directors and officers (D&O insurance). Insurers and brokers carefully monitor legislative and judicial developments to see if a new product might be marketed successfully.[131]

Of course the matching is not perfect. First, unanticipated liabilities may be imposed without warning, giving rise to uninsured loss, although inevitably there will be either general market or specific discussions to see whether policy wording should be adjusted

[125] The need for insurance is reported to have been noticed by the founders of the first employers' liability insurers during the process of parliamentary debates on the Employers' Liability Act 1880.

[126] The early history of motoring is covered in LJK Setright, *Drive On: A Social History of the Motor Car* (London: Granta Books, 2004).

[127] Parsons, n 124, gives the examples of 'property owners' indemnities, scholars' indemnities (covering liability for injury to school pupils) and special policies for innkeepers, farmers and the like'.

[128] [1932] AC 562; [1932] All ER Rep 1.

[129] Parsons, n 124.

[130] *Bartoline v Royal & Sun Alliance Ins Plc* [2006] EWHC 3598 (QB); [2007] Lloyd's Rep IR 423.

[131] A clear example of this is the film finance insurance, devised by brokers, which facilitated investment by commercial lenders in film production: *HIH Casualty and General Insurance v Chase Manhattan Bank* [2001] EWCA Civ 1250; [2001] 2 Lloyd's Rep 483.

for the future. Second, anticipated liabilities may not arise, so that insurance cover may prove to be targeted at a phantom risk.[132] Third, some emerging liabilities may be regarded as uninsurable, so that there will be no insurance cover—or, if any, restricted by financial limits or exclusions—for particular liabilities laid down by the courts. Nevertheless, the starting point in addressing the relationship between liability and insurance is that insurance has emerged to meet new liabilities. We find no strong evidence that issues around the legality of liability insurance particularly held it back: the development of liability cover is much like the development of any cover.

There are, nevertheless, limits to the liabilities that insurance exists to meet, and the definition of these limits doubtless influences the law of tort in turn. The fact remains that the shape of tort liability is also influenced by parties and the disputes that they bring (and find it worthwhile to bring): private law remains focused on response to inter-party disputes and its principles are developed in this way. The non-availability of insurance for intentional harms, other than where the liability is purely vicarious, may very well account for the paucity of tort claims in respect of deliberate harm, for example. If so, then a little-observed factor is operating to affect the very shape of the law of tort. It does this because parties are influenced by recoverability issues.

This brings us to an important point. As Abraham has argued, a century of development in the law of tort has not fundamentally altered the truth of the observation that negligence is the dominant basis of liability for accidental harm,[133] even in the United States, where the availability of insurance has been used as a reason for shifting to stricter liabilities in some areas.[134] But on the whole, the growth of liability insurance has been accompanied by expansion in the range of negligence duties. Negligence and insurance fit closely together. 'Mere' negligence is not excluded from the realms of insurability by ideas of moral hazard; but, at the same time, the need to show fault holds the line against excessive liabilities and means that claimants are not entirely freed from responsibility. But the spread of negligence operates through expansion in the range of negligence duties. This too is achieved in part in response to the availability of funds to meet a claim. Where the perpetrator of a wrong is uninsured, or acts intentionally so that the loss falls outside the reach of insurance, or simply where the perpetrator's liability insurer sees an opportunity to offload some of the cost, the effect of insurance is to create an incentive to argue for new duties, drawing in new parties to the tort frame.

In Chapter 8 we will suggest that, in many contexts, English courts have been alive to these pressures; and that their reasoning around tort duties is more influenced by insurance arrangements than has been appreciated. In this context, awareness of the pressures for expansion related to insurance has produced not a broadening of tort

[132] A first-party illustration may be found in the mass of insurance policies sold in the run-up to the year 2000, to counter fears that 'Y2K' might cause widespread computer failure. In the event there was no recorded case of loss being suffered in this way.

[133] K Abraham, n 101, ch 6, 'Which Came First, the Liability or the Insurance?'

[134] In the US, strict liability premised openly on the availability of insurance has been advanced in relation to products liability (complete with the academic backlash referred to in Chapter 1); auto liability in around 12 states; and workmen's compensation.

duties, but a reason to hold the line against such expansion.[135] In the next two sections, we continue our exploration of the way that insurance cover interacts with tort liabilities.

3.5 Liability Insurance and Liability

3.5.1 Forms of liability insurance

Liability insurance today plays a crucial role in the law of obligations. The most general form is public liability, which is possessed by most businesses (and indeed by households, very often tucked away as an additional benefit of a property policy), and covers occupiers' liability and injury or property damage inflicted upon others from the conduct of business activities. Public liability insurance does not cover liability to employees or arising out of accidents on the roads; those are separate heads of insurance which are compulsory under the Employers' Liability (Compulsory Insurance) Act 1969 and the Road Traffic Act 1988. Businesses providing services will have in place professional indemnity insurance, and businesses supplying goods will have in place product liability insurance. Commercial operations will typically insure themselves against liability to clean up pollution through EIL insurance. Marine liability insurance for shipowners is normally written by P&I Clubs, and gives an indemnity for claims in respect, most importantly, of injury to crew, cargo losses, oil and other pollution, and collision damage to fixed or floating objects.

The importance of liability insurance in the operation not only of the law of tort, but also of party relations more generally, cannot be overstated. As we explain in Chapter 9, compulsory liability cover exists in relation to the overwhelming majority of personal injury claims.[136] Even where such insurance is not compulsory as a matter of law, it may be compulsory under professional rules.[137] Negotiations for major contracts will inevitably involve lengthy discussion of the supplier's liability cover, and a customer or client will often insist upon the extension of the scope or amount of the supplier's existing cover if it is regarded as in some way inadequate. The very existence of liability insurance thus plays a crucial part in the initial awarding of contracts, and—as we explain in Chapter 7—it will form the basis of risk allocation between the contracting parties. If a loss occurs, liability insurance is likely to be the single most important fund for meeting claims.

Valuable work by Parsons[138] suggests that liability insurance is problematic for insurers and, at least as regards coverage for personal injury claims, is rarely particularly profitable: employers' liability insurance in particular often produces operating loss, and general liability insurance fares a little better but is on occasion subject to massive unforeseen claims. Parsons identifies four types of moral hazard which are

[135] Consistent with Clarke, n 52, 333.

[136] Note also R Lewis, 'How Important are Insurers in Compensating Claims for Personal Injury in the UK?' (2006) 31 *The Geneva Papers on Tort and Insurance* 323.

[137] For example, accountants.

[138] C Parsons, 'Moral Hazard in Liability Insurance' (2003) 28(3) *Geneva Papers on Risk and Insurance*. See also Baker and Siegelman, n 102.

particularly relevant to this form of cover: (a) policyholder hazard—the risk that an assured will behave with less care when backed by insurance; (b) claimant hazard—the risk of unmeritorious or even fraudulent claims, each of which has to be investigated; (c) jurisprudential hazard—the risk of a change in the law which impinges upon liability insurers; and (d) underwriting hazard—the chase for premium.

3.5.2 Legality questions

It has been questioned whether liability insurance has always been regarded as lawful,[139] and the question has intuitive appeal to tort lawyers who are inclined to associate carelessness so strongly with fault and the very basis for responsibility. It is certainly the case that in England, liability policies did not emerge outside the marine context until the second half of the nineteenth century.[140] The case against legality is that judicial reasoning initially favoured responsibility (thus, 'moral hazard'), over compensation, so that liability insurance was regarded with suspicion. Responsibility thus appears to be an older response than transfer of risks, and there appears to be a struggle over whether to allow the displacement of responsibility threatened by insurance. Abraham argues that the attitude to negligence of the insured party in maritime cases changed at a tangible point in the nineteenth century, to allow indemnification of a negligent party where this would enable the compensation of an innocent party, thereby choosing compensation over moral hazard. If such a conceptual change did take place, it might be thought to capture the most critical ambiguity in the modern tort of negligence: recoverability depends on a falling short on the part of the defendant and indeed a breach of duty owed to the claimant; but protection of the claimant from the effects of this typically depends on the defendant being able to deflect the financial consequences of its wrong to a third party (an insurer). Has the modern approach to liability insurance genuinely reflected such deep change in the attitude to civil wrongs, observable in this transformation from prohibition to requirement, dovetailing with an accompanying shift in some areas of tort from emphasis on wrongdoing to emphasis on compensation? It is a neat theory but the evidence is not as compelling as might be expected if any settled view against the wisdom, morality, or legality of liability insurance existed. The issue was not really pressed. Where it was raised at all, the answers were very equivocal—much more equivocal then they are sometimes presented to be.

The slow development of liability insurance in the UK can be explained in other ways. One set of factors relates to the hesitant development of liability already illustrated, since insurance has followed liabilities. But equally important is the fact

[139] Abraham, n 101, 17, suggests that 'At common law, liability insurance was...understood to be against public policy, because it was thought to create moral hazard'. Note also the discussion by M Davies, 'The End of the Affair: Duty of Care and Liability Insurance' (1989) 9 LS 67.

[140] Cornelius Walford's *Insurance Cyclopaedia* (London: C and E Layton, 1871–80) notes however (vol 1, p 475) that the use of insurance 'as a means of indemnity' had been practised in France for longer, with the first carriage insurance in around 1840. Walford attributed this to the severity of the Code Napoléon in relation to persons causing injury to others (an illustration of liability insurance following liability). Walford explains that 'flat rates' for carriage insurance were ended in 1872 in England adding that 'more systematic "moral hazard" in this branch of business is very great'.

that insurance companies were not permitted to operate until the repeal of the Bubble Act in 1824, and Lloyd's engaged only in marine insurance, so that there was no expertise outside the marine context for the underwriting of liability risks. It may be, therefore, that the market took some time to develop, and in any event it was not until the dangers and liability risks arising from railway travel became apparent that there was any serious need for personal injury liability insurance.[141] There is no basis to assume that the fact that such insurance did not appear from the outset was the consequence of any objection to liability insurance at common law: there was no history of non-marine liability insurance when the risk became apparent, and railway companies may have posed special considerations: the special blame directed at the railways may have been one;[142] but another is that rail companies may have found that contingency funds and the development of in-house legal services were adequate.[143]

The evidence that the common law applicable to maritime policies regarded liability insurance with disfavour is weak. From the outset the law did not flinch from allowing an assured to recover from his first-party marine insurers despite his own negligence or that of his workers.[144] More specifically, although marine law requires an assured to take reasonable steps to prevent or mitigate his loss[145] the cases so deciding have been explained not as imposing any sanction for negligence but rather as laying down the principle that in exceptional cases the assured's own failure to act might break the chain of causation from the insured peril.[146] So, the notion that negligence could debar a first-party claim was never a part of the law, and the cases indeed favour the view that only wilful misconduct on the part of the assured personally provided a defence: wilful misconduct by the master and crew—barratry—was an insured peril from earliest times.[147]

The only direct authority put forward as evidence of the illegality of liability insurance is *Delanoy v Robson*,[148] from which, we suggest, too much has been drawn.[149] This was a running down action in which a shipowner claimed for damages

141 Davies, n 139, asserts that the policy was in place with an exception for maritime cases because of the importance of sea transport. This is unconvincing: marine was the rule, not the exception.

142 Discussed further in Chapter 5.

143 Discussed in the important Appendix to RW Kostal, *Law and English Railway Capitalism 1852-1875* (Oxford: Clarendon Press, 1994). If railways were the first processors of mass personal injury claims, then they rose to the occasion by devising systems of claims handling which are now at least largely in the hands of insurance companies. One statement—that the railway companies had asked an insurer to provide liability insurance but had been told that it was against the policy of the Board of Trade—has been produced as evidence that liability insurance was regarded as unacceptable in policy terms. This is rather weak evidence on which to hang an argument, which is probably accepted more for its intuitive appeal than for any hard evidence.

144 The cases on this point in the first half of the nineteenth century include: *Busk v Royal Exchange Assurance Co* (1818) 2 B & Ald 73; *Walker v Maitland* (1821) 5 B & Ald 171; *Hahn v Corbett* (1824) 2 Bing 205; *Bishop v Pentland* (1827) 7 B & C 219; *Shore v Bentall* (1828) 7 B & C 798n; *Dixon v Sadler* (1839) 5 M & W 405; *Redman v Wilson* (1845) 14 M & W 476; *Thompson v Hopper* (1856) 6 E & B 172.

145 Marine Insurance Act 1906, s 78.

146 *Masefield v Amlin Corporate Member Ltd* [2011] EWCA Civ 24; [2011] 1 WLR 2012.

147 For example: *Elton v Brogden* (1747) 2 Str 1264; *Nutt v Bordieu* (1768) 1 TR 323.

148 (1814) 5 Taunt. 605; and C Parsons, 'From Accident to Liability—A Brief History of Liability Insurance' (2002) 17 *Journal of Insurance Research and Practice* 23.

149 The case indeed is not even referred to in contemporary texts, eg successive editions of *Park on Marine Insurance* (n 103).

against the defendant shipowner following a collision between their vessels. The defendant obtained an order to have the case transferred from London to Durham. This was challenged by the claimant on the grounds that there were numerous P&I Clubs in Durham and it might be difficult to find a jury which was favourable to the claimant. The *defendant* asserted that the risk was not insurable so that there was no basis for the claimant's argument. The court dismissed the claimant's objection, noting that the members of a P&I Club, being a mutual association, were both insurers and assureds, so that there could not be said to be any bias. That is the core of the decision. The reporter refers to a *per curiam* statement that 'It would be an illegal insurance to insure against what might be the consequences of the wrongful acts of the assured', although it is impossible to tell from the report whether this was a general rally against liability insurance or whether the circumstances were such that there was a 'wrongful act' in the form of a deliberate running down and for which an indemnity ought not to be available. The former explanation is unlikely, given that marine liability cover on a mutual basis appears to have been common. What is certain is that *Delanoy* was not taken at its face value by the market, with the formation of the Indemnity Mutual Marine Insurance Co (Indemnity Mutual Marine) in 1824 immediately following the repeal of the Bubble Act 1720, offering three-fourths collision liability cover.[150] The remaining fourth was in part needed to ensure the incentives were in place for collisions to be avoided, in part an attempt to restrict the scope of cover and possibly in part a nod towards *Delanoy v Robson*.[151]

The first marine insurance of what might be seen as analogous to tort liabilities related to collision damage. Collisions were, it seems, initially perceived as akin to perils of the sea,[152] and were dealt with by early maritime codes from which English and other maritime laws developed. The English interpretation of these codes led to a position in which, in the event of a collision, and provided there was fault on both sides,[153] the total damage done by the ships was added together and divided equally. Therefore, one ship may have to pay a residue to the other ship, which had suffered greater loss. This rough and ready regime, which operated subject to the limitation of the liability to the total value of the ship causing the loss,[154] was famously slighted by the Court of King's Bench in *De Vaux v Salvador*:[155]

[150] J Hill, *O'May on Marine Insurance* (London: Sweet & Maxwell, 1993), 213. It may also be noted that the codification of marine principles, in the Marine Insurance Act 1906, specifically states in s 3(2)(c) that liability forms part of any marine adventure.

[151] *O'May*, n 150, 214.

[152] 'The rule probably had its origin, partly in the disposition of the medieval Courts to treat all collisions as perils of the sea, for which seamen and ship-owners could not properly be held responsible; and partly in their recognition of the extreme difficulty of ascertaining the facts necessary to enable them to arrive at a just decision in each case': RG Marsden, *A Treatise on the Law of Collisions at Sea* (London: Stevens & Sons, 1880), 51.

[153] Some versions of the rule in maritime codes were further removed from fault in that they applied the division wherever there was no wilful default.

[154] Which remains the basis of the right of a ship owner to limit liability for damage to third parties: *The Bramley Moore* [1964] 2 WLR 259; [1963] 2 Lloyd's Rep 429.

[155] (1836) 4 A &E 420.

> It turns out that the ship insured has done more damage than she has received, and is obliged to pay the owners of the other ship to some amount, under the rule of the Court of Admiralty. But this is neither a necessary nor a proximate effect of the perils of the sea; it grows out of an arbitrary provision in the law of nations from views of general expediency, not as dictated by natural justice, nor (quite possibly) quite consistent with it; and can no more be charged on the underwriters than a penalty incurred by contravention of the Revenue laws of any particular State.[156]

But the Court did not invalidate the insuring of collision liabilities. It merely ensured that they were not to be treated as 'perils of the sea' within the meaning of existing policies of insurance. The more or less immediate response was for marine insurers to add the 'Running Down Clause' (RDC) which, as with the earlier policies issued by Indemnity Mutual Marine, covered three-fourths of the liability.[157] Subsequently the remaining fourth was picked up on a mutual basis by P&I Clubs, although, as we have noted above, the modern tendency is for marine insurers to offer the remaining fourth in return for additional premium. *De Vaux v Salvador* is not evidence against the acceptance of liability insurance. It illustrates some disapproval of the rules relating to maritime collisions on the part of the Court of King's Bench, and a reluctance to treat the risk of legal rules which were seen as 'arbitrary' and rough (as opposed to principled, perhaps) as perils of the seas. It could be said that the concern of maritime law with the practical needs of the market was the subject of disapproval here—an illustration of legal pluralism operating in relation to the different various courts. It has been said that Lloyd's underwriters sought to outlaw the new clause,[158] but they were interested participants and this is not evidence of a general legal perception.[159] It was to meet the exposure to liability falling outside marine insurance policies sold by the underwriters that the first marine protection society was incorporated in 1854, providing precisely the form of insurance which has been described as so doubtful.[160]

The maritime example therefore illustrates the complexity of legal development. It becomes important to ask exactly who is said to have taken the view that liability insurance was illegitimate and/or creative of what would now be called 'moral hazard'.[161] There were no *legislative* interventions to make insurance of liabilities unlawful,[162] and the evidence on offer relates to a small number of court decisions,

[156] Lord Denham CJ, *De Vaux v Salvador* (1836), 4 AD & E 419, 431–2.

[157] The RDC was perfected by the Institute Hull Clauses (Time) 1888, and remained in much the same form until 1983 when it was replaced by the clearer wording of the Collision Liability Clause which appears also in the 1996 and 2003 revisions of the 1983 Hull Clauses.

[158] *O'May*, n 150, 214, states that representations were made by Lloyd's underwriters in 1850 and 1854 to outlaw collision liability insurance because it removed the incentive for care to be taken. The government was unmoved.

[159] D Thomson, 'Chairman's Introduction', *One Hundred and Fifty Years: The Britannia Steamship Association Limited* (London: The Britannia Steam Ship Insurance Association Ltd, 2005), 4.

[160] The Shipowners Mutual Protection Society, the predecessor of the Britannia Steamship Association. When cover of liabilities toward cargo owners was added, 'Indemnity' was added to 'Protection' and the first 'P&I Club' was created: W Reynardson, 'The History and Development of P & I Insurance: the British Scene' (1969) 43 *Tulane Law Review* 457, 467.

[161] Chapter 2 introduces the idea of moral hazard in the insurance context.

[162] Quite late in the nineteenth century, in 1883, a Private Members' Bill intended to outlaw collision liability was presented to the House of Commons, but it appears not to have been debated.

which do not relate to liability insurance at all.[163] Some are more concerned with the limits of the right to indemnity where there has been wilful neglect on the part of the insured (the shipowner) or his crew. Any observed disapproval of maritime practices may simply reflect vested interest on the part of insurers who were at this time fighting a battle against maritime insurance fraud, and in some instances a lack of sympathy or understanding on the part of common lawyers, who perhaps had a stronger attachment to liability according to fault.

The point, therefore, is that there is no evidence that liability insurance itself was regarded with suspicion by the common law. The validity of liability insurance on public policy grounds was not squarely raised until 1929, in *James v British General Insurance Co*,[164] where insurers sought to challenge the validity of their own policy insofar as it covered an intoxicated driver for manslaughter liability. Roche J decisively rejected the suggestion that the insurance was void on public policy grounds, following the earlier decision of Bailhache J in *Tinline v White Cross Insurance Association Ltd*[165] in which a driver convicted of motor manslaughter was held to be entitled to recover an indemnity for the damages awarded against him, and taking into account that at the time of the argument in *James* the Bill which was to become the Road Traffic Act 1930 making motor insurance compulsory was before Parliament so that any decision in favour of the insurers would be reversed by legislation. It is noteworthy that the argument in *James* was not directed to liability insurance generally, but only to its application to losses arising from criminal activity.[166] That is not surprising, since liability insurance for employee claims had become widespread since its origins in 1880, and familiarity with it had provided elements of the operation of the workmen's compensation schemes. It would be far-fetched to suggest that *James* and *Tinline* were needed to establish the legitimacy of liability insurance *per se*.

3.5.3 Triggers

An important feature of liability insurance policies whose significance has not always been grasped relates to the variety of possible triggers. In other words, to what does the policy respond? There are three broad possibilities, leaving aside the various subclasses: (a) the negligent act of the assured (causation); (b) the injury suffered by the third party (injury); or (c) the making of a claim against the assured (claims made). Claims made policies raise discrete questions considered in later paragraphs. Initially, we outline the differences between causation and injury.

The earliest marine and personal injury liability policies responded to liability for damage inflicted during the currency of the policy ('injury'). There was no need to distinguish between the negligent act and the injury, because the latter would follow the former more or less instantaneously where, for example, two ships collided or

163 So, for example, *Colbourne v Patmore* (1834) related to the enforceability of an indemnity on the part of someone instructing the claimant to publish a libel (which was a criminal offence)—not a third-party insurer promising to indemnify for accident liability.

164 [1927] 2 KB 311.

165 [1921] 3 KB 327.

166 Chapter 11 discusses the question of criminality and liability insurance claims.

a passenger was injured alighting from a train. It was not until the passing of the Employers' Liability Act 1880, when claims by employees against their employers became a realistic possibility, that the limitations of such wording became apparent.[167] An employee who was negligently exposed to a harmful substance in one year might not suffer injury until a later year, so that 'long-tail' claims raised the question of whether the policy attached to the exposure or to the injury. The problem was exacerbated by the passing of the Workmen's Compensation Act 1897, under which the courts construed the word 'injury' as including some forms of disease, and again by the Workmen's Compensation Act 1906 which for the first time recognized disease as a free-standing head of compensation. If the assured has a causation policy, the insurers will not be liable for injury suffered in the currency of the policy if it arose from a pre-policy act of negligence. By contrast, if the assured has an injury policy, the insurer is not liable for negligent acts committed in the policy year unless they result in injuries in the same year. The basis of the coverage depends upon the wording, and we discuss the point in full in Chapter 13. The law has concluded that employers' liability policies referring to 'injury sustained' are to be construed as causation wording[168] whereas public liability policies using the same phrase take effect as injury covers and thus, in long-tail cases, provide cover for negligence having taken place in the distant past.[169] The phrase 'disease contracted' appears to mean causation in both classes of cover.

The 'claims made' trigger has been developed for use in the professional indemnity market.[170] Under this form of wording the insurers face liability for claims made against the assured during the currency of the policy, even though the claims emanate from acts of negligence committed in earlier periods. Such policies are generally extended to cover circumstances which may give rise to a claim but which have not yet done so, if they are notified to the insurers during the currency of the policy, in which case any later claim against the assured is deemed to have been made when the circumstances were notified. This form of insurance has proved to be cheaper and easier to rate, given that it rests upon known previous conduct of the assured. Just how far back the acts of negligence may go depends upon policy wording, but claims made policies generally contain a 'retroactive date'[171] which excludes any earlier acts of negligence. Claims made policies, although in widespread use, give rise to a series of problems. First, although the primary form of cover is for a 'claim' *against the assured* within the policy period, in practice the assured is aware of a problem before a final claim is pressed by the third party and accordingly the vast majority of claims *by the assured* take the form of notification of circumstances of which the assured has become

[167] Chapter 9.

[168] *Employers' Liability Insurance 'Trigger' Litigation: BAI (Run Off) Ltd v Durham* [2012] UKSC 14.

[169] *Bolton MBC v Municipal Mutual Insurance Ltd* [2006] EWCA Civ 50; [2006] 1 WLR 1492, the correctness of which was left open in *Employers' Liability Insurance 'Trigger' Litigation: BAI (Run Off) Ltd v Durham* [2012] UKSC 14.

[170] It has been used in other forms of liability insurance, even employer's liability, but the modern trend is to confine claims made to the professional indemnity market.

[171] In some cases this may be the commencement of the policy period itself, so that cover is limited to acts of negligence which give rise to claims against the assured (or at least notifiable circumstances) but only where both occur in the policy period. It will be appreciated that very little insurance is in practice provided under a policy drafted in this fashion.

aware and which may give rise to a claim. That, however, has led to disputes[172] as to the meaning of knowledge, as to the person within the assured's organization who possesses that knowledge, and as to exactly when a circumstance may, or is likely[173] to, give rise to a claim. Second, a policy will typically exclude circumstances which have been, or could have been, notified in an earlier year, so that if an assured fails to appreciate that circumstances of which he is aware in year 1 might give rise to a claim, and they do in year 2, the year 2 insurers may rely upon such a clause to deny liability. Third, there may be difficulty in establishing a causal link between the circumstances notified and the later claim: by way of example, a notification to insurers by the insured designer of the circumstance that a building has developed flooding problems to its walkways is not enough to allow a later claim to be made against those insurers in respect of defective foundations, as there is no causal link between the notification and the actual damage for which liability may be incurred by the assured.[174]

In all forms of liability insurance there will be an obligation on the assured to notify insurers of an actual or potential claim. In the case of a causation or injury policy, failure to notify will constitute a breach of a policy condition, and such breach may[175] entitle insurers to deny liability. In the case of a claims made policy, failure to notify means that there is no coverage at all. Accordingly, it is unsurprising that a third party who has an actual or potential claim against a wrongdoer may urge the wrongdoer to inform his liability insurers forthwith, failing which—even if the third party succeeds in his action against the wrongdoer—there will simply be no insurance coverage in respect of the claim.[176]

3.5.4 Indemnity and aggregation

Policies, other than those on life, are designed to provide an indemnity against loss. If there is an assumption that the existence of insurance against the liability in question means that insurers will pay the bill whatever its amount, then it is misconceived. Insurers protect themselves against unlimited liability by two forms of financial restriction. The first is the deductible, which is the financial point at which the insurer's liability is triggered. A deductible is in part designed to guarantee that the assured bears some part of any claim so that the assured's care and responsibility are built into to the risk, and in part designed to protect the insurers against small claims. In general terms, the higher the deductible level is set, the lower the premium will be. In practice, where

[172] For these issues: *Kidsons v Lloyd's Underwriters* [2008] EWCA Civ 1206; [2009] 1 Lloyd's Rep 8.

[173] 'Likely' means more likely than not, ie, more than a 50 per cent chance, whereas 'may' is a wider concept which requires notification of events which are not necessarily likely to give rise to a claim but may well do so.

[174] *Kajima UK Engineering Ltd v Underwater Insurance Co Ltd* [2008] EWHC 83 (TCC); [2008] Lloyd's Rep IR 391. See also the controversial decision in *McManus Seddon Runhams v European Risk Insurance Co* [2013] EWHC 18 (Ch) allowing for the notification of all potential claims without identifying the claimants or the contracts.

[175] Discussed in later paragraphs.

[176] But note that notification clauses cannot be enforced in compulsory policies issued under the motor and employers' liability legislation. Further, when the Third Parties (Rights against Insurers) Act 2010 comes into force, breach by the assured of a notification clause (at least under a causation or injury policy—the position of claims made policies is unclear under the legislation) cannot be relied upon by the insurers as a defence to a direct claim by the third party following the assured's insolvency.

the assured or reinsured faces a large deductible, that deductible can be insured under a separate policy with other insurers or sometimes the same insurers.[177] The second is the policy limit, namely the maximum sum for which the insurers can be liable under the policy. All of this is straightforward enough when the assured has suffered just one loss or faces only a single claim from a third party. However, if there is more than one claim, it is necessary to determine whether the assured bears only a single deductible (in that he is able to aggregate the claims and treat them as a single claim) or, if the claims are substantial, whether the insurers can assert that the limit of indemnity applies to the total amount of all claims made against the assured so that he cannot claim a separate limit of indemnity for each claim.[178]

This, then, is the function of aggregation clauses: they determine how the policy responds to more than one claim. One of the initial points which should be made here is that in general terms the ability to aggregate claims for the purposes of a deductible works in the assured's favour, whereas the ability of the insurers to aggregate claims for the purposes of policy limits works in the insurers' favour. Given that the same words are often used to express how aggregation works in both contexts, there is plainly no possibility of applying the *contra proferentem* principle, because it is impossible to say which side of the argument the parties will be on in any given case, as all will depend upon the size and number of losses.

Examples may clarify the point. The Road Traffic Act 1988, s 145(4)(b) imposes a compulsory insurance requirement upon the users of vehicles on public roads in respect of third-party property damage to a minimum amount of £1 million caused by or arising out of out of 'any one accident'. A speeding driver loses control, spins into a parked high performance vehicle (written off at a cost of £100,000), and bounces into a shop window (causing damage to structure and contents totalling £950,000). Is there one accident or two? There is no obvious answer, as it depends upon whether the matter is looked at from the point of view of the assured or the point of view of the victims.[179] The same point arises under the Employers' Liability (Compulsory Insurance) Act 1969, where the minimum sum insured under a compulsory policy is £5 million in respect of 'a claim relating to any one or more . . . employees arising out of any one occurrence'.[180] An employer negligently exposes a large number of employees to a dangerous substance over a period of months and they all suffer injuries: are all the exposures to be regarded as the same occurrence because they have a common origin? These examples both relate to policy limits, but the same point arises with deductibles. In *Standard Life Assurance Ltd v Oak Dedicated Ltd*[181] the assured obtained a liability

[177] The latter form of cover is known as 'deductible buy-back'.

[178] Excess of loss reinsurance treaties are drafted on an aggregation basis, so that the reinsurers' liability attaches only when aggregate losses reach a given figure. Very often aggregation is defined in terms of all losses arising from a single event.

[179] The latter would seem to be correct, so that there are as many accidents as there are victims: *South Staffordshire Tramways Co Ltd v Sickness and Accident Assurance Association Ltd* [1891] 1 QB 402; *Allen v London Guarantee and Accident Co Ltd* (1912) 28 TLR 254. See also; *Tioxide Europe Ltd v CGU International Insurance plc* [2004] EWHC 2116 (Comm); [2005] Lloyd's Rep IR 114, affirmed on other grounds [2005] EWCA Civ 928; [2006] Lloyd's Rep IR 31.

[180] Employers' Liability (Compulsory Insurance) Regulations 1998, SI 1998/2573, reg 3.

[181] [2008] EWHC 222 (Comm); [2008] Lloyd's Rep IR 552.

policy for the sum of £75 million, with a deductible of £25 million 'each and every claim and/or claimant'.The concluding words 'and/or claimant' had been added on renewal, and they were held by Tomlinson J to mean that the deductible applied to each person with a claim against the assured. This meant that, although the assured had received some 97,000 claims and had incurred liabilities in excess of £100 million, nothing was recoverable because no single claimant sought to recover anything close to £25 million: indeed, the average claim was less than £10,000.

There are various terms which may be used to delimit whether losses can be aggregated, including accident, event, occurrence, loss, claim, and cause. It is impossible to be definitive as to the meaning of these words, because each has to be construed in the context of the policy in which it appears. However, it is possible to make some broad generalizations from the cases, which may hold good if the context does not dictate otherwise. The two terms most commonly used are event/occurrence (which are regarded as interchangeable) and 'cause'. An event is 'something which happens at a particular time, at a particular place and in a particular way' whereas a cause 'is something altogether less constricted. It can be a continuing state of affairs; it can be the absence of something happening'.[182] In other words, 'the word event or occurrence describes what has happened; the word "cause" describes why something has happened'.[183] In tort cases the point most commonly arises where the assured has adopted a course of conduct which has led to multiple losses. Thus: where the assured is a provider of financial products and has failed to train staff properly, resulting in them selling inappropriate products to consumers, the cause is the failure to train and the event is each individual sale;[184] where the assured Lloyd's underwriter has a blind spot which causes him to enter into a series of reinsurance agreements which cause loss to Syndicate members, the blind spot is the cause[185] and each contract of reinsurance is the event;[186] and where the assured is a manufacturer of goods, and in manufacturing does so using a negligent process or design, the negligence is the cause and each defective product is the event.[187] The same distinction between state of affairs and loss-causing incident is also found in property coverage cases.[188]

The effect of a per event deductible is, therefore, that the assured is only able to recover for individual losses which exceed the deductible. If it is pitched at a high level

[182] The quotations are from Lord Mustill in *Axa Reinsurance (UK) plc v Field* [1996] 3 All ER 517; [1996] 1 WLR 1026.

[183] *Countrywide Assured Group plc v Marshall* [2002] EWHC 2082 (Comm); [2003] Lloyd's Rep IR 195.

[184] *Countrywide*, n 183.

[185] *Cox v Bankside Members Agency Ltd* [1995] 2 Lloyd's Rep 437.

[186] *Caudle v Sharp* [1995] LRLR 433; also *American Centennial Insurance Co v INSCO Ltd* [1996] LRLR 407.

[187] *James Budgett Sugars v Norwich Union Insurance* [2002] EWHC 968 (Comm); [2003] Lloyd's Rep IR 110; *Seele Austria GmbH & Co KG v Tokio Marine Europe Insurance Ltd* [2008] EWCA Civ 441; [2008] Lloyd's Rep IR 739. In *IRB Brasil Resseguros SA v CX Reinsurance Company Ltd* [2010] EWHC 974 (Comm); [2010] Lloyd's Rep IR 560, Burton J upheld an arbitration award which held that a decision by an employer to install asbestos at its premises was an 'event'. The point was not discussed in detail and the decision may be explained on the grounds that the court was unwilling to overturn an arbitration award, but it does not seem consistent with authority.

[188] *Kuwait Airways Corporation v Kuwait Insurance Co SAK* [1996] 1 Lloyd's Rep 664; *Scott v Copenhagen Reinsurance Co (UK) Ltd* [2003] EWCA Civ 688; [2003] Lloyd's Rep IR 696; *Mann v Lexington Insurance Co* [2001] Lloyd's Rep IR 179; *Aioi Nissay Dowa Insurance Co Ltd v Heraldglen Ltd* [2013] EWHC 154 (Comm); [2013] All ER (D) 102 (Feb).

and the individual losses are small, then—as in *Standard Life v Oak*[189]—little or nothing may be recoverable. For that reason policies may use 'series' clauses designed to deem all events in a series to be a single event carrying only one deductible. There are many types of wordings found in practice, and to date they have been of limited success.[190] Some policies also contain aggregate extension clauses, which allow the assured to aggregate individual unrelated losses of the same type: it appears that this form of wording originated in the United States, to deal with the problem of lids popping off bottles of gaseous drinks.[191]

3.6 Does Liability Influence Liability Insurance?

In later chapters we consider whether the law of obligations has been influenced by the existence of liability insurance. Here, however, we flip the coin and pose the often-neglected question whether construction is influenced by the substantive liability which is faced by the policyholder.[192] Do the courts seek to construe insurance policies in a way which matches the law of liability? We suggest that the influence of liability upon policy construction is real but neither consistent nor straightforward. This is an appropriate context in which to observe the degree to which courts 'vacillate' between relatively formalistic, and contextual, substantive responses to relational disputes,[193] and the degree to which they are confident to reason purposively, in light of the liabilities concerned. In other words, is the existence of liability rather like public law regulation in its influence,[194] operating to inject a degree of purposiveness to the courts' interpretive role?

Potentially, a liability policy has two purposes which do not necessarily easily combine: to provide funds for the compensation of the third party; and to reduce the personal exposure to liability of the assured. To make matters more complex, social policy has produced a number of interventions into the operation of liability insurance directed at securing funds to satisfy tort claims,[195] in making insurance compulsory and in regulating the terms of insurance policies covering compulsory risks.[196] For these reasons, interpretation of liability insurance policies takes place in an environment affected by a hybrid of private law techniques and public ordering of private relations. Failures to provide expected coverage may either frustrate the purposes of liability; or expose the assured to a personal responsibility beyond convincing justification. It appears right, for example, that an assured who commits an act intended to

[189] *Standard Life v Oak*, n 181.

[190] *Lloyds TSB General Insurance Holdings v Lloyds Bank Insurance Co Ltd* [2003] UKHL 48; [2003] Lloyd's Rep IR 623; *Beazley Underwriting Ltd v Travelers Companies Inc* [2011] EWHC 1520 (Comm); [2012] Lloyd's Rep IR 78, the sequel claim against the brokers who placed the policy in *Standard Life v Oak* (n 181).

[191] Hence their popular name: 'Coca Cola Clauses'.

[192] J Steele, 'Tort, Insurance, and the Resources of Private Law', in S Degeling, J Edelman, and J Goudkamp (eds), *Torts in Commercial Law* (Sydney: Thomson Reuters, 2011).

[193] Collins, n 59, 196.

[194] Discussed in 3.3.

[195] Under the Third Parties (Rights against Insurers) Acts 1930 and 2010: Chapter 13.

[196] Chapter 9.

cause harm should not be able to recover an indemnity from insurers, but from the victim's point of view it is immaterial whether the injury was inflicted negligently or deliberately—or, indeed, deliberately inflicted injury may particularly require a remedy. Again, an assured who fails to cooperate with insurers in handling a claim may deserve little sympathy if the courts are considered to be engaged primarily in regulating the market relationship between assured and insurer, but the position is quite different if the assured has become insolvent and has no interest in the claim so that the main loser from the assured's diffidence is the victim whose injuries have generated the claim.

It may thus be asked whether there is any discernible difference between the approach of the courts to liability policies, and in particular to compulsory liability policies where insuring and other terms are to a greater or lesser extent fixed, and to other insurance policies, or indeed to contracts in general. There appears to be no wholly consistent view as to whether the predominant purpose of liability insurance is to protect the policyholder against potentially ruinous claims or to provide the third-party victim with a source of compensation in the event of the wrongdoer's insolvency.[197] This is, in part, because interpretation of the purpose of liabilities themselves is not necessarily straightforward. But it is also because it is unclear to what extent courts think it legitimate to adjust interpretation of policy terms in order to reflect the nature and purpose of the insurance. There are at least three reasons for this. First, the resolution of the tension between the two objectives is crucial only where the sole prospect of the claimant recovering any compensation awarded to him is from the defendant's insurance; if the defendant has his own resources, then recovery under the policy is equivalent to making good what is in essence a first-party loss, so the wider social function of liability has no part to play. Often it will be obvious into which category the defendant falls, but it would plainly be invidious for a court to adjust its conclusion based upon the perceived financial position of the defendant. Second, every judicial ruling creates a precedent as to the meaning of the words used, and again it would be wrong to adopt a strained construction to meet the facts of any one case when that construction could have implications for countless other policyholders, the market, and indeed reinsurers. Third, and related to the second point, construction can be a double-edged sword. Words of coverage in some policies may be express exclusions from others, so a constant meaning is required. A further example may be drawn from the concept of aggregation. As pointed out above, policies may restrict coverage both by imposing a policy deductible on, and by specifying the maximum sum recoverable for, every event, occurrence, cause, or claim. In *South Staffordshire Tramways Co v Sickness & Accident Assurance Association*[198] a public liability policy imposed a policy limit of £250 in respect of 'any one accident'. A tramcar overturned, injuring some forty people and giving rise to total liability of £833. The Court of Appeal,

[197] For example, the approach of Megaw LJ in his dissenting judgment in *Richardson v Pitt-Stanley* [1995] QB 123; [1995] 2 WLR 26. But contrast Stanley Burnton LJ in *Durham v BAI (Run-off) Ltd* [2010] EWCA Civ 1096; [2011] Lloyd's Rep IR 1 (though the decision of the Court of Appeal was reversed by the Supreme Court: Chapter 12).

[198] [1891] 1 QB 402.

accepting that the policy was ambiguous, construed the term 'accident' as referring to each individual injury rather than to the overturning of the tramcar, so that the policy cap applied to each claim separately rather to the aggregate of claims. At first instance Lawrence J made clear that the underlying reason for this approach was that

> the object of the policy was to provide for the assured an indemnity against claims made upon them for injuries resulting from the negligence of their servants. This being so, I think it more appropriate to hold that the preceding word, 'accidents,' is used from the point of view of the several claimants upon the assured for injuries, each of whom claims in respect of a specific accident to himself, and not from that of the insurers, and that therefore 'any one accident' means any accident to any one claimant upon the insured.[199]

But would the same result have been reached if the policy had required the assured to bear, for example, the first £50 of each accident? That would have given little or no recovery.[200]

The evidence of influence of wider considerations on liability policy construction is patchy. If motor insurance in the post-1930 compulsory era is discounted, liability insurance decisions constitute a relatively small proportion of the total body of insurance case law. It can at least be said that there are some decisions which are explicable only by reference to the desire to protect third-party claimants. A clear illustration of such influence is *Employers' Liability Insurance 'Trigger' Litigation: BAI (Run Off) Ltd v Durham*,[201] where—as is seen in Chapter 12—the Supreme Court interpreted the terms of an employers' liability policy in accordance with the perceived purpose of providing compensation to the victims of exposure injuries as well as to the victims of instantaneous injuries, though it did so through the mediating idea of the 'commercial purpose' of the insurance policies sold. Other illustrations can be seen in early cases on workers' compensation policies, where there have been narrow interpretations of the obligations imposed by policy conditions,[202] echoed in later cases.[203] However, there are many other cases on similar facts decided on entirely traditional grounds[204] without regard to their implications for third-party recoveries, although in at least some of them the courts have recognized and expressed regret as to the consequences of their rulings, particularly where the assured was insolvent and the outcome actually determined whether the victim would receive any compensation at all under the Third Parties (Rights against Insurers) Act 1930.[205]

[199] [1891] 1 QB 402.

[200] As in *Tioxide Europe Ltd v CGU International Insurance plc* [2005] EWCA Civ 928; [2006] Lloyd's Rep IR 31.

[201] [2012] UKSC 14; [2012] 1 WLR 867.

[202] *Re An Arbitration between Coleman's Depositories, Ltd and the Life and Health Assurance Association* [1907] 2 KB 798; *Re Bradley and Essex and Suffolk Accident Indemnity Society* [1912] 1 KB 415; *General Motors Ltd v Crowder* (1931) 40 Ll L R 87.

[203] *Lickiss v Milestone Motor Policies at Lloyd's* [1966] 1 WLR 1334; *Jacobs v Coster* [2000] Lloyd's Rep IR 506.

[204] *Aspen Insurance UK Ltd v Pectel Ltd* [2008] EWHC 2804 (Comm); [2009] Lloyd's Rep IR 440; *China Ping An Insurance (Hong Kong) Co Ltd v Tsang Fu Yin*, HKCFI, 19 March 2012.

[205] For example, *Pioneer Concrete v National Employers Mutual Insurance* [1985] 1 Lloyd's Rep 274.

It is also the case that the limits of tort law will explain the limits of coverage. Product liability policies have accordingly been construed to reflect tort liability, so that in the absence of some form of extension of coverage the assured cannot seek to rely upon a product liability policy for third-party claims which go beyond ordinary tort principles.[206] The courts have thus held that the insuring clause of a product liability policy will respond where the defective product is a component in a finished product which has been damaged by a defect in the component,[207] but it does not extend to business interruption claims arising from loss of custom for the finished product consequent on the defect in the component,[208] nor to the cost of remedying the defect itself,[209] or to diminution in the value of the defective product.[210]

3.7 Conclusions

In this chapter, we have explored some key features of the insurance contract and reviewed the development of the insurance market in response to new risks, including risks of liability. The close fit between obligations and insurance has been highlighted, and the link between insurance and the growth of negligence has been debated. We have explained that in relation to insurance contracts, until relatively recently the legislature has taken a back seat and the law has developed largely by way of response to the disputes of contracting parties. The recent superimposition of voluntary and then statutory controls over consumer and small business contracts, discussed in the next chapter, has served to correct the imbalances in the common law, but does not detract from our basic point that substantive insurance law in England is approached as essentially a private matter. This in turn reflects the fact that the degree of individual negotiation found in the market does not match the US perception of insurance contracts as quasi-legislation.

[206] The third-party claim against the assured may, for example, be for breach of contract, or for the costs of precautions necessary to prevent loss from defects in a product.

[207] *James Budgett Sugars Ltd v Norwich Union Insurance* [2003] Lloyd's Rep IR 114; *Tioxide Europe Ltd v CGU International Insurance plc* [2004] EWHC 2116 (Comm); [2006] Lloyd's Rep IR 31.

[208] *Rodan International Ltd v Commercial Union* [1999] Lloyd's Rep IR 495.

[209] *Rodan*, n 208; *Pilkington United Kingdom Ltd v CGU Insurance plc* [2004] EWCA Civ 23; [2004] Lloyd's Rep IR 891; *Horbury Building Systems v Hampden Insurance NV* [2004] EWCA Civ 418; [2007] Lloyd's Rep IR 247.

[210] *John Wyeth & Brothers Ltd v Cigna Insurance Co of Europe SA/NV* [2001] Lloyd's Rep IR 40 (drug which did not work but did not cause any harm), although contrast *Selected Seeds Pty Ltd v QBEMM Pty Ltd* [2010] HCA 37, where the High Court of Australia ruled that seed which was unfit for its purpose had damaged the land in which it had been planted, thereby giving the assured a claim against its product liability insurers for what at first sight seems to be a straight action for breach of contract.

4

Regulatory Dimensions

4.1 Introduction and Significance

The use of insurance to protect against contingencies is found in the earliest societies. It was seen in Chapter 3 that by the middle of the nineteenth century, life, marine, and fire insurance were firmly established in the UK, and thereafter as risks emerged new forms of insurance were developed to protect against potential losses from them. The significance of insurance for commerce and for the protection of families against loss of income was apparent to the legislature from an early stage: the Marine Insurance Act 1745 and the Life Assurance Act 1774, both designed to prevent the use of insurance as a means of gambling, may also have been seen as measures to protect the integrity of the activity.[1] Insurance calls for regulatory intervention more than almost any other class of commercial operation: there is an obvious risk of insurer insolvency if underwriting is based on incorrect principles and projections; the insurance fund, even if adequate, has to be protected against diminution on unrelated activities; the consequences for policyholders following an insurer insolvency are potentially more catastrophic than in any other field of commercial activity; business dealings are predicated upon the parties' respective insurance positions; and, as explored in particular in Chapters 1 and 9, private insurance has been utilized by successive governments to fund and otherwise support the tort system. Unsurprisingly, therefore, insurance regulation has been a key feature of government policy for close to 150 years. Indeed, solvency and prudential regulation is older and more extensive for the insurance industry than for any other.

The *laissez-faire* ideology of the nineteenth century, reflected in the 'light touch' regulation which prevailed until the financial crisis in 2007, produced a minimalist approach to regulation in the UK. A brief survey of the history of insurance regulation shows an *ad hoc* approach. Measures were introduced to counter particular problems demonstrated by insurance company failures, but in a manner designed to encourage rather than to stifle product development. Most importantly, it is a distinctive feature of the UK's approach that regulatory concern has been focused on the financial ability of insurers to pay policyholders rather than on whether insurers actually choose to do so. 'Material' regulation, in the form of control over policy terms and premiums was anathema. This may be contrasted with the position in many European civil law jurisdictions. However, the aim of the EU to create a Single Insurance Market changed the European picture. This was achieved by the harmonization of regulatory standards rather than substantive law. Those countries which operated material control were required to abandon it, in favour of harmonized regulatory standards which allowed an insurer regulated in one Member State to trade freely in all other Member States

[1] The first instance judgment of Langley J in *Feasey v Sun Life Assurance of Canada* [2002] EWHC 868 (Comm); [2002] Lloyd's Rep IR 807.

without intervention from any host State regulators. All of this was achieved in a succession of life and non-life directives beginning in 1973 before ultimate refinement in 2009.[2] EU policyholder protection[3] is instead found in conflict of laws rules under which consumer and small business assureds are given the benefit of their domestic substantive law irrespective of the nationality of the insurers.[4]

The traditional UK approach is also quite different from that in the United States, where state-level regulation embraces licensing requirements, regulation of policy terms, review of rates, and financial examination of insurers.[5] By statute Australia, and to a lesser extent New Zealand, similarly regulate the terms of insurance policies.[6] The US approach has led to a consumerist approach to the law of insurance, and judgments are replete with the statement that policy terms are to be interpreted by courts to accord with the reasonable expectations of assured parties,[7] a concept not recognized elsewhere in the common law world.

The public law contrast between complex solvency regulation and all but non-existent substantive law control is even more marked when set against the often draconian common law rules applicable to insurance contracts, as outlined in Chapter 3. It is only in recent years that eighteenth-century commercial principles have been removed from the consumer sphere, initially by self-regulation in the form of the Insurance Ombudsman Bureau and the Statements of Insurance Practice, subsequently by administrative regulation under the Financial Services and Markets Act 2000, and, most recently, by a limited piece of legislation in the shape of the Consumer Insurance (Disclosure and Representations) Act 2012. What is noteworthy from the following discussion is how it has been left primarily to public law administrative processes to resolve the difficulties and iniquities arising from private law. Insurance law as it appears in the books is, as a result of regulatory intervention, far removed from how it is applied in practice.

4.2 Regulating the Insurance Activity

4.2.1 Insurance companies

The Bubble Act 1720 had inhibited but not stifled the formation of insurance companies, although in the period up to the repeal of the Bubble Act in 1824 there was only

[2] European Parliament and Council Directive 2009/138/EC, the 'Solvency 2' Directive. This replaced the three non-life Directives (73/239/EEC, 88/357/EEC, and 92/49 EEC) and the Consolidated Life Directive (2002/83/EC, replacing three earlier life directives).

[3] The process was far from seamless, and a series of decisions of the CJEU (the 'insurance cases') made it clear that the Directives had to take account of the 'general good', so that member states were permitted to apply their general standards of consumer protection to insurance contracts. See: Case 205/84, *Commission v Germany* [1987] 2 CMLR 69; Case 220/83, *Commission v France* [1987] 2 CMLR 113; Case 206/84, *Commission v Ireland* [1987] 2 CMLR 150; Case 252/83, *Commission v Denmark* [1987] 2 CMLR 169.

[4] A principle now embodied in the Rome I Regulation 2009, reg 7.

[5] WK Sjostrom, Jr, 'The AIG Bailout' (2009) 66 Wash & Lee LR 943, 987, contrasting the different treatment of credit default swaps despite their fitting general descriptions of 'insurance'.

[6] Respectively: Insurance Contracts Act 1984 (Cth); Insurance Law Reform Acts 1977 and 1985.

[7] TL Hazen, 'Disparate Regulatory Schemes for Parallel Activities: Securities Regulation, Derivatives Regulation, Gambling and Insurance' (2005) 24 Ann Rev Banking and Fin L 375, 431 (referring to the 'paternalistic' and consumer-oriented element in US insurance contract interpretation).

one failure of the thirty-nine companies formed in that period.[8] From 1824 onwards companies began to appear, but many were not based on sound actuarial principles and a substantial percentage failed, that figure rocketing following the Joint Stock Companies Act 1844 and the opportunities conferred by new-found limited liability.[9] The trigger for action was the failure of the Albert Life Assurance Co in 1869, which on its insolvency took with it some twenty-four other life offices which it had absorbed in a rush of acquisitiveness. The outcome was the Life Assurance Companies Act 1870, which required any insurer carrying on life business, whether alone or in conjunction with non-life business, to deposit £20,000 with the Accountant-General as a guarantee of solvency.[10] This measure introduced a concept which remains to the present day, namely, the separation of life and non-life assets, with the former being ring-fenced to protect what was seen even then in terms of the long-term investment of the holders of life policies. The deposit system was extended to employers' liability insurance by the Employers' Liability Insurance Companies Act 1907, recognizing the widespread adoption of such insurance and its role as the prop for the workmen's compensation legislation and, by the Assurance Companies Act 1909, to fire, personal accident, and bond investment covers. The deficiencies of the deposit system were documented by the Clauson Committee Report in 1924,[11] but deposit was retained and indeed extended to compulsory motor insurance by the Road Traffic Act 1930, and also to industrial assurance[12] and aviation insurance.[13] The most important Clauson recommendation to be adopted was the grant of power to the Board of Trade to petition for the winding up of insolvent insurers and of insurers who failed to comply with statutory obligations.[14]

The shift away from deposit as a measure of solvency, and to licensing based on a measure of assets and liabilities, was finally implemented by the Assurance Companies Act 1946, following the recommendations of the Cassel Committee, reporting in 1937.[15] Although the Cassel Committee was set up in order to consider the new phenomenon of compulsory liability insurance, and was itself prompted by the failure of motor insurers undermining the purpose of the legislation,[16] all classes of insurance were now brought within the regulatory regime, and the test of authorization and continued trading was the establishment and maintenance of a solvency margin. The legislation was tightened following further failures, but a new and tougher financial regime was introduced by the Insurance Companies Act 1974 which was the immediate response to the failure of the Vehicle and General Insurance group, the collapse of which left over one million drivers without cover. That measure was consolidated by

[8] HE Raynes, *A History of British Insurance* (New York: Garland, 3rd edn, 1983), 353.

[9] Rising from around 45 per cent to 75 per cent. Some of the worst excesses are discussed in DEW Gibb, *Lloyd's of London: A Study of Individualism* (London: Macmillan, 1957), 80–81.

[10] The tale may be found in *Re Albert Life* (1871) LR 14 Eq 72.

[11] Cmnd 2820.

[12] Which provided low-level life and injury benefit, the premiums being collected door to door: Industrial Assurance Act 1923.

[13] Air Navigation Act 1936, a measure which was never brought into force.

[14] Insurance Companies (Winding Up) Act 1935.

[15] *Report by the Committee on Compulsory Insurance* (HMSO, 1937).

[16] Discussed further in Chapter 9.

the Insurance Companies Act 1982, but it was to last less than two decades. The Financial Services and Markets Act 2000 was prompted by three factors: the completion of the Single European Market for insurance; the need to repeal the failed self-regulatory system for investment contracts, including life insurance, established by the Financial Services Act 1986;[17] and the desire to regulate all financial services by a common regulator and using, so far as is possible, the same broad principles.

4.2.2 Financial Services and Markets Act 2000

The existing regulation of insurance companies in the UK set out in the Financial Services and Markets Act 2000 (FSMA 2000), as amended by the Financial Services Act 2012,[18] is a fascinating combination of public law, private law, and self-regulation. Elements of all of the earlier structures remain in place, but the overall pattern is novel. The legislation itself is supplemented by numerous statutory instruments and, most importantly, the Handbook published by the then regulator, the Financial Services Authority, the functions of which have been transferred by the 2012 amendments to the Prudential Regulation Authority (PRA) (which is concerned with solvency) and the Financial Conduct Authority (FCA) (which is concerned with market conduct and the treatment of customers). Each regulator now has its own Handbook. The 2000 Act is an all-embracing piece of legislation, catching all financial services, and it has a number of distinct themes: preserving solvency; regulation of marketing; supervision of conduct; resolution of disputes through the Financial Ombudsman Service;[19] and protection of investors under the Financial Services Compensation Scheme.[20] What is significant here is the spread of regulation from solvency to substantive law.

Each of the two regulators has statutory objectives relating to the financial system in general and insurers in particular.[21] The FCA has the strategic objective of ensuring that the financial markets work well, and the functional objectives of securing an appropriate degree of consumer protection, protecting and enhancing the integrity of the financial system and promoting competition in the interests of consumers.[22] The PRA's general objective is promoting the safety and soundness of the providers of financial services, and it has a specific insurance objective of contributing to the securing of an appropriate degree of protection for those who are or may become policyholders.[23] Supervisory powers are exercised by the regulators under a hierarchy of provisions: making general rules; preparing and issuing codes; giving general guidance in the form of information and advice about the operation of the Act and the rules; and determining general policy and principles.[24] All of this is contained in the Handbooks issued by the two regulators, which state into which category a provision falls and the consequences of its infringement.

17 The so-called 'Big Bang', which led to a disastrous period of product mis-selling.

18 The background is given in <http://www.hm-treasury.gov.uk/reform_and_regulation.htm>, accessed 23 April 2013.

19 Discussed in Chapter 3.

20 Examined in subsequent paragraphs.

21 The complex relationship between them is given in FSMA 2000, ss 3D–3Q.

22 FSMA 2000, ss 1B to 1E.

23 FSMA 2000, ss 2B to 2C.

24 FSMA 2000, ss 138–57.

There are eleven high-level Principles for Business set out in the PRIN section of the Handbooks, requiring a firm to: conduct its business with integrity; conduct its business with skill, care, and diligence; take reasonable care to organize and control its affairs responsibly and effectively, with adequate risk-management systems; maintain adequate financial resources; observe proper standards of market conduct; pay due regard to the interests of its customers and treat them fairly; pay due regard to the information needs of its clients, and communicate information to them in a way which is clear, fair, and not misleading; manage conflicts of interest fairly, both between itself and its customers and between a customer and another client; take reasonable care to ensure the suitability of its advice and discretionary decisions for any customer who is entitled to rely upon its judgement; arrange adequate protection for clients' assets when it is responsible for them; and deal with its regulators in an open and cooperative way, disclosing to the relevant regulator appropriately anything relating to the firm of which the regulator would reasonably expect notice.

There is a prohibition on the carrying on of a regulated activity in the UK[25] without the authorization of either the PRA or the FCA.[26] Regulated activities are set out in the Financial Services and Markets Act 2000 (Regulated Activities) Order 2001[27] and include effecting and carrying out contracts of insurance[28] in the UK.[29] Insurance authorizations are allocated to the PRA, although it will not grant authorization unless the FCA is also satisfied that grant should be made. A distinction is drawn between persons who have no authorization at all and persons who have limited authorization but exceed it. In the former case, a criminal offence is committed and contracts are enforceable only at the option of the client. By contrast, in the latter case there is no criminality and contracts are enforceable. As far as insurance is concerned, there are eighteen classes of general business and nine classes of long-term business, and authorization is required on a class-by-class basis. In order to obtain authorization, the applicant must be a body corporate with its head office in the UK, a fit and proper person meeting training and competence requirements,[30] and satisfying solvency requirements.

The regulation of post-authorization conduct falls under four broad heads. The first head is advertising and promotion. Here, the Handbooks lay down rules for long-term policies in the Conduct of Business Sourcebook (COBS) and rules for general policies in the Insurance Conduct of Business Sourcebook (ICOBS). A distinction is drawn between consumer and business clients, with tougher rules applying to the former. The general duties of an insurer under both ICOBS and COBS are: to take reasonable steps

[25] EU insurers authorized in their home states are exempt.

[26] FSMA 2000, ss 19–54, as amended. The formalities of application are detailed in FSMA 2000, ss 55A–55Z4.

[27] SI 2001/544.

[28] This includes receiving premiums, paying claims, administering policies, and holding out as having the capacity to do any of those things: *Bedford Insurance Co Ltd v Institutio de Resseguros do Brasil* [1985] QB 966; *Ackman and Scher v Policyholders Protection Board* [1993] 2 WLR 479; *R v Wilson* [1997] 1 WLR 1247; *Re Whiteley Insurance Consultants* [2008] EWHC 1782 (Ch); [2009] Lloyd's Rep IR 212.

[29] Pure offshore operations are excluded, although the fact that the insurer is offshore does not evade the prohibition if the activities carried out in the UK are a significant part of the overall activity: *DR Insurance Co v Seguros America Banamex* [1993] 1 Lloyd's Rep 120; *Re Great Western Insurance Co* [1999] Lloyd's Rep IR 377; *Financial Services Authority v Fradley and Woodward* [2005] EWCA Civ 1183; [2005] All ER (D) 314 (Nov).

[30] As set out in the Handbooks.

to ensure that any information is communicated in a fashion that is clear, fair, and not misleading; to comply with the requirements of the Distance Marketing Directive[31] and the E-Commerce Directive[32] where appropriate; to sell only policies under which policyholders can claim benefits; and to allow cancellation within fourteen days. The legislation itself imposes criminal sanctions where false or misleading statements are made or material facts are withheld.[33] The second head is concerned with the fitness and qualifications of persons employed by insurers, and in particular with securing the running of the insurer according to sound and prudent management criteria. The Supervision chapter of the Handbooks (SUP) contains statements of principle and a code of practice for persons approved by insurers to carry on functions for them. Third, the Handbooks include a Prudential Sourcebook for Insurers, INSPRU, which sets out in detail the prudential rules which apply to insurers, including the margin by which assets must exceed liabilities, the separation of long-term and general business, matching rules which require holding of 80 per cent of liabilities in local currency; accounting and actuarial requirements and the maintenance of a minimum guarantee fund representing one-third of the solvency margin. Finally, the 2000 Act[34] maintains the principle that the transfer of insurance business is permitted only with the sanction of the court. A proposed transfer has to be advertised to policyholders so that they have a chance to make comments, and the application to the court must be accompanied by an expert report. The regulator is also entitled to express its views. In practice transfer proposals are prepared with great care to ensure that they are as fair as possible to all parties, and the courts have taken the view that their absolute discretion is to be exercised by giving due recognition to the insurers' respective commercial judgments and ensuring that the reasonable expectations of policyholders are not adversely affected.[35] In practice schemes are always approved.

A variety of sanctions are open to the regulator. These include:[36] withdrawal of authorization where threshold requirements are no longer being met; public censure; the imposition of financial penalties; the right to apply to the court for injunctive relief; the issuing of a prohibition order against anyone who is not a fit and proper person; and the right to apply to the court for a restitution order to compensate persons who have been adversely affected by a contravention of the legislation or rules.

It should be added that the EU Directives referred to in the previous paragraph have been prospectively repealed and replaced by the Solvency 2 Directive of 2009.[37] Solvency 2 was initially scheduled to come into force at the end of 2012 but the earliest implementation date is now the end of 2014. The key features of Solvency 2 are the replacement of the existing test of solvency with an entirely new mechanism which assesses the present and future value of assets and liabilities by reference to modern

31 European Parliament and Council Directive 2002/65/EC.

32 European Parliament and Council Directive 2000/31/EC.

33 Financial Services Act 2012, ss 89 and 90 replacing FSMA 2000, s 397.

34 FSMA 2000, ss 105–14, supplemented by detailed secondary legislation.

35 *Re Allied Dunbar Assurance plc* [2005] EWHC 28 (Ch); [2005] All ER (D) 129 (Jan).

36 FSMA 2000, ss 45–7 and 205–11.

37 European Parliament and Council Directive 2009/138/EC 'on the taking-up and pursuit of the business of Insurance and Reinsurance' (Solvency 2).

actuarial principles and risk assessments; the introduction of a Supervisory Review Process (SRP) extending to strategies and compliance; and enhanced reliance on high-level supervisory principles rather than detailed rules including own risk and solvency assessment (ORSA).

4.2.3 Lloyd's

The origins of Lloyd's as a coffee house and its development into the leading centre for marine insurance in Europe were traced in Chapter 3. For some time the underwriters had no proper organization, but in 1769 a group of underwriters—in part disillusioned by the amount of wagering on lives in the form of insurance being conducted at Lloyd's[38] and in part as a response to increasing competition—broke away, and the future of Lloyd's proved to lie in their hands. In 1773 a Committee was elected and the great achievement of Lloyd's at that time was the formal adoption of the SG Policy in 1779, destined to last for over two centuries. In 1811, following criticism in a Parliamentary Report of 1810 concerning slow payment of claims and withholding of shipping information, Lloyd's formed itself into a Society with a proper management structure. Lloyd's shrugged off the repeal of the Bubble Act in 1824 and continued to dominate the marine market, and in the following years it took steps to secure the solvency of its members. Its failed attempt in 1870 to eject a member for alleged dishonesty[39] led to Lloyd's seeking and obtaining—by the Lloyd's Act 1871—incorporation as a self-regulating Society and Corporation. Thereafter Lloyd's extended its activities from marine to other forms of insurance, and in particular it accepted much business from overseas. Lloyd's own internal supervision secured exemption from the early insurance companies legislation and, with sporadic legislative amendments, the self-regulating status of Lloyd's was confirmed by the Lloyd's Act 1982, as amended by the Legislative Reform (Lloyd's) Order 2008.[40]

Lloyd's itself is not an insurance company, although it operates from a single set of premises in London. It is merely the facilitator and regulator of underwriters carrying on business under the Lloyd's banner. Lloyd's itself is not, therefore, liable to meet claims. The Lloyd's market is composed of underwriters, who are grouped into syndicates, and each syndicate operates independently and more or less in the same way as an insurance company, although some specialize in particular classes of insurance and reinsurance. In June 2013 there were ninety-eight active syndicates in operation. Until 1994 the underwriting members of Lloyd's were all individuals—known as 'Names'—and each bore personal liability for the syndicate's underwriting debts to the extent of his assets. In 1994 corporate capital was for the first time permitted by Lloyd's and the last individual member was admitted in 2003. Thus, today, some 96 per cent of underwriting capacity is in the hands of limited liability corporate members, either companies or limited liability partnerships. Those members are not permitted by Lloyd's rules to carry on any other activity. Each member remains

[38] Outlawed by the Life Assurance Act 1774, discussed in Chapters 3 and 5.
[39] *Forwood v Goschen* 1870, unreported.
[40] SI 2008/3001. This abolished the Committee of Lloyd's.

severally liable for claims.[41] Syndicates are controlled by managing agents, and those wishing to participate at Lloyd's will do so using the services of members' agents who advise on the proper level of investment in available syndicates.

Recent years have seen important developments from three main sources: changes to internal management structures; the EU solvency regime, which has required modifications to the solvency rules affecting Lloyd's; and the near-collapse of the Lloyd's market in the early 1980s following massive financial losses, mainly emanating from the United States from natural disasters and the asbestos claims. The latter resulted in the 'Reconstruction and Renewal' programme under which the slate was wiped clean for existing Names by requiring them to reinsure with a reinsurance company, Equitas, which was established for the purpose. The structure survived a series of ingenious challenges by Names unwilling to pay the substantial premium demanded by Equitas.[42]

Lloyd's itself has made a substantial contribution to tort law, in particular in *Henderson v Merrett Syndicates Ltd*,[43] a series of consolidated actions by Names against members' agents and managing agents. Some of the Names belonged to syndicates where the members' agent and managing agent was the same person (direct Names) and others belonged to syndicates run by managing agents to which they had been allocated by separate members' agents (indirect Names). The House of Lords found for the Names on a series of preliminary issues of law of key significance for the law of tort[44]: direct Names were owed a duty of care by their underwriting agent despite the existence of a contractual relationship between them, rejecting earlier authority for the proposition that the existence of a contract precluded a claim in tort; and indirect Names who did not have any contractual relationship with managing agents were nevertheless owed a duty of care by them even though the only loss capable of being suffered was economic, on the basis that there had been an assumption of responsibility. As to the content of the duty of care, the courts have ruled that a members' agent has to ensure that the member's portfolio is properly balanced and is not allocated mainly to high-risk syndicates. This point was made in *Brown v KMR Services Ltd*[45] where the Court of Appeal ruled that the appropriate measure of damages was based on the allocations that a properly advised member would have made, that the members' agent was liable for the appropriate proportion of the actual losses suffered by the member even though they were unprecedented in their amount, and (perhaps most controversially) that each year of membership constituted a distinct contract with the members' agent and had to be viewed separately so that profits made in one year could not be set off against losses in a later year even though the same negligent course of conduct had generated both. A members' agent is also under a duty to act with due vigilance when considering the underwriting policy of a syndicate,[46] although the members' agent is not responsible for the managing agent's defaults unless the members'

[41] Lloyd's Act 1982, s 8.

[42] The history of the Lloyd's litigation is traced in R Merkin, *Colinvaux's Law of Insurance* (London: Sweet & Maxwell, 9th edn with first supplement, 2012), para 13–038 ff.

[43] [1995] 2 AC 145; [1994] 3 WLR 761.

[44] Contract claims were time-barred, hence the importance of liability in tort.

[45] [1995] 2 Lloyd's Rep 513.

[46] *Aiken v Stewart Wrightson Ltd* [1995] 1 WLR 1281.

agent has failed to act with due diligence.[47] A managing agent's duty is to ensure that the syndicate's underwriting is prudent[48] and that there is adequate reinsurance in place.[49] Under current arrangements at Lloyd's, members have contractual relationships with both the managing agent and the members' agent, although the principles laid down in *Henderson* remain applicable.

One of the most interesting aspects of the structure of Lloyd's from a public law point of view is the statutory immunity conferred upon it from members, brokers and agents. Under Lloyd's Act 1982, s 14, the Society has no liability in damages for negligence, tort, breach of duty, or otherwise (other than defamation) for acts or omissions in relation to the performance of functions or exercise of duties or powers under the Lloyd's Acts or byelaws. It has thus been held that Lloyd's does not owe any common law or statutory[50] duty of care to its members to supervise the market with reasonable care and skill.[51] Further, the courts have ruled that, because Lloyd's does not carry out public functions, it is not susceptible to judicial review[52] or to the tort of misfeasance in public office.[53] Lloyd's has, however, established a procedure for the resolution of complaints by members, and this may ultimately be referred to the Lloyd's Members' Ombudsman Scheme.[54]

4.2.4 Insurance intermediaries

Various intermediaries operate in the insurance market. In the broadest terms, intermediaries may be divided into those acting for the insurers and those acting for the assured. Into the former category fall: employees; selling agents, including those providing insurance as part of a wider service, for example travel agents, motor dealers, banks, retailers, and solicitors; loss adjusters appointed by insurers to investigate loss; and underwriting agents, not in the Lloyd's sense described above, but rather in the sense of a person appointed by an insurer to accept risks on behalf of the insurer. Into the latter category fall brokers; and loss assessors appointed by the assured to assist with claims. The line is not, however, bright, because agents—and, in particular, brokers[55]—often act for both sides and the common law has done little to attempt to reconcile the activities of brokers with general legal and equitable principles.

[47] *Henderson v Merrett Syndicates Ltd* [1995] 2 AC 145; [1994] 3 WLR 761.

[48] *Berriman v Rose Thompson Young* [1996] LRLR 426; *Deeny v Gooda Walker Ltd* [1996] 1 WLR 426; *Wynniatt Hussey v Bromley* [1996] LRLR 310.

[49] *Aiken v Stewart Wrightson Ltd* [1995] 1 WLR 1281.

[50] Under the Supply of Goods and Services Act 1982.

[51] *Society of Lloyd's v Clementson* [1995] LRLR 307. Also *Ashmore v Society of Lloyd's (No 2)* [1992] 2 Lloyd's Rep 620.

[52] *R (on the application of MacMillan and Thompson) v Regulatory Board of Lloyd's of London* [1995] LRLR 485; *R (on the Application of West) v Lloyd's of London* [2004] EWCA Civ 506; [2004] Lloyd's Rep IR 755, holding that the position has not changed under the European Convention on Human Rights.

[53] *Society of Lloyd's v Henderson* [2007] EWCA Civ 930; [2008] 1 WLR 2255.

[54] <http://www.lloyds.com/The-Market/Operating-at-Lloyds/Regulation/Complaints/Corporation-complaints-guidelines>, accessed 25 April 2013, made in compliance with DISP 1.7 in the Disputes section of the FCA Handbook.

[55] Discussed in Chapter 3.

The scope of an agent's authority, and the rights of the agent and insurers, are matters of contract and, until recently, these matters have been untouched by external regulation despite some almost inexplicable decisions in which policyholders have been held to be responsible for the defaults of insurers' paid agents.[56] Partial relief was provided in the context of long-term investment policies under the Financial Services Act 1986, whereby insurers were required to answer for the acts or defaults of their appointed agents, and that principle has been maintained and extended to all forms of insurance under FSMA 2000, s 39. Indeed, under the FCA Handbook appropriate training of agents is a condition of authorization and its maintenance. Employed agents do not themselves require authorization under FSMA 2000, but independent agents—including underwriting agents—must be authorized.

By far the most important class of intermediary is the insurance broker. Brokers were used by merchants to place marine insurance from the earliest times of the practice in England, and were influential in the Chamber of Assurance operating in the Royal Exchange at the end of the seventeenth century. The broker's function was then much as it is now, to visit underwriter merchants and persuade them to subscribe to a proportion of the risk that he had been charged to place. The term 'broker' was not one that passed into general use at least until the beginning of the eighteenth century, as it had become a designation applied to receivers of stolen goods and, later, pickpockets,[57] and the description of 'office-keeper' was preferred. The role of brokers became of increased significance with the growth of the marine market in the eighteenth century, much of which consisted of foreign shipowners who had no direct access to the English market, and the decided cases in that era demonstrate that brokers were regularly used to place marine risks with Lloyd's underwriters. Gibb[58] estimates that in the Napoleonic era brokers accounted for about 50 per cent of placements. Thereafter the position of brokers was consolidated, and by the middle of the nineteenth century the use of brokers at Lloyd's had become the accepted form of dealing, and the gradual expansion of Lloyd's into the non-marine market gave brokers fresh lines of business. By the end of the nineteenth century there were many small broking firms operating in the Lloyd's market, and Lloyd's underwriters relied heavily upon brokers to find insurance business for them.[59] They were entirely unregulated, other than by Lloyd's itself. It was not until the twentieth century that major firms of brokers began to develop, and the provision of their services was extended to the non-Lloyd's market.

The activities of brokers remained all but unregulated until 1977. Up to that date the only controls on brokers had been imposed by Lloyd's, which would do business only

[56] There is a line of authorities typified by *Newsholme Brothers v Road Transport & General Insurance* [1929] 2 KB 356.

[57] Gibb, n 9, 18–19, citing an Act of 1603 regulating the activities of persons who called themselves 'brokers'.

[58] Gibb, n 9, 58.

[59] Even though the law at the time, and indeed now, regards brokers as agents of assureds and not underwriters. A broker acts as the agent of the assured when it comes to finding insurance, preparing the application, and drafting the wording, but is—without any special agreement with the assured—remunerated by the underwriters. This rule is long established, but generally regarded as indefensible: *Carvill America Inc v Camperdown UK Ltd* [2005] EWCA Civ 645; [2005] Lloyd's Rep IR 55, affirmed on other grounds [2006] Lloyd's Rep IR 1.

with brokers accredited by it. Lloyd's brokers were under a duty to comply with Lloyd's byelaws.[60] In 1977 the Insurance Brokers (Registration) Act, a Private Member's rather timid measure was passed. This established a system of self-regulation under the auspices of the Insurance Brokers Registration Council (IBRC). The IBRC promulgated a series of codes of practice on virtually every aspect of broking activities. Only persons who had registered with the IBRC were entitled to describe themselves by the term 'broker' and, as might be expected, those brokers who had given the most cause for concern chose not to register and carried on business under other descriptions. The legislation was ultimately repealed by the FSMA 2000, on the understanding that brokers would adopt a more rigorous form of self-regulation. This proved to be the short-lived General Insurance Standards Council (GISC). GISC, like IBRC before it, laid down standards of conduct for brokers, with sanctions—including expulsion—for non-compliers. Failure to join, or exclusion, were significant, because under GISC Rules those insurance companies which belonged to GISC (the vast majority) could not accept business through non-GISC brokers.

Ironically it was the exclusivity rule which proved to be the downfall of GISC, following a successful challenge under the Competition Act 1988 on the grounds that the rule was anti-competitive, so that GISC was unable to enforce its standards. The Government put GISC out of its misery in 2001 and announced the extension of FSMA 2000 to insurance brokers. That would almost certainly have happened anyway. In 1991 the European Commission had issued a recommendation suggesting minimum standards for brokers, and that paved the way for the Insurance Mediation Directive in 2002,[61] duly implemented in the UK partly by secondary legislation but mainly by changes to the FCA Handbook, the FCA being the sole regulator of brokers under the FSMA 2000 as opposed to the joint supervision of insurers by the FCA and the PRA. The relevant provisions are dotted around the FCA Handbook, but are collated in a tailored section entitled General Insurance Brokers (GIBKR). The effect of the Mediation Directive is to extend the EU single market to insurance mediation, using the familiar pattern of a single European Passport (freedom to open branches and freedom to provide services across EU borders) based on home state authorization and regulation, subject to compliance with minimum standards. In July 2012 the European Commission published a proposal for a Second Insurance Mediation Directive: its most important recommendation was a requirement on brokers to disclose commission levels paid by insurers.[62]

4.3 Protecting Policyholders: the Public Law Approach

4.3.1 Private law and public law solutions

Our survey of the regulation of insurance business has emphasized that the UK approach to regulation has been to make sure that insurers are in a financial position

[60] The restriction was modified in 2009, and any broker may apply to the Lloyd's Franchise Board for approval to act as a Lloyd's broker.

[61] European Parliament and Council Regulation 2002/92/EC.

[62] *Hobbins v Royal Skandia Life* [2012] HKFI 12 confirmed the rule that a broker, although engaged by the assured, is paid by the insurers.

to make payment, and not to require or encourage them to do so. Payment is a matter of private contract, governed almost exclusively by common law principles which for the most part have their origins in eighteenth-century maritime practice. The common law has lagged behind the development of new forms of cover and the expansion of the insurance market from business to consumers. Calls for reform of substantive law by the Law Reform Commission in 1957 and by the Law Commission in 1980 came to nothing,[63] and it took a seven-year investigation by the English and Scottish Law Commissions from 2006 to 2012 to produce—in the form of the Consumer Insurance (Disclosure and Representations) Act 2012—limited modification of the rules of utmost good faith.

Widespread dissatisfaction with the operation of the common law has, in the consumer context, led to two private initiatives by insurance companies to improve matters. The first was the introduction by the Association of British Insurers in 1977 of two Statements of Insurance Practice, one for general insurance and one for long-term insurance, a response to the exemption of the insurance industry from the Unfair Contract Terms Act 1977.[64] The Statements, which were renewed in 1986, prevented insurers from avoiding policies or denying coverage unless faced with unreasonable behaviour by the policyholders. The Statements were not legally enforceable,[65] but were given enhanced importance by the formation in March 1981 of the Insurance Ombudsman Bureau (IOB). The IOB in its inception was a small operation funded by the UK's leading insurance companies, the objects of which were 'To receive references in relation to complaints, disputes and claims made [and] to facilitate the satisfaction, settlement or withdrawal of claims', having regard to 'the terms of the contract... any applicable rule of law or relevant judicial authority [and] general principles of good insurance practice'. The IOB could make awards binding on members of up to £100,000. It was initially thought that one part-time ombudsman would suffice, but within a year there were three full-time decision-makers, and the gradual expansion of the IOB's membership—in particular to Lloyd's—led to an organization handling many thousands of claims every year and even to the publication of key decisions. On at least one occasion the views of the IOB pointed the way to legal development.[66] By the time of the passing of the Financial Services and Markets Act 2000 there was effectively a parallel regime in operation for the resolution of consumer disputes, and such disputes all but disappeared from the courts.

63 The very brief 1957 Report, Cmnd 62, was critical of the principles of utmost good faith and the use of warranties, and had one concrete outcome: insurers voluntarily agreed to abandon the use of arbitration clauses for liability (although not quantum) disputes, so that reliance on 'technical' (best defined as unrelated to the loss) defences was open to public scrutiny and not hidden behind an arbitral wall of confidentiality. The 1980 Report, Law Com No 104, considerably watered down in the consultation process from the Consultation Paper in 1978, was an attempt to pre-empt anticipated EU harmonization proposals again addressing utmost good faith and warranties. When the EU proposals evaporated, so did the impetus for implementing the Law Commission's proposals.

64 The argument for exemption put by insurers, and accepted by the government, was that it would be impossible for courts to determine the fairness or unfairness of exclusions from cover without themselves underwriting the risk.

65 *James v CGU Insurance* [2002] Lloyd's Rep IR 206.

66 *Sofi v Prudential Assurance* [1993] 2 Lloyd's Rep 559, the Court of Appeal holding that reasonable care exclusions in property policies were to be read as covering only deliberate or reckless acts.

FSMA 2000 gave statutory effect to both initiatives. The IOB, along with other ombudsman schemes including those set up by banks, building societies, and investment companies, were merged and given a statutory basis as the Financial Ombudsman Scheme (FOS).[67] The rules governing the jurisdiction of FOS are set out in FSMA 2000, ss 225–32 and sch 17, and the operation of FOS is set out in the Disputes section of the Handbooks (DISP).[68] FOS has compulsory jurisdiction where the complainant is a private individual or a business which has a turnover of less than €2 million and fewer than ten staff, and the policy is issued from a UK establishment; European insurers dealing predominantly with UK customers have voluntarily submitted to the jurisdiction of FOS. Since 2005 the jurisdiction of FOS has been extended to claims against insurance brokers. FOS may give binding awards of up to £150,000 plus interest, and an award for any sum in excess of that amount need not be honoured[69] although the complainant is free to bring judicial proceedings for any sum above the statutory maximum.[70] FOS determines disputes 'by reference to what is, in the opinion of the ombudsman, fair and reasonable in all the circumstances of the case'.[71] The common law may, therefore, be disregarded.[72] The Statements of Insurance Practice were superseded by the Handbooks issued under the authority of the 2000 Act, and the principles are now embodied in ICOBS Pt 8. FOS has indeed made significant changes to private rights under insurance policies falling within the Scheme.

Redress against insurers may be available independently of FOS. The Unfair Terms in Consumer Contracts Regulations 1999[73] apply to consumer insurances just as they apply to other consumer contracts, and render unenforceable terms which create a significant imbalance in the rights of the parties. The Regulations are aimed at ancillary provisions, in particular the obligations imposed upon the assured, rather than the fairness of coverage or exclusions as against the premium paid—which potentially would involve *ex post facto* judicial underwriting—unless the wording is not clearly expressed. There is little evidence that FOS pays much attention to the 1999 Regulations, as they are scarcely mentioned in the regular issues of *Ombudsman News* issued by FOS, and the most recent judicial authority on the application of the Regulations to insurance has taken the view that the protection afforded by FOS in many cases prevents insurance terms creating a significant imbalance in the rights of the parties.[74]

[67] The FOS, unlike the IOB, is thus subject to judicial review.

[68] J Summer, *Insurance Law and the Financial Ombudsman Service* (London: Informa, 2010).

[69] *Bunney v Burns Anderson plc* [2007] EWHC 1240 (Ch); [2008] Lloyd's Rep IR 198.

[70] *Clark v In Focus Asset Management & Tax Solutions Ltd* [2012] EWHC 3669 (QB); [2012] All ER (D) 232 (Dec).

[71] FSMA 2000, s 228(2).

[72] *R (on the application of IFG Financial Service Ltd) v Financial Ombudsman Service* [2005] EWHC 1153 (Admin); [2005] All ER (D) 301 (May); *R (on the application of Garrison Investment Analysis) v Financial Ombudsman Service* [2006] EWHC 2466 (Admin); [2006] All ER (D) 110 (Aug); *R (on the application of Heather Moor & Edgecomb Ltd) v Financial Ombudsman Service* [2008] EWCA Civ 642; [2008] All ER (D) 126 (Jun).

[73] SI 1999/2083.

[74] *Parker v National Farmers Union Mutual Insurance Society Ltd* [2012] EWHC 2156 (Comm); [2012] All ER (D) 23 (Aug). For analysis of the operation of the 1999 Regulations in the insurance sphere: A Carse and A Padfield, 'Consumer insurance: the risks of contracting on unfair terms' (2012) 125 BILA Journal 65; R Merkin 'Unfair Terms in Consumer Contracts: A Solution in Search of a Problem (2012) 23 Ins LJ 272.

More importantly, under FSMA 2000, s 138D, introduced by the Financial Services Act 2012 to replace the earlier provisions of FSMA 2000, s 150(1), breach of the regulatory rules may give rise to an action for damages for breach of statutory duty at the suit of a private person who suffers loss as a result of breach. Breach of an FCA rule is actionable unless the rule specifies otherwise, and breach of a PRA rule is not actionable (given the wider public policy nature of the PRA's functions) unless the rule so provides. Before the passing of the 2012 amendments, the FSA had exercised its powers to render breach of its general principles not actionable as breach of statutory duty, as they were regarded as high-level general propositions the interpretation of which should not be determined by the courts. That remains the position under the 2012 Act. That does not mean, however, the infringement of the Principles has no consequence. The regulators have the power, under FSMA 2000, s 404, to counter situations in which there has been a widespread or regular failure by firms to comply with regulatory rules resulting in loss to private persons. Here, the regulators may require firms to carry out a 'root cause analysis' of the problem and to implement a scheme for providing redress.

Ouseley J considered the relationship between these various remedies in *R (on the application of British Bankers Association) v The Financial Services Authority*,[75] which arose from the misselling of payment protection insurance (PPI). This type of cover is intended to provide funds for the assured to repay a loan if the assured defaults due to loss of employment. PPI policies were sold to many borrowers, but the selling process was riddled with a number of major faults. Most importantly, some borrowers were not told that it was included in the package, and assumed that their payments were purely related to the loan; others were told that PPI insurance was compulsory; and members of a third group purchased PPI cover even though they could never make a claim under it, for example if they were self-employed. On 10 August 2010 the FSA published Policy Statement 10/12 entitled 'The assessment and redress of Payment Protection Insurance Complaints'. The Policy Statement included amendments to Handbook rules and guidelines for settling claims and paying compensation. That led to a large number of successful complaints being made to FOS. The banks and other organizations who had sold these policies sought judicial review. The banks argued that the only breaches alleged were of high-level Principles, and those were not actionable under what is now the 2000 Act, s 138D. Ouseley J's ruling was that the section was concerned only with breach of statutory duty, and that infringement of the Principles did not preclude an award of compensation by FOS. Indeed FOS, in deciding whether or not to order compensation, was required to take into account regulatory rules, guidance, and good industry practice. That point aside, even in the absence of any regulatory policy statement, FOS would, in handling PPI complaints, have been bound to take into account the same considerations as had motivated the regulators. Second, the banks argued that the only obligation on a regulated person was to obey specific and actionable Rules in the Handbook, and to the extent that a Principle or general guidance contradicted a Rule there could be no liability. Ouseley J accepted that

[75] [2011] EWHC 999; [2011] All ER (D) 222 (Apr).

proposition as correct, but on the facts found no contradiction between the policy statement and the Rules. The learned judge regarded the policy statement as augmenting and explaining the Rules. He therefore regarded the argument as being the wrong way round, and that it was more appropriate to regard the Rules as doing no more than to lay down specific requirements from the high-level Principles. Thirdly, Ouseley J rejected the banks' argument that the only means by which redress could be secured was under a scheme promulgated under FSMA 2000, s 404.

What is apparent, therefore, is that FSMA 2000 has broken the regulatory tradition of confining attention to solvency. Substantive rights under insurance policies are now available, alongside the common law.[76] Indeed, ICOBS is having an increasing effect on the common law itself. In *Jones v Environcom (No 2)*[77] and *Harrison v Black Horse Ltd*[78] the courts were prepared to accept ICOBS as providing a definitive statement of the law relating to the duties of intermediaries, and in *William McIlroy Swindon Ltd and Rannoch Investments Ltd v Quinn Insurance Ltd*[79] Edwards-Stuart J ruled that the absence of a specific duty in ICOBS to warn the assured of a time bar in the policy effectively precluded a finding that the common law imposed such a duty. There is an as yet untested potential for proceedings to be brought under FSMA 2000, s 138D for damages for breach of ICOBS independently of a ruling by FOS.

4.3.2 Insolvent insurers

The preservation of the solvency of insurers has been the dominant objective of regulation at least since the first proper legislative measure in 1870. However, regulation has not proved to be foolproof, and there have been numerous insurance insolvencies over the years. Two quite separate questions arise here. The first is the modification of insolvency procedures where an insurance company is involved. Prompted by the requirements of EU law, the emphasis is on the protection of policyholders through the preservation of the insurers' business so that arrangements can be made for its transfer to a willing purchaser and so that any available assets go to policyholders by means of their statutory priority over other unsecured creditors.[80]

The second is the provision of compensation to the policyholders of an insolvent insurer where the sums due are irrecoverable from the company itself. Here the policyholder may claim under the Financial Services Compensation Scheme (FSCS). The adoption of a fallback scheme had been suggested at the end of the nineteenth century to support workmen's compensation, and the idea re-emerged at various points thereafter. However, it was not until the passing of the Policyholders Protection Act 1975 that the necessary provision was made. The legislation was repealed by FSMA 2000 and replaced by FSCS, the detail of which is set out in FSMA 2000, ss 213–24 and the Handbooks' Compensation (COMP) section. FSCS is operated by a scheme

76 Summer (2011) 121 BILA Journal 26.
77 [2010] EWHC 759 (Comm); [2010] All ER (D) 76 (Apr).
78 [2010] EWHC 3152 (QB); [2011] Lloyd's Rep IR 455.
79 [2010] EWHC 2488 (TCC), reversed on appeal on other grounds, [2011] EWCA Civ 825.
80 Insurers (Reorganisation and Winding Up) Regulations 2004. SI 2004/353, implementing European Parliament and Council Directive 2001/17/EC.

manager who is independent of the regulators, and the scheme itself is funded by a levy on insurers.

FSCS applies to policies issued by UK insurers on risks situated within the EU and by European insurers on risks situated within the UK. The default principle here is that a risk is situated where the policyholder has their habitual residence, although the risk on real property is situated where the property is located and the risk on a vehicle in most cases attaches to its place of registration. The claimant must be a 'policyholder', a term which means any of: an individual; a small business operated as a partnership; a beneficiary under a long-term policy; or a person with a direct claim against the assured's liability insurers under the Third Parties (Rights against Insurers) Act 1930 or 2010. FSCS thus has limited extraterritorial effect, and excludes companies, local authorities, and other organizations.

The amount payable by FSCS depends upon the nature of the policy in question and whether there has been any loss at the quantification date fixed by FSCS. The most straightforward is a first-party policy. Here, FSCS is liable for the first £2,000 of any loss (above any policy deductible) and 90 per cent of the remainder. If there has not been any loss, FSCS is liable for the unexpired proportion of the premium. Long-term policies are rather more complex. The primary obligation of FSCS is to seek to transfer the policy to, or at least to acquire an equivalent policy from, another insurer. If that cannot be done, compensation assessed on an actuarial basis is payable. The greatest difficulties are posed by liability policies. Where there has been a claim under a liability policy which has been established and quantified, FSCS must meet that claim 100 per cent for compulsory policies and 90 per cent for all others: compulsory insurance is differentiated from other liability insurance in this respect.[81] There is also liability for any claim made against the assured which has yet to be established and quantified, as such a claim is a contingent one. In all other cases, the assured is entitled merely to a return of premium representing the unexpired term of the policy. Once a claim by a policyholder has been settled, FSCS is required to make payment as soon as is reasonably practicable after the date of the winding-up order.

FSCS may also act before liquidation and where it becomes aware that an insurer is in financial difficulties.[82] This jurisdiction applies where an insurer is in provisional liquidation, has been shown in winding-up proceedings to be insolvent, or has proposed a scheme of arrangement under which benefits may be reduced. FSCS may then take steps to transfer the business to another insurer, provide funding to assist the insurer to overcome its problems, or—most usually—promote a scheme of arrangement under which policy benefits are reduced.

FSCS is designed to be an insurer of last resort, so that if there are available funds from any other source they must be taken into account in reducing FSCS's own liability. Thus FSCS will take an assignment of the assured's rights against the insurer in liquidation or at least exercise subrogation rights against the insurer, and payments made by any other insurer on risk are also to be deducted. The usual rule that two

[81] We review of the operation of compulsory insurance and its rationales in Chapter 9.
[82] FSMA 2000, s 217.

insurers on risk for the same loss are to divide it between them is thus dispensed with where the obligations of one of the insurers have been taken over by FSCS.

4.4 Conclusions

This chapter has outlined the importance of public law and public regulation in the insurance sector, and the nature of the mechanisms employed. We seek to show throughout this book that, in addition to its primary function of protecting persons against loss from all manner of contingencies, insurance underpins the law of obligations. By way of recognition of these considerations, statutory regulation has attempted to secure the solvency and prudential conduct of those operating in the market for longer and to a level beyond the rules applicable to any other industry; and regulation has also stepped in to mitigate the rigours of the common law in the relationship between insurer and assured. Public law has also pressed private insurance into use so that the tort system, where it recognizes compensation, does deliver that compensation. A study of the regulatory processes is a firm indication of the pervasive importance of insurance both generally and to our system of obligations.

PART 2

OPERATION

5

Subrogation

5.1 Introduction

5.1.1 The nature and influence of subrogation

'Subrogation', put simply, is a form of substitution, where one party is substituted for another. In the insurance context, the core subrogation remedy enables an insurer who has indemnified its assured to bring proceedings on its own account but in the name of its assured.[1] Though the practical effects of subrogation as operated by insurers have risen to the surface of consciousness from time to time, often attracting criticism as they do,[2] and in recent years there has been renewed classificatory discussion of its remedies,[3] obligations lawyers on the whole have not considered the profound impact of subrogation on the law of obligations itself. Here we begin to outline that impact. We will see further evidence of the influence of subrogation over the law of contract and tort in Chapters 7 and 8 respectively.

Insurance subrogation has often been criticized. To the extent that it allows substitution of the insurer for the assured, it changes the identity of one of the parties to a civil action, without this becoming superficially apparent.[4] One informed critic has described this as giving rise to a fiction, not appropriate for a modern legal system.[5] Related techniques have even been described as an 'obscenity' so far as insurers may seek to influence litigation by remaining disguised.[6] In English law however, the default

[1] Other related remedies for the insurer are considered in this chapter. The ability of a party suffering loss to bring proceedings *against* an insurer directly (exercising the rights of the assured) has also been described as a form of 'statutory subrogation' (AWB Welford, *Law Relating to Accident Insurance* (London: Butterworths, 2nd edn, 1932), 451–3), here the injured party being substituted for the assured who is insolvent. This originated in the Workmen's Compensation Act 1897 and was generalized to other forms of liability insurance (but not reinsurance) by the Third Parties (Rights against Insurers) Act 1930. Here, however, the claimant proceeds in his or her own name.

[2] Key instances are *Lister v Romford Ice and Cold Storage* [1957] AC 555 and *Morris v Ford Motor Co* [1973] QB 792. These are discussed in 5.6; less obvious cases of risk-shifting are debated in Chapter 8.

[3] In particular, moves have been made to explain the core subrogation remedy (above) in terms of unjust enrichment: C Mitchell, *The Law of Subrogation* (Oxford: Clarendon Press, 1994); C Mitchell and S Watterson, *Subrogation: Law and Practice* (Oxford: Oxford University Press, 2007); C Mitchell, P Mitchell, and S Watterson, *Goff and Jones: The Law of Unjust Enrichment* (London: Sweet & Maxwell, 8th edn, 2011); A Burrows, *A Restatement of the English Law of Unjust Enrichment* (Oxford: Oxford University Press, 2012), 175–6. We sound some notes of caution about this in subsequent paragraphs.

[4] For various reasons the defendant may also be an insurer standing in the shoes of its assured, also often described as 'subrogation', although the substitution there is to liabilities to a third party and not to rights against the third party; or an insurer may be administering the litigation.

[5] R Hasson, 'Subrogation in Insurance Law—a Critical Evaluation' (1985) 5 OJLS 416, 419–20, discussing the omission of modern fictions such as this from L Fuller, *Legal Fictions* (Stanford CA: Stanford University Press, 1967).

[6] Hasson, n 5, 421. Hasson here is referring particularly to the use of 'loan receipts' as a device to evade Federal 'real party in interest' provisions in the US, where juries are prevalent in civil cases. In a valuable discussion, R Derham, *Subrogation in Insurance Law* (Sydney: Law Book Co, 1985), Chapter 9, explains that although the loan receipt has developed to support such tactics, this was not its origin.

position is that an insurer who wishes to exercise subrogation rights is *required* to pursue the claim in the name of the assured,[7] though the policy itself may entitle the insurer to call for an assignment of the cause of action, displacing this default.[8] Nor are experienced judges likely to be misled as to the identity of the claimant. The disguise, however, may be inadvertently encouraged by theoretical accounts which make the two-party focus definitive of private law.[9]

Subrogation can be a powerful weapon, despite the limitations addressed in 5.4. Its influence is pervasive. For example, the existence of subrogation rights explains why, generally speaking, first-party insurance recoveries are to be left out of account in determining the defendant's liability to the claimant:[10] a feature of the law which might be taken to show the *irrelevance* of insurance is, rather, a manifestation of its impact on the nature of civil damages. Closer examination shows that a number of different but related remedies protective of the insurer's interest are bundled together under the umbrella of 'subrogation'. All of these, we suggest, respond to the indemnity nature of the contract. These remedies are wide-ranging. They enable the insurer to conduct litigation, whether the assured would be likely to seek alternative compensation or not; to reduce payments to the assured to reflect recoveries already made; to acquire an equitable lien over money received by the assured; and even to bring proceedings against an assured who has failed to protect the interests of the insurer. Lack of awareness of these remedies is doubtless heightened by their continued exclusion, in English courts, from first-party insurers offering life and personal injury insurance.[11] But as we will see, there is a need to control the operation of subrogation; and the route to controlling it begins with understanding it effectively.

5.1.2 Our argument

At least superficially, subrogation embodies and reinforces the principle of the defendant's personal responsibility for the claimant's loss, since it appears to ensure that liability is brought home in practice to a defendant who is liable as a matter of law. We suggest, however, that despite its intuitive appeal, personal responsibility is not necessarily a strong justification for subrogation remedies and certainly does not remove the

[7] This was the decisive issue in *London Assurance Co v Sainsbury* (1783) 3 Doug 245, where the insurer failed in its action purely because it had pursued that action in its own name.

[8] Which is commonly the case, given the potential limitations of subrogation which we discuss in 5.4. In most cases, however, insurers are content to rely upon subrogation and rarely invoke the right to call for an assignment.

[9] Most influentially, EJ Weinrib, *The Idea of Private Law* (New York: Oxford University Press, 1995), 1, 142–4.

[10] *Clark v Blything* (1823) 2 B & C 254; *Yates v White* (1838) 4 Bing NC 272. More recently, in *Bank of Nova Scotia v Hellenic Mutual War Risks Association (Bermuda) Ltd* [1988] 1 Lloyd's Rep 514, Hobhouse J denied that a defendant was discharged from liability because the claimant possessed first-party insurance against the loss in question. This cannot, however, be the reason why the same rule operates in personal injury cases (*Bradburn v Great Western Railway* (1874) LR 10 Ex 1), since ordinary personal injury policies do not give rise to a right of subrogation for the first-party insurer. This is discussed further in 5.5.

[11] The exclusion, and its uncertain limits, are discussed in 5.5, where we outline particular issues surrounding medical expenses insurance. The gradual expansion of subrogation into 'personal' and medical insurance in the US has led to deep controversy around the issues, as we explain in that section.

need for control mechanisms.[12] In particular, the responsibility justification bites hardest where the defendant is uninsured.[13] Here, and more generally, it is by no means clear that such a principle should be pursued in relation to ordinary instances of lack of care bringing about insured losses. It might be argued that personal responsibility for carelessly caused losses, rather than distribution by insurance, is the exception not the rule.[14] Certainly, carelessness is one of the risks most likely to be provided for *ex ante*, whether by contract or by legislative intervention. In addition, where the defendant is insured, the resulting picture is necessarily one of duplicated insurance, which has been condemned as wasteful.[15]

Our particular account of subrogation does not give primary place to personal responsibility. We suggest, rather, that considerations around the location of risk are more central in the law of subrogation than any supposed need to support the fault principle or personal responsibility *per se*. In subsequent chapters, we seek out the influence of risk allocation in the law of obligations more broadly. We suggest that parties often consider insurance in the *ex ante* allocation of risks associated with contracting (Chapter 7), a factor which remains fundamental to the interpretation of contractual principles by the courts, and that in tort cases too courts may consider liabilities in terms of their effect on existing allocations of risks, or as risk allocations in their own right (Chapter 8). In both contract and tort, subrogation emerges as a key factor. For example, it may either support or subvert the allocation preferred by the parties, or by the law, or by a combination of both. While the underpinning equitable origin of subrogation is now clear,[16] the basis of insurer subrogation nevertheless lies in the nature of the contract of insurance as an indemnity contract, and its proper

[12] A diverse range of commentators have doubted the value of an argument from fault. They include Hasson, n 5, 417, 423–5; T Weir, 'Subrogation and Indemnity' (2012) 71 CLJ 1 (a case note on *Morris v Ford Motor* (n 2) which was originally privately published), 4; P Atiyah, 'Collateral Benefits Again' (1969) MLR 397, and (with particular reference to 'deterrence') Mitchell and Watterson, n 3, 323. However, it seems unlikely that analysis of insurer subrogation in terms of unjust enrichment can operate without an idea that it is unjust for a party in breach to escape liability where an insurer has indemnified the party who suffers loss.

[13] There is, however, an element of retained responsibility where the defendant is insured, to the extent that the defendant is required to pay an insurance premium, and will have to bear at least part of the loss through deductibles and policy limits. More generally, corrective justice theory is not necessarily dependent on personal responsibility and it has been suggested that liability insurance poses no problems for corrective justice: eg J Gardner, 'What is Tort Law For? Part 1: The Place of Corrective Justice' (2010) 30 *Law and Philosophy* 1, 10–11, especially fn 25; and A Beever, 'Corrective Justice and Personal Responsibility in Tort Law' (2008) 28 OJLS 475. Nonetheless, corrective justice theories, once dissociated from personal responsibility, are formal in nature and contribute to the more general temptation to reduce the frame of vision through which the issues are perceived, squeezing out many significant issues related to insurance. See, for example, Chapters 10 (Vicarious Liability), and 11 (Illegality).

[14] See Chapters 6 and 9, and the cases discussed in this chapter, in 5.2 and 5.5. The boundaries of the distributive response, invoking fault of a greater magnitude than mere lack of care, are discussed in Chapter 11 and (raising the question of failure to insure) Chapter 9.

[15] Hasson, n 5.

[16] The House of Lords stated this decisively in *Napier and Ettrick v Hunter* [1993] AC 713. Any idea that subrogation was almost solely a creation of the common law of contract based upon implied terms, equity merely 'assisting' the common law, had arisen relatively recently, through a series of decisions of Lord Diplock: in particular *Yorkshire Steamship Ltd v Nisbet Shipping Co Ltd* [1962] 2 QB 330; *Hobbes v Marlowe* [1978] AC 16. While disapproving of this marginalization of equity, the House of Lords in *Napier* nevertheless recognized the central role of the parties' contractual arrangements.

scope—which may be modified by agreement—depends upon analysis of the relationships between various parties related to an insured loss. By definition, where an insurer seeks to bring an action in the name of the assured, it claims that another party should be the indemnifier in respect of the insured loss, and this is the claim to which the court must respond. This is an inherently multi-party question. Here, we assess the basis on which courts can and do respond to such claims, and therefore the actual and potential role of the courts in regulating subrogation practice.[17]

In pursuing this question, it is notable that English courts, unlike those in the United States, have generally not considered themselves free to exercise 'discretion' in awarding subrogation remedies, despite their equitable nature. Indeed, it has been said that the right to subrogation has 'ossified'.[18] Arguably, equity has been better at extending the insurer's remedies than at providing courts (and parties) with the resources to control them. The right of a surety, or other person providing an indemnity under some form of obligation, to exercise subrogation rights was recognized as early as the seventeenth century, albeit in a series of discrete situations of which insurance was the most important both in practice and in terms of contribution to legal principle. The later expansion of subrogation, largely prompted by the consideration that a subrogated claimant obtained a proprietary remedy which prevailed over unsecured creditors in insolvency, threw up a series of complex conceptual questions over, for example, the right of a surety to assert equitable ownership of securities posted for the discharged debt.[19] This is a long way from the straightforward concept of subrogation as it applies to insurance. The growth of such questions saw, in the last quarter of the twentieth century,[20] attempts to lay down, within a general framework of restitution, the principles applicable to subrogation claims. Subrogation is now firmly classified as a remedy based upon unjust enrichment.[21] It is not clear that this has helped in any way to explain insurance subrogation. It has been pointed out that the

[17] This is not intended to detract from discussion of the potential need for legislation to control subrogation, an issue returned to in 5.6.

[18] Derham, n 6, 26: 'Since insurance subrogation is equitable, it may be thought that the courts should have a discretion in determining whether to allow subrogation rights to be exercised in any particular case. However there has not been any real judicial recognition of such a discretion in insurance cases, and it would seem that the insurer's right has ossified to such an extent that there is little scope for its development.' In England, the exception is Lord Denning's approach in *Morris v Ford*, n 2, which has generally been dismissed as too broad and unworkable. Even so the failure to ask direct questions about the justness and fairness of subrogation led Weir, n 12, to make a despairing recommendation for statutory reform (which he also acknowledged was unlikely to occur, but which has been effected in Australia). See further 5.6. The position in the US is very different, and controls over remedies on the basis of 'equity' play a significant role.

[19] For example, *Paul v Speirway* [1976] Ch 220.

[20] Most influentially in England by the first edition of R Goff and G Jones, *The Law of Restitution* (London: Sweet & Maxwell, 1966).

[21] Mitchell, Mitchell, and Watterson, n 3, ch 39. This may be a particularly English phenomenon. JA Dieckmann has recently reported the fruits of comparative review of subrogation on the part of guarantors, concluding that civilian jurisdictions have not—despite their long adoption of unjust enrichment principles in the law more broadly—sought to explain subrogation in terms of unjust enrichment: JA Dieckmann, 'The Normative Basis of Subrogation and Comparative Law: Select Explanations in the Common Law, Civil Law and in Mixed Legal Systems of the Guarantor's Right to Derivative Recourse' (2012) 27 Tul Eur & Civ LF 49.

notion of 'unjust enrichment' operates at a potentially very general level.[22] Consistently with that observation, accounts of insurer subrogation based on unjust enrichment currently appear to use the same resources as our broadly contractual account. The leading work by Mitchell and Watterson, for example, describes the 'unjustness' in a case such as *Napier and Ettrick v Hunter*[23] as established through 'a combination of policy factors', which are also taken to explain the core subrogation right for insurers.[24] These 'policy factors' (namely the nature of the insured's relationship with the insurer and third party; and the identity of the person who is thought appropriate to bear the loss) are the very factors that we describe in terms of contextual analysis of party risk structures and of the purpose of relevant duties and liabilities. One question is whether it will clarify or obscure the position to describe these factors in terms of 'unjustness'.[25]

More positively, we suggest that analysis of risk allocation, particularly allocations effected by parties, offers the courts their most promising route to control of insurers' subrogation rights, and that they regularly take this up. While the insurer's remedies may have 'ossified' in certain respects,[26] this is not necessarily the end of the matter. The very *existence* of such remedies is dependent on showing that the assured, on proper construction of the various relationships in play, had a right of action for the insurer to take over. In many instances, the courts' approach to this question reflects the fact that insurance arrangements are a primary consideration for contracting parties, and we provide further evidence of this in Chapter 7. Outside the contractual context, the questions are more complex, but we suggest that risk allocation analysis remains significant. The effect of our argument is that insurance considerations directly affect the very existence of a contractual or tortious duty.

We argue, therefore, that English courts have not only shown awareness of the significance of subrogation despite the surface appearance that it is irrelevant to determination of rights between the assured and a potentially liable third party, but have also reached decisions which, in cases where there are contractual arrangements between the assured and the potentially liable third party, allow losses to be allocated in accordance with what they construe to be the parties' intentions. Since the role of the insurer is not always evident, a distorted view of the law may develop. In contract cases, and to a lesser extent in tort cases, the reader sees a decision which requires the risk of loss from an event to fall on one or other of the parties, but it will not be immediately

[22] See M Leeming, 'Subrogation, Equity and Unjust Enrichment', in J Glister and P Ridge, *Fault Lines in Equity* (Oxford: Hart Publishing, 2012), concerning subrogation generally, and arguing (consistently with our account) that (a) unjust enrichment may operate at too general a level to provide useful principles for disposing of the cases discussed and (b) that it is not well adapted to the multi-party context inherently involved in a subrogated action. The High Court of Australia has reiterated the view that unjust enrichment is not a principle that can be directly applied to dispose of particular cases in *Bofinger v Kingsway Group* [2009] HCA 44, discussed by Leeming (cited above in this note), and J Dietrich, 'Unjust Enrichment versus Equitable Principles in England and Australia', in the same collection.

[23] *Napier and Ettrick v Hunter*, n 16.

[24] Mitchell and Watterson, n 3, 10.27. See also A Burrows, n 3, 175.

[25] Discussed in 5.3.

[26] The expression used by Derham, n 6.

apparent that the claimant may be a subrogated insurer who has no interest in preserving the long-term relationship between the parties or even their objectively intended allocation of risk manifested in the insurance arrangements themselves, and whose claim is rejected on what would otherwise be inexplicable grounds. It would be wrong simply to assume that decisions are reached without considering the operation of subrogation. Indeed, it might be said that judicial disregard of subrogation, or of the parties' allocation of risk, has given rise to those decisions which have attracted the greatest criticism.[27] These cases have had the greater emphasis. But they stand out as the exception, rather than the rule.

5.1.3 Summary

The next part of this Chapter, 5.2, introduces a relatively simple and uncontentious illustration of subrogation in action, which illuminates its connection with risk allocation and with loss-spreading effects. We refer back to this illustration when we turn to exploration of the basis of subrogation and the means by which the courts may control its operation, in 5.3. In 5.4, we explore key features of subrogation in operation, drawing attention to some important limitations. The most important of these is its non-applicability to life insurance and standard personal injury policies. Because of the significant issues raised for the purposes of the law of damages and for the nature of subrogation itself, this limitation is explored in more detail in 5.5. Finally, 5.6 offers an interim assessment of the impact of subrogation in terms of risk allocation and loss distribution, drawing on particular cases where the effect of subrogation has been considered suspect, and shows how these stand out from the courts' general approach.

5.2 The Issues Illustrated

> In the complicated offshore drilling environment with its intricate divisions of responsibility and countless contractors and subcontractors, a simple slip-and-fall can turn into a multiparty morass of contribution cross-claims, third- and fourth-party defendants, reciprocal indemnity agreements, and the ever-popular warranties of workmanlike performance. The plaintiff in this litigation has long since departed but the other parties have chosen to remain on the field of battle to contest the appropriate share of the plaintiff's settlement to be borne by each of them.[28]

Lord Bingham quoted this remark from a US judge in *Caledonia North Sea Ltd v British Telecommunications Plc*.[29] This was no 'slipping and tripping' case, but the sequel to a multi-million pound settlement in respect of a major explosion with considerable loss of life. The judge's remarks themselves project a mixed picture. On one hand the injured party has 'long since departed'—compensated before the key legal battles ensue. On the other, the economic consequences appear to be the subject of

[27] For example *Lister v Romford Ice*, n 2.
[28] Judge Brown in the US Court of Appeals for the Fifth Circuit, *Fontenot v Mesa Petroleum Co*, 1209.
[29] [2002] UKHL 4; [2002] 1 Lloyd's Rep 553; 2002 SC (HL) 117, 122.

elaborate and costly litigation.[30] A key part of this 'multi-party' sequel is subrogation, and this was the main issue in play in *Caledonia* itself.

Since subrogation has often attracted criticism, *Caledonia North Sea Ltd* is a useful illustration that subrogation does not necessarily undermine but may both reflect, and underpin, contractual allocations of risk. But it also helps to illustrate the issues in play. The action was brought by the liability insurers of the operator of the oil platform 'Piper Alpha' nominally against contractors working on the platform. There had been a catastrophic explosion on board the platform, leaving many killed and injured. The insurers of the operator had promptly settled multiple claims for personal injury and loss of life brought by victims and families of the employees of contractors despite the fact that the contractual allocation of risk placed the duty to compensate, the duty to insure, and the duty to indemnify the operator against such claims, on the contractors themselves. Settlement of the tort claims by the operator's insurers enabled protracted questions about the destination of the financial burden of these losses to be determined between those insurers and the insurers of the various contractors whose employees had been killed or injured.[31] In this sense, the victims were assisted by being left out of the litigation process. Subrogation is, as we will see, sometimes alleged to provide windfall profits to insurers, in that relevant premiums are not set taking the availability of such actions into account: in other words, insurers pass on some of the risks which they are contracted to bear, and profit at the expense of policyholders.[32] In this instance, the operator of the oil platform could be said however to have gained the very benefit for which it had thought it worthwhile paying an insurance premium *in addition to* the negotiated contractual terms. That is, it escaped the responsibility and costs of litigation to ensure the risks lay ultimately where the contract placed them (with the contractors' insurers). The operator also had the benefit of an indemnity without the delays attendant on complex litigation.[33]

The claim in this case would make no sense without awareness of subrogation. On the face of it as we have seen, the claim was one by the platform operator, notwithstanding that it had been indemnified by its insurers and that the fault of one of its employees had contributed to the explosion. That claim was brought against contractors who had committed no breach of duty either personally or through their employees

[30] The prospect of litigation of this sort is one of the features of private law solutions to compensation questions which are said to make public provision more efficient. Hasson argues that much surrounding litigation is 'scandalously wasteful' and that '[i]t is difficult to believe that this kind of waste would be tolerated in the public sector' (Hasson, n 5, 427). The strength of arguments as to wastefulness is also recognized by Derham, n 6, 153; and referred to by P Cane, *Atiyah's Accidents, Compensation and the Law* (Cambridge: Cambridge University Press, 7th edn, 2006), 384 ('shifting losses around is costly').

[31] Because the claims were likely to be brought in a Texas court if not settled, the settlements were at a considerably higher level than a Scottish court would have awarded. The value of the actions expected to be settled after determination of the appeal was over £82 million, exclusive of interest and expenses (Lord Bingham, n 29, at [23]).

[32] See further nn 75, 76. Here, however, Lord Hoffmann assumed the contractual allocation of risk would have been reflected in lower premium costs, and in the context of a commercial deal on relatively standard terms this may well be the case.

[33] The operator was not contractually obliged, nor compelled by statute, to secure insurance, and as a contractual matter the liabilities fell elsewhere irrespective of fault; it had, nevertheless, purchased insurance as a matter of business prudence.

but who were liable for injury to or death of their own employees by virtue of the terms of the applicable contracts. Risk, not fault, was the parties' primary concern in choosing these terms. The contractual structure itself illustrates that in an industry where the risks of major harm caused by momentary carelessness are considerable, and where the chances are strong that any such harm will be caused by the employees of more than one contracting party, responsibility in relation to such harm is routinely perceived as an *ex ante* question to be approached in terms of liability to compensate as much as an *ex post* question of liability for breach.[34] The potential consequences of 'inadvertent negligence' of one or more individuals is routinely dealt with as part of contractual structures, just as legislative policy adopts a loss-spreading approach to the risk of carelessly caused harm in certain notable instances.[35]

We suggest that the House of Lords determined that the contractors, not the insurers, were to be treated here as the primary indemnifiers of the operator in respect of injury to or death of their employees. The court interpreted, and gave effect to, the risk allocation of the contracting parties, concluding that the operator's insurance policy was not the primary source of indemnity, and the insurers could themselves be indemnified. From the point of view of the contractors, the operator's insurance arrangements were irrelevant, and the contractors faced ultimate liability for claims by their own employees whether or not the operator was insured: were it otherwise, as their Lordships pointed out, the contractors would have received the benefit of a policy for which they had not paid any premium. This is frequently used as an argument in favour of subrogation but is often unpersuasive. Indeed, it is generally the case that the receipt of an unrequested benefit does not impose any obligation to pay for it.[36] Here, however, it actually does fit the contractual arrangements in that the contractors were to bear liability and to insure against it, so that the existence of the operator's own policy was (in terms of the agreed risk allocation for claims by contractors' employees) purely fortuitous. It is important to note, therefore, that the House of Lords did not *assume* that the contract was fortuitous, but argued towards this position in light of the contractual arrangements in relation to risk allocation. Before leaving *Caledonia North Sea*, let us also look briefly at the case in terms of loss distribution or spreading (the subject of Chapter 6, and also the source of much criticism of subrogation).

[34] The contractual structure was a familiar one in such undertakings: Lord Bingham in particular referred to leading works on oil and gas law.

[35] Examined particularly in Chapter 9.

[36] 'The general principle is, beyond all question, that work and labour done or money expended by one man to preserve or benefit the property of another do not according to English law create any lien upon the property saved or benefited, nor, even if standing alone, create any obligation to repay the expenditure. Liabilities are not to be forced upon people behind their backs any more than you can confer a benefit upon a man against his will': per Bowen LJ in *Falcke v Scottish Imperial Insurance Co* (1886) 34 Ch D 234, 248. Compare however the contested notion of 'free acceptance', applicable (if its supporters are correct) where a defendant 'should have known' that a claimant who rendered services expected to be paid for them, and where the defendant did not take a reasonable opportunity to reject the services. Evidence for the existence of such a principle is sometimes claimed to be implicit in the reasoning in *Falcke* itself: Mitchell, Mitchell and Watterson, n 3, 17–03. As the authors point out (17–05), the 'principle' was subject to convincing critique by A Burrows, 'Free Acceptance and the Law of Restitution' (1988) 104 LQR 576; and was subsequently abandoned as encapsulating an 'unjust factor' by its main proponent, Peter Birks: P Birks, *Unjust Enrichment* (Oxford: Oxford University Press, 2nd edn, 2005).

What may be seen at work in *Caledonia North Sea* is a judicial ruling which gave effect to the bargain reached by the parties. The parties doubtless regarded the arrangements whereby each employer took responsibility for injury to its own employees[37] as the most appropriate in terms of cost and availability of cover. Imposing liability on the operator for injury to contractors' employees would require extensive public liability (PL) insurance, given that the victims would not be the operator's own employees. By contrast, the contractors are required as a matter of law[38] to take out employers' liability (EL) insurance, and the parties doubtless decided to leave the losses to lie where the law placed the burden of insuring them. There is probably little difference in terms of ultimate loss-spreading, because both PL and EL insurers have extensive reinsurance arrangements in place and, irrespective of whoever paid the claims, they will to a greater or lesser extent be passed down the reinsurance chain, although these forms are quite different in nature despite similar wording in many instances.[39] So subrogation in this case simply ensured that the insurance arrangements which were required by the parties to be put into place operated according to their terms. Disregard of underlying arrangements or assumptions will, by contrast, cause difficulties. Indeed subrogation may, at its extreme and if it takes place in the absence of an understanding of contractual allocation, allow losses to be placed with uninsured individuals.[40] Probably more commonly, lack of attention to the legal context of tort liabilities may lead losses to be placed, through subrogation, with public bodies which may thus bear the burden of insuring, or absorb the loss.[41] In these cases, there is typically no relevant contractual allocation of risk, but the courts may nevertheless seek to interpret the policy of the law in relation to risk allocation, typically in relation to the question of whether there is a 'duty of care' on the part of the public body.[42]

Our general message is that subrogation is not uncontrolled by the courts, and that it does not always operate unfairly. However, we must recognize the potential for adverse effects. Even in a case similar to *Caledonia North Sea*, but with factual variation over the identity of negligent individuals and applicable contractual structure, it is possible to envisage tort claims being made against the contractors, to be settled by their insurers, and with a subrogation action by those insurers against the operator on the basis of the negligence of its employee. The result here would *not* be spreading of losses through the agreed insurance routes (except to the extent that contribution or reinsurance performs this role), and there would then be a stronger argument that subrogation

[37] Other than in case of injuries inflicted wilfully or recklessly.

[38] Employers' Liability (Compulsory Insurance) Act 1969, which has been extended to offshore drilling operations.

[39] *Employers' Liability Insurance 'Trigger' Litigation: BAI (Run Off) Ltd v Durham* [2012] UKSC 14; [2012] 1 WLR 867, considered in Chapter 13.

[40] This was the situation in *Lister v Romford Ice*, n 2. The case is critically explored in 5.6.

[41] This was the effect of *Home Office v Dorset Yacht* [1970] AC 1004. Subrogation rights were involved in the very origins of negligence liability of public authorities for failure to control other parties (Hasson, n 5; and for further discussion, Chapter 8).

[42] A key case raising issues of this type is *Stovin v Wise* [1996] AC 923, though this did not involve exercise of subrogation rights. This interpretation of risk allocation in the law of tort is explored further in Chapter 8. A general appreciation of subrogation is essential to the analysis.

might trigger the costly double insurance concerned. None of this would, however, be possible where the contractual structure is interpreted to give no such right of action to the contractor. And this in turn points to a key role for the courts, in determining what contractual obligations between the assured, and the third party, actually were, in light of their allocation of risk. The role of subrogation, as we have begun to explain, makes these questions more complex. But it is intimately connected with them.

5.3 The Basis of Insurer Subrogation

5.3.1 Classification and its implications

Subrogation is likely to evade effective control by the courts if its nature and rationale are not understood, since this lack of knowledge will tend to lead to inflexibility in remedies. This section is concerned, therefore, with the nature and basis of insurer subrogation. As we have seen, subrogation is very loosely translated as 'substitution'. Subrogation in our particular context may typically be identified as enabling an insurer, having indemnified its assured, to stand in the shoes of the assured and to exercise the legal rights of the assured in the assured's name against any third party who is responsible for the assured's loss. The principle is of some antiquity. In 1782, Lord Mansfield said that 'every day the insurer is put in the place of the assured'.[43] The right of substitution was codified in the Marine Insurance Act 1906, s 79, although the section is not a model of clarity. An insurer who pays any loss has transferred to it any right of suit which the assured might possess against a third party who has caused the loss (subrogation).[44] In addition, an insurer who has paid for a total loss[45] of subject matter is entitled on payment to assert the ownership of whatever remains of the subject matter (better referred to as salvage): in non-marine cases that is likely to be of little value because a total loss contemplates that nothing worth having has survived, but in marine cases the lesser concept of constructive total loss allows the assured to recover up to policy limits for less severe damage.[46] The only common feature of subrogation and salvage is that they confer rights upon the insurers which are exercisable on payment, but otherwise they have evolved to become separate concepts, though they share a common origin.[47]

It is clear that equity has played a central role in the development of insurer subrogation. One of the earliest reported subrogation cases, *Randall v Cochrane*,[48] refers to the 'plainest equity' on the part of the insurer. In a careful review of English decisions, Derham found only one case, *North of England Iron Steamship Insurance Association v*

[43] *Mason v Sainsbury* (1782) 3 Doug 61, 64.

[44] See the discussion of proprietary elements of subrogation by D Friedmann, 'Payment Under Mistake—Tracing and Subrogation' (1999) 115 LQR 195–8.

[45] There are no salvage rights where subject matter is damaged—the duty of the insurers is to pay the cost of repairs and plainly they cannot assert rights over the repaired subject matter.

[46] Marine Insurance Act 1906, ss 57 and 60.

[47] Lord Blackburn set out the distinction clearly before the 1906 Act in *Simpson v Thomson* (1887) 3 App Cas 279, 292. An insurer who acquired a ship as a total loss has ownership of it and therefore has all the rights of ownership (including receipt of payment of freight); but an owner who claimed for a partial loss could be indemnified for the loss sustained and retain 'all the benefits incident to the shipowner' (292).

[48] (1748) 1 Ves Sen 98; 27 ER 916.

Armstrong,[49] in which a right within the doctrine of subrogation was directly enforced by a common law court before the Judicature Acts.[50] Equally, however, courts have also accorded a very significant role to the nature of the parties' contract of indemnity in rationalizing this equitable response.[51] We return shortly to the continued importance of the contractual setting. There have however been recent moves to recast subrogation as a whole as an aspect of the law of unjust enrichment and therefore as providing an equitable remedy to reverse an unjust gain, and this merits consideration.[52] An attempt to recover the basic rationale of subrogation in coherent terms is in principle welcome. However, the language of unjust enrichment necessarily does not match the language used by the courts in the long history of insurer subrogation. More importantly, it is at this stage not clear whether the criterion of justness can assist, rather than obscure, the basis for controlling subrogation rights.

The central role of unjust enrichment in some instances of subrogation is irrefutable following the decision of the House of Lords in *Banque Financière de la Cité v Parc Battersea (Ltd)*, which offered a novel subrogation remedy in accordance with an unjust enrichment rationale.[53] That has not however been universally welcome; and some of the points made against the application of an unjust enrichment rationale in *Banque Financière* are resonant with the points we make in this chapter. For example, Michael Bridge argued that restitution or unjust enrichment is so focused on 'the doing of corrective justice between plaintiff and defendant that this function is in danger of subsuming all others' (particularly referring to neglect of 'distributive' issues including the rights of parties not before the court);[54] that the House of Lords in *Banque Financière* was not sufficiently alert to the need to avoid inconsistency between restitutionary remedies and contract remedies in the case of failed contracts;[55] that the idea of what is 'unjust' applied in the case was insufficiently defined and that parties would be subjected to a period of considerable uncertainty and insecurity before the courts managed to define what it means in such cases (at which point it would be confined to 'insignificant proportions');[56] and that it is 'highly questionable for the law of restitution to come to the aid in this way of a large financial institution that neglects

[49] (1870) LR 5 QB 244. [50] Derham, n 6, 13.

[51] In *Napier and Ettrick v Kershaw* [1993] AC 713, the House of Lords classified subrogation as an equitable remedy but the parties' contract formed the basis for its operation. In the US, the Supreme Court has limited legitimate contractual subrogation in the context of the Employee Retirement Income Security Act 1974 (ERISA) to those remedies that would be considered equitable 'in the days of the divided bench' (a reference to common law and equity): *Sereboff v Mid Atl Med Services*, 547 US 356 (2006). This is however just one among several routes to control of health insurer subrogation. BS Maher and RA Pathak provide critical comment on the operation of the standard (though support for the equitable analysis of subrogation): 'Understanding and Problematizing Contractual Tort Subrogation' (2008–9) 40 Loy U Chi LJ 49. Subrogation in this context (health insurance) is controversial and typically rests on express contractual provision. R Baron provides a highly critical review in 'Subrogation: A Pandora's Box Awaiting Closure' (1996) 41 South Dakota LR 237 ('Pandora's Box'), and more recently R Baron, 'The Revictimization of Personal Injury Victims by ERISA Subrogation Claims' (2011–12) 45 Creighton Law Rev 325 ('Revictimization'). The issues are further examined in 5.5.

[52] In particular Mitchell, n 3; Mitchell and Watterson, n 3; Mitchell, Mitchell, and Watterson, n 3.

[53] *Banque Financière de la Cité v Parc* [1999] 1 AC 221.

[54] M Bridge, 'Failed contracts, subrogation and unjust enrichment' [1998] JBL 323.

[55] Bridge, n 54, 324. [56] Bridge, n 54, 333.

to take proper precautions'.[57] We would argue that the interests of other parties, clarity of legal reasoning, fairness between parties, and even potentially principles of 'personal' responsibility, will most likely be enhanced by considering the parties' attempts to allocate risks rather than beginning with 'unjustness' viewed uniquely through attention to the parties before the court. Our core concern is of course with insurer subrogation. *Banque Financière* was not a case of the insurer's right of subrogation and, whatever the arguments for and against its use of unjust enrichment analysis, in our view that analysis was not said by the House of Lords to extend to insurance cases.[58] We should therefore consider the argument, contained in the most influential accounts of subrogation, that insurance cases were not in fact outside the reach of the comments of the House of Lords in *Banque Financière*, even if this is the most 'natural' meaning of those comments.

In this case, subrogation allowed a lending bank to acquire priority over other creditors (who were companies in the borrower's group) despite a lack of security offered by the borrower itself. It was an express condition of the advance offered that other companies in the group would 'postpone' their claims until after the lender had been paid. The other creditors did not know of the postponement letter; but this was irrelevant to a claim based not in 'contractual' subrogation (a category which in this context should be broadly understood for reasons set out below),[59] but in unjust enrichment. Most importantly, Lord Hoffmann distinguished the case of insurance from the kind of case represented by *Banque Financière*. Redefinition of insurer subrogation in terms of unjust enrichment is therefore inconsistent with Lord Hoffmann's discussion. Yet this discussion has been treated as the key authority for addressing insurers' subrogation rights (other than those based in express assignment) in terms of unjust enrichment.[60]

In the course of his judgment, Lord Hoffmann distinguished the issue in *Banque Financière* itself, already outlined, from the case of insurer subrogation. Lord Hoffmann made it plain that the basis of the insurer's subrogation remedies lay in the nature of the insurance contract and to this extent, in common intention.

> although in *Lord Napier and Ettrick v Hunter* [1993] AC 713[61] your Lordships rejected the exclusivity of this claim for the common law and assigned a larger role

[57] Bridge, n 54, 333.

[58] S Hedley, *A Critical Introduction to the Law of Restitution* (Oxford: Oxford University Press, 2005), 329, suggests that the attempt in this case to distinguish between insurance cases (based in contract), and other instances of subrogation (based in unjust enrichment) is unconvincing. We do not delve into that suggestion here, but we do seek to show that the distinction was made.

[59] The terminology is confusing because it may be thought to refer only to instances of subrogation provided for by express contractual terms, rather than through the law's interpretation (including equitable elements and the parties' intended risk allocation) of the contract.

[60] Mitchell and Watterson, n 3, 3–4. The authors state that 'Subrogation rights can be acquired by contract. They can also be awarded as a remedy for unjust enrichment.' It is clear that they consider subrogation rights conferred by law on insurers to fall in the latter category, as insurance is offered as the most important example of a type of subrogation provided 'by the law of unjust enrichment' to prevent double enrichment of a creditor (here, the assured); or the unjust enrichment of a defendant who is not pursued: Mitchell and Watterson, n 3, 6. This is not the classification adopted by Lord Hoffmann and we question whether it assists interpretation of the insurer's remedy, in what follows.

[61] n 16.

> to equitable principles, there was no dispute that the doctrine of subrogation in insurance rests upon the common intention of the parties and gives effect to the principle of indemnity embodied in the contract.

The potential for misclassification of the insurer's subrogation remedies probably arises from the continuation:

> Furthermore, your Lordships drew attention to the fact that it is customary for the assured, on payment of the loss, to provide the insurer with a letter of subrogation, being no more nor less than an express assignment of his rights of recovery against any third party. Subrogation in this sense is a contractual arrangement for the transfer of rights against third parties and is founded upon the common intention of the parties. But the term is also used to describe an equitable remedy to reverse or prevent unjust enrichment which is not based upon any agreement or common intention of the party enriched and the party deprived.

It is easy to see how it might be concluded that *only* express contractual terms are being contrasted with the form of subrogation which turns on unjust enrichment. But the earlier reference to subrogation arising from the nature of the insurance contract and thus from the parties' common intention makes this interpretation impossible given the clear contrast in the final sentence quoted. 'Common intention' is being used where, on the analysis previously adopted by Lord Diplock, the basis was in 'implied terms'. We agree that 'common intention' is a preferable and more flexible term than 'implied term'.[62] Remedies to reverse or prevent unjust enrichment are here contrasted with subrogation based upon 'any agreement or common intention' of the party enriched and the party deprived—the very basis of insurer subrogation as Lord Hoffmann had just outlined it.

Andrew Burrows has suggested that although Lord Hoffmann's words are 'most naturally interpreted' as suggesting that 'subrogation in indemnity insurance rests on common intention of the parties and is contractual', in fact this was not his intention.[63] In our opinion, however, Lord Hoffmann's emphasis on contract is not accidental. The very point of the distinction drawn by Lord Hoffmann in this passage is that party intentions were *not* to be considered relevant to the unjust enrichment category represented by this case. Turning this around, plainly, party intentions *are* relevant to the insurer's right of subrogation:

> The fact that contractual subrogation and subrogation to prevent unjust enrichment both involve transfers of rights or something resembling transfers of rights should not be allowed to obscure the fact that one is dealing with radically different institutions. One is part of the law of contract and the other part of the law of restitution. Unless this distinction is borne clearly in mind, there is a danger that the contractual requirement of mutual consent will be imported into the conditions for the grant of the restitutionary remedy or that the absence of such a requirement will be disguised by references to a presumed intention which is wholly fictitious. There is an obvious

[62] This is also demonstrated by our later discussion of *Lister v Romford Ice*, n 2, in 5.5.

[63] A Burrows, *The Law of Restitution* (Oxford: Oxford University Press, 3rd edn, 2011), 162; Burrows, n 3, 175.

parallel with the confusion caused by classifying certain restitutionary remedies as quasi-contractual and importing into them features of the law of contract.

The underlying problems, we suggest, are revealed by the fact that in this context, addressing the issue in terms of 'unjust enrichment' appears to leave the detailed business of determining whether and why subrogation remedies should actually operate to some rather indistinct ideas of 'policy'.[64] We suggest that it is better to look more closely at the resources available to the courts through broadly contractual analysis. This means looking at what the courts have actually been doing, and also at what they have been saying. Indeed in this instance, it is unjust enrichment which, with some irony, can be said to superimpose a new and over-generalized conceptual structure on to existing practice. To illustrate this further, on Burrows' account, the above statement of Lord Hoffmann 'purported' to support the statements of Lord Goff in the earlier case of *Lord Napier and Ettrick v Hunter*;[65] but failed to do so.[66] In our opinion, this rests on an unduly narrow interpretation of what is meant by the intentions of the parties.[67] Our approach in this chapter, and in later chapters, underlines the importance of the parties' allocation of risk beyond the narrow confines of express and implied terms. We interpret Lord Hoffmann's remarks as distinguishing between 'wholly fictitious' references to party intentions outside the ambit of subrogation on the basis of mutual intent; and the broad analysis of party intentions and allocations of risk which, in our view, appropriately underpins subrogation in the context of insurance. Although there is a question over what best to call these considerations, we would prefer the label which makes the questions more apparent. Taking the broader view of the resources available to contractual analysis adopted in this chapter, and reflecting the actual practice of the courts in relation to insurer subrogation as explored here and in later chapters, we can see that Lord Hoffmann's remarks are entirely compatible with the analysis of the House of Lords in *Lord Napier and Ettrick v Hunter*,[68] where the roots of the equitable response were also acknowledged to lie in the parties' contractual arrangement (hence, at a broader level, the intentions of the parties and the relationships between them). According to Lord Goff, the principle of subrogation in an insurance context 'has been regarded, both at law and in equity, as giving

[64] Burrows, n 63, 163, suggests that the 'unjust factor' in insurer subrogation is 'not straightforward', and 'is probably best explained as a policy-motivated unjust factor', adding that it 'appears to be unique to indemnity insurance' (n 63, 163 n 97). Also Burrows, n 3, 175, 'The injustice involved is the very specific one of adhering to the principle of indemnity by avoiding the over-indemnification of the insured/indemnified party'. Does the awkwardness inherent in this idea that 'adhering to the principle of indemnity' could itself be an 'injustice' suggest a flaw in the underlying approach? Why involve 'injustice' at all?

[65] n 16.

[66] Burrows, n 63, 163.

[67] The rival analyses here can be related to a long-running debate over the supposedly limited resources of contractual analysis. It has been suggested, in particular, that unjust enrichment theorists are too quick to dismiss analysis of contractual arrangements beyond the limits of express terms as inherently dealing in 'fictions' (eg Hedley, n 58, suggesting that the law of contract is too easily written off on the implausible basis that it has stood still since the Victorian era). See A Burrows, *Understanding the Law of Obligations* (Oxford: Hart Publishing, 1998), 101, replying to Hedley: 'Fictions and obscure jargon in the law are an abomination and must be sought out and excised. The law cannot fulfil its role of guiding behaviour if fictions, like the "implied contract" theory, survive'.

[68] n 16.

effect to the underlying nature of a contract of insurance, which is that it is intended to provide an indemnity but no more than an indemnity'.[69]

It is generally agreed, therefore, that the nature of the contract of insurance itself lies at the root of the subrogation remedies available to the insurer. It seems to us that the courts' opportunities for controlling the exercise of subrogation rights will be best understood in light of this. That is, in our view, exactly the point made by Lord Hoffmann—and also explains why the courts do not feel the need to refer to unjust enrichment principles when resolving cases involving insurer subrogation.[70] Equally, there are aspects of the insurer's rights in relation to subrogation which are not comfortably explained in terms of unjust enrichment, and which are more naturally explained in relation to the role of the insurer's contract of indemnity as understood and interpreted by the courts in relation to a wider web of party relationships. That is the interpretation which we pursue in this chapter.

5.3.2 Rationales for the insurer's right of subrogation

A very common justification for subrogation is that it ensures that in the case of 'indemnity' policies, the assured is not permitted to make a profit: this would amount to more than an indemnity.[71] Occasionally it is said that this is the sole purpose of subrogation. Where unjust enrichment analysis is applied, this is generally speaking the primary enrichment to be avoided. A more prosaic way of expressing the same point is to say that it prevents 'double dipping' by insured claimants.[72] Since as a matter of law, the insured party's rights against others remain intact despite the receipt of an indemnity, subrogation intervenes to ensure that the insured party does not benefit twice by then proceeding in respect of the same loss.[73] This stems from the same reasoning as the principle that if the assured has received any payment from the third party, the insurance claim is reduced by the amount of such payment: such payments reduce the loss for which the insurer contracts to provide indemnity.[74]

[69] n 16, 743–4.

[70] D Wright, 'The rise of non-consensual subrogation' (1999) *Conveyancer* 113–25, 115, therefore correctly categorizes insurers' subrogation remedies as instances of, in his terms, 'consensual' subrogation, even though it is clearly recognized that they can be operated without consent.

[71] *Castellain v Preston* (1883) 11 QBD 380 is the most widely cited authority. It is, however, a case where an insurer sought to recoup sums from an assured who had been indemnified twice for some of its losses, rather than a case where the insurer sought to take over the assured's right of action. Mitchell and Watterson (n 3) suggest that it should not be treated as a key case on the subrogation remedy, because it introduces confusion by conflating two different remedies. It only introduces confusion if remedial classification is given central importance, however. The point made by the courts is that the remedy stems from the same reasoning as the right to take over the assured's right of action, invoking the indemnity nature of the contract.

[72] This is the expression used by Kirby J when hearing an application for leave to appeal to the High Court of Australia in *Insurance Commr of Western Australia v Kightly* [2005] WASCA 154. The application was rejected. See further 5.5.2.

[73] Mitchell (n 3) and Mitchell and Watterson (n 3) argue that, generally, the rights of the assured against another party are not extinguished by the payment of the indemnity, so insurance cases are an instance of subrogation in relation to 'subsisting rights'.

[74] For example *Bovis Construction Ltd v Commercial Union Assurance* [2001] Lloyd's Rep IR 321.

This rationale is clearly insufficient, however, in that subrogation does not only operate to remove a surplus recovery from the insured. It may operate where the assured would not wish to bring an action, for example because the liable party is an employee or family member and is uninsured, or simply because he has been indemnified by his insurers. The argument then becomes that transferring the claim to the insurers and allowing them to recover removes any *possibility* of double indemnity. The emphasis is upon maintaining the integrity of insurance as a contract of indemnity. In these circumstances, enrichment of the assured is not a successful rationale, and further assistance is required. This is to be found in the indemnity nature of the contract of insurance.

A second rationale is that if a third party was discharged from liability simply because the claimant was insured and has been indemnified by his insurers, the third party would become an indirect beneficiary of a policy for which it has paid no premium. This is a second form of 'windfall' or enrichment—for the liable party (or its insurer). This too is not always convincing. First, the assured and the third party may have bargained to place the risk, and the burden of insuring against it, with the assured under a first-party insurance policy—and this may be the very reason for that insurance policy. This may be reflected in the contractual price; it may reflect the policy of the law; or it may reflect the reality of the third party's position as less able to insure and spread the loss. To argue that the third party is then 'enriched' by the assured's insurance policy (which is as agreed or expected) is not always appropriate. Subrogation, if exercised in such a case, is contrary to the parties' own risk allocation and exposes the third party to a liability which it has been agreed he should not bear. Further, it might be argued in exactly the same way that the subrogated *insurer* has acquired a windfall by finding a party to whom the loss may be shifted in a manner which defeats that party's own contractual rights.[75] In particular, it has been argued that premiums do not reflect the subrogation right, and if they did, they would also need to reflect the chance of subrogation *costs* after actions by other insurers,[76] leading to no benefit to assured parties but benefiting insurers as a whole through promoting duplication of insurance.

This is not to say that a subrogated insurer can always rightly be seen as receiving a windfall. Some insurers who recoup their losses may nevertheless have delivered the security for which the premium is paid.[77] But this argument against subrogation will

[75] Baron, 'Revictimization', n 51, cites the Third Circuit in *US Airways v McCutchen* (3rd Cir. 16 November 2011), as rejecting an insurance fund's claim for reimbursement as amounting to a windfall; but in this case the court also noted that the fund played no part in pursuing the third-party claim.

[76] Regularly cited still is WE Patterson, *Essentials of Insurance Law* (New York: McGraw Hill, 2nd edn, 1957): 'it plays no part in rate schedules'; Hasson, n 5; Baron, 'Pandora's Box', n 51, 244. In the specific case of ERISA subrogation, note also research by R Baron and D Druley, 'ERISA Reimbursement Proceeds: Where Does the Money Go?' *Minnesota Trial*, Spring 2010, cited in Baron, 'Revictimization', n 51, 334, suggesting that the money is not ploughed back to support employer health insurance schemes. A more sympathetic account (written in a different context and when the amount of case law was said to be modest) is SL Kimball and D Davis, 'The Extension of Insurance Subrogation' (1962) 60 Michigan LR 841, suggesting that 'rising loss ratios and vigorous price competition in some fields of insurance have led companies to seek for ways to effect marginal savings that may make the difference between a loss and a modest profit' (at 842–3).

[77] There were reasons why the operator's insurer in *Caledonia North Sea* (n 29), for example, might be thought to be supplying the benefit for which premiums were paid, discussed in 5.2.

tend to be strengthened if it should prove that the existence of subrogation rights encourages the search for liable parties, new or 'peripheral', to whom loss might be shifted,[78] and with an associated extension of liability. Rather, the insurer enjoys a 'windfall' if it can shift the loss in this way.[79] The idea of a windfall is a matter of perspective, therefore.[80] How can this line of argument be rejected? If there is no general agreement on the empirical question of how rates are set, it might be rejected on the basis that it is not in the nature of an indemnity insurer to be anything but the indemnifier of last resort. This, however, raises an evaluative question,[81] and it seems preferable to ask whether the indemnity insurer is or is not the primary indemnifier in a particular context. This justification therefore also needs support from the third rationale, discussed next.

Before considering the third rationale, it is important to note that neither the first nor the second rationale can explain the insurer's 'positive' right to proceed against an assured who has acted against the insurer's interests. We would argue that this also cannot be remedied by recasting the law in terms of unjust enrichment. The principle here is that an assured who has suffered a loss is under a duty, pending full indemnification by the insurers, to negotiate with the person liable for the loss in the interests of both himself and the insurers. Thus if the settlement reached by the assured is unduly favourable to the third party the assured faces personal liability to the insurers, which may amount to a reduction in the sum recoverable to reflect the insurers' loss or even denial of the entire claim.[82] It is apparent that such a settlement does not unjustly enrich the assured personally, and although it could be argued that there is unjust enrichment of the third party in that he has received the benefit of the assured's cover, it is rather curious that the insurers' remedy is not against the third party—because the settlement is binding as between the assured and the third party, and the insurers can have no greater rights—but against the assured himself. For this reason too, a further rationale is required.

That third rationale returns us to the fact just noted, that the role of indemnity insurers has been interpreted in such a way that they are typically considered indemnifiers of the last resort. Where this is the case, if the assured has a right to claim from any

[78] J Stapleton, 'Duty of Care: Peripheral Parties and Alternative Opportunities for Deterrence' (1995) 111 LQR 301. Our point here is that Stapleton's well-founded concerns about peripheral parties are illuminated by taking insurance into account—a step she rejected at the very start of her analysis, where she argued that 'alternative means of protection' available to parties 'could not mean self-protection for it could not mean protection by the purchase of first-party insurance' (at 301). There is further discussion of this aspect in Chapter 8.

[79] The 'windfall' explanation has been used in US courts when denying a subrogation remedy: *US Airways v McCutchen* (n 75), and other examples discussed by Baron, 'Revictimization', n 51, 334.

[80] Also Maher and Pathak, n 51, 58: 'The windfall argument can cut both ways' (commenting on the argument that there has been a windfall to the insured, and identifying the role of subrogation in rate-setting as the key issue).

[81] Notice also the question of whether the state in offering social welfare benefits, or liability insurers, should be seen as the insurer of last resort, and the legislative answers to this question: R Lewis, 'Recovery of State Benefits from Tort Damages: Legislating for or Against the Welfare State?', in TT Arvind and J Steele, *Tort Law and the Legislature* (Oxford: Hart Publishing, 2013), and Chapter 9.

[82] *Commercial Union Assurance Co v Lister* (1874) LR 9 Ch App 483; *West of England Fire Insurance Co v Isaacs* [1897] 1 QB 226; *Phoenix Assurance Co v Spooner* [1905] 2 KB 753; *Horwood v Land of Leather Ltd* [2010] EWHC 546 (Comm); [2010] All ER (D) 177 (Mar).

third party[83] then the loss is ultimately to be borne by the third party rather than by the insurers. While this may be interpreted as exemplifying the law's attachment to principles of fault, that is not necessarily the case, since the same reasoning has been applied whether the third party's liability is strict or fault based, statutory, contractual, or tortious—hence, potentially no different from the insurer's own liability.[84] This justification draws attention to the nature and role of the contract of insurance itself, and is entirely consistent with the comments of the House of Lords in the key case of *Napier and Ettrick v Hunter*, and of Lord Hoffmann in *Banque Financière*. The important point is that it also depends upon consideration of the role of the insurer in relation to the role of the potentially liable third party. This rationale is essential in moving beyond the limited possibilities derived from over-indemnity of the assured. It requires assessment of a tripartite (at least) set of relationships.

The root authority on the idea of primary indemnifier is *Mason v Sainsbury*.[85] This case does not exemplify the priority of fault, since the 'primary liability' was strict, falling by statute on the local community in a case of riot damage.[86] The case was interpreted and applied in *Caledonia North Sea Ltd v British Telecommunications plc*,[87] which, as we have seen, was a case of contractual indemnity where, like the statutory indemnifier in *Mason*, the contractual indemnifier was not at fault (and where the insured would, in terms of tort law alone, have been a vicariously liable party). Their Lordships ruled that the subcontractors were relegated to the rights of insurers even though they were, as contractual indemnifiers, in much the same position as the insurers. In *Mason v Sainsbury*, Lord Mansfield had identified the relevant question as who, as between the insurer and the 'hundred' (the local community) was 'first liable'.[88] In *Caledonia North Sea Ltd*, the House of Lords interpreted this as meaning not who was *chronologically* first liable, but who was to be regarded as the 'primary' insurer. It is important to note that this is plainly an evaluative question which looks at the two potential indemnifiers in relation to one another, in light of an overall structure of duties, liabilities, and risk allocation. Though over 200 years apart, in each of these cases, the legal context of the liabilities of the two indemnifiers (rather than general considerations of justice) was the focus for this evaluation. In *Mason v Sainsbury*, Lord Mansfield considered that the statute 'puts the hundred, for civil purposes, in the place of the trespassers'. In effect, he treated both potential indemnifiers as 'standing in the shoes' of another, and 'upon principles of policy', the case was to be approached as though no indemnity had been paid. In *Caledonia North Sea*, the structure of the relevant contracts was designed to place the responsibility of compensating employees with their employer in each case, irrespective of where fault lay, and it was for this reason that the operator's decision to insure these risks on its own part was to be regarded as an insurance *inter alios*, for its own unilateral benefit. The contractors (and thus their insurers) were intended to be the primary indemnifiers, and the operator's

[83] Excluding other insurers: this is the province of contribution, discussed in Chapter 6.
[84] Compare the discussion in 5.1.
[85] n 43.
[86] Discussed further in Chapter 6.
[87] [2002] UKHL 4; [2002] 1 Lloyd's Rep 553.
[88] n 43, 540.

insurer could exercise subrogation rights against the contractors. It is plain from the discussion of the House of Lords that not all first-party insurance is to be approached as 'fortuitous' from the point of view of the defendant.[89] We will suggest later that in some instances where the courts have not been so alert to the role of contractual structure and evaluation of the insurer's role in determining whether subrogation is appropriate, they have been led into error.[90]

5.4 Operation and Limits

The insurer's subrogation remedies are limited in important respects. It is largely because of the limitations that insurers often stipulate for the right to obtain an express assignment of any claim. But subrogation also supplies further remedies, beyond the right to bring the action in the assured's name.

So far as the right to conduct the action in the name of the assured is concerned, the assured's cause of action is transferred to the insurers only when they have fully indemnified the assured against the loss. One implication of this is that the insurers have no contingent right of subrogation, in the period between the assured suffering a loss and the assured being paid, which would allow them to take over the assured's claim. The action remains vested in the assured. For that reason some policies put the assured under an express duty to take all necessary steps to preserve the insurers' future subrogation claim, for example by issuing a claim form within the limitation period or seeking a freezing injunction against the third party's assets by way of security for any claim. In the same way, even if the insurers have paid up to the limits of the policy but the assured's loss is actually greater,[91] so that the assured has not been indemnified, the right to control the proceedings against the third party is retained by the assured. In these situations the assured is under an implied contractual duty to the insurers to take their interests into account in negotiating with the third party and handling the action against him. This is particularly important as a result of the ruling in *Napier and Ettrick v Kershaw* that sums received from the third party are allocated 'down'. By way of example, suppose that the assured claimant has insured property for the sum of £250,000, but the actual loss is £400,000, leaving a shortfall of £150,000. Any sum recoverable from the third party responsible for the loss will in the first instance be applied to the uninsured shortfall, with the balance—if any—going to the insurers. So, based on a recovery of £300,000, the first £150,000 goes to the assured and the remaining £150,000 is held by the assured for the benefit of the insurers under an equitable lien. That means that the risk that the third party is uninsured or otherwise of

[89] This is a very significant point because it has proved tempting to see first-party insurance in precisely these terms, particularly from the point of view of the law of tort, and particularly in respect of personal injury (further discussed in Chapters 8 and 9). Personal injury is the exception not the rule—and, even here, there are some doubts about the right approach to personal insurance (5.5).

[90] Thus the established approach, evident in both *Mason v Sainsbury*, n 43, and *Caledonia North Sea*, n 29, could have been used to reach a different outcome in *Lister v Romford Ice*, n 2 (discussed further in 5.6).

[91] Any excess, whereby the assured is required to bear the first £x of any claim, is to be disregarded, because the arrangement between the parties is that that sum is not a loss at all for insurance purposes: *Napier and Ettrick v Kershaw* [1993] AC 713, n 51.

limited means is borne by the first-party insurers.[92] The assured's implied duty towards the insurers accordingly requires him to negotiate with the third party in a bona fide fashion and not to settle for an unreasonably low amount: if he is in breach of that duty, then, as we have seen, he faces personal liability to the insurers for the amount that they might have recovered but for the settlement. Some policies indeed impose an obligation on the assured not to settle with the third party without the insurers' consent.[93]

Once there has been full indemnification, the right of subrogation arises.[94] The assured's cause of action becomes vested in the insurers and they are free to sue the third party. English law does not confer any new cause of action upon the insurers, and operates the fiction that the assured is the claimant. Accordingly, the insurers must bring their action in the name of the assured. From *London Assurance Co v Sainsbury*,[95] where this principle was clearly determined, a number of justifications can be gleaned, but avoidance of juror prejudice against the insurer is not one of them. First, the insurer must suffer 'all the disadvantages' of the assured, and bringing the action 'as' the assured is apt to secure this. It may be noted that it was not at that time possible to effect a legal assignment of a chose in action, including a cause of action,[96] so that any assignment could take effect only in equity and the claim had to be brought in the name of the assignee. Subrogation was thus consistent with established principle, albeit operating automatically rather than by way of equitable assignment. Secondly, Lord Mansfield noted that, 'As between the parties themselves the law has long supported it for the benefit of commerce; but the assignee must sue in the name of the assignor; by which the defence is not varied'.[97] It is clear that Lord Mansfield thought subrogation would facilitate the intentions of the contracting parties ('facilitate commerce'); while making the insurer proceed *as* the assured would *protect the defendant*. The defendant owes no duty to the insurer (and even in today's expanded law of negligence this remains correct).[98] In addition, Buller J stated a potential 'inconvenience' (policy consideration) in relation to the bringing of an action in the name of the insurer. Again this presents subrogation as devised to avoid prejudice to the *defendant*. Buller J suggested that if the assured has a number of policies, or is 'short-insured', there will be not one, but a range of actions in the name of various insurance companies, and a remaining action for the assured itself. The court, he added, 'ought to prevent a

[92] The recover down rule does not apply to marine insurance. Marine policies are, by the Marine Insurance Act 1906, s 81 presumed, unless otherwise agreed, to be 'subject to average', so that the assured is deemed to be his own insurer for the uninsured sum. Thus, using the example in the text, if a cargo worth £400,000 is insured for £250,000, all losses and recoveries are divided in the proportion 8 to 5, so that a recovery of £300,000 would be divided 8/13 to the insurers and 5/13 to the assured.

[93] *Horwood v Land of Leather Ltd* [2010] EWHC 546 (Comm); [2010] All ER (D) 177 (Mar), a ruling questionable on its facts, because the clause (in a liability policy) relied upon by the insurers appears to have been concerned with the settlement of claims against the assured and not the settlement of contribution claims against third parties by the assured.

[94] If there is a shortfall in insurance cover, in some cases insurers may simply pay the full amount of the loss beyond the policy limits so that they can exercise subrogation rights.

[95] (1783) 3 Doug 245.

[96] That did not occur until the Judicature Act 1873.

[97] n 95, 251.

[98] Weir, n 12, suggests that the effect of subrogation is to evade the restrictions on recovery of economic loss: only in the case of a close relationship (which clearly does not exist between the insurer and the third party) would the law recognize a duty not to cause such loss.

multiplicity of suits'. As we have seen, subrogation by no means prevents a multiplicity of suits today; but those suits are not brought against a single defendant. Whether or not these reasons remain sound, the rule has remained a feature of the law.[99]

Just as the action is brought in the name of the assured, so also the insurers are subject to all of the substantive and procedural duties and restrictions which would have applied had the assured been the actual claimant. Thus the insurers are bound by any arbitration, exclusive jurisdiction, or choice of law clause which operates between the assured and the third party;[100] the limitation period is that applicable to the assured's claim against the third party, so that there is no fresh limitation period running from the date of indemnification;[101] proceedings cannot be brought by the insurers of a dissolved company;[102] and costs of proceedings have to be assessed as if the claimant was the assured, so that it makes no difference that he was instructed to incur those costs by his insurers.[103] Again, it is irrelevant that the insurers have not incurred the full loss suffered by the assured: if they have indemnified the assured they are entitled to recover the amount of their payment from the wrongdoer even though (for example) they have received commission from a supplier of replacement goods to the assured.[104]

Subrogation, as opposed to assignment, does have some advantages for insurers. The fact that the action is being brought by them and not by the assured is at least superficially hidden from view, and a right of subrogation vests automatically on indemnification so that there is no need for the insurers to seek the assured's consent to bring the action or otherwise to take formal steps to perfect the right to claim. However, we have seen that legal subrogation also has limitations. It cannot be exercised until payment. It will be lost if the assured is a company which is ordered to be dissolved. The amount which the insurers may retain is limited to the precise sum that they have paid. If the insurance proceeds are paid in sterling but the subrogated action is brought in another currency, for example, adverse movements in the exchange rate could mean that insurers might suffer a shortfall.[105] For these reasons, the exercise of any express contractual right to call for an assignment of the cause of action from the assured to the insurers may remain valuable.

Although the most widely recognized aim of subrogation appears to be negative, to prevent the assured from making a profit in accordance with the indemnity principle,[106] we have pointed out that it has a positive aspect as well. If an assured, having been paid, enters into an arrangement with the defendant under which the defendant's

[99] Some jurisdictions however have abandoned it. For example, New York *compels* the insurers to sue in their own name as the true 'party in interest'.

[100] For example, *Whitesea Shipping and Trading Corporation v El Paso Rio Clara Ltda, The Marielle Bolten* [2009] EWHC 2552 (Comm); [2010] 1 Lloyd's Rep 648.

[101] *RB Policies v Butler* (1949) 65 TLR 436.

[102] *Re Ballast plc, St Paul Travellers Insurance Co Ltd v Dargan* [2006] EWHC 3189 (Ch); [2007] Lloyd's Rep IR 742.

[103] *Sousa v London Borough of Waltham Forest* [2011] EWCA Civ 194; [2011] 1 WLR 2197, a case involving 'after the event' insurance, a product now restricted in its efficacy: see chapter 13.

[104] *Bee v Jenson (No 2)* [2007] EWCA Civ 923; [2008] Lloyd's Rep IR 221.

[105] *Yorkshire Insurance Co v Nisbet Shipping Ltd* [1962] 2 QB 330.

[106] We have also noted the need for other justifications.

liability is waived or compromised for a lesser sum, the insurers have a cause of action against the assured for breach of contract.[107] Again, a pre-policy contract entered into between the assured and another person, which restricts the assured's ability to claim from that person in the event that he causes harm to the assured's property, is potentially a material fact which has to be disclosed to the insurers in the negotiations for cover. Failure to do so can lead to avoidance of the policy,[108] in that the absence of subrogation rights is clearly directly relevant to the amount which the insurers will ultimately have to bear in the event of a claim. On the other hand, such rights are limited. If such a contract postdates the policy, and there is no policy term which restricts the assured's freedom of action, then the insurers have no rights: there is no post-contractual duty of disclosure; there is no contingent right of subrogation prior to indemnification; and insurers are required to take the risk that the chances of loss may increase by reason of changed circumstances after the policy has been issued.[109] Though subrogation is a powerful weapon under some circumstances, the assured may circumvent it in its dealings with third parties. Again, these detailed considerations underline the complexity of the idea that an insurer may be an indemnifier of last resort and illustrate the influence of other party relationships on the reasoning of the courts as to whether this is indeed the case in the particular context. We return to this point in 5.6.

5.5 Exclusion of Life and Personal Injury Policies

5.5.1 The roots of double recovery: life insurance

The most important limitation on the subrogation right of insurers is that it does not operate for the benefit of an insurer whose policy provides compensation for death or personal injury, although in the latter case there is real debate as to the boundaries of the exclusion.[110] The practical implications of this are considerable, and the Law Commission took the view that while express contractual subrogation rights can enhance the rights of the insurer, they cannot be validly created outside the circumstances where the law would offer the right: such an agreement might be champertous,

[107] If there is no express term, one to this effect will be implied. In *Re Ballast plc* [2006] EWHC 3189 (Ch); [2007] Lloyd's Rep IR 742, it was confirmed that the insurers do not possess an equitable lien on the cause of action, an issue considered by the House of Lords in *Napier and Ettrick* (n 51) without firm conclusion. *Re Ballast* has been followed in *Dornoch Ltd v Westminster International BV* [2009] EWHC 889 (Admlty); [2009] 2 Lloyd's Rep 191.

[108] Potentially, because the duty of disclosure does not extend to facts which the insurers knew or ought to have known. If the contract is a standard one, insurers have no complaint: *Tate & Sons v Hyslop* (1885) 15 QBD 368.

[109] *State Government Insurance Office (Qld) v Brisbane Stevedoring Pty Ltd* (1969) 123 CLR 228.

[110] The Law Commission (LC) took the logical view that while personal accident insurance is non-indemnity insurance, 'medical expenses and permanent health insurance' are indemnity insurance: LC 262, *Damages for Personal Injury: Medical, Nursing and Other Expenses: Collateral Benefits* (November 1999), 10.73. P Atiyah stated the same view in 'Collateral Benefits Again' (1969) 32 MLR 397: personal accident insurance directed at protecting against income loss might be considered an indemnity policy if the issue should be tested in the courts. We visit the evidence of this, and potential controversies, later in this Section. Clearly subrogation does operate in favour of an insurer offering an indemnity for *liability* in cases of death and personal injury: liability policies clearly are contracts of indemnity.

and therefore void.[111] These issues also raise challenges for any understanding of subrogation in terms of legal principle or of policy. We return to these issues after seeking the reasons for the exclusion.

The root of the exclusion is that subrogation reflects the indemnity nature of the insurance contract, combined with the law's position that life and traditional personal injury policies are not contracts of indemnity. The exclusion has important consequences. Just as the goal of subrogation is at least in part to avoid double recovery, the exclusion of life and personal injury insurance from subrogation, when combined with the present situation whereby the liable party pays full damages irrespective of private insurance, has the implication that double recovery by the claimant here appears to be condoned. This conclusion can be avoided only if it is thought that there is not, in truth, over-compensation, or double recovery for the same loss.[112] Here we consider the reasoning behind the position that such contracts are not contracts of indemnity, and that insurance payments are not to be deducted, with resulting benefit to insured parties. This limitation in the process of subrogation makes an important contribution to the general position in personal injury law in which some benefits to the injured party are to be discounted, though it is by no means the sole manifestation of this approach.[113]

In relation to the 'non-indemnity' nature of the contract of life or personal injury insurance, the courts reached the current position in the nineteenth century. They did this by reasoning from life insurance, to insurance against personal injury. Authority for the proposition that life insurance is not a contract of indemnity derives from *Dalby v India & London Life Assurance Society*,[114] the most important decision on the arcane but still operative Life Assurance Act 1774 which demands that the policyholder under a life policy has an insurable interest in the life assured. This remains an important provision despite the archaic language of the statute. Indeed, in *Dalby*, much of the uncertainty of interpretation turned on the tense of the word 'hath'—did this point back to the point at which the contract was formed, or did it relate to the time at which payment under the policy was required?[115]

[111] LC 262, n 110, 10.77, referring however to J Birds, 'Contractual Subrogation in Insurance' [1979] JBL 124 as suggesting that such rights could be created. Developments in express assignment in relation to personal injury policies—and especially medical expenses insurance—are reviewed in subsequent paragraphs.

[112] Yet there *is* recoupment of certain state-provided benefits and expenses direct from the tortfeasor. The provisions are discussed by Cane, n 30, 390–4. R Lewis, 'Deducting collateral benefits from damages: principle and policy' (1998) *Legal Studies* 15, explores the general picture in respect of collateral benefits and possible rationales. In the US context, health insurance plans take a primary role in the funding of care and the question of subrogation on the part of such plans is closely entwined with the idea of collateral benefits. For discussion in relation to Medicaid, see E Pryor, 'Part of the Whole: Tort Law's Compensatory Failures Through a Wider Lens' (2007–8) 27 *Review of Litigation* 307, 323–5.

[113] Fleming described this wider phenomenon as having led to the opportunity to turn personal injury into a 'bonanza' for the injured party: J Fleming, 'The Collateral Source Rule and Loss Allocation in Tort Law' (1966) 54 Cal L Rev 1478. But this remains a controversial assessment. This is also discussed by the Law Commission, in CP 147, *Damages for Personal Injury: Collateral Benefits* (1997) and CP 148, *Claims for Wrongful Death* (1997); and n 110. Pryor (n 112) nevertheless describes tort damages as providing the 'cadillac' of compensation packages to injured claimants.

[114] (1854) 15 CB 364, applied in *Solicitors and General Life Assurance Society v Lamb* (1864) De GJ & Sm 251.

[115] Life Assurance Act 1774, s 3: 'And in all cases where the insured hath interest in such life or lives, event or events, no greater sum shall be recovered or received from the insurer or insurers than the amount of value of the interest of the insured in such life or lives, or other event or events.' This was interpreted in *Dalby*, n 114, so as not to work against the contingency nature of the policy—it could have been read in quite the opposite way, as essentially requiring the assured to be limited to an indemnity.

In *Dalby*, the claimant, an insurer, had taken out a policy for £1,000 payable on the death of Adolphus Frederick, Duke of Cambridge. At common law, policies on lives of those unrelated to the insured were accepted as a lawful form of gambling. The intention of the Life Assurance Act 1774 was to outlaw this practice, and to avoid what could be its unfortunate consequences:[116] its Preamble refers to a 'mischievous kind of gaming' which the Act would control. In this instance however, the policy had been secured by the claimant by way of 'cross-assurance', to minimize the exposure of his own company under existing policies on the life of the same Duke (which far exceeded the £1,000 payable).[117] This legitimate interest had ceased since those policies had been given up, but the claimant had continued to pay the premiums due. The court held that the requirement of insurable interest has to exist only at the date of the policy and not thereafter, so that if the policyholder has lost his interest[118] or the policy has been assigned to a third party without interest, the insurers cannot deny liability. The interpretation of a life insurance policy as not a contract of indemnity was integral to the decision, since the *extent* of liability was also not to be limited to the insured party's interest in the death (the section 3 point); and the court determined that the earlier decision of Lord Ellenborough in *Godsall v Boldero* (limiting the right of recovery of a creditor under an insurance policy on the life of his debtor to the amount of loss actually suffered as a consequence of the death) was wrong.[119] It may be noted therefore that the logical idea that some of today's life insurance policies protect against particular pecuniary losses, and ought therefore to be treated as indemnity policies,[120] formed the background to *Dalby* itself. We should notice that it was not the nature of the loss protected, but the nature of the bargain, which was crucial.

It is true to say that life insurance policies in general are very different in their form from the general run of indemnity policies. As the court in *Dalby* pointed out, they

[116] G Clark, *Betting on Lives: The Culture of Life Insurance in England, 1695–1775* (Manchester: Manchester University Press, 1999) identifies instances of 'ghoulish' behaviour—eg bets being taken on the number of German refugees stranded in Goodman's Fields, London, who would be left alive before charitable groups could be mobilized to help them; the running of one life against another; and the 'disturbing possibility' that a gambler 'might not let nature take its course' (50, 51). Of more concern to some it seems were the instances of policies taken out on lives of those already known to be ill, or the imposition of 'bad lives' on insurers (51). Alborn suggests that this included 'street betting' on the lives of the sick and impoverished, as insurers would write policies without ever seeing the person. Insurers did not always contest claims in court 'lest the world know that such a thing was possible' (a reference to the case of a woman found burned to death in the East End in 1909 with ten policies on her life) (T Alborn, 'A Licence to Bet: Life Insurance and the Gambling Act in the British Courts', in G Clark, G Anderson, C Thomann, and J-M Graf von der Schulenburg, *The Appeal of Insurance* (Toronto: Toronto UP, 2010), 114).

[117] It may be that the arrangement was one which would now be classified as reinsurance, but there is insufficient detail in the report to be certain of the point.

[118] The situation in *Dalby*, n 114.

[119] *Godsall* (1807) 9 East 72. Parke B noted that the case in *Godsall* had ultimately been determined on different grounds and that insurers had not subsequently chosen to rely on Lord Ellenborough's judgment, deciding that it would be against their interests (presumably, in selling life insurance policies) to do so. It has been suggested that the judgment in *Godsall* was typical of Lord Ellenborough's inclination to obstruct commercial arrangements (Alborn, nn 110, 116, drawing on PS Atiyah, *The Rise and Fall of Freedom of Contract* (Oxford: Clarendon Press, 1979)); and that *Dalby*, n 114, was much more conducive to commercial activity—and more representative of the Victorian courts' permissive attitudes in this regard. The inability of the 1774 Act to prevent gambling, and the deficiencies of *Dalby*, are examined in R Merkin, 'Gambling by Insurance: A Study of the Life Assurance Act 1774' (1980) 9 Anglo-American LR 331.

[120] For example Mitchell, n 3, referring to 'key man' policies covering employees.

generally involve a fixed premium throughout the period of the policy for which, at the end of the insured life, an agreed sum is paid, irrespective of any loss on the part of the premium payer. Such policies respond to a 'contingency' rather than a loss—a set event triggers a set payment. It is important that this is a point about the *form* of the policy, not the nature of the loss suffered by the dependants of a person who has died. In a contingency policy, cover is not calculated on the basis of loss. It is also true that at the time of the decision in *Dalby*, life insurance was typically also very different in its objectives from the ordinary indemnity policy—though as we have noted this was not the case with the creditor's policy on the life of his debtor in *Godsall v Boldero*. As Bramwell put it in argument (appearing as counsel for the claimant), 'Life assurance is, in effect, a contrivance for accumulating'.[121] How apt are these words today? Life assurance generally provides security to dependants. And yet, in a domestic setting, this security is often directed chiefly to the family's main means of accumulation, the family house. The core point is that life insurance proceeds are not measured by lost income, and the security provided by life insurance continues to resemble a benefit to dependants, rather than an indemnity for loss.[122]

At the same time, the treatment by the common law of statutory dependency damages in the event of fatal accident has since its origins recognized the pecuniary nature of the harm made good by such damages. Again this tends to underline that it is *the form of the insurance policy*, not the fact that it relates to a human life, which explains the categorization of such policies as 'non-indemnity' policies. Lord Campbell himself, architect of the first Fatal Accidents Act in 1846,[123] directed a jury in 1857 that in awarding damages under that Act, they should 'consider the pecuniary loss which the family has sustained by the death of the father', specifically pointing out that in a case where insurance policies in relation to *railway accidents* were concerned, the proceeds of these should be deducted from the damages.[124] On the other hand, Lord Campbell appears to have suggested that if there were policies on his life 'independently of accident', then the jury might wish to treat these differently, perhaps deducting only the cost of the premium from the damages to be awarded. A deduction of proceeds is inconsistent with any subrogation rights on the part of the insurer, a matter which had been determined of course by *Dalby*. But equally, the damages themselves (dependency damages) focused on *what had been lost*.[125] This defies any idea that it was thought that a life could not in *any* sense be the subject of indemnity. Fatal Accidents Act damages compensated for pecuniary losses; and in the case of fatal

[121] *Dalby*, n 114, 469. In *Parry v Cleaver* [1970] AC 1; [1969] 2 WLR 821, Lord Wilberforce described accident insurances as 'essentially wagers' (42).

[122] For exploration of the moral scruples associated with this aspect of life insurance in the US during the nineteenth century (that it seemed to create a profit for dependants), see the study by V Zelizer, *Morals and Markets* (New York: Columbia University Press, 1979).

[123] *Hicks v The Newport, Abergavenny and Hereford Railway Co*, 17 February 1857, noted in the very significant decision in *Pym v Great Northern Railway Co* (1863) 4 B & S 397.

[124] A contrary position was soon reached in respect of personal injury in *Bradburn v Great Western Railway* (1874) LR 1, which is addressed in subsequent paragraphs. *Hicks*, n 123, was affirmed as correct.

[125] This was to a large extent the controversy aroused by *Pym*, n 123, since this led to a very large award of damages based on the difference made to the claimant because of the nature of the settlement applicable on the death of the deceased. For discussion of the significance of *Pym* to the railway companies, see R Kostal, *Law and English Railway Capitalism 1825–1875* (Oxford: Oxford University Press, 1994), 295–8.

accidents, insurance payments operated to reduce these losses. This remains the case even if they do not take the form of an indemnity.

Statutory intervention soon altered the common law position. The decision in *Hicks* is said to have 'excited indignation in the minds of policy-holders', and led the Railway Passengers Assurance Company to write letters 'to the principal daily papers, sending a copy of s. 36 of their Act of 1849'.[126] This provided that compensation paid by the company 'was in no case to be taken in diminution of damages otherwise recoverable'. Eventually, in 1908, a similar provision was made applicable to all accident insurers.[127] This combination of non-deduction based on statutory policy, with absence of subrogation rights based on common law reasoning, led directly to double recovery, and this is the origin of today's position.

5.5.2 Double recovery in personal injury awards

Much more debatable is the extension of the reasoning in *Dalby* to personal accident policies in *Theobald v Railway Passengers Assurance Co*,[128] the key authority for the proposition that personal injury policies also are not contracts of indemnity. In truth, it is very fragile authority. After this case, courts also moved to their own conclusion that personal injury damages were non-deductible, on the basis of very limited reasoning,[129] and thus the courts themselves created the double recovery which in the case of fatal accidents is the product of common law and statute in combination. It will be noticed that *Theobald*, like *Hicks* and *Bradburn*, was a case against a railway company, and such cases may have raised particular concerns.[130] This is the context in which double recovery for personal accident in general had its origins. Despite the subsequent rise of liability insurance after the Employers' Liability Act 1880,[131] the basic positions set out have not been altered.

In *Theobald*, the assured was covered under a first-party policy for £1,000 for death as the result of railway accident, and a proportionate payment in the event of injury. This particular feature of the contract—that it expressed liability in the event of personal injury as a proportion of a life—may help explain the court's treatment of the nature of personal injury insurance as analogous to life assurance. This is very different from today's accident policies which provide a tariff for particular forms of injury. In any case, in other respects this short-term accident policy with one-off premium in no way resembled the long-term life insurance policies with set annual premiums which were the subject of *Dalby*.

[126] F Hayter Cox, *The Oldest Accident Office in the World: The Railway Passengers Assurance Co 1849–1949* (London: Fanfare Press, 1949), 32.

[127] Fatal Damages (Accident) Act 1908.

[128] (1854) 10 Ex 45.

[129] *Bradburn v Great Western Railway* (1874) LR 1, discussed in the text at n 140, which has been affirmed by the House of Lords in recent years.

[130] 'A railway was quite different from a colliery or cotton mill. Gentlemen and their families did not dig coal or drive the power looms. Only the railways, the great rolling transportation factories of England, presented an often deadly mixture of industrial production and consumption' (Kostal, n 125, 321).

[131] Examined further in Chapter 9.

The assured slipped and was injured, and the question[132] for the court was the measure of recovery. The insurers' argument was that the sum had to be in some way proportionate to the amount recoverable for death. The court rejected that argument, deciding that the true measure was the amount of injury, *capped* at the amount payable in the event of death. Therefore, this decision that personal injury policies are not contracts of indemnity concerned a policy which was recognized to offer some compensation for measurable losses, and it is hardly surprising that the exclusion has proved hard to rationalize with confidence. The jury's award of £34 19s for medical attendance and expenses was upheld, but its separate award of £100 for 'loss of time or loss of profit' was not. The main significance of the case has been taken to be Alderson B's comment that 'This is not a contract of indemnity because a person cannot be indemnified for the loss of life as he can in the case of a house or ship'.[133] This remark was made in the course of argument, not in the course of judgment. It is in any case by no means clear what Alderson B had in mind. If he meant that there could not be a *full* indemnity through insurance for a loss of life, in the same way as for loss of property, there is a case that this remains correct, though that question is not straightforward. Though damages are now awarded for non-pecuniary losses and, in the case of a fatal accident, for bereavement, it is unclear in the former case what the relationship is between these damages and 'full compensation'; in the latter instance, it is clear that the award is purely conventional.[134] However, the remark might be taken instead to imply that it is not *possible* for compensation for personal injury and death to be in the nature of an indemnity (a man 'cannot be' indemnified for a loss of life), because human lives are not to be valued as ships and houses are. This may be the most natural meaning of the words; but it would be inconsistent with some other aspects of the developing law at the time, and possibly even with the measure of damages in *Theobald* itself. As we have seen, even within a few years of *Theobald*, the courts clearly recognized the pecuniary element of damages for death in relation to the Fatal Accidents Act 1846.

The decision in *Bradburn v Great Western Railway Co*,[135] some years later, is the root authority for non-deduction of insurance payments in the case of personal injury. This was not a case where the accident policy covered the assured's full loss.[136] Bramwell B, faced with the suggestion that the amount paid under the accident policy should be deducted from damages, proclaimed that 'one is dismayed at this proposition'.[137] The policy was treated as analogous to that in *Dalby*, in that the claimant's right to be compensated was 'an equivalent for the premiums he has paid'. Pigott B put the same point still more clearly: the injured party 'does not receive that sum of money because of the accident, but because he has made a contract providing for the contingency'. This appears to make a questionable assertion based on causation, which has

[132] There was also a question whether this was a railway accident, the answer being yes.

[133] This is rather different from the reasoning in *Dalby*, n 114, which did not turn on whether there *can* be indemnification for a loss of life, but on the nature and form of life insurance contracts themselves.

[134] n 110.

[135] (1874) Ex 1.

[136] The damages were assessed at £217, and the accident policy provided £31.

[137] This may reflect the middle-class uproar caused by the decision in *Hicks*, n 123, though Bramwell described that case as correct in relation to Fatal Accidents Act damages.

been the subject of much debate. The 'causation' point was taken seriously enough to be dismissed by the House of Lords in *Parry v Cleaver*,[138] to be replaced with an argument that the sums were not deductible because the injured person had paid for them himself.[139] More important, we suggest, is that Pigott B here drew attention to the fact that this was to be seen as a *contingency* contract, and this meant that it was in effect similar to life insurance: the injured party had won a wager, and still had his claim for damages intact.[140] Personal accident policies of the contingency type are conceptualized not as making good the claimant's loss, but as supplying a particular sum in response to the 'contingency' of suffering an injury. There are cases in which subrogation has been permitted by medical expenses insurers, and the terms of health insurance contracts commonly contain subrogation clauses, but personal accident insurance in general continues to be considered a non-indemnity contract.

The point was argued before the Supreme Court of Western Australia in *Insurance Commission of Western Australia v Kightly*,[141] where a health insurer's claim for reimbursement out of settlement monies was allowed. More generally, there have been strong arguments that in modern conditions, the effects of *Dalby* and *Theobald* are to be questioned, and subrogation should be available in personal injury cases.[142] This would eliminate double recovery in cases where the subrogation right was exercised,[143] but it would not reduce costs to tortfeasors and their insurers. The basis for the argument is that it has been recognized for many years that the economic effects of personal injury and death are considerable and that damages and insurance both seek to ameliorate these effects. Equally, the boundaries of indemnity and non-indemnity insurance are not clear,[144] nor have they ever been: serious consequences are allowed to follow from the adoption of broad general 'rules of thumb', or classifications of convenience. We note however that there is some risk of elision here between different arguments. We have seen that it is not sufficient, to qualify as an indemnity contract, to show that the kind of harm to which the contract responds is pecuniary in nature. Rather, an indemnity contract provides benefits according to the amount of loss, rather than on a 'contingency' basis. Otherwise, the existence of an insurable interest would often ensure that the contract was not a contingency contract, and this is counter to *Dalby*.

[138] [1970] AC 1.

[139] LC 262, n 110, reviewed the inconsistencies associated with this line of argument. More recently, non-deduction has rested on the *existence* of subrogation rights, eg in *Horton v Evans* [2007] EWHC 315 (QB).

[140] *Bradburn* was affirmed by the House of Lords in *Parry v Cleaver* (n 138); also *Hussain v New Taplow Paper Mills Ltd* [1988] AC 514 and *Hodgson v Trapp* [1989] AC 807.

[141] n 72. The same appears to be more securely established in Canada, but *Kightly* has not been widely referred to in subsequent Australian decisions.

[142] Mitchell, n 3; C Sappideen and P Vines, *Fleming's The Law of Torts* (Sydney: Lawbook Co, 10th ed, 2011) (identifying double recovery, but noting a 'pervasive feeling' that tort damages never fully compensate for personal injury).

[143] If there was a deliberate policy of eliminating double recovery however, more than this would be required. For example, tortfeasors could be required to pay part of damages direct to insurers. This is the route taken for recoupment of state benefits and hospital expenses.

[144] For example *Feasey v Sun Life Assurance Co of Canada* [2003] EWCA Civ 885; [2003] Lloyd's Rep IR 637; J Birds, 'Insurable Interest—Orthodox and Unorthodox Approaches' (2006) JBL 224.

The potential problem is illustrated by *Kightly* itself. Here the majority of benefits under a health insurance policy took the form of lump sum payments expressed as a capital sum. Several of the benefits, however, related to expenses (medical, travel, and rehabilitative) which had actually been incurred, up to a cap. The tort claimant in this case had reached a settlement. The Supreme Court of Western Australia held that he had failed to take into account the health insurer's interests, which he had a duty to do irrespective of the absence of direct contract between tort claimant and insurer. Damages payable to the insurer were to be established, but might encompass 'the whole of what was paid to the respondent by the appellant'. The effect on the tort claimant in this case could be significant, depending on the generosity of the settlement. The potential effect on *future* tort damages awards is to increase them as cover is shifted from health insurers to liability insurers, while the likelihood of a concomitant reduction in health insurance premiums is, to say the least, uncertain. The risk is that subrogation will, as Hasson predicted more generally,[145] either reduce benefits or increase the costs of tort liability, though it may be good for health insurers' profit margins. Despite the *logic* of treating health insurance as an indemnity contract, its impact needs careful attention. It is notable that the Western Australia Supreme Court in *Kightly* cited the early, relatively positive appraisal of Kimball and Davis,[146] but none of the more recent, critical contributions to the debate over the impact of health insurer subrogation in the United States.

The possible implications are far-reaching, therefore, and here we consider the limited reported English authorities. The underlying picture cannot, of course, be tested by such authorities, particularly in relation to settled claims,[147] but they give an indication of the response of the courts to such developments. It is clear that health insurers expressly reserve rights of subrogation in their contracts, but less clear is how often these are exercised. Two reported cases where such express rights were held to be effective, and where (as in *Kightly*) the tort claimant had no direct contractual relationship with the insurer, were *Horton v Evans*,[148] where Keith J subsequently assessed damages to a high-earning claimant, taking into account the involvement of health insurers with reserved rights of subrogation,[149] and *Shulman v Simon*,[150] where Judge Mackie QC assessed damages in a case of mesothelioma where BUPA had reserved rights in relation to medical expenses. In both cases the subrogation rights were held to be relevant when assessing the claim despite the absence of contractual duties on the tort claimants to account to the health insurer for the sums they had spent on care. Notably, the effect in both decisions was to increase the damages award: the tort claimants could recover damages in respect of medical expenses which they had not personally paid, in order to enable them to repay the health insurers. The impact is

145 n 5. 146 n 76.

147 Consider for example the refusal of leave to appeal on quantum (liability having been agreed) in *Tandara v Watson* [2010] EWCA Civ 549: Carnwath J noted a dispute over a payment to BUPA of £4,470.41 out of a damages award of £7,349 plus interest, and concluded that this was a matter which could be 'sorted out by agreement between the parties' (at [4]).

148 [2007] EWHC 315 (QB); [2007] All ER (D) 97 (Mar).

149 Harvey McGregor, *McGregor on Damages* (London: Sweet & Maxwell, 18th edn, 2012), 35–225, makes a sharp distinction between health insurance policies, and personal accident policies, citing *Horton v Evans*.

150 [2010] EWHC 2762 (QB); [2010] All ER (D) 69 (Nov).

that the existence of the employer's health insurance scheme gives the claimant the benefit of additional care, at the expense of tortfeasors, their liability insurers, and all those who contribute to the costs of that insurance. Controversial though this may be, it is in line with the policy of the law as expressed in the Personal Injuries Act 1948 and subsequent case law of high authority. It extends here to a scheme for which the claimant has not personally paid the premium.

As we have seen, the effect of health insurer subrogation will not always take this form. It had potentially serious effects for the injured claimant in *Kightly*, and that experience is familiar in the United States.[151] In *Horton v Evans*,[152] there were two relevant health insurance policies. The potential for trouble ahead can be revealed by a close look at one of these, the Aetna policy, extracted in the judgment of Keith J. The Aetna policy provided that, if the assured had a right of action against a third party:

> this Plan is entitled to recover, in first priority, the full amount recovered from any third-party payer, up to the total benefits it has paid in connection with that injury or illness. The Plan may recover these amounts directly from the person or organization making or responsible for payment, or from proceeds paid to you or your dependants by that party. 'Any proceeds paid' includes all amounts recovered, regardless of whether the settlement or judgment specifically designates the recovery, or any portion of it, as including expenses for which this Plan has paid benefits. If necessary, the Plan may take legal action to recover its payments, or it may require you or your dependants to assert a claim for recovery from any available source.

The potential effect of this on tort claimants who are tempted to enter into discounted settlements is clear. If the prevailing view is that the extension of subrogation to health insurers is logical and clear[153]—so that, as Keith J put it, sums recovered are held 'in equity' for the Plan—then English courts may soon face the challenge of how to control their impact on settlements and on tort claimants, which is the story of developments in the United States. It is most likely that the continuing emphasis on state health care, rather than private insurance, in this jurisdiction has held back these developments to date.[154] Recalling our earlier discussion of the possible justifications for subrogation, it is clear that in a case such as *Horton v Evans*, there is no prospect of double recovery

[151] Note Ellen Pryor's (n 112) discussion of the US Supreme Court's efforts to control the recoupment of insurer expenses from settlements—many of which will be non-itemized—in *Arkansas Department of Health and Human Services v Ahlborn* 547 US 268 (2006). Subrogation may also have a negative impact on the incentive to settle—the opposite of the desired effect outlined in 5.2.

[152] n 148.

[153] It has been pointed out that the decision of the Court of Appeal in *Simpson v Norfolk and Norwich University Hospital NHS Trust* [2011] EWCA Civ 1149; [2012] 2 WLR 873—which recognized that a personal injury action is capable of being assigned, though in that instance the assignee had no legitimate interest in pursuing it—by implication further supports the notion that personal injury insurers can contract for subrogation rights: A Tettenborn, 'Personal injury claims and assignment: interesting times?' (2012) PN 61.

[154] Private Healthcare UK reports that 11.1 per cent of the UK population had private medical insurance in January 2011. This had fallen from 12.4 per cent in January 2009, a fall attributed to recession and redundancies. The majority of private medical insurance is employer funded (2.95 million employer-funded policies, compared with 1.01 million self-funded policies): Private Healthcare UK, 'Private Healthcare Key facts (February 2012)', available at <http://www.privatehealth.co.uk/service-to-industry/statistics-and-data/private-healthcare-key-facts/>, accessed 26 April 2013. Aetna is a US insurer founded in Hartford, Connecticut.

except to the extent that the court's decision to take account of subrogation rights and therefore to *include* medical expenses in the award (though not incurred by the claimant) creates it. Rather, this is a case where the likely enrichment is, somewhat notionally, that of the tort defendant, who would otherwise 'benefit' from the existence of the Plan—though only in the sense that the tort claimant is entitled to benefit from private medical care and the expense of this is thought *appropriately* to fall on the tort defendant. There is a value judgement at work therefore, or indeed more than one, for the total amount of loss is thought appropriately to be increased by the choice of private care, and the burden of this is thought appropriately to lie with tortfeasors and their indemnifiers, not on the providers of private Plans who have received the relevant premium. The implications of this in a jurisdiction with socialized health care is distinctive, namely that the existence of private Plans on the part of *some* tort claimants drives up the *overall* cost of tort liability (thus liability insurance). Tort claimants covered by such plans have no choice but to recoup the costs of private care from tortfeasors and their insurers, because they have a duty to do so; and settle claims at their peril. Given concerns over the cost of tort, it seems unlikely that this state of affairs would commend itself to government today if subjected to open policy debate. Here is an instance in which the health insurer's argument is that the tortfeasor and/or the liability insurer is the primary indemnifier, and this needs evaluation in light of distributive effects.[155]

It is useful to consider these developments against the general background assumption that subrogation is not available in relation to personal accident insurance, while the insurance proceeds continue to be non-deductible. This assumption has continued for over 150 years despite serious questions about the root authorities. Possibly, the conventional classification of insurance policies is used or maintained not because it is convincing, but because there is no incentive to question it, as the end result is consistent with the law's general position. If there is a starting point that victims of personal injury and bereaved relatives will never be fully or adequately compensated, it is possible to argue that it is legitimate for them to receive pecuniary benefits from more than one source: to reduce damages would be to introduce a false element of accuracy.[156] Inserting subrogation into the picture would inevitably mean single recovery where practised.[157] While the origins of double recovery, like the exclusion of subrogation, lie in the contingency nature of the bargain struck with the insurer, its continuation may rest on rather different ideas.

When it considered these issues, the Law Commission recommended that personal injury and death awards should be subject to compatible regimes. Private insurance payments were in each case not to be the subject of deduction. So far as insurance

[155] In effect this is a particular counter-argument to the distributive claim of Jane Stapleton, 'Tort, Insurance and Ideology' (1995) 58 MLR 820, namely that the burden of losses *ought* to fall on tortfeasors not claimants. This is discussed further in Chapter 8.

[156] The LC (n 110) aspired to remove this position by improving assessment of damages and increasing the non-pecuniary award, but this did not alter the position of consultees nor, in the event, the LC itself.

[157] The US experience of medical expenses insurance suggests that insurers might be very keen to practise subrogation rights, but the context is different, as these are actions designed to protect the exposure of an employer fund providing basic benefits to employees: Maher and Pathak, n 51. However, there is evidence (already reviewed) that health insurers in the UK also exercise their reserved subrogation rights.

payments under life and accident policies were concerned, these were justified by treating them as not meeting the same loss as damages for wrongful death. Such insurance policies were (still) to be regarded as 'essentially an investment' for the assured, or dependants.[158]

It is quite possible that the core idea that insurance policies do not cover the same damage is itself merely a rationalization, deployed in order to avoid looking too closely at the idea of double recovery. Indeed, the Law Commission itself argued that in the case of fatal accidents, only 'blatant' double recovery should be ruled out (thus accepting, by implication, that less blatant double recovery is inherent).[159] Perhaps it can only be said that this reflects the mixed nature of the law's response to personal injury liability in particular, in which economic well-being and security, fault and deterrence, and the encouragement of self-sufficiency, prudentialism, and investment for the future, all play a part, and in which little can be explained on the basis of simple 'principle' alone. The level of criticism levelled at use of insurer subrogation in relation to personal injury in the United States suggests that the creation of such rights, despite its inherent logic, might attract unwelcome critical attention to subrogation as a whole.[160] Given the sheer number of personal injury actions both in and out of the courts each year, it is tempting to see personal injury as typical of the law of tort in particular, and the law on personal injury as representative of the relationship between insurance and the law of obligations. The extent to which this is not the case is illustrated by the fact that standard policies relating to personal injury and death are shakily justified exceptions to the general approach to the insurance contract in terms of indemnity, and that the logic of subrogation threatens to bring to the surface some concealed debates about the nature of personal injury damages. These issues are also reflected in the discussion of 'state subrogation', and the balance between public and private provision. What seems clear is that in this context, logical classification of insurance policies and of remedies will not be enough.

5.6 Reflections on Risk Allocation and Loss Distribution

5.6.1 Critique

No matter how it is rationalized, subrogation faces criticism based on its overall effects. In particular, it has been asserted that subrogation is an expensive and wasteful process, the sole purposes of which are to switch loss from first-party insurers and to encourage duplicated insurance. But for subrogation, the argument runs, losses would be borne by first-party insurers, and the only beneficiaries of loss-switching are the lawyers who

[158] LC, CP 148, n 113, 3.90.

[159] LC 263, *Claims for Wrongful Death* (1999), 5.45: 'the exception should be construed narrowly and confined to instances of blatant double recovery'—eg claims for loss of a survivor's pension, when the claimant is in receipt of a survivor's pension (*Auty v NCB* [1985] 1 WLR 784).

[160] Documenting the extension of subrogation to personal policies in the US, see for example O Reed, 'Insurance Subrogation in Personal Injury Actions: the Silent Explosion' (1975) 12 Am Business LJ 111; DJ Srail, 'Insurance Subrogation in Personal Injury Torts' (1978) 39 Ohio LJ 621; Kimball and Davis, n 76. More recent, often critical, commentary has been referred to throughout this chapter.

represent first- and third-party insurers in subrogation proceedings.[161] Furthermore, the sole beneficiary of double insurance is the insurance industry. This is a far-reaching criticism. Here we consider the loss-distribution question, before turning to examine more closely the potential of risk allocation analysis.

Abolishing subrogation would eliminate tort claims for property and related losses where the victim has taken the precaution of taking out adequate first-party insurance. It seems logical that one inevitable consequence of such a switch would be to increase the cost of first-party premiums.[162] It is not immediately obvious how this would affect liability insurance premiums because liability cover for death and personal injury would have to remain in place, and parties may need to cover the possibility of actions by uninsured, or under-insured, claimants. Tort scholars who adhere to the concept of personal responsibility might not warm to a reform which tends to reduce the application of tort's principles in cases of breach of duty, though it is worth noting that here it is insurers who currently guarantee the continuation of the law of tort for property damage.[163] But in terms of loss-spreading, what would be the effect? Some evidence as to what might occur is provided by the history of 'knock for knock' agreements, at one time widely used in the motor insurance industry. The idea was that if two vehicles collided then each of the insurers would pay its own assured's property losses irrespective of the degree of blame attributable to each assured. The system was widely remarked upon by scholars who challenged the dominance of fault in the law's response to accidents.[164] It is salutary to note therefore that the agreement was abandoned in the 1980s following complaints that the innocent victims of collisions were worse off by having to bear the inevitable first loss excess applicable to the policy and also by having to pay higher premiums following the loss of no-claims bonuses. Such a conclusion needs to be compared with the rising price of motor insurance premiums associated with tort damages. But it is at least a possible result of abolishing subrogation claims that some assureds might be classified as bad risks for reasons beyond their own control.

A further criticism of subrogation is that it may allow first-party insurers to switch losses to uninsured third parties, or (in a variation of the argument) to 'peripheral' parties who may or may not be insured. At first sight this is a curious objection, because many scholars support the tort system on the very basis that its liabilities are attracted by personal responsibility and, as we have seen, one of the reasons offered for subrogation is that without it, third parties would be 'taking the benefit of' an insurance policy for which they have not paid. We have begun to question this point of view, and indeed the most widely accepted view is that there is something unjust in allowing insurers to recover from uninsured persons. This, we suggest, is best interpreted as

[161] Hasson, n 5; U Procaccia, 'The Effect and Validity of Subrogation Clauses in Insurance Policies' (1973) Ins LJ 573.

[162] Note, however, the common assertion that, as things stand, rate setting is not affected by subrogation: n 76.

[163] Insurers do not, of course, act for this reason, and their interests may lead them to undermine the law of tort in some contexts, such as in the case of 'first dollar' subrogation agreements found in the US.

[164] Explored by J Birds, 'Insurance and the Knock for Knock Agreement' (1978) 41 MLR 201; R Lewis, 'Insurers' Agreements Not to Enforce Strict Legal Rights: Bargaining in the Shadow of the Law' (1985) 48 MLR 275.

reflecting a general acceptance that negligence is a form of risk like any other—in fact, a classic insurable risk.[165]

5.6.1.1 Lister v Romford Ice

The decision in *Lister v Romford Ice and Cold Storage Co Ltd*[166] illustrates that some of the unfortunate distributive effects of subrogation (particularly the pursuit of uninsured parties) can be addressed through the risk allocation questions identified earlier in this chapter and which represent a settled aspect of the law of subrogation in the courts. This is a much-discussed case, and, oddly, it has been used as clear evidence of the irrelevance of insurance in the law of tort.[167] Our argument is that the case is both exceptional, and poorly reasoned, and that a better resolution was possible without the need to have recourse to broad policy factors. And in addition to this, it is not evidence of the irrelevance of insurance.

In *Lister*, an employee was injured by the negligence of a fellow employee who happened to be his son. The employers were vicariously liable towards the victim, and the employers' liability (EL) insurers, having indemnified the employers, commenced subrogation proceedings against the victim's son on the grounds that he faced liability to indemnify his employers. The House of Lords found for the employers/insurers. The majority judgments turned not on the fairness or otherwise of subrogation but on the narrower grounds that a contract of employment was not subject to an implied term that employers would refrain from seeking indemnity from their employees. The decisive analysis in both majority and minority decisions, and in the courts below—as is pointed out in Chapter 7—turned on the interpretation of the parties' contracts.[168] This is, as we have suggested, broadly the correct approach to subrogation questions, because subrogation is most fruitfully to be understood in terms of the question, 'who is the primary indemnifier?' This itself is best addressed by reference to the parties' various relationships and the context of the liability concerned.

The dissenting judges concluded (entirely reasonably) that an employed driver like the defendant could hardly be expected to enter employment on the basis that he alone among all drivers would personally, and without the benefit of insurance, take the pecuniary risks associated with his own negligence.[169] Nor would an implied term

[165] Welford, n 1, in the first volume on accident insurance law in the UK, pointed out that 'Negligence is the most usual cause of accident; and an assured, being but human, is as likely to be negligent as his servants' (169).

[166] [1955] AC 55.

[167] The judgment of Viscount Simonds is quoted to this effect by Stapleton, n 155, 823.

[168] The British Insurance Association (BIA, now the Association of British Insurers), in its evidence to the Inter-Departmental Committee set up to consider the implications of *Lister* (which were thought unsettling to labour relations) commented that the EL insurer was acting by virtue of a term in the insurance policy rather than through the subrogation right at law; that it was not a member of the BIA, which had already agreed not to proceed in such cases without the consent of the assured; that the motor insurer was not involved; and that in the Association's view, the problem stemmed fundamentally 'from the relationship between employer and employee': TNA LCO 2/5642; evidence dated 30 September 1957.

[169] This was also the view of McNair J, the first instance judge, expressed forcefully in a letter to the Lord Chancellor after the House of Lords decision: insurance would most likely be considered by both parties to the employment contract and it was 'wholly unrealistic' that the lorry driver would willingly take the whole

placing that risk with the employer's insurers be of any surprise to the insurers. The contractual route in *Lister* was therefore appropriate; but the method applied by the majority in addressing the question of where the parties had placed the risk was excessively formalistic, and is fairly described as unrealistic. Viscount Simonds argued that he could not recognize an implied term in the contract of employment if it could not be specified at what date such a term would first have been implied, and what its content would be,[170] because an implied term ought to be relatively certain. Yet, as we have seen, uncertainty and evaluation are normal aspects of the question to be asked by courts where a first-party insurer seeks reimbursement from a third party: who is the 'primary indemnifier'? In light of the existence not only of widespread motor insurance, but also of *compulsory* motor insurance, the idea that the parties would expect the risk of liability to fall on the individual driver is indeed unreal. Nor is it adequate to suggest, as Lord Morton did, that if subrogation were to be denied, the insurer would be disadvantaged by a term in a contract to which they were not a party. He even described this result as 'surprising'.[171] The analysis throughout this chapter should make plain that there is nothing surprising about it. It is of course entirely normal that subrogation rights are no more than the rights of the assured, and that the rights of the assured are a matter of express and implied terms, tort duties, equity, and much else besides, as in any other relationship governed by private law. It is perhaps fortunate that the courts, as exemplified by the House of Lords in *Caledonia North Sea*,[172] have edged away from the language of implied terms in favour of a more broadly evaluative approach to where the parties had placed the risk. There are many other instances of a similar approach in Chapter 7.

Apart from the poor quality of the majority judgments and their distance from the typical reasoning to be found in subrogation cases, it is astonishing that this case should have become emblematic of the suggested disregard of insurance in determining rights under a contract,[173] since the difference between the judges turned on what the parties would consider the agreed insurance position. Only fleetingly did Viscount Simonds appear to deny the relevance of insurance in any general sense to the rights and duties between the assured and other parties. His much-quoted remark that 'a man insures at his own expense for his own benefit and does not thereby suffer any derogation of his rights against another man' has created much misunderstanding. Even in the context of an overly rigid analysis, this statement was a starting point, to which Viscount Simonds himself admitted there would be 'possible exception'. More fundamentally, in light of the general approach to subrogation observable in the decisions of the courts,

risk: letter dated 14 January 1959: TNA LCO2/5642. McNair J reasoned by analogy with maritime liabilities and the recognized legitimate protection of masters of ships where they could be a tempting target in order to evade agreed restrictions on other routes to recovery. Again this recognizes that what is in issue is primarily risk, and that the presence of fault is scarcely a reason to trump the agreed balance. The ILO, too, took an interest in *Lister* in connection with the rights of employed drivers. The implied term was in no sense fanciful.

[170] Plainly Viscount Simonds did not think it adequate to suggest that the employer would be expected by both parties to 'take care of' all matters relating to insurance. But this seems well suited to describe the fact that an employed driver would not expect to insure himself against liability, or to be exposed to personal liability, and would expect his employer to put arrangements in place.

[171] *Lister*, n 166, Lord Morton at 584. [172] n 29. [173] n 166.

it is also misleading. *Mason v Sainsbury*,[174] cited as authority shortly before, raised the question of who is to be seen as the primary indemnifier. In modern case law, this is recognized as an evaluative question affected by parties' risk allocations and, where appropriate, by the policy of the law, expressed in the various liabilities themselves. It is not *necessarily* the case that a man insures only on his own account, and the minority was correct to say that it was not the case here. More fundamentally perhaps, even the much-quoted Viscount Simonds recognized that whether (or not) that was true in the circumstances was the very issue in this case. The misguided nature of assertions that insurance is generally fortuitous from the point of view of other parties is highlighted by the very case most commonly used to illustrate it.

5.6.1.2 Restriction of Lister

There was an immediate reaction to *Lister*. An Inter-Departmental Committee was established to consider its implications and clearly disapproved of its impact, but decided not to recommend legislation. Instead it accepted the option of an improved[175] agreement between insurers that EL insurers would not exercise subrogation rights against employees except in cases of collusion or wilful misconduct.[176] It appears from the nature of the discussions both within the Committee and by the Lord Chancellor's Department that reliance was placed primarily on the fact that insurers would not in future think it worth the political risk to bring such an action again. Legislation, in other words, was not worth the time and trouble.[177] But it is not only EL insurers who can misuse subrogation if courts fail to adopt sufficiently flexible reasoning, as the House of Lords failed to do in *Lister*. Even with reference to the employment context, it is interesting that the Ministry of Labour never did manage to comply with the insurers' request to secure the formal agreement of nationalized industries and local authorities not to employ subrogation rights.[178] One local authority (Lancashire County Council) expressly underlined its intention to use its right to seek indemnity against an employee on certain occasions. The Council self-insured for its liability to employees; but secured motor insurance to cover its employees' driving. The Council pointed out that the motor insurance policy entitled the employee driver to 'stand in the shoes' of the County Council if he were sued personally, and a full indemnity would be paid to the driver. Where the County Council was sued, it had taken

[174] n 43.

[175] A voluntary agreement was reached by the BIA in 1961, with the active encouragement of an Inter-Departmental Committee led by the Ministry of Labour and reporting in 1959. There was already a 1953 agreement in place but the insurer in *Lister* (a Lloyd's underwriter) was not a party to it. The earlier agreement was also weaker in that it only prevented the bringing of subrogation claims without the consent of the insured party: TNA LAB 10/1618. It is likely that the claim in *Lister* was seen as fishy because it was a father-son case, so that the damages payable and negligent act were within the same family.

[176] Gerald Gardiner (later Lord Chancellor) criticized this route to reform by agreement in (1959) 22 MLR 652–6, and indeed there are numerous problems with the 'agreement'. Refer also to Lewis, n 164.

[177] The Committee's Report considered various potential approaches to legislation and rejected them all as too troublesome.

[178] TNA LAB 10/1618. This contains correspondence following the Report of the Inter-Departmental Committee, documenting the relatively long-running and inconclusive attempts to arrive at a secure agreement, legislation having been rejected.

the course of entering third-party proceedings against the driver, which enabled the Council to take advantage of the driver's personal indemnity under the insurance policy. This was not, therefore, a case of proceeding against an uninsured employee; but a case of a self-insuring (uninsured) employer seeking the benefit of an indemnity for which it had paid, by proceeding against the employee.[179]

There is a real question whether, notwithstanding the majority decision in *Lister*, a future court would—should the issue arise—take the same view as in *Lister*, particularly since EL insurance became compulsory under the Employers' Liability (Compulsory Insurance) Act 1969. There is a strong indication to the contrary effect in *Morris v Ford Motor Co*,[180] which arose from one of the gaps in the post-*Lister* agreement, namely that it applies only where the claimant is a fellow employee and not a member of the public or other third party. We would submit that *Morris* is more in tune with the general reasoning of common law courts than the decision in *Lister*. Here, Ford entered into an agreement with a firm of cleaners, Cameron, for Cameron to provide cleaning services at Ford's Halewood site. Cameron was under a contractual obligation to indemnify Ford in the event that one of Cameron's employees was injured in the course of his work and obtained damages from Ford (the fairness of this provision has been doubted).[181] Mr Morris, who was employed by Cameron, was injured by one of Ford's employees, Mr Roberts. Mr Morris commenced proceedings against Ford, and Ford issued a third-party notice against Cameron in accordance with Cameron's contractual obligation to indemnify Ford. The claim was ultimately paid by Cameron (and, in all likelihood, Cameron's insurers), so the loss lay upon Cameron in accordance with the agreement. However, Cameron, having indemnified Ford, sought to use Ford's name to bring an action against Mr Roberts. The reality of this claim was probably that Cameron's liability insurers were exercising Cameron's own subrogation right (as contractual indemnifier) to use the name of Ford, and then Ford's subrogation rights to sue Mr Roberts, thereby undermining the agreed allocation of loss and seeking to impose that loss upon an almost certainly uninsured individual. The position was therefore somewhat similar to that in *Lister v Romford Ice* discussed in previous paragraphs. However, it fell outside the post-*Lister* agreement which precluded any subrogation action by an insurer against a negligent employee, because that agreement applied only to injuries inflicted by and against employees of the same employer.

The majority, Lord Denning MR and Stamp LJ, agreed that the loss should lie with Cameron (the contractual indemnifier) rather than with the negligent individual, but differed in their reasoning. Lord Denning's judgment is probably the only instance in

[179] The County Council set out this rationale in a letter to the Ministry of Labour dated 18 March 1963. This also pointed out that the insurers had been asked whether they might instead assess a premium to cover the liability 'from a limited EL aspect', but they had declined. Litigation following the pattern and rationale described was brought against the driver of a fire engine in respect of injury to a fellow employee before Elwes J on 30 January 1963: *Lancashire County Council v Robert John Swash* (QBD, Liverpool). The true nature of the litigation was revealed to Elwes J after his judgment of liability, in relation to the question of costs, the Council's legal representative stating that 'it is a dispute between the Insurance Company and the County Council, and Mr Swash obviously will not meet this judgment or costs'. The evident concerns of the judge were assuaged, and judgment and costs were awarded to the Council.

[180] [1973] QB 792. [181] See the strong remarks of Weir, n 12.

the English courts of a judge denying subrogation on the basis that subrogation was an equitable remedy, and that the equitable balance was against the party wishing to exercise the right. His reasoning was characteristically broad and succinct. 'Everyone knows that risks such as these are covered by insurance'; and if the servant makes a mistake while doing his employer's work, to make the servant personally liable would be 'positively unjust'. There has been general agreement that the breadth of Lord Denning's reasoning here is unsupported by any previous decision. But equally, some frustration has been expressed that addressing the issue of justice plainly—particularly if 'unjust enrichment' is supposed to be the basis of subrogation—should prove not to be possible.[182] Lord Denning added, as an alternative, that there would be no implied term that the cleaners should be able to use Ford's name.[183] James LJ took the far more promising route of construing the parties' contracts and concluded that 'the terms of this indemnity in the context of this contract' did not give rise to a right of subrogation. In the style of the time, he expressed there to be an 'implied term' excluding the subrogation right. More helpfully, he reached his conclusion by looking at the 'industrial setting', in which he held subrogation of the contractual indemnifier (Cameron) to the rights and remedies of the third party against their employees 'would be unacceptable and unrealistic'.[184] This was the contextual analysis, of the setting and the contractual terms as a whole, by which James LJ felt able to distinguish this case from *Lister*.[185] In the result, the fact that there was a third-party source of funding available to Ford—in the form of Mr Roberts—therefore did not undermine the loss allocation agreement.

Despite some difficulties with the reasoning in *Morris*, what it shows is that if subrogation is to be denied, it will typically be because the contractual relationship between the claimant and the defendant, properly construed, relieves the defendant from liability in the circumstances, so that there are simply no rights to which the insurers (or other indemnifiers) can be subrogated.[186] This amounts in many cases to the same question as whether the insurer is intended by the parties, or identifiable as a matter of law and legal policy, to be the primary indemnifier. The interpretation not only of the assured's contract with the insurer, but also of its relationship with potentially liable parties is therefore highly relevant to the insurer's rights, a matter discussed later in this work.[187]

[182] Weir, n 12.

[183] This is also not the question generally asked by the courts, which is addressed to what obligations are owed, rather than whether there is implied permission to be subrogated.

[184] n 180, 815.

[185] In dissent, Stamp LJ looked only at the terms of the indemnity contract itself, not at the contractual rights which the indemnifier, Cameron, sought to take over. This, we suggest, was unduly narrow.

[186] There is a parallel here with the partly dissenting opinion of La Forest J in the Canadian case of *London Drugs v Kuehne and Nagel* [1992] 3 SCR 299. While the majority carved out an exception to privity to provide an employee with the benefit of the employer's limitation of liability, La Forest preferred to say that under the circumstances no duty of care was owed by the employee to the (insured) contracting party, the implication being that there was no tort claim to which the first-party insurer could be subrogated. This is discussed further in relation to tort duties and risk allocation, in Chapter 8.

[187] Chapter 7.

5.6.2 A model for reform

These issues have been addressed in Australia by the Insurance Contracts Act 1984. Sections 65 and 66 remove the right of subrogation in the following cases:

(1) where the assured might reasonably be expected not to exercise a claim by reason of a family or other personal relationship between the assured and the third party;

(2) where the assured might reasonably be expected not to exercise a claim by reason of the assured having consented to use by the third party of the insured motor vehicle;

(3) where the third party is uninsured or only partly insured against liability, the subrogation recovery is limited to the amount if any of the liability insurance;[188]

(4) where the assured is an employer and the third party is an employee who acting in the course of his employment caused the employer to incur liability—this operates to reverse *Lister v Romford Ice.*

In all cases under this legislation a third party whose misconduct was serious or wilful loses subrogation immunity.[189] What is notable here is the distance that has been travelled from personal responsibility for negligence, and the acceptance that, in the presence of insurance to cover a risk, a third party should only face personal liability for the same risk where he has been guilty of serious or wilful misconduct.[190] This is in tune with the treatment of many liability risks, and indeed risks arising from negligence more generally, as quintessentially insurable. This approach remains in tension with any idea that tort principles in particular are primarily about personal responsibility or individual deterrence.

5.6.3 Subrogation and public bodies

Apart from potentially diverting liability to uninsured parties, subrogation may also enable an insurer to pursue another potentially liable party, who was not the primary tortfeasor, but may be said to have responsibility for the loss, or for the incident which leads to the loss, for some other reason. The most significant group of such cases involves public authorities, not least because these authorities have widespread positive duties to act (largely through statute), most of which are not the creation of contractual agreement, and because they are often regarded as having deep pockets. In reality, their resources are thinly stretched, and it is by no means obvious that the costs of tort compensation, especially where the subject of first-party insurance, are well placed with them.[191]

[188] This is similar to the solution suggested by Tony Weir, n 12, in response to the claim in *Morris v Ford Motor Co.*

[189] For example *Boral Resources (Qld) Pty Ltd v Pyke* [1992] 2 Qd R 25 and *Ingham v Vita Pacific Ltd* (1995) 8 ANZ Ins Cas 61-272 (drunken driving; both serious and wilful misconduct).

[190] If he does have liability insurance, his policy will not provide cover for such acts; so these are outside the range of loss-spreading. These issues are examined further in Chapter 11.

[191] Chapter 6 considers public and private roles in loss-spreading.

This issue, and its connection with subrogation, is not a new one, though its legal and policy setting has changed in fundamental ways. The foundational case of *Mason v Sainsbury*[192] concerned whether a first-party property insurer or the local community should be seen as the 'primary' indemnifier. The question of whether private insurers, or public purse, are to bear the brunt of particular losses continues to arise through the exercise of subrogation rights. But while *Mason* involved a statutory liability for riot damages (examined further in 6.5), in more recent times the right of subrogation has enabled liability insurers to push for expansion in the reach of the law of negligence.[193] On our analysis, this should not only require showing a duty on the part of a local authority; it should also require a court to consider whether the authority is to be considered the primary indemnifier. This, as we have seen, incorporates questions which have conventionally been thought to be irrelevant to the tort of negligence. The crucial step therefore is to consider whether this interpretation can be used to accommodate such concerns within tort decisions, particularly through analysis of the duty of care.

This is only one aspect of course of the complex set of questions relating to tort, and especially negligence, in relation to public authorities; but it is no departure from the proper concerns of the law of obligations to consider this in risk allocation terms—where does the law allocate the risk of injury, given the existence of alternative indemnifiers, and given the intentions, in the broadest sense, of the parties and of applicable legal duties? This is the approach subjected to analysis in Chapter 8, where we consider the relative strength of risk allocation, and of fault-based reasoning, in respect of the delineation of tort duties, and question the view that, of all considerations, insurance in particular is to be ruled out of account.[194]

5.7 Conclusions

We have illustrated here that subrogation has a deep influence on the nature of tort and contract liabilities, which will be clarified further over subsequent chapters. Having identified the rationale of insurer subrogation in the nature of the indemnity contract, we have suggested that the exercise of subrogation rights is not entirely uncontrolled by the courts. Courts typically address claims with awareness of subrogation, and by reference to the risk allocation intended by the parties or preferred by the law. Equitable discretion has not been developed by English courts to provide a similar method of control, and redefinition in terms of unjust enrichment has not provided any new means of responding appropriately to an insurer's claim to be the indemnifier of last resort, other than by turning to the contractual context.

Broadly contractual analysis focused on risk allocation can deal with some, but not all, of the potential unfairness of subrogation, not least by recognizing the *ex ante* nature of risk allocation whether that is performed by the parties or by legal and social policy. Analysis based on risk allocation is limited in certain ways. In particular, the parties' risk allocation is not necessarily substantively 'fair'. The fairness of imposing

[192] n 43. [193] Discussed generally in Chapter 8. [194] Stapleton, n 155.

the insurance burden on cleaning contractors working at Ford's sites is questionable, for example, and the imposition of risk on the purchaser of property in *Castellain v Preston* is worse.[195] But the adverse effects are multiplied by allowing insurers to unravel allocations for their own purposes. We suggest it is better to refer to the courts' existing resources for dealing with these issues in terms of 'contract' than in terms of 'justness', if no independent notion of justice comes into it. Equally, no approach based on risk allocation can entirely deal with broader concerns about wastefulness and social cost which focus on the scale of litigation sparked by subrogation and its tendency to create duplication. The latter considerations are properly defined as questions of 'policy'. We suggest however that *ex ante* risk allocation is at the core of the courts' reasoning in many cases about the relative rights and obligations of parties. As one aspect of this, insurance is not correctly described as inherently 'fortuitous' from the point of view of other parties: to assert this as a general rule is mistaken, because the nature of the insurance policy as fortuitous or not is often the very question in play for the court. These conclusions are at odds with the most widely held views about tort and, to a lesser extent perhaps, contract duties. They are further explored in the chapters that follow.

[195] n 71; MS Thompson, 'Must the Purchaser Buy a Charred Ruin?' (1984) Conv 43; also described by Weir, n 12, 6, as 'as inequitable as one can imagine'.

6

Loss-Spreading

6.1 Introduction

In Chapter 2, we explained that insurance is sometimes conceptualized almost entirely in terms of its function of spreading losses; and that this function is often understood, under the influence of an 'actuarial model', in terms of spreading losses across a discrete risk pool. But, as we began to explain in Chapter 2, the nature and extent of the loss-spreading effected by market insurance in practice, and the mechanisms through which it is achieved, do not resemble this picture.

In the present chapter, we focus on the means by which loss-spreading by insurance is achieved, and most particularly on issues of private law which arise in this process. We identify the involvement of a complex series of party transactions and relations and show that losses are spread much further and more widely through insurance than is typically appreciated. One of the key operating factors here is reinsurance, and some core elements of law relating to reinsurance are introduced in 6.4. The issues addressed in the chapter illustrate that risks are by no means spread simply within defined risk pools; and that the pattern of loss-spreading does not necessarily serve, or even match, any overarching purpose or method. The compatibility of loss-spreading with private law concepts is thus enhanced, but at the same time, this raises questions of cost, control, and substantive desirability (and the need for regulation) which are not apparent from the presuppositions of the actuarial model, which de-emphasizes private risk-shifting activity.

While insurance does indeed achieve loss-spreading on a significant scale, it spreads losses not just beyond like risk pools, but also beyond national borders and into different markets. This is one reason why the supposition that loss-spreading goals taken to their logical conclusion must imply that the state should spread losses is misconceived, and we explore some examples of market–state interaction in the final two sections. In this chapter, we touch on the allocation of losses within one or another insurance fund, and the intermingling of losses in different funds. This process becomes stronger as the number of insurer participants increases, and bears little resemblance to insurance in its widely (mis)understood sense of a payment in return for an indemnity from a like risk pool. Indeed, we seek to show that this image is generally speaking (and outside the realms of genuine mutuality) something of a fantasy.

6.2 Some Misconceptions About Loss-Spreading

Some tort scholars in particular have approached the risk-spreading effects of insurance in a restricted way, which overstates the tension between insurance and private law duties, and understates the intimate connections between them.[1] It has been said that insurance is a closed system which confines benefits to contributors;[2] that insurance creates a homogenous risk pool which divides members into groups and charges them risk-related premiums, so that in principle in the long run each member would recover what it has paid in—described as embodying a principle of 'insured pays', and thus in effect (in comparison with tort), 'victim pays';[3] and that each pool is self-financing and does not carry the potential for imposing financial penalties on outsiders.[4]

The difficulty is that none of this accurately reflects the way that the insurance market operates to spread risks.[5] Risk-spreading is much less bounded, and at the same time much more open to creating incentives, than this implies. Both first-party and third-party insurance policies confer benefits on other persons: first-party policies are often designed to protect a range of persons, including associated companies and other contracting parties; and third-party policies rarely make payment to the assured but rather payment is made directly to the assured's victim, a process required by statute where the assured is insolvent[6] or under various compulsory insurance statutes.[7] Insurance rarely consists of a homogenous risk pool, in that policies cover a variety of first- and third-party risks and there is no legal requirement, other than in respect of the separation of assets and liabilities attributable to life (long-term business) and non-life (general business), for premiums to be allocated to classes of risk.[8] Further, risks are to some or other extent inevitably reinsured, and reinsurance is made necessary by the fact that individual insurers cannot hope to gain the full benefit of the 'law of large numbers'. Even though it is acknowledged as the basis of modern underwriting and insurance pricing, the law of large numbers alone is not enough to ensure the survival of the insurer,[9] and it is a regulatory requirement in most jurisdictions that an insurer has adequate reinsurance. In practice, for risks to be spread, diversification is required. Even leaving aside the need for diversification rather than homogeneity in risk, the notion that members would in the long run ultimately receive benefits reflecting their premiums in the insurance risk pool is not borne out in practice, in that most policies

[1] We draw here on J Stapleton, 'Tort, Insurance and Ideology' (1995) 58 MLR 820, 821–2. Further discussion of the arguments is to be found in Chapters 8 and 9. Note also K Abraham, *Distributing Risk: Insurance, Legal Theory and Public Policy* (New Haven CT: Yale University Press, 1986), 64, on which Stapleton's article draws.

[2] 'A characteristic of insurance is that it is a closed system in the sense that a group of people who pay into the finance pool is identical to the group of people who are entitled to claim from it', Stapleton, n 1, 821.

[3] Stapleton describes this (n 1, 821) as 'the most fundamental characteristic of insurance', illustrating the influence of the actuarial heritage outlined in Chapter 2.

[4] Stapleton, n 1, 821.

[5] Reflections on the variation between theory and reality here are developed by R Merkin, 'Tort, Insurance and Ideology: Further Thoughts' (2012) 75 MLR 301.

[6] Third Parties (Rights against Insurers) Acts 1930 and 2010.

[7] Discussed further in Chapter 9.

[8] The regulation of insurance business was outlined in Chapter 4.

[9] Swiss Re's *Reinsurance Matters: A Manual of the Non-life Branches* (Zurich: Swiss Re, 2005; original edition published 1968) captures this in a matter-of-fact way in explaining the necessity of reinsurance: 'In practice, it is impossible to group similar risks, both by type and amounts insured, in sufficient numbers for the law of large numbers to operate' (16).

are short-term; the identity of insured persons changes from year to year; and insurance funds are often used up from large losses affecting a small number of persons.

From the point of view of the relationship between insurance and the law of obligations, perhaps the most important misunderstanding is the assumption that insurance does not impose financial penalties on outsiders and thus—unlike tort, and indeed, contract—cannot operate as a deterrent. A person suffering loss may decide to sue the wrongdoer, and if the claimant happens to be insured then his or her indemnity insurers will do it in their place (indeed, may be more likely to do it than the assured party acting on his or her own account).[10] First-party property claims in this way become third-party liability claims; and we dealt with the need to regulate this process and to moderate the way that insurers may seek responsible parties, in the previous chapter. Liability insurers for their part are able to exert a degree of control over policyholders by increasing premiums or, ultimately, withdrawing cover, sanctions which plainly have a significant deterrent effect; and may also involve themselves in the risk management process of their clients. As we saw in Chapter 2, 'moral hazard' is an idea which originated in insurance, and reflects the longevity of the idea that insurance must be accompanied by responsibility. Last but not least, it can also be argued that an uninsured person who has nothing to lose if he or she faces liability has less incentive to take care than an insured person who cannot continue their activities without insurance. Insurance, in principle, may be a powerful regulator.[11]

6.3 Contribution Between Insurers

Contribution exists in a variety of legal contexts,[12] and has been explained as a principle of fairness or equity: where many parties owe the same debt, it is inequitable for one to pay without contribution from the others.[13] In the context of insurance, it operates to allocate the burden of any loss to all insurers whose policies respond to that loss. The role played in the development of the principles of the law of contribution by cases to which insurers are parties is notable,[14] and the application of contribution to overlapping marine insurance policies can be seen as early as 1763.[15] Today, insurance contribution takes its place as a particular illustration of the wider equitable principle of

[10] Contrast Stapleton's assertion (n 1, 821) that 'deterrence of misfortune cannot be accommodated as a direct goal of insurance: for example, in first-party insurance the creator of the misfortune does not pay!'

[11] See for example C Heimer, 'Insuring More, Ensuring Less: The Costs and Benefits of Private Regulation Through Insurance', in T Baker and J Simon, *Embracing Risk: The Changing Culture of Insurance and Responsibility* (Chicago: University of Chicago Press, 2002). In the same collection, Baker and Simon refer to insurance as (potentially) a 'sleeping giant of power' (12).

[12] See the brief historical overview on the part of Lord Bingham in *Royal Brompton NHS Trust v Hammond* [2002] 1 WLR 1397, drawing on Goff and Jones, *The Law of Restitution* (London: Sweet & Maxwell, 5th edn, 1998).

[13] Lord Bingham suggested (n 12, [2]), that the 'common link' between all the situations where the law recognized entitlement to claim contribution 'was the obvious justice of requiring that a common liability should be shared between those liable'.

[14] A review of the table of cases to the leading work, C Mitchell, *The Law of Contribution and Reimbursement* (Oxford: Oxford University Press, 2003), illustrates this point.

[15] *Newby v Reed* (1763) 1 Wm Bl 416.

contribution, recently restated by the High Court of Australia in *Friend v Brooker*,[16] in the context of ensuring equity as between mutual debtors of the same creditor. Although subrogation and contribution have common equitable roots, a key difference is that insurers make and defend contribution claims in their own right, and thus in their own names.

Contribution between insurers is particularly pertinent to our analysis of loss-spreading, and allows liability relating to a single loss to be divided and the shares to be shifted to different risk pools. There can, for example, be contribution between a motor insurer and an insurer of domestic goods if they happen to cover the same subject matter. Contribution is not the only process through which losses, translated into liabilities, are divided and spread between insurers, but it has a significant role in division and dispersion. Insurers typically seek to avoid the consequences of contribution by express policy terms.

6.3.1 Double insurance

The trigger for contribution is double insurance, a concept which may be defined as any situation in which two or more policies cover a single claim. The practice of taking out overlapping policies developed in the early years of insurance for good and bad reasons. The good reason was the fear that one underwriter might not be able to pay to the full limit of his subscription, so that a second policy might be taken out by way of security. The bad reason was furthering a fraud by deliberately scuttling a vessel and claiming from each insurer, a practice which led at the end of the seventeenth century to the compulsory registration of policies in the Chamber of Assurances in order to pick up cases of double insurance. The growth of prudential supervision has minimized the risk of insurer insolvency, and today double insurance tends to arise 'incidentally', or by accident. 'Incidental' double insurance occurs where two policies are different in scope but happen to converge in specific circumstances, as where a motorist is insured under his own policy to drive any vehicle, and borrows a vehicle from a friend whose own policy covers any person driving with the friend's consent. 'Accidental' double insurance occurs where the assured is unaware that he has a perfectly good policy and obtains another. This can occur where, for example, a person is unaware that his household policy provides litigation funding cover (before the event, BTE insurance) and takes out a litigation funding policy (after the event, ATE) in respect of a claim that he wishes to bring. It can also occur where travel cover is provided by the assured's bank account and also by his employers.[17]

The common law abandoned any objection to double insurance in the middle of the eighteenth century,[18] and the marine authorities were codified by the Marine Insurance Act 1906 s 32. The effect of the section is that the assured is entitled to insure as many times as he wishes, and he can claim against one or more of the insurers in such

[16] [2009] HCA 21; [2009] 4 LRC 635.

[17] In *O'Kane v Jones* [2003] EWHC 2158 (Comm); [2004] 1 Lloyd's Rep 389, a second policy was taken out in the mistaken belief that the first had been cancelled.

[18] *Godin v London Assurance Co* (1758) 1 Burr 489.

proportions as he wishes, but the principle of indemnity dictates that the total amount recovered can never exceed his actual loss. There is no implied term in a policy that an insurer is only liable for its own proportion of any loss.[19]

All of this is, however, subject to express agreement. Insurers remain wary of double insurance and seek to control it by contract provisions of three main types. First, the insurers may seek to come off risk entirely in the event that other cover is taken out: there may be a condition precedent to cover that no other insurance exists at the time, and there may be a cancellation clause if some other policy is subsequently taken out. Such terms are known as 'escape' clauses. Second, the insurers may adopt a lesser provision under which their liability is postponed to that of other insurers, so that if at the time of the loss there is another insurance in place, that insurance has to pay up to the limits of its cover and only if there remains uncompensated loss does the policy respond. The policy thus becomes an excess layer policy, responding only where other policies are exhausted. Third, insurers may insert a rateable proportion clause, under which the insurer is only liable for a proportion of the loss rather than its full amount.

These clauses work without undue difficulty where only one policy contains them,[20] but give rise to intriguing and difficult questions where each of the policies seeks to 'escape', to postpone liability or to apportion liability. It suffices here to say that: concurrent 'escape' clauses cancel each other out, as otherwise there would be the absurd position that the assured could not recover from either insurer;[21] concurrent excess clauses are similarly self-cancelling, as it is plainly not possible for each policy to operate in excess of the others;[22] and an escape or excess clause in policy A trumps a rateable proportion clause in policy B, because the former negatives cover entirely under policy A whereas the rateable proportion clause in policy B operates only where policy A remains in force.[23]

6.3.2 The contribution principle

The Marine Insurance Act 1906 s 80, which codified the common law rules on contribution between insurers,[24] provides as follows:

[19] *Phillips v Syndicate 992 Gunner* [2003] EWHC 1084 (QB); [2004] Lloyd's Rep IR 426; *International Energy Group v Zurich Insurance* [2013] EWCA Civ 39; [2013] All ER (D) 52 (Feb).

[20] One exception is where the assured has a series of consecutive policies and the claim falls within each of them. It has been held that a rateable proportion clause applies only to concurrent and not consecutive policies, so that an insurer against whom a claim is brought remains 100 per cent liable. There is discussion of *Phillips v Syndicate 992 Gunner* [2003] EWHC 1084 (QB); [2004] Lloyd's Rep IR 418 in Chapter 12.

[21] *Weddell v Road Traffic and General Insurance Co Ltd* [1932] 2 KB 563; [1931] All ER Rep 609; *Structural Polymer Systems Ltd and Structural Polymer Technologies Ltd v Brown* 1999, unreported. Contrast *National Employers Mutual General Insurance Association Ltd v Haydon* [1980] 2 Lloyd's Rep 149, where the principle was recognized but held not to be applicable on the facts, adopting *Gale v Motor Union Insurance Co* [1928] 1 KB 359; [1926] All ER Rep 170.

[22] *Austin v Zurich General Accident & Liability Insurance Co Ltd* [1945] KB 250; [1945] 1 All ER 316.

[23] *National Farmers Union Mutual Insurance Society Ltd v HSBC Insurance (UK) Ltd* [2010] EWHC 773 (Comm); [2011] Lloyd's Rep IR 86. These 'other insurance' clauses are prohibited in Australia under the Insurance Contracts Act 1984 (Cth), s 45, so as to allow the assured a completely free hand in making a claim.

[24] Subject to one doubt relating to calculation, discussed in subsequent paragraphs.

> **80.**—(1) Where the assured is over-insured by double insurance, each insurer is bound, as between himself and the other insurers, to contribute rateably to the loss in proportion to the amount for which he is liable under his contract.
>
> (2) If any insurer pays more than his proportion of the loss, he is entitled to maintain an action for contribution against the other insurers, and is entitled to the like remedies as a surety who has paid more than his proportion of the debt.

Contribution between insurers operates independently of the terms of the contract of insurance (except to the extent that those terms vary the rights of the parties) and indeed of the statutory right of contribution between joint wrongdoers in the Civil Liability (Contribution) Act 1978. That Act entitles a paying defendant to recover from another person liable for 'the same damage'. It has been suggested that the proper approach to contribution *between* insurers is now to treat them as subject to the 1978 Act on the basis that their indemnity to an assured is treated as a matter of law as remedying a failure to protect the insured from harm.[25] However, it may be said that the 1978 Act was not designed to supersede existing equitable principles and appears to add nothing to them in the context of double insurance. In *Bovis Construction Ltd v Commercial Union Insurance Co Ltd*,[26] David Steel J held (with only brief discussion) that the 1978 Act did not apply to a contribution claim by an architect against a property insurer: in this case, the property insurer was not liable for the same 'damage' as the architect, which had breached a duty of care, leading to 'damage' consisting of a propensity to flooding. The insurer only owed a duty to pay, not to avoid the damage: this was, therefore, not a liability for 'the same' damage. The House of Lords approved that reasoning in *Royal Brompton NHS Trust v Hammond*.[27] In *Greene Wood McClean LLP v Templeton Insurance Ltd*,[28] Cooke J held that a claim lay under the 1978 Act against a liability insurer whose failure to pay a claim against the assured for costs triggered the liability of the claimant solicitors under a guarantee in respect of the assured's costs. However, the action was not between two insurers liable for the same loss, and the claim was in essence for an indemnity up to policy limits. It is of interest to note that Cooke J held that the same result was reached by the application of the equitable principle that a person who under a legal obligation discharges the debt of another is entitled to recover that sum from the primary obligee.

'Double insurance'—the trigger for contribution between insurers—requires that: the policies cover the claim, whether it be for damage to property or in respect of the assured's liability; the policies exist concurrently rather than consecutively;[29] the person making the claim is an assured under the policies; and the same interest is insured under the policies. Thus there is no double insurance where the owners of a cargo and the warehouse holding that cargo each insure it under separate policies; not only are the policyholders different people but also their interests in the cargo are quite

25 Mitchell, n 14, 4.43.

26 [2001] Lloyd's Rep IR 321.

27 [2002] UKHL 14; [2002] 1 WLR 1397, [34], preferring the reasoning of David Steel J to that of Judge Anthony Thornton QC in *Bovis Lend Lease v Saillard Fuller and Partners* (2001) 77 Con LR 134.

28 [2010] EWHC 2679 (Comm); [2011] Lloyd's Rep IR 557, applying the analysis of the Court of Appeal in earlier proceedings seeking permission for service out of the jurisdiction: [2009] 1 WLR 1397.

29 *Phillips v Syndicate 992 Gunner* [2003] EWHC 1084 (QB); [2004] Lloyd's Rep IR 426.

distinct. In such a case, if the cargo is destroyed through the negligence of the warehouse, and the owners' insurers are called upon to pay, they have a subrogation rather than a contribution action against the insurers of the warehouse.[30] There can, however, be contribution even though the policies differ in nature, for example, as between a household policy on goods and a motor policy which happens to cover the same goods while in the assured's vehicle,[31] and differences in the amounts of deductible and financial limits do not affect the principle of contribution although they will affect its amount.

Contribution is only available as between policies which were both in force and enforceable at the date of the loss, so that if one of the insurers has a right to avoid cover or some defence under the terms of the policy, it is immune. The point here is that the assured must have been able to make a claim against an insurer at the date of the loss before contribution is possible. What remains controversial is whether events after the loss affect contribution claims so that contribution is possible only if all of the insurers are liable when contribution is actually sought. To give a simple example, suppose that the assured's business premises are insured by insurer A and insurer B at the date of the loss, and that each policy contains a condition precedent that the assured notifies any claim within fourteen days of the occurrence of the insured peril. A fire then occurs and the assured notifies A, but not B, within fourteen days. Plainly A is liable to meet the claim, but if A pays and then brings a contribution action against B, B may assert that although it was liable when the fire occurred it ceased to be liable fourteen days later so that there is no basis for a contribution claim. The cases on the point are divided, some favouring the view that a contingent contribution claim arises as soon as the fire occurs and crystallizes when A makes payment,[32] whereas others assert that the assured has to have a valid and subsisting claim against B at the date that A makes payment.[33] The latter view can draw some analogy with the rules of subrogation and salvage in that the loss suffered by the assured does not from the outset give the insurers any contingent equitable right over subject matter which has been totally lost (salvage) or the assured's cause of action against a third party for causing the loss (subrogation) and that those rights become vested only on payment,[34] but the analogy with salvage at least is weak because if the assured disposes of the subject matter prior to payment his indemnity

[30] *North British and Mercantile Insurance Co v London, Liverpool and Globe Insurance Co* (1877) 5 Ch D 569.

[31] *American Surety Co of New York v Wrightson* (1910) 103 LT 663 appears to require something more than an incidental overlap, but the modern cases do not limit contribution in this way, eg *Bovis Construction Ltd v Commercial Union Insurance Co Ltd* [2001] Lloyd's Rep IR 321.

[32] *Legal and General Insurance Society Ltd v Drake Insurance Co Ltd* [1992] QB 887, [1992] 2 WLR 157; *O'Kane v Jones* [2003] EWHC 2158 (Comm); [2004] 1 Lloyd's Rep 389.

[33] *Monksfield v Vehicle and General Insurance Co Ltd* [1971] 1 Lloyd's Rep 139; *Eagle Star Insurance Co v Provincial Insurance plc* [1994] 1 AC 130; [1993] 3 WLR 257; *Bolton Metropolitan Borough Council v Municipal Mutual Insurance Ltd* [2006] EWCA Civ 50; [2006]; 1 WLR 1492 [2007].

[34] There is a possible exception in marine insurance, in that if the subject matter is the subject of a constructive total loss, in that it cannot be repaired or recovered at a cost lower than the repaired or recovered value, the assured is entitled to give a notice of abandonment to the insurers, and acceptance of that notice is thought to confer an equity on the insurers over the subject matter, which crystallizes into a right of salvage on actual payment. It is uncertain, however, whether the combined effect of the Marine Insurance Act 1906 ss 62 and 63 operates in this way, and the point is in practice unimportant because hull insurers rarely, if ever, accept notices of abandonment for fear of being required to assume ownership of

will be reduced by that amount. The former view disregards the independence of contribution from the policy itself, and recognizes that in many cases the assured will only claim against one insurer meaning that the insurer's contribution will be defeated almost from the start unless there is a policy term[35] which insists upon claims being made against all insurers.

On occasion, an insurer will pay a claim *ex gratia* in full or in part where another insurer which is liable for the loss is refusing to make any payment. This may typically happen where insurer A's policy contains a rateable proportion clause so that it is liable for only a part of the claim, but insurer B has denied liability entirely: insurer A may then do the decent thing—pay the entire claim and seek a rateable contribution from insurer B. The difficulty with this approach is that insurer A, having paid as a volunteer, is, as a result of the maxim that 'equity will not assist a volunteer', unable to rely upon the equitable right of contribution. Fortunately, the most recent English decisions recognize that if insurer A unsuccessfully argues with insurer B to honour its obligations, insurer A cannot be described as a volunteer and is entitled to be indemnified.[36] By way of extension it has been held that if insurer A faces no liability at all under its own policy, but nevertheless makes payment because it is the right thing to do, then insurer A has, by analogy with contribution, an equitable claim for recoupment against insurer B.[37]

There are at least three main methods of calculating the amount payable under a contribution claim. Which is used varies depending upon whether the policies are of the same type or only incidentally cover the same loss, but that which is most widely used for marine[38] and liability[39] claims is 'independent liability'. Here, the sums for which each insurer would, if it was the sole insurer, face liability, are determined, and the total loss is apportioned accordingly. The alternatives are 'maximum liability', which apportions on the basis not of actual liability for the claim but of each insurer's potential maximum liability under the policy, and 'common liability', which apportions the loss equally up to the point at which the maximum liability of one of the insurers is reached, and the balance is then taken up by the others. It would seem that common liability is not available for marine policies, as the Marine Insurance Act 1906 s 82 requires a proportional approach.[40]

6.4 Reinsurance

The most significant means by which insurance markets operate to spread risks beyond like risk pools is reinsurance. The operation of reinsurance is rarely discussed outside

onerous subject matter once they have paid. The issues are discussed in *Dornoch Ltd v Westminster International BV (No 2)* [2009] EWHC 889 (Admlty); [2009] 2 Lloyd's Rep 191.

[35] Seen in some policies, eg travel, but not in most.

[36] *Drake Insurance Co v Provident Insurance Co* [2003] EWCA Civ 1834; [2004] 2 WLR 530. The earlier decision in *Legal & General Assurance Society v Drake Insurance Co Ltd* [1992] QB 887; [1992] 2 WLR 157, where contribution was denied, is now unlikely to be followed.

[37] *Limit (No 3) Ltd v ACE Insurance Ltd* [2005] EWCA Civ 383; [2005] Lloyd's Rep IR 552; *SHC Capital Ltd v NTUC Income Insurance Co-operative Ltd* [2010] SGHC 224; [2011] Lloyd's Rep IR 271.

[38] *O'Kane v Jones* [2003] EWHC 2158 (Comm); [2004] 1 Lloyd's Rep 389.

[39] *Commercial Union Assurance Co Ltd v Hayden* [1977] QB 804; [1977] 2 WLR 272.

[40] *O'Kane v Jones*, n 38.

specialist literature, and illustrates more than any other feature of insurance that the legal principles by which insurance operates are disproportionately overlooked, compared to their significance.[41] This section offers an introduction to key features of reinsurance, and some of the sources of complexity in the legal issues that arise. In their very nature, these illustrate the relational or transactional nature of the process through which losses are spread; and the intrinsic relevance of private law to this process.

6.4.1 The nature of reinsurance

Reinsurance may be defined loosely as the insurance of insurers. The earliest definition of reinsurance, by Mansfield CJ in *Delver v Barnes*,[42] referred to 'a new assurance effected by a new policy on the same risk which was before insured in order to indemnify the underwriters from their previous subscriptions'. This definition has not stood the test of time, in that reinsurance is often arranged in advance of insurance; although reinsurance is often a further policy on the same risk[43] that is not necessarily the case, and reinsurance may be akin to a liability cover for the reinsured; and reinsurance can cover risks faced by the reinsured which do not arise under insurance contracts but under, for example, bonds.[44] The practice of reinsurance is as old as insurance itself. The purposes of reinsurance are to expand the financial capacity of an insurer so that it can accept risks which would otherwise be beyond its resources, and to protect an insurer against insolvency if faced with a plethora of claims. The London market is still the focus for much of the world's reinsurance, excluding that written internally in the US and Japan,[45] and the international spread of reinsurance facilitates the insurance of risks in countries whose markets are of insufficient capacity or are otherwise underdeveloped to absorb the risk locally. Reinsurance agreements are normally subscribed to by a number of reinsurers each taking a percentage (or line), and those reinsurers will themselves be reinsured (retrocession), so in that way risks can be spread amongst many underwriters and across national borders. Reinsurance may be written on a facultative or treaty basis.

Facultative reinsurance is written to protect a single large insurance risk. The researches of Dr Golding[46] uncovered a facultative marine reinsurance policy written in 1370. Not much is known about the early history of facultative reinsurance other than it was at one time regarded as little more than wagering, and marine reinsurance was outlawed by the Marine Insurance Act 1745 s 4. That measure was repealed by the

[41] A similar point is made in respect of the regulatory potential of reinsurers, and the lack of regulatory attention to reinsurance, by A Abramovsky, 'Reinsurance: the Silent Regulator?' (2008–9) 15 Conn Ins LJ 345: reinsurance agreements 'likely lead to the institutionalisation of systems beyond and not necessarily congruent with many of the expectations and avowed purposes of some regulatory activities' (405).

[42] (1807) 1 Taunt 48.

[43] *Wasa International Insurance Co v Lexington Insurance Co* [2007] EWHC 896 (Comm); [2007] Lloyd's Rep IR 604.

[44] *Travellers Casualty & Surety Co of Europe Ltd v Commissioners of Customs and Excise* [2006] V & DR 230; [2006] Lloyd's Rep IR 63.

[45] Lloyd's of London has the fifth-largest market share of global reinsurance business, with Munich Re dominating: Standard & Poor's *Global Reinsurance Highlights*, 2011 edition, 46. Available at <http://www.standardandpoors.com/spf/upload/Ratings_EMEA/GRH_2012.pdf>, accessed 28 April 2013.

[46] C Golding, *A History of Reinsurance* (London: Waterlow & Sons, 1927).

Stamp Act 1861 s 4, which probably did little more than reflect what was going on in the market.[47] Where insurance cover is sought, and it is apparent that reinsurance protection will be required, the brokers involved may well seek to place facultative reinsurance first,[48] as it becomes easier to persuade insurers to accept a risk if the security of reinsurance forms a part of the package. Facultative reinsurance is generally written on a proportional basis, so that the reinsurers accept an agreed proportion of any loss for an equivalent proportion of the premium.[49] What that proportion will be varies from case to case. In some instances the reinsured may cede 100 per cent of the risk to reinsurers. This will typically be the case where the risk is from overseas and the law of that jurisdiction requires the business to be written by a local insurer: reinsurance arrangements will be put into place, and then a local insurer will be pressed into use as a 'front'. Again, many large commercial concerns operate, for tax and other efficiency reasons, wholly owned 'captive' insurers which accept risks from their parent and associated companies and then reinsure them into the market.

Treaty reinsurance allows an insurer to reinsure its risks on a collective basis. A treaty may cover specific accounts (for example, marine or motor), specific forms of loss (for example, earthquakes), or even the insurer's whole account. The first traceable reinsurance treaty was entered into in 1821 between the Compagnie Royale of Paris and the Compagnie des Proprietaires Réunis (of Brussels) and the first treaty case decided in England was *Re Norwich Equitable Fire Assurance Society* in 1887.[50] Treaties may be proportional or non-proportional. Under a proportional quota share treaty the reinsured and the reinsurers agree to bear all losses in the parties' respective agreed proportions, and under a proportional surplus treaty the reinsured will bear the first agreed monetary amount of losses and only the balance is allocated to the parties in their agreed proportions. Excess of loss treaties are non-proportional, in that the reinsured bears all losses until in aggregate they reach an attachment point (the ultimate net loss) and the reinsurers then provide cover for sums in excess of that amount. A typical excess of loss treaty covers many different classes of policy written by the reinsured, and provides cover when an event or occurrence has given rise to multiple losses and the total of those losses reaches the attachment point. A variation is the stop loss treaty, which operates in much the same way as an excess of loss treaty except that when losses reach the attachment point the reinsurers become liable for all sums and not just those in excess of the attachment point. The distinction between proportional and non-proportional treaties is important. The relationship between the parties in the former case is much closer in that the wording of the two contracts is generally the same and the reinsurers accept a proportion of the risk matching the premium paid to them by the reinsured. For that reason there is a presumption that a

[47] The decision in *Rooke v Thurmond* 1769 (unreported) indicates that marine policies were written irrespective of the measure.

[48] In which case the reinsurers are regarded as having made standing offers to the insurance market whereby any insurer who subscribes to the insurance agreement can at the same time accept the offer of reinsurance: *General Accident Fire and Life Assurance Corporation Ltd v Tanter, The Zephyr* [1985] 2 Lloyd's Rep 529.

[49] Minus a percentage, often around 10 per cent, by way of 'ceding commission' for the reinsured.

[50] (1887) 57 LT 241.

proportional reinsurance is to be construed 'back to back' with the underlying policy, whereas no such presumption operates in non-proportional reinsurance.[51] The back-to-back presumption is of particular significance where the two contracts are identically worded but governed by different applicable laws which would otherwise give rise to different outcomes.

Most treaties are 'obligatory' in that any policy written by the reinsured automatically attaches to the reinsurance, so that there is no need to obtain consent from the reinsurers and there is simply a formal obligation on the reinsured to notify the reinsurers of the issue of new policies. There is accordingly one contract between the parties, the treaty. A small number of treaties are 'non-obligatory', which means that the treaty itself just provides a mechanism for the submission of individual proposals for cover to the reinsurers. The treaty will, therefore, apply only to risks which are individually accepted by the reinsurers, and each individual declaration is a policy of reinsurance in its own right.[52] The distinction has important implications for the duty of utmost good faith, in that as regards an obligatory treaty there is only one contract and the duty comes to an end when the treaty is agreed,[53] whereas in the case of a non-obligatory treaty each individual declaration is a separate contract which exists independently of both the treaty and other declarations.[54]

There are distinct contractual relationships between the assured and the insurer, and between the insurer and reinsurers. This raises the question of whether the assured has a cause of action against the reinsurers if the insurer fails to pay claims. The point is of particular significance where the insurer has become insolvent. The English cases have rejected any suggestion that a proportional treaty is a partnership between insurer and reinsurers even though in one sense the parties have agreed to share the risk,[55] and the mere fact that the insurer is simply a front for the reinsurers and that all settlement negotiations are conducted by the reinsurers is not enough to create a contractual nexus.[56] Some treaties, particularly those governed by New York law, contain cut-through clauses under which the assured is given a direct claim against the reinsurers if the reinsured becomes insolvent.[57] Those clauses are doubtless enforceable by the assured as beneficiary under the Contracts (Rights of Third Parties) Act 1999, but there is an unresolved question about whether a cut-through clause operates as a charge on the reinsured's assets which has to be registered under the Companies Act 2006 in order to be enforceable against the reinsured's liquidators. A further—as yet

[51] *Axa Reinsurance (UK) plc v Field* [1996] 1 WLR 1026.

[52] Facultative/obligatory treaties, whereby the reinsured can decide what to declare and the reinsurers have no discretion to refuse, are rarely found these days, as they allow the reinsured to 'cherry pick' the best risks.

[53] *Limit No 2 v Axa Versicherung AG* [2008] EWCA Civ 1231; [2009] Lloyd's Rep IR 396.

[54] *SAIL v Farex Gie* [1995] LRLR 116.

[55] *Re Norwich Equitable Fire Assurance Society* (1887) 57 LT 241.

[56] *Grecoair Ltd v Tilling* [2004] EWHC 2851; [2005] Lloyd's Rep IR 151. It was suggested, without success, in *Equitas v Wave City* [2005] EWHC 923; [2006] Lloyd's Rep IR 577, that where the insurance provided that the insurer was required to pay only on being paid by the reinsurers (a typical fronting arrangement), the reinsurers' refusal to make payment to the reinsured amounted to the tort of inducing breach of the (insurance) contract.

[57] More commonly, such clauses are found in retrocession agreements, the cut-through clause designed to operate as security for the reinsured in the event of the reinsurers' insolvency.

unanswered—question is whether a cut-through clause, by conferring secured status on the assured, infringes the rule that all unsecured creditors of an insolvent company have to be treated equally. There is no provision for statutory cut-through in the UK: the Third Parties (Rights against Insurers) Act 1930, which confers the right of a claimant against an assured to bring proceedings against the insurers in the event of the assured's insolvency, does not apply to reinsurance.[58] Accordingly, the policyholders of an insolvent insurer have no direct claims against reinsurers and have to prove in the insurer's liquidation (albeit protected to a limited extent by the priority given to policyholders over other unsecured creditors by the Insurers (Reorganisation and Winding Up) Regulations 2004).[59] By contrast, it has recently been held in New Zealand that the statutory charge procedure does apply to reinsurance[60] and Australian law imposes a charge on any sums owed by reinsurers to an insolvent reinsured.[61]

The following paragraphs are designed to give some insight into how tort claims are fed into the international chain of insurance and reinsurance and how they are paid. What should be obvious, particularly from the discussion of treaties, is that the ultimate liability for a tort claim is almost certainly untraceable. So much for the 'closed risk pool'.

6.4.2 Terms of reinsurance contracts

All reinsurance contracts make provision for insured perils; excluded perils; obligations imposed upon the parties; and dispute resolution. Treaties tend to be detailed, but they cover multiple risks, and complex provisions for premium and loss calculation are required. Facultative reinsurance, by contrast, is typically written on the same terms as the underlying insurance, which normally means that the only specific reinsurance wording is contained in a single sheet to which the direct policy is appended (or to which the policy may even just refer). The reinsurance wording will usually impose an obligation on reinsurers to accept settlements entered into by the reinsured although that may be tempered by an obligation on the reinsured to allow the reinsurers to be kept informed of (claims co-operation), or even take over (claims control), settlement negotiations. Facultative contracts are usually expressed to be 'as original', wording which the courts have assumed[62] operates to incorporate the terms of the direct policy into the reinsurance insofar as the terms are germane to the reinsurance, make sense in the reinsurance context, are consistent with the express terms of the reinsurance, and are apposite for incorporation.[63] The numerous cases on incorporation show that the courts are, in the interests of back-to-back cover, prepared to incorporate coverage and exclusion clauses, but that they are not prepared to incorporate dispute resolution provisions (arbitration, jurisdiction, and choice of law clauses) as those provisions

[58] The 1930 Act s 1(5), a principle adopted by the Third Parties (Rights against Insurers) Act 2010 s 15.

[59] SI 2004/353.

[60] *Ruscoe and Thorn v Canterbury Policyholders* [2012] ANZ Ins Cas 61-921.

[61] The Corporations Act 2001 s 562A provides that, in the event that an insurer goes into liquidation, its reinsurance recoveries are held for the benefit of insurance creditors in priority to other creditors. For the allocation of those sums amongst the insurer's policyholders: *Amaca Pty Ltd v McGrath* [2011] NSWSC 90.

[62] This is typically common ground between the parties, as in *WASA International Insurance Co v Lexington Insurance Co* [2009] UKHL 40; [2009] 3 WLR 575. An authoritative ruling is awaited.

[63] *HIH v New Hampshire* [2001] EWCA Civ 735; [2001] 2 Lloyd's Rep 161.

require express consent,[64] and that they may incorporate contractual obligations imposed by the direct policy (for example, notice of loss clauses) if they can be made to work sensibly in the reinsurance context.[65]

Insofar as the contract is silent on particular matters, the courts have in recent times proved to be reluctant to imply terms which the parties could have inserted themselves. Thus they have denied that there is any implied term under which the reinsurers are to pay the costs incurred by the reinsured in defending claims by the assured,[66] and although there is first instance authority to the effect that reinsurers under a proportional treaty benefit from implied terms relating to underwriting, claims investigation, and record keeping by the reinsured,[67] more recently in *Bonner v Cox Dedicated Corporate Member Ltd*[68] the Court of Appeal implicitly doubted the correctness of this interventionist approach but held that it did not apply to non-proportional reinsurance so that there was no basis for implying a term requiring the reinsured to write business which was profitable independently of reinsurance coverage.

6.4.3 Losses under facultative reinsurance contracts

6.4.3.1 Establishing a claim against reinsurers

The reinsured is entitled to recover from the reinsurers if two conditions are satisfied: the reinsured has suffered a loss within the terms of the direct policy; and the loss falls within the terms of the reinsurance coverage.[69] The reinsurers' liability to make payment is triggered by the satisfaction of these two requirements, and there is no further obligation at common law on the reinsured to make payment as a condition of receiving the reinsurance proceeds.[70] There have been attempts to oust the rule by stating that payment is not due until the reinsured 'shall actually have paid',[71] but in *Charter Re v Fagan*[72] the House of Lords held that the words were inconsistent with the basis on which the contract was written, namely that it responded to liability rather than to payment, and accordingly that they were to be construed in that context. The most important implication of this decision, of which the House of Lords was clearly aware, was that the prepayment provision would deprive an insolvent reinsured of a right of indemnity, conferring a windfall benefit upon the reinsurers and depriving the reinsured's policyholders of an important source of funding.

[64] *Tryg-Hansa v Equitas* [1998] 2 Lloyd's Rep 439; *AIG Group UK Ltd v The Ethniki* [1999] Lloyd's Rep IR 221; *Gan Insurance Co Ltd v Tai Ping Insurance Co Ltd* [1998] EWHC 1210 (Comm); [1999] Lloyd's Rep IR 229.

[65] *Home Insurance of New York v Victoria-Montreal Fire* [1907] AC 59.

[66] *Baker v Black Sea* [1998] UKHL 18; [1998] 1 WLR 974.

[67] *Phoenix General Insurance of Greece v Halvanon Insurance* [1987] 2 WLR 512.

[68] [2005] EWCA Civ 1512; [2006] 2 Lloyd's Rep 152.

[69] *Hill v Mercantile and General* [1996] LRLR 341.

[70] The rule here is the same as for ordinary liability policies, eg *Firma C-Trade SA v Newcastle Protection and Indemnity Association, The Fanti* [1991] 2 AC 1; [1990] 3 WLR 78, although in that case the parties had made prepayment a condition.

[71] Wording typically used in excess of loss treaties.

[72] [1997] AC 313; [1996] 2 WLR 726.

6.4.3.2 Proof of the reinsured's liability

The first of the two trigger requirements is that the reinsured's liability to the assured has been established and quantified. This can happen in one of three ways: the assured has obtained a judgment against the reinsured; the assured has obtained an arbitration award against the reinsured; or the assured and reinsured have entered into a settlement. A judgment is strong evidence of the reinsured's liability, although the reinsurers are at the very least able to argue that a judgment is not binding if the reinsured did not contest the assured's claim properly or—particularly in the case of a foreign judgment—the court did not possess jurisdiction over the reinsured or the court's judgment was 'manifestly perverse'.[73] Similarly, if there is an adverse arbitration award against the reinsured then, subject to these possible exceptions, the reinsurers are bound to accept it.[74] A settlement, by contrast, is of less weight: many settlements are not based on legal liability or even on arguable legal liability, but are made because the reinsured does not wish to prejudice a good commercial relationship with the assured or because the size of the claim is too small to justify the cost of investigating it fully. Accordingly, if the reinsured has entered into a settlement, and the reinsurers refuse to accept it as proof of the reinsured's liability, the reinsured's only means of doing so is to bring proceedings against the reinsurers in which the reinsured asserts that, had the assured's claim been litigated, the reinsured would have been liable for at least the amount of the settlement.

The principles above were laid down in *Commercial Union Assurance Co v NRG Reinsurance Ltd*,[75] in which the reinsured was faced with property damage and pollution claims in Texas from Exxon following the *Exxon Valdez* oil spill in 1989. The reinsured was convinced that it had a good defence under the policy but, following powerful advice from a local lawyer indicating that a Texas jury would almost certainly find against it and probably award punitive damages as well, chose to settle the claim on what were indisputably favourable terms in the circumstances. The Court of Appeal refused summary judgment to the reinsured, holding that reinsurers were liable for a settlement only if it replicated the position at law. Accordingly, the scope of the policy was subsequently litigated in the English courts some years later[76] and the Court of Appeal concluded that the reinsured had not faced any liability to Exxon.

[73] These exceptions were noted in *Commercial Union Assurance Co v NRG Reinsurance Ltd* [1998] EWCA Civ 467; [1998] 2 Lloyd's Rep 600 Potter LJ. In *WASA International Insurance Co v Lexington Insurance Co* [2009] UKHL 40; [2009] 3 WLR 575, Lord Mance noted that the idea that a judgment against the reinsured was automatically binding on the reinsurers had not been the subject of a final decision in England, and it now appears from *AstraZeneca Insurance Co Ltd v XL Insurance (Bermuda) Ltd* [2013] EWHC 349 (Comm) that a foreign judgment is only prima facie evidence of the reinsured's liability whether or not one of Potter LJ's exceptions applies.

[74] *Lincoln National Life Insurance Co v Sun Life Assurance Co of Canada* [2004] EWCA Civ 1660; [2005] 1 Lloyd's Rep 606.

[75] [1998] EWCA Civ 467; [1998] 2 Lloyd's Rep 600. See also *AstraZeneca Insurance Co Ltd v XL Insurance (Bermuda) Ltd* [2013] EWHC 349 (Comm), where Flaux J rejected the suggestion that the wording of the reinsurance agreement required the reinsurers to provide an indemnity in cases where the liability was merely alleged rather than proven.

[76] *King v Brandywine* [2005] EWCA Civ 235; [2005] 1 Lloyd's Rep 655.

6.4.3.3 *Follow settlements clauses*

It has been recognized for well over a century that a reinsured who settles faces the risk of having to initiate legal proceedings against the reinsurers simply to show that the settlement was justifiable as a matter of law. Reinsureds demanded a form of wording which bound the reinsurers to accept settlements which were made on sensible business grounds even though they did not necessarily reflect legal liability. After a search for an appropriate wording,[77] the parties alighted upon the formulation 'follow the settlements',[78] and this was tested in *Insurance Co of Africa v Scor (UK) Reinsurance*.[79] There the Court of Appeal held that the requirement to reach a settlement reflecting the law was replaced by one to settle in a bona fide and businesslike fashion, taking all proper and businesslike steps, including legal advice on local law and undertaking a full investigation of the facts giving rise to the claim.[80] Other forms of wording are also used from time to time. Some cut back on the reinsurers' duty, by excluding settlements stated to be *ex gratia* or without prejudice.[81] Others have purported to confer upon the reinsured a right to be indemnified in all cases, for example that settlements will be followed 'without question',[82] 'whether liable or not'[83] or regarded as 'in every respect unconditionally binding'[84] but the cases have been consistent in rejecting the suggestion that the reinsured can recover even though the settlement has not been reached in a bona fide and businesslike fashion.

6.4.3.4 *Proof of the reinsurers' liability*

The reinsured, having established and quantified its own liability to the assured by judgment, award, or settlement (in the latter case, with or without the benefit of a 'follow the settlements' clause), has to proceed to the second requirement of showing that the claim also fell within the scope of the reinsurance wording. In facultative reinsurance cases this is not a common source of dispute, because the two contracts are generally written on the same terms so that proof of liability under the direct policy

77 'To pay as may be paid thereon' was held in *Chippendale v Holt* (1895) 65 LJQB 104 merely to replicate the common law.

78 In the US these words are used interchangeably with 'follow the fortunes', although there is no authority on whether they mean the same as a matter of English law.

79 [1985] 1 Lloyd's Rep 312. The case also decides that if the reinsurance agreement contains a claims clause expressed in terms of a condition precedent to the reinsurers' liability, failure by the reinsured to comply with the clause will override the 'follow the settlements' clause. This can give rise to the situation in which a reinsured has acted in a bona fide and businesslike fashion but has failed, for example, to keep the reinsurers informed of the process of negotiations, and thereby loses the claim. See also *Lexington Insurance Co v Multinacional De Seguros SA* [2008] EWHC 1170 (Comm); [2009] Lloyd's Rep IR 1; *Gan Insurance Co v Tai Ping Insurance Co (No 3)* [2002] EWCA Civ 248; [2001] Lloyd's IR 667; *Eagle Star Co Ltd v Cresswell* [2004] EWCA Civ 602; [2004] Lloyd's Rep IR 537.

80 *Gan Insurance Co Ltd v Tai Ping Insurance Co Ltd (No 3)* [2002] EWCA Civ 248; [2001] Lloyd's IR 667.

81 *Faraday Capital Ltd v Copenhagen Reinsurance Co Ltd* [2006] EWHC 1474 (Comm); [2007] Lloyd's Rep IR 23.

82 *Assicurazioni Generali Spa v CGU International Insurance plc* [2004] EWCA Civ 429; [2004] Lloyd's Rep IR 457.

83 *Charman v Guardian Royal Exchange Assurance plc* [1992] 2 Lloyd's Rep 607.

84 *Hiscox v Outhwaite (No 3)* [1991] 2 Lloyd's Rep 524.

more or less automatically provides proof of liability under the reinsurance.[85] Nevertheless, there will be cases in which the reinsurers have deliberately chosen to use different and narrower wording, in which case that wording is paramount.[86] The international nature of reinsurance business may give rise to the unexpected complication that the insurance and reinsurance contracts, while identically framed, are governed by different laws which give rise to different outcomes on the same wording. Such a case was *Forsikringsaktieselskapet Vesta v Butcher*,[87] in which insurers issued a policy governed by Norwegian law on a Norwegian fish farm, and reinsured on the same terms under a facultative agreement governed by English law. Each of the contracts thus contained a warranty that the assured would maintain a twenty-four hour watch over the farm. The assured failed to do so, but that did not give the insurers a defence because under Norwegian law breach of warranty is operative only where it is causally linked to the loss. However, the English law of warranties remains that any breach of warranty automatically determines the risk whether or not it is causally linked to the loss. The House of Lords, faced with the situation in which the parties plainly intended the two contracts to be back to back but were thwarted in their attempt to do so, concluded that it was necessary to construe the reinsurance agreement in the same manner as it would have been construed by a Norwegian judge, giving rise to the novel proposition that a contract can be governed by English law but construed in accordance with some other law.

The *Vesta* case was distinguished by the House of Lords in the much-discussed decision in *WASA International Insurance Co v Lexington Insurance Co*.[88] The direct policy in this case was one of a consecutive series taken out by Alcoa to indemnify it against property damage. The policy was operative in the years 1977 to 1980 and contained a service of suit clause under which the insurers agreed to submit to the jurisdiction of any US court of competent jurisdiction. It was matched by a facultative reinsurance for the same period, governed by English law. Losses occurred at various of Alcoa's sites, and proceedings were ultimately brought in Washington. The Washington Supreme Court, applying its own conflict of laws rules, held that the policy was governed by the law of Pennsylvania and that Pennsylvania law had from the 1980s onwards recognized the 'continuous trigger' theory of liability[89] under which if any damage occurred in the policy year then the insurers were liable for all loss. The effect

[85] See the discussion in *Assicurazioni Generali Spa v CGU International Insurance plc* [2004] EWCA Civ 429; [2004] Lloyd's Rep IR 457.

[86] *GE Reinsurance Corporation v New Hampshire Insurance Co* [2003] EWHC 302 (Comm); [2004] Lloyd's Rep IR 404 (specific warranty in the reinsurance agreement not appearing in the direct policy); *Aegis Electrical and Gas International Services Co Ltd v Continental Casualty Co* [2007] EWHC 1762 (Comm); [2008] Lloyd's Rep IR 17 (narrower definition of 'explosion').

[87] [1989] 1 All ER 402. Also *Groupama Navigation et Transports v Catatumbo CA Seguros* [2001] Lloyd's Rep IR 141.

[88] [2009] UKHL 40; [2009] 3 WLR 575. Discussed in R Merkin, 'Wasa International Insurance Co Ltd v Lexington Insurance Co: commercial certainty in the reinsurance market' (2010) 126 LQR 24; A Mecz and A Bailey, 'Wasa International Insurance Co Ltd v Lexington Insurance Co: buyer beware' [2010] JBL 1; A Schaff, 'Wasa International Insurance Co Ltd v Lexington Insurance Co: the limits to the "back to back" presumption' [2010] JBL 9; O Gurses, 'The Construction of Terms of Facultative Reinsurance Contracts: Is Wasa v Lexington the Exception or the Rule?' (2010) 73 MLR 119.

[89] Originally derived from asbestos cases.

of the judgment was that the insurers were liable for losses occurring before, during, and after the policy years, amounting to some forty-five years of cover. The reinsurers unsurprisingly refused to meet the claim for indemnity, and the House of Lords held that they were not under any obligation to do so. *Vesta* was distinguished on the narrow grounds that the law applicable to the direct policy was in *Vesta* known from the outset, so that the reinsurers were aware of the liabilities that they faced, whereas in *Wasa* the law which was going to be applied to the direct policy could not be known until a dispute arose, so that the reinsurers were entitled to the certainty of English law. It is clear from the reasoning that *Wasa* is the exception rather than the rule, and that if there had been a choice of law in the direct policy then a subsequent change in the law leading to greater liability than had originally been contemplated would not have discharged the reinsurers.

6.4.4 Losses under treaties

As far as treaties are concerned, the position is necessarily more complex, because the reinsured's proof of loss is not confined to a single policy but rather extends to an entire portfolio of policies. Consider, for example, a reinsured that has issued many hundreds of employers' liability policies and is faced with defending many thousands of claims by employees alleging injury from exposure to asbestos. If the treaty is in excess of loss form, the reinsured has to establish that its aggregate liability based on individual claims has reached a particular trigger level, and if the treaty is proportional then the reinsured can recover for any one loss only by showing that it is covered by the relevant direct policy. In either case it is obviously impractical for the reinsured to prove that every single claim made against the employer was valid and correctly valued, particularly given that the overwhelming majority of those claims would themselves have been settled rather than resolved in legal proceedings. In practice, therefore, treaty reinsurers do not often take coverage points relating to underlying policies, although they do from time to time assert that the treaty wording does not cover the reinsured's claims.

The problem of contesting underlying claims has come before the English courts in two cases, each involving excess of loss treaties which contained a 'loss settlements clause' under which the reinsurers agreed to follow settlements provided that such settlements were 'within the terms and conditions of the original policies' and also 'within the terms and conditions of this reinsurance'. It was common ground that the 'loss settlements clause' replicated the common law.[90] The first of the cases, *Equitas Ltd v R & Q Reinsurance Co (UK) Ltd*,[91] was in part a sequel to the *Exxon Valdez* litigation and in part a sequel to litigation involving the seizure of Kuwait airport on the invasion by Iraq in August 1990. In each case there were many hundreds of layers of excess of loss reinsurance in what was known as the London Market Excess (LMX) Spiral. Claims from both events were fed into the Spiral and were paid at its lower levels, but litigation intervened and showed that the amount recoverable was up to 20 per cent

[90] *Hill v Mercantile & General* [1996] 1 WLR 1239.
[91] [2009] EWHC 2787 (Comm); [2010] Lloyd's Rep IR 600.

less than had previously been assumed. Claim payments stopped, and the market ground to a halt because it was impossible to reconstruct the Spiral and thus impossible to determine whether the financial trigger for the attachment of successive layers had been reached. Gross J, opting for practicality rather than legal principle, held that it sufficed for a reinsured to prove its liabilities on the balance of probabilities, and this had been achieved by the production of an actuarial model which purported to replicate, as far as possible, the pattern of policies in the Spiral and the relevant attachment points.[92]

This approach was followed in *IRB Brasil Resseguros SA v CS Reinsurance Co Ltd*,[93] where holders of liability policies in the US faced a mass of claims for asbestos exposure, defective breast implants, and contamination of foodstuffs by genetically modified crops. Class actions were brought against the insurers, and they were settled on a global basis so that each qualifying claimant received a proportion of the insurance proceeds. Outwards claims were then presented to reinsurers, who contested them on the grounds that the underlying claims had not been established. Once again it was held that the loss settlements clause required no more than that the reinsured prove its loss on the balance of probabilities, and in the absence of any evidence challenging the basis of the global settlements the reinsured had done just that.

6.4.5 Alternatives to traditional reinsurance

Reinsurance remains the most important form of loss-spreading by insurers. In recent years, however, concerns over capacity, the impact of catastrophic losses, and the short-term nature of most reinsurance contracts have led to the adoption of other mechanisms. New forms of reinsurance contracts have been developed. The earliest class was 'financial reinsurance', which in some of its forms is closer to a banking transaction than a reinsurance arrangement and amounts to little more than a loan of the premium and its return if investment income exceeded losses. These types of transactions distorted the apparent financial position of the reinsured, and were a major factor in the collapse of the HIH Group in Australia in 2001.[94] Passing reference has already been made to the use of captives, by which a company (or, more often, group of companies) establishes an in-house insurer which then seeks reinsurance: by this means the assured can obtain bespoke cover and take advantage of low tax rates in the jurisdiction where the captive is established. In addition, a series of mechanisms designed to bring the financial power of the capital markets into the equation have been adopted. These mechanisms, collectively known as Alternative Risk Transfer (ART),

[92] See J Steele, 'Satisfying Claims? Money, Tort, and "Consumer Society"' (2011) 20 *Social and Legal Studies* 516, discussing Pat O'Malley's argument in *The Currency of Justice: Fines and Damages in Consumer Societies* (Abingdon and New York: Routledge-Cavendish, 2009) and suggesting that the divisibility of both money and risk in a commercial reinsurance setting illustrates disjuncture between the realities of loss-spreading, and 'consumer society' theories premised on control through pricing signals (522).

[93] [2010] EWHC 974 (Comm); [2010] All ER (D) 63 (May). See also *New Zealand Local Government Corporation Ltd v R+V Vershcherung AG [2013] NZHC 690.*

[94] The full grim story is told in <www.hihroyalcom.gov.au/finalreport/index.htm>, accessed 28 April 2013. There is a general discussion of financial and finite reinsurance at <http://rmcsinc.com/articles/JACF173.pdf>, accessed 28 April 2013.

encompass a range of market solutions.[95] Catastrophe bonds[96] are bonds issued to the capital market by a body established for the purpose (a Special Purpose Entity—SPE) whose affairs are managed by a trustee.[97] Bondholders can deal with the SPE only through the trustee, and if a dispute arises, the bondholders can, by the specified majority, require the trustee to take action against the SPE.[98] The SPE will make payments to the reinsured either on proof of loss (the indemnity model) or on proof of the occurrence of a particular trigger event, for example, an earthquake or a run of bad weather making it inevitable that the reinsured will face claims in the future (the parametric model).[99] It is in part through new forms of reinsurance that the global insurance market is able to survive repeated shocks from major catastrophic events, with the number and magnitude of such events increasing.[100] Since 2001, according to Kunreuther and Michel-Kerjan, 'we have entered a new era of catastrophes'.[101] But this does not mean that risks and losses cannot be absorbed. The potential for diversification opened up by reinsurance, most particularly through new forms of reinsurance, helps to explain the resilience of insurance, largely due to the ways in which the market is able to diverge from the bounded model of loss-spreading assumed by the actuarial model.

6.5 Riot Damages: Market or Community Loss-Bearing?

The final two sections of this chapter raise, in different ways, the question of how insurance markets and states may interact in relation to the spreading of losses, and how insurance contract law is implicated in this process. The present section deals with the long-standing issue of how to distribute the costs of damage caused by riot. The final section illustrates the ways in which the state may be engaged where new forms of insurance are made necessary by particular risk events.

The Riot (Damages) Act 1886, a relic of a bygone age and successor to the Riot Acts of 1714 and 1827 (and more ancient statutes before them), remains an important but controversial mechanism. The 1886 Act, s 2(1), imposes upon a local police authority

[95] Any interested reader can obtain a wealth of information from the most basic Google search. There are some papers collected at <http://www.artemis.bm/library/intro_to_art.html>, accessed 28 April 2013. There is further detailed discussion at Clyde & Co, *Reinsurance Practice and the Law* (looseleaf, 2012) paras 1.203–1.261.

[96] Discussed in the presentation by David Greenwald to the Reinsurance Working Party of the International Association of Insurance Law (AIDA) in Lisbon in May 2011, available at <http://www.aida.org.uk/workpart_reinsurance_nextmeeting.asp>, accessed 28 April 2013.

[97] The use of SPEs and trustees is now the established model for securitization.

[98] For the relationship between bond issuer, trustee, and investors, see: *Citibank v QVT* [2007] EWCA Civ 1; [2007] 1 All ER (Comm) 475; *Electrim v Vivendi* [2008] EWCA Civ 1178; [2009] 1 Lloyd's Rep 59.

[99] The notion that payment is triggered by an event rather than by a proven loss is in principle difficult to reconcile with the notion that insurance provides indemnity. However, this type of arrangement was held to be lawful under insurable interest rules relating to life policies in *Feasey v Sun Life Assurance Co of Canada* [2002] EWHC 868 (Comm); [2002] Lloyd's Rep IR 807, and the EU regulatory principles applicable to reinsurance recognize the validity of the use of SPEs as long as they satisfy the usual solvency and prudential requirements.

[100] The largest insured losses in recent years include damage caused by major hurricanes, earthquakes, and acts by terrorists.

[101] H Kunreuther and E Michel-Kerjan, *At War with the Weather: Managing Large-Scale Risks in a New Era of Catastrophe* (Cambridge MA: MIT Press, 2009).

the obligation to pay for damage to a house, shop, or building caused 'by any persons riotously[102] and tumultuously assembled together'.[103] Liability is strict, although subject to deduction to the extent that the claimant has failed to take precautions or has been involved in the assembly. Once a claim is made,[104] the police authority must fix such compensation as appears to them just.[105] A person aggrieved by a refusal to fix compensation, or by the amount of compensation fixed, may bring proceedings to recover the amount of the claim.[106] Payment is to be made out of the police fund.[107] The background to the legislation, starting with the Statute of Winchester 1285, through the Riot Act 1714, and then to the 1886 Act, is traced in the judgments of Walker J in *Bedfordshire Police Authority v Constable*[108] and Beatson J in *Yarl's Wood Immigration Ltd v Bedfordshire Police Authority*.[109] In placing liability with the police authority in these cases, the 1886 Act, like its predecessors, placed losses with the local community and in this confined sense spread them beyond the initial victim of the damage. In focusing on those whose role would naturally include control of riots, there is doubtless an element of intended deterrence or incentive, so that these statutes shared some of the traditional objectives of insurance in policy terms. But the move toward police funding from general taxation,[110] the potential for private insurance on the part of both parties, and the increased contracting out of some relevant services such as prison security,[111] raise different aspects of loss-spreading, illustrating the ways in which complexity in loss-spreading effects may arise.

Turning to the claimant's arrangements, first-party insurance recoveries are to be taken into account in fixing the amount of compensation, so that an insurance payment reduces the sum to that extent. However, if an insurance payment is made, the insurer is given statutory subrogation rights against the police authority.[112] Ultimately, therefore, the police authority bears responsibility to make payment for losses irrespective of the claimant's insurance position. Insurers' swift action in settling the most recent riot damage claims in 2011 may not be all that it seems, therefore. This in turn raises the liability insurance position of police authorities. In *Constable* Walker J

[102] A riot requires at least twelve persons: Public Order Act 1986, s 1, modifying the common law rule that three or more persons sufficed. It was held in *London & Lancashire Fire Insurance Co v Bolands* [1924] AC 836 that a robbery at a bakery by four armed men constituted a riot and thus was excluded from a property cover, a result which, gratifyingly, could not be reached today.

[103] s 2(1).

[104] Under the Riot (Damages) Regulations 1921 (SR & O 1921/1536), a claim had to be made in statutory form and within fourteen days. Following the Tottenham riots in July 2011, the 1921 Regulations were amended, removing the need for a statutory form: (Riot (Damages) (Amendment No 2) Regulations 2011(SI 2011/2009)), and extending the time period for a claim to forty-two days (Riot (Damages) (Amendment) Regulations 2011 (SI 2011/2002)).

[105] s 3(1).

[106] s 4(1).

[107] s 5(1).

[108] [2008] EWHC 1375 (Comm); [2009] Lloyd's Rep IR 39.

[109] [2008] EWHC 2207 (Comm); [2009] 1 All ER 886.

[110] D Feldman, 'Rioting Detainees: Who Pays? Statutory Interpretation and the Shackles of the Past' (2010) CLJ 433.

[111] Yarl's Wood Immigration Centre was built and run by a limited company under contract with the government, employing Group 4 Security to keep order; the Act is drafted on the basis that it is the police who have responsibility for maintaining order.

[112] s 2(2).

and the Court of Appeal[113] held that a public liability policy held by the claimant police authority, which provided—using wording commonly found in such policies—indemnification for 'all sums which the assured may become legally liable to pay as damages', covered compensation payable by the police under the 1886 Act. The Court of Appeal ruled that the phrase 'liable to pay as damages' had to be construed in its commercial context, and that although compensation under the 1886 Act might not be described as 'damages' by a lawyer, it was not unreasonable to start with the premise that a public liability policy indemnified against liability to the public at large, and the liability imposed upon the police was in respect of their notional failure to maintain law and order. In that context, the term 'damages' encompassed compensation. Thus, a link was made with tort liability, rather than solely with loss-spreading *per se*.[114] That ruling meant that the police authority's insurers were in principle liable to indemnify the authority for the claim made against it by the operators of the Yarl's Wood detention centre following riots by persons being held there, a very sizeable claim subsequently upheld by the Court of Appeal in *Yarl's Wood Immigration Ltd v Bedfordshire Police Authority*.[115]

The market responded to the *Constable* ruling by excluding liability for compensation under the 1886 Act from public liability policies issued to police authorities. Accordingly, the source of funding for riot damages payments is, these days, taxation. Riot damages therefore represent a form of community loss-spreading, rather than market loss-spreading, and this result is maintained despite the efforts of the courts. The saga is a reminder that whatever the social benefits of insurance, market insurers do not generally act for non-market reasons. It also illustrates the existence of competition between public and private sources of compensation to avoid bearing loss.

6.6 State and Market

By no means all interactions between state and market in relation to loss-spreading are uncooperative. Loss-spreading is often desired or needed but in some of the cases where it is needed most, the insurance market is justifiably wary. This is particularly the case in relation to perils which are potentially unlimited in the amount of havoc and loss that may result. Obvious examples are war, terrorism, and natural catastrophes. Some private insurers are content to write business covering these perils, protecting themselves by reinsurance or other forms of contractual loss-spreading. The cost of such cover may, however, be prohibitive. It may also be pointed out that in relation to large, infrequent risks, calculation on the basis of past experience is less promising as an avenue for risk management: insurers (and particularly reinsurers) must, instead, work on the basis of available models, including scientific models where appropriate. This requires a rather different form of expertise from the traditional basis of actuarialism in probability, and will necessarily involve insurers in new exercises in hedging or

113 [2009] EWCA Civ 64; [2009] Lloyd's Rep IR 607.

114 An interesting analogy was drawn with liability in *Rylands v Fletcher* (1868) LR 3 HL 330.

115 [2009] EWCA Civ 1110; [2010] 2 WLR 1322 reversing Beatson J and holding that the 1886 Act extended to protect private bodies exercising, by delegation, public duties.

dispersing their own risks.[116] Government has intervened in time of crisis to ensure that commerce has the insurance backing necessary to continue. Various models are found in operation.

First, the state may act as insurer of last resort or, more accurately, reinsurer. The War Risks Insurance Act 1939, subsequently extended by the War Damage Act 1941, required insurers to maintain insurance on vessels, cargo, and buildings against war damage, with the government acting as 96 per cent reinsurer.[117] The earlier legislation was replaced by the Marine and Aviation Insurance (War Risks) Act 1952, under which the government is empowered to act as war risks reinsurer for vessels, aircraft, and cargo, and also to act as a direct marine insurer if there is no available market. The same technique was adopted following the IRA bombing campaign in London, culminating in a major bomb in 1992 which led property insurers to withdraw terrorism cover for commercial and indeed all other buildings. Under threat of major financial institutions decamping from London, the government rushed through the Reinsurance (Acts of Terrorism) Act 1993. This Act established a state-backed reinsurer, Pool Re, which acts as reinsurer, on commercial rates, of property insurers willing to underwrite terrorism risks. Emergency state-backed reinsurance arrangements were similarly put into place in the immediate aftermath of the events of 11 September 2001 in New York, following the immediate withdrawal of insurance cover for aircraft.[118]

Second, the state may take over as primary insurer. This parallels the model provided by the UK's industrial injuries scheme, where National Insurance contributions pay a basic level of benefit for injuries incurred in the workplace and additional sums may be obtained from private accident insurance (often provided by employers). A more complex illustration is the scheme adopted in New Zealand for compensating the victims of earthquakes and other natural catastrophes.[119] Under the Earthquake Commission Act 1993 any policy taken out by the owner of residential premises will automatically attract cover for damage to the land itself and buildings up to the sum of NZ$150,000 and for goods up to NZ$20,000 provided by the Earthquake Commission (EQC), a body funded partly by a levy on the premium and supplemented by a state guarantee. The EQC has in turn reinsured a substantial proportion of its potential liabilities.[120] Commercial policies on buildings and

[116] R Ericson and A Doyle, *Uncertain Business: Risk, Insurance, and the Limits of Knowledge* (Toronto: University of Toronto Press, 2004), illustrate their points about the persistence of insurance in relation to uncertain risks, and the relationship between insurance and mechanisms of risk pre-emption, by reference to earthquake and terror risks. In relation to terrorism, they make the point that 'Even in exorbitant conditions of uncertainty, insurance is a crucial technology in search of more security' (42).

[117] The Restriction of Advertisements (War Risks Insurance) Act 1939 banned private advertisements for war risks insurance without Treasury permission. The Liability for War Damage (Miscellaneous Provisions) Act 1939 negatived various contractual obligations to insure against damage to property caused by war risks.

[118] The various responses of states to the withdrawal of terrorism cover from buildings are discussed in R Merkin and J Kullmann, *The Insurance and Reinsurance of Terrorism Risks*, 2006, published on the website of AIDA: <http://www.aida.org.uk/default.asp>, accessed 28 April 2013.

[119] R Merkin, 'The Christchurch Earthquakes: Insurance and Reinsurance Issues' [2013] Canterbury LR (forthcoming).

[120] EQC has an aggregate loss retention of NZ$1.5 billion, with sums in excess of that amount being reinsured up to NZ$2.5 billion for each 'loss occurrence' (defined in terms of each earthquake): *Tower Insurance Ltd v Earthquake Commission* [2011] NZHC 943.

goods[121] are accordingly written as covering only losses in excess of these figures. It will be appreciated that under this scheme, losses from natural catastrophes are distributed away from those at risk: all policyholders insuring their dwellings by private insurance are required to pay the EQC levy even though they live in areas of New Zealand which are unaffected by earthquakes; the EQC's payments are for the most part reinsured; and the amount actually payable by the EQC from its own resources is supplemented by general taxation to the extent that there is a shortfall between the reinsurance deductible and the sums gathered in from the levy. Other approaches to earthquake risk which place part of the risk with insurers and leave the state with remaining losses exist in states such as Mexico, Japan, and Taiwan.[122]

Third, the state may simply require particular forms of loss to be covered by direct insurance. An illustration of this possibility is found in Australia in the 2012 amendments to the Insurance Contracts Act 1984 (Cth), passed in the wake of the Queensland floods at the end of 2010. The legislation sets out a statutory definition of 'flood', so that flood coverage in a policy must cover catastrophic flooding. Of course, the further risk is that insurers will simply leave the market, and such requirements are perhaps workable only if they form part of a wider set of arrangements and negotiations.[123] In the UK, widespread flooding after the excessively wet summer of 2007 created the most costly UK insurance event ever, with insured losses estimated at £3bn. The losses were largely spread through the private insurance market, as flood insurance was, and remains, a part of typical property insurance for households and businesses. The response was the production of an agreed statement between the ABI and government in 2008, due to be replaced in July 2013. The stated principles target the government's resources on flood protection expenditure; though it was suggested even before the 2007 floods that the need for explicit agreement might imply the breakdown of a more implicit 'gentlemen's agreement'.[124] As has been widely reported, after further extensive flooding in 2012, insurers and the government are in the process of negotiation over renewal of the agreement, and there is much argument about the interpretation of fairness in relation to the pricing of flood insurance, raising significant questions about the use of the market to provide security against risks on an equitable basis.[125] The response of government and the insurance industry to flooding in the UK illustrates a very particular variety of state–industry 'partnership', in which appropriate roles are in the process of negotiation.

[121] Land is not privately insurable, so that cover is provided only by the EQC.

[122] Swiss Re, *Sigma* No 3/2011, *State Involvement in Insurance Markets*, 13–21. Available at <http://www.swissre.com/sigma/>, accessed 28 April 2013.

[123] Such a requirement was a stage in the development of the California Earthquake Authority—with funds committed by property insurers who were thereby permitted to discontinue their own earthquake coverage, and with 'capped' liabilities implying that the state would act as insurer of last resort. The story is reviewed by D Moss, 'Courting Disaster? The Transformation of Federal Disaster Policy since 1803', in K Froot (ed), *The Financing of Catastrophe Risk* (Chicago: University of Chicago Press, 1999), 339–40.

[124] M Huber, 'Reforming the UK Flood Insurance Regime: The Breakdown of a Gentlemen's Agreement', ESRC Centre for Analysis of Risk and Regulation, Discussion Paper No 18, January 2004.

[125] See J O'Neill and M O'Neill, *Social Justice and the Future of Flood Insurance* (York: Joseph Rowntree Foundation, 2012), arguing for a solidaristic approach to the availability of flood insurance. Note also the excellent discussion by J Morgan and M Stallworthy, 'Indemnifying against Flood Loss in a Changing Environment' (2013) 33 LS 239: the authors identify the tension inherent in the use of commercial arrangements to deliver socially important protection, in light of broader issues surrounding climate change and justice. Our discussion here has indicated that such issues are encountered in a range of contexts.

7

Allocation of Risk in Voluntary Arrangements

7.1 Introduction: Contracting and Insurance

7.1.1 Contract, insurance, and risk allocation

This chapter examines the part played by insurance arrangements in contracting. The chapter develops two important themes from the account in Chapters 1 and 2: namely, that insurance may be addressed not as an extrinsic factor but as an inherent aspect of party relationships, in which uncertainty is, as far as possible, addressed by risk allocation;[1] and that obligations between parties may be better understood by expanding the frame of analysis beyond two parties to incorporate wider contractual arrangements.[2] As we explain, this multi-party picture is, in practice, highly pertinent to the resolution of contractual disputes, many of which concern the question of where particular risks lie, or should be treated as lying, within the contractual relationship.

It is common ground between businessmen and economic theorists that contracts are made because each of the parties expects to derive some benefit from the arrangements. Contracting is, however, unavoidably and pervasively subject to future uncertainty both from the conduct of the parties themselves and from matters beyond their control. As we saw in Chapter 1, a continuum of arrangements has been identified where the approach to future uncertainties varies from close planning in which contractual terms are designed to be authoritative in relation to specified risks (and where those terms may be the very point of the contract), to a more flexible approach in which the 'paper deal' is less significant. Such arrangements have been charted from the most discrete and 'transactional', to the most co-operative and 'relational'.[3] At the transactional pole there is an effort to address all possible contingencies (to 'presentiate the future'); while at the relational pole there is looser planning or 'preparation for' the future. Contracts may, moreover, have significantly transactional and relational aspects.[4] Here we deal not with every type of contract, but with a range of commercial arrangements—not just insurance arrangements—which could be said, in Macneil's terms, to 'presentiate' the future.[5] Our key point is simple, namely that one of the most crucial and ubiquitous features of such forward planning—insurance arrangements—has been largely excluded from analysis. This is the omission we seek to redress.

It is not that insurance contracts themselves have been entirely neglected in theoretical debate. The contract of insurance has, with justification, been held up as the most

1 Chapter 2. 2 A theme developed in Chapter 1.

3 I Macneil, 'The Many Futures of Contract' (1973–4) 47 S Cal L Rev 691.

4 n 3, 745, by reference to an employment contract.

5 Macneil (n 3, 732) pointed out that even the purest of transactions, such as futures exchanges, occur 'against a backdrop of regulations, customs, and ongoing relations'.

obvious example of risk allocation between contracting parties, often with 'adhesive' qualities.[6] Here however we go further, looking beyond the two-party insurance contract itself, to show how insurance arrangements pervasively underlie decisions by contracting parties as to the risks that they are prepared to accept. The same is also true of insurance contracts themselves: an insurer is unlikely to be willing to accept a risk if there is no available reinsurance.[7]

We should say a little more about our focus on party intentions. This is derived from attention to the market context in which insurance operates, and not from an exercise in neo-liberal will theory.[8] As we have explained, the focus of this chapter is on transactional aspects of commercial contracting, and we suggest that, even here, party arrangements have been too narrowly read. Even as a starting point however, the notion that the law of contract reflects the decisions of the parties is itself not a given amongst theorists. While some scholars take the view that the law supports and recognizes the needs of members of the business community, others have preferred to stress the autonomy of law and its priority in creating norms around which market activity is ordered. For the latter group, law comes first in every sense. Such theorists are more likely to pay attention to principles of responsibility than to questions of intended risk allocation, for example; and the hold of this approach has implications for our analysis both here, and in subsequent chapters.

The issue can be illustrated by reference to Fuller and Purdue's uniquely influential article on the subject of contract damages.[9] The parties' search for benefit remains the acknowledged starting point in English law when assessing such damages, which seek to place the claimant in a position which would have been reached, had the contract been performed.[10] This measure has been widely associated with the 'executory contract'.[11] Fuller and Purdue nevertheless relegated protection of the 'expectation interest' to the bottom of their list of remedial priorities, beneath the 'reliance' and the 'restitution' interests.[12] They offered (and then dismissed) a potential explanation of the protection of expectation interests:

> The essence of a credit economy lies in the fact that it tends to eliminate the distinction between present and future (promised) goods. Expectations of future values become, for purposes of trade, present values. In a society in which credit has

[6] F Kessler, 'Contracts of Adhesion' (1943) 43 Columbia LJ 629; discussed also in Chapter 3.

[7] Discussed in Chapter 6.

[8] We discuss 'dynamic market individualism' and its relationship to our approach in Chapter 8, 8.2. J Adams and R Brownsword, *Understanding Contract Law* (London: Sweet & Maxwell, 4th edn, 2004), ch 6, 'The Concept of Risk', address exclusion clauses in particular (contractually allocated risks) in terms of formalist, market individualist, and welfarist approaches. 'Dynamic market individualism', or market contextualism, represents an important addition to these possibilities: R Brownsword, 'After *Investors*: Interpretation, Expectation, and the Implicit Dimension of the "New Contextualism"', in D Campbell, H Collins, and J Wightman (eds), *Implicit Dimensions of Contract* (Oxford: Hart Publishing, 2003).

[9] L Fuller and WR Purdue Jr, 'The Reliance Interest in Contract Damages' (1936) 46 Yale Law J 52.

[10] Parke B in *Robinson v Harman* (1848) 1 Ex 850, 855.

[11] P Atiyah, *The Rise and Fall of Freedom of Contract* (Oxford: Clarendon Press, 1979), ch 22, 'The Wheel Come Full Circle', especially at 764; in relation to insurance contracts: M Clarke, *Policies and Perceptions of Insurance* (Oxford: Clarendon Press, 2005), 172–3.

[12] For criticism see D Friedmann, 'The Performance Interest in Contract Damages' (1995) 111 LQR 628 (arguing that beneficial performance is the point of the contract on both sides).

> become a significant and pervasive institution, it is inevitable that the expectancy created by an enforceable promise should be regarded as a kind of property, and breach of that promise as injury to that property.

This point can be generalized and extended to many facets of market behaviour, including insurance contracts themselves, and we have seen that such issues have subsequently begun to play an important role in contract theory.[13] Fuller and Purdue, however, quickly rejected the point on the basis that future values are tradable only *because* the law protects them: law, they alleged, has priority over practice and this can be illustrated as a matter of chronology. Considerable evidence against this chronological claim has subsequently been presented;[14] but the influence of a 'juridical' account continues nevertheless.

The significance of this is that the emphasis on doctrine removes the focus from what the parties have (or are taken by rules of construction to have) intended in making their contract, including their attempts to deal with uncertainty and allocate risk. Instead, attention has been directed to the development of counter-currents in the law such as those relating to substantive fairness, protectionism including consumer protection, and the imposition of duties bringing contract closer to the law of tort:[15] contextual approaches became welfarist in orientation. Analysis of party intentions including risk allocation was cast as an emanation of liberal individualism which would play a reduced role in light of these developments. Patrick Atiyah, writing in the late 1970s,[16] specifically predicted that the role of party intentions, and in particular the role of contract in securing expectations and allocating risk, would be further diminished over time. He later freely admitted that the immediate rise of neo-liberalism proved that prediction wrong.[17] In particular, his argument that party expectations would not be so fully protected by contract, and that at the same time expectations of, for example, future employment and other forms of security would be increasingly provided by social measures and not by private law, has been largely demolished by the rise of market measures.[18] The important point is that this does not prove that Atiyah's focus

[13] For example Macneil, n 3. Note our discussion of lending, security, and credit risk insurance at 7.3. As we saw in Chapter 2, futures trading and derivatives of all kinds strongly exemplify the value and dangers of future-present trade-offs.

[14] See for example AWB Simpson 'The Origins of Futures Trading in the Liverpool Cotton Market', in P Cane and J Stapleton, *Essays for Patrick Atiyah* (Oxford: Clarendon Press, 1991); O Prausnitz, *Standardisation of Commercial Contracts in English and Continental Law* (London: Sweet & Maxwell, 1937); RB Ferguson, 'Commercial Expectations and the Guarantee of the Law: Sales Transactions in Mid-nineteenth Century England', in G Rubin and D Sugarman, *Law, Economy and Society* (Abingdon: Professional Books Ltd, 1984).

[15] Most influentially by G Gilmore, *The Death of Contract* (Columbus OH: Ohio State University Press, 1974). Chapter 8 turns this around and reflects on the influence of risk allocation in tort.

[16] Atiyah's focus in *The Rise and Fall of Freedom of Contract*, n 11, was on the decline of *enforcement* of contractual terms in the absence of reliance, but (expressly acknowledging the influence of Fuller and Purdue, n 9) he made an explicit link between the rationale for enforcement, and the measure of damages, suggesting that expectation *damages* were likely to be further whittled down as a consequence of the decline in inclination to enforce promises *per se* in the absence of (for example) reliance (754–64).

[17] P Atiyah, 'Contract and the New Right', in *Essays on Contract* (Oxford: Clarendon Press, 1990); 'Personal Injuries in the Twenty-First Century: Thinking the Unthinkable', in P Birks (ed), *Wrongs and Remedies in the Twenty-First Century* (Oxford: Oxford University Press, 1996).

[18] This is directly linked to the discussion in Chapter 2.

on the social and economic context of the law of contract was misguided. Rather, it suggests that context must always be carefully assessed and is subject to reversal. Atiyah was correct in anticipating the ever-increasing legislative regulation of contracts to which there is an appreciably weaker party, of which employment contracts, consumer sales, and consumer services are paradigm examples. As we have seen, there are tribunals and ombudsmen to deal with those disputes, in the latter case by the rejection of strict principles of law. But, as regards commercial contracts—and it is those where risk allocation is to the fore—we suggest the law's desire to give effect to the intentions of the parties has been and remains the starting point. Footnoting judicial support for this proposition would require us to list virtually every commercial case decided in England.

7.1.2 Contract law and market context

Here we make two points: that the common law was fashioned to meet the needs of commerce; and that the modern approach to contractual interpretation involves an analysis of the context in which the contract was made. Experienced commercial judges are rarely unaware of the context or implications of what they are deciding.

Turning to the first point, the origins of modern English commercial law are often traced back to the appointment of Lord Mansfield to the King's Bench in 1756. Lord Mansfield sat with merchant advisers, and the legal principles developed in the eighteenth century were, to a significant extent, an endorsement of market practices. Obvious examples are the recognition of the principles applicable to bills of lading, bills of exchange, sale agreements, marine insurance, and agency.[19] The later root doctrinal cases on matters which today form the headings of chapters in textbooks on contract arose to a large extent out of discrete (often non-commercial) disputes or novel situations, and many of the exceptions to doctrine enumerated in current texts pre-date what is stated to be the general rule and far outweigh its practical relevance. To take two illustrations, the doctrine of privity of contract, before its modification by the Contracts (Rights of Third Parties) Act 1999, never played much part in the operation of market practices involving shipping, agency, or negotiable instruments, even though its emergence later disrupted attempts to confer benefits upon family members, and want of consideration has rarely defeated a commercial transaction. Thus, subject to overriding matters of policy, such as misrepresentation,[20] illegality, and duress, the common law reflects market practice, and contract rules are essentially default provisions which come into play in the absence of agreement or in case of the unforeseen. The law reports for the past 250 years are replete with cases in which the courts have recognized market practice as law. An extreme and very recent illustration is *Hobbins v*

[19] Of the examples in n 14, note particularly Prausnitz (detailing how the law in these fields has been a crystallization of commercial practice).

[20] But even that can be regulated by contract, in the form of 'four corners' and similar clauses which exclude liability for misstatements in negotiations or other than by specified individuals, unless there is fraud involved: *HIH Casualty & General Insurance v Chase Manhattan Bank* [2003] UKHL 6; [2003] Lloyd's Rep IR 230.

Royal Skandia Life Assurance Ltd,[21] in which Reyes J gave effect to two centuries of decisions recognizing the market practice that an insurance broker, while the agent of the assured, is remunerated by the insurers, even though in any other context such an arrangement would infringe basic fiduciary principles.

Turning next to the question of interpretation, one of the last acts of the House of Lords before its conversion to the Supreme Court, in *Chartbrook Ltd v Persimmon Homes Ltd*,[22] was to confirm that the process of interpretation is objective[23] and that the test is 'what a reasonable person having all the background knowledge which would have been available to the parties would have understood them to be using the language in the contract to mean'.[24] The 'factual matrix' focuses not on the reasonable person but on the reasonable market participant.[25]

The outcome is that the law is analysed as responding to the context in which it operates,[26] even though it also regulates the activities that make up that context. This does not suggest that law is subordinate to the market and cannot seek to guide it. But it does indicate that law is responsive to the market; and the law of contract would cease to be fit for purpose if it were not. We endorse the need to analyse law in relation to its context but we argue that in the context of law's relationship with market activity, the activity of insuring the risks associated with contracting is not sufficiently explored. Any form of contextual response to market arrangements can, we suggest, benefit from an appreciation of this, even if the core role of insurance appears to be a traditional one: permitting the parties to anticipate and allocate risks.

7.1.3 The relevance of insurance

It will be obvious that our approach rejects the suggestion that insurance arrangements should be disregarded in the interpretation of contracts. That suggestion is an extension of the argument that the law should disregard insurance arrangements in determining the existence and scope of tortious liability.[27] The reasoning behind this is that a court has little or no knowledge of the private insurance arrangements adopted by the parties, or indeed of the potential insurability of a first-party loss or third-party liability for that loss, so assumed insurance arrangements cannot provide accurate guidance as to the practical implications of a judicial ruling. If insurance is not to influence tort, then by analogy it should not influence contract either, so whether one or other party is insured against the loss that has occurred is not a valid inquiry in the determination of

[21] [2012] HKCFI 10; [2013] Lloyd's Rep IR 42.

[22] [2009] UKHL 38; [2009] 1 AC 1101.

[23] The English courts have rejected subjectivity on the pragmatic grounds that relevant evidence could be both open-ended and tailored to justify the outcome sought.

[24] Per Lord Hoffmann at [14], applying the principles settled in *Investors Compensation Scheme Ltd v West Bromwich Building Society* [1998] 1 WLR 896.

[25] See, for a recent example, *Gard Marine & Energy Ltd v Tunnicliffe* [2011] EWHC 1658 (Comm); [2011] All ER (D) 03 (Jul), where the expert testimony of energy risk underwriters as to the flexible meaning of '100 per cent' in that form of cover won the day for the reinsured.

[26] H Collins, *Regulating Contracts* (Oxford: Oxford University Press, 1999), ch 8, 201, contrasts contextual approaches aimed at enhancing the capacity of the parties for self-regulation with the impact of the 'virus of legal formalism'.

[27] J Stapleton, 'Tort, Insurance and Ideology' (1995) 59 MLR 820. Discussed further in Chapters 6 and 8.

the incidence or amount of liability.[28] In Chapter 8 we express reservations about the denial of the relevance of insurance to tort but, those reservations aside, that analysis cannot be extended to contract disputes where there is a pre-existing relationship between the parties and they have had the opportunity to stipulate which of them is to bear loss in given circumstances. The court will have access to the arrangements and can ascertain from them what was intended. Key to those arrangements will be insurance provisions.

7.2 Common Concerns

As we have said, contracting is a purposive activity in which parties seek to gain a benefit. Nevertheless, these benefits are uncertain, and contracting creates more or less identifiable risks of loss. We identify three common concerns of contracting parties here. The first concern could be said to have determined the development of many of the mechanisms used by commercial lawyers, namely, how is a contracting party to protect itself against the risk of the other's insolvency? An obligation on the supplier of goods or services to put defects right, or to indemnify the purchaser if liability to a third party is incurred, is only worth having if the supplier is good for the money; the same point arises where goods are supplied to a customer who subsequently proves unable to pay for them. The second concern is, which of the parties bears responsibility to make good losses if something goes wrong? Risk-allocation clauses, which may be used to supplement the basic obligations undertaken by the parties,[29] are central to commercial contracting. A contract improperly performed may have direct and indirect effects on a variety of the claimant's interests, including damage to property, loss of business, and damage to customers' goodwill, and it will be sensible to determine from the outset to what extent the defendant is liable to make good such losses rather than to rely upon rules of remoteness. Equally, improper performance may cause physical damage to third parties or their property, as where employer A's employee is loaned to employer B and injures one of employer B's own workmen; it is a common arrangement that employer B is to answer for any liability without recourse to employer A. The third concern is that external events may render performance of the contract uneconomic for one of the parties or pointless for the other: the law of frustration does not provide any relief as long as performance remains physically possible, but a *force majeure* clause may excuse performance or a refusal of the tender of performance.

In each of these areas, insurance has a key part to play. As regards insolvency, a variety of contractual mechanisms may be used to protect the parties, including reservation of title in sale contracts and the demand for guarantees and other forms of security in others, but insurance features high on the list. The contract may require

[28] Stapleton, n 27, 830.

[29] Compare Moore-Bick LJ in *Seadrill Management Services Ltd v OAO Gazprom* [2010] EWCA Civ 691; [2011] 1 All ER (Comm) 1077, [18]. Moore-Bick described the express contractual risk-allocation clauses as operating independently of negligence or other fault, but not supplanting entirely 'the basic contractual obligations undertaken by each party' (including an implied obligation of performance with due care). Notably, Moore-Bick LJ explained that, in what he described as the more traditional approach to contractual terms, the parties set out their obligations, 'leaving it to the general principles of law to allocate loss'. This makes the link between general principles of contract law, and express contractual risk allocation clauses—these are two (often supplementary) ways in which the risk of loss may be allocated.

one or other party to insure; in other cases insurance is taken out as a unilateral safeguard. Insofar as the risks of loss arising from defective performance are foreseeable, the contract will make provision for their allocation either expressly or not, and such allocation is again usually supported by an insurance arrangement of one or other type. Again, insurance may be secured against the 'frustration' (in the widest sense) of contractual obligations.

The cost of insurance is crucial here. To take an obvious situation, if employer A and contractor B enter into an agreement under which contractor B is to bear the risks of liability for defective performance and injury to third parties, contractor B will build into the price the cost of insurance that he has to take out in order to allow him to bear that risk. Conversely, if all is at the risk of employer A, then A will wish to insure and the price paid to contractor B will be reduced accordingly. To insure the risk is to make it proportionate to the benefit gained from the contract. The same process operates less obviously but with equal force in other contexts. All of this is reflected in the statutory and judicial approach to exclusion clauses in commercial contracts. It may be perfectly reasonable for a supplier to exclude liability if the price charged for performance reflects the fact that the customer will bear, and insure against, loss. Equally it is unreasonable for a supplier to use comprehensive exclusion clauses where the price reflects an assumption of risk on his part.

Given that the risks of insolvency, defective performance, and the occurrence of external events are crucial to commercial contracting, many (regrettably, far from all) agreements are drafted with care—and often with lengthy negotiation—to ensure as far as possible that there is consensus and understanding as to where risks and losses should fall. Some contracts are standard form, promulgated by trade organizations or other institutions,[30] others are individually negotiated either afresh or on the basis of standard terms by the parties or their lawyers.[31] The allocation of risks by contract imposes a cost on one or other of the parties, not only a possible future cost, but more immediately an insurance cost. Thus, insurance affects the price of the contract as a whole. Accordingly, contracts are frequently designed to ensure that the cost of insurance is not duplicated. This would raise the overall cost of contracting and reduce the benefit to both parties. To revert to the above example, if the risks flowing from a construction contract are borne by contractor B so that the cost of B's insurance is reflected in the price paid by employer A, the arrangements must be such that A does not feel the need to take out his own insurance to counter the possibility of a court ruling that B is not liable to A for a particular form of loss. If there is a danger that the courts will not give effect to the contractual allocation of risk as reflected in the insurance arrangements, A may feel the need to pay twice, once in the price charged by B and once for his own cover in the event that B's insurance fails. It is for that reason that the manner in which the courts construe contracts has to reflect agreed risk

[30] For example, the Joint Contracts Tribunal (JCT) for construction contracts and the International Underwriting Association for some insurance and reinsurance contracts.

[31] Contracts of the latter class tend to be lengthy and to cover almost every conceivable (and many inconceivable) eventualities. It is the inclusion of the latter that makes too many lawyer-drafted contracts almost incomprehensible.

allocation. This is not necessarily a product of philosophical commitment to free will, but recognizes the importance of anticipating risks.[32]

Atiyah has argued that 'in contracts which really are risk-allocation arrangements' (a category in which he included certain forms of insurance contract), 'to hold the contract binding must, in general, favour the party who has the better skill and knowledge for assessing future risks' so that inequalities are sustained.[33] Some care should be taken before using this as the basis for viewing risk-allocation provisions with scepticism when construing contract terms. Many 'pure' risk-allocation arrangements of this sort are the result of careful negotiation between the parties, and commercial insurance contracts in particular tend to follow a lengthy period of proposal and counter-proposal from the insurers on one side and the assured's broker on the other. Consumer contracts, where there is a palpably weaker party, are these days subject to statutory regulation to ensure that the customer does not bear the risk of payment for goods and services which are dangerous or worthless. We have already suggested that the point about rising consumerism is well made. But the wider point is that most commercial contracts have at their core a central element of risk allocation in the broader senses that we have just described even though they are not—as with insurance contracts—solely or primarily about transferring particular risks. Rather they specify how losses, if they occur, should be allocated. Disregarding pricing for the risks assumed is a potential distortion of the assumptions of the parties. Any suggestion that risk allocation should be overturned because the parties may have different degrees of expertise would require courts to rewrite commercial contracts to take account of what has actually happened even though the contractual risk-pricing will have taken into account a variety of things that might have, but did not, happen.

7.3 Insuring Against the Risk of Insolvency

In this and the following section, we outline a range of possible party arrangements dealing with key concerns of contracting parties, and highlight the role of insurance in those arrangements. We also begin to identify the part played by insurance arrangements in the response of the courts when faced with relevant disputes. This section incorporates discussion of insolvency risks; the next focuses on the risk of loss caused by non-performance, or defective performance.

7.3.1 Insurance and lending

Unsecured creditors must be treated equally, and contract clauses which seek to confer priority on an unsecured creditor in the event of the debtor's insolvency are void in that they offend the *pari passu*[34] and 'non-deprivation'[35] principles. The common law has

[32] Contrast Atiyah, n 11, 6: '[p]romise-based liability rests upon a belief in the traditional liberal values of free choice'.

[33] Atiyah, n 11, 6.

[34] *British Eagle International Air Lines Ltd v Compagnie Nationale Air France* [1975] 1 WLR 758.

[35] *Folgate London Market Ltd v Chaucer Insurance plc* [2011] EWCA Civ 328; [2011] Lloyd's Rep IR 623.

nevertheless been generous in recognizing a range of securities in favour of a creditor. A distinction may be drawn between general loans and purchase money loans.[36] A general loan permits the borrower to use the money for general purposes, and security will be found in a charge on the debtor's assets or in the form of a personal guarantee provided by, for example, the directors of a company to which sums have been loaned. A purchase money loan is designed to allow the borrower to obtain real or personal property, typical securities consisting of the mortgage and, where the purchaser is obtaining the subject matter from the seller, a retention of title provision whereby the buyer gets title when the seller is paid[37] or the use of hire-purchase terms whereby the seller retains ownership of the subject matter until full payment has been made. Equipment leases based on a rental which reflects the useful life of the machinery in question[38] fulfil the same function.

The creditor's ability to recover a loan in the event of default is, however, as strong as his security. A mortgaged house may catch fire and a mortgaged vessel may sink, and it is likely that the house or ship is the debtor's only significant asset, so it is a standard term of any mortgage that the borrower takes out insurance against the risk of damage and the borrower may also be required to obtain life cover with the lender as nominated payee or even assignee. A guarantee given to a bank by the directors of a debtor company is of no value if the directors are as insolvent as their company, and so there may be an obligation on the directors to provide additional security for the guarantee, possibly in the form of insurance coverage. Goods transferred under a hire-purchase or equipment lease may be damaged or destroyed, and so equipment leases impose an obligation on the lessee to insure the equipment. In short, even secured lenders need to have recourse to the insurance market.

A lender who has loaned money in return for a mortgage on land or an equivalent security on goods, and who has required the borrower to insure the secured property, is still far from safe. The assured person under the policy is the borrower. If the property is destroyed and the policy for whatever reason does not respond, for example because the assured borrower is in breach of his pre-contractual duties to answer questions accurately or—in the commercial market—to disclose material facts, is in breach of policy conditions, or is guilty of arson, the lender will lose out. Some lenders may seek letters of undertaking from the insurers, requiring notification if the insurance is cancelled,[39] so that at the very least the lender can refrain from making future advances which are effectively unsecured, but that does not protect the lender in respect of sums

[36] The distinction is rather more carefully defined in the Consumer Credit Act 1974 in terms of restricted- and unrestricted-use loans and in terms of debtor-creditor-supplier and debtor-creditor loans: the 1974 Act, ss 11–13.

[37] The *Romalpa* clause, first tested in *Aluminium Indusrie Vaassen BV v Romalpa Aluminium* [1976] 1 WLR 676. There is now a mass of complex case law on such provisions.

[38] Often entered into on a sale-and-leaseback basis, so that the borrower can raise capital on existing assets.

[39] Wording which gave rise to problems in *Bank of Nova Scotia v Hellenic Mutual War Risks Association (Bermuda) Ltd, The Good Luck* [1992] 1 AC 233. In that case the risk was terminated automatically by a breach of warranty, and the bank's complaint that it had not been notified was rejected on the grounds that there had not been any cancellation within the ordinary meaning of that word.

previously loaned. For this reason lenders adopt a variety of techniques, with varying degrees of safety.

First, the lender may require the borrower to inform the insurers of the lender's interest in the property, or the lender may do so itself. A creditor who insists that his interest is 'noted' on the policy probably gains nothing by it. Noting does not make the lender a party to the policy nor confer any rights on him in the event of a loss.[40] The practice is nevertheless widespread.

Second, the policy may contain a provision whereby the lender, although not a party to the insurance, is deemed to be the loss payee under the policy, so that the proceeds are to be paid not to the borrower but directly to the lender. Such clauses have been used for many years, and insurers have generally complied with them, although it is only since the implementation of the Contracts (Rights of Third Parties) Act 1999 that the clause became enforceable by the lender. The clause protects the lender against the risk that the borrower will obtain payment and then disappear, leaving the debt unpaid, but it does not overcome the problem that if the insurers are under no obligation to pay under the policy for any of the reasons given above then there are no proceeds to be paid to the lender. Some policies contain extended loss-payee clauses under which the insurer agrees to pay the lender free of all defences under the policy, and in such a case the insurers may reserve to themselves a right of recourse against the borrower (for what that may be worth).

The third insurance device to guard against insolvency is mortgagees' interest insurance (MII). This form of cover is of particular significance in shipping cases, and there are standard London Market clauses for the purpose.[41] The essence of MII is that it provides fallback insurance in the event that there is non-payment or partial payment under the shipowner's own policy where an insured peril has occurred. The sum payable to the mortgagee is the amount irrecoverable from the primary insurers.[42] MII insurers have express subrogation rights, so in the event of a payment to the mortgagee, the insurers have the right to attempt to recoup their payment from the mortgagor's own insurers and, ultimately, from the mortgagor himself in those rare cases where the mortgagor possesses any other assets.

The final device, and perhaps the most important in practice, is co-insurance. Under this approach the lender and borrower are both named as assureds under the policy for their respective rights and interests. The law accepts that it is perfectly possible for two or more persons who have an interest in the insured subject matter to be co-assureds. A distinction is to be drawn between joint insurance, which arises where the parties have the same indivisible interest in the insured subject matter, and composite insurance, which arises where the parties have distinct interests in the insured subject

[40] *First National Commercial Bank plc v Barnet Devanney (Harrow) Ltd* [1999] Lloyd's Rep IR 43.

[41] Institute Mortgagees' Interest Clauses 1997.

[42] It was held in *Continental Illinois Bank & Trust Co of Chicago v Bathurst, The Captain Panagos* [1985] 1 Lloyd's Rep 625 that an MII policy is a marine policy, so that, unless the policy otherwise provides, the sum recoverable is the market value of the vessel assessed immediately before the loss. That sum is generally less than the amount loaned, and accordingly the MII Clauses were modified to break the link between the value of the vessel and the amount recoverable under the policy.

matter.[43] The best (and possibly only) example of the former is jointly owned property, typically by husband and wife or other cohabitees. Because the interest is the same, any defence open to the insurers against one joint assured is equally available against the other: thus, if the husband is guilty of fraud, his wife has no claim in her own right.[44]

However, in the case of composite insurance the rule is different. Each party is treated as having a separate contract with the insurers for their respective insurable interests. Thus a borrower has an insurable interest in the value of the mortgaged property, by virtue of his ownership, and the lender has an insurable interest in the mortgaged property to the value of the debt, and each may insure his own interest.[45] The same principle applies to hire purchase.[46] The benefit to the lender is that, because he has a separate contract with the insurers quite distinct from that between the borrower and the insurers, defences which the insurers may have against the lender will not prevail against the borrower. Thus, if there has been non-disclosure,[47] breach of condition,[48] or fraud[49] by one co-assured, the rights of the other are unaffected.

For these reasons, co-insurance is perhaps the most secure form of contractual arrangement between borrower and lender, but it is not free from difficulty. There is some doubt about whether a breach of warranty by one co-assured leaves the rights of other co-assureds intact, in that a warranty is regarded as a statement of the circumstances in which the insurer faces liability, and if those circumstances have ceased to exist then there can be no liability.[50] Further, in the context of ship mortgages,[51] the deliberate grounding or sinking of the vessel by the borrower will defeat any claim under the policy by the lender. In such a case there is simply no insured peril and thus there are no recoverable policy moneys[52]: the definition of perils of the sea requires a fortuitous loss and not a deliberate one.[53] The lender can only hope that, if the

[43] Confusingly, composite insurance taken out in the construction industry is referred to as 'joint names insurance'. That phrase should be understood as merely reflecting the fact that two or more names appear on the policy: it is composite because the interests of the parties are different. The construction industry is discussed in 7.6.

[44] *Direct Line v Khan* [2001] EWCA Civ 1794; [2001] All ER (D) 476 (Oct), although there the Court of Appeal rested its judgment on its finding that the husband had acted as the agent of his wife in making a fraudulent claim. Other common law jurisdictions have rejected the indivisibility of interest in husband and wife cases, although the English and Scottish Law Commissions in their joint Consultation Document of December 2011 (Eng LCCP No 201; Scottish LCCP No 152) felt that the problem was not sufficiently common to justify legislation to bring the UK into line with other jurisdictions.

[45] *Samuel & Co Ltd v Dumas* [1924] AC 31; *General Accident Fire and Life Assurance Co Ltd v Midland Bank Ltd* [1940] 2 KB 388; *Woolcott v Sun Alliance* [1978] 1 WLR 493.

[46] *Lombard Australia v NRMA Insurance* [1969] 1 Lloyd's Rep 575.

[47] *First National Commercial Bank plc v Barnet Devanney (Harrow) Ltd* [1999] Lloyd's Rep IR 43; *Woolcott v Sun Alliance* [1978] 1 WLR 493; *Arab Bank plc v Zurich Insurance Co* [1999] Lloyd's Rep IR 262; *Brit Syndicates Ltd v Italaudit SpA* [2008] UKHL 18; [2008] Lloyd's Rep IR 601.

[48] *King v Brandywine Reinsurance Co (UK) Ltd* [2004] EWHC 1033 (Comm); [2004] 2 Lloyd's Rep 670 (affirmed on other grounds [2005] EWCA Civ 235); *Tate Gallery (Trustees) Ltd v Duffy Construction Ltd* [2007] EWHC 361 (TCC); [2008] Lloyd's Rep IR 159.

[49] *New Hampshire Insurance Co v MGN Ltd* [1997] LRLR 24; *National Oilwell (UK) Ltd v Davy Offshore Ltd* [1993] 2 Lloyd's Rep 582; *State of Netherlands v Youell* [1997] 2 Lloyd's Rep 440.

[50] Rix J left this point open in *Arab Bank plc v Zurich Insurance Co* [1999] Lloyd's Rep IR 262.

[51] A significant proportion of vessels are mortgaged to banks.

[52] *Samuel & Co Ltd v Dumas* [1924] AC 31.

[53] Marine Insurance Act 1906, sch, para 7; *Global Process Systems Inc v Berhad, The Cendor Mopu* [2011] UKSC 5; [2011] 1 Lloyd's Rep 560.

borrower is intent upon destroying his own ship, he has the decency to do so by setting fire to it, as fortuity is not a part of the definition of fire.[54] The insurers would of course have a right of recourse against the borrower in those circumstances, but they and not the lender bear the risk of his insolvency. The practical difficulty with co-insurance is that the parties' interests are not just different, but may be competing, in that one co-assured may cause the insured loss suffered by the other, and the insurers may then wish to exercise subrogation rights. Subrogation is excluded against a co-assured who, while responsible for the loss, could have recovered in respect of it (typically where there has been negligence), but subrogation actions against co-assureds regularly reach the courts.

7.3.2 Credit insurance

The risk of bad trade debts is the most consistent fear of businesses. Credit factoring, whereby a trader sells future debts to a credit factor at a discount (generally between 75 per cent and 90 per cent of the value of the debt), is a useful way of ensuring cash flow and guaranteeing that at least some money is received.[55] This illustrates the prevalent use of risk allocation, employing trade-offs between present and future value, in market activity of many sorts. Once a debt has fallen due and is not paid, many businesses either assign their debts at a discount or appoint debt recovery agencies. However, private credit insurance is a regularly used alternative. Various forms of credit insurance are available in the market. Policies may cover the creditor's whole account, in which case premiums will be based upon trading figures,[56] or they may be confined to specific customers or to a number of key customers.[57] Insurers may impose requirements as to the assured's lending criteria or may require that the assured does not act inconsistently with its ordinary lending criteria,[58] particularly where the assured has advanced credit to 'sub-prime' debtors.[59] Policies may be confined to domestic transactions, they may extend to international transactions, or they may include both domestic and export transactions. As an illustration of the points made in Chapter 2 about the necessity of insurance for commerce, insurance may have an impact on the market itself; if insurers take the view that trading with a particular customer is too risky to underwrite, that may well have the effect of precipitating the financial demise of that customer.[60]

[54] *Schiffshypothekenbank Zu Luebeck AG v Compton, The Alexion Hope* [1988] 1 Lloyd's Rep 311.

[55] The purchaser of book debts can obtain insurance to protect itself against fraud by the assignor, who may assign 'phantom' debts: *Fortisbank SA v Trenwick International* [2005] EWHC 399 (Comm); [2005] Lloyd's Rep IR 464. The issue in *Fortisbank* was whether the purchaser had given timely notice of its discovery of fraud to the insurers.

[56] *Kazakhstan Wool Processors (Europe) Ltd v Nederlandsche Credietverzekering Maatschappij NV* [2000] Lloyd's Rep IR 371, where the assured's failure to comply with policy conditions as to the timely submission of trading returns was held to give the insurers a defence in respect of claims arising out of non-submitted returns but did not affect claims arising out of properly submitted returns.

[57] Illustrated by *Moore Large & Co v Hermes Credit & Guarantee Co plc* [2003] EWHC 26 (Comm); [2003] 1 Lloyd's Rep 163.

[58] *Svenska Handelsbanken v Sun Alliance* [1996] 1 Lloyd's Rep 519.

[59] *College Credit Ltd v National Guarantee Corporation Ltd* [2004] EWHC 978 (Comm); [2004] 2 All ER (Comm) 409.

[60] The troubles of a famous high-street retailer were enhanced in 2010 when credit insurers announced that they were no longer prepared to provide insurance to persons trading with the store.

The risks insured vary from case to case. Where whole account insurance is provided, the risk insured is generally non-payment by the due date or some other specified date, depending upon the nature of the underlying transaction,[61] and generally the reason for non-payment is irrelevant.[62] Policies insuring against non-payment by individual customers often rest upon the occurrence of one or more trigger events, most importantly the commencement of an insolvency procedure against the customer.[63]

The role played by insurance here is not merely passive; it may facilitate commercial transactions which would not otherwise have taken place. The film finance story is illustrative here. In the 1980s and 1990s film production companies wished to find a means of financing the making of films. A scheme was developed with the assistance of London Market insurance brokers under which banks and other institutions would advance the necessary funds to the film production companies, and the banks would be repaid out of the revenues earned by the films. If, however, the revenues failed to meet the sums repayable on a given date, the lenders would be covered by insurance issued by a number of underwriters including Australian insurers HIH.[64] The insurance policies covered the difference between the revenues and the sums repayable. HIH was reinsured by major London Market reinsurers. Although the contracts were described as being of insurance, in fact they bore little resemblance to traditional contracts, in that HIH waived, by express clauses,[65] the lenders' ordinary duty of disclosure.[66] The lenders incurred substantial losses and HIH made payment[67] even though it was aware that the warranties in the insurance contracts had been broken because the production companies had not made the promised number of films and revenue losses were almost inevitable. In a series of sequel decisions, HIH was held to be unable to recover from its reinsurers[68] because it had in effect paid the lenders on an

[61] *British Credit Trust Holdings v UK Insurance Ltd* [2003] EWHC 2404 (Comm); [2004] 1 All ER (Comm) 444, where the insured creditor provided motor vehicles on hire purchase and there were various trigger dates, depending upon whether the vehicle had been repossessed and, if so, subsequently sold.

[62] *Governor and Company of the Bank of Scotland v Euclidian (No 1) Ltd* [2007] EWHC 1732 (Comm); [2008] Lloyd's Rep IR 182, where the sum was irrecoverable as a matter of law.

[63] *Merrill Lynch International Bank v Winterthur Swiss Insurance Co* [2007] EWHC 893 (Comm); [2007] Lloyd's Rep IR 532, in which Gloster J held that various French protective measures ordered by the French courts in respect of the assured bank's customer, Eurotunnel, constituted insolvency events for the purposes of the bank's credit insurance policy.

[64] This company and its associates, constituting the second-largest insurance group in Australia, went into spectacular insolvent liquidation in 2001, with liabilities exceeding assets by some A$7 billion. The London Market trading in film finance insurance was loss-making, but only a small part of the reason for the overall insolvency. This led to a Royal Commission, whose 2003 Report is fascinating and instructive reading: <http://www.hihroyalcom.gov.au/>, accessed 28 April 2013.

[65] The House of Lords considered the so-called 'Truth of Statements' clauses in detail in *HIH Casualty and General Insurance v Chase Manhattan Bank* [2003] UKHL 6; [2003] 2 Lloyd's Rep 61.

[66] For analysis of the types of policies used, refer to *Screen Partners v VIF Filmproduktion GmbH* [2001] EWCA Civ 2096.

[67] Partly prompted by the desire of HIH not to be seen to default and thereby to prejudice its credit rating and produce a loss of confidence. In fact HIH was insolvent at the time anyway, so it was merely postponing the inevitable.

[68] In separate proceedings, *GE Reinsurance Corporation v New Hampshire Insurance Co* [2003] EWHC 302 (Comm); [2004] Lloyd's Rep IR 404, insurers were held to be in breach of a warranty to the reinsurers that the artistic director of the film production company would remain employed. In fact he left shortly afterwards. There was no equivalent warranty in the insurance policy, with the effect that the insurers

ex gratia basis: the reinsurers were held not to have waived HIH's disclosure obligations even though HIH had waived the lenders' disclosure obligations;[69] and the reinsurers were also held not to have waived the underlying breaches of warranty.[70] A claim by HIH against the brokers, for failing to keep HIH informed of the problems relating to the making of the films and thereby prejudicing HIH's ability to recover from its reinsurers, was rejected on the grounds that HIH was fully aware of those problems when it chose to make payment so that it had caused its own loss.[71] Although the saga is a sorry one, it does demonstrate that many commercial transactions would simply not take place but for the backing of insurance arrangements, and the problems have had the incidental effect of unveiling the underpinning effect of insurance.

Brief mention should also be made of the state credit insurance scheme operated by the Export Credit Guarantees Department (ECGD) under the authority of the Export and Investment Guarantees Act 1991.[72] This is a state scheme which offers bad debt and war risks cover, in the form of insurance or (if insurance is in place) reinsurance, up to the sum of £35,000,000 in the aggregate, to persons carrying on business in the UK and supplying goods or services to persons outside the UK.[73]

7.3.3 Summary

The above account illustrates not only the shifting of credit risks by express contract terms or other arrangements but also the central role of insurance as a risk-shifting mechanism. There is scarcely a contract entered into by a commercial concern which does not provide in some way for protection against default by reason of insolvency and/or which is unsupported by first-party insurance against such default. These arrangements show the extent to which awareness and allocation of risk underpins contractual relationships. This is seen equally clearly when, as we proceed to do, attention is focused on losses flowing from the performance of contracts.

7.4 Risk Allocation and Insurance in Contracts

In this section, we address a core question facing contracting parties and the law of contract, namely the location of responsibility for making good losses on the part

had no defence against the lenders but the reinsurers had a defence against the insurers. Without doubt the insurers would have turned their attention to the brokers who arranged these policies.

[69] *HIH Casualty and General Insurance Ltd v New Hampshire Insurance Co* [2001] EWCA Civ 735; [2001] 2 Lloyd's Rep 161.

[70] *HIH Casualty and General Insurance Ltd v Axa Corporate Solutions* [2002] EWCA Civ 1253; [2003] Lloyd's Rep IR 1.

[71] *HIH Casualty and General Insurance Ltd v JLT Risk Solutions Ltd* [2007] EWCA Civ 710; [2007] 2 Lloyd's Rep 278.

[72] See also European Commission Directive 98/29 on the provision of export credit by member states. The ECGD scheme can be traced back to a scheme introduced immediately after the First World War under which government aid was provided to exporters through the Board of Trade. The function was transferred to the ECGD in 1926.

[73] For the detail of the scheme refer to <http://www.ecgd.gov.uk/>, accessed 28 April 2013.

of contracting parties where things go wrong. This was the second form of risk identified in 7.2. Here we identify the role of insurance in relation to this question.

7.4.1 The role of insurance in risk allocation

As we explained in 7.1, risk allocation is pervasive in commercial contracts[74] and risk allocation and future planning often have no necessary connection with fault or blame. To the extent that the parties have failed to allocate risks and liabilities the law provides a series of default rules. Discussion of those rules is beyond the bounds of this work and, illustrating the centrality of the question, would amount to a textbook on the law of contract. It may be said in general terms however that legal default rules have little part to play unless the intentions of the parties cannot otherwise be ascertained or interpreted.[75] Judicial recognition of risk allocation by the parties is patent in some cases. Steyn J, in *Associated Japanese Bank (International) Ltd v Credit du Nord*,[76] speaking of a contract allegedly void for mistake commented that '[O]ne must first determine whether the contract itself, by express or implied condition precedent or otherwise, provides who bears the risk of the relevant mistake'.[77] The importance of risk allocation in decisions reached by the courts may be less obvious, or even hidden, because courts do not always use that language. Questions which may be raised include which of the parties is to bear the loss when an acceptance is not delivered;[78] one party has a mistaken view of the nature of the agreement, either self-induced[79] or induced by the words or deeds of the other;[80] circumstances change so that the contract cannot be performed profitably;[81] circumstances change so that the contract cannot be performed at all;[82] the law forbids the type of performance adopted by the defendant;[83] the

[74] Academic discussion of the law of contract as a risk-allocation mechanism tends to focus on the more obvious situations in which an allocation of risk is called for, for example, mistake or frustration, and there is a good deal of law-and-economics consideration of the concept of 'efficient breach' in circumstances where market changes make performance less desirable from the point of view of one of the parties. For example: RE Scott and JS Kraus, *Contract Law and Theory* (Albany NY: LexisNexis Matthew Bender, 4th edn, 2007); RA Posner and AM Rosenfield, 'Impossibility and Related Doctrines in Contract Law' (1977) 5 JLS 83; JD Wladis, 'Impracticability as Risk Allocation: The Effect of Changed Circumstances Upon Contract Obligations for the Sale of Goods' (1988) 22 Georgia LR 503; GG Triantis, 'Unforeseen Contingencies. Risk Allocation in Contracts' University of Virginia, 1998.

[75] Virtually every commercial case begins with a discussion of this matter. The number of citations of the leading cases on construction, *Investors Compensation Scheme v West Bromwich Building Society* [1998] 1 WLR 896 and *Chartbrook Ltd v Persimmon Homes Ltd* [2009] UKHL 38; [2009] 3 WLR 267, speaks for itself.

[76] [1989] 1 WLR 255.

[77] [1989] 1 WLR 255, 268.

[78] *Adams v Lindsell* (1818) 1 B & Ald 681.

[79] *Associated Japanese Bank (International) Ltd v Credit du Nord* [1989] 1 WLR 255; *Great Peace Shipping Ltd v Tsavliris Salvage (International) Ltd, The Great Peace* [2002] EWCA Civ 1407; [2003] QB 679; *Butters v BBC Worldwide Ltd* [2009] EWHC 1954 (Ch).

[80] *Taylor v Hamer* [2002] EWCA Civ 1130.

[81] *Williams v Roffey Brothers* [1991] 1 QB 1.

[82] *McRae v Commonwealth Disposals Commission* (1951) 84 CLR 377; *Pioneer Shipping Ltd v BTP Tioxide Ltd* [1982] AC 724. The complex law of frustration leads many commercial parties to include *force majeure* clauses in their contracts rather than leave the matter to litigation.

[83] *St John Shipping v Joseph Rank* [1957] 1 QB 267.

claimant suffers losses by reason of a breach by the defendant;[84] and the contract is ambiguous or opaque in its language.[85] Judges are always aware of the fact that a rise or fall in the market, rendering performance by one or other party undesirable, will be manifested in court proceedings on an entirely different issue, such as alleged short delivery or some technical variation in the description of the subject matter.[86] In such cases, wherever possible, the courts will reject these defences and allow the risk to lie where it was originally intended to fall.[87]

Our point here is simply that risk allocation is a pervasive theme of the law of contract, and the intention of the parties plays a special role. It is therefore important to note that insurance is highly significant to the manner in which risks are allocated, because risk allocation is, as we have said, often accompanied by insuring obligations. Moreover, a contracting party may be constrained by insurance considerations from entering into an agreement under which the risk of loss is borne by or transferred to him. If a contracting party A has entered into an agreement under which the other party B is held harmless, then the fact that A's insurers do not have subrogation rights against B on the indemnification of A may be a material fact which has to be disclosed to them, failing which they may have the right to avoid the policy.[88] If A has insurance and then enters into a contract with B, A may be constrained by the policy terms from giving immunity to B.[89] Insurance considerations may also affect the settlement of contract disputes: any settlement reached by the assured with a third party whereby the third party is relieved from liability to the assured (or whereby the assured assumes the other's liability to third parties) may lead to the insurers refusing to indemnify the assured for breach of an express policy term or, if there is no such term, prejudice to the insurers' subrogation rights.[90]

There are two particular forms of risk which are commonly the subject of express allocation: the risk of non-performance or defective performance by one contracting party, causing loss to the other; and the risk of external injury being inflicted on a third party. Our focus in the next section is on the former. Of the latter it is necessary only to comment that the parties may agree that one of them is to bear the ultimate burden of any third-party claim whichever of them the third party chooses, or has the right, to sue. An occupier of land may insist that any liability incurred by him to a neighbour as the result of works on his land is borne by the contractor responsible for those works, by means of an indemnity to the occupier.[91] Again, where an employee of B is loaned to employer A and is injured by negligence for which A is liable either personally or

[84] *Transfield Shipping Inc v Mercator Shipping Ltd, The Achilleas* [2007] EWCA Civ 901; [2007] 2 Lloyd's Rep 555.

[85] *Chartbrook Ltd v Persimmon Homes Ltd* [2009] UKHL 38; [2009] 3 WLR 267.

[86] *Reardon Smith Line Ltd v Yngvar Hansen-Tangen* [1976] 1 WLR 989.

[87] A classic example is *Pao On v Lau Yiu* [1980] AC 614.

[88] *Tate & Sons v Hyslop* (1884–5) LR 15 QB 368. There is a right to avoid only if B's immunity is of a type which would not normally be found, because insurers need only be told of matters which they could not otherwise know.

[89] For example, *Argo Systems FZE v Liberty Insurance (Pte)* [2011] EWHC 301 (Comm); [2011] 2 Lloyd's Rep 61.

[90] *Horwood v Land of Leather Ltd* [2010] EWHC 546 (Comm), where both defences found favour.

[91] The converse arrangement is the issue in *Slocan Forest Products Ltd v Trapper Enterprises Ltd* 2011 BCCA 351.

vicariously, it is common for B to agree to hold A harmless, by means of an indemnity, often backed by an obligation on B to insure. In the absence of agreement as to allocation of risk, the general assumption is that the loss lies where it falls,[92] although the fact that one of the parties is required to be insured against third-party claims may, depending upon the circumstances, be a strong or weak indication that he is to carry the risk.[93] We confine discussion of such provisions to our case study of construction contracts in 7.6, and to the following chapter on tort duties.

7.5 Risk Allocation and Defective Performance

7.5.1 The problem and some possible solutions

The problem to be addressed here can be expressed simply by reference to the decision of the Supreme Court in *Jones v Kaney*,[94] as indeed can the potential solutions. Here, the Supreme Court by a five-to-two majority lifted the previous immunity from suit conferred upon expert witnesses.[95] If an expert witness is negligent, and the negligence causes loss to the client of that witness, there is a loss which has to be borne by somebody. The majority view was that the loss should, if negligence and causation can be shown, be borne by the expert. In that case a doctor appointed by the claimant in a personal injury action as an expert witness signed a joint report which, the claimant alleged, substantially understated the degree of the claimant's psychological injuries and accused the claimant of deception, and thus led to the claimant's advisers agreeing to a settlement which was much lower than the sum that might otherwise have been received. The doctor subsequently admitted that she had not agreed with much of the analysis in the joint report but had signed it anyway. The majority of the Supreme Court decided that the immunity long thought to have been granted to expert witnesses was not justified and that, if negligence could be proved, liability would follow to the extent that loss was suffered. The majority felt that the role of an expert witness was closely analogous to that of an advocate, with advocate's immunity having been removed a decade earlier.[96]

There are strong views about this ruling,[97] and these are expressed in the opposing judgments given by the Supreme Court. The majority thought that the supply of expert

[92] *Professional Financial Services v Dick* [2010] ScotCS CSOH 131.

[93] *Beazley Underwriting Ltd v Travelers Companies Inc* [2011] EWHC 1520 (Comm); [2012] Lloyd's Rep IR 78.

[94] [2011] UKSC 13; [2011] 2 WLR 823.

[95] The immunity of witnesses of fact, who are required to give evidence as opposed to an expert witness who agrees to do so voluntarily, is unaffected by the decision. However, as Lady Hale pointed out, the distinction between these two classes is not always clear.

[96] *Arthur JS Hall & Co v Simons* [2002] 1 AC 615; [2000] 3 WLR 543.

[97] Readers might wish to conduct an Internet search of the many tens of law firms and expert witness organizations which have commented on this. There is little or no support. The overwhelming majority of comments are adverse, taking the view that the role of the expert as a 'hired gun', caricatured by the majority, is outmoded, and that these days most experts accept that their duty is to the court or tribunal and not to the party who has paid them: the Civil Procedure Rules 1998 (CPR) Part 35 codifies *The Ikarian Reefer* [1993] 2 Lloyd's Rep 68, which specifically states that: '(1) It is the duty of experts to help the court on matters within their expertise. (2) This duty overrides any obligation to the person from whom experts have received instructions or by whom they are paid.' The present trend is for courts and arbitrators to insist

witnesses would not dry up, that they would not be deterred from giving honest evidence in compliance with their overriding duty to the court, and that—like barristers—they voluntarily assumed their duties. Lord Collins also indicated that liability already existed in the form of prosecution for perjury, wasted costs orders, or professional disciplinary proceedings for misconduct. The minority was primarily concerned to maintain the overriding duty of the expert witness, namely, that of assisting the court, although Lord Hope also referred to the risk that the expert, shorn of immunity, might face damaging even though fatally flawed litigation. Lady Hale added that a lifting of immunity raised complex issues where the expert was appointed by the court[98] or was a joint appointment.[99] However, the important point for our analysis is to look at the impact of the decision on an expert witness and to treat this as a microcosm of contracting generally. Suppose that a doctor, lawyer, surveyor, accountant,[100] or other person is approached to be an expert for a party in judicial or arbitral proceedings. What is her response going to be in the light of *Jones v Kaney*? There are five possibilities: (1) the risk of liability is such that it is inappropriate to accept instruction to act as an expert witness; (2) the risk of liability is so remote that it is to be ignored in the agreement between the client and the expert, so that each party privately decides how to cover potential losses or liabilities as the case may be, in which case the expert is almost certain to take out private liability insurance and to charge the cost to the client, generally by a boost of fees; (3) the expert will agree to serve but only on the basis that the client takes out first-party insurance against the risk of negligent advice; (4) the expert will agree to serve but is required to take out liability insurance, the cost of which will—expressly or in the form of a top-up to the fee—be borne by the client;[101] or (5) the expert will agree to serve but the contract with the client is required to exclude all possible liability to the client in the event of negligence.[102]

Even in the light of *Jones v Kaney* (1) is a relatively remote possibility unless there are factors at work other than potential *Jones v Kaney* liability.[103] After all, expert witness work is lucrative, and in many areas there are more potential witnesses than available work. It is almost certain, therefore, that the expert will want to accept the engagement

upon joint expert reports which identify the areas of agreement and narrow the areas of disagreement (the very situation in *Jones v Kaney*), and an imposition of liability in that situation seems contrary to the objectives of the CPR. Interestingly, the general view is that the vast majority of expert witnesses are at little risk of liability as long as they comply with their CPR role.

[98] Note the Arbitration Act 1996, s 37, which empowers an arbitrator to appoint an expert to advise him. In practice the expert may enter into agreements with the parties or he may be appointed by the arbitrator and his costs and fees are then charged to the costs of the arbitration. Whoever the agreement is with, it is far from obvious that such an expert owes a duty of care—contractual or otherwise—to the parties, given that the role is to advise the arbitrators in the assessment of the evidence put forward by the parties' own experts. It is likely that an expert appointed by an arbitrator—typically a lawyer, forensic accountant, or surveyor—would be covered by professional indemnity insurance relating to his business activities, but an exclusion of liability may still be insisted upon to forestall the possibility of litigation.

[99] The decision does not deal with the possibility that the expert may face a negligence action from the other party. It would seem sensible now for an expert witness to obtain insurance against that possibility.

[100] The most common classes of expert witness in civil litigation involving commercial disputes.

[101] Either exclusively, or possibly spread amongst all of the expert's clients.

[102] Liability incurred by deliberate wrongdoing is not a risk capable of exclusion.

[103] The usual considerations, for example, that the expert is unable to give an opinion which is likely to further the client's cause, or conflict of interest.

but at the same time to shuffle off potential liability, and the client will in effect be required to pay for that shift, but the question becomes, how is this to be done?

The solution under possibility (2) is that the contract is silent and that the expert chooses either to accept the limited risk of liability or to insure against it,[104] charging the client accordingly. If the expert does rely upon professional liability insurance, he or she is at risk that for one or other reason the policy does not respond to the claim so that he or she faces the burden of liability. Moreover, the very existence of the cause of action might, as Lord Hope commented in *Jones v Kaney*, expose the expert witness to 'worthless but possibly embarrassing and time-consuming proceedings by a disgruntled and disaffected litigant in person'.

Possibility (3), first-party insurance, is a device which is used in a variety of contexts, but is fraught with danger, because a clause of this type may not be recognized judicially as requiring the client to hold the expert harmless and to look only to the client's own insurers in the event of negligence, because insurers may have a good defence under the policy or, alternatively, having paid, may choose to exercise subrogation rights against the expert.[105]

Possibility (4), compulsory insurance by the expert, shares with the possibility of optional liability insurance under (2) the problems that there may be coverage issues under the policy and also that there may be unjustified litigation which causes damage to the expert's reputation and activities.

Possibility (5), exclusion of liability, is a valid approach to overcome the risk of litigation, but the expert has to be satisfied that the courts will recognize that the commercial purpose of the clause is to ensure that the risk of negligence rests with the client and not with the expert: it is at this point that problems potentially arising under the Unfair Contract Terms Act 1977 have to be recognized. These are however relatively minimal in that the courts are unlikely to go behind an exclusion clause reached in an arm's length transaction even though the expert's terms may be standard.[106] Nevertheless, there is always the risk that the validity of the exclusion clause may be challenged, however hopeless the case, causing the expert witness to incur defence costs in fighting off the action.

In the following paragraphs, we consider the viability of possibilities (2), (3), (4), and (5) for risk allocation in a variety of other everyday and commercial contexts. But to return to expert witnesses for a moment, it should be said that there are two forms of expert: the professional expert, whose living[107] is fully or partly made up from such work; and the occasional expert who appears from time to time.[108] Their responses may be different. Professional experts often belong to one or more of the various expert witness organizations and have terms of engagement—those terms, even prior to *Jones v Kaney*, excluded liability for professional negligence. A good number of such experts

[104] Lord Dyson emphasized the availability of insurance. Contrast Lord Hope (dissenting), who said of expert witnesses: 'Some may be academics, and some may come forward to give expert evidence only once in a lifetime. It seems to me that it would be unwise to assume that they all have insurance cover against claims for negligence.'

[105] Chapter 5 discusses the nature of subrogation.

[106] If they are not, the 1977 Act will not apply.

[107] Or, very often, pension.

[108] Such as Dr Kaney.

also possessed liability insurance before *Jones v Kaney*, by way of coverage for defence costs in the event of perjury actions, wasted costs orders or disciplinary proceedings,[109] and against the risk of a negligence suit for advice given prior to the trial,[110] and many more now do. The cost is thus spread amongst clients. The response of the occasional expert will depend upon the particular circumstances of an instruction, and there may in particular be a difference in the availability and cost of insurance coverage for a 'professional' expert and for one who performs the function on a one-off basis, but these two devices will doubtless be used increasingly by all experts. More generally, it will be seen that although the parties may reach agreement on the way in which risks are to be allocated (thus, the limits of liability), it is not necessarily easy to make that agreement stick. Most particularly, the courts may adopt reasoning processes which are, possibly inadvertently, at odds with the process of risk allocation.

7.5.2 No agreement on risk allocation

Commercial contracts are rarely silent on risk allocation. *Force majeure* clauses are standard if there is a fear that performance may be disrupted by outside events, particularly direct or indirect political intervention; and an obvious risk that the contract may be incapable of performance or impose significant additional costs[111] is often subject to express terms. Selling land without making provision for responsibility for pollution clean-up costs would be foolhardy.[112] If the allocation of risks is express by the terms of the contract, the parties may make their own decisions on whether possible risks or liabilities should be insured.

In other cases however the manner in which risk and liability is to be allocated is not obvious from the contract. All manner of considerations may be in play, and different theories may point to different outcomes,[113] but our concern in the present chapter is the key and much-neglected role of insurance. Our basic point is that the allocation of risks and liability by the courts does not occur in an insurance-free vacuum. It is almost inevitable that one or both of the parties will be carrying relevant insurance, or at least that such insurance is commonly available but has not been taken up. The question then becomes, to what extent will the courts take note of actual or potential insurance in deciding which of the parties is to bear liability? The same issue arises in tort cases, and we discuss this in the following chapter.

[109] Professional indemnity policies might cover such defence costs, although in many cases they would be repayable if liability was actually established. Policies do not cover fines, and as a matter of public policy they cannot do so: Chapter 11.

[110] Such liability was recognized before *Jones v Kaney*, in *Palmer v Durnford Ford* [1992] QB 483; *Stanton v Callaghan* [2000] QB 75; [1999] 2 WLR 745.

[111] *William Sindall plc v Cambridgeshire CC* [1984] 1 WLR 1016 (purchaser of land to bear the risk of third-party rights existing over the land).

[112] A Waite, G Jones, T Jewell, and M Woods, *Environmental Law in Property Transactions* (Haywards Heath: Tottel, 3rd edn, 2009).

[113] Scott and Kraus, n 74, p 88, note that the court may: (a) apply default rules; (b) impose an *ex ante* equitable solution; or (c) let the loss lie where it falls.

The possible range of insurance positions is as follows: (a) the claimant is insured against first-party loss and the defendant is insured against liability; (b) the claimant is insured against first-party loss and the defendant is not insured against liability; (c) the claimant is not insured against first-party loss and the defendant is insured against liability; (d) neither party is insured, either by conscious choice or because insurance is unavailable. Experienced judges will be aware of the likely insurance position. They will know that banks insure against fidelity losses and that householders insure against damage to their houses and contents, and they also know that insurance is compulsory in the professions. However, different expectations of the insurance position may give rise to different outcomes. *Jones v Kaney* is a perfect illustration: for the majority, expert witness liability was in part justified by the availability of insurance; for the minority, the fact that insurance was available did not mitigate the risk to the expert of facing damaging litigation if immunity did not exist.

Where the defendant has agreed to indemnify the claimant against loss, the fact that the claimant has taken out a fallback policy to protect itself should obviously not in any way affect the indemnity, because that policy is plainly not intended to be the claimant's primary security.[114] A typical illustration is an ordinary contract for the sale of real property. Risk passes to the purchaser on exchange, so that there is a liability to pay the purchase price on completion even though the property to be sold has become a smouldering ruin in the period between contract and completion. The undoubted existence of the seller's insurance policy is irrelevant to the matter, because the obligation to pay remains with the buyer. If the seller chooses to look to his insurers, they will pay him and thereby acquire subrogation rights against the buyer.[115] Given that the buyer retains primary liability to make good the loss, it is sensible for him to take out his own insurance on the property to cover this very eventuality.[116] The position is less obvious if there is no risk allocation in the contract. The courts have, for example, held that a landlord is not to be taken to have agreed to bear the loss in the event that the tenant negligently sets fire to the premises even though it is almost certain to be the case that the landlord is insured against fire damage but the tenant is not insured against liability. The law casts the burden on the negligent tenant, and private insurance arrangements do not affect the position.[117] This is true even though the tenant has paid the insurance premiums by way of service charges.[118]

What emerges from these cases is that the existence (or non-existence) and incidence of first-party insurance rarely plays an explicit role in determining risk allocation where the contract itself is silent, because it may not be obvious whether the policy is intended to be the primary source of recovery or a fallback source.

[114] *Caledonia North Sea v British Telecommunications plc* [2002] UKHL 4; 1 Lloyd's Rep 553, discussed in Chapter 5.

[115] *Castellain v Preston* (1882–3) 11 QBD 380.

[116] Some property policies extend cover to the purchaser if he does not possess his own insurance: eg *National Farmers Union Mutual Insurance Society Ltd v HSBC Insurance (UK) Ltd* [2010] EWHC 773 (Comm); [2011] Lloyd's Rep IR 86.

[117] The bizarre facts of *University of Western Ontario v Yanush* 56 DLR (4th) 552 (1988) are a fascinating diversion.

[118] *Lambert v Keymood Ltd* [1999] Lloyd's Rep IR 80.

7.5.3 Risk allocation by first-party insurance

Some contracts provide that a party is to take out first-party insurance against the risk of loss. Typical are bailment agreements[119] and certain forms of contracts of carriage, where the insuring party has undertaken that the goods will be handed over safely and thus bears the risk of loss or damage. In that situation, first-party insurance matches the risk allocation.

However, there may be a difficulty with this form of contractual arrangement where the insured subject matter is damaged by the other party to the contract: that party may be uninsured in anticipation of immunity, or it may have fallback liability insurance, but in either case the expectation is that the owner will bear his own first-party loss. An obligation on a party to procure first-party insurance is not, however, necessarily sufficient to amount to an agreement whereby the insured party agrees to look only to the insurers if there has been a loss which is the fault of the other party. The courts have noted that 'It is a fallacy to assume that an obligation to insure can, without more, throw [a] loss on the insured when, by another provision of the contract, it is to be borne by another party',[120] and 'insurance provisions are primarily in a contract in order to provide a fund in the event of the risk eventuating; they are not there primarily for defining the obligations of one party to the other'.[121] But such statements do not render insurance provisions irrelevant. The question is one of context. The effect of an insurance provision depends upon whether the contract, construed as a whole, shows an intention that the risk of loss should be borne by the insured party alone. As Lord Atkin said in *Canadian Transport Co Ltd v Court Line Ltd*,[122] 'a man may contract with another on the terms that if he is injured by that other then, if he happens to be insured, he will look to the insurers in relief of the wrongdoers'. So an express term to that effect removes the difficulty. But if there is no such express term, all will turn upon the intention of the parties. In the absence of an intention to relieve the wrongdoer from liability, the insured party retains a cause of action against the wrongdoer for breach of contract. That cause of action will doubtless be exercised by the insurers who, having paid the assured, are granted subrogation rights. It is apparent that the potential use of subrogation can undermine the agreement between the parties. If party A has agreed to insure against the risk of loss, any prospect that B may be sued for negligence by way of subrogation will cause B to take out his own policy and charge the premiums to A, who will therefore pay twice. The device of subrogation, the legal rationale of which was explored in Chapter 5, threatens to unsettle contractual risk allocation between two other

[119] Insurance policies taken out by bailees may cover the value of the goods, or they may cover the amount of the bailee's liability for the goods (which may be substantially less, given the use of exclusion clauses). The presumption is in favour of the former, so that the bailee is entitled to recover the full sum insured and will then hand over to the bailor the policy moneys in excess of the bailee's own interest: *Ramco Ltd v International Insurance Co of Hannover* [2004] EWCA Civ 675; [2004] 2 Lloyd's Rep 595 is illustrative of the many cases on the point.

[120] *National Trust v Haden Young* (1974) 72 BLR 1, per Nourse LJ. The same issue arises where there is a co-insurance clause: discussed in 7.6.

[121] *Casson v P J Ostley Ltd* [2001] EWCA Civ 1013; [2001] All ER (D) 340 (Jun), per Schiemann LJ at [25].

[122] [1940] AC 934.

parties, as indeed we saw in that chapter. The parties or the courts may therefore use two devices to prevent subrogation proceedings from undermining what has been agreed.

The first is that the insurance policy may specifically exclude any right of recourse against the wrongdoer. Examples of subrogation waiver are: in respect of a contract for the carriage of goods, the insurers of the cargo owners may waive subrogation rights against the carrier in the event of damage to the goods, particularly common where the owner and carrier are in the same corporate group;[123] in respect of charter parties, hull insurers generally waive subrogation rights against charterers associated with the owners unless the charterers have their own insurance;[124] and composite policies issued in the construction industry contain subrogation waiver clauses.[125] Since the implementation of the Contracts (Rights of Third Parties) Act 1999, a subrogation waiver clause is enforceable by way of defence to a subrogation claim even though the defendant is not a party to the policy.[126]

The second device is to treat the insuring clause as a risk-allocation provision, to be supplemented by an express or implied term that the insured party has agreed to exempt the other from liability covered by the policy. If there is no express term, whether such a term is to be implied is a matter of the proper construction of the contract as a whole. On this important question, the cases do not send out a clear message. In the context of landlord and tenant, the leading authority is *Mark Rowlands v Berni Inns Ltd*.[127] Here, a lease imposed an insuring obligation upon the landlord, and the tenant paid the premiums for the cover by way of service charges. Following a fire caused by the alleged negligence of the tenant, the insurers indemnified the landlord and exercised subrogation rights against the tenant. The Court of Appeal's view was that the parties had intended that the landlord should bear the risk of fire losses, whether accidentally caused or the result of the tenant's negligence, and that there was to be implied in the lease a term that the tenant was immune from liability. The effect of the implied term was to preclude the subrogation action. *Mark Rowlands* may be distinguished from the other landlord and tenant cases, already discussed, where there was no obligation on the landlord to insure so that it could not be said that the parties intended the landlord to bear the risk of the tenant's negligence. The same reasoning has been applied in contracts involving the bailment of goods.[128]

The difficulty in ascertaining whether a first-party insurance clause operates as a risk allocation has caused particular difficulty in construction cases. It may be a requirement that the employer take out first-party insurance against all risks or, depending upon the contract, only specified risks, of loss of or damage to new structures and site

123 *The Surf City* [1995] 2 Lloyd's Rep 242.

124 International Hull Clauses 2003, cl 28.

125 JCT Building Contracts are discussed in 7.6.

126 Even before the implementation of the 1999 Act the orthodox view that a third party could not rely upon a subrogation waiver clause (adopted in *National Oilwell (UK) Ltd v Davy Offshore Ltd* [1993] 2 Lloyd's Rep 582) was sidestepped on the basis that an insurer would be acting inequitably in seeking to exercise an equitable right when it had agreed not to do so (*The Surf City* [1995] 2 Lloyd's Rep 242).

127 [1986] QB 211. Compare *Quirkco Investments Ltd v Aspray Transport Ltd* [2011] EWHC 3060 (Ch).

128 *Coupar Transport (London) Ltd v Smith's (Acton) Ltd* [1959] 1 Lloyd's Rep 369; *Deltamax Freight Service (HK) Ltd v Tung Tat Transportation Ltd* [2010] HKCFI 359. But contrast *Amoi Electronics Co Ltd v Kin Cheung Transportation (Hong Kong) Co Ltd* [2010] HKDC 31.

materials.[129] In such a case, if the contractor negligently damages the new structure or site materials, it has to be determined whether the risk of contractor negligence is transferred to the employer and subsumed into the insuring obligation. If it is, the insurers have no subrogation rights against the contractor and the loss lies with the insurers. A case in point is *Tyco Fire & Integrated Solutions (UK) Ltd v Rolls-Royce Motor Cars Ltd*,[130] in which the Court of Appeal construed the construction contract as one under which the employer was required to obtain first-party insurance in respect of existing structures against loss by specified perils. There was damage covered by the policy caused by the negligence of the contractor, which was paid by the insurers who then exercised subrogation rights against the contractor. The Court of Appeal held that the agreement did not imply that the employer would look only to the insurers to make good the loss, and that the agreement was no more than a promise by the employer that first-party insurance would be in place so that in the event of loss by a specified peril the employer would have sufficient funds to reinstate the works. No conferral of immunity was intended. This decision may be contrasted with rulings on earlier versions of the standard construction contracts under which it was the employer who was required to insure, and at its 'sole risk', loss from specified perils. That wording was held to mean that the risk of the contractor's negligence from those perils[131] was borne by the employer and, in particular, the employer's insurers.[132]

Each case of course turns on its own facts, but it is apparent that the underlying principle adopted by the courts is the presumed intention of the parties as to where the risk should lie and for whose benefit any insurance is ultimately to enure. The courts may not always reach a result which is unarguably correct, but the process is at least readily apparent.

7.5.4 Risk allocation by liability insurance

By contrast with allocating risks through first-party insurance, parties may instead seek to allocate risks by means of liability insurance. Here, the supplier of goods or services does not seek to pass liability back to the customer/client but accepts liability and insures against it.

Most forms of liability policy do not cover pure breach of contract claims. The general rule is that liability policies—often expressed as covering legal liability by way of damages—respond only to imposed rather than assumed liability. This is the case as a matter of law,[133] and there is often express wording excluding liability assumed by the assured under contract or agreement and which would not have attached in the absence of such contract or agreement. The leading authority is *Tesco Stores Ltd v*

[129] JCT Contracts are discussed in 7.6.

[130] [2008] EWCA Civ 286; [2008] Lloyd's Rep IR 617. Contrast *Surrey Heath Borough Council v Lovell Construction* (1990) 48 BLR 108; *National Trust v Haden Young* (1994) 72 BLR 1.

[131] But not other perils. If the loss was caused by a peril which is not within the insuring obligation or 'sole risk' provision, and the contractor was at fault, the contractor faced liability in the usual way.

[132] *James Archdale & Co Ltd v Comeservices* [1954] 1 WLR 159; *Scottish Special Housing Association v Wimpey Construction (UK) Ltd* [1986] 1 WLR 995; *Norwich City Council v Harvey* [1989] 1 WLR 828.

[133] *Furness Withy & Co v Duder* [1936] 2 KB 461; *Hall Brothers SS Co Ltd v Young* (1939) 63 LlLR 143.

Constable,[134] in which the claimant provided a contractual indemnity to a train operator for any disruption caused to the track from building works being carried out by the claimant. The reason why a contractual indemnity was required was that the operator had no possessory title, being a bare licensee, so that its loss from events causing damage to the land and track would be in the nature of pure economic loss. No tort claim was likely to succeed. The train operator duly called in the indemnity when a bridge collapsed and blocked the line, and a claim was made by the claimant against its public liability insurers. The Court of Appeal held, in line with general principle, that 'public liability' does not mean liability voluntarily assumed towards a particular party. A pure contract liability—a case of contractually assumed liability where no tort claim existed—was therefore excluded. The position is different if the assured's breach of contract also gives rise to a parallel claim in tort, such claims being within the wording of an ordinary public liability policy, but that was not the position in *Tesco Stores* because the operator had suffered pure economic loss in circumstances where it would not be recoverable in tort. Accordingly, if pure contract claims are to be insured, there will have to be specific agreement by the insurers on the point.[135] Tuckey LJ accepted that Tesco's rights against the insurer would have been different if the rail operator had also owned or leased the land and track; but also made the point that having expressly accepted a contractual liability, Tesco could (and should) have sought additional cover, at an additional premium, to cover the liability.[136]

There are isolated illustrations of cases in which a contracting party who is to perform services for the other requires that other to take out liability insurance for the benefit of the performer. The best example is that of directors' and officers' (D&O) insurance. Since 1989 it has been lawful for companies to take out insurance to cover the potential liabilities of directors both to the company and to third parties. D&O cover is now taken out by many companies on behalf of their directors, and it is commonplace for directors—particularly non-executive directors—to refuse to take up office unless the company has arranged liability insurance for them.

Mechanisms other than pure insurance arrangements are regularly put in place to protect one party against non-performance or defective performance by the other. Again, these mechanisms illustrate the continuity between contracting for insurance, and contracting in other ways to minimize risk.[137] Letters of credit issued by banks are universally used in overseas sales transactions. Their function is to give immediate payment to a supplier who has parted with possession of the goods by delivering them to a carrier for transmission to the purchaser. The purchaser is required to open a letter of credit against which the seller may make a call as soon as transport documents complying with the contractual requirements of the sale agreement are presented to the

[134] [2008] EWCA Civ 362; [2008] Lloyd's Rep IR 636.

[135] For example: *M/S Aswan Engineering Establishment Co v Iron Trades Mutual Insurance Co* [1989] 1 Lloyd's Rep 289; *Enterprise Oil Ltd v Strand Insurance Co Ltd* [2006] EWHC 58 (Comm), [2006] 1 Lloyd's Rep 500.

[136] *Tesco Stores*, n 134 at [31].

[137] These mechanisms are also discussed in Chapter 2.

bank.[138] The goods are generally at the risk of the purchaser as soon as they are shipped, and are either insured by the purchaser or, if the contract so provides, by the seller under a policy which is assigned to the buyer as soon as payment has been received.[139] If the goods are lost or damaged before arrival, the buyer's claim is against the insurers under the relevant policy. A letter of credit is not insurance as such, but it fulfils the same purpose as a liability policy in that it provides a fund from the customer against which the supplier has a claim.

Similarly, as far as a purchaser is concerned, the most common form of security for performance is the performance bond, in widespread use in particular in the construction industry.[140] A bond of this type may be issued by a bank or insurance company,[141] and is issued to the customer. It allows the customer to make a call for payment under the bond where a breach of contract on the part of the supplier is alleged. The supplier will subsequently be required to indemnify the bond issuer. Bonds are generally 'on demand',[142] which means that the bond issuer is required to make payment when a call is made, and the bond issuer is not required to demand evidence of an actual breach of contract on behalf of the supplier.[143] The real difficulty relating to the use of performance bonds is that a call may be made when there is no suggestion of any breach of contract by the supplier. In the earliest cases on performance bonds, it was established that such bonds are not guarantees but autonomous and entirely distinct from the construction or supply contract to which they relate, so that it is not open to the bank to refuse payment nor is it open to the supplier to seek an injunction against the bank to restrain payment. Thus in *Edward Owen Engineering v Barclays Bank International Ltd*[144] the English court refused to grant an injunction against payment even though there was a clear breach of contract not by the supplier but by the customer who had made the call. The point has been confirmed in a series of subsequent cases.[145] Accordingly, a call must be satisfied as long as it has been made in the right form alleging a breach of contract by the supplier,[146] the only recognized exceptions being clear evidence of fraud on the part

[138] The best analysis is in E McKendrick, *Goode on Commercial Law* (Harmondsworth: Penguin, 4th edn, 2010), ch 35.

[139] The CIF contract.

[140] McKendrick, n 138.

[141] A performance bond is not strictly an insurance contract as a matter of law, because the risk is ultimately passed back to the supplier rather than being borne by the bond issuer, but it is treated as a class of insurance business for which authorization is required under the FSMA 2000: Financial Services and Markets Act 2000 (Regulated Activities) Order 2001, SI 2001/544, sch 1, class 15.

[142] *Meritz Fire and Marine Insurance Co Ltd v Jan de Nul NV* [2011] EWCA Civ 827; [2011] 2 Lloyd's Rep 379.

[143] International performance bonds are now generally made on the terms of the ICC Uniform Rules on Demand Guarantees (URDG), first issued in 1978 and revised in 2010: URDG 758.

[144] [1978] QB 159.

[145] *R D Harbottle (Mercantile) Ltd v National Westminster Bank Ltd* [1978] QB 146; *Howe Richardson Scale Co Ltd v Polimex-Cekop* [1978] 1 Lloyd's Rep 161; *Uzinterimpex JSC v Standard Bank plc* [2008] EWCA Civ 819; [2008] 2 Lloyd's Rep 456; *Rainy Sky SA v Kookmin Bank* [2009] EWHC 2624 (Comm); [2010] 1 All ER (Comm) 823.

[146] *AES-3C Maritza East 1 EOOD v Credit Agricole Corporate and Investment Bank* [2011] EWHC 123 (TCC); [2011] All ER (D) 30 (Feb).

of the customer[147] or clear evidence that the bond is ineffective or has been terminated.[148] The risk of unfair calling is such that insurance is available against the risk. The availability of ECGD insurance cover for suppliers, against unfair calling was noted earlier.

7.5.5 Risk allocation by exclusion of liability[149]

By far the most obvious method of allocating responsibility for loss is by means of contract terms which delimit the responsibilities of the parties or which exclude liability in the event of breach. Very often exclusions of liability are coupled with the types of insuring obligations or expectations outlined earlier, though equally often they are discussed in complete isolation from considerations of insurance, with an adverse impact on the degree to which they are fully understood. Illustrative of the issues is the decision of the Supreme Court of Canada in *London Drugs Ltd v Kuehne & Nagel International Ltd*.[150] The claimant entered into a contract with the defendant for the custody of the claimant's goods and under which the defendant's liability was limited to $40. The claimant specifically declined the offer of insurance by the defendant, and it can therefore be presumed that the claimant had either obtained its own insurance (most likely, and identified in the judgments as being the case) or otherwise had agreed to bear the risk of loss through self-insurance. The property was damaged and a direct action was brought against the defendant's two employees allegedly responsible for the loss. It is straightforward to guess what was going on here. The claimant's insurers were unable to sue the defendant or its insurers by way of subrogation for more than $40, and so picked upon the employees, for whom the defendant was vicariously liable and against which liability the defendant was insured: by this sidestepping, the claimant's insurers would be able to avoid the $40 limitation. The majority of the Supreme Court held that the employees owed a duty of care, but that it was necessary to fashion an exception to the doctrine of privity of contract and to hold that the employees were entitled to the benefit of the limitation clause and thus their liability was limited to $40.[151] The attempt to sidestep the contractual arrangements was at the heart of the ruling. The dissenting judgment of La Forest J went further, rejecting the notion that the employees owed any duty of care at all, and we discuss this in relation to tort duties, in the following chapter. Here we would focus on the words of Iacobucci J, holding that the privity rules should be relaxed:

> Holding the employees liable in these circumstances could lead to serious injustice especially when one considers that the financial position of the affected employees

[147] *Enka Insaat ve Sanayi AS v Banca Popolare Dell'alto Adige Spa* [2009] EWHC 2410 (Comm); [2009] All ER (D) 61 (Oct), which makes it clear that it is not enough for the supplier to show that he has a real prospect of success in establishing fraud.

[148] *British Arab Commercial Bank plc v Bank of Communications* [2011] EWHC 281 (Comm); [2011] 1 Lloyd's Rep 664; *Simon Carves Ltd v Ensus Ltd* [2011] EWHC 657 (TCC); [2011] All ER (D) 260 (Mar).

[149] See the English and Scottish Law Commissions, *Unfair Terms in Contracts*, Cm 6464, February 2005 and the appended Draft Bill.

[150] [1992] 3 SCR 299. This case is discussed further in Chapter 8.

[151] A remarkable leap, not the least because the clause made no mention of employees.

> could vary [considerably] such that, for example, more well off employees would be sued and left to look for contribution from their less well off colleagues. Such a result also creates uncertainty and requires excessive expenditures on insurance in that it defeats the allocations of risk specifically made by the contracting parties and the reasonable expectations of everyone involved, including the employees.[152]

The first sentence is an appeal to the emotions, because it is hardly credible that a subrogation action would have been brought against manual labourers unprotected by insurance. But the second sentence gets to the heart of the matter: if limitation clauses can be so easily sidestepped, then both sides will have to insure come what may, increasing the costs of both. In Chapter 8, we take the analysis further, and address the extent to which duties of care are rightly affected by insurance arrangements.

Exclusion clauses were traditionally read at face value by the English courts, but, with the growth of consumerism from the 1940s onwards and an increasing number of cases coming before the courts involving, by any standards, blatantly unfair attempts by suppliers to evade their responsibilities under the Sale of Goods legislation or otherwise in respect of poor service, the courts developed a series of devices to restrict the use of such clauses. These included rulings that such clauses had not been validly incorporated into the contract;[153] or were to be construed narrowly so as not to extend to negligence unless clearly expressed to do so;[154] or that the performance by the supplier was so flawed that it amounted to something quite different to what the exclusion clause had contemplated.[155] The numerous decided cases, many by or under the influence of Lord Denning, spoke of unfairness rather than risk allocation, and that tendency has been maintained in legislative developments which have more or less superseded the common law in business to consumer agreements. The Unfair Contract Terms Act 1977 (the 1977 Act) controls exclusion clauses in most standard-form contracts and consumer sales;[156] the Unfair Terms in Consumer Contracts Regulations 1999 (the 1999 Regulations) [157] render unenforceable unfair contract terms in consumer agreements;[158] and the Consumer Protection from Unfair Trading Regulations 2008[159] coupled with the Business Protection from Misleading Marketing Regulations

[152] [1992] 3 SCR 299 at 446.

[153] *Olley v Marlborough Court Ltd* [1949] 1 KB 532; *Thornton v Shoe Lane Parking Ltd* [1971] 2 QB 163. The more unusual and extreme the term, the more that has to be done to bring it to the other's attention: *Interfoto Picture Library Ltd v Stiletto Visual Programmes Ltd* [1989] QB 433.

[154] *Canada Steamship v R* [1952] AC 192; [1952] 1 Lloyd's Rep 1; *Hollier v Rambler Motors (AMC) Ltd* [1972] 2 QB 1; *E E Caledonia Ltd v Orbit Valve Co plc* [1994] 1 WLR 1515; *HIH Casualty and General Insurance Ltd v Chase Manhattan Bank* [2003] UKHL 6; [2003] 2 Lloyd's Rep 61.

[155] So-called 'fundamental breach', as applied in *Harbutt's 'Plasticine' Ltd v Wayne Pump & Tank Co Ltd* [1970] 1 QB 447; [1970] 2 WLR 198, a doctrine which was finally put out of its misery by the House of Lords in *Photo Production Ltd v Securicor Transport Ltd* [1980] AC 827 after an earlier unsuccessful attempt in *Suisse Atlantique Société d'Armenement Maritime SA v NC Rotterdamsche Kolen Centrale* [1967] 1 AC 361.

[156] Insurance being a notable exception.

[157] SI 1999/2083, implementing the EU's Unfair Terms in Consumer Contracts Directive, EC Directive 1999/13/EC.

[158] These two measures sit uncomfortably together and overlap in significant respects. The Law Commission has recommended a unified scheme: *Unfair Terms in Contracts*, Law Comm No 292, February 2005, Cm 6464, and modified its views on points of detail in advice presented to the Department of Business, Innovation and Skills in March 2013.

[159] SI 2008/1277.

2008[160] (each implementing EU law)[161] introduce criminal sanctions against misleading contract terms and unfair practices.

The cases on exclusion clauses and the provisions of the subsequent legislative measures are examined fully in standard works on contract, though the role of insurance remains largely unexplored. Here, we briefly note the entirely different approaches that are adopted in consumer and commercial cases, and we particularly flag the neglected insurance issues.

Where the contract involves a consumer, the 1999 Regulations impose a fairness test on all terms other than those which have not been individually negotiated or which define the subject matter or the price paid, and even those may be regulated by a statutory *contra proferentem* rule if not expressed clearly. In addition, the 1977 Act, ss 6–7, prevents any exclusion of the rights of a purchaser of goods or services.

In a business to business transaction, the law is quite different. The 1999 Regulations have no application, and the 1977 Act imposes a reasonableness test only where one party is seeking to rely upon his written standard terms of business to render performance substantially different from what was reasonably expected (the 1977 Act s 3), where one party is purporting to exclude liability for misrepresentation (Misrepresentation Act 1967, s 3, as amended by the 1977 Act) or when a supplier purports to exclude his statutory obligations in respect of the sale or supply of goods (the 1977 Act, ss 6–7). The cases on business to business exclusion clauses expressly or impliedly recognize the right of commercial parties to allocate risks as they think fit.[162] Many of them also recognize that allocation is generally based upon, or incorporates, insurance arrangements. The courts' approach may be illustrated by reference to three sets of cases.

First, the scope of the 1977 Act has been restricted. The courts have drawn a distinction between clauses which simply define a contracting party's obligations and those which purport to exclude liability, holding that the former are outside the 1977 Act.[163] A similar distinction has been made between clauses excluding liability for misrepresentation and clauses which specify that no misrepresentation has actually been made.[164] Further, although there is an absolute rule in the 1977 Act, s 2(1), that a person may not by contract term or notice exclude liability for death or personal injury, it has been held that a clause which requires the employer to indemnify the contractor against liability for injury suffered by an employee of the contractor working under the employer's control is not within s 2(1) at all, as it merely allocates liability for the

[160] SI 2008/1276.

[161] European Parliament and Council Directive 2005/29/EC on unfair commercial practices.

[162] Discussed by J Adams and R Brownsword, 'The Unfair Contract Terms Act: A Decade of Discretion' (1988) 104 LQR 94, particularly emphasizing the dangers of striking down exclusion clauses in business to business contracts without due regard to the commercial context (at 118). The authors mention the dangers of decisions made on the basis of 'possibly inaccurate information about the insurance background' (at 118). We suggest here that the insurance position is an inherent aspect of the commercial context.

[163] *Titan Steel Wheels Ltd v Royal Bank of Scotland plc* [2010] EWHC 211 (Comm); [2010] 2 Lloyd's Rep 92.

[164] *Raiffeisen Zentralbank Osterreich AG v Royal Bank of Scotland plc* [2010] EWHC 1392 (Comm); [2011] 1 Lloyd's Rep 123. But contrast 'entire agreement' clauses, which have been construed as not preventing one party asserting that the other had made a false statement: *Axa Sun Life Services plc v Campbell Martin Ltd* [2011] EWCA Civ 133; [2011] 2 Lloyd's Rep 1.

employee's claim between the parties and leaves unaffected the employee's right to make a claim.[165]

Second, in those cases which remain governed by the common law, and a substantial proportion of business to business contracts are in this category—because they are not made on standard terms or because the standard terms are those of a trade association or other independent body—the judicial approach is exemplified by the analysis of Lord Wilberforce in *Photo Production Ltd v Securicor Transport Ltd*.[166] His Lordship commented that:

> in commercial matters generally, when the parties are not of unequal bargaining power, and when risks are normally borne by insurance, not only is the case for judicial intervention undemonstrated, but there is everything to be said, and this seems to have been Parliament's intention, for leaving the parties free to apportion the risks as they think fit and for respecting their decisions.

The courts now recognize that clauses which merely restrict the obligations of one of the parties have to be construed in the context of the allocation of risks under the contract, the price paid, and also the insurance arrangements contemplated by the parties.[167]

Third, where the 1977 Act does apply, the court has to apply statutory reasonableness guidelines in respect of the sale and supply cases (s 11(2) and sch 2), and, although there are no such guidelines in respect of standard-term exclusion clauses, the judicial tendency is to apply them by analogy. There is nothing in the guidelines about risk allocation or insurance as such.[168] They refer only to matters such as comparative bargaining strength and the availability of better terms elsewhere in the market. And yet, risk allocation—and in particular insurance—features in judicial decisions under the 1977 Act. Further, s 11(4) specifically provides that if an exclusion clause limits a party's liability to a specific sum, the court is required in assessing reasonableness to take into account the extent to which that party could have insured itself against liability. Insurance thus features at two levels: in general terms, in assessing reasonableness in the courts; and specifically, where s 11(4) is applicable.[169] It is clear from the cases that if the clause is considered to form part of a carefully constructed agreement under which risks are allocated according to the commercial view taken by the parties and their respective insurance arrangements, then, unless there is significant imbalance in the parties' bargaining position or one party is seeking to rely upon his own default, there is no real basis for judicial intervention under the 1977 Act.[170] This is particularly

[165] *Thompson v Lohan (Plant Hire) Ltd* [1987] 1 WLR 649.

[166] [1980] AC 827.

[167] *Ailsa Craig Fishing Co Ltd v Malvern Fishing Co Ltd* [1983] 1 WLR 964; *E E Caledonia Ltd v Orbit Valve Co plc* [1994] 1 WLR 1515.

[168] But compare the reasonableness criteria set out in the Law Commissions' Draft Bill 2005 (n 149), which include 'the possibility and probability of insurance'.

[169] As opposed to excluding all liability: *Watford Electronics Ltd v Sanderson CFL Ltd* [2001] EWCA Civ 317; [2001] 1 All ER (Comm) 696.

[170] *R W Green Ltd v Cade Brothers Farms* [1978] 1 Lloyd's Rep 602; *Watford Electronics Ltd v Sanderson CFL Ltd* [2001] EWCA Civ 317; [2001] 1 All ER (Comm) 696; *Macquarie International Investments Ltd v Glencore (UK) Ltd* [2008] EWHC 1716 (Comm); [2008] All ER (D) 276 (Jul). The most recent case is *FG Wilson Engineering Ltd v John Holt & Co (Liverpool) Ltd* [2012] EWHC 2477 (Comm); [2012] 2 Lloyd's

the case if it is understood that the customer or client is able to obtain first-party cover[171] or has been advised to procure it,[172] or where it is not possible for the supplier to take out appropriate liability insurance because it has no information about how the products supplied are going to be used.[173] However, if there is significant imbalance, the supplier is seeking to rely upon his own default[174] and it is clear that the supplier was required to insure his own liability,[175] had done so,[176] or was able to do so,[177] then there is plenty of potential for a finding of unreasonableness.

The leading authority is *George Mitchell (Chesterhall) Ltd v Finney Lock Seeds Ltd*,[178] in which the House of Lords struck down a clause limiting the liability of a supplier of seeds to the purchase price in the event that they proved to be defective. Two key considerations were that the supplier could have insured against such risks without significantly increasing their price,[179] and that the supplier was seeking to escape liability for its own negligence. This approach was followed in *St Albans City and District Council v International Computers Ltd*,[180] Scott Baker J holding that a clause limiting the liability of a software supplier to £100,000 was unreasonable because the supplier was in a powerful negotiating position and was protected by liability insurance. This approach emphasizes the point made by this chapter, that contractual risk allocation and insurance obligations or expectations are closely linked in the commercial world, and in some contexts—such as construction contracts—they are inseparable.

Even though liability is stated to be excluded by a contract term, that does not necessarily mean that a contracting party will not take out liability insurance. This may happen either because of misunderstanding or because of a fear that the 1977 Act may lead a court to strike the clause down. There may be liability insurance even where the immunity is not subject to the discretion of the court. For example, an arbitrator presiding over an arbitration with its seat in England or Wales has statutory immunity from suit in proceedings brought by either party to the arbitration,[181] unless he has acted in bad faith,[182] for much the same reasons that judges have immunity from suit: there is fear of restraint on decision-making; and any claim would require the entire

Rep 479, where a no-set-off clause was held to be valid under the 1977 Act in part because, without such a clause, the supplier's trade credit insurance would not have attached.

[171] *Monarch Airlines Ltd v London Luton Airport Ltd* [1998] 1 Lloyd's Rep 403; *Frans Maas (UK) Ltd v Samsung Electronics (UK) Ltd* [2004] EWHC 1502 (Comm); [2004] 2 Lloyd's Rep 251.

[172] *Regus (UK) Ltd v Epcot Solutions Ltd* [2008] EWCA Civ 361; [2009] 1 All ER (Comm) 586.

[173] *Sterling Hydraulics Ltd v Dichtomatik Ltd* [2006] EWHC 2004 (QB); [2007] 1 Lloyd's Rep 8.

[174] *Smith v Eric S Bush* [1990] 1 AC 831; [1989] 2 WLR 790; *Britvic Soft Drinks v Messer UK Ltd* [2002] EWCA Civ 548; [2002] 2 All ER (Comm) 321; *Bacardi-Martini Beverages Ltd v Thomas Hardy Packaging* [2002] EWCA Civ 549; [2002] 2 All ER (Comm) 335.

[175] *Overseas Medical Supplies Ltd v Orient Transport Services Ltd* [1999] 2 Lloyd's Rep 273.

[176] *St Albans City and District Council v International Computers Ltd* [1995] FSR 686.

[177] *George Mitchell (Chesterhall) Ltd v Finney Lock Seeds Ltd* [1983] 2 AC 803; [1983] 3 WLR 163; *Balmoral Group Ltd v Borealis (UK) Ltd* [2006] 2 Lloyd's Rep 629.

[178] [1983] 2 AC 803.

[179] It is perfectly possible that the supplier was indeed insured and that the defence was run by its product liability insurers.

[180] [1995] FSR 686, varied on appeal on the issue of damages, [1996] 4 All ER 481.

[181] Arbitration Act 1996, s 27.

[182] Which is uninsurable anyway.

arbitration to be reheard. However, arbitrators regularly take out liability insurance and there are underwriters who advertise it. It would seem from the many articles written in response to *Jones v Kaney*, particularly by experts themselves, that many professional experts possessed liability insurance before the decision even though it was (thought to be) clear that no cause of action lay against them. As noted earlier, there were always some risks, including that of incurring defence costs should an action be brought misguidedly and that of disciplinary proceedings before the relevant professional body of which the expert was a member. The use of exclusion clauses is not foolproof, and it is likely that experts will seek insurance as a fallback.

7.5.6 Concluding thoughts

We have discussed in the above paragraphs the various ways in which the parties to a contract can allocate the risk of loss or third-party liability. That allocation is inevitably underpinned by insurance. Insurance may not be explicit in the arrangements but it plays a central part: retention or assumption of first-party loss by a customer or client will be undertaken without serious demur only where the loss is one which can be covered by affordable insurance or at least borne without major financial impact. Retention or assumption of liability—often characterized by the absence of a contractual exclusion of liability—operates in the same way. However, whenever there is an assumption or allocation of liability, the customer or client may demand that the other take out liability insurance to counter the risk of the supplier's insolvency. To take an obvious example, it will not be enough for occupier A, who faces potential liability to a neighbour as a result of the activities of contractor B, to require B to indemnify A against any third-party claim: if B becomes insolvent and has no insurance, the loss will lie with A. Equally, a public authority which retains a firm of solicitors will insist upon scrutinizing the solicitors' public liability insurance to make sure that it is adequate to cover any claims which may be made against the authority in respect of which it has the right to seek indemnity. All of the situations discussed in the preceding paragraphs are based upon allocation choices by the parties, and all of them depend upon express or implicit insurance assumptions. To disregard those assumptions in the construction of the parties' rights and liabilities in favour of a paramount legal doctrine carries the risk of rewriting and distorting the bargain. To so act by way of extension from theories of non-relational tort liability may be thought simply dogmatic.

7.6 Construction Contracts: a Case Study

At various points in the above analysis we have referred to problems arising under construction contracts. Nowhere are the risks of liability, and insurance for them, more intricately allocated than in the world of building and construction. This partly reflects the complexity of the contractual structures in place, but it also illustrates some particular implications of that complexity in light of the purposive nature of the structures as a whole. Hugh Collins has described construction contracts as exemplifying a particular form of complex multilateral association resembling a 'hub and spokes' where the 'spokes' consist of chains of bilateral contract.[183] English law, as Collins points out, is clear that it treats such associations as taking the form of a series of contracts, and not as analogous to business organizations in their own right, even if the contracts are coordinated to serve a common purpose. He argues however that a number of features of the legal response to such contracts illustrates that certain pressures are felt in this respect; and signs may be found that the related nature of the contracts is relevant to allocation of risk and intermittently recognized when dealing in particular with insurance issues.

A particular example used by Collins is *Norwich City Council v Harvey*,[184] one of many cases illustrating the related nature of tort and contract liabilities in respect of risk allocation.[185] Here, it was thought not to be fair, just, and reasonable for a duty of care to be imposed upon a subcontractor towards the Council, where the liability of the head contractor to the Council was excluded by a contractual term. Although the subcontractor was not a party to the contract containing the exclusion, there had been negotiations between all parties, and (in particular) the Council had assumed the responsibility to insure. It is a fair bet that the parties had acted accordingly, and that if there was insurance in place then it was held by the Council, and if that was the case then the action was one brought by the Council's insurers by way of subrogation in an attempt to shift their loss on to a party who had been led to believe that it was unnecessary to insure against liability. But for the agreement, the subcontractor would almost certainly have insured and, through the price charged to the contractor, passed the cost of that insurance back to the Council. If the parties had decided for themselves that the Council was best placed to secure the relevant insurance, or to self-insure, it makes little sense for a court to overturn that finding and to impose liability on the subcontractor with the implication that it should have carried insurance. The analysis underlines that the test for a duty of care in negligence cases, when it operates in a contractual context, allows consideration of risk-allocation questions. And such questions are inextricably linked to insurance, as our analysis has explained. We continue this discussion in Chapter 8.

So far as the detailed insurance position is concerned, there are standard forms for the various forms of contract used in the UK market, published by the JCT. These were revised most recently in 2011 and came into force in April 2012. The terms discussed in what follows are drawn from clauses 5–6 of the Prime Cost Building Contract 2011, although similar provisions are found in other standard forms.[186] The 2011 wordings to some extent deal with the problems of risk allocation and insurance identified earlier.

[183] H Collins, 'Introduction', in G Teubner, *Networks as Connected Contracts* (Oxford: Hart Publishing, 2011), 10. Note also H Collins, 'Ascription of Legal Responsibility to Groups in Complex Patterns of Economic Integration' (1990) 53 MLR 731, dealing primarily with the problem of imposing responsibility towards third parties on complex associations.

[184] [1989] 1 WLR 828.

[185] Other cases discussed are *Lister v Romford Ice* (Chapter 5); and *Jones v Kaney* and *London Drugs* (this chapter, nn 94 and 150 respectively).

[186] Including: Major Works Construction Contract; Management Building Contract; Intermediate Building Contract; Minor Works Building Contract; Measured Term Contract; and Design and Build Contract. A full list of contracts can be found on the JCT website.

The JCT Contract deals separately with liability for injury to persons and damage to property, and with damage to the building works themselves as well as existing works and site materials. As far as injury to persons is concerned the contractor is liable for, and must indemnify the employer against, claims for death or personal injury, the indemnity being removed only where the liability is incurred due to the act or neglect of the employer (or persons for whom the employer is responsible). Thus, the risk of liability for death or personal injury is borne by the contractor unless the employer is at fault. As regards property damage, the contractor's liability is confined to the case in which the contractor is personally or vicariously liable by reason of negligence, breach of statutory duty, omission, or default, so that the risk of loss other than by reason of the contract's default is borne by the employer. To make certain that the contractor is good for his indemnity, or that he is able to satisfy third-party claims so that the employer does not have to meet them, the contractor is required to insure against the risks imposed upon him by these provisions. The contractor may be required to take the policy out in the joint names of the contractor and the employer, so that if the third party chooses to sue the employer alone, or the employer and contractor jointly, there is insurance in place.

Liability to third parties as the result of employer negligence is retained by the employer, and is not required to be covered by the policy taken out by the contractor. For that reason, the JCT Contract provides that the employer can instruct the contractor to take out a joint names policy which covers the employer's own liability, but only in respect of injury or damage to property caused by collapse, subsidence, heave, vibration, weakening or removal of support, or lowering of groundwater arising out of or in the course of carrying out the works. The costs of that insurance are to be borne by the employer. There is no provision for the employer to insure against liability for his own negligence, and there is no obligation on the employer—just an option—to require the contractor to insure the employer's liability for these special losses. The insuring obligation does not in any event extend to loss attributable to errors or omissions in the designing of the works, loss which could reasonably be foreseen to be inevitable, and pure contract claims.

Subcontractors are entitled to be named as co-assureds or to benefit from a subrogation waiver in all cases, up to the date of completion, but only in respect of the specified perils.

7.6.1 The use of composite insurance

The general principle underlying the JCT policies is that they are 'joint names' policies as between the employer and the contractor, including subcontractors for existing works and site materials. The rights of the parties under a composite policy are entirely separate and—with some (as yet not fully defined) exceptions—the acts or defaults of one co-assured do not prejudice the rights of others. The wording of the policies contains a definition of joint names, as meaning 'a policy of insurance which includes the employer and the contractor as composite[187] insured and under which the insurers

[187] The terminology 'joint names' here therefore does not mean joint insurance, it means composite insurance taken out in two (or more) names.

have no right of recourse against any person so named as an insured'. The significant point is that this definition makes it clear that, where there is a joint names policy, the insurers have no subrogation claim against an insured party who is responsible for the loss. The absence of subrogation action is designed to ensure that if the risk is to be borne by the party carrying insurance, the insurers cannot, having indemnified that party, undermine the arrangement by bringing proceedings against the other (who is intended under the arrangements to be uninsured). Insurance arrangements, here, are collaboratively designed by the contracting parties to take the risk outside the contract, with the cost of this transfer being allocated to the parties.

The use of composite insurance to provide subrogation immunity in construction cases was to some extent facilitated by a series of court decisions on earlier versions of the JCT Clauses. The courts, by a tortuous process of reasoning, reached the conclusion that co-insurance status may give each co-assured immunity from suit by way of subrogation.[188] We will look at this in terms of two ways of categorizing co-insurance clauses.

7.6.2 Co-insurance clauses as loss-allocation provisions

The starting point is whether a co-insurance clause in a construction contract amounts to a contractual waiver of suit by the employer, so that the employer is thereby undertaking to look only to the insurers and not to the co-assured contractor. If the clause has that effect, there is no need to go any further: the insurers can have no better rights than the employer, and the employer necessarily has no rights. The message from the cases is that a co-insurance clause taken alone is not conclusive, and that it is necessary to examine the contract as a whole. The leading authority is the decision of the House of Lords in *Co-operative Retail Services v Taylor Young Partnership Ltd.*[189] In this case the employer, CRS, appointed a main contractor, Wimpey, and the main contractor in turn appointed a subcontractor, Hall. In accordance with the contractual arrangements, Wimpey took out a joint names co-insurance policy naming itself, CRS, and Hall as co-assureds. CRS subsequently appointed two other subcontractors, who were outside these insurance arrangements, and those two subcontractors were found to be liable for fire damage to the works. The joint names insurers provided indemnification to CRS, and exercised subrogation rights against the two subcontractors. The subcontractors sought contribution from Wimpey and Hall on the basis that they were liable for the 'same damage' under the Civil Liability (Contribution) Act 1978. Their Lordships were firmly of the view that Wimpey and Hall were, under the arrangements with CRS, not liable for any damage to CRS and that the joint names insurance clause held them harmless from any claim. Accordingly, the contribution action could not succeed. This decision was applied in *Scottish and Newcastle Plc v GD Construction (St Albans) Ltd*,[190] in which a joint names clause was held to exclude the liability of the

[188] The significance of this is explained in Chapter 5, where we discuss the way that subrogation is capable of undermining party risk allocations, if uncontrolled.

[189] [2002] UKHL 17; [2002] 1 WLR 1419.

[190] [2003] EWCA Civ 16; [2003] Lloyd's Rep IR 809. Another similar case is: *Ossory Road (Skelmersdale) Ltd v Balfour Beatty Building Ltd* [1993] CILL 882 and contrast *John F Hunt Demolition Ltd v ASME Engineering Ltd* [2007] EWHC 1507 (TCC); [2008] 1 All ER 180 (Chapter 8).

contractor to the employer for negligence, thereby requiring the employer to look to the insurers and depriving the insurers of subrogation rights[191] against the contractor. In these cases the construction contracts were construed as casting the risk of the contractor's negligence on the employer, there being nothing in the contracts to contradict that analysis. By contrast, where the contract provides that the employer will procure joint names insurance, and the contract also provides that the contractor is to indemnify the employer for losses caused by the contractor's negligence, it is apparent that the joint names insurance clause does not remove a claim by the employer (ie, a subrogated claim by the insurers) in the event of the contractor's negligence.[192] One important undecided issue is whether a co-insurance clause which is construed requiring the employer to look to the insurers for its loss holds good where the insurers have a defence under the policy so that there is no recovery. In such a situation:

> It may be the true construction that a provision for insurance is to be taken as satisfying or curtailing a contractual obligation, or it may be the true construction that a contractual obligation is to be backed by insurance with the result that the contractual obligation stands or is enforceable even if for some reason the insurance fails or proves to be inadequate.[193]

7.6.3 The effects of a co-insurance policy

The inquiry thus comes to an end if the joint names insurance clause operates as a negligence waiver. However, if the clause does not so operate, that does not necessarily mean that the contractor is subject to a subrogation action. The fact remains that he is co-assured under the policy, and his status as co-assured may operate to give him immunity. Such immunity depends upon the operation of the policy.

An assured who negligently damages or destroys the insured subject matter is not by that reason alone precluded from recovering under the policy. Negligence is not a defence to a claim open to the insurers, and even if they expressly stipulate by a policy condition that the assured must exercise reasonable care, that has been taken to mean—for both liability and first-party policies—no more than that the assured must avoid recklessness.[194] So, if the assured is able to recover because he can show loss from an insured peril, for example fire, then he is able to recover even though the fire was his fault: insurers do not have the right, having paid, to recoup their payment because the assured negligently caused his own loss.

If, therefore, the negligent contractor is a co-assured, what effect does that status have on a potential subrogation claim by insurers who have indemnified the employer? A co-insurance policy is one which insures the parties' property interests in the subject

[191] In fact the employer had failed to take out the requisite insurance, but it was common ground that this did not affect the analysis.

[192] *National Trust v Haden Young* (1974) 72 BLR 1; *Surrey Heath Borough Council v Lovell Construction Ltd* (1990) 48 BLR 108; *Dorset County Council v Southern Felt Roofing Co Ltd* (1990) 48 BLR 96; *London Borough of Barking & Dagenham v Stamford Asphalt Co Ltd* (1997) 82 BLR 25.

[193] *Surrey Heath Borough Council v Lovell Construction Ltd* (1990) 48 BLR 108, per Dillon LJ at 121.

[194] *Fraser v Furman* [1967] 1 WLR 898; *Sofi v Prudential Assurance Co Ltd* [1993] 2 Lloyd's Rep 559.

matter. If, therefore, there is damage to the subject matter, any insured person is entitled to recover to the extent of his interest in the subject matter, irrespective of his negligence. On this analysis it would be inconsistent with the contractor's status as co-assured if insurers could, having paid the employer, then exercise subrogation rights against the contractor who was himself insured against that very loss. The contractor must, therefore, be immune from suit. Early attempts to explain the immunity were based on circuity, i.e. the notion that insurers cannot exercise subrogation rights against a person entitled to recover under the policy.[195] Later cases moved away from this reasoning and focused instead on the fact that an assertion of subrogation rights by insurers would be to subject the contractor to the very loss that co-insurance was intended to cover, and that to avoid that possibility there was to be implied into co-insurance policies a subrogation waiver clause to the effect that the insurers would not exercise subrogation rights.[196] The courts in such cases have placed significant emphasis on the parties' allocation of risk, and have given effect to the parties' intention, through the contract, to remove risk to the insurer through payment of the relevant premium by one of the parties. This approach has not been universally accepted, and there are important and persuasive dicta to the effect that a co-insurance policy does not give subrogation immunity as such, and that the sole question is whether the contract between the employer and the contractor confers such immunity so that there are no rights to which a subrogation claim can attach.[197] On this reasoning, the sole purpose of a co-insurance clause is to allocate responsibilities between the employer and contractor, and the fact that the contractor is co-assured is of no benefit to him if he otherwise bears the risk of negligence. Once again, it is the location of the risk of negligence which takes priority, not the location of blame. The point is of less significance than was the case before the revision of the JCT Terms initially in 2005, as maintained in 2011. The requirement for a joint names policy is now that 'the insurers have no right of recourse against any person so named as an insured' whether or not the construction contract itself is to be construed as casting the risk of the contractor's negligence on the employer. It may be thought that this definition also operates to make it clear that the employer is, by implication, agreeing to hold the contractor harmless.[198]

[195] *The Yasin* [1979] 2 Lloyd's Rep 45; and *Petrofina (UK) Ltd v Magnaload Ltd* [1984] QB 127; [1983] 3 WLR 805, in which Lloyd J explored different versions of the circuity theory.

[196] *National Oilwell (UK) Ltd v Davy Offshore Ltd* [1993] 2 Lloyd's Rep 582; *Stone Vickers Ltd v Appledore Ferguson Shipbuilders Ltd* [1991] 2 Lloyd's Rep 288, reversed on appeal on other grounds, [1992] 2 Lloyd's Rep 578.

[197] In particular the judgment of Lord Hope in *Co-operative Retail Services v Taylor Young Partnership Ltd* [2002] UKHL 17; [2002] 1 WLR 1419 and the judgment of Rix LJ in *Tyco Fire & Integrated Solutions (UK) Ltd v Rolls-Royce Motor Cars Ltd* [2008] EWCA Civ 286; [2008] Lloyd's Rep IR 617. Contrast *Hopewell Project Management Ltd v Ewbank Preece Ltd* [1998] 1 Lloyd's Rep 448.

[198] If that is wrong, complex issues arise, because there is a risk that although the joint names clause precludes a subrogation action by the insurers using the name of the employer, it would not prevent an action by the employer in his own name in the event of negligence by the contractor. That gives rise to the risk that the employer is paid twice, once by the insurers and once by the contractors. The risk disappears if the claim is made against the contractor first, because any sums received from him go to diminish the employer's loss and thus reduce any insurance claim to that extent. However, if the claim is made against the insurers first, it is trite law that the insurance recovery is to be disregarded in assessing damages, leading to the situation that the employer has accumulated his recoveries. In that situation the insurers would

7.6.4 Limits on co-insurance protection

The subrogation immunity conferred by the co-insurance policy is available only if the contractor is covered for the loss caused. That depends upon the scope of his insurable interest. As discussed in Chapter 3, although it is now lawful for a person who does not possess insurable interest to insure property,[199] he cannot make a claim under the policy unless he can show that he has suffered loss. That flows from the indemnity nature of insurance contracts. If, therefore, an employer hires a contractor to carry out services on a small part of the works, and by his negligence the contractor damages the entirety of the works, he can only claim to be a co-assured for that part of the works in which he has insurable interest. Lloyd J addressed that problem in the root decision on the matter, *Petrofina v Magnaload*.[200] It was there decided that each of the various contractors or subcontractors working on site possessed a 'pervasive' insurable interest in the entire works. This is a fiction, and the courts have been able to reach that conclusion by asserting that a contractor who is responsible for only a small part of the site will nevertheless suffer loss if there is damage to other parts of the site, because there is a risk that building work has to stop and, accordingly, the contractor runs the risk of not being able to carry out future work for which he can be paid: in a different context the majority of the Court of Appeal adopted this analysis in *Feasey v Sun Life Assurance Co of Canada*.[201] This provides evidence that the interconnected and purposive qualities of the contracts in construction cases have some influence in the courts. The shared interests of the contractors help here to justify, as a matter of legal principle, externalization of the risks through insurance rather than allowing the costs to be reallocated within the contract.

The insurable interest problem has in this way been resolved. But that does not mean that the contractor is protected in all situations, and once again English law is drawn back to the full force of its 'series of contracts' analysis. The contractor has to show that he is insured against the loss which has occurred. Subrogation is possible where the contractor is outside the range of persons protected by the policy;[202] the policy does not cover the contractor for the particular form of loss which has occurred;[203] the interest

probably be entitled to recoup their payment from the employer, because the employer will arguably have been unjustly enriched, and it is far from obvious that such recoupment can be described as 'subrogation' prohibited by the policy. While this uncertainty remains, the only sensible option for the contractor is to obtain separate liability insurance to cover the possibilities that the employer may seek to sue him despite having all risks cover, or that the all-risks insurers may choose to do so in circumstances where there is no cover for the contractor under the all-risks policy.

199 Unless the policy is governed by the Marine Insurance Act 1906.

200 [1984] QB 127; [1983] 3 WLR 805. Insurable interest is also discussed in 3.3.

201 [2003] EWCA Civ 885; [2003] Lloyd's Rep IR 637. The policy was a property policy and not a liability policy. Here, although the contractor may face liability if he damages the insured subject matter, he is not insuring against that liability. He is insuring against property damage, hence the need for a search for some interest he may possess in the property itself.

202 *Appledore Ferguson Shipbuilders Ltd v Stone Vickers Ltd* [1992] 2 Lloyd's Rep 578. Contrast *BP Exploration Operating Co Ltd v Kvaerner Oilfield Products Ltd* [2004] EWHC 999 (Comm); [2005] 1 Lloyd's Rep 307.

203 *National Oilwell (UK) Ltd v Davy Offshore Ltd* [1993] 2 Lloyd's Rep 582.

of the subcontractor in the works has come to an end;[204] the contractor has deliberately caused loss to the insured subject matter, thereby taking himself outside the terms of the cover;[205] or the contractor is in breach of policy terms which render him uninsured.[206] Subrogation, evidently, poses a vital challenge to the capacity to allocate risks.

7.7 Conclusions

In the course of this chapter, we have outlined the central role of insurance arrangements in commercial contracting. We have underlined that commercial parties use contractual terms as a means of allocating risk, including the risk of insolvency and of the parties' own default. This reflects the element of futurity, and thus of uncertainty and risk, in commercial contracts. It is not surprising that courts addressing disputes begin their analysis with the parties' intentions in respect of risk allocation. Such intentions provide an essential starting point if parties are to order contractual risk. Most importantly, we have shown that risk allocation and risk pricing do not proceed in an insurance-free vacuum. The contractual structure is inherently extended through the addition of one or more insurance contracts and attendant legal regulatory and remedial issues. Insurance, as we pointed out in Chapter 2, is inherent in party relationships, and not foreign to private law.

Though contracting for insurance is just one mechanism of risk management, it is widely used in the context of commercial activity. Contracting parties often collaborate to set the terms of their contracts, including linked contracts in multilateral cases, in order to avoid replication of insurance costs or, more importantly, in order to ensure that the risk of loss is successfully transferred outside the contract. At times this is in tension with the equitable principle of subrogation within the insurance contract itself; and is achieved through the mechanism of adjusting the insured party's rights of recourse. In sum, the phenomenon of risk allocation, and thus the core of much contract law, is less securely understood by ignoring insurance and what may often be the parties' mutual objective of successfully locating insurance costs and insured risks. Importantly for our discussion in the following chapter, the risk of negligence by either party (including of course its employees) is itself one of the risks which are routinely allocated through contractual terms, including contractual obligations to insure.

[204] *Deepak Fertilisers & Petrochemical Corporation v Davy McKee (London) Ltd* [1999] 1 Lloyd's Rep 387; *TWF Printers Ltd v Interserve Project Services Ltd* [2006] EWCA Civ 875.

[205] *State of Netherlands v Youell* [1997] 2 Lloyd's Rep 440.

[206] *Matalan Discount Club (Cash & Carry) Ltd v Tokenspire Properties (North Western) Ltd* 2001, unreported; *Tate Gallery (Trustees) v Duffy Construction Ltd* [2007] EWHC 361 (TCC); [2007] Lloyd's Rep IR 758.

8

Allocation of Risk and Tort Law

8.1 Introduction

In this chapter, we turn our enquiry from contract to tort. Our concern here is with the role of insurance in determining the existence and ambit of tort duties.[1] The chapter extends the concerns of Chapter 7, but the terrain is more diverse, and in terms of received opinion we face a much bigger challenge. That is because, quite simply, influential accounts have denied that insurance plays any role at all in determining the existence and ambit of tort duties.[2] Indeed, some of the same accounts suggest that it makes no sense to say that tort duties have such a thing as 'ambit' at all, except in special cases where they are restrained on '*ex post*' grounds.[3] In conventional cases, they are simply duties to act in particular ways. We will explain our disagreement with these views in the course of the chapter. However, such is the entrenched acceptance of the doctrinal irrelevance of insurance to tort duties, we should be clear from the start that there are certain assertions about insurance which are the target of these exclusionary views, and which are *not* part of the analysis which we offer. We are, in other words, hoping to move the debate to new terrain, where positions need not be so sweepingly stated and assumptions may be questioned.

In particular, the received view that insurance concerns as a whole are and should be irrelevant to determination of principles of tort liability may be based on a fear that consideration of insurance will lead either to a simple 'deep pockets' argument (thus to circularity, as insurance follows liability, which follows insurance), or to tort being swallowed up in its entirety by loss-spreading concerns. Both of these tend to associate insurance concerns with an *ex post* search for deep pockets. This is not our account of

[1] This by no means exhausts our consideration of the relationship between tort and insurance. The role of insurance, and insurers, in funding litigation is explored in Chapter 13; the influence of insurance over tort damages is also explored in Chapter 5. Consideration of compulsory insurance is deferred to Chapter 9, and other dimensions of the connection between insurance and the substantive law of tort are considered in more detail in Chapters 10 (vicarious liability) and 11 (illegality).

[2] The best known instance is Jane Stapleton, 'Tort, Insurance and Ideology' (1995) 58 MLR 820. The focus of that article was on resisting the idea that first-party insurance and tort liability are direct equivalents. That is not the core focus of this chapter, but is directly relevant to the discussion in Chapter 9, dealing with cases where the existence of a duty of care is clear. See also the response to Stapleton by Rob Merkin, 'Tort, Insurance and Ideology: Further Thoughts' (2012) 75 MLR 301, pointing out that the argument does not map well on to claims involving contractual elements (Chapter 7). For discussion of the focus on first-party insurance in Stapleton's article, and the existence of a broader range of questions, see J Steele, 'Tort, Insurance, and the Resources of Private Law', in S Degeling, J Edelman, and J Goudkamp (eds), *Torts in Commercial Law* (London: Sweet and Maxwell, 2011). The complexity of questions surrounding tort and insurance, and the need to respect contractual arrangements which include insurance issues, is also identified by J Allsop and L Dargan, 'The Central Role of Insurance in Modern Society and in the Development of the Law' (2013) 24 Ins LJ 1.

[3] J Stapleton, 'Evaluating Goldberg and Zipursky's Civil Recourse Theory' (2006–7) 75 Fordham Law Rev 1529 (discussed in 8.2).

the role of insurance. In fact, we suggest that the role of insurance is complex and context-dependent, and not reducible to one sweeping proposition. Most particularly, it is not to be reduced to an *ex post* search for a compensation fund, in which duty becomes irrelevant.

The received view (that insurance is doctrinally irrelevant to tort) retreats from the fear that tort will be reduced to a search for deep pockets by suggesting that insurance is essentially a private matter between assured parties, and their insurers. Insurance is best seen as something parties can choose to obtain, or must obtain in some contexts, in order to deal with the liabilities, and is irrelevant to tort questions. An olive branch is proffered, in that it is suggested that insurance may have a role in supporting tort in achieving its goals;[4] but the end result is that this merely cements its doctrinal irrelevance.[5] In our view, just as insurance does not offer a single knock-down source of rational answers to tort questions, neither should it be excluded from the doctrinal picture. A starting point to our departure from the received view is that *ex ante* bargaining around risks is not outside the frame of tort reasoning, and that from this point of view, insurance is by no means to be written off as 'fortuitous' as far as other parties are concerned.[6] Given the centrality of insurance to contractual arrangements, charted in Chapter 7, it is simply impossible to ignore insurance while taking account of party risk arrangements. The extent to which the courts do take account of such arrangements has been understated, whether claims arise as between contracting parties, or on the part of others exposed to risk by the parties' arrangements. We will further suggest that the risk-allocation analysis of tort duties is more variable and extends further into the law of tort than is generally appreciated, as too does the role of insurance.

Given the entrenched hostility to including insurance considerations in the determination of tort duties, we should underline that we do not consider insurance to be an overriding factor which 'explains' the entire law of tort, nor even those parts of the law of tort which are most closely associated with making good material losses. Nor do we consider that the law of tort (or significant parts of it) should be seen as collapsing into one large loss-spreading device operated by the courts: the job of the courts is not to seek the 'best loss-spreader' in each case, and they are not equipped to do so.[7] Nor is our analysis likely to show that tort is a poor relation of insurance in the distribution of losses, for it shows that in practice the relationship is symbiotic. Rather, our enterprise is focused on understanding the internal operation of the law of obligations, and in relation to tort as in relation to contract we find that in many instances risk allocation,

[4] A Beever, 'Corrective Justice and Personal Responsibility in Tort Law' (2008) 28 OJLS 475, proposes that a 'corrective justice' account of tort can accommodate liability insurance in this way, whereas an approach based on 'personal responsibility' cannot.

[5] We pause to point out that even in this 'supporting' role, insurance richly deserves study, as it shapes litigation and thus inevitably influences the development of the law: T Baker, 'Liability Insurance as Tort Regulation: Six Ways that Liability Insurance Shapes Tort Law in Action' (2005) 12 Conn Ins L J 1; R Lewis, 'Insurance and the Tort System' (2005) 25 LS 85; and Chapters 11 and 12.

[6] For illustration see the discussion in Chapter 5, 5.2, of *Caledonia North Sea Ltd v British Telecommunications Plc* [2002] UKHL 4; [2002] 1 Lloyd's Rep 553, where contractual structure was well understood.

[7] For agreement on this point, see Stapleton, n 2; Merkin, n 2; M Clarke, *Policies and Perceptions of Insurance in the Twenty-First Century* (Oxford: Oxford University Press, 2005), 308.

and thus (as we have explained in the previous chapter) inevitably insurance, is inherent to this operation.

We would point out that to consider the role of risk allocation in this way is not to deny that tort liabilities are dependent on duties; nor that these duties are imposed by law and reflect a variety of normative concerns. On the contrary, we suggest that those cases where duty is a key issue in tort litigation have frequently raised issues about risk allocation, and about the relationship between tort and other forms of ordering of risk. Through the remedies for harm occasioned by their breach, tort duties have the effect—and are approached by parties, courts, and legislators as having the effect—of allocating various risks to those who bear them. Courts treat this as a reason to be circumspect in the extension of duties.[8] The fact that the duties are not simply duties to 'insure' against loss, but set various standards of behaviour, by no means undermines this point.[9] In fact, the rich variety of tort duties indicates that risk allocation is a complex matter. Where the duty is to take reasonable care, the risk allocated is of carelessly caused harm, to the extent that it is attributable to the breach and falls within the scope of the duty. So, for example, where the law seeks an 'assumption of responsibility' as the prerequisite of a duty of care, the required assumption *may* (depending on the parties' relationship) be interpreted as an assurance that the claimant need not worry about the risk of the defendant's negligence—not just that the defendant will take care.[10] Even in the case of duties which approach the absolute in their content,[11] issues arise surrounding the ambit of the duty and whether the particular instance of harm falls within, or outside, the risk thus allocated to duty-bearers; and whether the defendant is a person owing such a duty to the claimant.[12] The existence of different duties throughout the law of tort is not inconsistent with the idea that tort law allocates

[8] An enlightening argument that it is philosophically coherent to emphasize the effects of a duty (liability) when justifying the duty is given by J Gardner, 'Backwards and Forwards with Tort Law', in J Keim-Campbell, M O'Rourke, and D Shier (eds), *Law and Social Justice* (Cambridge MA: MIT Press, 2005). Much of this chapter evidences that outcomes are included in the courts' reasons when defining duties.

[9] Gardner, n 8, points out that not every criterion producing desired liability outcomes can coherently be an obligation, even if outcomes are relevant to the decision whether to impose an obligation, or not. It must make sense to regard oneself as bound by a legal duty (even if courts have outcome-based reasons for the way that duties are defined). Being insured or in possession of deep pockets obviously cannot be confused with being under a duty.

[10] A point made by J Blom, 'Economic Loss: Curbs on the Way Ahead?' (1986–87) 12 Can Bus Law Journal 275, 292. This has similarities with the restrictive modern view of the *volenti* defence in the context of negligence: it operates only where the claimant intends to absolve the defendant of liability.

[11] For example the Provision and Use of Work Equipment Regulations 1998, SI 1998/2306, reg 5, imposing a duty on employers to ensure that work equipment is maintained in an efficient state, efficient working order, and good repair. This was described as an absolute duty in *Ball v Street* [2005] EWCA Civ 76, [59], referring to earlier authorities interpreting predecessors of reg 5, particularly *Starck v Post Office* [2000] ICR 1013, [42] (Waller LJ). These authorities were referred to by Lord Hope in *Smith v Northamptonshire CC* [2009] UKHL 27; [2009] 4 All ER 557, [8], as providing the background to that appeal. Recently enacted legislation means that in future, breach of such duties will not give rise to civil liability unless expressly prescribed by regulation: Enterprise and Regulatory Reform Act 2013, s 69. For discussion of this provision and its background, see n 191 and related text.

[12] The philosophical coherence of strict duties, and particularly of duties not only to try but also to succeed, are defended by J Gardner, 'Obligations and Outcomes in the Law of Tort', in P Cane and J Gardner (eds), *Relating to Responsibility* (Oxford: Hart Publishing, 2001). See further the discussion in 8.2.

risk. Duties are a key determinant of the risks to be allocated to various parties, and are often quite deliberately tailored to this effect.[13]

8.1.1 Trajectory: risk structures from contract to tort

In Chapter 7, we argued that courts applying contractual principles attach particular significance to the parties' allocation of risks, and that insurance and the transfer of risk have been under-emphasized features in these allocations. We argued that predictions of the demise of party risk allocation as a core concern in the law of contract had been overstated and indeed were misconceived. However, our analysis of party risk structures departed from the traditional bipartite frame of classical contract theory. In particular, our analysis underlined the involvement of multiple parties which is inherent where risks involved in contracting are insured,[14] and we emphasized the role of the courts in supporting party arrangements—particularly in respect of the allocation of risks—in their market context. Linked to our analysis in Chapter 5, which indicated the extent of issues surrounding subrogation and the need which often arises for courts to consider insurers in relation to other indemnifiers, this will include evaluative choices about the appropriateness of holding an insurer, or another contracting party, to be the 'primary indemnifier' in light of planned risk structures, an issue which is submerged from view because the very existence of an insurer may remain at least superficially concealed, and because traditional bipartite analysis encourages this state of affairs.

We saw in Chapter 7 that predictable liability risks are typically allocated by parties, with varying degrees of sophistication depending upon the nature of their contract. This is significant, in that parties often anticipate and deal with risks caused by fault whether their own, or that of their employees, or of others. It makes sense, in other words, to discuss the risk of fault as one of the risks to be allocated. Certainly, parties do not focus uniquely on deterrence when determining how to deal with such risks. Equally, the law is perfectly ready to support parties when they negotiate around the financial burden of their liabilities and structure their relationships accordingly. Thus, our general portrayal of the role played by the law of contract has affinity with the paradigm of 'dynamic market individualism' outlined by Roger Brownsword as typical of the courts' approach to commercial contracts,[15] in which courts interpret and

[13] In the case of product liability, the Consumer Protection Act 1987, implementing Council Directive 85/374/EC *expressly* allocates risks as between manufacturer and consumer, particularly through the 'development risks defence'.

[14] Through the involvement of insurers.

[15] R Brownsword, *Contract Law: Themes for the Twenty-First Century* (Oxford: Oxford University Press, 2nd edn, 2006); R Brownsword, 'Static and Dynamic Market Individualism', in R Halson (ed), *Exploring the Boundaries of Contract* (Aldershot: Dartmouth, 1996). This is also related to 'new contextualism', which departs from the formalist interpretation of classical contract theory and has been identified as the now dominant paradigm of contract in the courts: R Brownsword, 'After *Investors*: Interpretation, Expectation and the Implicit Dimension of the "New Contextualism"', in D Campbell, H Collins, and J Wightman (eds), *Implicit Dimensions of Contract* (Oxford: Hart Publishing, 2003). Contextual analysis of the 'implicit' dimension of contracts has been justified both as an appropriate means of protecting party expectations and as welfare-enhancing in its own right: D Campbell and H Collins, 'Discovering the Implicit Dimension of Contracts', in Campbell, Collins, and Wightman, at 47–9.

support party agreements. We saw that not all accounts accept that legal principles are designed to support party risk arrangements. The very idea of a mutual risk structure across a number of parties will remain suspect when viewed within the strongly bipartite frame associated with classical contract doctrine (or with some approaches to the law of tort). Beyond this, it is in any event much less widely recognized that the location of insurance is a key factor in these risk allocations; and a number of cases prove on examination to be brought by insurers whose claim for indemnity would, if it succeeded, upset a planned risk allocation. We argued that the involvement of insurance in the parties' structuring of risks and duties has been underestimated in theoretical accounts of such cases. But where do tort duties fit into this analysis?

Tort duties are generally conceived of as creations of law and legal policy, rather than as springing from party agreement. As we saw in 7.1, this provided the essence of a 'welfarist' argument, developed particularly during the 1970s, that tort was gaining dominance over contract: given the particular approach to tort adopted by its proponents, this was effectively also an argument that legal policy was dominant over party intention.[16] Courts have, however, been vigilant in restraining the potential impact of tort in unravelling contractual allocations of risk. A recent expression of the basic difference can be found in the judgment of Jackson LJ in *Robinson v PE Jones (Contractors) Ltd*:

> Contractual obligations spring from the consent of the parties and the common law principle that contracts should be enforced. Tortious duties are imposed by law, as a matter of policy, in specific situations.[17]

It will be noticed that Jackson LJ refers here to 'specific situations'. We suggest that this well reflects the current position of the courts, and indicates that it is misleading to suppose that tort duties are also different from contract duties in being owed to 'persons generally'.[18] A first key question, therefore, is whether the existence and definition of such duties are capable of being affected by party arrangements. This can be easily answered, because in at least some instances, it is perfectly clear that they are.[19] It is widely recognized (though with differing degrees of enthusiasm) that party

[16] Most influentially: G Gilmore, *The Death of Contract* (Columbus OH: Ohio State University Press, 1974); P Atiyah, *The Rise and Fall of Freedom of Contract* (Oxford: Clarendon Press, 1979).

[17] [2011] EWCA Civ 9; [2011] 3 WLR 815 [75]. We also discussed public liability policies, and the exclusion from these of voluntarily assumed liabilities, in Chapter 7.

[18] This is the 'standard account' outlined by R Brownsword, 'Themes for the Twenty First Century', ch 7 in R Brownsword, *Contract Law*, n 15, 197, before exploring the disputed boundary: 'the standard modern account of the distinction between contract and tort has it that, whereas in tort the duties are fixed by law and are owed to persons generally, in contract the obligations are fixed by the parties themselves and are owed to specific persons' (197–8). It is also a view attacked by R Goldberg and B Zipursky, 'The Moral of *MacPherson*' (1998) 146 U Pa L Rev 1733. Jane Stapleton (n 3) has suggested that the 'duty to the world' view is *correct* in what she calls 'traditional' tort cases (variously described in terms of direct physical injury, or as arising between strangers), though she concedes that Goldberg and Zipursky's 'relational' view (in which duties are owed only to specific claimants or classes of potential claimants) provides a convenient analysis of various problematic areas of negligence liability. This issue is examined further in 8.2.

[19] Key English authorities are *Pacific Associates v Baxter* [1990] 1 QB 993 (CA); *Henderson v Merrett* [1995] 2 AC 145; *Simaan v Pilkington Glass* [1988] QB 758; *Norwich City Council v Harvey* [1989] 1 WLR 828 (discussed in 8.3). All have been subsequently approved and applied. A key Canadian authority is *London Drugs v Kuehne and Nagel* [1992] 3 SCR 299 (Chapter 7). Party arrangements have also been relevant where the defendant is not party to the contractual structure: 8.4.

arrangements, particularly party risk allocations, have influenced decisions about the existence and nature of tort duties where the parties 'come together' against the background of a contractual structure. Such cases have been loosely captured in the idea that the duties fall to be considered within a 'contractual matrix', a term explained in 8.3. Broadly, 'contractual matrix' cases are those where contractual structuring of risks forms the background to the proposed tort duty.

The expression 'contractual matrix' is generally used outside those cases where the claimant and defendant are directly related by contract ('concurrency' cases). Claimant and defendant may, instead, be related by a series of contracts, whether these are best referred to in terms of a 'chain', or (borrowing Hugh Collins' description of construction contracts), in terms of a 'hub and spokes'.[20] In either case, arrangements are in place which structure the location of risks among more than two parties; and the argument is that tort duties fall to be considered against the background of such arrangements. It might be added, however, that the role of the claimant in such cases may vary widely, in that the claimant might be a participant in a common risk structure, or outside that structure and adversely affected by it. The response of the law is rightly sensitive to these differences; and in this respect, sensitivity to party arrangements is not incompatible with protection of consumers or others.[21] Reasoning associated with the 'contractual matrix' may even be relevant where the defendant is not a contracting party, and the question arises of how far such issues extend into the law of tort.[22]

That being the case, our second key question is: what role is played in the determination of such duties by insurance arrangements? This question has not had the emphasis it deserves in existing accounts. The analysis in Chapter 7 has shown how deeply insurance concerns are implicated in party allocations of risk; and we draw further on this analysis in 8.3 and 8.4. Continuing the themes of Chapter 7, but extending them to analysis of tort duties, we show that insurance *arrangements* present different issues from the mere presence, or even possibility, of insurance; and that these are generally part and parcel of the prevailing risk structure, even if there is silence on such issues on the part of most scholars.

It is widely recognized that tort duties are often proposed in such circumstances because the law of contract is hampered by its concept of privity from responding appropriately to multi-party arrangements. The question is whether tort is able to be sensitive to the notion of a planned, multi-party transaction, where the law of contract falls short. It is suggested that tort will hinder, rather than help, in this context if it too is overly fixated on two parties rather than the existence of a multi-party context; if it proves insensitive to existing risk structures; and if its goals are inflexibly defined. Simply shifting from a classical, bipartite analysis of contract, to an equally doctrinaire, bipartite reading of tort, will only succeed in producing a hierarchy of rules or values in which either tort or contract trumps the other, preferred risk structures being the

[20] Discussed in 7.6. The 'hub and spokes' image has the advantage of suggesting a shared enterprise (a series of contracts leads to a common centre).

[21] For example *Smith v Eric Bush* [1990] 1 AC 831; *London Drugs v Kuehne and Nagel*, n 19.

[22] Further discussed in 8.4 and 8.5.

victim. Hence, the turn to tort law to overcome contract's limitations where third parties were concerned has also necessitated some flexible reorientation of the reasoning to be deployed in relation to tort duties.[23] That reorientation has plainly occurred, even if there is continued scholarly resistance to it. It is not surprising that this has had an effect in other areas of the law.

In relation to 'contractual matrix' cases, our goal is to highlight the continued importance of insurance when the focus shifts to tort. This will itself be resisted by some.[24] Over a series of articles, Jane Stapleton has consistently rejected any role for insurance in determining whether tort duties are owed in all categories of case,[25] sometimes by reference solely to previous work of her own.[26] Such is the influence of this body of work that we must engage with it here. As one part of the general project, Stapleton has proposed that a claimant's alternative opportunity for protection may be a valid reason for refusing a tort duty, but only if that opportunity was consistent with enhanced deterrence of negligent conduct.[27] Highlighting (by contrast) our point in the preceding paragraph, this approach rests on a stark division between the purposes of tort and contract duties, while elevating a single proposed purpose of tort duties (deterrence) over that associated with contract (which is more often recognized as structuring of risk).[28]

[23] For example, by letting go of the idea of a 'hierarchy' of interests in which economic losses are restricted subject to special rules. Acceptance of such changes is gradual: there is resistance to this in Lord Lloyd's dissenting judgment in *Marc Rich v Bishop Rock Marine Ltd, The Nicolas H* [1996] AC 211 (8.4); and in the failure to acknowledge ideas of financial reliance, rather than reliance on performance, in Lord Nicholls' dissenting judgment in *Stovin v Wise* [1996] AC 923 (8.5).

[24] Stapleton, n 2.

[25] Tom Baker has described Stapleton's position as a 'jeremiad' against the place of insurance in tort reasoning: T Baker, 'Insurance in Socio-Legal Research', University of Pennsylvania Institute for Law and Economics, Research Paper No 10-07, May 2010, referring particularly to Stapleton, n 2. In addition, see J Stapleton, 'Duty of Care Factors: A Selection from the Judicial Menus', in P Cane and J Stapleton, *The Law of Obligations: Essays in Celebration of John Fleming* (Oxford: Clarendon Press, 1998) ('Judicial Menus'), where (at 64) she dismisses the existence of liability insurance along with 'deep pockets' thinking more generally as an unconvincing factor. The reason here is that tort is premised on 'personal responsibility' and deterrence (the kind of inflexible reading which we have said is likely to be obstructive in the contractual matrix cases). In J Stapleton, 'Duty of Care: Peripheral Parties and Alternative Opportunities for Deterrence' (1995) 111 LQR 301 ('Peripheral Parties'), 301, the author singles out insurance for exclusion, offering the reason that tort duties must be compatible with deterrence (an equally inflexible view). We challenge this view in later sections of this chapter.

[26] Stapleton, n 3, at n 22, takes the opportunity to point out that in her multidimensional approach to tort duties, in which a 'wide array' of concerns is taken into account, the one factor that is not 'legitimate' is insurance. There is no justification for singling out insurance in this way, nor for adding the stigma of 'illegitimacy' specifically to insurance in the context of an approach which is generally open to policy considerations. In many instances, as we explain in this chapter, the inclusion of insurance is less deserving of the 'policy' label than other relevant factors.

[27] In cases where the defendant was 'causally peripheral', Stapleton considers it is easier for denial of a duty to be consistent with deterrence, because there is less necessity to deter the defendant's conduct (the defendant is not the principal generator of risk). But the designation of a party as 'causally peripheral' entails a value judgment, which may itself be informed (it seems to us) by some of the same considerations which we would see as more directly involved in determination of duty questions.

[28] Stapleton, 'Peripheral Parties', n 25, 310, concedes that defendants can no longer be seen as 'peripheral' where the parties have bargained and the claimant has paid for protection from the risk on the part of the defendant, citing *Smith v Eric Bush*, n 21. This appears to come somewhat closer to our position, but it underlines the value judgments involved in designation as 'peripheral' or not. Stapleton does not enter into discussion of cases where the parties have bargained and arrived at an expectation that the claimant will insure, and in this sense take the risk of negligence, which would evidently test the dominance of deterrence more strongly.

Rejecting these arguments, we begin by seeking to redress the neglect of insurance in 'contractual matrix' cases involving tort duties. But we also raise some questions about the general depiction of tort law involved in Stapleton's critique, and contemplate the influence of risk allocation, including insurance issues, beyond a small subset of tort duties. It is salutary to be reminded that the bulk of tort litigation is conducted away from the appellate courts—away from the courts at all. But we would point out that what Stapleton describes as core instances of 'traditional' tort claims—road traffic accidents between strangers[29]—are themselves deeply shaped by insurance and by distributive concerns. They present a very poor paradigm of tort law if what is desired is to expunge the influence of insurance. Both ends of the spectrum—cases where parties have structured risks, and cases between strangers—therefore raise insurance issues, albeit in different ways, and we do not find the existing prohibition of discussion of insurance to be helpful at any point along it.

Reaching further from the domain of contractual structures, we ask whether the existence and shape of specific tort duties is influenced by a much more general recognition that the imposition of tort duties, just like the interpretation of contractual duties, itself has the effect of allocating risk. Even if the source of tort duties is recognized to be conceptually different from the source of contract duties, the impact of such duties is in important respects the same.[30] Both tort and contract duties oblige parties to behave in particular ways; but both also, inescapably, allocate the risks associated with a failure to do so. This is the very purpose of many contractual terms. That it is also an inescapable result of tort follows from the fact that the consequence of recognizing a tort duty is that liability will follow as of right where relevant harm is caused by its breach. With a particular focus on the English courts, we suggest that there is increasing emphasis on *ex ante* allocation of risks, as part of the process of determining the existence and the ambit of tort duties; and we explore the relevance of insurance in this process.

8.1.2 Summary

Shifting our attention from contract duties to tort duties considerably broadens and diversifies the range of our enquiry. The relationships which give rise to tort duties are varied, and so too are the ways in which questions relating to insurance may arise. Our analysis across the course of Chapter 7 and this chapter reflects a spectrum of relationships in which questions of risk allocation arise. Our spectrum is in the reverse order from Stapleton's analysis,[31] which begins with stranger cases, and treats this as the paradigm by which other cases are to be judged. At one end of our spectrum are those cases where the two parties themselves are in a contractual relationship,[32] or

[29] n 3; also discussed in Chapter 9, 9.1.

[30] 'Tort' and 'contract' therefore provide alternative means of approaching the issues in a range of cases: see for example B Markesinis, 'Eternal and Troublesome Triangles' (1990) LQR 556, drawing attention to the German law focus on contract in what for English law are 'contractual matrix' cases in tort; and more generally B Markesinis, 'An Expanding Tort Law—the Price of a Rigid Contract Law' (1987) 103 LQR 354; Peter Cane, *Tort Law and Economic Interests* (Oxford: Clarendon Press, 2nd edn, 1996).

[31] n 2.

[32] As in *Henderson v Merrett*, n 19, in relation to the 'direct names'.

a relationship akin to contract.[33] Close to these are other cases where there is no privity of contract between the parties, but their arrangements are linked through a contractual risk structure.[34] In these circumstances, the parties' risk arrangements have been understood to affect tort duties, or to affect the courts' reasoning as to the ambit of such duties; but the role of insurance has been underplayed. These cases, beyond concurrency, have been more or less firmly understood in terms of the 'contractual matrix' within which the parties' relationship is to be considered; but the significant link with contextual analysis of contracting, and the need to soften tort's own two-party frame, has been much less securely acknowledged; and the role of insurance least recognized of all.

Further along the spectrum of tort duties, there are cases where party arrangements are less obviously relevant, or where only one of the litigants in the tort claim is party to a contract purporting to allocate risks.[35] In these areas of law, the challenge is to show how courts are still influenced in their approach to tort duties by awareness that they are allocating risks; and to consider what role the pattern of insurance arrangements (rather than the fortuitous presence of insurance) plays in determining such duties. This may mean that structuring of risks by parties remains significant. Or it may mean that society's preferred response to risks can be discerned through statutory and other arrangements, and that tort duties are thought to destabilize these arrangements, or to be unnecessary. A key point is that even at the 'traditional' end of the spectrum there is a concentration of claims in a few categories, including claims against public authorities (though these are varied in their nature); claims against employers (which, of course, is not an instance of claims between 'strangers'); and claims in relation to road traffic accidents. Cases of the former sort have tested the appellate courts in many jurisdictions, as is well known, and some are explored here. In the latter two instances, as in a number of others, liability insurance is compulsory. The influence of insurance is inclined to be quite different in such cases, but is still not straightforward. We explore the nature of that influence in Chapter 9. But the recognition that there are risk structures in place far beyond contractual matrix cases has also enabled questions of risk allocation to be patently discussed in relation to the duty of care even in some personal injury actions. It is perhaps in relation to personal injury that the reversal of an expected trend to increased welfarism seems most stark. But these cases show that the reasons for the restraint of tort may as readily be products of perceived social preferences about the allocation of risk in pursuit of social goals, as of party arrangements.[36] The complex mixing of, and cross-fertilization between, varied social and private goals, legal forms, and associated working concepts (one could also say,

[33] As in *Hedley Byrne v Heller* [1964] AC 465, where there was direct communication but no consideration.

[34] As in *Pacific Associates v Baxter*, n 19, and similar cases (8.3).

[35] This is often the defendant: an example is *Donoghue v Stevenson* [1932] AC 562; but also *Woodland v Essex County Council* [2012] EWCA Civ 239 and other cases of alleged or actual non-delegable duty. However, it could be the claimant, in a case where it is clear from the factual matrix that the claimant was required to bear the risk of property/economic loss or liability. A key case here is *Marc Rich v Bishop Rock Marine*, n 23.

[36] The same may be said about contract. There may be social reasons, and reasons of fairness, for supporting party risk structures, particularly once the role of insurers is taken into account.

'ideologies')[37] in relation to supposedly 'traditional' tort claims is addressed in detail in Chapter 9, with a particular focus on compulsory liability insurance.

Uniting these examples is the observation that tort duties are disciplined—and increasingly so—by reference to other forms of ordering of risks. This can be seen in different ways across the spectrum of cases, leading from concurrency, through contractual matrix cases, to 'stranger' or 'direct physical injury' cases of one sort or another, which occur with regularity in respect of particular risks where insurance implications are well recognized. Discounting this can lead to the undermining of settled or preferred risk structures, particularly where the identity of insurers themselves as litigants is thereby overlooked.

During an important, restrictive phase in the evolution of tort duties, John Fleming proposed that the extension of tort into the domain of contract had worked in two directions. As had been predicted, contract had been socialized, absorbing some of tort's facility with the imposition of duties.[38] But at the same time, tort had 'learned to respect the important message of private ordering'.[39] In other words, tort has been part of the same movement noted in Chapter 7, in which the law of contract has developed a contextual approach to assessment of the parties' allocation of risks in light of their arrangements as a whole.[40] According to Fleming, this sense of discipline in the law of tort arose in line with the shift from expansionist and generalizing, to restrictive approaches to the ambit of the law of negligence in particular.[41] We agree; and we find the same pattern of restriction, and of concentration on *ex ante* ordering (private or not), still reflected far beyond the recognized 'contractual matrix' cases. Some such cases may reflect 'private ordering'; others may reflect alternative, publicly mandated, or preferred responses to risk. This process, by which tort duties are restrained in the light of *ex ante* ordering of risk, and most particularly the role of insurance within that process, are the core themes of this chapter.

8.2 Overview: Tort Reasoning and Risk Allocation

8.2.1 Negligence duties

The very idea that tort duties are to be seen as influenced by questions of risk allocation, even without the additional focus on insurance, will appear incompatible with some influential views. It has been tenaciously argued, for example, that a 'duty of care' must be understood as simply a duty to be careful. Courts therefore cannot 'know' what the extent of the duty is or what risks fall within it (or 'which consequences of its breach were those to which the imposition of that duty was directed'), for its meaning is simply

[37] Stapleton, n 2, rightly notes that reforms shifting between one legal form and another (say, from tort to first-party insurance) involve ideological as well as practical implications.

[38] n 16.

[39] J Fleming, 'Tort in a Contractual Matrix' [1995] Osgoode Hall LJ 661, 678.

[40] n 15, and particularly the point made by Campbell and Collins that this may be welfare enhancing in its own right.

[41] n 39, 678: 'These developments surfaced at a time of growing judicial concern for ways to rein in the expansive, indeed explosive, potential of tort liability, especially the law of negligence'.

to require a certain standard of conduct.[42] Associated with this is a view that tort duties essentially *are* owed to the world in general, and simply specify how parties should conduct themselves ('act with due care'; 'do not defame'). We disagree with this reading of tort duties. The portrayal of a duty of care as solely an obligation to be careful has been deployed in order to resist analysis of what have been more typically called 'remoteness' issues in terms of the 'scope' of particular duties.[43] Our core concerns are different, but the assertion is nevertheless related to our themes, because the recognition of tort duties, on our account, allocates particular risks, often between particular parties, and does so with due regard to existing risk structures.[44]

The specific and relational nature of tort duties are important elements of our account of their role in allocating risks: if negligence duties did simply give instructions to be careful,[45] the duty concept could have no risk-allocation function. Stapleton has argued, in support of the idea that negligence duties are merely duties to act carefully, that the denial of a duty to some claimants but not others is 'discriminatory' and 'distasteful' because it suggests that the defendant is 'allowed' to act negligently towards those who are not owed a duty.[46] We leave aside our doubts about whether this is really so when compared with alternative avenues for defining the limits of negligence liability,[47] and further doubts as to whether duty-owers are really 'allowed' by the law not to act carefully towards certain people simply because they do not owe tort duties in respect of particular risks. More fundamentally, we suggest the courts use the idea of 'duty of care' to mean a duty to take care *of* certain interests. This is captured in the very idea of being careless 'towards' someone. The duty is owed to particular people, in respect of particular interests, and is a duty to take care *of* their interests. Boundaries are therefore inherently important to any statement of a tort duty, and are not merely to be seen as constraints upon those duties.

That duties are not simply defined by their content is a clear implication of the approach in *Caparo v Dickman*.[48] That approach is too well established to be dismissed as a consequence of one particular decision, or a handful of decisions. For example, it is clear that the duty of care is owed only to some people, not to others;[49] only for some

[42] Stapleton, 'Occam's Razor Reveals an Orthodox Interpretation for Chester v Afshar' (2006) 122 LQR 426, 433.

[43] Stapleton urges that the better terminology is 'scope of liability', in order to underline that the enquiry is (in her view) to do with the extent of liability rather than the nature of the obligation. For example: J Stapleton, 'Cause-in-Fact and the Scope of Liability for Consequences' (2003) 119 LQR 388; J Stapleton, 'Legal Cause: Cause-in-Fact and the Scope of Liability for Consequences' (2001) 54 V and LR 947.

[44] Evaluative questions are a part of this, and need not be 'hidden' or concealed when approached in terms of duties of care rather than in terms of 'scope of liability'.

[45] It seems to us that at the very least, D needs to be instructed to be careful *of the interests of* some people, perhaps those who are reasonably foreseeable. But then the duty immediately becomes relational albeit towards a large class, and we face the problem that in *Donoghue v Stevenson*, it was thought necessary to temper the argument with proximity. The duty was owed only to some.

[46] n 3, 1531.

[47] Rather like the reasoning in *Osman v Ferguson* [1993] 4 All ER 344, or the second stage of the test in *Anns v Merton* [1978] AC 728, restraining duties and liabilities on *ex post* grounds may give the impression that the law is refusing to give effect to existing rights in particular circumstances.

[48] [1990] 2 AC 605.

[49] In *Caparo*, n 48, this was existing shareholders rather than those planning to purchase shares.

purposes;[50] and only in respect of certain harm.[51] Stapleton acknowledges that the first of these observations is correct.[52] But she continues to maintain that the *ex ante* role of negligence duties in particular is simply to offer guidance to act (here, to audit accounts) with due care. How can the duty be limited to particular recipients (as in *Caparo*) while its *ex ante* effect (simply to require due care) is said to be so general? Stapleton acknowledges constraining factors, which limit the duties owed by a careless defendant, but prefers to treat them all as *ex post* 'control factors'. Is this simply an alternative route to the same end? For the reasons set out in this chapter, we think that it is important to reject the idea that tort duties are merely guidance directives, and to accept the portrayal of tort duties as relational.

Defamation can be offered as an illustration. Stapleton argues that Goldberg and Zipursky's argument has 'insuperable problems' with torts other than negligence, and illustrates this with reference to defamation. We are not convinced that the 'relational' approach faces insuperable problems accounting for defamation. On the contrary, defamation torts depend on statements made of an individual or a limited class in which the individual is identifiable, and are not best understood as duties owed to the world. Defamation duties are at least as 'relational' as negligence duties: they are duties not to publish statements defamatory of X or Y. They are not easily understood as duties 'not to make defamatory statements' in the abstract, as the idea of a defamatory meaning or statement cannot exist without reference to an affected party. Defamation underlines the relational nature of tort duties. Similar points may be made about other torts, such as deceit: there must be an intention to mislead the claimant specifically, in such a way that they act in reliance. The relational approach does not struggle to account for torts other than negligence.

Equally, we do not accept that strict duties in general demand any different analysis. It may certainly be doubted whether it is true that there are *no* strict tort duties to succeed,[53] even if statutory provisions are for some reason excluded from the ambit of 'tort'. Apart from the possibility that negligence imposes such duties,[54] it is arguable that there is a strict duty to succeed in not falsely imprisoning someone, for example, in that an imprisonment which is false remains false even if the defendant was reasonable in his or her belief that it was lawful: *R v Governor of Brockhill Prison, ex p. Evans*.[55] That trespass torts (such as false imprisonment) are viewed as requiring a breach of duty is now settled in English law, at least for the purposes of interpreting provisions of

[50] So far as the shareholders were concerned, the valuation could be relied upon for the purpose of general governance of the company—not for the purpose of buying and selling shares.

[51] Thus, liability will not extend beyond the scope of the duty: *Banque Bruxelles Lambert v Eagle Star* [1997] AC 141 (the effects of a market fall on the value of property were outside the scope of the duty to value the property carefully).

[52] n 3.

[53] Stapleton asserts, n 3, 1560: 'Nowhere does the law of torts impose a strict obligation to achieve a result'. The source of this is given as Stapleton's own article, 'The Normal Expectancies Measure in Tort Damages' (1997) 113 LQR 257. That article had very different concerns from the discussion here, namely the conceptualization of a core measure of tort damages. Stapleton sought to distinguish the nature of tort damages from the 'reliance measure' in contract. But to the extent that this requires or underlines a distinction between tort and contract, it has implications for the analysis of tort duties, with which we engage here.

[54] n 12. [55] [2001] 2 AC 19.

the Limitation Act 1980, and it may therefore be concluded that here is not only a strict liability, but a clear instance of a strict *duty* to succeed.[56]

It is consistent with a relational view of tort duties to propose that to be owed a duty of care is for the risk of negligence within the ambit of the duty to be placed with the person who owes the duty, so far as a pattern of legal rights and duties can do it.[57] The 'risk allocation' view of tort law does not collapse into a denial of duty or a reduction of duty to mean only the risk of liability.[58] Put simply, courts and legislatures take seriously both the nature of obligation (tort duties must be consistent with the sense of being under a duty, even if it is a strict duty to avoid a particular result); and the impact of liability which is a necessary corollary of recognizing or imposing a tort duty. Across the spectrum of tort, duties are determined on the basis of a wide variety of reasons (or criteria). At the more restrictive end of the negligence spectrum, it can be argued that duties are imposed where it is concluded that the risk was one that the claimant could treat as taken care of by the defendant.[59] Across the spectrum, not merely in exceptional cases, the impact of liability is reflected in the definition of tort duties. To think in terms of risk allocation is not to negate duties, nor even to subject them to policy restraint, but is an important element in the reasoning process behind the creation of those duties as a matter of law.

8.2.2 Evolving styles of reasoning

Decisions of the courts will express the issues just debated to different degrees, but risk allocation questions are no longer hidden beneath the surface of judgments. Equally, it has become more difficult to deny that insurance is relevant to judicial decision-making as it is discussed as a factor in an increasing number of instances and, as we show throughout, at pivotal moments in the law's development.[60] This partly reflects the more general way in which judicial reasoning styles have gradually evolved where tort duties are concerned. A formal style of reasoning can be recognized in which relatively abstract categories such as 'foreseeability', 'proximity', or more detailed ideas such as 'control', are applied to the case in hand. English courts have in the past been criticized for adopting a formalistic approach along these lines, and for not grappling with policy concerns, or failing to make plain what the motivating reasons were.[61] It is our suggestion that English courts now adopt a more pragmatic style of reasoning around tort duties, despite the existence of umbrella terms such as 'proximity'. In

[56] *A v Hoare* [2008] UKHL 6; [2008] 1 AC 844.

[57] In reality of course, this is achieved only if litigation follows, and is successful.

[58] Goldberg and Zipursky have been motivated in part to rescue the notion of negligence 'duties' from oblivion in US tort law: J Goldberg and B Zipursky, 'The Restatement (Third) and the Place of Duty in Negligence Law' (2001) 54 Vand Law Rev 657.

[59] Blom, n 10.

[60] Note also J Morgan, 'Tort, Insurance and Incoherence' (2005) 67 MLR 384.

[61] This is a reasonable criticism of, for example, the reasoning in *Murphy v Brentwood* [1991] 1 AC 398, which appeared to treat as decisive the definition of the loss as 'economic'. Its formalism has contributed to the poor reputation of that authority throughout the Commonwealth. However, English courts seem, in general, not to have had cause to regret the decision itself.

particular, courts have drawn attention more confidently to the impact of allocating risks to defendants through imposing a duty.

We should clarify that our point about pragmatism does not amount to a general argument about the incorporation of 'policy considerations' in all their multiple guises. Indeed, if 'policy' is chiefly concerned with considerations beyond the parties, some of the pragmatism to which we refer is not properly described in terms of policy at all (unless a particularly hard-line bipartite approach is adopted to the question of what 'relates to the parties' and their relationship). This reflects the fact that in relation to insurance, we do not think that courts are primarily reaching for 'community welfare' in a direct sense,[62] although they may of course be influenced by the existence of legislative structures which reflect judgments about community welfare.

The issues here go back once again to changing understandings of the context in which the law of obligations operates, and of the social and economic role of this aspect of private law. We have already touched here on a shift from welfarism (in which tort trumps contract) to market contextualism, in which the significance of party intentions is reinstated and the law's role becomes more reflexive, encouraging and supporting party self-regulation. In terms of the law of tort, this shift was adeptly captured by Sir Anthony Mason, writing the Preface to the 9th edition of Fleming's *Law of Torts*.[63] He fittingly observed a reorientation from 'economic "welfarism"' to 'economic "rationalism"', which he perceived as a vindication of John Fleming's scholarship. He described this reorientation as strikingly illustrated by *Stovin v Wise*,[64] a decision of the House of Lords in which attempted risk-shifting by insurers was, as we explain below, centrally implicated.[65] We explain why we consider this an astute depiction, in 8.4. This trend has continued. The most recent edition of *Fleming's The Law of Torts* continues the theme, containing a Foreword[66] which makes express the transition made by the English courts from formalism to overt recognition of the implications of liability. Lord Hoffmann describes a 'different style of judgment-writing, in which judges are more open about the real reasons for their decisions and less inclined to think that the authority of their priesthood requires concealment of the inner mysteries of the craft'. This further encourages our view that risk-allocation questions are among the 'real reasons' for decisions, and are not to be dismissed as mere 'makeweight' arguments.[67]

Quite possibly, the road map to duty of care questions offered by *Caparo v Dickman* has turned out to be better adapted to certain forms of pragmatism than the rival approaches of Australian, Canadian, and New Zealand courts, as they have diverged from the English approach in relation to duties of care, despite (or because of) their more open embrace of wide-ranging policy concerns. Tort rarely, if ever, represents the

[62] For discussion see A Robertson, 'Justice, Community Welfare and the Duty of Care' (2011) 127 LQR 370.

[63] Sydney: Law Book Company, 1998. This was the last edition to be written by Fleming himself.

[64] n 23.

[65] This was not a subrogation case, but has much in common with the observations we make in Chapter 5 about the subversion of existing risk structures. Here, those structures are publicly mandated but privately operated (motor insurance).

[66] Lord Hoffmann, 'Foreword', in C Sappideen and P Vines (eds), *Fleming's The Law of Torts* (Sydney: Law Book Company, 10th edn, 2011).

[67] Stapleton, n 2, 833.

only response to risk in operation,[68] and this is increasingly recognized by the pragmatic style articulated by the House of Lords in *Caparo*. As concern with the impact of expansive tort liability in all contexts has mounted, English courts have offered more express justifications for the restrained shape of liability. These reasons are, quite rightly, not necessarily labelled 'policy'. In this process, insurance concerns, among others, have been at work in restricting, rather than only expanding,[69] liabilities, because insurance arrangements often reflect existing forms of ordering, whether public or private.

In the remainder of the chapter, we begin our analysis with 'contractual matrix' cases, and explore the role of insurance in relation to party risk structures (8.3). We then extend our examination into the area of advice (8.4), and beyond that to the varied category of local authority liability (8.5). These are among the recognized pressure points for delineation of tort duties. As we move along the spectrum, risk allocation increasingly becomes one of a variety of considerations; and yet we suggest that it does not become irrelevant. Deferring our analysis of the non-paradigmatic paradigm—running-down cases—for the next chapter, we nevertheless consider one area where duty relationships are both well recognized and backed by compulsory insurance, and where the structure of duties is complex. This is the area of employers' duties to employees (8.6), where we briefly examine the structure of duty and the roles of insurance in order to give a sense of the variety and depth of influence of insurance in relation to tort duties.

8.3 'Contractual Matrix' Cases: Tort and Party Risk Structure

It has been widely recognized that tort duties may be embedded within market arrangements, raising pertinent questions about the nature of those duties and their relationship with the law of contract. On the tort side, such issues have been approached in terms of a category of 'contractual matrix' cases, where parties 'come together against a background of contract', or where the risks involved are generally planned, even where the parties to the tort action do not themselves contract directly with one another.[70] Initially, the issues were thought relevant only to a special category of 'pure economic losses'. The key point however is that the parties make provision for the economic cost of various harms, so that it is really the pattern of relationships and of risk allocations which offers these cases their complexity, not the category of loss involved. Referring in particular to recovery in tort for purely 'economic' losses, such cases have been described as raising particular issues precisely because they are more likely than other cases to be associated with 'planned transactions', and 'contractual

[68] Note also the discussion in Chapter 6.

[69] We refer here to the argument that liability insurance is an expansionist influence in the law of tort because it makes bearable not only more extensive duties, but also more substantial damages, than could possibly be supported without it. For example *Imbree v McNeilly* [2008] HCA 40, Kirby J; and R Lewis, n 5, 92: without insurance, 'The very nature of tort law would have to change'. This argument cannot be brushed aside but we suggest here that the doctrinal influence is also real.

[70] Where the parties to the tort action are also directly linked by contract, the case is generally seen as one of '(true) concurrency'.

expectations'.[71] More recently, it has become much clearer that these factors may also be present in cases of physical damage.[72]

Use of the term 'contractual matrix' in this context is most associated with John Fleming,[73] who drew it from the judgment of La Forest J in the Supreme Court of Canada in *London Drugs v Kuehne & Nagel*.[74] Here, the Supreme Court held that a contracting party who had agreed to a limitation in liability in respect of damage to its goods could not evade this contractual limitation by proceeding in tort against an employee of the company with whom it had contracted. The limitation of liability operated also for the benefit of the employee. This has been treated as a significant relaxation in the privity requirement in contract, and has subsequently been deployed in different circumstances by the same court.[75] La Forest J, agreeing in the result, dissented on the separate question of whether the employee owed any duty of care at all: in his view, no duty of care arose in the context of the particular allocation of risk observable in the contractual matrix. It appears that the claimant had taken the obvious course when faced with a limitation of liability—indeed, the expected course—and insured against loss above the contractual limit. The action was brought by the claimant's insurer, and the approach of La Forest J is therefore in accordance with our analysis in Chapter 5, namely, his approach to relevant duties identified the insurer as the primary indemnifier against the background of the contractual structure or matrix. La Forest in turn referred to the reasoning of the English Court of Appeal in *Pacific Associates v Baxter* as exemplifying the influence of the 'contractual matrix' in tort reasoning.[76]

It is not an accident that the expression 'contractual matrix' recalls the idea of the 'factual matrix' which recurs in contextual analysis of contract terms and their meaning.[77] Like the 'new contextualism' which has become orthodox in relation to the English law of contract, the logic of analysis of tort duties against the background of a 'contractual matrix' seeks a purposive interpretation of the risk structure adopted by the parties. That being the case, it is not really to the point that in some (though by no means all) instances,

[71] J Blom, 'Fictions and Frictions on the Interface between Tort and Contract', in P Burns and S Lyons (eds), *Donoghue v Stevenson and the Modern Law of Negligence* (Vancouver: University of British Columbia, 1991).

[72] *Norwich City Council*, n 19, and *Marc Rich v Bishop Rock Marine*, n 23, discussed further in 8.3 and 8.4.

[73] J Fleming, 'Employee's Tort in a Contractual Matrix: New Approaches in Canada' (2003) 13 OJLS 430; Fleming, n 39; Fleming's *Law of Torts*, 9th edn, n 63, 206, referring particularly to 'planned transactions' and also Fleming, 10th edn, n 66, 214 (8.360). Stapleton, 'Peripheral Parties', n 25, 301, uses the term, but generally prefers to refer to cases involving 'unbroken contractual chains'.

[74] [1992] 3 SCR 299, 327: 'it was concurrent in the broader sense that I prefer to refer to as tort liability in a contractual context or matrix' (referring to *Rivtow Marine v Washington Iron Works* [1974] SCR 1189, and to the reasons of Purchas LJ in *Pacific Associates v Baxter*, n 19).

[75] *Fraser River Pile & Dredge Ltd v Can-Dive Services Ltd* [1999] 3 SCR 108.

[76] n 19. Discussed further in 8.3. Notice that, if the employee in *London Drugs* (n 19) was covered by the employer (defendant's) insurance, this would only reinforce the point being made: it would divert the risk to the 'wrong' insurance policy as agreed between the parties. The point that the employee may have been covered is made (in an article sceptical of interpretations based on 'commercial realities' or party intentions, amongst others) by J Neyers, 'Explaining the Principled Exception to Privity of Contract' (2007) 52 McGill LJ 757, 773. The article proposes an alternative two-party route to the outcome in *London Drugs* and subsequent extension in *Fraser River*, deploying estoppel rather than a relaxation of privity.

[77] *Investors Compensation Scheme Ltd v West Bromwich Building Society* [1998] 1 WLR 896. We discuss the significance of this in Chapter 7.

literal agreement to waive or exclude rights in tort cannot be found: intentions may legitimately be inferred from existing patterns of risk allocation, even if this is avowedly an interpretive exercise. This is inherent to the difference between literalism and contextualism.[78] In this light, Stapleton's doubts about the expression 'contractual matrix', and preference for the terminology of unbroken contractual 'chains', is itself significant.[79] We suggest that this terminological preference reflects unease with the idea of multi-party structuring of risks which is also reflected in reluctance to allow risk structures falling short of contractual terms to override the perceived functions of tort duties (in Stapleton's account, primarily deterrence).

Even among those existing analyses of 'contractual matrix' cases which share some ground with our position, looking at liability and associated risks in *ex ante* terms, insurance has not been fully absorbed within the process, despite the significant role demonstrated for insurance in Chapter 7. Some have particularly resisted the softening of tort's focus on two parties, and the implication that responsibility and deterrence in relation to careless behaviour do not necessarily trump the allocation of risks associated with that behaviour, simply by turning from contract to tort.

In particular, while proposing that the ability of claimants to achieve alternative protection than from the defendant is a key factor in determining duty questions, Jane Stapleton has forcefully limited the range of acceptable opportunities, to encompass only those which are consistent with enhanced deterrence. It is on this basis that she claims that insurance in particular cannot be a consideration.[80] This rests on a strict, verging on absolute, interpretation of the nature of the law of tort as aimed at achieving deterrence, which is deployed particularly forcefully at the exclusion of insurance. Stapleton argued that the idea of alternative opportunities of *protection* open to the claimant is too crude a concept to be relied upon in the limitation of tort duties without refinement. For example, 'it could not refer to *any* means of self-protection for it could not mean self-protection by the purchase of first-party insurance'. The footnote to this statement continues, 'In deciding whether to protect a plaintiff the law of tort does not take his or her insurability into account, nor could it do so and also seek coherently to promote deterrence of defendant carelessness'.[81] We argue here that 'insurability' does not exhaust the relevant questions in relation to insurance, so that the blanket exclusion is far too general. But we also note that the footnote is circular: the reason for requiring consistency with deterrence (hence rejection of insurance as a consideration) is that without it the law would be inconsistent with deterrence. The priority of

[78] Neyers (n 76) draws on R Stevens, 'The Contracts (Rights of Third Parties) Act 1999' (2004) 120 LQR 292 in this respect. Focusing (at 293) on frustration of party intentions and doubting the rationale for the 1999 reform of privity, Stevens argues that only the *promisee's* intentions are frustrated if the third party is not benefited. The promisor could always perform the contract. The argument in the text is that the parties have structured their obligations and the action *against* a third party is inconsistent with that structure: indeed the promisor here did as expected and covered the risk through insurance, an arrangement which the action against an employee threatens to unravel. Equally, no lack of intention on the part of the promisee can be inferred from inaction since the promisor's action may not be in breach of contract (and more particularly if an insurer has the right to conduct the defence). The approach is in this sense more 'literal' than our own.

[79] Stapleton, 'Judicial Menus', n 25, 79: cases where the parties are linked by a 'chain' of contracts are referred to as 'the so-called "contractual matrix" cases'.

[80] 'Peripheral Parties', n 25. [81] 'Peripheral Parties', n 25.

deterrence is simply assumed. We would like to challenge that assumption, and its particular effect on the relevance of insurance. Not only is deterrence merely one feature of the law of tort, whose value is highly questionable in many instances,[82] but the accent on who will bear the cost of liability if things should go wrong is of independent significance in many areas of tort. 'Momentary carelessness' amounting to breach of duty is after all a familiar risk to be planned.

At the same time, as John Fleming pointed out, Stapleton expressed herself willing to allow opportunities for deterrence to be missed, in order to prevent claimants 'free-riding' on the law of tort. Fleming identified this as a 'value judgment', starker even than the old law of contributory negligence (which at least required some fault on the part of the claimant).[83] Even here, when discussing the capacity for free-riding on tort and defining its avoidance as more important even than deterrence, Stapleton took the trouble to define insurance as irrelevant: apparently, a failure to purchase first-party insurance, no matter how widely available, cannot amount to 'free-riding' so as to overwhelm deterrence arguments. We have already argued that the existence and scope of insurance to match contractual risk allocation is a key element in the negotiation of commercial arrangements. We suggest that support of party risk allocation is more deeply engrained in the law than a fear of 'free-riding'. On this basis, the contractual matrix cases do not exclude insurance from consideration, but bring them into the fold without the feared consequence of simply suggesting that liability follows insurance.

A great many tort cases could be approached in terms of the relationship between tort duties, and the limits of contract. In particular, some of the most high-profile cases in which claimants have sought to expand the boundaries of the duty of care could be characterized as having been brought by third parties, seeking a remedy where there has been a breach of a contract to which they are not a party.[84] That contract will define which of the parties to it is to bear risks and, in some contexts, it may well contain insuring obligations, but in each case this generally occurs within two-party limits. A third-party action may seek to expand the liability which was intended to be assumed and which was probably not anticipated by the insurance arrangements or by the policy itself. Since in many cases, the courts do not overtly express the point in insurance terms, the question arises to what extent decisions relating to the influence of contractual terms over duties to third parties should be tempered by the terms of the contract to which they were not a party. Those cases which do consider the insurance position are not exceptions to general processes of reasoning, as we hope to show. Further, the involvement of insurance emerges as a natural feature of the determination of tort

[82] Cases where tort's (assumed) deterrent effect has been thought likely to be perverse or unhelpful include *Marc Rich v Bishop Rock Marine* (n 23); *Stovin v Wise* (n 23); *Transco v Stockport* [2003] UKHL 61; [2003] 3 WLR 1467 (all discussed here) and, more broadly, *Hill v Chief Constable of West Yorkshire* [1989] AC 53; *Brooks v Commissioner of Police of the Metropolis* [2005] UKHL 24; [2005] 1 WLR 1495; *Tomlinson v Congleton* [2003] UKHL 47, amongst others.

[83] Fleming, n 39.

[84] Apart from *Donoghue v Stevenson* itself and the cases explored here, see for example *White v Jones* [1995] 2 AC 207 (intended beneficiary under a will successfully bringing a claim in negligence against careless solicitor), where Steyn LJ made the point explicitly in the Court of Appeal that in the absence of privity, the claim is in tort or does not exist. It is unlikely that the present Contracts (Rights of Third Parties) Act 1999 would have assisted in a scenario such as *White v Jones*.

duties once it is seen that the latter frequently are considered in terms of the effect they have in allocating risks.

8.3.1 Construction and engineers

The influence of contractual structure on tort duties has arisen particularly plainly in construction and engineering cases. The significance of the issues arising is by no means confined to this context, however. For example, the decision in *Marc Rich v Bishop Rock Marine* has been influential here,[85] though the case is removed from the core 'contractual matrix' category since one of the parties was not a contractor. We consider the case further in 8.4.

In Chapter 7, we saw that in the construction industry, contractual structures are complex as many parties are often involved in one project. Contractual structure as a whole may be seen in terms of a common purpose and is governed by relatively standard terms whose overall intention can be made out.[86] The vital role in these structures for insurance, and the potential complexity of its operation, was discussed in Chapter 7. So far as the influence of contractual structure on the law of tort is concerned, a much-cited 'position' statement is that of Purchas LJ in *Pacific Associates v Baxter*.[87] Where the parties 'come together against a contractual structure which provides for compensation', the court would be 'slow to superimpose an added duty of care beyond that which was in the contemplation of the parties'. Purchas LJ acknowledged the different starting points for duties in tort and in contract (the latter being founded on the objective intention of the parties); but added,

> in order to determine whether a duty arises in tort it is necessary to consider the circumstances in which the parties came together in the initial stages at which time it should be considered what obligations, if any, were assumed by the one in favour of the other and what reliance was placed by the other on the first.

Contractual structures are therefore part of the backdrop against which the existence of tort duties must be addressed. In *Pacific Associates v Baxter* itself, the claimant was a participant in the contractual 'matrix', entering into a contract with the employer to provide dredging work. The defendant was a supervising engineer whose role included certification of the completion of the claimant's work. Claimant and defendant were therefore related by a contractual structure of the 'hub and spokes' variety; but did not contract with one another. The claimant's contract provided for remedies against the employer, in the event of error in this process. Indeed the claimant had pursued its contractual remedy against the employer through arbitration. Dissatisfied with the quantum of the award, the claimant commenced proceedings in tort against the engineer, in the absence of a contractual route.

The Court of Appeal held that no duty in tort arose in this context, where it would 'cut across' the contractual structure. Among contract scholars, the case sparked

[85] n 23.
[86] J Adams and R Brownsword, 'Privity and the Concept of a Network Contract' (1990) 10 *Legal Studies* 12.
[87] n 19. Cited, for example, by members of the Supreme Court of Canada in *London Drugs*, n 19.

discussion because of its qualification of the impact of privity of contract: a party gained protection through limitation of its own liability in a contract to which it was not a party. The absence of direct contract between A and B did not necessarily mean that a clause in a contract between B and C, limiting A's liability, would have no effect on *tort* duties owed by A to B.[88] Tort here had managed to reflect the contractual risk structure. Moreover, it had done this by looking at the structure as a whole. The court had therefore avoided the trap of approaching both contractual duties, and tort duties, in a bipartite frame, where the risk structure involved more than two parties. This is a step toward recognizing the role of insurance, which inherently involves one or more additional parties. It is also, of course, resisted by the traditional frame of analysis of both contract, and tort. Roger Brownsword has recently underlined this, arguing that even after the relaxation of privity,[89] 'we continue to be fixated with contract as a bipolar transaction', and that this has blocked us from seeing what is 'staring us in the face': recognition of 'networks' does not supplement contract with something more like tort. Rather, the freedom to opt into rules operating across a network of parties is a 'paradigm of authentic contractual activity'.[90] If tort is viewed in a bipartite frame, parties (including insurers) will employ it in order to avoid the multi-party arrangements which fit so much less comfortably into the mould adopted for the law of obligations.

It is clear that in *Pacific Associates v Baxter* the planning of contractual liabilities *ex ante* was considered relevant to the existence and ambit of tort duties. But turning to general implications for tort, we can be more specific about the nature of the risk allocation which the Court of Appeal considered to be involved, and thus the nature of tort duties as the Court perceived them. It was pointed out that although there was no doubt reliance in one sense on the engineer performing its role with due care, the *remedies* for failure in this role lay against the employer: this was the basis on which the claimant had been willing to contract, and there was 'no reason to infer that the contractor was relying on any right to recover damages' for breach of this duty, other than by pursuing remedies against the employer under the contract. The kind of reliance that the Court of Appeal had in mind as justifying a duty of care was, therefore, reliance not merely on careful performance but on the availability of a remedy, in the event of loss. Only this would justify supplementing the contractual remedies. Again, this clearly makes the link between tort duties and allocation of risk. The parties in this instance had entered into contractual arrangements in relation to such risk, albeit not directly with one another.[91]

[88] Purchas LJ, n 19, 1022G. [89] Contracts (Rights of Third Parties) Act 1999.

[90] R Brownsword, 'Network Contracts Revisited', in M Amstutz and G Teubner (eds), *Networks: Legal Issues of Multilateral Co-operation* (Oxford: Hart Publishing, 2009), 31, 51–2. We do not suggest that the contractual relationships in this instance amounted to a network, but the points made by Brownsword remain pertinent.

[91] It should be clear therefore that contractual intentions in such cases can be observed from the parties' written agreements, and perhaps from the structure of standard contracts, rather than being a matter of guesswork—though in another case, more interpretation may certainly be required. P Cane, *Tort Law and Economic Interests*, n 30, 319–21, expressed doubts on this issue, and also suggested that appeals to a shared expectation are overstated if the relationship has broken down sufficiently for litigation to ensue. The latter point is perhaps wide of the mark in any event in the sense that contractual disputes are generally resolved

As we showed in Chapter 7, insurance is an inherent element of contractual planning. Indeed, discussing the contractual structures in these cases without reference to insurance, while focusing on *ex ante* planning, is like missing the key plotline to the agreements. Yet that is precisely how tort lawyers—and even to some extent contract lawyers—are wont to discuss the cases. Since we have exhaustively treated the wider role of insurance as a technique of party risk allocation in Chapter 7, here we focus on a core example, and its later development, in order to demonstrate how the contractual risk allocation, and particularly the insurance position, directly affects the tort duties themselves; and to indicate how the issue in relation to duty of care has been subjected to academic analysis without reference to insurance, despite the increasingly patent centrality given by the courts to insurance.

In *Norwich City Council v Harvey*,[92] the claimant employed contractors in the extension of its building; the defendant was a subcontractor through whose alleged fault a fire had damaged the building. In reality, it was the employer's subrogated fire insurer who pursued the claim: the 'claimant' had insured against the loss in accordance with the risk structure adopted by the parties. That is the risk structure that the insurer's claim in tort would subvert. This decision of the Court of Appeal has been deployed to show that the courts are willing to create exceptions to strict 'privity' rules within arrangements amounting to a 'network'.[93] Unlike the earlier decision in *Junior Books v Veitchi*,[94] which was also taken to indicate obligations (without direct privity) within a network, the decision in *Norwich CC* placed the risk with the party who had agreed to insure, and was thus consistent with the contractual structure intended by the parties. *Norwich*, unlike *Junior Books*, has subsequently been approved. Indeed, later decisions have continued its work in treating the nature of the contractual setting as relevant to the existence of duties of care in tort which might run parallel with, or cut across, contractual structures.

Referring to the brief discussion of change in the nature of tort reasoning in 8.2, we should note that *Norwich CC* was decided relatively 'early' in the recent (and prolonged) restrictive phase of negligence—at around the same time as the decisions of the House of Lords in *Murphy v Brentwood* and *Caparo v Dickman*.[95] Restriction in the scope of tort remedies had emerged as an important issue for the courts but appropriate justifications were more uncertain. Most importantly, the 'pragmatic' style of reasoning and its emphasis on risk allocation had not so confidently emerged. The

by looking at what the parties agreed (even though they now disagree), but is particularly so where it is an insurer, rather than a participant in the construction contracts, who seeks to subvert the risk structure. This point is missed because the identity of insurers is treated as irrelevant.

92 n 19.

93 Adams and Brownsword, 'Privity and the Concept of a Network Contract', n 86, 19, refer to the case as incorporating a 'counter-doctrine' (to privity) in the 'emerging idea of the background "contractual setting"'.

94 [1983] 1 AC 520. Here a nominated subcontractor was held to owe a duty in tort to an employer in relation to a defective floor, despite absence of physical damage to other property and absence of direct contractual relationship. The emphasis was on reliance in performance, rather than on contractual risk structure (reliance in relation to risk). This factor differentiates the unsuccessful tort analysis in *Junior Books*, from the analysis in later cases involving a 'contractual matrix'.

95 nn 61, 48.

consequence is that the whole purpose of the claim—through which a subrogated insurer sought reimbursement—and the whole substance of the contractual structure in relation to fire—through which the parties sought to place the risk with the insurer in return for a premium—are not illuminated by the manner in which the reasoning was presented, despite its apparent focus on the nature of the parties' intentions in relation to risk. The absence of overt reference to insurance arrangements in the court's reasoning, in particular, has proved to be misleading.[96] In Chapter 7, we explained why *Norwich CC v Harvey* can only be satisfactorily understood by reference to the insurance provisions in the parties' contracts. This has been more confidently and openly accepted as an aspect of the reasoning of later courts deciding similar points. Indeed it clearly appears from those later decisions how central the role of insurance is in such cases. This explanation of *Norwich CC* can be contrasted with those contemporaneous explanations which omit the insurance dimension. For example, our focus on the insurance position and exploration of later cases leads us not to place too much weight on the doubts expressed by Peter Cane, who asked whether parties' expectations might more profitably be seen as shaped by the law in such cases, rather than vice versa; and wondered whether the idea of party expectations in such cases (in the sense of structuring of risks) is simply a rationalization of decisions reached on other grounds.[97] By contrast, we think recognition of party expectations was genuinely the most influential factor. At the same time, our approach also contrasts with some of those accounts which included reference to insurance. We are happy to accept that this is because we write with the benefit of hindsight, since more recent cases have made more apparent the points we make here.

As we have seen, the employer (claimant)'s subrogated fire insurer pursued the claim in *Norwich CC*. The main contract specified that the existing structures were to be at the sole risk of the claimant, and the claimant was to maintain adequate insurance against the risk. This is, therefore, an illustration that the parties' intentions may be easily and clearly observable, and that the parties may employ the support of the law of contract in structuring foreseeable risks, including the risk of negligence. It therefore placed an obligation to insure with the claimant. We have explored the implications of such obligations in Chapter 7. The difficulty of interpreting the case and its influence on the interpretation of duty is that the insurance issues were presented as a mere background issue which in terms of doctrinal analysis did not need to be dealt with.

The defendant subcontractor argued that it did not owe a duty of care in light of the contractual structure; and, in the alternative, that it was not a suitable case for the exercise of subrogation rights. The Court held there was no duty of care, and therefore that it did not have to comment on the issues of 'insurance and subrogation'. This obscures the fact that its decision plainly was about insurance. The location of the obligation to insure was important to the absence of duty of care—and indeed the

[96] Apart from the analyses by Adams and Brownsword, n 86, and Collins, Chapter 7, 7.6, Cane, n 30, 479, interprets *Norwich CC* as a case giving effect to the parties' contractual intentions, and indicating the priority of contract, but without reference to the insurance obligation or the parties' intentions in relation to insurance of the risk. Insurance is then discussed in relation to its impact on incentives to avoid harm.

[97] Cane, n 30, ch 6, Pt 7.

absence of an action on the part of the assured is the key means of denying subrogation rights. If this appears circular, the explanation lies in the allocation of risks which is relevant both to the denial of the tort duty, and the consequent absence of any action on the part of the subrogated insurer: the risks, in the contractual structure which the parties adopted, were placed with insurers, not subcontractors.[98] For contract scholars, the exciting implication was, as with *Pacific Associates v Baxter*, that the subcontractor obtained protection *from* liability in tort 'which the rules of privity do not provide'. It benefited from the contractual structure, which placed the obligation to insure with the employer. Beneath the surface, the court thus succeeded in placing the risk with the insurer: there was no claim to which the insurer could be subrogated, and only in that sense did the court not deal with 'issues of insurance and subrogation'.

The received interpretation of *Norwich CC* does not emphasize the role of insuring obligations or of risk allocation. From the tort side, most accounts focus on mutual reliance within a contractual chain. By contrast, in a note of the case Basil Markesinis emphasized the insurance dimension while also pointing out that the judgments contained merely a tantalizing 'hint' at the role of insurance.[99] More recent decisions are not so coy, as we will see. While Markesinis pertinently identified the involvement of a subrogated insurer in bringing the claim, he also suggested that the role of insurance here could only be in the nature of a 'policy' argument, which might therefore not be to everyone's taste. This was informed by his general perception that insurance considerations were indeed pertinent policy concerns, in contrast to the prevailing view that they were irrelevant; and that more overt argument as to the outcome of decisions in general ought to be seen in judicial decisions relating to tort liability. We suggest that the regulation of subrogation rights by courts in line with party arrangements is so core to the questions resolved by the law of obligations that it makes sense not to see it as an extraneous policy concern, nor certainly as a matter of taste, but as inherent to the reasoning which is indeed central to the cases. Indeed, in relation to *Norwich CC* we would suggest that the incidence of insurance which gave effect to the parties' intended allocation of risk demonstrably was core to the reasoning of the court, despite the contrary impression that it gave.

Not all is as it seems on the surface of tort decisions. Far from removing protection from contracting parties, the effect of denying the duty of care in *Norwich CC* is to *improve* their protection by interpreting the overall intention of the parties as being to place responsibility for indemnifying the employer with the insurer, not with subcontractors. The parties, between them, have then succeeded in insuring against risk, in the sense that the risk is ousted from the contract or network itself (in return for the insurance premium). If contractual structures are to be studied in terms of common purpose, then their common purpose in insuring in this way needs more emphasis.

[98] May LJ drew at 837C on the decision of the House of Lords in *Scottish Housing Association v Wimpey Construction UK Ltd* [1986] 1 WLR 995, a decision relating to contractors but also interpreting the contractual provisions as placing the whole risk with employers, with reference also to subcontractors.

[99] 'Eternal and Troublesome Triangles' (1990) 106 LQR 556. Given the involvement of the subrogated insurer, the case had more than three corners, in fact.

These factors can help illuminate the shortcomings of *Junior Books*.[100] One problem with *Junior Books* was that it imposed a bipartite analysis onto a wider contractual structure. Another is that, equally fundamentally, it emphasized reliance between parties in the form of expectation of good performance. Comparing this with the approach in *Pacific Associates v Baxter* and *Norwich CC*, we see that in the latter cases, reliance is associated with an expectation that the risk, therefore specifically the liability and the responsibility to insure, would lie with particular parties, on the basis of the contractual structure against which the parties 'came together'. Those expectations can be derived from the express terms of the contracts themselves in these particular cases; and there is no question of depriving the court of the capacity to question the underlying fairness of the arrangement, should this appear relevant.[101] Primarily, the expectations in question are about risk, not performance, and the significant issue on which to focus is the allocation of *risk* between the parties, not reliance on performance between parties who are working together through a contractual chain. The way in which the reasoning in *Norwich CC* itself was presented does not help to highlight this, but it is the only way to explain the action that was brought, and the best explanation of its impact. The role of risk allocation and of insurance specifically is made much plainer by later cases interpreting the role of tort duties, arising in different ways, but in the context of similar contractual structures.

An example is the decision of the House of Lords in *British Telecommunications plc v James Thomson & Sons Ltd*.[102] Here, as in *Norwich CC*, a contractual structure in relation to building work placed an obligation on the employer to insure existing structures against fire. However, the contracts in this instance extended the benefit of insurance or a subrogation waiver to nominated subcontractors. Here, a fire appears to have been started by a 'non-nominated' or 'domestic' subcontractor, and the insurer brought a claim against the subcontractor in negligence. *Norwich CC* was distinguished on the basis of interpretation of the particular contractual terms, and most specifically the terms of the obligation to insure, and the Court held that a duty of care was indeed owed to the employer. As a result, the subrogated insurer therefore could seek indemnity against the domestic subcontractor. As we will see, the decision can be criticized, since it is arguable that the House of Lords did not adopt a sufficiently general understanding of the parties' intentions in relation to the location of risk. Even so, the court reached its conclusion through explicit consideration of the contractual obligations in relation to insurance, and the influence of these provisions on the existence of a duty of care in tort is, in this instance, clear and undeniable. The contractual term as to insurance was not held to oust a duty of care owed by it to the employer. This was not in itself enough to *justify* such a duty, but as Lord Mackay put it, the structure of insuring obligations was relevant to whether it was 'unfair, unjust, or unreasonable' to impose the obligation. Lord Mackay went on to assert that

[100] n 94. [101] The two arguments raised by Cane, n 91.

[102] [1999] 1 WLR 9. Part of the significance of the decision was that it accepted the approach in *Caparo v Dickman* (n 48) to be applicable in Scotland even where the claim was not one for pure economic loss but also for damage to property—a point later accepted in relation to failure to prevent physical assault in *Mitchell v Glasgow City Council* [2009] UKHL 11; [2009] 2 WLR 481.

the existence of a subrogation right against the subcontractor 'will legitimately affect the question of premium'.[103] In determining whether the duty was fair, just, and reasonable, all of the contractual terms were relevant, and Lord Mackay thought the distinction between 'nominated' subcontractors, who had the benefit of the employer's insurance obligation, and 'domestic' subcontractors such as the claimants, who did not, was decisive.

Unusually perhaps, if the House of Lords in this case was in any way influenced by more abstract considerations—such as whether it is right for parties to be protected by contractual provisions to which they are not a party—it is this which was merely hinted at,[104] and the key considerations presented related to insuring obligations. Insurance was, therefore, the crucial issue and the determining factor in recognition that a duty lay on the subcontractor. This probably explains the absence of discussion of the case in tort texts, though as the Court impliedly recognized, it was merely doing more expressly what had been done in *Norwich CC*, namely assessing where the insuring obligation lay. All that was missing (unfortunately) was a sense of the general intentions of the parties. Thus, Convery has criticized the case not only because of its failure to engage with broader issues of principle, but also for its failure to meet Lord Rodger's view in the Outer House, that it was legitimate for the *defenders* (subcontractors) to have proceeded on the basis that they did not need to insure the existing structures and for them to price their contract accordingly.[105] This case illustrates that the general intentions of the parties are indeed open to interpretation.[106] But evaluative interpretation is an inevitable part of decision-making in relation to tort duties, and in relation to contract duties, no pretence is made that a focus on party risk structures will provide an escape from this. That is part and parcel of any contextual approach to construction.

A more recent first-instance decision, which plainly illustrates that insurance issues are deeply embedded and well recognized in tort claims arising within the matrix of construction contracts, is *John Hunt Demolition Ltd v ASME Engineering*.[107] It is plain that in this decision the purpose of the contractual structure as a whole was analysed in order to answer the question of whether the subcontractor owed a duty of care to the employer. In doing this, the insurance provisions were vital. Indeed Judge Peter Coulson QC pointed out (following *Keating on Construction Contracts*[108]) that 'the clear intention of the JCT Forms as a whole was that the risk of damage due to a specified peril should fall upon the insurers, rather than the parties to the relevant contracts'. This is more than a reference to the general intention of connected parties in relation to risk: it also goes to the location of that risk *with the insurers*. The decision is

[103] This assumption has been questioned, as discussed in Chapter 5.

[104] *BT v Thomson*, n 102, 16E–G: 'It is unnecessary for the purposes of the present case to consider these arguments': this is the very mirror image of the reasoning pattern in *Norwich CC*, n 19, yet ironically it is *Norwich CC* which appears more likely to have achieved the parties' intentions in relation to insurance.

[105] J Convery, 'Standard Form Building Contracts and Duty of Care' (1999) 62 MLR 766, 773, quoting Lord Rodger, 1997 SLT 767, who had dismissed the insurer's claim against the subcontractor (as did the Inner House).

[106] This is therefore a case which shows that party intentions are not always easy to glean: see our discussion of Cane's view, text to n 101.

[107] [2007] EWHC 1507 (TCC); [2008] 1 All ER 180.

[108] London: Sweet & Maxwell. The current edition is the 9th edn, 2012.

compatible with *Norwich CC* but, like *BT v James Thomson*, its interpretation of insuring obligations is express. Here that interpretation was deployed to show that a subcontractor should not have settled a claim against the employer, and therefore could not claim reimbursement from the subsubcontractor. Whilst in *Pacific Associates v Baxter*, the contractor (claimant) had to settle for the contractual remedies which formed the background to its relationship with the defendant, despite the lack of direct contract between them, in *John Hunt v ASME* it was concluded that the contractual structure was not intended to place the risk with subsubcontractors, but with the employer's insurer. The general intention of such contracts in relation to the displacement of risks to insurers, and the impact on subrogation, is missed by most interpretations from the tort side, and some from the general contracts perspective also, possibly through a continuation of the misguided argument that considerations of subrogation and the placing of risk with insurers must be 'policy' questions, and outside the proper scope of tort reasoning. In fact, they are essential to the questions arising in relation to the existence of a duty of care between parties linked by a contractual 'matrix', even if not by a direct contract.

In summary, contractual structures between commercial parties have been treated in academic discussion as raising particular issues of risk allocation in the determination of tort duties, even when the centrality of insurance has been overlooked. But the lessons relating to risk allocation have generally been seen as specific to limited 'contractual matrix' scenarios, even leaving aside the neglect of insurance issues; and tort scholars have not always acknowledged that the analysis of party purposes and arrangements is more contextual and less focused on the expressed will of individual parties than classical contract theory would propose. It is not only that privity is evaded; the contract is also purposively construed.[109] Do these cases (illustrating how tort duties can have similar implications to contract duties, and both can be influenced by insurance structures) point to any more general issues beyond the boundaries of the recognized 'contractual matrix' considerations?[110] Particularly pertinent, we suggest, is the notion of reliance in relation to risk, rather than performance, that can be taken from these cases, and the recognition that the effect of tort duties is, as with contract duties, to allocate particular, definable risks.

8.4 Advice

Taking one step beyond the commercial parties involved in construction contracts leads to consideration of the situation where *purchasers* of premises are concerned. Here, English law in relation to builders has held to the line in *D & F Estates v Church*

[109] Note the recognition by Campbell and Collins, n 15, that general standards of fairness will not provide solutions in many commercial contexts, 'for in the allocation of risks in commercial contracts the touchstone is not fairness but the efficient allocation of insurable risks. It would be better for the court to discover evidence of practice, perhaps revealed in the insurance arrangements, in order to determine the application of limitations on recovery of damages' (at 46).

[110] Stapleton, 'Judicial Menus', n 25, lists as a special consideration courts' justified reluctance to allow the law of tort to be used to circumvent parties' agreed arrangements, incorporating these cases. No mention is made of insurance, and there is an implication that the issue is generally extraneous to tort, which is simply *not* to be used to disturb the structure.

Commissioners,[111] that there is no duty owed in negligence to the purchaser unless the breach causes damage to other property. Purchasers cannot rely on builders beyond the protection of contract, including the incorporation of protection through schemes such as the National House-Building Council (NHBC).[112] This position was reinforced in relation to a purchaser who entered directly into a contract with the builder, in *Robinson v PE Jones*.[113] If purchasers cannot rely on builders however, they take a risk. Beyond the limits of contractual protection, this risk can be dealt with by taking advice in relation to a purchase.[114] That advice, of course, should be carefully given. But if it is not, and liability follows, it is also the gateway to professional liability insurance. It is recognized that duties are owed not only in contract, but also in tort; and tort has on key occasions been allowed to circumvent the restrictions of contract.[115] Just as the tort duties have centred on advice rather than supply of products, so also relevant professional indemnity policies have been interpreted as restricted to liability for negligent advice.[116]

The cases explored in this section form a very loose category, including some of the most significant cases in the evolution of negligence liability. There is no existing, settled label to define the cases. However, we suggest that it is helpful to approach them as instances where the defendant is offering 'advice' to the claimant (calling attention to *their relationship*), rather than as cases involving 'statements' (calling attention to the particular form of the *defendant's conduct*).[117] The leading authority on how to approach novel claims in relation to duty of care in English law is a claim where the relationship did not amount to one of 'advice' for the relevant purposes: *Caparo v Dickman*.[118] To return to our general analysis in 8.2, the House of Lords in this case conceptualized the various duties owed by the defendant as having limited purposes. This reflected the fact that a duty in tort (to take care of the claimant's interests) has different implications from other duties, for example under the Companies Act. In this sense, public authorities are not the only defendants whose liability in tort falls to be interpreted against the background of a range of statutory powers and duties.[119] Equally, a duty in tort to particular individuals (shareholders) does not necessarily extend to all purposes (here, it did not extend to reliance in buying and selling). The

[111] [1989] AC 177.

[112] Though subject to limits, this adds value to common law remedies in that the remedy is underwritten by NHBC itself—preventing exposure to the (considerable) risk of builder insolvency within the limits of the scheme. There is however no direct contractual relationship between the purchaser and the NHBC, and the limits of the scheme are therefore significant: *Crest Nicholson (Eastern) Ltd v Western* [2008] EWHC 1325 (TCC).

[113] n 17. Stanley Burnton LJ (though not the other judges) described as wrongly decided a few first-instance decisions holding that an 'assumption of responsibility' justified a duty in tort in relation to defects.

[114] We defer consideration of local authorities' position to 8.5. In England, it is clear that local authorities do not owe duties to prospective purchasers when conducting building inspections: *Murphy v Brentwood District Council*, 61.

[115] *Smith v Eric Bush*, n 21, where there was no privity, and *Henderson v Merrett*, n 19, where there were privity issues and the contract claims which did exist were time-barred, are the key instances.

[116] *Encia Remediation Ltd v Canopius Managing Agents Ltd* [2007] EWHC 916 (Comm); [2008] Lloyd's Rep IR 79; *Timetech Chemicals Ltd v QBE Insurance (International) Ltd* [2012] NZCA 274.

[117] The latter appeared to be a pertinent factor in *Hedley Byrne v Heller* [1964] AC 465, which initiated the stream of cases relating to advice.

[118] n 48.

[119] A parallel drawn by Sedley LJ in *O'Connor v Surrey* [2010] EWCA Civ 286; [2011] QB 328, [119].

particular implication of a duty in tort, as we saw also in relation to *Pacific Associates v Baxter*, is that it might form the basis of a claim in damages; and this would effectively shift the risk of a careless report on the value of a company from purchaser (here, of a company), to valuer.

As we have already argued (in 8.2), the denial of duty in *Caparo* amounted to a clear endorsement of the idea that the function of a duty is not merely to instruct people to be careful. Tort duties are not owed to people generally nor even to specific people for unlimited purposes. The reference to purposes effectively draws attention to whether one can rely, in the particular sense identified in relation to 'contractual matrix' cases—in other words, where the financial risk is acknowledged to lie in the light of the *ex ante* plans which were made, or should reasonably have been made, not just where the law seeks to draw a line in 'restraint' of tort duties. All of this made the decisive difference to whether the auditors, and their insurers, bore the risk of the over-valuation, and recalls the formulation adopted by Blom: was this a risk which the claimant could reasonably have thought was taken care of by the defendant?[120] The answer—with that of the House of Lords—is plainly 'no'. This is not a case where claimant and defendant were linked by contractual purpose; but the question of whether risk is shifted to the defendant continues to operate effectively.

Another significant case standing outside the contractual matrix, but importing some of the same contextual reasoning, is *Marc Rich v Bishop Rock Marine*.[121] In *Marc Rich*, an unsuccessful attempt was made to shift risk to an unpaid classification society, operating on a non-profit basis and outside the applicable contractual structure, where liabilities on the part of other potential parties were successfully limited by contract. The role of the society was to inspect ships and certify them as seaworthy in order to protect life and property. That role would benefit those whose property might otherwise be at risk; but was there a duty to take care of those interests when performing the duty? It is natural to see the tort claim here as seeking a shifting of risks not least because the contractual structure between shipowners and cargo owners (which was a creation of international Convention) was recognized to be the basis on which parties would insure their risks; and because the property involved was clearly a commercial asset. The case has been referred to in a number of 'contractual matrix' cases, and is of wide influence. And, indeed, the decision marks a significant point in the evolving approach of the House of Lords to questions of tort duty.

The Court of Appeal's decision—that no duty was owed—prompted considerable comment.[122] One question, consistent with a traditional 'bipartite' frame of analysis, asked why the allocation of risks as between certain parties (shipowners and cargo

[120] n 10. [121] n 23.

[122] In favour was Malcolm Clarke. Citing Saville LJ in the Court of Appeal, he explained that the Hague Rules place the primary burden of caring for the cargo (thus also liability for failure to do so) on the shipowners. To place an identical obligation with the classification society, but without the internationally recognized and accepted balancing factors (particularly compensation limits), would be unnecessary, and unreasonable. More generally, tort will not be used to 'break' an established pattern of liability: M Clarke, 'Negligence—Under Control and Under Contract?' (1994) 53 CLJ 220, 222. By contrast, Jane Stapleton considered the decision 'opaque', but also urged (recalling her reduction of the 'contractual matrix' to the idea of a 'contractual chain') that the decision might rest on an assumption that all parties had accepted that the Hague Rules would be 'exhaustive' of their rights: 'Peripheral Parties', n 25, 331.

owners) should affect the duties owed as between shipowners and an entirely different category of parties, namely classification societies.[123] In the House of Lords, Lord Steyn accepted this as a 'cogent criticism' of the Court of Appeal's approach, but nevertheless went on to explore a 'further dimension of the problem'. That further dimension was that the agreed liability limits formed the basis for the insurance of international trade. Not only could the claimants readily insure, but the recognition of a duty on the classification societies would have an impact on international trade, as they would in turn take steps to shift risks to shipowners, entirely circumventing the international risk regime. The parallel with contractual matrix cases in which all parties are engaged in a series of contracts is clear, provided those cases are not too rigidly analysed in terms of express individual agreement:

> The result of a recognition of a duty of care in this case will be to enable cargo owners, or rather their insurers, to disturb the balance created by the Hague Rules and Hague-Visby Rules as well as by tonnage limitation provisions, by enabling cargo owners to recover against a peripheral party to the prejudice of the protection of shipowners under the existing system. For these reasons I would hold that the international trade system tends to militate against the recognition of the claim in tort put forward by the cargo owners against the classification society.[124]

This approach is consistent with the analysis of contractual matrix cases offered in 8.3, in that it identifies a risk structure involving a range of parties and takes care not to disrupt that structure by imposing tort liabilities between two parties considered in isolation. Notably, seeing those parties in isolation is held up as a desired characteristic of decision-making on a bipartite view. The House of Lords chose to investigate the broader risk structure, which was not trumped by faulty performance by one party. More than this, Lord Steyn's significant judgment in this case also plainly invalidates Stapleton's then very recent statement that the possibility of self-protection through insurance is a consideration 'which no appellate court has asserted is a coherent reason for denying the protection of tort'.[125] That is precisely what the House of Lords did assert here. That it occurred not in some general way but within the specific framework of a recognized structure of risks is entirely as we would predict: the role of insurance is highly variable and dependent on context. But it is certainly not to be written off if other features of 'self-protection' are written in. Equally, while Stapleton argued that opportunities for self-protection are only of relevance where they enhance deterrence, the House of Lords in this case sought to avoid *over*-deterrence of the activities of classification societies. This illustrates that deterrence is not always a desired goal. Equally, while Stapleton fears that attention to party risk arrangements may 'slide into

[123] P Cane, 'The Liability of Classification Societies' [1994] LMCLQ 363.

[124] Lord Steyn, *Marc Rich*, n 23, 240B–C. Lord Steyn has also made an important contribution to the 'new contextualism' in the English law of contract: eg Lord Steyn, 'Contract Law and the Reasonable Expectations of Honest Men' (1997) 113 LQR 433 ('Reasonable Expectations'). Despite his arguments being deployed by the majority, Peter Cane, n 30, subsequently questioned the impact of the decision in terms of incentives on the classification society to take care (a 'deterrence' argument), and on the basis of 'fairness'. It is suggested that the fairness objection is less compelling given the existence of a clear allocation of risk, limitation of responsibility, and capacity to insure on this basis.

[125] 'Peripheral Parties', n 25, 333.

fiction',[126] the House of Lords was—consistently with developments in the construction of contractual terms—willing to glean information about those intentions from the surrounding matrix.[127] And to underline the *core* nature of such concerns, Lord Steyn did not designate all issues of insurance as 'policy' matters, and rightly so. He listed *additional* policy concerns relating to insurance and litigation—complexity in claims, and the likelihood that 'an extra layer of insurance' would be purchased—under a separate heading of 'policy factors'.[128] The need to respect existing ordering of risks by contrast was an inherent element of the decision. The decision in *Marc Rich* therefore perfectly illustrates many elements of our argument here.

Leaving commercial claimants behind, a further very significant advice case is *Smith v Eric Bush*.[129] While the claimants in *Caparo* and *Marc Rich* were commercial entities well placed to purchase their own advice or (more directly in the latter case) insurance, the claimant in *Smith* was very differently placed. Here, absence of contract is synonymous with absence of influence over the risk structure adopted. The issues raised by the case overlap with the 'contractual matrix' cases considered above, in the loose sense that the tort duty is to be considered against the background of a contractual chain which did involve both of the parties to the tort claim. But this claimant may be judged to have had no real part in the structuring of risk associated with that chain. In *Smith*, it was held that a tort duty was owed to a purchaser of property at the lower end of the domestic market. The reasoning was preoccupied chiefly with the validity of an exclusion of liability, where the claimant was the intended recipient of advice, and had paid for it. This is pertinent in itself: the question was whether the contractual arrangements entered into by two commercial parties could exclude liability to a third, a consumer.[130] But the prior question is whether a duty was owed without the exclusion. The existence of the duty in this case was justified on the basis of the vulnerability of ordinary purchasers in this position. Although this departs from the defendant's expectations as to the location of risk, it is not an incoherent or one-off response.[131] It places the risk of misvaluation with valuers and their insurers, not with ordinary domestic purchasers,[132] and indicates that in considering risk allocation, the law does not in all circumstances elevate party intentions *above* considerations of substantive fairness. Rather, party intentions, and party relationships, are relevant factors in determining substantive fairness. Here, the claimant could be called a 'vulnerable

[126] 'Peripheral Parties', n 25, 337, suggesting this is a problem with the 'anti-circumvention principle' (a somewhat reductionist description of the contextual analysis of existing risk structures).

[127] See also Lord Steyn, 'Reasonable Expectations', n 124.

[128] *Marc Rich*, n 23, 241. We argued in Chapter 5, and in 8.3, that not all issues relating to insurance arrangements are best seen as 'policy' questions, since they are not extraneous to the relationships between parties.

[129] n 21.

[130] This is different from the situation in *Pacific Associates v Baxter*, n 19, where a contract to which the claimant was a party excluded liability on the part of the defendant, and the defendant could in effect rely on this despite absence of privity.

[131] The case is described as exceptional—but with approval on the basis of awareness of the reality of the purchaser's position—by Fleming, n 39.

[132] This may not be a 'bright line' category (discussed in relation to *Scullion v Royal Bank of Scotland*, in text at n 136). But few categories in the law of negligence are. Equally, the question of *which* risks are and are not within those shifted in this way is open to a range of different answers.

party',[133] but that vulnerability is specifically related to the contractual risk allocation. This calls attention to the evaluative element which we have stressed throughout or, if preferred, it shows that the emphasis on 'private ordering' is not an absolute and may be overridden by considerations of fairness where those considerations are pertinent. So, the protection of an ordinary domestic purchaser who had already paid for the mortgage company's valuation and could not reasonably be expected to pay for advice (and thus insurance) twice, was significant enough to override the expectations of the commercial parties involved; in *Norwich CC*,[134] the interests of a fire insurer in seeking indemnity for an insured risk from a subcontractor was not justified in the same way, and was not allowed to frustrate the parties' allocation of risks. Both decisions are appropriate, and indeed both placed risk with an insurer. Neither requires courts to guess about the insurance situation; both rest on interpretations of the contractual structure, bearing in mind the quality of the relationships involved.

The reality of the purchasers' situation in *Smith v Bush* was that they could not be expected to pay twice for advice about the same issue. It is plainly understood that with 'advice' comes insurance of the risk concerned. Advice is aimed at security; and careless advice is covered by liability. The reasoning in *Smith v Bush* was contextual and plainly pragmatic in the sense we have observed, namely that it is oriented to *ex ante* risk considerations and the unreasonableness of expecting a domestic purchaser of limited means to acquire protection against the risk of over-valuation by paying twice for a valuation. We are suggesting here that the protection the purchaser is seeking does not only take the form of professional advice (a careful report), but specifically entails the availability of an indemnity should that advice be substandard. This is therefore an exercise in risk allocation, with or without insurance, and this is so even where the negligence standard applies. In fact, liability beyond negligence might not be successfully insured.[135] Negligence and insurance are hand in glove. As with developments since *Norwich CC*, so with developments since *Smith v Bush*, the insurance dimension has recently come more expressly to the surface.

The Court of Appeal returned to the issues in *Scullion v Bank of Scotland plc (Colleys)*.[136] The duty in *Smith v Bush* was not owed to a 'buy to let' purchaser, given that such a purchaser will generally have the means to acquire independent advice. Those who argue against the relevance of insurance considerations will doubtless seize on the closing remarks of Lord Neuberger of Abbotsbury MR, namely that the outcome gave little satisfaction given that the claimant had been badly misled and that the defendants' liabilities would, he strongly suspected, 'be footed by insurance'—despite which, no duty was owed.[137] Clearly, the likely existence of liability insurance was not sufficient to establish a duty. But we have already pointed out that our analysis of the

[133] Stapleton has urged that vulnerability of the claimant is a significant factor in identifying tort duties, but has not incorporated insurance issues into the definition of vulnerability: J Stapleton, 'The Golden Thread at the Heart of Tort Law: Protection of the Vulnerable', in P Cane (ed), *Centenary Essays for the High Court of Australia* (Sydney: LexisNexis Butterworths, 2004). Debating the link, see T Carver, 'Insurance and the Law of Negligence: An Influential or Irrelevant Persuader?' (2011) 22 ILJ 51.

[134] n 19.

[135] Chapter 11.

[136] [2011] EWCA Civ 693; [2011] 1 WLR 3212. Leave to appeal to the Supreme Court was granted, but it appears that a settlement has now been reached.

[137] [2011] EWCA Civ 693, n 136, at [70].

role of insurance does not suggest that courts seek insurance funds as a form of 'deep pocket' (though doubtless litigation is framed for this purpose). Rather, the key questions surround the appropriate allocation of risks associated with negligence. On this basis, the more pertinent reflections on the connection between duties of care on the part of advisers, and insurance, are contained in an earlier part of the reasoning. Here, Lord Neuberger rejected an argument that the low figure paid for the report (£35) was of any weight against the claimant. As he put it, £35 was the amount accepted by the defendants for providing the report and, significantly, 'all that it entailed'. They had, in fact, already made their inspection and perhaps drawn up the report, in order to advise another prospective mortgagee. What Lord Neuberger meant by 'all that it entailed' was, explicitly, the possibility that there may be liabilities stemming from reliance upon it:

> It [the fee] may have represented little more than the equivalent of an insurance premium for exposing themselves to liability for negligence in providing the report, but if Mr Scullion effectively did no more than pay for such insurance, that is enough to satisfy the principle behind the requirement that he paid for the report.[138]

Negligence duties, as *Caparo* itself makes plain, are not merely duties to be careful, but duties bringing the implication of liability should there be a failure to take due care. To take on a task which gives rise to a duty is to take on a risk of liability. The shifting meaning of the 'assumption of responsibility' to some extent reflects the degree to which the courts take into account that they are considering whether to impose the risk of liability as a corollary of taking on a role in relation to the claimant.[139] We entirely agree with Jane Stapleton that the parties' opportunities to protect themselves are pertinent considerations in attaching the risk of liability outside agreed patterns, and that there is scope to explain the divergence between building and advice claims in these terms. But we depart from her view that patterns of insurance are irrelevant to this question; and that only opportunities of protection which enhance deterrence can be relevant to the law of tort. To consider risk allocation without reference to insurance is entirely unrealistic. The sweeping exclusion of insurance from the array of 'legitimate' concerns in all circumstances has become an article of faith with no compelling foundation.

8.4.1 Concluding remarks on contractual matrix and advice cases

One of the key objections to including insurance in tort reasoning is that it will lead to incoherence depending on the happenstance of whether or not the parties are insured; or involve the courts in the task of deciding who was the best insurer. That is not the way that insurance is involved in the categories explored so far. There are patterns of insurance at work, and these patterns are well known to the courts. Some is compulsory; some is standard form. These patterns of insurance reflect purposes, goals, and policies of more than one party (the assured) or even two (including the insurer) to one

138 [2011] EWCA Civ 693, n 136, at [57].

139 The concept nevertheless remains among the most protean in the tort of negligence.

degree or another. This in itself is a departure from the received view of the irrelevance of insurance. Further, courts are quite prepared to reason pragmatically in relation to tort duties, and rationally discernible risk structures give coherence to their pragmatism. Some of this has been recognized in some—but not all—accounts of the cases examined so far. The additional key point is that insurance arrangements are a vital part of what courts consider when they reason. This is not the same as seeking deep pockets; it reflects the very *ex ante* approach recommended by Stapleton herself, though she (wrongly in our view, for reasons discussed) proposes that insurance be excluded from the *ex ante* concerns legitimately to be considered, and also suggests that those concerns are merely restraining factors which in 'conventional' tort claims will not operate—without 'special' concerns, the duty of care simply instructs those who owe it to be careful. In many instances, such as those governed by the JCT standard contracts, and other instances where similar issues surrounding liability risks arise, to think about parties' risk allocation without reference to insurance is to enter the realms of fiction. *Ex ante* risk allocation and insurance are too closely entwined for this to be recommended. Through advice cases, we can see similar issues arising in cases where, for one reason or another, the parties do not share in the mutual structuring of risk, or are not part of a contractual matrix.

Some of the most significant staging posts in the development of the law of negligence have arisen from cases which raise issues of this kind (for example *Caparo v Dickman*, *Henderson v Merrett*, *Smith v Bush*).[140] Given the influence of these cases, it is not surprising that some of the more general features of the approach in these cases—the inclination to think about negligence liabilities in terms of the location of risks, and the associated pragmatic form of reasoning—should have made progress in other areas of the law. In the next section we explore these features of the courts' reasoning in the (apparently) very different context of public authority liability, though we have chosen not to focus on building inspection cases (*Anns v Merton* and *Murphy v Brentwood*).[141] Given the similarities between these claims, and the claim against the classification society in *Marc Rich*, we suggest that the analysis in these cases has in any event been improved upon now by the English courts. The analysis in the next section does not purport to be complete. Rather, it raises the question of how far risk allocation extends in the realms of tort duties, and particularly to what extent courts are prepared to extend the logic of risk allocation into the domain of very different kinds of damage.

8.5 Public Authorities and Risk Allocation

Public authority liability is an area of some complexity, on at least two levels. First, the activities of public authorities are influenced by a range of statutory powers and duties and although it is settled that duties of care may be owed, there is a need to reconcile those duties with the wider obligations imposed upon them. Second, the courts have on occasion expressed a fear that imposition of liability on a public authority is effectively a

[140] nn 48 (*Caparo*); 19 (*Henderson*); 129 (*Smith v Eric Bush*).

[141] nn 47, 61.

charge on council or general tax payers, and that it may be more appropriate for the claimant either to bear his own loss or to insure against it himself.[142]

Some care is needed with the latter point. Public authorities may or may not insure against their own direct liabilities. They have exemption from certain duties to insure, on the basis that they do not pose the same risk of insolvency as other defendants, but in practice they may choose to carry insurance against these, and other liabilities.[143] Equally pertinently however, local authorities frequently carry out their functions through contractors, and where there is a risk that contractor negligence may give rise to a claim against the public authority itself—as in the case of liability for non-delegable duties—the contract will routinely impose upon the contractor the twin obligations of providing an indemnity to the public authority and insuring against the risk of having to meet it. The importance of this is, if anything, increasing with the greater use of voluntary organizations to supply services previously directly operated by public bodies. The effect is to shift the cost of covering the risk from a public authority or its insurer if any, to insurers of smaller, sometimes charitable organizations.[144] In such a case, liability would involve no charge to the public as a whole (other than, indirectly, the amount set aside in the contract for the purchase of insurance) unless the public authority itself remained liable in the same manner as employers subject to recognized 'non-delegable' duties.[145] In relation to direct liability, as we have seen, public authorities may insure or 'self-insure', a euphemism for assessing potential claims and setting aside funds for them. But again, some risks may be uninsurable: following the decision in *Bolton v MMI*[146] public liability policies exclude liability for claims for exposure to diseases; and following the riots in the summer of 2011 it is increasingly difficult for the police to obtain insurance to cover their liabilities under the Riot Damages Act 1886.[147]

For these reasons amongst others, public authority cases in many instances raise similar issues to those already explored, even though the identity of the claimant and nature of the loss are potentially far more variable. But beyond this point, public authority cases take a number of very different forms, and by no means all involve subcontracted functions. All of this reflects an important point, that settled or desirable risk allocations, including those involving insurance, are not solely a function of the parties' mutual arrangements. Courts may consider issues of risk allocation to be pertinent to the existence or non-existence of duties on a much broader canvas, and in doing so they may employ some of the same techniques addressed above. Here, we

[142] As in *Lamb v Camden* [1981] QB 625; [1981] 2 WLR 1038.

[143] Chapter 9 discusses local authority exemptions from duties to insure in the Road Traffic Act 1988 and Employers' Liability Act 1969; and Chapter 5 examines the attempt to include local authorities in the post-*Lister* agreement not to bring actions against careless employees.

[144] *Insurance Age*, February 2012 reports on the implications of a 'shift of governmental responsibility into the charity sector'. The tendering process by the NHS and local authorities 'goes hand in hand with a transferring of risk and an insurance requirement [including] public liability, professional indemnity and Employers' Liability. These are areas where the NHS and local authorities have, more often than not, self-insured'. The result is a growing market for insurance among contractors, including charities.

[145] This was the issue in *Woodland v Essex* [2012] EWCA Civ 239, discussed below in this section.

[146] [2006] EWCA Civ 50; [2006] 1 WLR 1492. Critically discussed in Chapter 12.

[147] Chapter 6.

explore how the issues already identified have either risen to the surface, or operated beneath the surface, in a range of claims against public authorities.

As in contractual matrix cases, so also in public authority cases, the courts have taken a journey from expansion to restriction. This is evidenced across a wide range of cases. True, a notable feature of public authority liability in the UK is that such authorities are now subject to new potential liabilities under the Human Rights Act 1998 s 8. To date however, the influence of the Human Rights Act (HRA) has seen further restriction in tort law, rather than extension of protection, as might have been (and generally was) envisaged.[148] Here we track the influence of insurance considerations at some vital points of this journey and relate them to the arguments above.[149] In particular, it is plain that in this context 'deterrence'—the overriding consideration in tort law on Stapleton's account, as we have seen—is afforded considerable scepticism and regarded, at best, as a blunt instrument (at worst, as positively unhelpful).[150] The increased emphasis not only on the pure costs of liability, but also on appropriate *ex ante* planning for those costs, is notable. The ambit of duties in tort has increasingly been set with reference to the particular financial implication of the tort remedy, which makes it singularly appropriate to consider in the light of alternative avenues of dealing with (and avoiding) the risk. This is far from excluding insurance. So here, too, the downplaying of deterrence, and embrace of insurance, are notable deviations from the pattern argued for by Stapleton—and, in our view, understandably so, because the normative basis of the exclusion of insurance and elevation of deterrence is highly questionable.

We begin our exploration with *Dorset Yacht Co v Home Office*,[151] which was decided in the middle of the expansionist phase of negligence and was one of the key cases referred to in *Anns v Merton* as evidencing that duties of care are owed according to general principles.[152] Here Edmund-Davies LJ argued in the Court of Appeal that the successful claimants (later successful again before the House of Lords) 'blaze no trail and can lay no claim to be pioneers. Nor would success in the present action be likely to place the plaintiffs at the head of a long line of litigants'. Though he was thinking chiefly of claims against the Home Office in respect of Borstal inmates, on a broader

[148] The path to restriction is explored by J Steele, 'Damages in Tort and Under the Human Rights Act' (2008) CLJ 606, and '(Dis)owning the Convention in the Law of Tort', in J Lee (ed), *From House of Lords to Supreme Court* (Oxford: Hart, 2010). Substantively, the first sign of green shoots of change in the Supreme Court may appear to be *Rabone v Pennine Care NHS Foundation Trust* [2012] UKSC 2; [2012] 2 WLR 381, where it was accepted that 'tort-like' liability had been developed by the jurisprudence of the European Court of Human Rights in relation to breaches of the state's positive duty to protect life under the European Convention on Human Rights art 2, and damages were awarded under the HRA. But the damages awarded in *Rabone* did not shift a risk. The damages were bereavement-style damages, whose significance is not in seeking to replace what has been lost, but in offering a conventional measure of compensation reflecting both the loss, and the wrong suffered.

[149] We will not directly consider *Murphy v Brentwood*, n 61, which was caught up with the definition of the loss as 'purely economic' and is not particularly helpful for that reason.

[150] The cases may to one extent or another fit the description of claims against 'peripheral parties', where Stapleton accepts that deterrence is less significant. But the inapplicability of the guiding principle in yet another significant category is notable in itself.

[151] [1970] AC 1004 (House of Lords); [1969] 2 QB 412 (CA).

[152] *Anns v Merton* [1978] AC 728 (n 47). *Anns* is no longer treated as authoritative in English law. In Canada, however, its approach to the duty of care is still adopted, albeit with modifications.

canvas he was proved quite wrong, and with hindsight *Dorset Yacht* stands at the start of a major expansion in claims for public authority liability. These have been subject to determined restriction by the courts more recently. It is possible to address this in terms of the concentration at the time of *Dorset Yacht* on relatively simple principles of justice and a restricted range of concerns about negligence liability, innocent of later concerns about the 'explosion' of liability. The chief question is whether the contrast with later cases involves a greater focus on the location of risks and possibility for alternative precautions. We would argue that this is indeed the case, and that this is related to increasing focus on the need to justify the risk allocation achieved by imposing tort duties.

Given its significance for the law of negligence, it is worth highlighting that the action in *Dorset Yacht* was not brought by the yacht owners, but by their first-party insurers, who had reimbursed the owners and were subrogated to the claim. The cost of repairs to the yacht, for which the insurers sought reimbursement from the Crown, was £1,303 1s 8d. Survey fees added a further £12 12s. Thus the origins of the expansionist phase in public authority liability lay in a small claim brought by first-party property insurers.[153] The expense involved in pursuing this shifting of cost from insurer to Crown has been criticized as a fiasco, not least because the tort claim was acknowledged not to be the place to investigate the policy issues surrounding the supervision of Borstal boys.[154] Indeed it seems unlikely that if the insurers shared the view of Edmund-Davies LJ that they would not be trail-blazers, they would have pursued a sum of this kind to the House of Lords. Leaving aside the issue of proportionality and cost, it would be good to be able to say that argument in *Dorset Yacht* surrounded the proper scope for an insurer to protect its own interests against the Home Office, in the context of risks associated with a scheme aimed at the rehabilitation of young offenders. But that was not the case, because as Lord Denning bluntly pointed out (and the other judges simply got on and did), the court was to treat the very presence of the insurer as irrelevant.[155]

Both in the Court of Appeal and in the House of Lords,[156] the reasoning in *Dorset Yacht* was focused in relatively formal terms on certain issues relating to duties of the public authority defendant. Did the statutory and discretionary nature of its activity remove it from the reach of the tort of negligence? Could it be required to bear responsibility for the acts of a third party? The case was not conceptualized in terms of whether it was right for risks to be borne by the authorities in a context where first-party insurers had already indemnified the notional claimant. Yet here was a case in

[153] Note Lord Hoffmann's reference to such issues in *Transco v Stockport BC* [2003] UKHL 61; [2004] 1 AC 1, discussed later in this section.

[154] R Hasson, 'Subrogation in Insurance Law—a Critical Evaluation' (1985) 5 OJLS 416, 426, referring particularly to Viscout Dilhorne's dissent. His views on this would now, we suggest, gain wider judicial acceptance, evidenced by the developments discussed next.

[155] It was Lord Denning's practice to set out the insurance position even if he did not decide it was relevant to the determination of the case, thus going some way to clarify what was at stake for the parties in the case, and why the litigation was framed as it was: for example *Photo Production v Securicor Transport Ltd* [1980] AC 827; *Morris v Ford Motor* [1973] QB 792; *Nettleship v Weston* [1971] 2 QB 691; *Denham v Midland Employers Mutual Assurance* [1955] 2 QB 437: who is the employer/which insurance policy responds?

[156] n 151.

which, to adopt the analysis above, the claimant had indeed taken up an 'alternative means of protection', and in which there might well be public policy arguments *against* deterrence, or which would undermine the acceptability of deterrence as a goal. Though the Court of Appeal sought to play down the potential impact of this by recourse to the need to show genuine negligence (an issue of breach), two sceptical responses are possible. First, and as already noted, a claim in negligence for property damage may not be the right place to review the desirability of Home Office policy in relation to rehabilitation. Only if it was could the tort liability be said to be more desirable than the cheaper alternative of first-party insurers taking the loss. Second, 'no duty' is a more effective way of avoiding exposure of defendants to litigation than the factual enquiry relating to breach. The courts' analysis in later cases has increasingly recognized this, matching the evolution of the role of the duty of care from a 'control device', to a necessary criterion requiring positive justification in terms of who bears the risk of negligence.[157] To omit from consideration not only the availability of insurance, but also its actual existence and the presence of an insurer in the litigation, is hard to justify in light of the current approach.

Dorset Yacht is not, in these respects, symptomatic of all public authority cases. In particular, claims for failure to control third parties have more recently appeared in relation to physical assaults,[158] where issues of insurer subrogation do not arise. The same is also true of cases of educational welfare and failures in care provision. Such cases illustrate that people do not only bring actions against public authorities in circumstances where they (and/or their insurers) want to shift risk. Indeed issues about public liability to individuals now also find expression in actions under the HRA 1998, and claims in tort raising parallel issues. Even so, the approach of the courts has become more restrictive in the years since *Phelps v Hillingdon*.[159] The latest serious success in a novel claim against a local authority in the English courts, *O'Connor v Surrey CC*,[160] involved a recognized relationship of employer and employee. Even here, extensive analysis was devoted to justifying compensation of the claimant against a background of statutory powers and duties.

Leaving aside *Murphy v Brentwood*,[161] the most decisive cases leading to this more restrictive position certainly do involve express questions about the location of risk. These are *Stovin v Wise*,[162] and *Gorringe v Calderdale*.[163] In these cases, the House of Lords plainly perceived the public authority as a 'peripheral party' whose power to remove or ameliorate hazards was translated through the arguments of litigants into a

[157] Also *HM Customs and Excise Commissioners v Barclays Bank* [2006] UKHL 28; [2007] 1 AC 181.

[158] *Mitchell v Glasgow City Council* [2009] UKHL 11; [2009] 2 WLR 481. Note also *Smith v Littlewoods* [1987] AC 241—not a public authority case but Lord Goff's approach emphasizing the absence of a duty of care was used, and vindicated, in *Glasgow*.

[159] [2001] 2 AC 619.

[160] [2010] EWCA Civ 286; [2011] QB 328. Beyond local authorities, note also the decision of the Supreme Court in *Smith & Others v Ministry of Defence* [2013] UKSC 41, identifying the limits of the specific doctrine of combat immunity, and identifying the potential for a duty of care in negligence accordingly.

[161] n 61. The reasoning in *Murphy* deserves the criticism it has received, as it was largely confined to defining the kind of damage suffered; yet it is clear from the cases discussed in 8.3 and 8.4 that 'pure economic loss' is a recoverable form of damage in some instances.

[162] n 23. [163] [2004] UKHL 15; [2004] 1 WLR 1057.

tort duty to bear certain risks associated with those hazards. Having framed the question in this way, the House of Lords rejected the attempted transformation.

The role of insurance in *Stovin v Wise* was made patent by Lord Hoffmann. The role of the insurer in *Stovin* was referred to again by him in *Gorringe* nearly ten years later, explaining how the local authority came to be a defendant in the earlier case, though questions of risk allocation in the latter case were addressed more openly by Lord Rodger, as we will discuss. The claimant in *Stovin* had settled a claim for personal injury against the defendant driver. Insurance to cover liability to third parties in road traffic claims is compulsory, and we can assume that this settlement was reached by the defendant's insurer. But the defendant (which is likely to mean the defendant's insurer), applied to join the Council as a second defendant, on the basis that the junction at which the accident happened was a dangerous one, and that the Council ought to have exercised its statutory powers, and improved it. Indeed, it had decided to do so, but had failed to act. The 'defendant'/insurer, therefore, not the injured party, argued that the local authority owed the claimant a duty at common law, to make the junction safe, that this duty had been breached, and that the local authority should therefore bear part of the liability.

This argument was accepted in the courts below, and the Council's share in damages assessed at 30 per cent. The majority of the discussion in the House concerned the relationship between statutory powers, and alleged positive duties in negligence to take steps in line with the powers. On this issue, *Stovin* and *Gorringe* between them are key authorities. How much significance therefore should be attached to the role of insurance? A pertinent feature of the case is that, as with *Dorset Yacht*, it was the insurers who sought to shift part of the burden of compensating to the public purse. In *Dorset Yacht*, this did not affect the court's decision, and indeed, that decision seems to neglect arguments about bearing the risk of a readily insurable, and relatively small harm. In *Stovin*, Lord Hoffmann mentioned insurance as a consideration militating against liability. Should this be dismissed as a 'makeweight' argument?[164] We argue that it was not a mere makeweight argument, partly because its importance is supported by the fact that it forms part of a discernible pattern in leading cases, of attention to the burdens of liability, and the responsibilities of others (including sometimes individual claimants) to bear their own risks. It would be more accurate to say that insurance issues are among a continuum of factors which bear on the question of whether compensation—the financial burden of making good a loss—should flow, and it is here that the depiction of this case in terms of 'economic rationalism', rather than 'economic welfarism', is most pertinent.[165] Lord Hoffmann's judgment in *Stovin*, like many other decisions of the highest court in the latest, restrictive period of tort liability, notably emphasizes the financial consequences of tort liability—the fact that the substance of the remedy is to transfer a financial burden. In this instance of course, the location of insurance is far from unknown, incidental, or fortuitous, since it has been placed on particular parties by legislation; and the 'rationalism' concerned does not operate to undermine the welfare of the injured party, whose claim has settled. In

[164] Stapleton, n 2, 833. [165] 8.2, n 63.

this sense, and in its protection of public funds, it may ultimately be considered more compatible with 'welfarism' than forms of analysis (based on policy or on principle) which ignore the allocation of risk and, most pertinently, the role of insurance.

The key point, therefore, is that Lord Hoffmann's judgment approaches tort *duties* in terms of the potential *liabilities* that follow from their recognition, and thus with the financial burden that they impose.[166] The nature of this approach to tort duties can be highlighted by contrast with the dissenting judgment of Lord Nicholls. Lord Nicholls presented tort duties as essentially duties to be careful. Recognizing that positive duties in tort are potentially objectionable, he attributed this to their invasive requirement to do something. Lord Nicholls made the point that this was less objectionable where there was a (public law) duty to act in any event. References to the burdens of action, and reasonableness of the claimant's reliance on action, pervade the judgment. This is in marked contrast to Lord Hoffmann's approach, which is preoccupied with the burden not of action, but of liability. For Lord Nicholls, a positive duty to act might not impose an additional burden, 'in the sense of requiring an authority to act differently from the course already required by its public law obligations'.[167] Equally, and relating to our earlier discussion of reliance within a contractual structure, Lord Nicholls approached reliance in terms of the claimant's reliance on the authority 'acting in a particular way'; and assumption of responsibility in terms of whether the authority had assumed responsibility 'to act in a particular way'.[168] Neither is likely to distinguish sharply between tort duties, and public law powers and duties, because the emphasis is on action rather than on the parties to whom the duties are owed, and the consequences of breach. As we have said, in the pragmatic style, tort duties are recognized to be specific, and not reducible to an obligation to act.[169] They are owed to specific people in respect of specific risks. This is clearly observable in Lord Hoffmann's account, which emphasizes very different burdens—not simply the burden of acting, but the financial burden of liability—in considering the existence of a duty which is distinctively a *tort* duty. This, in fact, is explicit:

> It is one thing to provide a service at public expense. It is another to require the public to pay compensation when a failure to provide the service has resulted in loss.[170]

Lord Hoffmann here is discussing the existence of tort duties where powers and duties are set out in a statute, and it may be thought that this raised distinct issues. But an approach to tort duties as imposing financial burdens, and implying financial reliance, can be seen at work throughout his judgment, and has broader significance. For example, the difference between reliance on action and reliance in relation to financial risks is spelled out by reference to the risk of fire. 'In one sense', Lord Hoffmann argued, the fire service is there to protect people where they could not be expected to protect themselves. But on the other hand, property owners 'can and do protect themselves by insurance against the risk of fire'. He continued:

[166] These points are discussed in 8.2 and 8.3. [167] n 23, 935. [168] n 23, 937.

[169] The pragmatic style is not alone in recognizing this. The same is true of certain other approaches to the idea of duty, such as the 'rights-based' approach of R Stevens, *Torts and Rights* (Oxford: Oxford University Press, 2007).

[170] n 23, 952.

> It is not obvious that there should be a right to compensation from a negligent fire authority which will ordinarily enure by right of subrogation to an insurance company. The only reason would be to provide a general deterrent against inefficiency. But there must be better ways of doing this than by compensating insurance companies out of public funds.[171]

The nature of a duty of care in tort, on this approach, is not solely that it requires action or conduct of a particular sort, but that it places potential liabilities with the duty-ower, and that this is something on which claimants may rely when planning around risks. The general availability of insurance in known categories of case—and the fact that subrogation will operate on behalf of insurers to shift risks to those who owe a duty—are relevant to the contemplation of tort duties. We would underline once again that tort duties are clustered in areas where insurance arrangements have become familiar and in some instances are statutorily mandated.

Connected to this last point, equally significant is Lord Hoffmann's emphasis on legislative policy in relation to the burden of losses. Compulsory motor insurance expresses a legislative policy—consistently advanced over many years—about where burdens should lie.[172] Lord Hoffmann's comments mark a clear contrast between his analysis of this particular case, and the Australian courts' elaboration of liability to those who would otherwise be without protection in a range of circumstances. In this instance, he pointed out, 'denial of liability does not leave the road user unprotected'. Nor does the road user rely in general terms on the roads being entirely free of hazards ('[e]veryone knows that there are hazardous bends, intersections and junctions')—a reference to the theory of general reliance adopted in New Zealand. Rather, Lord Hoffmann concluded his opinion by expressing the view that it is 'primarily the duty of road users to take due care'; and that if they do not, 'there is compulsory insurance to provide compensation to the victims'. It is suggested that this is not a makeweight argument but a high-level encapsulation of what duty questions in this type of case are considered to be driving at—the determination of whether there is sound reason to say that the risk of harm should, through the instrument of liability, be placed with the defendant. The pattern of insurance, particularly where it is legislatively mandated, to some extent defines settled ideas of self-reliance and reliance on others in respect of risk. Tort remedies, in those cases where tort responds to losses (including non-pecuniary losses), have a special character when compared with public law remedies or other means of covering risks, because they seek to shift the loss, through the medium of money. These explanations show insurance to be 'in the thick of it' when it comes to tort duties, not because insurance is a special consideration, but for the entirely opposite reason.

Lord Hoffmann's reference to liability for fire, noted earlier, invites comparison with tort duties beyond negligence. Issues similar to those already discussed can be observed in relation to the remnants of strict liability for escape of dangerous things, in the

[171] n 23, 955.

[172] The consistency of the pattern is underlined by S Hedley, 'Tort and Personal Injuries, 1850 to Present', in TT Arvind and J Steele, *Tort Law and the Legislature: Common Law, Statute and the Dynamics of Legal Change* (Oxford: Hart Publishing, 2013). For analysis, see Chapter 9. See also Carver, n 133.

'action in *Rylands v Fletcher*'.[173] In *Transco plc v Stockport Metropolitan Borough Council*,[174] the most authoritative recent statement of the English law in this area, Lord Hoffmann again drew attention to common patterns of insurance, arguing that these were relevant to the question of which accumulations were sufficiently exceptional to give rise to the strict liability. Drawing attention to express statutory liabilities, accompanied by duties to insure,[175] in some of the most dangerous undertakings, he argued that:

> so far as the rule does have a residuary role to play, it must be borne in mind that it is concerned only with damage to property and that insurance against various forms of damage to property is extremely common. A useful guide in deciding whether the risk has been created by a 'non-natural' user of land is therefore to ask whether the damage which eventuated was something against which the occupier could reasonably be expected to have insured himself. Property insurance is relatively cheap and accessible; in my opinion people should be encouraged to insure their own property rather than seek to transfer the risk to others by means of litigation, with the heavy transactional costs which that involves. The present substantial litigation over £100,000 should be a warning to anyone seeking to rely on an esoteric cause of action to shift a commonplace insured risk.[176]

Plainly, the allocation of financial risks, and particularly insurability, is here regarded as a key element in the recognition of when the strict tort duty should arise—a risk can hardly be called exceptional or extraordinary if it is both commonplace, and habitually insured. These are not isolated remarks, but employ ideas which have provided important decision-making resources in other areas where the boundaries of tort duties have needed definition. In the more recent case of *Stannard (t/a Wyvern Tyres) v Gore*,[177] the Court of Appeal subjected common law liability for fire to the approach in *Transco*, with the result that damage by fire beginning on the defendant's premises will rarely be the subject of a strict duty in tort. Ward LJ summarized the 'moral of the story' not only in that case, but also in *Transco* itself, as 'taken from the speech of Lord Hoffmann: make sure you have insurance cover for losses occasioned by fire on your premises'.[178] Of course, this also recalls Lord Hoffmann's comments about fire risks in *Stovin v Wise*, and this in turn is a reminder that the liability of public services for failure to attend in order to put out fires has been the subject of litigation, despite the widespread presence of property insurance against fire.[179] The point is not that

[173] Derived from the celebrated case of *Rylands v Fletcher* (1868) LR 3 HL.
[174] [2003] UKHL 61; [2003] 3 WLR 1467.
[175] This is significant because it once again draws attention to a willingness to respect existing distributive responses to risk, rather than to superimpose functions specific to the law of tort which would cut across these—akin to the arguments about private ordering in contractual matrix cases.
[176] *Transco*, n 174, [46].
[177] [2012] EWCA Civ 1248; [2013] 1 All ER 694.
[178] n 177, [50]. The 'moral' of a story is generally a lesson that can be taken from it (rather than, for example, an explanation of why the events happened). But it is also an encapsulation of one of its most important (not peripheral) features.
[179] For example *Capital and Counties Plc v Hampshire CC* [1997] QB 1004.

insurance will always be in place; but that it is *reasonable* to place an insurance risk with property owners.[180]

In *Gorringe v Calderdale*,[181] a unanimous House of Lords confirmed the restrictive approach of the majority in *Stovin v Wise*, underlining growing unanimity in the need to protect risk allocations. Here, the claimant had failed to slow down sufficiently approaching the brow of a hill, and was in collision with a bus coming the other way. The bus driver was not at fault and the bus had not strayed from its carriageway. In the absence of any fault on the part of the other driver, the claimant sought compensation from the local authority, on the basis that despite the obviousness of the hazard, it ought to have repainted warnings on the road which had previously been visible. In this instance, it is the legislative emphasis on third party, rather than first-party insurance which encourages the attempt to shift risk to a local authority. Lord Rodger's judgment dealt expressly with this aspect of risk allocation, and with its underlying policy. The fault principle means that drivers must 'look out for dangers themselves' and not rely on others beyond the bounds of due care. If they fail to drive carefully, and *others* are injured, those others 'can recover compensation from the drivers' insurers or from the Motor Insurers' Bureau'. Neither a driver at fault, nor other injured parties, can recover from the local authority for failure to paint a warning sign. Notably, Lord Rodger expressed this as a 'settled pattern' which should not be changed by the courts, and in respect of which 'additional funding' for authorities to meet and handle claims would need to be approved.[182] Not only in the emphasis on duties as reflecting responsibility for financial risks, but also in the emphasis on settled and understood risk structures or patterns, both *Stovin* and *Gorringe* have much in common with the 'contractual matrix' and advice cases referred to in 8.3 and 8.4. These cases illustrate that the courts are prepared to maintain their focus on the financial implications of tort liability not only where there is property damage, but even where the actions in question are for personal injuries and, in the case of *Gorringe*, where it would appear that the claimant lacks other sources of compensation. This brings us to a much more testing case for the reach of economic rationalism. What happens to deserving claimants, with no influence over risk allocation structures, when the intended source of compensation fails them?

8.5.1 *Woodland v Essex County Council*: non-delegable duties and risk allocation

There is much to be said about non-delegable duties,[183] and we do not aim to override those discussions here. Rather, we deal with the claim in *Woodland v Essex County*

[180] For discussion, see J Steele and R Merkin, 'Insurance Between Neighbours: *Stannard v Gore* and Common Law Liability for Fire' (2013) JEL (forthcoming). In *Transco*, the prevalence of insurance against fire was expressly rejected by Lord Hobhouse as a reason against the imposition of *Rylands* liability. Lord Hobhouse was the most enthusiastic supporter of the rule in *Rylands v Fletcher* in this case.

[181] n 163.

[182] n 163, 93.

[183] See for example the discussions by J Murphy, 'Juridical Foundations of Common Law Non-Delegable Duties', and Robert Stevens, 'Non-Delegable Duties and Vicarious Liability', in J Neyers, E Chamberlain, and S Pitel (eds), *Emerging Issues in Tort Law* (Oxford: Hart Publishing, 2007).

Council[184] as an individual and deeply unhappy case raising the question of how far economic rationalism as to risk might extend. The case before the Court of Appeal represents an instalment in a lengthy battle for compensation fought by parents of a child who suffered terrible injuries during a swimming lesson. This is not, ordinarily, the kind of risk for which families provide *ex ante* through insurance. But the case nevertheless shows the breadth of potential risk allocation issues. For the risk is exactly the sort of reason why members of the Swimming Teachers' Association are required to carry liability insurance.

The school attended by the claimant did not have its own swimming pool, nor were its staff trained in providing swimming lessons. In delivering these lessons, it contracted with Beryl Stopford, trading as Direct Swimming Services, who arranged swimming teaching and the availability of the pool. The pool itself was run by Basildon Council, not by Essex County Council (the education authority). The claimant had begun an action against three defendants: Beryl Stopford; a swimming teacher employed by Beryl Stopford; and the Swimming Teachers Association, of which both were members. On the side of these defendants, the claim was handled by Assitalia, who provided block insurance for the Swimming Teachers Association. For reasons whose obscurity was described by the Court of Appeal at an earlier stage of the litigation as 'deeply depressing',[185] it took around six years of apparent inactivity before Assitalia accepted liability. In 2009, nine years after the incident and after at least one interim payment and protracted negotiation over quantum, that admission of liability was revoked.[186] It was in these circumstances that a new claim was pursued against the education authority, arguing that it had breached a non-delegable duty to ensure that reasonable care was taken for their daughter's safety in the conduct of swimming lessons, irrespective of lack of negligence in the selection of the contractors,[187] and despite the fact that there was every reason to suppose that liability insurance was in place.

Clearly, this was a vulnerable claimant who had not neglected to take appropriate steps to secure her own safety or to provide in other ways for the risk. Equally clearly, the claim was pressed against the education authority only because problems appear to have arisen in the claim against parties who would be expected to guard against the risk both by avoiding it (by taking care), *and* by providing insurance in case it should eventuate. The education authority was a 'last ditch' hope for the claimant. Of the three opinions in the Court of Appeal, two offer no obvious sense that the case might raise issues of risk allocation or of insurance, despite the role of both of these in the arrangements entered into by the school and in the (highly unsatisfactory) process of the claim to date.

Influenced by Australian case law and, no doubt, by the vulnerability of the claimant, Laws LJ in dissent would have held that this was a proper case in which to recognize

[184] [2012] EWCA Civ 239.

[185] *Woodland v Stopford and others* [2011] EWCA Civ 266 [10] (Ward LJ).

[186] The Court of Appeal, n 185, accepted that this was in accord with practice protocols and validly made.

[187] A claim that there was negligence in selection was rejected by a judge and was not the subject of appeal; so also was an argument that the education authority was vicariously liable for the swimming teacher.

a 'duty to ensure that care is taken' on the part of the school. Despite its terminology, it is worth saying that such a duty does not seem likely to have any true incentive or deterrence function, other than in respect of financial provision. There was no realistic suggestion that the school had failed to put proper structures in place whether in terms of selection of the contractor or oversight of the lessons. It is tempting to conclude that the real purpose of a non-delegable duty here is not to ensure that care is taken but that a remedy is available where care is not taken. This is a possible way of dealing with the risks inherent in swimming, which is a prescribed aspect of the National Curriculum; but as we have seen, other structures were already in place. In the relatively formal style of reasoning we have described as distinguishable from reasoning openly around the allocation of financial risks, this was not referred to. Rather, the criteria would be that a hospital or school would owe such a duty where a child or patient (a) is 'generally in its care'; and (b) is receiving a service which is part of the institution's 'mainstream function' (of education or tending the sick, for example).[188] The result is that the school (education authority) would not escape responsibility for the risk of harm when it provided such services through those other than its servants. For the majority, Kitchin LJ reached the opposite conclusion using somewhat similar, but more targeted resources, noting that the environment in which the accident occurred was not under the 'control' of the defendants (presumably marking a distinction from cases where independent contractors work on school premises); and that they did not undertake the care, supervision, or control of the pupils while they were taking swimming lessons.

The remaining majority judgment was that of Tomlinson LJ. This was quite different in style, and expressly focused on *ex ante* issues about the economic risks, should the physical risk not be sufficiently avoided. Noting that the second and third defendants (Beryl Stopford and her employee) were required to hold liability insurance, Tomlinson LJ plainly thought this a reason why it was inappropriate to recognize a duty on the education authority which would go beyond any that had been recognized before. Indeed this is unmissable given his statement that 'the days are long gone when we ignored the incidence of indemnity insurance'. Consistently with what we have said about the influence of existing arrangements in determination of the boundaries of tort, as well as contract duties, Tomlinson LJ added that he would expect that the price for the service provided by the second defendant to the school would reflect the cost to the second defendant of arranging adequate insurance. Of course, those arrangements did not involve the claimant. Bluntly, he added that 'The only purpose of the present appeal is to ensure that liability is brought home to a defendant with sufficient resources to meet the possible award'. No criticism was, or can be attached to a claimant of this sort for pursuing such a purpose; but if the approach of Tomlinson LJ is accepted, a non-delegable duty in this situation would appear to be chiefly a duty to make provision for the financial consequences should care not be taken.[189] And since in this instance, unlike the familiar

[188] [2012] EWCA Civ 239, Laws LJ at [30].

[189] Tomlinson LJ also provided a 'pragmatic' explanation of the Australian case law from *Commonwealth v Introvigne* (1982) 56 ALJR 749 onwards as essentially filling in specific gaps in the availability of compensation, and as largely involving dangers on premises which were controlled by those who owed the duties.

employment instance,[190] there is no existing duty on the local authority to insure the pupils, and the primarily liable party is itself required to hold insurance, it is also an invitation to duplicated insurance, and at odds (as Tomlinson LJ pointed out) both with the contractual structure entered into by the defendant (but not the claimant), and—arguably—with the desired pattern of incentives.

Needless to say, this case does not reflect at all well on the law of tort as an avenue for providing compensation where it is most needed. However, it may be argued that the creation of novel duties on the part of the public authority would shift the financial consequences of these obvious shortcomings to public funds, given the failure of a recognized avenue of compensation. That failure might be blamed on insurers who revoke an admission of liability; it might be blamed on civil procedure rules; or it might be blamed on the existence of a fault principle which had worked against settlement. But in any case, the discussion of insurance by Tomlinson LJ cannot realistically be described as a mere 'makeweight'. The role of insurance in his discussion is entirely consistent with that discussion as a whole. His judgment poses the challenge of how far preferred risk allocation structures will constrain the creation of novel tort duties.

8.5.2 Concluding remarks: public authority liability

There is no entirely consistent pattern to whether public authorities are insured in respect of various liability risks. Why then is judicial reference to insurance becoming more discernible in this context? Part of the answer is that public authorities are attractive defendants either for subrogated insurers, or for those whose more obvious route to accessing a liability insurer is blocked for some reason (whether that is under-insurance, their own fault, or some other reason). So it is the insurance arrangements of others which often count—and in the examples we have seen, there have been important indications that these arrangements are the key to securing—or at least enabling—the distribution of risks. Local authorities remain targets when insurance fails, as well as being, sometimes, the target of loss-shifting by insurers. In *Woodland*, for example, the court was faced with the kind of situation where public authorities routinely insist on insurance as part of the contracting process; but where appalling delay in the process of a claim against the insured contractor deflected attention to the authority itself. More fundamentally, we see that these cases have placed particular emphasis on tort liability in its financial sense, reflecting and allocating risks.

8.6 Duties to Employees

So far, we have focused on doctrinal 'pressure points' in the higher courts, which have arisen from attempts by parties to expand the range of tort duties, and thereby to shift risk to others. But the pattern of tort duties as a whole can of course be seen as a pattern of responsibility for risk. Even in areas where insurance is widespread (or indeed mandated), gaps in cover will arise. This does not invalidate the argument that insurance

[190] 8.6.

is an influence on the law. Courts are willing to endorse patterns of duty which will produce overall suitable results, rather than responding with excessive particularity.

Here, we briefly illustrate some of these different aspects of the relationship between tort duties, risks, and insurance, through a focus on duties owed by employers to their employees. This has been one of the areas of compulsory liability insurance in English law since commencement of the Employers' Liability (Compulsory Insurance) Act 1969. Our focus is specifically on the structure and nature of duties in the presence of insurance. English law dismantled its statutory regime of Workmen's Compensation at the end of the Second World War in favour of a more general scheme of national insurance incorporating a special industrial injury scheme. But where obligations and liabilities are concerned, it has not of course returned to the limited approach of the nineteenth-century common law in relation to workplace injuries. On the contrary, the workplace is the site of many overlapping duties, some originating in the courts, others the creation of statute and legislation. In both instances, some of the duties are of a strict or even absolute nature.

Fundamental change in the relationship between civil liability and these strict or absolute duties is now on the horizon. The present coalition government has stated an intention to ensure that even where such strict or absolute duties exist, they should be actionable in damages only according to a negligence standard. The means by which this objective has been pursued is, in fact, still more far-reaching: the Enterprise and Regulatory Reform Act 2013, s 69 (which received Royal Assent on 25 April 2013) provides that breach of a duty imposed by health and safety regulations or legislation—including existing provisions—will not be actionable unless regulations under the section so provide. When in force, this provision will amount to a reversal of settled patterns of liability, and in view of the stated purpose behind the change it seems most likely that regulations made under the section will be aimed at removing strict liability.[191] If anything, this significant change of policy in relation to civil liability for breach of strict duties highlights the value of paying attention to employers' duties as strict duties to succeed in bringing about particular results. A key point is that the duties themselves aim at shaping employer behaviour, whether or not they are accompanied by civil liability. Civil liability for breach of such a duty does not mean abandoning the idea of a defensible obligation—no matter how strict—to secure

[191] Enterprise and Regulatory Reform Act 2013, s 69, amends the Health and Safety at Work Act 1974, s 47. The government's press release states in relation to this section that it 'establishes the principle that an employer should always have the opportunity, even where a strict duty applies, to defend themselves on the basis of having taken all reasonable steps to protect their employees': <https://www.gov.uk/government/news/enterprise-and-regulatory-reform-bill-receives-royal-assent> (accessed 21 May 2013) (in fact, it does this only in the sense that it removes civil liability from the regulations altogether unless there is regulation to the contrary). The reform was presented as the government's response to the Löfstedt Report: R Löftsedt, 'Reclaiming Health and Safety for All' Nov 2011, Cm 8219. Few lawyers were involved in that review. The relevant provision (then clause 62) was initially removed from the Bill by the House of Lords, but on a second vote it was passed. Particularly pertinent are the remarks of Lord Brown of Eaton-under-Heywood in the first House of Lords debate, 6 March 2013, Col 1513–14, emphasizing that 'There is nothing like strict liability, or its civil equivalent, to induce employers to take proactive steps to ensure that the risks and dangers are reduced to a minimum. Employers' insurers therefore, since 1974, have had altogether fewer claims to meet and have certainly incurred far fewer legal costs in meeting them.'

the safety of workers, in favour of a distribution of losses. These duties will remain even when civil liability in relation to their breach has been removed or limited, even if an important route to enforcing them will have been demolished. On the other hand, and consistently with our argument throughout, the fact that liabilities depend on defined duties means that only particular risks have been distributed through liability. This may well be a necessary feature of a scheme which continues to operate the full measure of tort damages across routine (rather than exceptional) risks.[192]

In 8.1, we gave the example of the Provision and Use of Work Equipment Regulations 1998, reg 5 as an instance of an 'absolute' duty. Other duties under these and similar regulations are strict, without being absolute. Such duties may indeed oblige those who owe a duty to achieve particular outcomes, though other duties are qualified by what is 'reasonably practicable'. Employers are under duties to carry out risk assessments and to anticipate risks; and also to take steps to protect employees from the specific risks identified. Without the first step, the employer may fail in its claim to have acted reasonably—in respect of which risk?[193] Therefore, there are duties to be *proactive* in protecting employees. The key point from our point of view is that these are duties which both guide behaviour, and have provided the route to liability and (through insurance) remedies. Not only do such duties coherently exist, but they relate to particular risks, and are owed to particular categories of people (whether employees, or those 'at work'), and by some parties, but not others.[194]

It is plain that the presence of insurance in such cases has a profound influence on the pattern of litigation. Examples vary from the high profile, such as *Chandler v Cape*,[195] to the more routine, such as *Hyndman v Brown*.[196] However, the direction and content of *particular* duties is the focus for the analysis of the courts, and the idea of strict liabilities backed by insurance does not collapse into a sea of undifferentiated liability for all injuries suffered at work—an important reminder that the existence of insurance does not destroy the role of legal duties, nor their ambition to secure improvement in the level of care taken. The influence of insurance is regularly to be seen in the detailed operation of the law in relation to workplace accidents. For example, interim payments can be ordered in the most serious cases, in a defined range of circumstances. One condition is that the potential parties, if two 'employers' are joined, are both or all insured: for example *Berry v Ashtead Plant Hire Co Ltd*.[197] This exemplifies how well it is understood that insurance is a significant factor in

[192] The contrast is with national insurance and workers' compensation of other forms: further discussed in Chapter 9.

[193] *Threlfall v Kingston-upon-Hull City Council* [2010] EWCA Civ 1147.

[194] Ordinary householders were held not to owe the relevant duties in *Kmeicic v Isaacs* [2011] EWCA Civ 451 (a claim motivated, as is not unusual in cases questioning the boundaries of recognized duties whether statutory or not, by failure of employers' liability insurance in the particular case).

[195] [2012] EWCA Civ 525; [2012] 1 WLR 3111, concerning a duty of care in negligence. A parent company owed a duty of care directly to the employees of its subsidiary in all the circumstances. The subsidiary had insurance, but this did not respond to the particular disease suffered. The parent did not have insurance, but did have deep pockets.

[196] [2012] NICA 3: a flaw in the employer's insurance led the claimant to pursue a claim against a different party, who had loaned to the employer the work equipment which caused the injury. That party however was held to have lacked sufficient control at the time of the accident for liability to be established.

[197] [2011] EWCA Civ 1304.

securing the compensation mandated by the duties created by the courts and the legislature; but these cases also show the persistence of flaws and uncertainties in the extent of duties even where strict duties and compulsory insurance are involved. Even so, duties define the risks that are placed with duty-owers. Insurance does not 'override' duties; and neither does the ambition to provide compensation necessarily undermine them.

8.7 Conclusions: Duties, Remedies, and Risks

Market arrangements and private ordering have their place in the determination of tort duties, as of contract duties. So too do other ideas—including protection of the vulnerable,[198] and deterrence; and the existence of social and political choices as to the ordering of risks. Welfarism and economic rationalism coexist as potential objectives in the law. These ideas do not replace moral argument; but equally, there is little basis on which to conclude that fault or responsibility are themselves sufficiently powerful ideas to displace concerns about these risk structures. Rather, we have observed an increased attention to the financial burden of negligence liability *when determining what duties lie*, which extends beyond cases where existing risk allocations are a matter of private ordering, to those where they are a matter of social (or legal) policy—such as compulsory or simply routine insurance. Insurance can plainly be admitted to be a relevant factor in the definition of tort duties without according it one general and dominating role. Rather, insurance is relevant in a host of different ways. These ways, in turn, reflect the courts' appreciation that to impose a duty on A in relation to B's interests is itself to allocate a risk.

Although we have ended this chapter by outlining the compatibility between tort duties and insurance with particular reference to employers' duties, we have generally not emphasized the role of insurance in cases where duties of care are well established, which make up the most 'high-volume' areas of tort claiming (empirically). These have also been seen (in theory) as the most 'conventional' and, to the extent that they occur between strangers, as more 'distinctive' of tort than of contract. These are the focus of our next chapter.

[198] This is not unique to tort, as the adaptation of contract to consumer protection illustrates.

9

Compulsory Liability Insurance

9.1 Introduction

This chapter explores the phenomenon of compulsory liability insurance, and its implications. The existence of compulsion plainly demonstrates the significant role of public purpose in securing the satisfaction of tort liabilities through insurance. We have already begun to consider the influence that this tangible purpose may have on judicial analysis of tort claims. However, the desired result is achieved through the insurance market. It is the interaction between tort liability, insurance market, and public purpose that we investigate here.

In the previous chapter, dealing with the role of insurance in shaping tort duties, we largely confined our remarks to 'novel' cases, deferring discussion of more 'conventional' cases. The relevance of insurance to 'conventional' cases has been more hotly debated, and resistance to insurance as a relevant factor has been strong, by reason of focus on the argument—particularly influential in the US—that tort should be analysed *as* a form of insurance. Responses to that argument deny that tort is simply a gateway to insurance and that liability rules operate on that basis; and (expanding slightly) that liability and first-party insurance should be seen as interchangeable policy options, so that the choices between them (including the choice between tort and insurance measures of compensation) are a matter purely of logic or efficiency. Whatever the cogency of 'tort as insurance' arguments,[1] we do not propose the reform of tort whether along the lines of a first-party insurance regime or otherwise. Rather, our goal is to explore the part played by insurance in the operation of the law of obligations, and to consider its implications once better understood. At the moment, such an investigation is largely locked out by the strength of normative objections to 'tort as insurance', and that poses the risk of misdescription, and hence misunderstanding.

9.1.1 Insurance at the heart of tort liability: 'conventional' claims and their operation

Compulsory insurance has a notable effect in relation to what have been called 'conventional' or 'traditional' tort claims. These have been identified as claims 'where

[1] For a particularly cogent exposition of the strongest reasons in favour of addressing first-party insurance and liability as alternatives in the context of products liability, see M Trebilcock, 'Comment on Epstein' (1985) 14 J Leg Stud 675. This refers to R Epstein, 'Products Liability as an Insurance Market' (1985) 14 J Leg Stud 645, and includes a defence of rethinking compensation levels along the lines of what parties would contract to secure. That argument is isolated for particular criticism by Ellen Pryor, 'The Tort Law Debate, Efficiency, and the Kingdom of the Ill: A Critique of the Insurance Justification of Tort Law' (1993) 79 Virginia Law Rev 91, as well as by Jane Stapleton, 'Tort, Insurance and Ideology' (1995) 58 MLR 820. Trebilcock himself was critical of existing efforts to secure insurance effects through judicial interpretation (deploying tort law itself as a means to access insurance): M Trebilcock, 'The Social Insurance-Deterrence Dilemma of Modern North American Tort Law: A Canadian Perspective on the Liability Insurance Crisis' (1987) 24 *San Diego Law Review* 929.

the defendant's own positive careless act directly causes physical injury to the plaintiff'.[2] In the directness of infliction, such cases are defined as occupied with acts rather than failures to act or to prevent harm. In their focus on direct physical injury, whether to persons or property, they are connected with harm rather than failure to protect or benefit. In both of these respects, the identification of these 'conventional' cases is intended to identify the core of the law of tort so that it is distinct from contract.[3] One of the reasons for this is to deny a key starting point of influential accounts of 'tort as insurance', namely the hypothetical 'opportunity to bargain' between the parties.[4] The goal is to maintain tort's distinctiveness in *imposing duties* (and thus defining wrongs), not sinking into a reflection of party agreement, real or hypothetical. The threat is the 'death of tort' through its interpretation as a surrogate for insurance.[5] Consistently with this goal, in addition to these hallmarks of 'conventional' tort claims, a 'distinctive' feature of tort duties is said to be that they are capable of arising between strangers.[6]

According to this view, the paradigm of tort liability, displaying both 'conventional' and 'distinctive' features, is a road traffic claim between strangers. Introducing the 'paradigm tort case', Stapleton suggested that

> [o]ne of the most remarkable features of these cases, such as the pedestrian run down by a careless driver, is that the plaintiff may not even know of the defendant's existence, let alone 'rely' on him in any meaningful sense.[7]

In its context, this point was made in order to underline that the normal measure of tort damages cannot be said to be a 'reliance' measure of the sort encountered (and often described as 'tort-like') in the law of contract.[8] But for our purposes, it is pertinent that recovery for these very paradigm claims largely depends on an insurance market and therefore on contracting, operating in a heavily regulated form. If we consider 'reliance' in terms of a source of protection against risk (a possibility discussed in Chapter 8), it will be clear that claimants in these situations may very well rely upon defendants to carry liability insurance. In a considerable number of jurisdictions, the paradigm has been removed from tort either in part, or altogether.[9] Consistently with

[2] J Stapleton, 'Evaluating Goldberg and Zipursky's Civil Recourse Theory' (2006–7) 75 Fordham Law Rev 1529 ('Evaluating Civil Recourse') at 1530.

[3] Although Stapleton refers to infliction by the defendant's own act, it is clear from the accompanying reference to *Palsgraf v Long Island Railway* 162 NE 99 (NY 1928) that this includes vicarious liability, as indeed it must if not to narrow the range of traditional cases immeasurably. In our view, for the reasons explored in Chapter 10, it is hard to combine vicarious liability with clean division between the domains of tort and contract.

[4] Stapleton, n 1, identifies this starting point and isolates it for criticism.

[5] In parallel with the misplaced supposition that contract would eventually be reabsorbed into tort, as proposed by G Gilmore, *The Death of Contract* (Columbus OH: Ohio State University Press, 1974) (and also discussion in Chapter 7).

[6] n 2, 1560.

[7] J Stapleton, 'The normal expectancies measure in tort damages' (1997) 113 LQR 257, 257.

[8] n 7.

[9] For an illustrative review of Michigan's renowned no-fault plan, enacted in 1973, and of its origins in academic debate during the 1920s: J Mellon and D Kowalski, 'The Foundations and Enactment of Michigan Automobile No-Fault Insurance' (2009–10) 87 *University of Detroit Mercy Law Review* 653. For an empirical review of North American regimes, comparing tort with no-fault compensatory alternatives and other approaches to deterrence: D Dewees, D Duff, and M Trebilcock, *Exploring the Domain of Accident Law: Taking the Facts Seriously* (New York: Oxford University Press, 1996). For a comparative

the fears of those who criticize the 'tort as insurance' model, this has generally meant a cap on the damages payable, as the price of expansion in the number of those to whom compensation is delivered.

Since 1930 (in the UK) the apparently 'paradigmatic', and certainly routine, liabilities arising from road traffic have been secured through compulsory liability insurance. Public and private law have been combined purposively (though not necessarily always with consistently purposive judicial support) to secure payment of damages. The tort–insurance relationship has created loss-spreading on a significant scale. Just as motor cases constitute the largest single group of tort claims for personal injury, so also payments in respect of motor claims constitutes a highly significant proportion of those made by the UK insurance industry overall, and the single largest line both of accident and of liability insurance.[10] As we explain in 9.3, the legislature has been centrally involved not only in requiring such insurance, but in mandating its terms. More recently, EU law has increased the reach and stringency of the applicable requirements. Beyond insurance contracts themselves, different contractual agreements operate to constitute a 'safety net', operated by the Motor Insurers' Bureau (MIB). The 'hybrid' (public–private) nature of these arrangements is abundantly clear.

Motor cases combine both 'conventional' and 'distinctive' features, and in their routine operation between strangers they may claim to be the *most* distinctive example of conventional tort claims operating on a large scale.[11] Where else should we seek the paradigm of tort? In the UK, in terms of volume, a further significant category consists of work accidents. This category too is backed by compulsory liability insurance. And, as with motor insurance, there are many jurisdictions which have departed from tort altogether, and have adopted exclusive 'no-fault' schemes. The UK has operated non-exclusive no-fault liability or (more recently) national insurance schemes for such injuries running alongside the law of tort since 1897,[12] and although the liability-based regime of workmen's compensation was abolished in the UK in 1946, no-fault liability for accidents at work remains in common law jurisdictions either the exclusive (as in New Zealand) or the basic (as in each of the Australian states and territories, Hong Kong, India, and Singapore) source of recovery for workplace injuries.

Employers' liability falls short of the suggested paradigm of tort liability only to the extent that it does not arise between 'strangers' (though it might be pointed out that the

review of the history of automobile liability in European jurisdictions: W Ernst (ed), *The Development of Traffic Liability* (Cambridge: Cambridge University Press, 2010).

[10] ABI News Release, 27 September 2012. Motor insurance payments outstripped other accident and liability lines but lagged behind endowment payments, pensions, investment bonds, and life insurance policies.

[11] Some may well deny that these cases are paradigmatic of tort, rather than negligence. For example they may urge with some justification that trespass fits the paradigmatic structure already set out more readily than negligence, and that negligence is a relatively recent and unfortunately vigorous intruder which blossomed partly because of its facility for dealing with indirect harm (and for enlarging the scope of existing contractual duties)—not at all fitting the suggested paradigm. For readers taking this view, the present chapter may be relatively peripheral, or illustrative of the consequences of over-emphasis on negligence; we refer such readers to Chapter 11.

[12] R Lewis provides an excellent analysis of the current position: 'Employers' Liability and Workers' Compensation: England and Wales', in K Oliphant and G Wagner (eds), *Employers' Liability and Workers' Compensation*, vol 31, *Tort and Insurance Law* (Berlin: de Gruyter, 2012).

same is true of a wide range of motor cases). It is therefore 'conventional' (provided vicarious liabilities are included in this category), but not 'distinctive' in the same way. This is significant to its history: analysis of these liabilities in terms of opportunities to bargain (the rejected starting point for critics of 'tort as insurance') was the *dominant* approach of the common law in the mid-nineteenth century, before (and to some extent even after) the intervention of legislation.[13] Though not 'distinctive' in this sense, employers' liability has however been described as *more* typical of the law of tort in another important respect. In her important critique of 'tort as insurance', Jane Stapleton has argued that in terms of the choice between first-party insurance and tort liability (supported by insurance), road traffic accidents may raise unique issues because of the broad-based and reciprocal nature of the risks involved. Historically, including the period when the current road traffic regime was initiated, this has not always been the case as motoring was initially the preserve of a few.[14] It may be more broadly the case today, but even so we would need to consider claimants who are cyclists and pedestrians and not at the same time paying motor insurance premiums,[15] and—perhaps more significantly—the drivers of public service vehicles excluded from the insurance requirement. If, however, we do accept this as at least broadly the case, then the distributive implications of shifting the cost of insuring to injurer or injured is not strong in motor cases—or at a minimum, not as strong as in certain other instances—because both form part of the same group.[16] For these reasons, Stapleton suggested that road traffic accidents are in fact 'atypical' or exceptional, and that employer liability and products liability are *more* typical of tort, in that they involve the infliction of risk on a class of claimants by a separate class of defendants who are, in addition, generally businesses.[17] Thus the 'paradigm' of tort liability she had identified is conventional and distinctive, but at the same time 'atypical'.

In the course of this chapter, we take seriously the argument that tort, private insurance, and social insurance may operate to embody different 'ideologies' and that choices between them are not merely practical but also ideological.[18] Our point, however, is that there is a long history of mixing these solutions. Some have argued

[13] Discussed in 9.4.

[14] Peter Bartrip, 'No-Fault Compensation on the Roads in Twentieth Century Britain' (2010) 69 CLJ 263, 263, mentions the 'widespread perception that roads were places of social conflict where rich and selfish male drivers killed and maimed impecunious pedestrians', and identifies a significant motoring lobby, with particular reference to the 1930s.

[15] Some statistics suggest that up to 25 per cent of UK road traffic fatalities were of pedestrians and cyclists, who may or may not be the owners of motor vehicles: <http://www.makeroadssafe.org/publications/Documents/road-traffic-injuries-kevin-watkins.pdf>, accessed 1 May 2013.

[16] Against this view, it may be argued that if we are thinking distributively there is a stronger argument in favour of the shift, which is that more would be compensated. This also does not depend on an exaggerated assumption of reciprocal risk between different road users.

[17] Stapleton, n 1, 842: referring to consumer products and an employer's liability to its workers, 'Here it is not true that the classes of potential defendants and plaintiffs are roughly the same', so that replacement of tort with first-party insurance would enrich business defendants as a class, remove deterrence incentives, and burden potential victims with the need to purchase insurance. Though note also the presence of business vehicles on the roads. 'Fleet' insurance is a separate and growing branch of motor insurance.

[18] The key message of Stapleton, n 1.

that cross-fertilization at the level of legal concepts, no matter how pragmatic the motivations of those deploying and developing those concepts, has deep effects on the conceptual development of the law over time.[19] Looking at the core instances in which compulsory liability insurance operates provides a focus for this cross-fertilization and its implications for understanding both liability and insurance. Because the concepts have been mixed so thoroughly, their ideological implications are also fuzzy. In a sense, compulsory insurance—which had been a topic of debate even before liability insurance had spread beyond the marine market[20]—is merely a reflection of a wider set of policy choices, though it may be found uniquely acceptable by the courts as an admissible point of reference. An implication is that insurance is not to be perceived in 'conventional' or paradigm cases, any more than in cases where party risk structures are in issue,[21] solely as a matter between the assured, and the insurer. That suggestion is in fact a very long way from the truth.

Although we do not recommend expansion of liability to fit available insurance, nor propose the reshaping of compensation to resemble an insurance market, we disagree with some of the more general remarks of those who have sought to refute such moves. Professor Weinrib has suggested that even those who take a 'public law' approach to the issues should 'feel some disquiet at the intrusion of a mediating factor such as insurance into the plaintiff's claim against the defendant'.[22] As we have seen in the previous two chapters, insurance may not be a mediating factor but the very point of a dispute. One or both of the parties, at least in cases not involving personal injury, may very well be an insurer seeking to place loss elsewhere. That is not a point about public law or even necessarily public interest, but about the law of obligations. But taking into account the prevalence of compulsory insurance at the heart of conventional tort claims, we also depart from his further suggestion that '[a] coherent pattern of state action hardly seems likely to emerge from the judicial grafting of a public purpose onto a series of fortuitous relationships between pairs of litigants'.[23] In the context of compulsory insurance, and perhaps more broadly, public purpose is not judicially grafted but plainly observable; the identification of a 'pair of litigants' may as ever be misleading; but, most of all, the insurance relationship as we will show is very far from fortuitous.

[19] S Deakin, 'Evolution for Our Time: a Theory of Legal Memetics' (2002) 55 *Current Legal Problems* 1; and S Deakin, 'Tort Law and Workmen's Compensation Legislation: Complementary or Competing Models?' ('Complementary or Competing Models?'), in TT Arvind and J Steele, *Tort Law and the Legislature: Common Law, Statute, and the Dynamics of Legal Change* (Oxford: Hart Publishing, 2013).

[20] H Robinson, *The Employers' Liability Assurance Corporation Ltd: Jubilee Book, 1930* (London: Waterlow & Sons, 1930) reveals that several contributors to debates on the Employers' Liability Bill of 1880 proposed that the liabilities would require a form of compulsory insurance, whether this was underwritten by the government or secured through groups of employers—but it could not be envisaged how such a system of insurance would operate. According to the author, the founders of the Corporation discussed the idea of forming such a body (recognized to have been the pioneer of liability insurance in both England and the US) even before the debates on the Bill had concluded: ch 1. The significance of this is examined in 9.4.

[21] This was the core of the analysis in Chapters 7 and 8.

[22] E Weinrib, 'The Insurance Justification and Private Law' (1985) 14 J Leg Stud 681, 687.

[23] n 22, 687.

9.2 Significance and Extent

9.2.1 Legislation and liability insurance

Compulsory insurance necessarily represents a legislative choice. Generally speaking, behind the choice is a decision to ensure (to one degree or another) that a person suffering harm receives indemnity or compensation. In the UK, the only existing instances of compulsory insurance by legislation (referring here to private rather than national insurance) relate to liabilities.[24] The choice of compulsory liability insurance also amounts in some sense to choosing *liability*.[25] Where liability is delivered through the law of tort and analogous regimes, with the choice of liability comes not only a reliance on breach of duty (defining the risks to be distributed), but also, unless it is adapted by legislation, a choice of the tort measure of damages.

The introduction of compulsory liability insurance, assuming that both liability and the tort measure of damages are to be retained, nevertheless brings with it further legislative choices. Apart from compulsion itself, will further legal resources be deployed to ensure that insurance *does* mean cover?[26] In this respect, a first question surrounds policy defences. As a matter of ordinary insurance contract law, insurers may have one of many defences to a claim, including breach of the duty of utmost good faith, lack of coverage, or failure by the assured to comply with policy terms, and the operation of these defences may remove the source of funds for compensation. An important question is whether legislation allows the insurers to rely upon their defences or whether it modifies rights under the policy so that the proceeds are payable to meet a third-party claim even though they are not so available in respect of first-party loss. Where this occurs, it is plainly a further step away from the idea that insurance relationships are 'fortuitous', and that they are a matter between assured and insurer, not concerning the tort claimant. It is a step which has clearly been taken in the UK. As will be seen below, compulsory policies issued in respect of road traffic losses and injury at work both modify policy terms. Partial relief is also given under the Third Parties (Rights against Insurers) Acts 1930 and 2010 to a claimant who brings an action

[24] William Beveridge, *Voluntary Action: A Report on Methods of Social Advance* (London: Allen & Unwin, 1948), 74, identified some old instances of compulsory *first-party* insurance, applicable to those involved in particular trades in the eighteenth century (referring to coal heavers in London in 1757, and skippers and keelmen in the coal trade on the River Wear in 1792, both operating through deductions from wages), but described these as precursors of state insurance in the National Insurance Act 1911. In the same paragraph he described the Workmen's Compensation Acts as not taking the 'form' of insurance, suggesting that they 'simply imposed a new legal liability on employers'. As we see below, the liability was itself planned as a form of insurance and it was intimately associated with the further rise of liability insurance which began in 1880 in response to new employer liabilities. Beveridge's *Voluntary Action* as a whole is an interesting supplement to his better known *Report on Social Insurance and Allied Services*, Cmnd 6404 (1942) and is occupied with what individuals had done and should do independently of the state, to help themselves and others. The 1942 Report made clear that the state should not 'stifle incentive, opportunity, responsibility', to make provision beyond the national minimum (quoted at 7), and in *Voluntary Action*, 'private' action is defined as 'non-State' action, including mutuality.

[25] That this understates the impact of insurance is illustrated by the relative lack of claims for more serious wrongdoing, other than vicariously, where insurance is generally unavailable either on grounds of illegality or of intention (or both): see Chapter 11.

[26] Paraphrasing Gleeson CJ, *Imbree v McNeilly* [2008] HCA 40.

against an insolvent assured when the assured has failed to comply with his post-claim obligations under the policy. The latter point is not confined to compulsory insurance. This in turn illustrates a general point, that legal actors and policy-makers have learned progressively through the interactions of tort and insurance against the backdrop of evolving social policy.[27] Component parts of different solutions—themselves sometimes pragmatically oriented to grasping the advantages of existing market responses—have been translated to and absorbed by new contexts, increasing the cross-fertilization to which we have already referred.

A further issue comes into play where liability and a claim under the policy are established, but the assured cannot satisfy the judgment. The issue here is whether the victim can enforce the insurance claim against the insurers. English law, via the 1930 and 2010 Acts,[28] confers a direct claim in all cases, and not only in relation to compulsory insurance, although there are special provisions relating to motor vehicle insurance. Here, an innovation which was initially prompted by the move to compulsory insurance has changed the nature of liability insurance in general, recognizing its role in compensating tort claimants, not only in indemnifying assured parties. It takes us a further step along the path away from insurance as a private and fortuitous relationship.

A yet further legislative choice concerns situations where liability is established and where insurance is required to be in place but where, for whatever reason, the insurance is ineffective. That may be because no policy has ever been taken out or because the law allows the insurers to rely upon their ordinary defences in respect of third-party claims and they have successfully done so. The question here is whether some form of fallback fund exists for paying compensation. In England, as regards personal injury and property damage, that is the case only for motor insurance.

9.2.2 Compulsory insurance: the current picture

In the UK, it is no exaggeration to say that compulsory insurance plays a central role in the operation of tort law in action. Accidents on the roads account for the vast majority of personal injury claims, and accidents at work though recently overtaken by public liability claims are in third position: both of these are covered by compulsory insurance.[29] The large majority of tort claims are met by insurers,[30] and most of tort law in relation to personal injuries functions on the understanding that insurance is in place, either because it is compulsory by legislation, or because insurance is known to be

[27] S Hedley, 'Tort and Personal Injuries, 1850 to the Present', in Arvind and Steele, n 19.

[28] Explored in Chapter 13.

[29] R Lewis, 'How Important are Insurers in Compensating Claims for Personal Injury in the UK?', (2006) 31 *The Geneva Papers on Risk and Insurance* 323, presents figures derived from the Compensation Recovery Unit. In 2004/5, over 400,000 of 579,282 personal injury accident (as opposed to disease) claims notified were road traffic claims (around 70 per cent). The figures for employment and public liability claims in the same year were 77,765 and 86,966 respectively. Only 4,463 claims fell outside these categories and medical liability.

[30] Lewis, n 29; the *Report of the Royal Commission on Civil Liability and Compensation for Personal Injury*, Cmnd 7054 (1978), concluded that 94 per cent of personal injuries compensation in tort was paid by insurers.

routine or required by the rules of professional associations.[31] In the current reforms of personal injury litigation and costs, the intention is that 85 per cent of personal injury claims will be dealt with through an extended version of the electronic 'portal' which was initially established to deal only with road traffic claims up to £10,000. It is expected that the portal will be extended to employers' liability and public liability claims up to £25,000.[32] Routine, insured liabilities cover the majority of tort claims for personal injury, and these liabilities extend beyond the area of compulsory insurance into the zone of common insurance (specifically public liability).[33] So far as the present incidence of compulsory insurance is concerned, and working on the assumption that the 2010 Act will be implemented and replace the 1930 Act some time in 2013 or 2014, the position may be tabulated,[34] noting the variables discussed in the preceding section.

Risk	**Tort rules intact**	**Policy defences intact**	**Direct action against insurers**	**Fallback fund**
Motor vehicles[35]	*Mostly*[36]	*No*	*Yes, two different types*	*Yes*
Employers' liability[37]	*Yes*	*No*	*2010 Act only*	*No*
Riding establishments[38]	*Yes*	*Yes*	*2010 Act only*	*No*
Nuclear installations[39]	*Strict liability*	*Yes*	*2010 Act only*	*No*
Dangerous animals[40]	*Yes*	*Yes*	*2010 Act only*	*No*
Aircraft operators[41]	*Yes*[42]	*Yes*	*2010 Act only*	*No*

[31] R Lewis, 'Insurers and Personal Injury Litigation: Acknowledging "The Elephant In The Living Room"', (2005) *Journal of Personal Injury Law* 1.

[32] Ministry of Justice, 'Analysis of Responses to the Call for Evidence in Relation to Extension of the Road Traffic Accident Personal Injury Scheme' (19 October 2012), also available at <https://consult.justice.gov.uk/digital-communications/extension-rta-scheme>, accessed 1 May 2013. At the time of writing, the timescale for extension of the portal to non-road traffic claims has been moved to 1 August 2013. This follows an application for judicial review of the government's reforms of portal work (including a cut in fixed fees, in force from April 2013) on the part of the Association of Personal Injury Lawyers (APIL) and Motor Accident Solicitors Society (MASS). That application was heard by the Divisional Court (Elias LJ and Cranston J) on 1 March 2013, but was unsuccessful. The argument put by APIL and MASS turned in part on the government's 'summit' with representatives of the insurance industry on 14 February 2012, to which no claimant representatives were invited. The Court concluded that the decision to cut costs had already been made before this 'summit'.

[33] 'The claimant view' reported in Ministry of Justice, n 32, is that there is an 'infinite number of variables between each case' and that there should be no extension along these lines—an argument in favour of treating each case as individual, rather than routine.

[34] Also R Lewis, 'The Duty to Insure' (2004) 19 *Journal of Insurance Research and Practice* 57.

[35] Road Traffic Act 1988.

[36] Discussed in 9.3.

[37] Employers' Liability (Compulsory Insurance) Act 1969.

[38] Riding Establishments Act 1964, as amended by the Riding Establishments Act 1970.

[39] Nuclear Installations Act 1965.

[40] Dangerous Wild Animals Act 1976. The outgoing Labour government proposed in March 2010 that there should be compulsory insurance for injury caused by dangerous dogs. That proposal disappeared along with the government in May 2010.

[41] Civil Aviation Insurance Regulations 2005, SI 2005/1089, implementing European Parliament and Council Regulation 785/2004/EC on insurance requirements for air carriers and aircraft operators.

[42] By virtue of the Warsaw Convention 1929, as amended.

Cargo oil pollution[43]	*Strict liability*	*Yes*	*Yes*	*No*
Bunker oil pollution[44]	*Strict liability*	*Yes*	*Yes*	*No*
Other maritime risks[45]	*Yes*	*Yes*	*2010 Act only*	*No*
Wreck removal[46]	*Strict liability*	*Yes*	*Yes*	*No*
Maritime passengers[47]	*Strict liability*[48]	*Yes*	*Yes*	*No*
Solicitors[49]	*Yes*	*No*[50]	*2010 Act only*	*No*
Insurance brokers[51]	*Yes*	*Yes*	*2010 Act only*	*No*

There is a rather different form of compulsory insurance set out in the Health and Social Care (Community Health and Standards) Act 2003, under which tortfeasors are required to pay the costs of NHS treatment incurred by the victims of accidents: if the tortfeasor has a liability policy, then the Act, s 164, implies into that policy a term under which there is coverage for that liability. The insurance device has thus been used to shift the costs of medical treatment from the NHS to the private market. There are other International Conventions which impose compulsory insurance on a strict liability basis with direct claims against insurers—the Civil Liability for Oil Pollution Damage resulting from Exploration for and Exploitation of Seabed Mineral Resources Convention 1977 and the International Convention on Liability and Compensation in Connection with the Carriage of Hazardous and Noxious Substances by Sea 1996—but these are not yet in force. The Health Act 1999, s 9, confers upon the Secretary of State the power to require those providing general medical services, general dental services, general ophthalmic services, or pharmaceutical services to carry liability insurance but that power has not been exercised, although there are statutory schemes for

[43] Merchant Shipping Act 1995, implementing the International Convention on Civil Liability for Oil Pollution Damage 1992 (CLC).

[44] Merchant Shipping Act 1995, as amended by the Merchant Shipping and Maritime Security Act 1997, implementing the International Convention on Civil Liability for Bunker Oil Pollution Damage 2001 (the Bunkers Convention).

[45] European Parliament and Council Directive 2009/20/EC on the Insurance of Shipowners for Maritime Risks.

[46] Nairobi Wreck Removal Convention 2007, due to come into force at the end of 2011.

[47] Athens Convention Relating to the Carriage of Passengers and their Luggage by Sea 1974, amended in 2002 and implemented by European Parliament and Council Regulation 392/2009/EC on the Liability of Carriers of Passengers by Sea in the Event of Accidents, implemented in the UK by the Merchant Shipping (Compulsory Insurance of Shipowners for Maritime Claims) Regulations 2012, SI 2012/2267.

[48] For personal injuries only. Liability for property damage rests on fault.

[49] Solicitors Indemnity Insurance Rules 2010, made under the authority of the Solicitors Act 1974, s 37.

[50] Policies must comply with minimum terms and conditions.

[51] By virtue of European Parliament and Council Directive 2002/92/EC on insurance mediation. The provisions of the Directive have been implemented in the Financial Conduct Authority's Handbook: Prudential Rules. Under those Rules brokers and other financial advisers have to obtain liability insurance as a condition of authorization under the FSMA 2000.

osteopaths[52] and chiropractors.[53] A similar power in relation to estate agents with regard to client money is dormant.[54] The statutory provisions are supplemented by professional rules which require liability insurance to be taken out as a condition of membership of professional organizations, as found, for example, in accountancy. Why then is compulsory insurance so attractive?

9.2.3 Why compulsory insurance?

There is little pattern to the range of duties to insure.[55] Apart from international Conventions, which seek to harmonize through minimum standards, compulsory insurance schemes may protect the vulnerable and operate where insolvencies are particularly likely or where confidence needs to be maintained. They are not confined to liabilities in respect of personal injury. Some cover property damage, but a number protect against recoverable categories of 'pure economic loss' (particularly in the case of professional advisers of one sort or another). In a general sense, compulsory liability insurance may be thought to have three main strengths. First, it goes some way to ensuring that there is a compensation fund for victims against which claims may be made.[56] Second, it protects assured parties from bankruptcy or insolvency. And third, if every person carrying on the relevant activity has to take out insurance, the sums paid by insurers are funded by premiums contributed to by all, so that there is no disproportionate premium burden resting on those who choose to insure. A potential objection—that the deterrent function of tort liability is thereby lost—has little basis and may even be turned into a further advantage of compulsory schemes: where liability insurance is a condition which has to be satisfied to carry on an activity, a bad claims record may lead to a refusal of cover or to unaffordable premiums and thus a loss of livelihood, and the fear of that consequence is no less an incentive to take care than the fear of potential liability faced by an uninsured person. This rationale depends on the market to supply desirable incentive patterns. The potential for this is not confined to compulsory insurance;[57] but the *need* to be insured heightens its likely effect.

Tort backed by compulsory liability insurance, when viewed as a purposive arrangement, is a form of insurance solution. Tort is one of the factors determining what is distributed. In the road traffic context, fault is the gatekeeper, but the process of distribution is indispensable. As currently achieved, this distribution extends beyond the bounds of individual responsibility, and the role of contract in this context is not

[52] Osteopaths Act 1993, s 37. [53] Chiropractors Act 1994, s 37.

[54] Estate Agents Act 1979, ss 16 and 17. This appears to have been superseded by the implementation of a statutory redress scheme in 2008.

[55] See also Lewis, n 34: the obligations have arisen in an *ad hoc* fashion.

[56] Note however the significance of boundaries (the outer limits of the scheme), gaps (such as failures to insure or insolvency of insurers), and limits (generally policy terms).

[57] See for example the research by Halliday, Ilan, and Scott on the behaviour of local authorities in Scotland in response to liability risks. This is explored by S Halliday, 'The Governance of Compliance with Public Law' (2013) *Public Law* 312, in terms of alternative forms of governance. Tangible effects are detected for market governance through the intervention of liability insurers.

wholly separable from the objectives of tort nor wholly (even predominantly) a private matter. We say this despite the fact that the measure of damages remains the tort measure, and despite heeding due warnings about treating tort as somehow 'about' insurance,[58] although we would additionally comment that, but for insurance, many tort claims giving rise to serious injuries would not otherwise be satisfied. Indeed tort claims are frequently compromised at the policy limit of indemnity.[59] The present arrangements may simply mark the most extensive form of distribution of the specific risks associated with motoring which are countenanced in the UK.[60] In the next section, we examine those distributive arrangements.

9.3 Compulsory Insurance for Motor Vehicles[61]

9.3.1 Motor insurance and tort liability

As we saw in 9.1, road traffic accidents have been described as the paradigm of tort cases, at least where they occur between strangers. Passenger cases initially tested the depth of the loss-spreading intent behind compulsory insurance, but these and most other issues have gradually been resolved in favour of securing insurance cover. The increasing completeness of the distributive impact of motor insurance is submerged in standard accounts of tort lawyers, and indeed by many critical approaches, both of which focus instead on the relatively orthodox and conventional state of the tort liabilities themselves. Here we show that the distributive impact of the arrangements goes far beyond the portrayal of insurance as merely providing a private route to satisfying conventional tort liabilities, despite the fact that the distributive intent is inevitably limited by the need to establish the relevant liability criteria. An important question is how far these criteria actually function as 'bargaining chips' which operate to reduce damages in the process of settlement:[62] the issue becomes not so much whether there was or was not causation of harm, for example, but what chance there is that a court would find that there was or was not causation. If that is accurate, then the tort process in this sphere is more thoroughly distributive than so far presented, with a wider distribution of somewhat reduced amounts operating despite the apparent presence of traditional legal criteria. Naturally, insurers are primary among such negotiators, so that actuarial logic is directly connected to the application of tort rules in practice.

Nevertheless, the starting point is that the general tort rules are largely intact in relation to road traffic liability, even if these rules typically do not fall for application by courts but influence negotiation. Few motor cases raise 'duty questions', unless there is

[58] Stapleton, n 1.

[59] Personal injury claims in motor cases are the sole exception, as insurance against such claims must be unlimited. Again this underlines the exceptional nature of the supposed paradigm of tort.

[60] P Bartrip, n 14, provides an account of the debate.

[61] See generally R Merkin and J Stuart-Smith, *The Law of Motor Insurance* (London: Sweet & Maxwell, 2004).

[62] The expression 'bargaining chips' is derived from D Harris et al., *Compensation and Support for Illness and Injury* (Oxford, Clarendon Press, 1984).

an attempt to extend liabilities to additional parties (such as public authorities).[63] Turning to the standard of care, the courts have held drivers to an objective standard irrespective of whether the driver in question could have satisfied it. This is seen in *Nettleship v Weston*,[64] where a learner driver was held to be liable for injuries inflicted on the passenger (her instructor), on the basis that she had failed to meet the standards of a fully qualified driver.[65] The role of compulsory insurance was, other than in the judgment of Lord Denning MR in *Nettleship*, not explicit in these cases. In the High Court of Australia, Kirby J has recently made the policy reasons explicit, in the learner driver case of *Imbree v McNeilly*[66]:

> If such compulsory insurance were *not* part of the legal background to the expression of the applicable common law, and if it were the case, or even possible, that someone in the position of the driver (or the owner) of the vehicle would, or might, be personally liable for the consequences of that person's driving affecting a passenger (such as the appellant) or other third party it is extremely unlikely, in my view, that the courts would impose on them liability, as in the case of the appellant's claim, sounding in millions of dollars.

It must be said that in English law, the objective standard itself is well established and of general application, and that it can be defended on grounds other than the existence of liability insurance. But Kirby J's point remains powerful even so: the operation of the objective standard in the road traffic context, against ordinary individuals in many instances, would have quickly become intolerable without such insurance. It is precisely when tort operates between individuals that it most needs distributive support.

The impact of insurance on tort may also be seen to some extent in the context of defences to tort claims. The defence of *ex turpi causa* has been applied in motor insurance cases in much the same way as in other cases, and we explore its hidden significance in Chapter 11. The defence of voluntary assumption of risk is removed by the Road Traffic Act 1988 itself: an agreement to exclude liability is void under s 149(2); and the fact that a passenger has willingly accepted the risk of negligence is not to be treated as negativing the driver's liability under s 149(3), for example, where the passenger is aware that the driver is intoxicated.[67] It should be admitted once again that *volenti* has in any event become a defence of very limited application in English negligence law.

Contributory negligence was reformed into a proportionate defence almost entirely to deal with the perceived unfairness of the total defence in road traffic claims.[68] In this guise there have been some generous decisions involving the victims of motor accidents,[69] but

[63] 8.5. [64] [1971] 2 QB 691.

[65] Also *Roberts v Ramsbottom* [1980] 1 WLR 823. A counter-example, though involving lack of volition, is *Mansfield v Weetabix* [1998] 1 WLR 1263.

[66] n 26.

[67] *Pitts v Hunt* [1991] 1 QB 24. James Goudkamp, 'Statutes and Tort Defences', in Arvind and Steele, n 19, charts the drastic and sometimes ill-reasoned tightening of tort defences in Australian law. This tightening is linked to a perceived insurance crisis.

[68] J Steele, 'Law Reform Contributory Negligence Act 1945: Collisions of a Different Sort', in Arvind and Steele, n 19.

[69] For example *Jones v Lawrence* [1969] 3 All ER 267 (no deduction for contributory negligence where a boy ran in front of a motor vehicle); *Booth v White* 2003, unreported (accepting lift from an intoxicated driver).

there are also contrasting outcomes on similar facts.[70] The distributive implications of contributory negligence in this context certainly deserve critical scrutiny. Contributory negligence operates to reduce damages and is particularly susceptible to being applied by parties (mainly insurers) reaching settlements, rather than by courts. Its impact, like that of other legal rules, is not easily charted since settlements are often not itemized.[71] It is most likely that contributory negligence simply acts as an additional qualifier on the extent to which full compensation is achieved through settlements, or indeed through court decisions in those instances where a court is involved.[72]

The more significant changes to tort law in action have come within the law of motor insurance, rather than in the liabilities to which it responds.[73] The nature of these changes is entirely unnoticed by accounts which simply assume motor claims are conventional tort claims in which insurance plays a secondary role.

9.3.2 Background to the Road Traffic Act 1988

Although motor insurance was the first compulsory liability insurance in the UK, the scheme had some pedigree. Liability insurance was already being sold to motorists; and this in turn was made possible by the historic creation of liability insurance (outside the maritime context) as a response to employers' liability risks from 1880 onwards. The way that the legislature dealt with dangers on the roads in 1930 was informed by fifty years of experience of insurance as a vehicle of *public policy* in the employment context. This included some detailed borrowing of techniques to enhance protection of the injured. In this light, it is not only no-fault compensation that shows the influence of workmen's compensation (discussed in the next section). Conventional fault-based liabilities also operate with the support of techniques learned from that regime.

The first UK motor insurance policy was issued in November 1896, covering first- and third-party losses arising from participation in the London to Brighton rally, organized to celebrate the passing of the Locomotive and Highways Act 1896. This measure, popularly known as the Emancipation Act, repealed legislation including the Highways Act 1865 which in its original form required any steam-powered vehicle to follow sixty yards behind the bearer of a red flag. 'Emancipation' was accompanied by the first recorded fatality, also in 1896. Accident levels reached disproportionately high levels for the number of vehicles. Records were not kept until 1926, but in that year there were 4,886 fatalities and 134,000 cases of serious injury, all arising from only 1,715,421 vehicles.[74] The casualty figures had risen in 1929 to 7,000 fatalities and 200,000 serious injuries.

[70] *Morales v Eccleston* [1991] RTR 151 (driver only 25 per cent to blame for failure to anticipate that a boy might run out in front of his vehicle).

[71] For this reason the research by Harris et al., n 62, remains an essential source.

[72] Steele, n 68, comments on the Law Revision Committee's neglect of the insurance context as it related to personal injury (as distinct from the marine insurance regime in the context on which the reform was modelled).

[73] Note however the blurring of these lines as a consequence of EU law, discussed in subsequent pages.

[74] At the end of 2011 there were 34.2 million vehicles licensed for use on the road: Vehicle Licensing Statistics, April 2012, available online.

The Road Traffic Act 1930[75] introduced compulsory insurance into English law, as part of a package of measures designed to improve road safety, including minimum standards for vehicle construction and for roads. A parallel measure, the Third Parties (Rights against Insurers) Act 1930, was passed to support the Road Traffic Act 1930 by giving the victim of a negligent policyholder the right to enforce any judgment against the insurers. This measure is clearly not designed to protect assured parties, and is solely aimed at protecting those to whom the assured is liable. The Third Parties Act 1930 itself ceased to be of significance in motor claims following the passing of the Road Traffic Act 1934, under which the victim of a motor accident was given a specific right to enforce a judgment against the driver's motor insurers, leaving the Third Parties Act in place to deal with other forms of third-party liability claim.[76] The 1934 Act also removed the right of insurers to rely upon non-compliance with claims conditions and certain other policy restrictions where the claim arose from third-party injury, and limited the ability of insurers to rely upon the defence of breach of the duty of utmost good faith, thereby emphasizing the status of insurance as something other than a purely private matter.

The road traffic legislation was reviewed alongside other areas of compulsory insurance by the Cassel Committee in 1937.[77] The Committee was appointed to review and improve the operation of compulsory insurance (though it decided that the extension of compulsory insurance, for example to workmen's compensation as a whole or to cyclists, was outside its terms of reference). It worked on the understanding that the purpose of such insurance was new, and, importantly, that it constituted an exception to the general rule that insurance exists to benefit the assured. It was perceived to be transformative, even if in the context of workmen's compensation it was hardly a new idea (as to which see 9.4):

> Our main recommendations involve a marked departure from the conditions which have hitherto governed insurance business in this country and they are made solely as a result of the special considerations which arise from the element of compulsion.[78]

The immediate cause for the Committee's investigation was the failure of several motor insurance companies, and this concentrated minds not only on the need for greater security of insurance; but also on the very purpose of compulsory liability insurance. Plainly, this was primarily considered to be for the benefit of the injured party to whom the assured was liable, and secondarily for the benefit of the assured:

[75] Implementing the recommendations of the Royal Commission on the Control of Traffic on Roads, Cmd 3365 (1929).

[76] Other than workers' compensation claims, as those had, since the introduction of the scheme in 1897, been enforceable against the insurers of insolvent employers (even though insurance was not compulsory). That provision was expressly the model for the new statutes on this point (a plain instance of cross-fertilization). The 1930 Act accordingly had relatively little significance after 1934 until the development of other forms of tort liability.

[77] *Report of the Committee on Compulsory Insurance*, Board of Trade, Cmd 5528 (July 1937).

[78] n 77, 8 [10]. The Committee took careful note of the recommendations of the Clauson Committee in 1907 and the resulting Assurance Act 1909, which it encapsulated in terms of 'freedom with publicity' (at 10 [18]). The Cassel Committee proposals departed from 'freedom' in response to the fact of compulsion.

> The object of compulsory insurance against third-party risks is to secure that an award of damages to an injured third party is not rendered nugatory by inability to pay on the part of the person responsible for the injury and this object is defeated by failures such as these.[79]

Three instances of compulsory liability insurance were by then in place, all enacted during the same decade.[80] Compulsion was seen as a generic development with important implications. The Committee did not only consider insolvency, but also (*inter alia*) the effect of policy terms. Here it was particularly clear that the contractual and private basis of insurance had to be rethought in the light of compulsion in support of liabilities. What is interesting is that compulsion came first, and some of its implications were spelled out later—an instance of practice running ahead of theory:

> The basis of voluntary insurance is the protection of the insured by means of a contract between himself and the person whom he selects as an insurer; but the person for whose benefit compulsory insurance has been introduced is not a party to the contract of insurance and has no voice in the framing of its terms. It is in the main the securing of protection for a stranger to the contract which has given rise to the problems which we have had to consider.[81]

The Cassel Committee was not a committee of lawyers, but it encapsulated the necessary shift beyond a two-party frame which much obligations theory still resists. It is often tort lawyers who decline to recognize the extended purpose of contract in such an instance—to secure protection for third parties whatever the intention of the assured.

Pursuing this logic, the Committee made two key recommendations: the extension of the solvency deposit system to motor vehicle insurers (adopted in 1937); and the creation of a fallback fund to pay compensation to the victims of drivers who were uninsured or otherwise unable to recover under their policies (referred to by the Committee as the 'Central Fund'). This was eventually achieved by an agreement between the government and an industry body—the MIB—in 1946 (now 1999).[82]

[79] n 77, 7.

[80] These were motor insurance under the Road Traffic Act 1930; insurance of workmen's compensation liabilities in relation to coal-mining under the Workmen's Compensation (Coal Mines) Act 1934 (referred to as 'the Nicholson Act' reflecting its introduction as a Private Member's Bill); and insurance of liabilities arising from the use of aircraft under the Air Navigation Act 1936, though the latter was never implemented: n 77, 14.

[81] n 77, 7.

[82] It has been suggested that the threat of nationalization, one of the defining themes of the post-war Labour government, was instrumental in producing this agreement: DB Williams, 'Chasing the Uninsured and Hit-and-Run Motorist' (1973) 59 *ABA Journal* 75, though the best documented threat was of nationalization of industrial insurance companies specifically. That plan was ultimately rejected for a number of reasons including the complexities of dealing with millions of existing policies, the destruction of considerable invisible exports through insurance of overseas risks, and the possibility that alienated insurance agents from 'the Pearl and the Pru' would effectively become Tory agents knocking on the doors of millions of homes (K Morgan, *Labour in Power: 1945–1951* (Oxford: Oxford University Press, 1985), 125–7). Certainly, however, the agreement emerged from recommendations of an official committee, and not spontaneously, although even in 1937 the Cassel Committee thought the ABI was fully behind the scheme; it was recognized as an important step in light of insurer insolvencies, and it might be thought that liability insurers as a whole ultimately gained protection from the need for compulsory insurance to be offered only by MIB members.

The existence of the MIB encapsulates the hybrid function of insurance under the compulsory scheme: proposed by a departmental committee in order to further the legislative and social purpose of compulsory insurance, it was nevertheless an attraction of the scheme that it would need no government involvement or resources for its operation. This is a counterpoint to tort lawyers' assertions that the logical conclusion of loss-spreading arguments is that the state should take the burden of the losses: loss-spreading requires resources and organization, and the state will often prefer to allow market actors to achieve this goal.[83]

The structure established by the 1930 and 1934 Acts and the 1946 MIB Agreement remains embedded in the current governing legislation, the Road Traffic Act 1988. There have been frequent amendments and consolidations. A further MIB Agreement extended compensation to the victims of hit-and-run drivers in 1969 (now 2003). However, the vast bulk of the amendments have been the result of the European Union's free movement programme; in the context of motor insurance this has led to a harmonized insurance structure for the provision of compensation to the victims of motor accidents. The EU legislation evolved over a series of five Directives between 1972 and 2005, and progressed from an initial requirement of compulsory insurance coupled with the abolition of border checks, an obligation to establish compensation bodies for the victims of uninsured and untraced drivers, single premium coverage for all EU risks, and a direct cause of action against insurers, culminating finally in steps to protect the victims of cross-border accidents. These measures were codified in European Parliament and Council Directive of 16 September 2009, 2009/103/EC 'relating to insurance against civil liability in respect of the use of motor vehicles, and the enforcement of the obligation to insure against such liability'.

The EU measures have transformed the original concept from insurance against the liability of the driver to insurance against liability arising from the use of an insured vehicle. That is still liability based on fault in the sense that driving has fallen below a relevant standard; but it means that insurance as the source of compensation has been manipulated to extend beyond the reach of personal responsibility of the driver, notably without recourse to traditional ideas of vicarious liability or agency.

The legislative structure is intended to provide compensation in all but exceptional cases (notably those of passengers who consent to be carried in stolen or uninsured vehicles) and it has been necessary to construe the Act in accordance with EU requirements. Together, the legislation does much more than simply make liability insurance for motor accidents compulsory. First, it regulates the terms of insurance policies themselves, preventing insurers from denying liability in given circumstances whatever policy wordings might say. Second, although the 1988 Act and the EU Directives are not designed primarily to affect common law liability rules, they may

[83] Notice also that in 1960, Spencer Kimball reported that in comparison with the US, Germany, and Sweden, England committed far fewer government resources to insurance regulation, commenting that 'The English carry the distaste for compulsion and for cumbersome administrative machinery as far as anyone'. As at that time, 'A mere handful of people at the Board of Trade, no more than a score at most, regulate insurance in one of the world's most important insurance markets': S. Kimball, 'The Purpose of Insurance Regulation: A Preliminary Inquiry in the Theory of Insurance Law' (1960–61) 45 Minn L Rev 471, 505–6. Kimball's point was that insurance was nonetheless an instrument of public policy everywhere.

do so indirectly. But more generally, we can observe a state of affairs where potential gaps in *cover* have been progressively filled. On the surface, tort appears to remain unchanged; but this is misleading, as notions of personal responsibility are qualified, or recast, in significant fashion.

9.3.3 The obligation to insure

Compulsory insurance entails significant new obligations of its own, carrying the weight of criminal liability in the event of breach. There are two basic strict liability offences set out in the 1988 Act, s 143(1): (a) using a motor vehicle on a road or other public place without insurance or security[84] complying with the requirements of the Act; or (b) causing or permitting such uninsured use.[85] The term 'use' refers to control, generally that of the driver but on occasion a passenger.[86] A 'motor vehicle' is one intended or adapted for use on roads even though it has some other primary purpose. A 'road' is 'any highway and any other road to which the public has access, and includes a bridge'.[87] The accepted view that anything other than private land was a 'road' was rejected by the House of Lords in *Cutter v Eagle Star Insurance Co* and *Clarke v Kato*,[88] holding that a car park open to members of the public and with road signs and markings was not a 'road' because it was a destination in its own right rather than a thoroughfare. That curious and non-purposive ruling was rapidly reversed by an amendment to the 1988 Act[89] which inserted the phrase 'or other public place', a wider term meaning a place to which the public have access.[90]

9.3.4 Civil sanction for infringement

The 1988 Act imposes criminal sanctions for failure to insure, but it is silent on civil consequences. At a very early stage, in *Monk v Warbey*,[91] the Court of Appeal held that failure to insure was actionable as breach of statutory duty. That was at best cold comfort to the victim of an uninsured tortfeasor, but it mattered where the uninsured use of the vehicle had been caused or permitted by an insured person who otherwise faced no liability for the victim's injuries. The concept of 'causing or permitting' use accordingly became of increased significance as a result of *Monk v Warbey*, and it is

[84] Security as an alternative to insurance is provided for by s 146 and the Motor Vehicles (Third-Party Risk Deposit) Regulations 1992, SI 1992/1284. This is of little practical significance.

[85] There are exceptions in favour of some public authorities: 1988 Act, s 144.

[86] *Brown v Roberts* [1965] 1 QB 1 (passenger opening car door, outside the insurance obligation).

[87] 1988 Act, s 192.

[88] [1998] 4 All ER 417; [1998] 1 WLR 1647. Car and caravan parks which are not designed to provide through access for vehicles are not roads, even though pedestrians do in practice use them as through routes: *Director of Public Prosecutions v Vivier* [1991] 4 All ER 18.

[89] Motor Vehicles (Compulsory Insurance) Regulations 2000, SI 2000/726.

[90] *DPP v Vivier* [1991] 4 All ER 18.

[91] [1935] 1 KB 75. Also: *Richards v Port of Manchester Insurance Co Ltd* (1933) 152 LT 413; *Daniels v Vaux* [1938] 2 KB 203; *McLeod v Buchanan* [1940] 2 All ER 179; *Lees v Motor Insurers Bureau* [1952] 2 Lloyd's Rep 210; *Martin v Dean* [1971] 2 QB 208.

now settled that any person with control of a vehicle who allows another to use it is liable unless an insurance condition is imposed upon the user.[92]

The tort of breach of statutory duty has lost most of its significance as far as the victim is concerned, for three separate reasons. First, many policies extend liability coverage to a third party who is using the vehicle with the owner's consent, and where coverage is extended to a third party by the owner's policy the user is entitled to seek indemnification from the insurers in his own right.[93] Second, under the MIB Uninsured Drivers Agreement 1999 the MIB is required to satisfy a judgment given against an uninsured user, so the victim has a direct claim against the MIB. The MIB may, nevertheless, bring the action against the owner by using its rights of subrogation or by taking an assignment from the victim.[94] To that end the MIB may insist, as a condition of payment, that the victim brings a *Monk v Warbey* action against the owner for the benefit of the MIB.[95] Third, if the owner does have a policy but cover does not extend to third-party use, the victim has no need to rely on a claim against the MIB, because—by reason of amendments to the 1988 Act, s 151(2)(b) to comply with EU law—the insurers are liable for any use of the vehicle which gives rise to liability. An insurer who is required to make payment under this provision has a statutory right of recourse against the person causing or permitting the uninsured use.[96]

An attempt to use *Monk v Warbey* to defeat the rights of a victim was rejected by the Court of Appeal in *Bretton v Hancock*.[97] Here, the claimant was injured in a collision with a vehicle driven by the defendant while a passenger in her own vehicle being driven by her uninsured fiancé. He was killed in the collision and his estate was impecunious. The claimant obtained judgment against the defendant, although the court gave judgment to the defendant for a 25 per cent contribution representing the fault of the claimant's fiancé. The defendant (or really the defendant's insurers) asserted that the claimant was liable in damages for the amount of the contribution, in that she had permitted her fiancé to drive her car uninsured and had caused the defendant to incur a loss for which he could not recover. The Court of Appeal's view was that *Monk v Warbey* did not confer an action for breach of statutory duty for anything other than personal injury or property damage. Rix LJ noted that

> [I]t would be undesirable if a wife who could in some sense be said to be the user of the household car could lose 90 per cent of her recovery because her husband, who told her he was insured, was not insured and was found 90 per cent responsible for a collision involving another driver and tortfeasor.

92 As shown by the very odd facts of *Lloyd-Wolper v Moore* [2004] EWCA Civ 766; [2004] 1 WLR 2350, where a father allowed his son to use a car on the mistaken assumption that the son was of age (in fact he was only 16) and thus covered by the father's policy.

93 1988 Act, s 148(7).

94 It is clear that the tort has survived the implementation of the MIB Agreement: *Corfield v Groves* [1950] 1 All ER 488; *Norman v Aziz* [2000] Lloyd's Rep IR 52.

95 This gave rise to a fatal problem for the victim in *Norman v Ali* [2000] Lloyd's Rep IR 395, as the claim against the owner—which was held to accrue at the date of the accident—had become time-barred.

96 1988 Act, s 151(8).

97 [2005] EWCA Civ 404; [2005] Lloyd's Rep IR 454.

This observation necessarily steps outside the two-party frame, to acknowledge the real setting for the tort claim and the implications of any other finding. Tort liabilities are here shaped in response to the complexity of the insurance implications, and in light of the purpose of that insurance.

9.3.5 Liabilities to be insured

The 1988 Act, s 145(3) lists the five heads of liability which an insurance policy is to cover. Two of these relate to cross-border issues within the EU.[98] We consider the remaining three here.

The first head of liability is that 'which may be incurred ... in respect of the death of or bodily injury to any person ... caused by, or arising out of, the use of the vehicle on a road or public place in Great Britain'. Legislative intent is underlined by a requirement that the policy must not have financial limits. The phrase 'any person' does not include the driver[99] but covers passengers. The law relating to passengers has been transformed in recent years. The legislation prior to 1971 did not require compulsory insurance for passengers other than those 'carried for hire or reward'.[100] In this sense, it reflected the distinction between strangers (to whom tort liability may be said to have been particularly relevant), and those with an existing relationship with the driver. However, the Motor Vehicle (Passenger Insurance) Act 1971 extended cover to all passengers, including the assured if carried as a passenger.[101]

The second head of liability is that 'which may be incurred ... in respect of ... damage to property'.[102] A key distinction is that financial limits may be imposed: the policy may limit cover to £1,000,000 'in respect of all such liabilities as may be incurred in respect of damage to property caused by, or arising out of, any one accident involving the vehicle'.[103] This figure is a generous one where property is concerned and is likely to be reached only where damage is caused to a building, even though the term 'any one accident' is defined as including two or more causally related accidents.[104] Insurance need not cover damage to the vehicle itself (a matter for first-party cover); damage to the property of an employee; or contractual liability.[105]

Finally, the policy 'must also insure ... in respect of any liability which may be incurred under the provisions of [the Road Traffic Act 1988] relating to payment for emergency treatment'.[106] At one time, the 1988 Act, ss 157–61, imposed liability upon motor insurers for relatively small sums representing part of the costs of treatment for motor accident victims. All changed on the implementation of the Road Traffic (NHS Charges) Act 1999, which introduced a policy of full recoupment of costs. The effect of the legislation was to confine the 1988 Act to private hospitals, so

[98] 1988 Act, s 145(3)(aa); s 145(3)(b).

[99] *R v Secretary of State for Transport Ex p National Insurance Guarantee Corporation plc* (1996) *The Times*, 3 June; *British Waterways v Royal & Sun Alliance Insurance plc* [2012] EWHC 460 (Comm); [2012] Lloyd's Rep IR 562.

[100] The rationale being to protect passengers on public service vehicles.

[101] *Limbrick v French and Farley* [1990] 11 CL para 329.

[102] 1988 Act, s 145(3)(a).

[103] 1988 Act, s 145(4)(b).

[104] 1988 Act, s 161(3).

[105] 1988 Act, s 145(4).

[106] 1988 Act, s 145(3)(c).

that private hospitals could recover only the relatively small sums set out in the 1988 Act whereas NHS hospitals could recover the full costs of treatment. The position changed again with effect from 28 January 2007: in respect of accidents occurring on or after that date, the Health and Social Care (Community Health and Standards) Act 2003 replaced the 1999 Act with a general provision under which all liability insurers, including motor vehicle insurers, are required to pay the full cost of NHS treatment. The sums recoverable by private hospitals are limited by the 1988 Act to £2,865.00 for each inpatient and £286.00 for each outpatient.[107] The provision is aimed directly at insurers.

There is no requirement for other forms of loss. The most obvious is the cost incurred by the claimant of hiring a replacement vehicle pending repairs to his own. Although this form of liability is not yet compulsory,[108] it is very commonly covered by motor policies.

9.3.6 Causation

The statutory liabilities to be insured are those 'caused by or arising out of' the use of a motor vehicle on a road or other public place. This raises an interesting causation issue, which is repeated in other jurisdictions.[109] Outside the road traffic context, there is a conflict of authority about whether these phrases are interchangeable formulations of the proximate cause principle or whether the expression 'arising out of' in insurance policies encompasses more remote causes.[110] In the context of UK motor insurance the authorities are consistent that the use of 'or' has created a separate head of liabilities 'arising out of' the use of a vehicle which is wider than ordinary causation. Thus the obligation to insure extends beyond pure driving, to accidents which occur while the car is stationary[111] and indeed when the assured is not even in it.[112] There are, however, limits,[113] as where a motor vehicle is used as a place to carry out sexual assaults.[114]

[107] R Lewis provides a critical assessment: 'Recovery of State Benefits from Tort Damages: Legislating for or Against the Welfare State?', in Arvind and Steele, n 19.

[108] It has yet to be tested before the European Court of Justice (CJEU) whether insurance against such liability is compulsory.

[109] See the analysis of Canadian jurisdictions by E Knutsen, 'Auto Insurance as Social Contract: Solving Automobile Insurance Coverage Disputes Through a Public Regulatory Framework' (2010–11) *Alberta Law Review* 715.

[110] *Beazley Underwriting Ltd v Travelers Companies Inc* [2011] EWHC 1520 (Comm); [2012] Lloyd's Rep IR 78 and *British Waterways v Royal & Sun Alliance Insurance plc* [2012] EWHC 460 (Comm); [2012] Lloyd's Rep IR 562, where the authorities are discussed. In that particular context the words 'arising out of' were held to give rise to a test wider than proximate cause.

[111] *Cutter v Eagle Star Insurance Co Ltd* [1998] 4 All ER 417; [1998] 1 WLR 1647, where injuries occurred in a parked car.

[112] *Dunthorne v Bentley* [1999] Lloyd's Rep IR 560.

[113] *Slater v Buckinghamshire County Council* [2004] Lloyd's Rep IR 432, where the claimant dashed across the road to board a minibus.

[114] *AXN v Worboys* [2012] EWHC 1730 (QB); [2012] All ER (D) 212 (Jun), discussed in Chapter 11.

9.3.7 Obtaining compensation where the Act applies

There is a general mechanism under the Third Parties (Rights against Insurers) Acts 1930 and 2010 for enforcing judgments obtained against insolvent policyholders.[115] Since 1934 there has been a specialized procedure for enforcing judgments in motor insurance cases, now enshrined in the 1988 Act, ss 151 and 152. In essence, the claimant must initially obtain a judgment against the person responsible for his injury or loss.[116] Armed with the judgment, the claimant is entitled to enforce it against the insurers of the vehicle.[117] The right of enforcement is largely free of policy defences that the insurers might otherwise have possessed. Significantly, a majority of the Court of Appeal (obiter) concluded in *Charlton v Fisher*[118] that, in the absence of any exclusion for deliberate acts, the insurers are required to meet liability for injury or damage deliberately inflicted by the user:[119] while a person who deliberately or recklessly causes loss has no personal claim under an insurance policy, the liability is nevertheless one which has to be covered by insurance.[120] It emerges clearly that the purpose of liability insurance extends beyond protection of the assured to the extent that it imposes obligations on liability insurers, where they would have been entitled not to indemnify their assured. It has already been commented that amendments to the 1988 Act, s 151 in accordance with EU law mean that the insurers have to satisfy a judgment against any person responsible for the loss, whether or not that person was insured under the policy. In that way, liability incurred by a person driving without consent, including a thief or joyrider, has to be satisfied by the insurers, subject only to the consideration that the claimant was not allowing himself to be carried knowing or having reason to believe that the vehicle had been stolen or unlawfully taken.[121] Participating passengers thus have no rights. It may be noted that the Directive refers only to actual knowledge, and the English courts have accordingly held that the words 'or reason to believe' are to be construed as being confined to 'blind eye' knowledge.[122] In a situation where insurers have been required to make payment when they would, but for the operation of the legislation, have had a defence to the claim, they may recover their payment from

[115] Chapter 13.

[116] The action may go ahead even though the assured has become insolvent in the meantime: the 1988 Act, s 153.

[117] Procedural requirements in the 1988 Act, s 152, have given rise to significant case law: *Nawaz and Hussain v Crow Insurance Group* [2003] EWCA Civ 316; [2003] Lloyd's Rep IR 471; *Stinton v Stinton* [1999] Lloyd's Rep IR 305; *Harrington v Link Motor Policies at Lloyd's* [1989] 2 Lloyd's Rep 310.

[118] [2001] EWCA Civ 112; [2001] 3 WLR 1435.

[119] But note the decision of the Court of Appeal in *EUI Ltd v Bristol Alliance Partnership Ltd* [2012] EWCA Civ 1267; [2012] All ER (D) 120 (Oct), ruling that an express policy term which excludes the liability of the insurers for damage inflicted deliberately is binding on the third party.

[120] *Hardy v Motor Insurers Bureau* [1964] 2 QB 745; [1964] 3 WLR 433; *Gardner v Moore* [1984] AC 548; [1984] 2 WLR 714. The issue of illegality and insurance claims is discussed at length in Chapter 11.

[121] 1988 Act, s 154(4). The Directive refers only to theft, so there is an argument that the passenger of a joyrider or other person who has no intention to steal the vehicle should be protected under EU law. However, the English cases have held that the legislation in its reference to 'unlawfully taken' is consistent with the Directive: *McMinn v McMinn* [2006] EWHC 827 (QB); [2006] Lloyd's Rep IR 802; *Stych v Dibble* [2012] EWHC 1606 (QB); [2012] All ER (D) 82 (Jun).

[122] *Stych v Dibble* [2012] EWHC 1606 (QB), not following *McMinn v McMinn* [2006] EWHC 827 (QB); [2006] Lloyd's Rep IR 802 where the Directive was seemingly overlooked.

the person whose liability triggered the claim. If the user was the assured, then the claim may be against the assured.[123] If the user was an uninsured person, then the claim may be made against either him or the assured if the assured caused or permitted him to use the vehicle, although the right of recourse will generally be excluded where the assured was himself the injured passenger.[124] Insurance of liabilities for the benefit of injured parties remains the primary goal of the law here: but insurers may deploy the fault principle provided the satisfaction of the tort claim is not thereby threatened. The implications for understanding whether the existence of liability insurance does, or does not, dilute the operation of the fault principle, and to what extent, should not be overlooked.

The procedure in the 1988 Act, s 151, has itself to a large extent been superseded by the European Communities (Rights against Insurers) Regulations 2002.[125] The idea of a direct action against motor insurers was first adopted in the Fourth Motor Insurance Directive in 2000,[126] and was designed to protect EU citizens injured outside their home territories by allowing them to sue the assured's liability insurers in the place where the accident occurred without having first to sue the assured. The EU's Fifth Motor Insurance Directive in 2005[127] took matters further and conferred a direct action in all cases. Anticipating the Fifth Directive, the UK implemented the Fourth Directive more generously than was at the time required by providing in the 2002 Regulations for a generalized right of direct action. Unlike the position under the 1988 Act, there is just one set of proceedings, against the insurers, although the insurers are entitled to raise (a) any defences to the claim that the assured may have possessed, and (b) any defences that they may have under the policy. The 2002 Regulations are speedier and cheaper, and are now in widespread use. Tortfeasors have faded further from the scene in that they are under the Regulations not even the nominal defendants.

9.3.8 Coverage

In the UK the state neither provides insurance nor drafts insurance policies. Rather, it provides the parameters for the drafting of contracts by private actors. The policy may be confined to a single driver, or it may extend to named drivers or other persons identified by class, but in all cases every person who is stated as being insured has—despite the absence of any contract with the insurers—a claim against the insurers in the event of liability being incurred.[128] All of this is largely irrelevant, because if there is a third-party claim against a driver, the insurers are required to meet it whether or not

[123] 1988 Act, s 151(7)–(8): *Lloyd-Wolper v Moore* [2004] EWCA Civ 766; [2004] 1 WLR 2350.

[124] *Churchill Insurance Co Ltd v Wilkinson and Evans v Equity Claims Ltd* [2012] EWCA Civ 1166.

[125] SI 2002/3061. A third enforcement mechanism is conferred upon EU visitors injured in the UK (and also UK residents injured elsewhere in the EU) which removes the need for legal proceedings: Motor Vehicles (Compulsory Insurance) (Information Centre and Compensation Body) Regulations 2003, SI 2003/37, as amended.

[126] European Parliament and Council Directive 2000/26/EC.

[127] European Parliament and Council Directive 2005/14/EC.

[128] 1988 Act, ss 145 and 148(7).

the driver is authorized to do so by the policy (for example, because he is a thief); the principle is that cover attaches to the vehicle, not to the driver.[129]

In order to comply with the legislation, the assured must be in possession of a certificate of insurance.[130] There is no legal need for a policy as such, although the issue of policies is universal practice. Certain terms which are commonly found in motor policies which seek to restrict coverage are rendered unenforceable by the 1988 Act, s 148, where a claim is made by a third party but not where the claim is for first-party damage to the assured's own vehicle. The list was first included in the 1934 Act (s 10) after it had become apparent that the 1930 Act could easily be sidestepped by the use of contractual restrictions.[131] As regards claims provisions, the 1988 Act, s 148(5), modifies the common law by stipulating that breach of any condition after the happening of the insured event does not give the insurers a defence in respect of a third-party claim; the insurers are however entitled by s 148(6) to insert into the policy a recourse clause allowing recovery from the assured in the event that payment is required despite the assured's breach.

As regards coverage, the effect of s 148(2) is to prevent reliance by insurers on many of the most common forms of restrictions found in motor policies, although an insurer unable to rely upon any such restriction has a statutory right of recourse under s 148(4) against the assured himself. The list of affected provisions is: (a) the age or physical or mental condition of persons driving the vehicle; (b) the condition of the vehicle; (c) the number of persons that the vehicle carries; (d) the weight or physical characteristics of the goods that the vehicle carries; (e) the times at which or the areas in which the vehicle is used; (f) the horsepower or cylinder capacity or value of the vehicle; (g) the carrying on the vehicle of any particular apparatus; and (h) the carrying on the vehicle of any particular means of identification other than any means of identification required to be carried by or under the Vehicles Excise and Registration Act 1994. The list is extended by the Act, s 150, to encompass restrictions on not-for-profit car-sharing agreements. It does not cover one particularly common restriction, namely use for 'social, domestic and pleasure' purposes only. The history of the legislation indicates that the list is exhaustive. The Cassel Committee on Compulsory Insurance, reporting in 1937,[132] took the view that the 1934 Act did not provide sufficient protection for a victim, and recommended that all policy terms restricting use, other than those removing cover for business and sporting use, should be void. That recommendation was not implemented. The legislation is nevertheless ambiguous, in that s 143 requires insurance to extend to 'any liability' for death and personal injury whereas s 152(2) requires an insurer to meet a judgment only where the assured's liability is 'covered by the terms of the policy to which the certificate relates', the latter indicating that policy terms are, unless otherwise stated in s 148, enforceable. The ambiguity has been explained by the Court of Appeal in *EUI Ltd v Bristol Alliance Partnership Ltd*[133] as

[129] 1988 Act, s 151(2)(b). The insurers will, however, have a right of recourse against the unauthorized driver.

[130] 1988 Act, s 147.

[131] *Zurich General Accident & Liability Insurance v Morrison* [1942] 2 KB 53, 61.

[132] n 77. [133] [2012] EWCA Civ 1267; [2012] All ER (D) 120 (Oct).

meaning that it is the duty of the assured not to incur liability while driving without insurance rather than for the insurance to cover all liability. Here an exclusion for 'deliberate' acts prevented the insurers themselves from incurring any liability to a third-party victim. In the vast majority of cases the victim is unaffected because reliance on a permitted policy term means that the assured has no cover and the liability has to be picked up by the MIB under the Uninsured Drivers Agreement 1999.[134]

The ruling is unconvincing[135] as a matter of statutory interpretation. It is also vulnerable under EU law. In *Criminal proceedings against Rafael Ruiz Bernaldez*,[136] the CJEU struck down a policy exclusion which removed coverage for property damage caused by an intoxicated driver,[137] and in so doing expressed itself rather more widely by stating that 'compulsory motor insurance must enable third-party victims of accidents caused by vehicles to be compensated for all the damage to property and personal injuries sustained by them' and that EU law 'precludes an insurer from being able to rely on statutory provisions or contractual clauses to refuse to compensate third-party victims of an accident caused by the insured vehicle'. In *EUI* the Court of Appeal, without giving clear reasons, confined these words to the specific case of intoxicated drivers, a restriction for which there is no obvious legal or policy justification.

9.3.9 Avoidance of the policy

The defence that insurers most commonly employ is that of breach of the duty of utmost good faith. The legislation has, since 1934, restricted this right in compulsory motor insurance cases. The procedure, which has been described as a 'fair compromise'[138] is now laid out in the 1988 Act s 152(2)–(4). The effect is to require insurers to act promptly if they wish to rely upon an avoidance defence. Again, the law has now developed further, and this point is not confined to motor insurance and its compulsory regime. The Consumer Insurance (Disclosure and Representations) Act 2012 in any event prevents avoidance by insurers against consumer assureds in the absence of fraudulent misrepresentation.

9.3.10 The Motor Insurers Bureau

As early as 1937 the Cassel Committee noted the need for a source of compensation if for whatever reason the driver was uninsured.[139] The recommendation was implemented in 1946, with the establishment of the MIB as the provider of fallback cover. The Uninsured Drivers Agreement of 1946 between government and the industry stated that the MIB would provide compensation if the judgment against the driver was

[134] 9.3.11. However, *EUI* (n 133) was exceptional, in that the claim was brought by subrogated first-party property insurers, and subrogation actions are excluded from the MIB Agreement. So if the policy did not respond, there was no recovery other than from the uninsured driver.

[135] M Hemsworth, 'Insurance Obligations, the Road Traffic Act 1988 and Deliberately Caused Damage' [2013] JBL 354.

[136] Case C-129/94, [1996] ECR 1–1929.

[137] A matter covered by the 1988 Act, s 148(4).

[138] *Merchants and Manufacturers Insurance Co Ltd v Hunt* (1941) 68 Ll LR 117, per Scott LJ at 120.

[139] n 77.

not covered by insurance. The Agreement has been revised over the years, the most recent version applying to accidents occurring on or after 1 October 1999. The Uninsured Drivers Agreement applies only where the victim has obtained a judgment against the driver, which left a major gap where the injuries were sustained by the victim of a hit-and-run driver. In *Adams v Andrews*[140] in 1964, Sachs J described this as lamentable. The point was finally addressed in the first Untraced Drivers Agreement in 1969, the most recent version applying to accidents occurring on or after 14 February 2003.

The Agreements do not have statutory force, but they do have statutory recognition, since membership of the MIB is a condition of authorization for the carrying on of motor insurance business in the UK. An issue has also arisen as to the consequences of any failure of the Agreements to comply with the requirements of the Consolidated Motor Insurance Directive. Under ordinary principles of EU law, a directive is binding on the state or any 'emanation of the state', which means that the state cannot rely on domestic law insofar as it conflicts with EU law. By contrast, a directive does not have an automatic binding effect on relationships between private persons. The view of the English courts is that the MIB is not an emanation of the state so that the Agreements are not automatically overridden by the Consolidated Motor Insurance Directive,[141] but this point awaits determination at European level.

The Agreements are between the state and the industry, so that victims are not parties to them. However, Diplock LJ made clear in *Gurtner v Circuit*[142] that the court would refuse to counter any defence based on privity, and it has been held that the Untraced Drivers Agreement is enforceable as a matter of law by victims under the Contracts (Third Parties) Act 1999.[143] Again, the purpose of the contracts—and of the insurance which they secure—is recognized to be the protection of the claimant.

9.3.11 The Uninsured Drivers Agreement 1999

The 1999 Agreement applies where the victim has obtained a judgment in Great Britain in respect of a liability which has to be covered by insurance but which has not been satisfied by the insurers either because the defendant has no insurance at all or because the insurers have a defence under the policy. There are relatively few situations in which, if a policy has been issued, the insurers will have a defence, and the gradual erosion of insurers' rights has led to a corresponding diminution in the significance of the Untraced Drivers Agreement in that respect. The MIB's obligation arises if the judgment has not been satisfied within seven days, and the amounts payable are the same as under statute: unlimited for death and personal injury cases; up to £1,000,000 for property damage,[144] plus interest and costs; and the cost of social security benefits recouped under the Health and Social Care (Community Health and Standards)

[140] [1964] 2 QB 347. [141] *Mighell v Reading* [1999] Lloyd's Rep IR 30.

[142] [1968] 2 QB 587; [1968] 2 WLR 668.

[143] *Carswell v Secretary of State for Transport and the Motor Insurers Bureau* [2010] EWHC 3230 (QB); [2011] Lloyd's Rep IR 644. The Uninsured Drivers Agreement 1999 predates the legislation.

[144] The MIB operated a £300 deductible for property damage cases, but that was removed in 2008.

Act 2003. Other than in respect of social security payments, the MIB is an insurer of last resort, so if the victim has obtained payment from any other source then the MIB does not face liability.[145] It has now been settled that if the assured has suffered property damage for which he has been indemnified by a first-party policy, the property insurers do not have a subrogation claim against the MIB.[146] This reflects our general argument in Chapter 5, that courts considering claims where subrogation rights are exercised should not neglect consideration of the role of the insurer as compared with the role of an alternative potential indemnifier.

There are various exceptions to the MIB's liability in the 1999 Agreement cl 6. If negligence is the gatekeeper to distribution, these exceptions may be taken to mark the outer limits of the distributive scheme. The first of these relates to damage to the victim's vehicle at a time when he knew or ought to have known that it was uninsured. The second relates to personal injury to a victim who was voluntarily allowing himself to be carried in the vehicle and could reasonably have been expected to have alighted from it,[147] where he knew or ought to have known that the vehicle had been stolen or unlawfully taken, or was being used in furtherance of a crime, or was being used as a means of escape from, or avoidance of, lawful apprehension. The third, and the most important in practical terms, is where the victim, who was voluntarily allowing himself to be carried in the vehicle and could reasonably have been expected to have alighted from it, knew or ought to have known that the vehicle was being used without the insurance required by the 1988 Act. This final derogation is permitted by the Consolidated Motor Insurance Directive, but only where the victim 'knew' that it was uninsured. The additional words 'or ought to have known' in the Agreement were accordingly construed by the House of Lords in *White v White*[148] as meaning subjective knowledge rather than objective constructive knowledge.

Actual claims-handling is a matter for the internal rules of the MIB. Special provision is made for an insurer who has issued a statutory policy but who has a defence to the victim's claim. In such a case the insurer will be required by the MIB to handle the claim, not as a statutory insurer but rather as the nominee of the MIB under the MIB's Articles of Association, art 75. Thus, an insurer who is not liable to meet a judgment under the 1998 Act, s 151, will normally find itself liable to do so as the 'Article 75 insurer'.

9.3.12 The Untraced Drivers Agreement

The various versions of the Untraced Drivers Agreement have given rise to a series of judicial challenges which have led to substantial changes over the years. This may be put down to the intrinsic difficulty with the Agreement, which is that it is not simply a means of enforcing a judgment but rather a means of establishing liability and, by

[145] It takes priority, however, over criminal compensation orders: Powers of Criminal Courts (Sentencing) Act 2000, s 130(6).

[146] *EUI Ltd v Bristol Alliance Partnership Ltd* [2012] EWCA Civ 1267; [2012] All ER (D) 120 (Oct).

[147] But contrast *Pickett v Motor Insurers Bureau* [2004] Lloyd's Rep IR 513; [2004] 1 WLR 2450, where a majority of the Court of Appeal laid an impossibly high burden of proof on the victim.

[148] [2001] Lloyd's Rep IR 493.

definition, in the absence of the defendant. The 2003 Agreement[149] applies where the victim has suffered personal injury and, unlike its predecessors, property damage. There had been understandable reluctance to include property damage because of the belief that the ability of a victim to claim for damage to his vehicle caused by an untraced vehicle would be a licence for fraudulent conduct by motorists looking to obtain free repairs and upgrades for wear and tear. The safeguard adopted by the 2003 Agreement is that the vehicle which caused the damage has to be identified, so recovery is restricted to the limited case in which the vehicle but not the driver can be traced. It would seem that this does not comply with the requirement of the Consolidated Motor Insurance Directive for compensation for property damage as long as there are also 'significant personal injuries' in the same accident.

In order to claim from the MIB, the victim must show that the insurance would have been required, that the driver cannot be traced, and that, had he been found and sued, on the balance of probabilities the driver would have been liable. The MIB is then liable for the sum that would have been awarded against the driver, excluding damages for loss of earnings (unless there is no other source of compensation) and for property damage subject to a £300 excess and a cap of £250,000. The MIB must also pay social security costs under the Health and Social Care (Community Health and Standards) Act 2003. The MIB is the indemnifier of last resort, and so any payments are net of other recoveries made by the victim. Until 2003 interest and costs were not payable, but the decision of the Court of Appeal in *Evans v Secretary of State for the Environment, Transport and the Regions*[150] to make a reference to the CJEU produced a ruling that these deficiencies—in the then 1996 Agreement—were in contravention of the Directives, and the 2003 Agreement was amended to include both. Interest is discretionary (as it is in judicial proceedings). The CJEU's ruling in *Evans v Secretary of State for the Environment, Transport and the Regions*[151] was handed down after the 2003 Agreement had come into force, and indeed confirmed that interest and costs were included in the Directives. It was subsequently held in *Carswell v Secretary of State for Transport and the Motor Insurers Bureau*[152] that the 2003 provisions on costs did comply with the Directives.

The most important exclusions from coverage mirror those in the Uninsured Drivers Agreement. Thus there is no compensation for a passenger who was allowing himself to be carried in or on the vehicle when he knew or ought to have known that it had been stolen or unlawfully taken, or was being used without insurance, or was being used in the course or furtherance of crime, or was being used as a means of escape from or avoidance of lawful apprehension.[153] Loss caused by terrorism (for example, car

[149] The Department of Transport's Consultative Document, published in July 2000, provides the background.

[150] [2001] Lloyd's Rep IR 1.

[151] n 150.

[152] n 143.

[153] In a remarkably generous decision in *Phillips v Rafiq* [2007] EWCA Civ 74; [2007] 1 WLR 1351, the Court of Appeal ruled that a claim by a widow under the Fatal Accidents Act 1976 was not barred by the fact that the deceased himself, had he lived, could not have claimed for one of these reasons.

bombs) is also excluded, that being the province of the Criminal Injuries Compensation Scheme.

The claims procedure is perhaps the most controversial aspect of the 2003 Agreement, because the MIB effectively operates as both adjudicator and defendant. The CJEU considered the procedure in *Evans v Secretary of State for the Environment, Transport and the Regions*,[154] handing down the preliminary rulings that the use of a non-statutory body to implement the Directives was valid, and that the arbitration procedure was broadly fair. The inquisitorial role of the MIB was considered in *Carswell v Secretary of State for Transport and the Motor Insurers Bureau*,[155] and was given a clean bill of health. Negotiations for a revised version of the 2003 Agreement were at an advanced stage at the end of 2012.

9.3.13 A general approach to construction?

It will be seen that the motor insurance regime has developed slowly into one which more or less guarantees payment if there is liability in tort. There are very few loopholes; rather, there are limits to the distributive scheme and its ambitions, though these operate far from the heart of fault in the negligence sense.[156] A question which emerges here is whether it is possible to glean any overall *judicial* policy from the approach of the courts to the interpretation of the legislation, for example, whether there is a trend of expansive interpretation which seeks to maximize its ambit. The answer is, probably not. There are certainly cases which are overtly purposive, for example, the causation and deliberate running-down decisions, and there are others which take a diametrically opposed approach, for example, the rulings on the meaning of 'road'. Rather, the clarity of legislative intent is itself the key factor. Apart from this, an overriding consideration is that the 1988 Act takes effect as the UK's implementation of the EU Motor Insurance Directives and that the English courts are required wherever possible to construe the legislation in accordance with EU law. Many of the generous interpretations are explicable on this basis, and in this sense EU technicalities (completion of an internal market) have been driving the completion of tort's distributive turn in its paradigm instance.

9.3.14 Liabilities and insurance: a blurring of lines?

To what extent does this reflect back on the meaning and interpretation of tort liabilities themselves? We began this section by pointing out that no general picture of stricter liabilities can be gleaned. Neither should such a picture be expected, as the choice of compulsory liability insurance is to some degree dependent on the retention of tort as the gatekeeper.[157] But EU law may very well lead to the blurring of lines

[154] Case C-63/01, [2004] Lloyd's Rep IR 391.

[155] n 143. Also *Moore v Secretary of State for Transport* [2007] EWHC 879 (QB); [2007] Lloyd's Rep IR 469, although there the claims for damages were held to be time-barred.

[156] We review these limits in Chapter 11. See, in particular, *Delaney v Pickett* [2011] EWCA Civ 1532; [2012] 1 WLR 2149.

[157] Note also our discussion in 9.4, illustrating that stricter duties are not always a guide to distributive intent.

between liability and insurance. The Consolidated Motor Insurance Directive was not intended to harmonize the law of tort, only to harmonize insurance coverage where liability is established under the relevant domestic law. However, it has proved impossible to separate the two entirely. Statements by the CJEU that the Directive does not affect liability rules are qualified:[158]

> [N]ational rules, formulated in terms of general and abstract criteria, may not refuse or restrict to a disproportionate extent the compensation to be made available . . . by compulsory insurance against civil liability in respect of the use of motor vehicles solely on the basis of his contribution to the occurrence of the loss which arises. It is only in exceptional circumstances that the amount of compensation may be limited on the basis of an assessment of that particular case.

The effect of this qualification is that if a rule of domestic liability law automatically deprives a victim of compensation it thereby undermines the effectiveness of the compulsory provision of compensation under the Directive and is of no effect. Instead, a rule is valid only if it operates in a proportional fashion and in exceptional circumstances. The principle has been applied by the CJEU in a series of cases[159] and the Court of Appeal considered at length the blurring between tort and insurance in *Churchill Insurance Co Ltd v Wilkinson and Evans v Equity Claims Ltd.*[160] These joined cases concerned the 1988 Act, s 151(8), under which insurers who are required to indemnify the victim of a negligent uninsured driver have a right of recourse against any person who caused or permitted the uninsured use of the vehicle. The section operates in a straightforward fashion where the assured owner of a vehicle allows its uninsured use and the driver injures a third party: the insurers have to pay the victim but may then exercise their rights of recourse against the driver or the assured. That has no impact on insurance coverage. However, its application is more problematic where the assured owner has allowed uninsured use of the vehicle and is himself the victim of the driver's negligence. Although the assured has a right to recover from the insurers, any compensation that he or she might obtain is cancelled out by the obligation to reimburse the insurers. On a reference from the Court of Appeal, the CJEU proceeded on the basis that s 151(8) operated as an exception to the right of an injured passenger to recover compensation, and that it could be valid only if was not absolute and could be applied in a proportional fashion which did not undermine the effectiveness of the EU's compulsory insurance requirement. Just how those principles were to be applied was remitted to the Court of Appeal for determination. The parties did not ask the Court of Appeal to give a substantive ruling, but rather they sought a statement of principle. Aikens LJ, noting that the distinction between civil liability rules and insurance coverage rules was one which called for further clarification, stated the principle as follows:[161]

[158] *Churchill Insurance Co Ltd v Wilkinson and Evans v Equity Claims Ltd* Case C-442/10.

[159] *Storebrand Skadforsikring AS v Finanger* [2000] Lloyd's Rep IR 462; *Candolin v Vahinkovakuutusosakeyhtio Pohjola* [2006] Lloyd's Rep IR 209; *Santos v Companhia Europeia de Seguros SA* Case C-484/09, [2012] Lloyd's Rep IR 60; *Lavrador v Companhia de Seguros Fidelidade-Mundial SA* Case C-409/09, [2012] Lloyd's Rep IR 236.

[160] [2012] EWCA Civ 1166.

[161] n 160, [45].

> As a general rule, if the relevant national provision is a rule governing '*civil liability*' then the only limitation on their applicability is that such provisions must not deprive the Directives of their effectiveness. But if the national provision is one that concerns the extent to which a passenger can benefit from civil liability insurance cover, then that does directly concern the Directives and the national law must not conflict with their objectives and provisions.

Aikens LJ classified s 151(8) as having elements of both civil liability (where the victim was a third party, in which case s 151(8) had no effect on insurance coverage) and insurance coverage (which was the case where the passenger was the assured, as s 151 (8) precluded recovery). Applied to the latter case, s 151(8) had the automatic effect of removing compensation. It was accordingly necessary to construe the provision in a fashion which covered both possibilities and which confined it to permitting a right of recourse only where 'proportionate and determined on the basis of the circumstances of the case'.[162] It is apparent that this formulation raises more questions than it answers, and will require a court to examine issues such as the causal link between the permission given by the assured and the ultimate loss, and the state of knowledge of the assured as to the driver's insurance position and driving capabilities.

However, the point which we draw from the cases is that the distinction between civil liability rules and rules which preclude insurance coverage is unclear, and that even if a distinction can be drawn then civil liability rules cannot be enforced to the extent that they undermine the effectiveness of the Directive. Substantive tort law is to that extent driven by insurance requirements.

9.4 Compulsory Employers' Liability Insurance

The provision requiring compulsory insurance of liabilities for bodily injury to employees is both much more recent, and considerably less comprehensive, than the equivalent provision for road traffic.[163] But this is no indication that legislative engagement in this area has been shorter, less intense, or less purposive. On the contrary, there is a lengthier history of legislative engagement in this area, and insurance has played a key but varied role. It has been central to policy debates; to actual and proposed solutions to the threat of accidents; and to the arrangements put in place by participants independently of legislative action. Insurance, therefore, has been both a fact, and a policy tool, in respect of workplace accidents since the latter part of the nineteenth century. This is a useful context in which to challenge the supposed divisions between these various responses, particularly if any hierarchy in favour of personal responsibility and deterrence is implied.[164]

[162] n 160, [76].

[163] Employers' Liability (Compulsory Insurance) Act 1969 (the 1969 Act). The *first* compulsory liability insurance on employers followed quite closely after the Road Traffic Act scheme, in 1934, but was limited in scope and related to workmen's compensation: Workmen's Compensation (Coal Mines) Act, 1934.

[164] Chapter 8.

9.4.1 The early common law position: common employment and other barriers

The doctrine of common employment is a suitable starting point for analysis, since it operated as a catalyst for the far-reaching changes (including insurance solutions of various types) charted here. Through this doctrine, employees were locked out of tort remedies. Judicial reasoning was purposive and, ultimately, probably welfare oriented in its own right.[165] The doctrine was not fully expunged from the law until its legislative abolition in 1948.[166] By then, courts had reacted to the doctrine by enhancing primary duties of the employer (through the idea of non-delegable duties), or by attaching civil liability to statutory safety duties (through the action for breach of statutory duties); and the legislature had not only enacted such duties but also created workmen's compensation liabilities operating independently of the doctrine. Common employment thus helped to promote an extensive range of strict duties in this context, as a substitute for negligence actions, a duality still seen today. The most recent legislative reform in this area—a sweeping withdrawal of civil liability from health and safety regulations unless and until mandated by new regulations under the section—therefore marks a reversal of over a century of legal development both in the courts, and through legislation.[167]

The early common law position was that risk of injury by the negligence of a co-worker was treated as voluntarily borne, in the absence of a special contract.[168] This principle first emerged in *Priestley v Fowler*,[169] where it was held that an employee was unable to recover when injured while being carried in an overloaded delivery van by a co-worker. Lord Abinger, delivering the judgment of the court, held that an employer did not owe any duty of care to a worker to protect him from injury arising from defects unknown to the employer: it would be 'alarming' if an employer faced liability 'for the negligence of all his inferior agents'; and a worker would be relieved of responsibility for his own welfare.

[165] A response to the disastrous impact of the Poor Laws has been identified as underlying the theory of free contract in the labour market. For deep discussion of the history and the impact on legal conceptualization of the contract of employment, refer to S Deakin and F Wilkinson, *The Law of the Labour Market: Industrialization, Employment, and Legal Evolution* (Oxford: Oxford University Press, 2005). We discuss the origins of today's vicarious liability principles in Chapter 10.

[166] The doctrine was very clearly not abolished by the Workmen's Compensation Acts (which is the account given by L Friedmann and J Ladinsky, 'Social Change and the Law of Industrial Accidents' (1967) 67 Columbia Law Rev 50, in relation to the US position). In the UK, some regarded workmen's compensation as a substitute for tort actions, and even defended the doctrine as a quid pro quo for the existence of limited strict liability.

[167] Enterprise and Regulatory Reform Act 2013, s 69 (not yet in force). See further Chapter 8, n 191, explaining that the government's stated intention is to ensure that there is liability only when there has been a failure to take reasonable care or reasonable precautions.

[168] Chapter 10.

[169] (1837) 3 M & W 1. Terence Ingman suggests that there were earlier authorities which established that an employer did owe a duty of care: T Ingman, 'A History of the Defence of Volenti Non Fit Injuria' (1981) 25 JR 1; T Ingman, 'The Rise and Fall of the Doctrine of Common Employment' (1978) 23 JR 106. For forensic dissection of *Priestley v Fowler*: MA Stein, 'Priestley v Fowler (1837) and the Emerging Tort of Negligence' (2003) 44 BCL Rev 689; PWJ Bartrip and S Burman, *Wounded Soldiers of Industry* (Oxford: Clarendon Press, 1983), 103–6, citing the pre-1837 authorities at 103, n 20. Friedman and Ladinsky, n 166 discuss the emergence of workmen's compensation in the US largely in terms of the abolition of common employment.

The principle was later applied in respect of railways and coal companies. In *Hutchinson v York, Newcastle, and Berwick Railway*[170] a railway worker, injured in a collision of trains due to the negligence of a driver, was held to have no cause of action. The House of Lords put the matter beyond doubt in *Bartonshill Coal Co v Reid*.[171] The principle became classified as an implied term in the contract of employment that the worker would not hold the employer liable for injuries inflicted by a fellow worker. The effect of these and subsequent rulings[172] was that an employer owed higher duties to 'strangers' (a category which included some with whom the employer had a contractual relationship, such as passengers) than he did to his own workers.[173]

Other restrictive doctrines also operated against the worker. The doctrine of contributory negligence, unlike the doctrine of common employment, was not specifically created to prevent employees' claims, but it affected them nevertheless. *Volenti* or willing assumption of risk was more directly aimed at employees and shared with the doctrine of common employment a focus on the employee as a free contracting agent. The courts themselves decisively limited the impact of *volenti* towards the end of the nineteenth century, though not without dissentients.[174]

It was however the specific doctrine of common employment which continued to provide the backdrop to later solutions and its core was not completely demolished by either the statutory or the judicial exceptions which followed.

9.4.2 The Employers' Liability Act 1880 and the 'insurance' solution

Parliamentary pressure for abolition of the doctrine of common employment emerged as early as 1862, and a series of unsuccessful Bills was introduced.[175] The government ultimately favoured a limited measure, which became the Employers' Liability Act 1880. This adopted the liability solution in favour of arguments for an alternative, namely that accidental injuries themselves should be covered by insurance, generally on a contributory basis rather than entirely at the expense of the employer. The emergence of a debate on this issue is significant because it indicates a rival development to freedom of contract at the level of economic theory, namely the

[170] (1850) 5 Exch 343. [171] (1858) 3 Macq 266, a Scottish appeal.

[172] For example: *Lovell v Howell* (1875–76) LR 1 CPD 161; *Burr v Theatre Royal, Drury Lane Ltd* [1907] 1 KB 544; *The Napier Star (No 4)* [1939] P 330; *Alexander and Another v Tredegar Iron & Coal Co Ltd* [1945] AC 286; [1945] 2 All ER 275. Note that the last three underline the continued existence of the doctrine long after the Employers' Liability Act 1880 ('the 1880 Act') and into the twentieth century.

[173] The effect in respect of liability of the railways after accidents was particularly glaring, since these would frequently result in injury or death to both passengers and employees: R Kostal, *Law and English Railway Capitalism 1825–1875* (Oxford: Clarendon Press, 1994), ch 7. In the US, such was the high profile of the dangers associated with the railways that favourable treatment was extended to employees, by statute, in this one industry. The legislation survived the introduction of workmen's compensation and the effect was that railway workers alone enjoyed common law rights, but were excluded from the compensation regimes: Friedmann and Ladinsky, n 166.

[174] Bartrip and Burman, n 169, 183–4, particularly discuss Lord Bramwell's dissent from this trend.

[175] Bartrip and Burman, n 169, 111, 126–30. The authors suggest that the frequency with which Bills were proposed to abolish the doctrine is a useful barometer of political feeling. During the passage of the Law Reform (Contributory Negligence) Act 1945, there were at least two attempts to introduce such an abolition into the Bill.

possibility of an actuarial and distributive response to risks, based on their increasingly observed regularity.[176] This was a key advance in thinking during the latter part of the nineteenth century, and underpins the shift from (in Witt's terms) 'free labor' to 'risk and insurance' in many jurisdictions (thus also a legal shift, from freedom of contract, to a degree of distribution of risks, both being intended to alleviate or avoid hardship).[177] These actuarial advances were deployed both in the markets, underpinning new developments in insurance business, and progressively in social and welfare policy.[178]

A blueprint for the insurance idea had been promoted in a paper delivered by a barrister, James Brown, at a meeting of the Social Sciences Association (SSA), chaired by Lord Shand, in June 1878.[179] His proposal was not for liability insurance but for first-party accident insurance, the cost of which would be shared between employer and employee,[180] to replace the common law. The insurance would offer protection to the worker in the event of any injury sustained at work, and not simply from the effects of those injuries which could be blamed on the negligence of others. The benefits of such a scheme would be that injured workmen would be compensated without the need to establish negligence, that employers would no longer face litigation costs, and that losses would be spread amongst the working population and employers, thereby keeping premiums low.

By contrast, the 1880 Act[181] sought to improve the lot of injured workmen by giving access to some of the remedies—within limits—enjoyed by other citizens. There is some evidence that the insurance solution was preferred by high-ranking lawyers (because it was separable from common law), and employers, and the liability solution (even to the extent in some instances of objecting to insurance of liabilities) by certain trade unionists.[182] From the point of view of the law of obligations, it is important to be clear that both these potential solutions (insurance of the workman, and opening up of

[176] Chapter 2.

[177] JF Witt, *The Accidental Republic* (Cambridge MA: Harvard University Press, 2004), 140–2 recounts the rise of actuarial science in the late nineteenth century, based on observation of regularity in misfortunes and accidents. Refer also to Chapter 2.

[178] For review of early uses of insurance techniques in social welfare provision, and particularly the influence of German social insurance developments, refer to the collection by WJ Mommsen and W Mock (eds), *The Emergence of the Welfare State in Britain and Germany 1850–1950* (London: Taylor and Francis, 1981), and particularly the contribution of P Hennock, 'The Origins of British National Insurance and the German Precedent'; and for reflections on the role of private law see W Steinmetz (ed), *Private Law and Social Inequality in the Industrial Age: Comparing Legal Cultures in Britain, France, and the United States* (New York: Oxford University Press, 2000).

[179] Discussed by Bartrip and Burman, n 169, 140–5. The paper is published in *Sessional Proceedings of the National Association for the Promotion of Social Science 1877–78*, 169–208, together with a record of two debates on the paper, one deferred for a week. Lord Shand, as Brown pointed out, had shortly before helped reinforce the doctrine of common employment in *Woodhead v Gartness* (1877) 4 R 469. He was for a separate route, not for reform of the law of obligations.

[180] In this latter respect it differed from workmen's compensation as later enacted, but in many respects it amounted to an argument for such a scheme. Lord Shand's contribution to the debate drew heavily on German precedents for workmen's insurance along these lines.

[181] AH Ruegg, *A Treatise Upon the Employers' Liability Act, 1880 (43 & 44 Vict. Cap 42)* (London: Butterworths, 1882).

[182] Bartrip and Burman, n 169, Chapters 5–7, present a rich body of evidence in relation to the political debates behind successive reforms. For compatible approaches in respect of contributory negligence and its reform refer to Steele, n 68.

common law liabilities) can be seen in terms of reorientation of the contract of employment, since the barriers to tort claims were constructed on the basis of contractual agreement; while the introduction of contributory insurance of employees would adjust the rights and duties associated with employment and pave the way for the employment contract to be a means of delivering social welfare objectives.[183] At the point where tort became an available route to compensation, at least where harm was done by a fellow employee, it was perceived that all progress in respect of liabilities and compensation adjusted the nature of the contractual relationship between the injured party and the employer. Tort and insurance solutions had this feature in common.

None of this is apparent from the wording of the Act, s 1 of which simply removed the defence of common employment in certain circumstances where a workman had died or was injured as the result of negligence, so that he was to be treated for the relevant purposes 'as if' he had been a stranger rather than an employee.[184] The Act listed various different situations in which the doctrine of common employment was to be disapplied, each of which gave rise to complex litigation involving the drawing of fine and technical distinctions. The Act was confined to 'workmen', defined to exclude clerical workers, shop workers, and transport workers other than railwaymen. Significantly, the amount recoverable was limited to estimated earnings during the three years preceding the injury.[185] The form of liability could be referred to as a hybrid, since it did not give access to the tort measure, despite being premised on (vicarious) fault. Despite its limitations, the principle gained some adherence among trades unions, on the basis that it raised the prospect that employers may have financial incentives to reduce the rate of accidents.[186] A link between tort liability and safety incentives was established.

A greater weakness of the 1880 Act lay in the continued dominance of freedom of contract in the courts. Fears (and hopes) expressed in debates before the Act, that its effects could be negatived by agreements between employer and workers, rapidly proved to be accurate.[187] Many employers used contracting out as a condition of future employment, but often provided, as an alternative, membership of a mutual accident compensation scheme which offered fixed compensation for injuries at work. These schemes were for the most part contributory and paid for by deductions from wages.[188] Indeed the operation of such schemes in practice was avowedly the inspiration for Brown's paper.[189] But the 1880 Act, which did not expressly mention the

[183] Deakin and Wilkinson, n 165.

[184] This expression was considered in *Griffiths v Earl of Dudley* (1882) 9 QBD 357. It has intriguing resonance with much earlier fictional arguments designed to bend the common law to the purposes of litigants: SFC Milsom, *A Natural History of the Common Law* (New York: Columbia University Press, 2003), discussing 'as if' clauses in pleadings.

[185] The 1880 Act, s 3. Minus sums payable under other legislation: s 5.

[186] Bartrip and Burman, n 169, chs 5 and 6.

[187] Bartrip and Burman, n 169, recount that the objections of one member of the House of Lords were withdrawn on the basis that contracting out would be permitted.

[188] For the scope of contracting out, and the nature of the schemes, see Bartrip and Burman, n 169, ch 6, who note that the most extensive contracting out was in those industries with the worst accident records.

[189] n 179.

issue, required neither the existence of such a scheme, nor its adequacy. This was a major flaw, and indicates that the imposition of liabilities was not intended as a matter of law to trump alternative, insurance-style arrangements. Once again, contract, insurance, and the limits of tort have been connected since the earliest days of what are now called 'conventional' tort liabilities.

The legality of contracting out was tested very soon, in *Griffiths v Earl of Dudley*.[190] The scheme run by the defendant colliery owner consisted of a benefit society which established a fund consisting of weekly levies on workers deducted from their wages. In the event of death or injury, the fund managers—the defendant's agents—had discretion as to whether payment of benefits should be made. The evidence showed that on the day the 1880 Act came into force, 1 January 1881, the employer made membership of the fund and a waiver of rights under the 1880 Act conditions of employment. In the case itself a claim was brought under the Fatal Accidents Act 1846 following the death of a worker in the colliery. The Divisional Court dismissed the claim and rejected the argument that contracting out was contrary to public policy. Field J indeed turned the argument on its head by noting that a prohibition on contracting out would cause injustice to the employer, 'because the workman might obtain the benefit of the contract for years in the form of higher wages to cover the risk of injury, and then claim full additional compensation when he was injured'. More generally, the decision indicates that 'public policy', as grounds for interfering with freedom of contract, was viewed extremely narrowly by the court. With extraordinary narrowness from today's perspective (but also, one would have thought, from the reformist perspective which had led to the Act), Field J implied that all elements of society should benefit directly in order for a public policy argument to be established: public policy was not in issue here because 'the interest of the employed only would be affected'.[191]

Inadvertently, the liability solution in the 1880 Act provoked the commercialization of industrial insurance arrangements. Existing companies, which for the most part were not at this stage composite and confined their activities to specific forms of cover, proved to be unwilling to expand into a new market which was expected to be characterized by 'fishy' claims and excessive legal costs,[192] thereby rendering rate-fixing at best an imprecise science.[193] The familiar pattern of the emergence of new specialist insurers was once again seen. On this occasion the spread of employers' liability insurance alongside other forms of accident insurance had a decisive effect on the shape of the insurance industry itself.[194] This effect was magnified by the introduction of the Workmen's Compensation Act 1897 and, above all, by the extension to all trades (including domestic servants) in 1906.

[190] n 184.

[191] n 184, 363. Field J also, in this case, asserted that 'workmen as a rule were perfectly competent to make reasonable bargains for themselves'—an instance of the common law's reluctance to engage in protectionism during this period of its history, while legislation was effecting significant social change. Inequality of bargaining power apparently did not enter into common law thinking, at least where workmen were concerned.

[192] Robinson, n 20, 40–1, referring to the costs caused by 'pettifogging lawyers', as well as fishy claims.

[193] HE Raynes, *A History of British Insurance* (London: Sir Isaac Pitman & Sons, 2nd edn, 1964), 305.

[194] B Supple, *The Royal Exchange Insurance: A History of British Insurance 1720–1970* (Cambridge: Cambridge University Press, 1970), 224–37.

9.4.3 Workmen's compensation

The champion of the previously rejected insurance solution was Joseph Chamberlain, who, from the unlikely office of Colonial Secretary, engineered the passing of the Workmen's Compensation Act 1897.[195] The legislation was the subject of frequent reviews, refinement, and many hundreds of judicial rulings. Virtually all of the commentators on the legislation, and many judges, criticized it for its complexities and incongruities. Employers accepted it because its liabilities were essentially moderate and predictable, and by the same token eminently insurable; and the unions accepted it largely on the basis that it would leave common law rights and remedies intact. They did not embrace it as a working through of collectivist ethos, perhaps because, looked at in its own distributive terms, the legislation clearly did not place the whole cost of accidents with employers.[196] The logic of the legislation, like the logic of Brown's paper to the SSA, was modelled on first-party insurance rather than on fault or even breach of strict duty. But the assurance was to be paid for by employers, without employee contributions. It was delivered through no-fault liabilities, without the need to show breaches of duty or a 'falling short', on the part of employers. It was avowedly designed to place responsibility for *assurance* of workmen with business, rather than with the community, and in this sense it was a form of (limited and insurable) 'enterprise liability'.[197] Once the issues were seen in terms of accident insurance and 'compensation', however, rather than in terms of fault of individual employers, the pressure grew to make the scheme more comprehensive and to secure compensation more effectively, generally speaking through further insurance of the liabilities. These issues arose repeatedly in the history of the legislation and its successors. Like the 1880 Act, the Workmen's Compensation Act 1897 ('the 1897 Act') created a hybrid, building on concepts from different areas of law, and mixing the identities of tort, contract, insurance, and emerging social insurance arrangements.

The 1897 Act introduced the obligation of an employer, or an undertaker who had sub-contracted the worker, to pay compensation to a worker injured by accident[198] arising out of and in the course of his employment on the basis of no-fault liability. The sum was payable weekly but limited to half of the worker's annual average wage and capped at £1 per week. A worker with a long-term injury could, after six months, opt for a lump-sum payment approved by the local County Court.[199] In the case of death, the sum payable to dependants wholly supported by the deceased was based on average weekly wages, subject to minimum and maximum payments. If there were no dependants, funeral expenses of £10 were payable. The worker had to choose between damages

[195] For the processes leading to the Act, refer to Bartrip and Burman, n 169, ch 7. PWJ Bartrip, *Workmen's Compensation in Twentieth Century Britain: Law, History and Social Policy* (Aldershot: Gower, 1987), 12, categorizes the 1897 Act as 'the solution which least divided the various interest groups'.

[196] A point made by economist J Cohen in his review of the operation of workmen's compensation: J Cohen, *Workmen's Compensation in Great Britain* (London: Post Magazine, 1923), 30: two-thirds of the cost of accidents was borne by the worker.

[197] Though this more modern expression was not used, it fits the declared objectives of the reformers and those who supported the legislation.

[198] The 1897 Act, s 1(1). [199] The 1897 Act, Sch 1.

in tort from the employer where available or a claim under the 1897 Act,[200] a decision which necessarily turned upon the amount of his weekly wages.

The 1897 Act was subject to numerous restrictions. Employment had to be by an undertaker in an industry regarded as particularly dangerous, the list including railways, factories,[201] mines, and quarries.[202] Crown employment was within the Act, although there was no cover for those employed on naval or military service.[203] By extension in 1900,[204] agriculture was brought into the list, though insurers were never comfortable with its inclusion.[205] The parties could agree to contract out of the Act, but—in a provision which shows the influence of earlier debates concerning contracting out under the 1880 Act—only where a scheme approved by the Registrar of Friendly Societies which was at least as favourable as that under the 1897 Act was in place.[206] The employer had a defence to a personal injury claim if serious and wilful misconduct on the part of the worker could be shown[207] although, short of gross negligence, *volenti non fit injuria* and contributory negligence were not defences to a claim. Insurance against liability under the 1897 Act was not compulsory; it was itself a form of mandatory insurance, achieved through and in the form of liability of the enterprise.

In 1906, the experiment represented by the 1897 Act was given much more general effect. Under the Workmen's Compensation Act 1906 ('the 1906 Act'),[208] coverage was extended beyond 'dangerous' occupations to 'any person who enters into or works under a contract of service or apprenticeship with an employer, whether by way of manual labour,[209] clerical work or otherwise'. Non-manual workers were, however, protected only if they earned less than £250 per year. Coverage was still not comprehensive, in that outworkers, casual workers not a part of the employer's overall activities, independent contractors,[210] partners,[211] the police, employees in the naval

[200] The 1897 Act, s 1(2)(b). Under s 1(4), if a claim brought in tort was dismissed, the worker could nevertheless seek compensation from the court in the same proceedings, but subject to any costs awarded to the employer in respect of his successful defence of the tort claim.

[201] A word which proved problematic: *Barrett v Kemp Brothers* [1904] 1 KB 517.

[202] The 1897 Act, s 7.

[203] The 1897 Act, s 8.

[204] Workmen's Compensation Act 1900.

[205] According to the author of the ELAC Jubilee book, H Robinson (n 20, 54), 'no class of insurance has been so unprofitable'. The reasons given were variously the far-flung nature of the work, the carelessness of agricultural workers and lack of basic safety provision, and the increased complications following ordinary injuries caused by lack of medical attention.

[206] The 1897 Act, s 3. This had been floated by a Commission on the operation of the 1880 Act, but not accepted. There was much continuity in policy debate across the liability and insurance 'solutions'.

[207] The 1897 Act, s 1(2)(c).

[208] There were many thousands of decided cases under the 1897 and 1906 Acts, so much so that a discrete set of law reports—BWCC—was introduced to accommodate them all. This was despite the ambition for such disputes to be resolved by private arbitration, so that many of the issues which arose have remained disguised: FR Batt, *The Law of Master and Servant* (London: Pitman & Sons, 1933).

[209] Which was held to refer to unskilled work (*Simpson v Ebbw Vale Steel, Iron, and Coal Co* [1905] 1 KB 453) performed with hands (thereby excluding drivers (*Morgan v London General Omnibus Company* 13 QBD 832)).

[210] The distinction between employees and independent contractors has generated a mass of case law under a wide variety of legislation. An extra dimension has been added in respect of legislation which implements EU directives, in that there is now a good deal of CJEU authority on the matter.

[211] *Ellis v Ellis* [1905] 1 KB 324.

or military service of the Crown,[212] and family members remained excluded, although 'masters, seamen and apprentices to the sea service and to apprentices in the sea-fishing service', on UK-registered vessels, excluding share fishermen, were brought in. Any claim was to be made against the employer or, in the case of a workman loaned to another employer, the latter employer. The employer also faced liability for injuries to workmen 'on or in or about' his premises[213] if employed by a subcontractor, but with a right of recourse against the subcontractor.[214]

The 1897 legislation had been confined to 'accidents'[215] in the sense of sudden occurrences, so that physical injury, psychological injury, or disease brought about by an incident which was both untoward[216] and accidental from the victim's point of view[217] was covered. Disease[218] and disability[219] contracted by continual exposure to a hazard had been excluded from the 1897 Act because there was no loss caused by 'accident'. The 1906 Act removed this restriction and extended protection to those industrial diseases specified in the Act[220] and also other diseases subsequently brought within the scheme by statutory instrument.[221] The extension of coverage to exposure to diseases raised the problem, all too familiar in modern law, of identifying which of a number of employers responsible for exposure should bear liability. The solution adopted by the 1906 Act, s 8(1), was to allow a claim to be brought against any employer who had last employed the worker in the twelve months immediately prior to the onset of disease[222] as long as the worker could show that the disease was one due to the risks posed by the nature of the employment.[223] That employer, however, had a right of recourse from other employers who had been guilty of exposure.[224] It should be noted that this was several decades ahead of the breaking of the need to prove a causal

[212] The 1906 Act, s 9(1).

[213] This phrase was held to mean that there had to be a close geographical connection between the premises and the injury: *Powell v Brown* [1899] 1 QB 157.

[214] Thereby casting the burden of the subcontractor's insolvency on the employer: the 1906 Act, s 4, subject to an exception where the subcontractor provided farm machinery.

[215] These decisions stretch the boundaries of 'accident' and causation to their limits, and later insurance cases construing the terms 'accident' and 'accidental injury' have expressly rejected any analogy with the cases decided under the 1897 and 1906 Acts: *De Souza v Home & Overseas Insurance Co Ltd* [1995] LRLR 453.

[216] *Fenton v Thorley & Co* [1903] AC 443; *Wilson v Chatterton* [1946] KB 360.

[217] So that injury caused by the deliberate acts of third parties was covered: *Nisbet v Rayner* [1910] 2 KB 689; *Trim Joint School v Kelly* [1914] AC 667.

[218] *Walker v Lilleshall Coal Co* [1900] 1 QB 481; *Steel v Cammell Laird & Co* [1905] 2 KB 232; *Broderick v London County Council* [1908] 2 KB 807.

[219] *Marshall v East Holywell Coal Co Ltd, Gorley v Backworth Collieries* 21 TLR 494.

[220] Sch 3. These included anthrax and ankylostomiasis.

[221] Under s 8. Regulations were duly made bringing in a variety of diseases arising from specified processes. The list included cancers, poisoning by chemicals such as lead, phosphorus, and mercury, cataracts, cramp, problems with joints, and the effects of dust.

[222] If the worker did not fulfil this requirement, he had to prove that the employment was the cause of his disease: *Dean v Rubian Art Pottery Ltd* [1914] 2 KB 213.

[223] *Leaf v Furze* [1914] 3 KB 1068; *Mayer and Sherratt v Co-Operative Insurance Society Ltd* [1939] 2 KB 627; *Blatchford v Staddon* [1927] AC 461; *Ellerbeck Collieries Ltd v Cornhill Insurance Co* [1932] 1 KB 401.

[224] Anticipating the system now adopted by the Compensation Act 2006 whereby an employee who has contracted mesothelioma can pin liability upon any one employer (although, unlike the position under the 1906 Act, not necessarily the last) and it is left to the employers and their insurers to fight out allocation as between themselves. Quite how liability is to be apportioned, both then and now, remains a mystery: Chapter 12.

link between the totality of the victim's injuries and the degree of exposure,[225] and also of the first contribution legislation in the law of tort,[226] illustrating the way in which workmen's compensation played its part in generating new legal resources and techniques. It could be said that it developed the law of tort, during a period when tort itself was largely ineffective. This is a variation of Wex Malone's recognition of the 'contagious' principle of workmen's compensation in the United States,[227] for it does not refer to export of the grander 'principles', such as strict or enterprise liability, on which it was based. Rather, it shows the infectiousness of detailed and practical solutions which have been pragmatically adopted and translated to contexts governed by tort. Our point is that pragmatic development even at this detailed level gives rise to variations in working concepts, which are capable of influencing the law to an extent which has not been fully appreciated.[228]

As under the 1897 Act, the accident giving rise to the loss had to be one arising out of and in the course of employment.[229] This was interpreted liberally by the courts, which eschewed ordinary causation rules in favour of a wider search for more remote causes.[230] The serious and wilful misconduct of a worker in bringing about his own fate,[231] although not mere negligence or disobedience to orders,[232] precluded recovery. An important change from the 1897 Act (and a significant contrast with the common law, even under successive Fatal Accidents Acts) was that serious and wilful misconduct was to be disregarded in death and serious and permanent disablement cases,[233] the view being taken that the true beneficiaries were the worker's dependants.

The compensation rules were set out in the intricately drafted 1906 Act, Sch 1, and took the form of weekly payments for incapacity. In the event of death, persons dependent upon the deceased[234] were entitled to compensation for a three-year period, again subject to a minimum and a cap. The workman retained his right to sue the employer at law 'where the injury was caused by the personal negligence or wilful act of the employer or of some person for whose act or default the employer is responsible'

[225] Compensation Act 2006, s 3, discussed in Chapter 12.

[226] Law Reform (Married Women and Tortfeasors) Act 1935.

[227] W Malone, 'Damage Suits and the Contagious Principle of Workmen's Compensation' (1952) 9 Natl Association of Claimants' Compensation Attorneys LJ 20, cited by J Witt, n 177, 197.

[228] Deakin, 'Complementary or Competing Models?', n 19. This is a counter-balance to lawyers' usual search for the most general of principles as organizing and classifying ideas.

[229] The 1906 Act, s 1(1). As Earl Loreburn LC commented in *Warner v Couchman* [1912] AC 25, 'There cannot be imagined a more difficult part of this difficult Act to determine'.

[230] *Thom v Sinclair* [1917] AC 127.

[231] The employer bore the burden of proving such conduct: *Johnson v Marshall Sons & Co Ltd* [1906] AC 409.

[232] *Harris v Associated Portland Cement Manufacturers Ltd* [1939] AC 71. Disobedience to statutory obligations did not necessarily take the worker outside the course of employment. Contrast *Bourton v Beauchamp* [1920] AC 1001 and *Moore & Co v Donnelly* [1921] 1 AC 329 (outside course of employment) with *Bist v London and South Western Railway* [1907] AC 209. *Barnes v Nunnery Colliery Co Ltd* [1912] AC 44; *Wilsons and Clyde Coal Co v M'Ferrin* [1926] AC 377; *Hannaby v Llay Main Collieries Ltd* [1931] 1 KB 602; and *Thomas v Ocean Coal Co Ltd* [1933] AC 100 (course of employment).

[233] The 1906 Act, s 1(2)(c): *Johnson v Marshall* [1906] AC 409; *John George v Glasgow Coal Co Ltd* [1909] AC 123; *Williams v Llandudno Coaching and Carriage Co Ltd* [1915] 2 KB 101.

[234] The test for dependency was a pragmatic one, the question being whether the applicant relied for all or part of his support (or the support of his family) on the money which the deceased was earning: *Main Colliery v Davies* [1900] AC 358; *Senior v Fountains and Burnley* [1907] 2 KB 563.

but could not recover under both the common law or 1880 Act and the 1906 Act.[235] He had to choose one or the other.[236] By way of contrast to the provisions of the 1897 Act, the workman was entitled to retain compensation paid to him under other safety legislation.[237] Further, the phrase 'personal negligence or wilful act of the employer' was held not to encompass the case in which an employer was liable for breach of statutory duty, so that it was possible for an injured workman to claim under the 1906 Act and then top up his damages with a claim for breach of statutory duty.[238]

The contracting-out principles of the 1897 Act were further developed by the 1906 Act.[239] Regulations made by the Chief Registrar of Friendly Societies set out the rules for the minimum content of schemes and for the holding of worker ballots for the approval of schemes. Thus, the legislation dealt with both of the key objections to contracting-out provisions of the 1880 Act, namely the adequacy of alternative compensation, and the inequality of bargaining power. Freedom of contract was therefore heavily qualified in pursuit of welfare goals. A decision to join the scheme did not preclude any claim for damages at common law,[240] but it did preclude a claim for damages under the 1880 Act, as the agreement amounted to an option not to bring an action under that Act.[241]

All disputes were in principle to be resolved by arbitration rather than judicial proceedings,[242] a procedure which was thought to be speedy, cheap, and non-adversarial. However, the good intentions were not borne out in practice. Arbitration proved to be the first rather than last stage in the process. The mass of case law under the 1906 Act indicates the failure of this particular provision, although it appears that the number of contested claims dropped significantly after 1921, down by some 30 per cent on pre-war figures.[243]

It has already been noted that the development of employers' liability insurance was prompted by the 1880 Act. Continuity in this need for insurance was at least as significant as the formal shift from liability to workmen's compensation, not least because both forms of liability were subject to statutory limitation. Many employers[244] rapidly took advantage of the new form of cover, though it appears that the

[235] *Unsworth v Pease and Partners Ltd* [1937] 2 KB 504; *Selwood v Townley Coal and Fireclay Co Ltd* [1940] 1 KB 180; *Young v Bristol Aeroplane Co Ltd* [1946] AC 163.

[236] The 1906 Act, s 1(2)(b). The advice given by the Fabian Society was that a claim under the 1880 Act should be pursued only: '(i) if the workman's wages were £2.10s a week; (ii) if the action is almost certain to be successful because of the employer or his foreman being clearly and seriously to blame; and (iii) if the workman's injuries are very serious and likely to continue for some considerable period or for life', *Fabian Society Tract No 82*, 1901, relating to the 1897 Act.

[237] The 1906 Act, s 1(5). The relevant measures under which penalties imposed upon an employer could be distributed to the victim or his family were the Metalliferous Mines Regulation Act 1872, the Coal Mines Regulation Act 1887, and the Factory and Workshop Act 1901.

[238] *Wheeler v New Merton Board Mills Ltd* [1933] 2 KB 669.

[239] The 1906 Act, s 3.

[240] *Coe v London and North Eastern Railway Company* [1943] KB 531, overruling *Taylor v Hamstead Colliery Co Ltd* [1904] 1 KB 838 on the point.

[241] *Taylor v Hamstead Colliery Co* [1904] 1 KB 838.

[242] The 1906 Act, s 1(3) and Sch 2.

[243] Bartrip, n 195, 133–5.

[244] One of the objections to extension of the 1906 Act to domestic servants was that individuals who employed servants but who were not otherwise in business, and who might be of comparatively modest means, would be under pressure to insure. Many chose to do so.

competition between insurance companies was intense and the profitability of the business doubtful. The extent of such insurance can be seen from the fact that those who did not insure against liability to workmen became known as 'self-insurers'.[245] To be of value, policies had to cover liability at common law, under the 1880 Act and under the 1897 Act[246] even though insurance was not compulsory. Following the passing of the 1906 Act, the extension of liability to disease meant that policies were amended to cover specified diseases, and there is evidence to show that when new diseases were added to the 1906 Act insurance cover was adjusted accordingly.[247] Premiums were calculated by reference to wages paid, given the link between pay and the level of compensation under the 1906 Act. One interesting insight into the significance of insurance to employers is shown by *Mackenzie v Iron Trades Employers' Insurance Association Ltd*,[248] in which a workman claimed damages from an insurance company on the basis that it maintained a list of workmen who were not to be employed and that as a result he had been dismissed by two employers and refused employment by a third. The truth of the claim was never tested, as the court ruled that there was no actionable wrong in the circumstances, but the allegation suggests that employers would go to great lengths to maintain their insurance cover.

By the time of the Holman Gregory Committee Report in 1920,[249] there were some sixty-five insurance companies writing employers' liability business, and forty-eight of those had formed themselves into the Accident Offices' Association which had adopted 'tariff' wording.[250] Both in policy terms, and in terms of market share, the services of insurance companies, and of mutual insurers, were in competition. Insurance companies were by 1928 estimated to have something around one-quarter of the potential market (based on payments), with most companies being enrolled in mutual associations and the remainder being self-insurers.[251] Some of the contracts taken out by employers with mutual associations were not true insurance at all, and required the employer to repay the mutual if there had been payment of a claim, and so proved to be of dubious value,[252] not only to the insurer, but also to the injured worker or his dependants.[253] Yet mutuality also offered a route to insurance without the overheads necessitated by profits and expenses for the companies, and encouraging mutuality remained a tempting policy option for this reason.

[245] Raynes, n 193, 299.

[246] See the policy wording in *Lancashire Insurance Company v Commissioners of Inland Revenue* [1899] 1 QB 353.

[247] *Smith & Son v Eagle Star & British Dominions Insurance Co* (1934) 48 Ll LR 67; *Ellerbeck Collieries Ltd v Cornhill Insurance Co* [1932] 1 KB 401, in each of which policies were construed so as to ensure that cover matched the statutory liability for disease.

[248] (1910) SC 79.

[249] Report of the Departmental Committee on Workmen's Compensation, Cmd 816 (July 1920).

[250] The meaning of that wording has proved to be crucial in resolving current coverage disputes in respect of liability for asbestos exposure, as we discuss in Chapter 12.

[251] Bartrip, n 195, 130.

[252] *Pailin v Northern Employers' Mutual Indemnity Co Ltd* [1925] 2 KB 73.

[253] It became particularly apparent that mutual insurers sometimes might not assist at just the point where, in policy terms, they were most needed, namely on the insolvency of the liable employer: Cassel Committee, n 77, 35–43: mutual arrangements were largely satisfactory for the employer but the employee's security depended on continued solvency of the members (the very problem the compulsory insurance regime was designed to remedy). See also TNA PREM 1/149, relating to the Nicholson Act.

Workmen's compensation was not administered by the state, but it remained under close governmental scrutiny. The Report of the Holman Gregory Committee in 1920[254] made a series of important recommendations aimed at enhancing the scheme, ranging from increase in death benefits to widows and children to the introduction of a requirement on insurers that at least 70 per cent of premiums should be repaid in the form of benefits (only 48 per cent of premiums were repaid in benefits at the time). The recommendations were largely not implemented, though the latter was dealt with not by law but by agreement with the insurance industry, and it provided only for 60 per cent of premium income to be paid as benefits, rising to 62.5 per cent from 1927.[255] This illustrates the involvement of the state in reviewing the effect of market insurance as an instrument of social policy—and also the importance of negotiation between government and the industry.[256] Significantly, among the recommendations was a proposal for compulsory liability insurance across the sector. It came to nothing, but limited compulsory insurance was later achieved for the coal industry in particular, in 1934. This was however a compassionate response to hardship following insolvencies in an industry in decline, engineered by an individual Conservative MP who managed to outflank the party leadership and secure somewhat reluctant support—not unlike the more general provision enacted in 1969.[257]

9.4.4 The origins of the modern system

The most significant turning point came with the appointment of the Beveridge Committee in 1941. Its goal was to survey 'existing national schemes of social insurance and allied services, including workmen's compensation, and to make recommendations'. Since the focus was national insurance, tort damages became designated the 'alternative remedy'—a rather different hierarchy from that encountered in theoretical accounts today.[258] So far as workers' compensation was concerned,[259] Beveridge regarded the system as beneficial but flawed. His solution was to deliver benefits via the state, removing the idea of liability, with contributions to the insurance fund being made by employers and employees.[260] The 'insurance' solution remained a constant factor in the shift from liability to state provision. But it appears that the shift from liability has meant a shift out of legal consciousness.[261]

[254] n 249.

[255] *Employers' Liability Insurance: Undertaking given by the Accident Offices Association*, Cmd 1891, 1925.

[256] R Lewis, 'Insurers' Agreements Not to Enforce Strict Legal Rights: Bargaining with Government and in the Shadow of the Law' (1985) 48 *Modern Law Review* 275; also our discussion of the MIB at 9.3.10; the response to *Lister v Romford Ice and Cold Storage* (Chapter 5); and the ABI-governmental agreement on flood insurance (Chapter 6).

[257] Workmen's Compensation (Coal Mines) Act 1934. The Act was prompted by Conservative MP Donald Nicholson, who represented the mining district of Morpeth. He had observed that even at this date, after decades of 'security' through workmen's compensation, men who were entitled to pensions under the Workmen's Compensation Act had been thrown on to the poor law due to the insolvency of employers.

[258] For a perspective on the hierarchy: Lewis, n 12.

[259] Beveridge Report, n 24, [77]–[105].

[260] On the eventual removal of a separate fund: Lewis, n 12.

[261] Lewis, n 12.

By the National Insurance (Industrial Injuries) Act 1946,[262] the post-War Labour government repealed the Workmen's Compensation legislation and replaced it with a state scheme of social insurance built upon Lloyd George's National Insurance Act 1911, thus transferring the burden of industrial injuries, and the administration of the scheme, to the state.[263] The scheme is now enshrined in the Social Security Contributions and Benefits Act 1992, the Social Security Administration Act 1992, and the Social Security Act 1998,[264] supplemented by a myriad of statutory instruments. The current legislation is labyrinthine,[265] but many of its concepts reflect the issues that arose under the Workmen's Compensation Act.[266]

Beveridge had raised but not answered the question of whether there should be an additional right to claim damages in tort.[267] As we have seen, the fate of tort liability in the proposed new structure was debated by a Departmental Committee chaired by Sir Walter Monckton QC. The Committee's recommendation that the doctrine of common employment should finally be abolished was implemented by the Law Reform (Personal Injuries) Act 1948 (s 1(1)), which also repealed the Employers Liability Act 1880 which had thereby been rendered redundant (s 1(2)), prohibited contracting out (s 1(3)), and resolved the double recovery dilemma raised by Beveridge by opting for a compromise position under which damages awarded[268] were to be reduced by the amount of one-half of any benefits to be received by the worker under the industrial injuries scheme for a five-year period (s 2).[269] The most significant subsequent change came with the Social Security Act 1989, which introduced the idea that the prohibition on double recovery should enure to the benefit of the state and not (through reduction in damages) the tortfeasor. Thus the insurance market distributes a share of the cost of medical treatment, through third-party liability insurance. Again these provisions are generally under-emphasized by tort lawyers. They are important in that they express the balance between state insurance and liability insurance, as a source of indemnity for the burden of losses, and as a mechanism for their distribution, envisaging a hierarchy between state and market in the distribution of the costs of treatment.[270] The current legislation, the Social Security (Recovery of Benefits) Act 1997, ensures that any social security benefits received by the victim of a tortfeasor are recouped from the tortfeasor by the Compensation Recovery Unit (CRU) of the Department for Work and Pensions

[262] AF Young, *Industrial Injuries Insurance* (London: Routledge & Kegan, 1964), 98–146.

[263] *Royal Commission on Civil Liability and Compensation for Personal Injury*, Cmnd 7054 (1978) ('Pearson Report'), ch 17.

[264] Replacing the National Insurance (Industrial Injuries) Act 1965.

[265] NJ Wikeley and AI Ogus, *Wikeley, Ogus and Barendt's Law of Social Security* (Oxford: Oxford University Press, 6th edn, 2005); P Cane, *Atiyah's Accidents, Compensation and the Law* (Cambridge: Cambridge University Press, 7th edn, 2006), 338–62.

[266] Lewis, n 107, provides a critique.

[267] Beveridge, n 24, [258]–[264].

[268] But, rather curiously, not if agreed by settlement.

[269] The Monckton Committee had recommended 100 per cent deduction. There was no deduction for the value of NHS provision, and if there was any apportionment by way of contributory negligence—under the newly implemented Civil Liability (Contributory Negligence) Act 1945—then the deduction was from gross and not net damages.

[270] Lewis, n 107.

(DWP). Under this scheme the victim does not obtain double recovery, and the full cost of damages falls to the tortfeasor (and the tortfeasor's insurer).

9.4.5 Moves towards compulsory insurance

The idea of compulsory liability insurance had been suggested in 1920 by the Holman Gregory Report in relation to Workmen's Compensation. During the 1930s, it was enacted in the three specific areas reviewed by the Cassel Committee: road traffic, private aircraft, and workmen's compensation in the coal industry. The Cassel Committee's discussion of the generic idea suggests that the appeal of compulsory insurance, and its recognized significance, was wider than its implementation. The idea recurred in connection with employers' tort liabilities. Governments consistently rejected it, apparently not on ideological or political grounds but rather because they thought it could be difficult to enforce, and that the enforcement costs would be disproportionate because most employers were insured.[271] The legislature, after years of involvement in establishing and reviewing workmen's compensation and related compensation schemes, declined to devote the same legislative resources to securing liabilities.

The turning point was an individual tragic event. On 18 November 1968, a fire occurred in a warehouse in Glasgow.[272] It was destroyed and twenty-two workers were killed. Security bars at the windows, designed to keep thieves out, prevented escape by all but three victims. The employer was insured, but the insurers avoided the policy on the grounds of non-disclosure, so that little compensation was paid. The fire gave rise to questions in Parliament, and led to a Private Member's Bill, introduced by David Watkins MP, which was afforded a fair wind by the government. The resulting legislation was the Employers' Liability (Compulsory Insurance) Act 1969, a short measure duly supplemented by rather more detailed secondary legislation, but not of the length or complexity which the government had predicted two years earlier. A deep irony is that the right of insurers to avoid the policy for breach of the duty of utmost good faith—the very situation following the Glasgow fire which ultimately led to the Act—was left untouched. However, the Act added a new layer of protection by making compulsory what had, for close to a century, been a practical choice for employers.

The 1969 Act was an uneasy compromise.[273] Industry pressure in 1969 made sure that the measure did not go too far. The government guaranteed that there would not

[271] The files suggest that in effect a form of words was handed down from one government to the next to deal with constituency MPs' questions on the matter: TNA LCO 2/8391 (employers' liability, 1951–65). The level of hardship was regularly said not to justify the difficulty and expense of compulsory insurance legislation. During this period, Lord Gardner was asked (LCO 2/8392, letter, 26 July 1965) to remove from the first Law Commission programme proposed consideration of the notion of compulsory insurance to 'supplement or replace' the right to sue for damages for personal injury. He complied, but expressed himself 'suspicious of those who say that something desirable is administratively impossible' (letter, 4 August 1965)—well capturing the nature of the arguments put up against the idea.

[272] <http://urbanglasgow.co.uk/archive/james-watt-street-fire-1968__o_t__t_737.html>, accessed 2 May 2013.

[273] R Hasson, 'The Employers' Liability (Compulsory Insurance) Act 1969—A Broken Reed?' (1974) 3 Indus Law J 79. Hasson suggested that the provisions should be tightened rather than 'waiting for Pearson'—suggesting that some took for granted that the Report of the Pearson Commission (n 263) would lead to broader changes.

be a levy upon the insurance industry to pay the bills of uninsured employers, the model adopted in the context of motor insurance through the MIB Agreements.[274] Tort law was to be left almost, but not entirely, unscathed.[275] As will be seen in the following outline, the 1969 Act is a pale reflection of its motor insurance counterpart.

9.4.6 Compulsory insurance under the 1969 Act

The legislation is supplemented by the Employers' Liability (Compulsory Insurance) Regulations 1998 ('the 1998 Regulations').[276] The basic insuring obligation of the 1969 Act, s 1(1), requires every employer carrying on any business in Great Britain to insure, and maintain insurance, under one or more approved policies with an authorized insurer or insurers against liability for bodily injury or diseases sustained by his employees,[277] and arising out of and in the course of their employment in Great Britain. Exempted employers are for the most part official bodies, including the health service and local authorities,[278] although the most significant exemption, added in 2004, removes from the legislation a company which employs only its owner, aligning the position with a sole trader operating other than in corporate form.[279]

The coverage of the policy is liability, including liability under the Fatal Accidents Act 1976,[280] for bodily injury or disease, although not for damage to any employee's property. The minimum sum insured is £5 million in respect of claims relating to any one or more of his employees arising out of any one occurrence, including defence costs.[281] The figure may seem high, but the phrase 'any one occurrence' refers to an incident which gives rise to multiple losses. It is the practice to insure for £10 million for losses arising from any one occurrence. There is a prohibition of any policy deductible,[282] but insurers often overcome this prohibition by requiring the employer to repay a sum equivalent to a deductible once the insurers have satisfied a claim. Such liability may be separately insured.[283] Insurers will also be liable for the costs of NHS treatment in accordance with the Health and Social Care (Community Health and Standards) Act 2003.

[274] HL Hansard, 14 October 1969.

[275] The Employers' Liability (Defective Equipment) Act 1969 reversed the effect of *Davie v New Merton Board Mills* [1959] AC 604, thus imposing strict liability on employers where an employee is injured by defective equipment supplied by the employer. Extensive liabilities were created in the Provision and Use of Work Equipment Regulations 1998, SI 1998/2306 but, as noted in earlier discussion and in Chapter 8, the Enterprise and Regulatory Reform Act 2013, s 69, will remove civil liability for breach of these and other health and safety regulations.

[276] SI 1998/2573.

[277] Independent contractors are excluded by the definition in s 2(1), although separate (voluntary) public liability cover is generally obtained.

[278] The 1969 Act, s 3 and the 1998 Regulations, Sch 3.

[279] The employer will almost certainly have separate public liability cover which protects against legal liability to any person. Such cover is not, however, compulsory.

[280] *Re T&N Ltd (No 4)* [2006] EWHC 1447 (Ch).

[281] 1998 Regulations, reg 3(1).

[282] 1998 Regulations, reg 2(2).

[283] As arranged in *T&N v Sun Alliance* [2002] EWHC 2420 (Ch); [2004] Lloyd's Rep IR 102; and *T&N v Sun Alliance (No 2)* [2003] EWHC 1016 (Ch); [2004] Lloyd's Rep IR 106.

The employer's obligation is to 'insure, and maintain' insurance. As was seen in Chapter 3, liability policies can respond to the event which ultimately gives rise to injury; the injury; or the claim against the assured. Most injuries are the consequence of a single immediate event, so that it matters little which of the three types is used. However, the position is different where the employee suffers a disease or injury as the result of an event occurring at some earlier point, and becomes even more complex when the injury is latent and does not become manifest for many years (a long-tail injury). In *Employers' Liability Insurance 'Trigger' Litigation: BAI (Run Off) Ltd v Durham*,[284] the Supreme Court ruled that the Act required coverage based on exposure rather than injury; the implications are explored in Chapter 12.

To be 'approved', the policy has to comply with the timid control on policy terms set out in the Regulations. Regulation 2 prohibits any condition which prevents or restricts liability under the policy by reference to: (a) any obligation after the event giving rise to the claim; (b) failure to take reasonable care; (c) failure to comply with protective legislation; and (d) failure to keep employment records. This goes little further than the common law.

In contrast with the road traffic position, the sanction for failure to insure is solely criminal.[285] The Court of Appeal in *Richardson v Pitt-Stanley*[286] ruled that the 1969 Act was not designed to give rise to civil liability; thus, if an employer failed to insure there was no possibility of an action for breach of statutory duty against the defaulting directors. There is no body equivalent to the MIB to provide fallback compensation to the employees of uninsured employers. Two relevant problems may face an injured employee. The first is that the employer might be entirely uninsured. The second is that the employer is insured but the insurers cannot be traced. There are no plans for the establishment of a compensation body to cover injuries sustained by the employees of uninsured employers, and instead the focus has remained on untraced insurers. In November 1999 a Code of Practice was agreed between the government, the ABI, and the Lloyd's Market Association for tracing employers' liability insurance policies, and the vast majority of insurers are now capable of being traced. If an insurer which has been traced has ceased to exist, its liability will be picked up by the FSCS. A DWP Consultation Paper issued in February 2010 proposed formalizing the position by the establishment of an Employers Insurance Bureau (EIB) to pick up the liabilities of employers with untraced insurers, and in April 2010 the government established the Employers' Liability Tracing Office charged with the functions of maintaining an electronic register of policies and assisting victims with the process of tracing. Since February 2011, employers' liability insurers have been required by rules made under the FSMA 2000 to maintain an Employers' Liability Register of new policies. In July 2012 the coalition government announced that the idea of establishing an EIB had been abandoned. In its place, legislation is to be introduced to impose a levy on insurers to meet mesothelioma claims only, and—pending legislation[287]—under an agreement taking effect on 25 July

[284] [2012] UKSC 14; [2012] 1 WLR 867.

[285] The 1969 act ss 5, 5A, and 5B.

[286] [1995] QB 123.

[287] The Mesothelioma Bill 2013 (a measure with cross-party support) had its first reading in the House of Lords on 9 May 2013. Clauses 13–14 deal with the proposed levy on insurers.

2012 the ABI agreed that payments will be made on a voluntary basis to the sufferers of mesothelioma. The Compensation Bill was introduced into the House of Lords in May 2013 to implement this undertaking. Under the Bill, any employee who is first diagnosed with mesothelioma on or after 25 July 2012 but who is unable to bring an action against an employer or insurer for any reason (in particular because they cannot be traced or no longer exist) will be entitled to recover compensation under the Diffuse Mesothelioma Compensation Scheme. The Scheme is to be funded by levies on insurers.

The story of the influence of employers' liability insurance and of the public policy context in relation to this disease is picked up in Chapter 12.

9.5 Conclusions

We have been absorbed here with some of the most 'conventional' of tort claims, relating to personal injury. The identification of traditional tort claims with 'stranger' cases, and the consignment of the insurance relationship to a separate, private, and supporting role, is more than a little misleading. These paradigm cases of tort liability interact closely with contractual arrangements. In both cases, underlying contractual relationships—both the insurance relationship, and the employment relationship—have themselves been reconceived. Road traffic represents the peak of both compulsion and distribution of risks according to the tort measure of damage (so far as that measure is not itself translated into a function of litigation risk), despite the misleading presence of the fault principle as the gatekeeper to distribution. Compulsion is in addition supported and accompanied by a range of other steps, many of which operate beyond the compulsory insurance domain though initially devised to support its purpose.

Despite the relative weaknesses of the employers' liability insurance regime, this context too reminds us that compulsion is not the sole indicator of public policy in operation, and powerfully illustrates that distributive intentions do not necessarily mean state distribution. Rather, a choice between private and public mechanisms has operated for around 150 years in achieving the distribution, to some level, of the risk of accidental injury in the workplace. Oddly perhaps, the relatively half-hearted nature of compulsory insurance in the employment context may have its explanation in the very imbalance between employer and employee (the 'typical' state of affairs according to Stapleton)[288] which also explains the growth of new, stricter duties in the last half-century, up until the changes of 2013. These duties have been aimed primarily at enhancing safety and placing responsibility for risks with employers. In other words, stricter duties are here more fully illustrative of *primary* responsibility (to keep safe) than are negligence duties.[289] Strict duties do not necessarily imply that distribution has taken priority over responsibility, even where civil liability attaches to harm done through their breach. This is not however a reverse of the 'halting paradigm

[288] n 1. [289] That there is no necessary correlation is illustrated by the table in 9.2.2.

shift from free labor to risk and insurance'.[290] Rather it shows a distinct emphasis on progressive reductions of risk, in which the negligence standard has not been demanding enough, and which has redefined the nature of obligations related to employment and to some extent beyond. It has marked a supplementing of the notion of responsibility in relation to risk, which has also been noted by scholars of insurance.[291]

[290] JF Witt, n 177, 211, referring to the US.

[291] Chapter 2. This amplifies the significance of recent legislative reform (s 69, Regulatory Reform and Enterprise Act 2013), which seeks to snuff out the involvement of civil liability in this process.

PART 3

APPLICATIONS

10

Vicarious Liability

10.1 Introduction

The chapters in this final section of the book address a number of discrete topics, applying our earlier analysis to uncover the role played by insurance in important aspects of the law of obligations. The chapters do not purport to provide exhaustive treatments, but aim to further the discussion embarked on in the previous chapters, and to contribute a new perspective to existing debates. Some of the topics covered in these chapters have been widely recognized as important, though the role of insurance has not been fully investigated;[1] others have been relatively neglected in proportion to their significance.[2] The present chapter falls into the first of these categories. It examines the relationship between insurance and vicarious liability, and explains what light may thus be shed on the legal principles in operation.

In this introduction, we set out four aspects of the argument to come. First, we suggest that when the contribution of insurance, and indeed of insurance law, is taken into account, it becomes plain that vicarious liability is, as most scholars have suggested, a form of secondary liability. It attaches to one party (most often an 'employer') in respect of the torts of another (most often an 'employee').[3] We offer reasons for suggesting that this is more accurate than an alternative theory (sometimes called the 'master's tort' theory), holding that vicarious liability is a form of 'primary' liability, where the tort itself is attributed to the vicariously liable party.[4] Critically, the 'primary liability' theory is inclined to squeeze vicarious liability into a bipartite form, in order to protect theoretical models.[5] We have challenged bipartite readings of private law in earlier chapters, calling attention to a larger, multi-party picture in which insurance plays a key role, and which offers a truer representation of the law of obligations in operation. Vicarious liability in its contemporary form is an important illustration of this larger picture.

At this stage, we should add a little more information about the reasons why we perceive vicarious liability to be secondary liability. The treatment of companies is of particular importance. A company, being a legal fiction, has no identity other than in

[1] Chapter 12. [2] Chapters 11 and 13.

[3] For other instances, and for a new flexibility surrounding relationships possessing sufficient similarity to employment for the purposes of vicarious liability, refer to 10.2.

[4] E Weinrib espouses such an approach, *The Idea of Private Law* (Cambridge MA:, Harvard University Press, 1995), 185–7; as does R Stevens, *Torts and Rights* (Oxford: Oxford University Press, 2007), 257–74; R Stevens, 'Vicarious Liability or Vicarious Action?' (2007) 123 LQR 30–34. G Williams adopted a mixed theory, 'Vicarious Liability: Tort of the Master or of the Servant?' (1956) LQR 522, arguing that both theories might be useful in different circumstances.

[5] Weinrib, n 4, 186: '*respondeat superior* construes (indeed, constructs) the doer as a composite: the employer-acting-through-the-employee'. This is required to fit the corrective justice model of tort law. Stevens, *Torts and Rights*, n 4, adopts the primary liability theory because liability for wrongs attaches, in his view, to those breaching rights. Secondary liability would evidently be an exception to this (244).

law and is incapable of acting other than through human agency. One question which arises is whether the relevant conduct can be attributed to the company. This is not the same question as whether the company is vicariously liable. Attribution depends upon the nature of the conduct and the status of the corporate agent, and there is no fixed standard: all depends upon why the question is being asked.[6] The key point is that if there is attribution, the liability imposed upon the company is primary and not secondary, so that the company is a tortfeasor in its own right. An employer who is vicariously liable is not a wrongdoer but nevertheless has to answer for the acts of others, whereas a company facing personal liability is regarded as a wrongdoer in its own right and is answerable for its own attributed misdeeds. This distinction may appear merely technical, but it has important implications for post-liability loss-spreading. There is no objection to a vicariously liable employer seeking recovery under a contract of insurance or in some other way, but there may be public policy reasons justifying refusal to allow a company which faces primary liability from seeking indemnification;[7] some such liabilities may well be outside contractual cover. Finally, there is no doubt that this may affect the way in which tort claims are framed.

This brings us to a second aspect of our argument. While some writers have taken the view that in general it makes little difference whether vicarious liability is to be seen as primary or secondary,[8] we show that the classification does matter, both in practice and as a matter of principle. In fact, we argue that it is when the distinction between primary (or personal) and secondary liability matters most, that the law responds by showing the generally accepted view of vicarious liability (as secondary liability) to be correct. For example, 'attribution' of acts to a company is a far narrower idea than the looser sense of 'group unity' which has often been thought relevant to acceptance of vicarious liability,[9] and which may be seen reflected in the present development of vicarious liability beyond the bounds of employment relationships as they have hitherto been understood (and, indeed, beyond the bounds of employment relationships at all).[10]

The third, and most important aspect of our argument links the secondary nature of vicarious liability to the issues of risk allocation and loss-spreading which have been debated throughout earlier chapters, and thus expands on the reasons why it is significant. Plainly, the current principles of vicarious liability were developed before the rise of liability insurance charted in Chapters 3 and 9. In this chapter, we show that

[6] *Meridian Global Funds Management Asia Ltd v Securities Commission* [1995] 2 AC 500. Also: *Lennard's Carrying Co v Asiatic Petroleum* [1915] AC 705; *Tesco Supermarkets v Nattrass* [1972] AC 153; *El Ajou v Dollar Land Holdings plc* [1994] 2 All ER 685; *Royal Brunei Airlines Sdn Bhd v Tan* [1995] 2 AC 378; *Mahmud v BCCI* [1998] AC 20; *McNicholas Construction Co Ltd v Customs and Excise Commissioners* [2000] STC 553; [2000] All ER (D) 819.

[7] *Moore Stephens v Stone & Rolls Ltd* [2009] UKHL 39; [2009] 3 WLR 455.

[8] For example, P Atiyah, *Vicarious Liability in the Law of Torts* (London: Butterworths, 1967), 7: in the 'vast majority of cases' it makes no difference; where it does matter, courts are likely to be 'influenced by pragmatic considerations' rather than 'doctrinaire legalism'.

[9] Williams, n 4; Atiyah, n 8, 20.

[10] *Various Claimants v Catholic Child Welfare Society and Others* [2012] UKSC 56; [2012] 3 WLR 1319; and before that *JGE v Trustees of the Portsmouth Roman Catholic Diocesan Trust* [2012] EWCA Civ 938; [2012] PIQR P19 (see further 10.2).

these principles were the product of nineteenth-century exercises in risk allocation between parties. They operated as restrictions on potential liability. These exercises however laid down a framework of risk-bearing which soon became the basis for loss-spreading:[11] the impact of vicarious liability was transformed by the considerable changes occurring relatively soon after its core concepts were set out, as the idea of loss-spreading through liability insurance (particularly on the part of employers), workmen's compensation, and national insurance all took hold. This phenomenon is demonstrated in 10.3.

Insurance, however, while a significant means of channelling and distributing risks, is of course not the sole means. A feature of the modern 'enterprise' is that it too 'operates as a mechanism for absorbing, controlling and spreading social risks'; and the boundaries of the enterprise from this point of view are in part defined by notions including the definition of 'employee' or (more inclusively) 'worker'.[12] Employment, the enterprise, and vicarious liability, are all related, and their relationship is strongly associated with the potential for channelling (controlling and spreading) risks.

Finally, a fourth aspect of our argument is that we address the limits of the process of loss-spreading. In particular, we see that in many cases it is the operation of insurance law, together with the division between primary and secondary liability, which determines whether losses are susceptible to being spread. This function of insurance and insurance law, in setting the boundaries of loss-spreading, is premised on ideas of responsibility and fault, though not in the negligence sense. The risk of negligence is a highly distributable one. This important theme is further developed in the following chapter.

10.1.1 Summary

The argument of the chapter is structured as follows: 10.2 briefly outlines the key parameters of vicarious liability and some different views about its nature and rationale, and indicates the place of loss-spreading within this general picture. The following section, 10.3, considers the origins of vicarious liability in its modern form and illustrates that the principles we use today originally effected not an extension, but a restriction, of potential liabilities. We underline that this restriction initially included exercises in (originally contractual) risk allocation. This section also introduces the question of primary and secondary liability in this formative period; and illustrates the rising influence of loss-spreading.

In 10.4 and 10.5, we focus on contemporary issues, and the contribution of insurance law. Beyond the tort cases raising issues of vicarious liability is a further body of law

[11] In *Various Claimants* (n 10), Lord Phillips suggested that the policy basis of vicarious liability is 'to ensure, so far as it is fair, just and reasonable, that liability for tortious wrong is borne by a defendant with the means to compensate the victim. Such defendants can usually be expected to insure against liability, so that this risk is more widely spread' (n 10, [34]). That was evidently not the policy objective of the courts which laid down the working concepts, as we show in 10.3; but with related changes in the role played by the contract of employment these concepts became particularly suited to such loss-spreading purposes.

[12] S Deakin, '"Enterprise-risk": the Juridical Nature of the Firm Revisited' (2003) ILJ 97, 112. The notion of 'workers' rather than 'employees' was used for example in minimum wage legislation in order to avoid limiting its protective effect (109); National Minimum Wage Act 1998, s 54.

determining whether the principal's insurance policy will indeed respond to the liabilities imposed. This body of legal decisions underlines that for some vicariously liable parties, insurance is an available option only where the tort is *not* attributed to the insured party. But equally, insurance contracts may be designed to have the effect of preventing the spreading of certain losses, or of deflecting the burden of spreading losses to another party. Both of these phenomena return us to the idea that the consequences of everyday fault—even, in this instance, some fault which goes beyond negligence[13]—are the basic stuff both of risk allocation, and of loss distribution. However, we also see that legal notions of fault, strategic contracting activity, and the law's response to contractual allocations may operate to limit the spreading of losses. These limits chiefly operate beyond the two-party model, but they affect relevant duties and liabilities, and should be brought within the analytical frame.

10.2 Nature and Boundaries

10.2.1 Essential features

Vicarious liability is a deeply entrenched feature of the law.[14] In fact for the most part it is so familiar that it operates without note.[15] In *Various Claimants*, Lord Phillips drew attention both to the extensive use of vicarious liability principles, and by implication to their generally uncontroversial application: '[a] glance at the table of cases in *Clerk & Lindsell on Torts*, 20th edn (2010), shows that in the majority of modern cases the defendant is not an individual but a corporate entity'.[16] Courts resolving these cases generally have no need to bring into play theories of 'attribution', but the result is straightforward secondary liability in the sense described in 10.1.

The effect of vicarious liability is therefore to attach liability to one party for the torts of another. This is captured in the terminology of *respondeat superior*: the vicariously liable 'superior' answers for the torts of a servant or agent. As we have seen, some scholars argue instead that the tort is treated as that of the superior, though the act is that of the servant or agent, because the law attributes the act to the principal, or treats the principal and agent together as one actor (taking quite literally another dictum, *qui facit per alium facit per se*—who acts through another acts for himself).[17] We have amplified our preference for the first approach, and its significance for our argument, in 10.1.

In its core instance, vicarious liability has traditionally attached to an employer ('master') for the torts of an employee ('servant'), provided these are committed in 'the

[13] Thus, the 'close connection' test is willing to envisage that there are risks of violence, abuse, and fraud connected with at least some types of employment. There is no bright line which defines them as incapable of allocation or distribution.

[14] Similar rules (with variations) apply very widely across common law and civil jurisdictions: for comparison with German and French law: P Giliker, *Vicarious Liability in Tort: A Comparative Perspective* (Cambridge: Cambridge University Press, 2010).

[15] G Schwartz, 'The Hidden and Fundamental Issue of Employer Vicarious Liability' (1995–1996) 69 S Cal Law Rev 1739.

[16] n 10. [17] n 4.

course of employment'.[18] That core instance is however 'on the move'.[19] The category of employees, or of people who are to be treated as employees, has been subject to extension,[20] and considerable stretching,[21] and it has now been recognized that the idea of 'employment' for the purposes of vicarious liability is 'fluid'[22] and will reflect the purposes of vicarious liability itself; indeed, liability for non-employees is now recognized to be possible where the necessary 'incidents of employment' are present, so that it is 'fair and just' to treat the relationship as sufficient to give rise to vicarious liability.[23] Despite these developments, the key distinction with which the law continues to work is between vicarious liability for the torts of an 'employee', and no vicarious liability for the torts of an 'independent contractor', and this distinction provides the backdrop to the law's current development.

The latter distinction was set down before the middle of the nineteenth century,[24] and has been a key element in the subsequent operation of the law.[25] An unsatisfactory feature of this division is that the label 'independent contractor' has, prior to the most recent developments, been used to refer to anyone with whom one contracts for work, who is not an employee. This problematic dichotomy was by no means entirely a creation of the law of tort, although it was adopted in nineteenth-century tort cases in the formative period both of vicarious liability, and of the employment contract.[26] The distinction between those who are employed and those who are not employed is also found in much legislation (including, close to our themes, the statutory requirement for employers to insure). The tensions, also, are by no means restricted to tort.[27]

[18] For history of the 'course of employment' concept in common law and under the Workmen's Compensation Acts, refer to S Deakin, 'Tort Law and Workmen's Compensation Legislation: Complementary or Competing Models?', in TT Arvind and J Steele, *Tort Law and the Legislature: Common Law, Statute, and the Dynamics of Legal Change* (Oxford: Hart Publishing, 2012).

[19] Lord Phillips, n 10, [19].

[20] For example the attachment of liability to chief constables for the torts of police officers under the Police Act 1966.

[21] Problems arise from the general fragmentation in employment and other related changes. For identification of issues around casual work: E McKendrick, 'Vicarious Liability and Independent Contractors—A Re-examination' (1990) 53 MLR 770, cited as significant by Ward LJ in *JGE*, n 10. In relation to volunteers in particular: Phillip Morgan, 'Recasting Vicarious Liability' (2012) CLJ 615.

[22] *JGE*, n 10, Ward LJ at [59], warning against the use of statutory construction of provisions aimed at a different context. This marks the end of any unified concept of employment for all purposes and has been adopted by the Supreme Court in *Various Claimants*, n 10.

[23] *Various Claimants*, n 10, [35] sets out five 'incidents' of employment in this sense. The first of these is that 'the employer is more likely to have the means to compensate the victim and can be expected to have insured against liability'.

[24] *Quarman v Burnett* (1840) 6 M & W 499.

[25] Many English cases have been preoccupied with determination of whether an individual tortfeasor is to be treated as an employee, or an independent contractor, for the purposes of attaching vicarious liability. Key examples over the decades are *Mersey Docks and Harbour Board v Coggins* [1947] AC 1; [1946] 2 All ER 345; *Stevenson, Jordan, and Harrison v Macdonald* [1952] 1 TLR 101; and *Viasystems v Thermal Transfer (Northern) Ltd* [2005] EWCA Civ 1151; [2006] QB 510. The first and last of these are concerned with 'borrowed employees' and therefore with *who is the employer*, rather than with the question of whether the relevant individual is an employed worker.

[26] 10.3.

[27] S Deakin, 'Does the "Personal Employment Contract" Provide a Basis for the Reunification of Employment Law?' (2007) ILJ 68, discussing M Freedland, *The Personal Employment Contract* (New York: Oxford University Press, 2006).

In light of the variety of different relationships which may be involved, the need for a more positive and more flexible way of understanding the problematic dichotomy has been increasingly recognized as desirable both in relation to tort, and more generally. So far as tort is concerned, the Court of Appeal achieved new flexibility in *Viasystems v Thermal Transfer*.[28] Prioritizing function over form made it possible for the Court to recognize an idea of dual employment. A more recent Court of Appeal has described this as a 'William Ellis moment', where 'their Lordships picked up the ball and ran with it thereby creating a whole new ballgame—vicarious liability even if there is strictly no employer/employee relationship'.[29] The Supreme Court in *Various Claimants* took up and clarified the rules of this new game in terms of the purpose of vicarious liability. Consistently with the discussion in this chapter, one route to understanding this new game is to consider 'employees' as those who form part of the risk-bearing enterprise associated with the employer, whereas independent contractors are risk-bearers in their own right.[30] It is quite possible that insuring obligations and expectations may emerge as relevant factors in interpretation of the intended relationship, as the existence of a classic 'contract of employment' becomes increasingly inadequate as a guide. While more traditional approaches have focused on tests such as 'control' and 'integration', the law has now arrived at a position where there is no set list of factors which will determine an employment relationship for the purposes of vicarious liability.

The second limb, the 'course of employment', has been subject to equally significant development in recent years. Before *Lister v Hesley Hall*,[31] English courts focused on whether the servant was conducting the master's business, or carrying out authorized acts, albeit in an unauthorized (or even prohibited) fashion.[32] Since *Lister*, the focus has shifted. Courts have asked whether there is a relevant 'close connection' between the tort and the employment.[33] That test is apt to include more instances of deliberate and self-seeking wrongdoing than earlier formulations.[34] Equally, the idea of a 'close connection' may be seen as resting on a different underlying approach. Whereas the 'employer's business' approach may be thought to be a mixed idea, which could operate either because the employer retains a degree of control at some level, or because the employer is the intended beneficiary (however misguidedly) of the act, the 'close connection' test can be seen as relating more directly to the identification of risks which can fairly be described as incidental to the

[28] [2005] EWCA Civ 1151; [2006] 2 WLR 428.

[29] *JGE*, n 10, Ward LJ at [60].

[30] In *JGE*, for example (n 10), Ward LJ thought that a priest may not entirely fit the existing definition of an employee but was even less like an 'entrepreneur' ([79]). Equally, the vow of poverty was thought in practical terms to be inconsistent with the priest taking out insurance (while the religious organization would carry insurance) [83].

[31] [2001] UKHL 22; [2001] 1 WLR 1311.

[32] Different questions arose in cases of fraud, where *Lloyd v Grace Smith and Co* [1912] AC 716 clearly recognized liability for the agent's purely self-seeking actions, which were entirely against the interests of the principal.

[33] In this respect, English courts expressly took their lead from Canada, citing *Bazley v Curry* (1999) 2 SCR 534.

[34] Thus bringing other self-seeking acts closer to the approach to fraud (n 32).

employment.[35] Whether such risks may be absorbed, or distributed, by the employer, depends on other features of the multi-party picture.

Finally, and very importantly, courts will increasingly consider the issues relevant to the 'close connection' or 'course of employment' criterion to be relevant also to definition of a relationship as one effectively of employment,[36] and courts increasingly feel the need to identify the underlying functions of the concepts involved, in order to determine their boundaries.[37] Both of these developments reveal the extent to which the established concepts have been under pressure. This is not surprising. Surrounding legal changes include the development of loss-spreading as a widespread technique, and alterations in the nature of contracting for work. To this may be added changes in tort law itself which facilitate the division, transfer, and spreading of risks. To suggest that courts have simply been confused into thinking that vicarious liability has some association with the handling of risks misrepresents the extent of legal, not just social, change.

10.2.2 Incidence of vicarious liability

The operation of vicarious liability is not entirely confined to employment cases, even including their extensions. For example, a similar principle also applies to make one partner liable for the torts of another partner. The position is currently enshrined in legislation, though it appears this was intended as codification of the common law position.[38] Given the professional context of most partnerships, the provision tends to have its greatest application in cases of fraud or deceit. In cases of fraud more generally, outside partnership cases, the language employed is that of 'principal' and 'agent'. It seems that only in cases of fraud, or the driving of vehicles, is the language of principal and agent used in this context in English law, and these two cases have little in common. In cases of fraud, liability attaches within the agent's authority: actual, usual, or apparent.[39] It is of very long standing.[40] Liability for fraud illustrates some

[35] Lord Millett, *Lister v Hesley Hall* [2001] UKHL 22; [2001] 1 WLR 1311, n 31, [107]; and *Dubai Aluminium v Salaam* [2003] 2 AC 366. For critique of uses of 'risk' in *Lister* and subsequent cases: P Morgan, 'Distorting Vicarious Liability' (2011) 74 MLR 952. Ernest Weinrib, n 4, 186, on the basis of Canadian case law employing the language of 'close connection', focuses rather on the closeness of the connection 'between the assigned task and the tortious act'—thus continuing to emphasize the involvement of the employer in relation to the act as a means of making 'plausible' the primary liability theory.

[36] It was suggested at first instance in *JGE v English Province of Our Lady of Charity* [2011] EWHC 2871; [2012] 2 WLR 709 that the factors relevant to the course of employment could also be used to redefine what counts as a relevant employment-style relationship. In *Various Claimants*, n 10, both the Court of Appeal and the Supreme Court spoke in terms of a 'synthesis' of the two limbs. Refer also to Phillip Morgan, n 21; Deakin, 'Complementary or Competing?', n 18.

[37] A particularly clear judicial statement is that of Rix LJ in *Viasystems v Thermal Transfer* (n 28): the tests 'have developed in a way which has gradually given precedence to function over form' (at [55]). This was taken up by the Court of Appeal in *JGE*, n 10, and by the Supreme Court in *Various Claimants*, n 10.

[38] Partnership Act 1890 s 10. Atiyah argued that the 'codification' in this provision actually removed a degree of doubt in relation to tort liability (Atiyah, n 8, 116, citing *Ashworth v Stanwix* (1860) 3 E & E 701).

[39] Usual and apparent are collectively 'ostensible'. Usual authority is the authority that an agent of that class would have in the ordinary course of business so that hidden limitations on that authority are to be disregarded. Apparent authority is a type of authority which an agent of that class would not normally have, so what is required is a holding out by the principal: apparent authority is, therefore agency by estoppel. Cases of fraud on the part of agents have turned on ostensible authority: *Lloyd v Grace, Smith and Co*, n 32.

[40] Often cited is *Hern v Nichols* (1708 1 Salk 289).

of our general points in 10.1. Lord Mcnaughten in *Lloyd v Grace, Smith & Co* referred to the early idea that of two innocent parties, the principal who appointed the agent and clothed the agent with authority should bear the loss, rather than an innocent stranger,[41] proceeding to add that principals (in this case solicitors) could insure the 'fidelity' of their employees or could require employees with relevant functions to secure insurance.[42] This is an excellent illustration of the way that loss-spreading rationales may supplement principles based essentially (in this instance) in fairness.[43]

Vicarious liability has operated in a range of ways beyond the established category of employment, in particular in relation to the vicarious liability of unincorporated associations.[44] Beyond this, it has also been argued that it operates in special circumstances to make an employer liable for the torts of an independent contractor. This appears to break through the basic dichotomy between employees and independent contractors, even with its newly recognized flexibility.[45]Although there clearly is some liability where harm results from the acts of independent contractors, such cases can arguably be conceptualized as involving breach of a primary (typically, 'non-delegable') duty attached to the defendant, so that they are not instances of vicarious liability at all.[46] They have, in other words, been differently analysed by the courts, and while Ward LJ in *JGE* hinted that the development of such duties in English law is possible,[47] it is arguable that the new flexibility in vicarious liability itself will make this less likely.

In risk-allocation terms, the law's position is that independent contractors are held responsible for the risks of their own activities (they are independent risk-bearers); but non-delegable duties (whether contractual, statutory, or at common law) may nevertheless place the same risks with other parties, who cannot escape liability by contracting for the duty to be discharged.

[41] This was the subject of a well-known dictum of Holt CJ in *Hern v Nicholls*, n 40, quoted with approval by the House of Lords in *Lloyd v Grace, Smith and Co*, n 32: 'for seeing someone must be a loser by this deceit, it is more reason that he that employs and puts a trust and confidence in the deceiver should be a loser than a stranger'.

[42] n 32, 738: and 10.4.

[43] M Lunney, 'Insurance and the Liability of the Legal Profession: a Case Study' (1995) Leg History 94, finds evidence that the legal profession accepted the decision in *Lloyd* with relative equanimity, and suggests that the requirements of the National Insurance Act 1911 (as well as workmen's compensation legislation) will have made the idea of insuring in respect of employees a familiar one for partnerships. The terminology of agency is also used in respect of road traffic but it is generally agreed this is *sui generis* (*Clerk and Lindsell on Torts* (London: Sweet & Maxwell, 20th edn, 2010), 6–78). As we showed in Chapter 9, this area is in any case suffused by insurance questions.

[44] This is one of the major extensions to the reach of vicarious liability over the last fifty years mentioned by Lord Phillips in *Various Claimants*, n 10 [20], by reference to cases including *Heatons Transport (St Helens) Ltd v Transport and General Workers' Union* [1973] AC 15, and *Dubai Aluminium v Salaam* [2003] 2 AC 366.

[45] Morgan, n 21, suggests the possibility of an additional category between the two.

[46] R Stevens makes the argument that liability for the torts of independent contractors is primary liability: 'Non-delegable duties and vicarious liability', in J Neyers et al., *Emerging Issues in Tort Law* (Oxford: Hart Publishing, 2007). As already explained, we part company with the author's analysis in respect of vicarious liability itself. Analyses which treat liability for independent contractors as part of vicarious liability, justified on the same policy grounds include Atiyah, n 8, and D Brodie, *Enterprise Liability in the Common Law* (Cambridge: Cambridge University Press, 2010). The latter suggests that theories of 'enterprise liability' are capable of justifying extension of liability for independent contractors given current societal approaches to the responsibility of corporations.

[47] n 10, and discussion in 8.5.

10.2.3 Justifications and the role of loss-spreading

Most authors who accept that vicarious liability is secondary liability also embrace the idea that justifications for the doctrine of vicarious liability are varied, overlapping, and largely policy oriented;[48] and this appears also to be the position adopted by the English courts.[49] Paula Giliker, in a recent comparative study of the operation of vicarious liability in a number of jurisdictions, found support in case law for rationales falling into four broad categories. These were: first, fault and 'identification';[50] second, victim compensation and loss distribution, including distribution through insurance; third, deterrence (in this instance, the idea that liability will encourage precautions); and fourth, fair allocation of risk given that enterprises create risks and gain from them.[51] Both aspects of the second are closely linked with insurance. Patrick Atiyah, writing in 1967, also identified 'social insurance' as a relatively modern justification, to be added to earlier rationales.[52]

It has been objected that 'loss-spreading' is an incoherent explanation of vicarious liability because its logical conclusion is social insurance for accidents via the state, negating any role for tort law.[53] We think it important to rebut this suggestion, which in our view generally misstates the part played by loss-spreading in the law of obligations in a number of ways. First, state involvement is a more complex question than this argument suggests, for reasons explained in Chapter 6. Even to the extent that loss-spreading is adopted as a social goal, the state may have significant reasons for leaving some loss-spreading to the market. In particular, loss-spreading is not costless, and priorities in the spreading of losses must be set. Not surprisingly, many aspects of the loss-spreading function, and indeed the determination of loss-spreading priorities beyond a certain range, are left to the private sector.[54] Second, the private interest in loss-spreading is illustrated by the fact that parties have engaged in loss-spreading and insurance for several centuries, often it seems despite the inclinations of the law and of social policy.[55] Private parties devote considerable resources to achieving loss-spreading or resisting its burden, and the law of obligations has necessarily responded to such efforts.[56] Third, and related to this, the loss-spreading effects of the law of obligations are not reducible to a single collective purpose. Rather, they emerge from an amalgamation of multiple layers of risk allocation, and of legal response.

[48] Not surprisingly, primary liability theorists dismiss this as likely to lead to incoherence: R Stevens, *Torts and Rights*, and 'Vicarious Liability or Vicarious Action?', n 4, and G Williams, 'A Servant of Two Masters' n 4, (2006) 122 LQR 201.

[49] *Various Claimants* and *JGE*, n 10.

[50] Giliker dismisses this as a fiction (n 14, 234). See KW Wedderburn, 'Negligence—Standard of Care—Vicarious Liability' (1955) 13 CLJ 151, a note on the decision of the Court of Appeal in *Jones v Staveley Iron and Chemical Co Ltd* [1955] 1 QB 474. Wedderburn objected to the attempt made by Denning LJ in that case to treat the relevant liability as arising from the master's own failure to see that work was properly and carefully done, considering this to be 'further from reality even than the old rules' (153), but added that the 'metaphysical notion' that the servant's acts are those of the master, whether or not it remained convenient, 'surely cannot be used to sweep away in a judicial side-wind the fundamental concept of vicarious liability' (154).

[51] Giliker, n 14, ch 8.

[52] Atiyah, n 8.

[53] Stevens, *Torts and Rights*, n 4, 258.

[54] Analysed in Chapters 6 and 9.

[55] Chapters 2 and 3.

[56] Chapters 5 and 7.

Despite these observations, it is perfectly clear that neither loss-spreading, nor the availability of insurance funds, has been the sole rationale for vicarious liability. It is also clear that loss-spreading rationales were not behind the initial articulation of the core concepts still employed, albeit in adapted form. But it is also true to say that the approach of courts even at that formative stage approached liabilities essentially in terms of risks; and that judicial policy in respect of the likely burden of liability suffused this process.[57] Like the idea of fault, these exercises set boundaries to the broad potential liabilities then emerging. These factors help to frame our subsequent discussion.

10.3 Risk Allocation and Loss-Spreading

10.3.1 Contractual origins

Mid-nineteenth-century expressions of the underlying concepts of vicarious liability were exercises in the allocation of risk, and consciously so. They clearly contained purposive elements, most plainly in the context of employment. They were not (yet) related to liability insurance, as such insurance had not yet emerged outside the maritime context; but common conceptual roots made the interlocking of vicarious liability and liability insurance a natural development. Indeed it was the partial resolution of issues raised by vicarious liability in the Employers' Liability Act 1880 which led directly to the existence of liability insurance business.

In the middle of the nineteenth century, many claims were made against individuals, including individual householders and employers. However, in the same decades that key concepts were laid down, the railways were transforming the country both physically and economically.[58] In the courts, actions against railway companies were taking on particular importance. There are different views over the degree to which this impacted upon the emerging principles of vicarious liability. Robert Kostal suggests that the courts particularly pressed home liabilities against railway companies, much to the resentment of the latter, and that this included recognition of wide vicarious liability.[59] Equally, damages awards in fatal cases reached startling levels.[60] Michael

[57] Illustrated in 10.3.

[58] M Robbins, *The Railway Age* (London: Routledge & Kegan Paul, 1962; Manchester: Manchester University Press, new edn, 1998) refers to the period to 1850 as the 'heroic age' of railway expansion. By the end of 1850, there were 6,000 miles of railway open for public traffic in Great Britain. In 1830 there had been fewer than 100 miles. Between 1846 (also the year of the first Fatal Accidents Act) and 1850 alone, 3,600 miles were laid. The extraordinary expansion is graphically mapped by R Kostal, *Law and English Railway Capitalism 1825–1875* (Oxford: Clarendon Press, 1994), 19, 146. These dates should be compared with those of the key decisions discussed in this section. The restrictive decisions in *Quarman v Burnett*, n 24, and *Reedie v London and North Western Railway; Hobbit v London and North Western Railway* (1849) 4 Ex 244 were handed down in 1840 and 1849 respectively.

[59] Kostal, n 58, chs 7 and 8. Kostal argues that 'Drawing on a diverse array of social, economic, and legal considerations', the courts rigidly separated passenger claims and employee claims. By 1850, 'Railway companies bore an all but unlimited vicarious liability to passengers, and an all but non-existent liability to workers. The choices of Victorian judges had at once saved and cost English railway capitalism enormous amounts of money' (313–14).

[60] Particularly *Pym v Great Northern Railway* (1861) 2 B & S 761 (QB), where a jury award to dependants under the Fatal Accidents Act 1846 was reduced from £13,000 to a still considerable sum of £9,000. As Kostal, n 58, 295, observes, most railway labourers at this time earned less than £52 per year.

Lobban, however, has also identified judicial anxiety over the potential for broad liability, and a sense on the part of the courts that applicable principles had to operate fairly in all cases.[61] The early cases reviewed here certainly do not signify an expansion in existing principles to reach deep pockets, even where the defendant was an enterprise,[62] but a restriction, consistent with Lobban's analysis.[63] What can be agreed is that personal injury actions against large enterprises would almost always involve the railways, since factories tended only to injure their own employees, and here the route to compensation was blocked as soon as it was attempted.[64] Railways injured and killed not only their own employees, but also passengers, passers-by, and other companies' employees.

Further, in the formative period of the vicarious liability concepts still in use today, those concepts operated to delimit the liability both of individuals as employers, and of enterprises as employers. Many of the arguments used today about the justice and fairness (rather than the proposed loss-spreading function) of vicarious liability can be seen in outline in early (pre-1850) case law regarding the liability of individuals performing the role of employers,[65] householders contracting for work,[66] or owners of a carriage hiring a driver.[67] The current principles behind vicarious liability of *employers* stem from cases which dealt sometimes with individuals, sometimes with corporations (especially rail companies) of one sort or another. The most decisive of these cases was *Quarman v Burnett*,[68] a case against householders who owned a carriage and were found not to be liable for accidental damage caused by the neglect of the coachman who had been hired, with horses, to drive the carriage for them.[69] This case, which established the need for a contract of employment rather than a contract

[61] M Lobban, 'The Development of Tort Law', in W Cornish, JS Anderson, R Cocks, M Lobban, P Polden, and K Smith, *The Oxford History of the Laws of England: Vol XII* (Oxford: Oxford University Press, 2010), quoting Pollock CB in *Roe v Birkenhead Lancashire and Cheshire Railway* (1851) 7 Exch 36, 895.

[62] Undoubtedly, more actions were brought in response to the existence of the railway company defendants, but this also reflected the mixed class base of those killed and injured. Kostal, n 58, 321, points out that the middle classes did not 'dig coal or drive the power looms', but that they were exposed to risks by the railways: '[o]nly the railways, the great rolling transportation factories of England, presented an often deadly mixture of industrial production and consumption'.

[63] Lobban, n 61: as he puts it, the courts' attitude 'reveals a narrowing of the scope of vicarious liability' (897).

[64] *Priestley v Fowler* (1837) 3 M & W 2 1030, whose link with vicarious liability is explored in this section.

[65] *Priestley v Fowler*, n 64.

[66] *Bush v Steinman* (1799) 1 B & P 404 (householder liable where contractors working on his property left obstacles on the highway, causing injury). Note that this was overruled fifty years later by *Reedie*, n 58, in favour of a more restrictive rule derived from *Quarman v Burnett*, n 24, and discussed in text at n 68. This was found to apply to fixed as well as to moveable property.

[67] *Laugher v Pointer* [1826], where the judges could not agree; and *Quarman v Burnett*, n 24, where Parke B explained that the court was deciding the point left open by the former case.

[68] n 24.

[69] He had left it unattended while returning his uniform to the defendants' hall. Contrast the position today where owners of motor vehicles are concerned. Today's position depends heavily on the existence of compulsory liability insurance, but looking further back, extensive liability for owners of vehicles where they were driven with authority was of long standing before *Quarman*, n 24. Atiyah, n 8, suggests this was derived from maritime law treating vessels as a conglomerate (125, citing *Moreton v Harden* (1825) and *Stables v Eley* (1825)—the latter being overruled by *Smith v Bailey* [1891] 2 QB 403). In maritime cases, insurance has been a familiar feature for much longer (Chapter 3). On the other hand Pollock ('Review' (1916) 32 LQR 226) relates the position of the domestic coachman to 'a severe but narrow liability for a man's personal depend[a]nts' in contrast to the 'wider but less harsh one' for affairs conducted 'under his

for services (with an independent contractor) in this sort of context, was treated as authoritative by subsequent courts.[70]

The contractual elements of the analysis entered into by the courts—used, as we have said, in order to limit the potential reach of pre-existing principles in new conditions—deserve to be underlined.[71] Development in vicarious liability at this stage was not some sort of 'deep pockets' counter-current to the strongly *laissez faire* character of the common law during this period. The development of the case law of this time suggests that it was the delimitation of vicarious liability, rather than the existence of the core principle, which typically exercised the courts.[72]

Michael Lobban has suggested that the emerging challenge for English tort law in general during this period related to a shift in paradigm from that of the 'Englishman in his home' (a question of the private domain where due care did not enter into the definition of rights and their limits), to that of 'the Englishman in the world' (where strict liabilities would be potentially ruinous given the nature and variety of interaction).[73] Strict liabilities in relation to property on the first paradigm worked both ways. Property rights defined ownership and were protected irrespective of fault; at the same time, there was strict liability for the consequences of what was *done* on the property in a range of instances, no matter who carried out the work, and this would not be thought of as 'secondary' liability. The shift described by Lobban is the background to a more generally developing unease with liability beyond the boundaries of fault—including, of course, vicarious liability—bearing in mind that this was not yet the heyday of loss-spreading. It is true that a range of devices (some contractual) was used to extend the liability of railway companies beyond the limit of the 'employment' criteria which had just been firmly set out—for example through implied terms that carriages would be in fit working order throughout the route (benefiting passengers, but not of course employees), and through the idea of 'non-delegable duties'.[74] However, the general picture shows not a deliberate extension of liability on the part

control', which developed as the nineteenth century progressed. Similar patterns of liability in different eras may express entirely different underlying rationales.

[70] The judges left open the possibility that cases where the defendant was the owner of fixed rather than moveable property may be different (on which basis *Bush v Steinman*, n 66, would continue to be correct), but such cases were brought within the general principle by the decision in *Reedie*, n 58. Even then, it was left open whether nuisances might be treated differently.

[71] Some such interpretation was of course plainly based in judicial policy—including the preference for freedom of contract itself, in some classes of case but not others. Pollock, n 69, 227, entertained the 'amusing speculative question' of what would have happened if vicarious liability had been abolished, concluding that '[d]enial of the "superior's" liability in tort would surely have led to a luxuriant and perplexed growth of contracts implied in law'.

[72] Note the shifts from earlier, more expansive positions in *Reedie*, n 58, and *Quarman*, n 24, as well as the position taken (and later strengthened, as we saw in Chapter 8) in *Priestley v Fowler*, n 64. Since *Reedie* was a case against a railway company, whereas *Bush v Steinman*, n 66, had been a claim against the owner of a house on which contractors were working, the more restricted approach to liability in the later case does not suggest an expansion of liability to make the most of growing corporate resources.

[73] M Lobban, n 61, 889.

[74] Lobban, 'Daniel v Metropolitan Railway Company (1871)', in C Mitchell and P Mitchell (eds), *Landmark Cases in the Law of Tort* (Oxford: Hart Publishing, 2010), 95, discusses *Daniel v Metropolitan Railway* (1871) LR 5 HL 45 (where the railway company was not liable), and other railway cases of the period.

of employers, but a struggle between different perspectives on how far such liability should be *limited* given the problems now troubling the courts.

Returning to *Quarman v Burnett*,[75] the requirement of a contract of employment was authoritatively set out by Parke B, who is thought of as one of the more committed individualists on the bench.[76] This underlines the connection between vicarious liability, and the employment contract, as a device for delimiting the reach of liability of employers. The contractual *allocation* of risks, and the potential for this to affect the unwary stranger,[77] was a key issue in these cases. That remains the case in present-day law. Plainly this is not the same as adopting *loss-spreading* as a direct policy goal for the principles of legal liability. Parke B sat in both *Priestley v Fowler* and the case which secured the extension of its key principle, *Hutchinson v York, Newcastle and Berwick Rly*,[78] both of which declined to spread the risks of employment beyond those arising from the personal fault of the employer, in those instances where the claimant was not a 'stranger', but an employee in the course of employment. Given the centrality of employment to vicarious liability in its core instance, and given the close relationship in both time and authorship between *Priestley* and *Quarman v Burnett*, it is well worth considering the connection between these cases.

As we showed in Chapter 9, the 'doctrine of common employment' derived from the decision in *Priestley v Fowler*[79] held that the employer was not vicariously liable to his employee if he was injured in the course of his employment through a tort not of the master, but of a fellow servant. Superficially, it may appear that *Priestley v Fowler* treated the servant as 'identified with' the master, and indeed with his fellow employees, but this was neither its reasoning nor its effect. Equally, *Priestley* might be thought to indicate doubt on the part of the judges about basic vicarious liability principles, since it prevented the application of those principles in a wide range of cases (injuries to one employee through the fault of another). Again, this appears not to be the case. Rather, the court distinguished the employee (who was injured while riding in his master's cart) from an ordinary passenger, partly on the basis of the greater knowledge the employee could be taken to have had of the relevant danger (on the facts of this case), and partly because of a supposed difference in the nature of his contract. While the employee was thought to be free to negotiate higher wages for higher risks, and to refuse to run risks of which he was aware, Abinger CB commented in argument that by contrast 'The passenger pays his money in his consideration of being carried, and there is an implied contract that he shall be carried safely'.[80] There would, therefore, be liability to the passenger, though at this stage, implied contract provided the simplest route—just as the supposed understanding of the parties to the employment contract

[75] n 24.

[76] P Atiyah, *The Rise and Fall of Freedom of Contract*, (Oxford: Oxford University Press, 1979), 369–70, discusses Parke's role.

[77] Contracting parties (but most particularly employees) were assumed to have a much greater degree of prescience about the risks involved in the contract than would be the case with individuals today.

[78] *Priestley v Fowler*, n 64, *Hutchinson v York, Newcastle and Berwick Rly* (1850) 5 Ex 343. The court here went further than in *Priestley*, evading the need for awareness of the particular risk and asserting that parties would have contracted on the basis that the servant would run the risk of a fellow servant's negligence, *knowing* only that 'between himself and his master, he would run this risk' (351).

[79] n 64, 1030. [80] n 64, 1031.

provided the route to *no* liability on the part of the master. As we have seen, if implied contract was the route to liability to passengers, liability on the part of the employer—who was the relevant contracting party—raised no puzzles. There was no need for a distinct doctrine of vicarious liability at all. The cases which brought about the core approach to vicarious liability of employers seen today were the work of the same court, in the same period.[81] Despite the emphasis on contract in Abinger CB's comments in *Priestley* just quoted, only a year later, the same judges (Abinger CB and Parke B, this time with Bolland B) seem to have had no principled difficulty in *Bridge v Grand Junction Railway Co*[82] with upholding a claim against a railway company on the part of a passenger of a *different* railway company. The claim was based on the claimant's proposition that 'the said company [the defendants], by their said servants, so carelessly, negligently, and improperly behaved and conducted themselves' that their train collided with his, destroying (apparently) the carriage in which he was travelling. The weight of the case is limited however by the fact that it disposed of the defendant's motion on the basis of insufficiency in its pleadings. The case was seen as closely related to *Butterfield v Forrester*,[83] and the insufficiency stemmed from the existence of the doctrine of sole legal cause, which in turn underlay the total defence of contributory negligence before its reform in 1945.[84] In the brief judgments, no adverse comment was passed in relation to this claim against a railway company, based clearly on the negligence of its servants, on the part of a stranger with no contractual link to the defendant (the passenger of another railway), and judgment was entered for the claimant.

The more problematic question, unresolved in the case because of the insufficiency of the pleadings, surrounded the impact on a claimant such as this of negligence on the part of his carrier. But, as we have seen, in the common employment case of *Hutchinson*, a few years later, it was thought uncomplicated to state the position of a stranger without reference to contract: 'It is admitted that if by the unskillfulness of A [an employee] a stranger is injured, the master is responsible.' Indeed the same would be true of a servant *not* acting in the service of his master at the time of the injury, for then he would be 'substantially a stranger, and entitled to all the privileges he would have had, if he had not been a servant'. Degrees of knowledge, and implied contractual terms

[81] The inconsistency of treatment between employees and passengers in a substantive sense gradually became glaringly apparent however: why was one contract said to contain an implied term for safety, while the other did not? The answer may well lie in the association between labour and the poor law, which was in the minds of the judges, and the route based on freedom of contract was a conscious choice to avoid protectionism. The same concerns blatantly did not apply to passengers.

[82] (1838) 3 M & W 245, 1134. The language of pleadings from the period tends to be rather intense. The carriage was 'broken to pieces, and destroyed', and 'thereby three of his the plaintiff's ribs were fractured and broken, and he was otherwise greatly wounded, bruised & injured, &c'. Kostal (n 58) identifies this as the earliest reported case in which a railway company was found liable to the passenger of another railway. Its authority is limited however by the peculiarities of the legal context as explained in the following paragraphs.

[83] (1809) 11 East 60.

[84] The live issue was not vicarious liability at all, but the role of contributory negligence, here on the part of the servants of the railway company of which the plaintiff was a passenger. It did not suffice for the defendant to allege negligence on the part of the other railway company (P's carrier), because this might not prove to be an 'operating cause'. *Bridge* is not representative of modern law.

related to employment, appear to have made the difference—not the attribution of the servant's acts to the master, nor the identification of two servants with one another. To talk in the latter terms would indeed seem inconsistent with the contractual analysis prevailing in respect of employees.

In conclusion, the selection of employment as the relevant link between tortfeasor and vicariously liable party in the mid-nineteenth century was itself a reflection of the courts' focus on contractual issues as a starting point when analysing parties' relationships. This may be understood as a response to the much broadened nature of potentially injurious interaction, and provided the courts with a means of delimiting the liabilities of 'principals'. Passengers might be given the benefit of implied contractual terms, and strangers might be permitted to assume that the acts of a servant were those of a master. But in the core instance of employee claims relating to injuries in the course of employment, it was clear that the law did not identify servants' acts as those of the master. This was a question of what a particular individual could be expected to know, to accept, and to assume.

10.3.2 The growth of loss-spreading

As we have seen, the core concepts of vicarious liability facilitated exercises in risk allocation, which were undoubtedly affected by the courts' sense of the consequences of attaching liability too broadly given the extension of potential claims. A key subsequent factor is the growth in spreading of losses both as a practice, and as a social goal. So too is the rise of the enterprise as the key focus of many social risk-spreading devices, as well as a loss-spreading device in its own right.[85] These developments responded to some of the same pressures that required the courts to set out new principles of vicarious liability. Vicarious liability was, in turn, itself closely implicated in the growth of loss-spreading. We have seen in Chapter 9 that the creation of exceptions to the common employment doctrine in the Employers' Liability Act 1880 led directly to the growth of liability insurance business. The larger exception that followed, workmen's compensation, was implicated in the very growth of corporations and in their new 'social' risk-spreading role. In both instances, chiefly vicarious liability was covered. Beyond the law of accidents, growing economic risks were also dealt with through loss-spreading devices such as insurance.[86]

One of the few authors to have proposed abolition of the doctrine of vicarious liability was Thomas Baty, writing in 1916.[87] A lot can be learned from his arguments. His approach was, to say the least, not representative of its time, but deeply resistant to contemporary developments. That Baty was plainly reacting against the rise of loss-spreading (thus equally plainly demonstrating its existence) is illustrated by his subsequent article, 'The Rights of Ideas—and of Corporations'.[88] In this article, Baty began

[85] On the risk-processing functions of corporations (particularly as employers), refer to S Deakin and F Wilkinson, *The Law of the Labour Market* (Oxford: Oxford University Press, 2005).

[86] *Lloyd v Grace, Smith and Co*, n 32.

[87] T Baty, *Vicarious Liability* (Oxford: Clarendon Press, 1916).

[88] (1919–20) 33 Harv Law Rev 358.

by polemically decrying the rise of the welfare state in its 'social insurance' guise: one of the 'relics of German misty theorizing' which he felt ought to be swept away was 'that huge Brocken-spectre, the State Grandmother—the thin and incoherent dream that Universal Insurance can take the place of Universal Responsibility'.[89] This sufficiently puts into perspective his failure to discuss loss-spreading in relation to vicarious liability, while underlining the importance of its influence over his views, by way of reaction. Pollock, reviewing Baty's critique of vicarious liability, recognized this, and emphasized the significant rise of risk-spreading. Baty, he pointed out, had neglected to explore *Priestley v Fowler*,[90] which he referred to as 'a curious piece of both legal and economic history, and a remarkable illustration of the modes of thought prevalent in the middle period of the nineteenth century'—conveniently ignoring that the doctrine developed from *Priestley v Fowler* was at that stage still part of the common law. Pollock added that this had led Baty not to notice an important factor in the operation of vicarious liability. He associated this factor with workmen's compensation, which had of course largely superseded common law within the remit of *Priestley*, and probably explains Pollock's sense of happy distance from that case:

> otherwise he [Baty] might have been led to notice another thing which he ignores—the factor of insurance in the practical aspect of these questions. It has been remarked by Mr Justice Holmes and others that the aim is not a strict ethical judgment, but such a distribution of loss as will produce a minimum of hardship. The Workmen's Compensation Act had the merit of frankly acknowledging this principle.[91]

While the abolition of workmen's compensation was accompanied by the repeal of the doctrine of common employment, so that *Priestley v Fowler* is no more, we have seen that the core principles of vicarious liability are the work of the same group of judges,[92] during the same era, and dealing with issues which they will have correctly perceived to be related. While lawyers like Pollock treated the first as an outdated curiosity[93] which had been superseded by loss-spreading even by 1916, the second continues to provide

[89] n 88, 358. It is no coincidence that Baty's main objection in this later article was to the treatment of corporations as persons, and indeed he took the opportunity in *Vicarious Liability* (n 87) to link vicarious liability with the rise of limited liability. Both may be seen as routes to loss-spreading; and Baty's objection to both was premised on the need to retain individual responsibility.

[90] n 64.

[91] Pollock, n 69, 227. It may be just possible to dismiss Pollock's view as that of a 'proto-realist', as Stevens, *Torts and Rights*, n 4, 257, has dismissed Harold Laski's arguments of the same year (referring to H Laski, 'The Basis of Vicarious Liability' (1916) 26 Yale LJ 105), but it seems much more plausible that the views of both writers indicate how far loss-spreading had become a familiar aspect of legal and social policy by this time (see also Lunney, n 43).

[92] Though Parke B did not deliver the judgment in *Priestley* (n 64), he was part of the court, and is reported as having commented in argument that 'I apprehend the contract would only be to carry as safely as could be, in the condition in which the passenger knew the vehicle to be'—a reference to the allocation of risk to the servant on the basis of knowledge. It was suggested in *Limpus v London General Omnibus Company* (1862) 158 ER 995 that another judgment presented by Lord Abinger after a trial before Parke B, *Huzzey v Field* (1835) 2 Cr M & R 432, had been written by Parke ('Lord Wensleydale'). The case incorporates an elucidation of 'course of employment'.

[93] It was far more than this to the labour movement, and campaigns for its abolition continued throughout its life. It is not far-fetched to say that the English unions' commitment to the remedies offered by the law of tort owe much to being excluded from the 'usual' remedies for over a century: workmen's compensation never had the full support of the unions: Chapter 9.

the core working concepts of vicarious liability. The allocation of risks was the initial purpose behind the carving out of these concepts, yet any broader allocation has been advanced cautiously. The doctrine of common employment was repealed by statute; but in vicarious liability, common law continues to work with related concepts laid down in precisely the same era.

The introduction of workmen's compensation, among other social risk-spreading devices,[94] undoubtedly enhanced the awareness of loss-spreading as a potential response to accidents (though it did not spread all employment risks, as we have seen). It was also highly significant in requiring the spreading of losses primarily at the level of the enterprise, encouraging further (though often imperfect) risk-spreading through insurance of one sort or another. In the UK, workers' compensation was accompanied, and superseded, by state loss-spreading and has not dominated legal consciousness in relation to liability as it appears to have done in the US. But in the US, factors of this sort inspired a lasting theoretical transformation in respect of the law of torts associated with the rise of 'enterprise liability'.[95] The import of loss-spreading to liability principles therefore strongly reflected social policy goals. But loss-spreading has also long been prevalent in private arrangements. Here too, the practice of loss-spreading was enhanced by the broadening impact of vicarious liability.

On both sides of the Atlantic, a refinement of the point expressed by Pollock is therefore required. This relates to his treatment of insurance as a *practical* aspect of the questions, not (for want of a better word) as a juridical one. This was a comfortable position when loss-spreading was conducted through workmen's compensation, and therefore formally outside the common law.[96] But we have seen that issues of risk have been inherent to the development of common law concepts. It was in respect of workers' claims that the choices made by the common law courts prevented the evolution of a loss-spreading response, for the losses were left by common law to lie with the individual employee. Social policy rapidly took a very different position from that of the common law. When tort claims became accessible to workers, the possibility and indeed suitability of loss-spreading through liability was nevertheless an established aspect of the legal landscape which undoubtedly left its imprint in the law. With the development of many forms of liability insurance, this sort of perspective acquires much broader potential application. However, loss-spreading is not unlimited, and its boundaries are as ever influenced by the response of the law. We review the present role of loss-spreading in the next section, which turns to some features of vicarious liability as it currently operates.

[94] For example, the National Insurance Act 1911.

[95] The story is critically told by G Priest, 'The Invention of Enterprise Liability: A Critical History of the Intellectual Foundations of Modern Tort Law' (1985) 14 J Leg Stud 461. Priest focuses on product liability. Workmen's compensation claims were however acknowledged as having a significant influence on product liability. The link is also acknowledged and critically explored by DG Gifford, 'The Death of Causation: Mass Products Torts' Incomplete Incorporation of Social Welfare Principles' (2006) 41 *Wake Forest Law Review* 943, 948–9.

[96] Chapter 9 examines cross-fertilization.

10.4 Loss-Spreading and Insurance in Vicarious Liability

10.4.1 The basis of insurance cover for vicarious liability

We have emphasized at various points in this book that the spreading of liability risks is achieved largely through contractual structures. Much litigation surrounds the insurance of vicarious liabilities, but little academic attention is given to such litigation, which lies beyond the traditional focus of the law of tort. Here we address the legal questions which surround this side of the operation of vicarious liability. The issues, as will be seen, are clearly recognizable as features of private law.

It is certainly the case both historically and today that, but for vicarious liability, many—and possibly most—tort claims would be brought against persons of straw. The late Tony Weir expressed this in his own inimitable style:

> Now if there is one class of persons who are unlikely to carry insurance, it is the working class, and it is they who are especially likely to be guilty of torts, since liability attaches to people who do things badly and only people who do things at all can do them badly.[97]

A quick glance at the established heads of vicarious liability discussed in 10.2 shows this to be the case. Moreover, much early liability insurance was a response, initially, to vicarious liability.

Not surprisingly, almost all liability policies protect the assured against both personal and vicarious liability. Where insurance is compulsory, coverage of vicarious liability is also compulsory. All of this enhances the risk-spreading potential of vicarious liability. In the employment field, the Employers' Liability (Compulsory Insurance) Act 1969 draws no distinction between personal and vicarious liability and simply requires insurance for both in respect of injury to an employee in the course of the employer's business. The Road Traffic Act 1988 goes even further, and tosses aside the concept of vicarious liability by rendering the assured's insurers liable to a third-party victim for loss caused by the conduct of any person using the vehicle, whether or not they have been authorized to do so by the assured.[98]

As we have indicated already, whether liability is personal or vicarious matters a great deal however, because an insurer's liability to indemnify a policyholder for vicarious secondary liability is potentially more extensive than for personal liability. This is the result of the defence open to insurers of *ex turpi causa*, a principle as deeply rooted in insurance law as vicarious liability is in the law of tort. During the long history of this principle in insurance law, there are further clear instances underlining that the acts of the employee are not attributed to the master, whether or not he is liable to others for the effects of their actions. In particular, Lord Mansfield treated 'barratry'

[97] T Weir, 'Subrogation and Indemnity' (2012) 71 CLJ 1–7, 4 (originally written in 1973 and privately published at that time).

[98] Road Traffic Act 1988, s 151, which covers liability for injury caused by a thief. If the assured has caused or permitted an uninsured person to use the vehicle contrary to s 145, he is personally liable to the victim for breach of statutory duty (*Monk v Warbey* [1935] 1 KB 75) and may also face criminal sanctions.

(fraudulent wrongdoing on the part of a ship's crew) as a wrong *against the owner*, so that it did not enable insurers to deny indemnity under the owner's insurance policy.[99]

An assured who has personally committed an act which has led to the imposition of a criminal or administrative fine upon him has no claim against his or her insurers, and equally there is no claim if the assured's personal conduct, while not criminal, has given rise to loss in circumstances where the provision of indemnity would be offensive to public policy.[100] All of this may set limits to the loss-spreading possibilities of vicarious liability. However, if the act is of an employee or other person for whom the assured faces vicarious liability, the insurers have no such defence. This important principle in insurance contract litigation illustrates clearly that the law does not attribute the employee's act to the employer. What it does is to place the liability with the employer, and the employer must deal with the risk—but is also free to do so. An illustration, though a controversial one, is the law's treatment of punitive damages. A party who is personally liable for punitive damages and who seeks to recover the amount of that liability from an insurer would almost inevitably fail, because the exceptional circumstances which can attract the award of such damages by implication attract an *ex turpi causa* defence. Thus, if the agents of a company act in a fashion which imposes a personal liability for punitive damages on the company, the loss will lie where it falls.[101] However, an employer who faces vicarious liability will also be responsible for any punitive damages.[102] The suggestion that such liability is explicable only because the employee's acts are attributed to the employer is unsound. The result may also be justified by the consideration that the monetary consequences of employees' abuse of power is one of the risks that employers, especially those of public servants who are particularly susceptible to punitive damages awards, may be expected to manage in the same way as other liability risks (for example, by acting to reduce the risk). That is a debatable proposition. However, the insurance position underlines that the employer's responsibility is secondary and not personal. This is clear from *Lancashire County Council v Municipal Mutual Insurance*,[103] in which the insured local authority was held to be able to recover from its insurers exemplary damages awarded against it by reason of its vicarious liability for the deliberate violent conduct of police officers. Had the local authority's liability been based upon an attribution of the conduct itself, plainly the insurers could not have been called upon to respond.

[99] *The Rachette*, 1786: discussed in F Martin, *The History of Lloyd's and of Marine Insurance in Great Britain* (London: Macmillan, 1876), 257–62. This seems to have set English law apart from some other jurisdictions (notably France), although the common law definition of barratry—now enshrined in the Marine Insurance Act 1906, Sch, rule 11—is also now enacted in that form in most common law jurisdictions.

[100] The dual test laid down in *Safeway Stores v Twigger* [2010] EWCA Civ 1472; [2011] 1 Lloyd's Rep 462, discussed in Chapter 11.

[101] See the lengthy discussion by the House of Lords in *Stone & Rolls v Moore Stephens* [2009] UKHL 39; [2009] 3 WLR 455, a tort claim brought by a company against its accountants for failing to pick up the fraudulent conduct of the company's controller. The majority view was that the controller's conduct was imputed to the company so that it was personally and not vicariously responsible, thereby debarring its claim. The minority view was that the company was itself a victim.

[102] *Thompson v Commissioner of Police for the Metropolis* [1998] QB 498; [1997] 3 WLR 403.

[103] [1997] QB 897; [1996] 3 WLR 493.

This is far from an isolated decision. The distinction between primary and vicarious liability permeates the insurance cases, and these demonstrate that there is no question of the tortious acts themselves being 'attributed' to the employer. In *Hawley v Luminar Leisure Ltd*[104] a security operative (bouncer) employed by the assured nightclub dealt violently with a member of the public, and caused him serious injuries. The bouncer was convicted of inflicting grievous bodily harm. The victim brought a civil claim for damages against the nightclub, which in turn claimed indemnity from its liability insurer. On the insurance point, the Court of Appeal held that the assured was entitled to recover under its liability policy, because it had not itself been guilty of any wrongful or deliberate act giving rise to liability. Although cover was limited to 'accidental injury', what constitutes an 'accident' has to be looked at from the point of view of the assured rather than the bouncer himself. Once again, this underlines the treatment of faulty conduct as one of life's risks for all those other than the perpetrator of some types of deliberate harm. The liability was vicarious, and there was no question of the conduct of the bouncer being imputed to the assured. All that was imputed was responsibility for that conduct. It was therefore an essential aspect of the decision that the nightclub and its employee were to be treated as separate. The position would have been otherwise had the nightclub authorized or turned a blind eye to the bouncer's activities. In such a case the nightclub's liability would have been personal and not vicarious and the injuries could not have been regarded as 'accidental' from the nightclub's point of view. Insurance cover would have been excluded. This clearly underlines that not every act of a 'servant' satisfying vicarious liability tests can be attributed to his or her employer. Questions of vicarious liability and attribution of acts to a corporation are distinct issues and the consequences of the distinction are highly significant both for assured parties, and for the victims of torts.

The distinction between primary and secondary liability emerges still more clearly when the position of companies is analysed more closely. Corporations, of course, raise particular issues of personality and action. But in insurance litigation, this has decisively not been thought to mean—as the strong forms of 'attribution' need to suggest—that the torts of any employee in the course of employment are the torts of the company. Rather, the question has been whether the individual guilty of the deliberate misconduct is of a status, or performing a role, within the company which allows his or her conduct to be attributed to the company itself for the purpose of the legal rule under examination. This question has taxed the courts and been closely examined in a way which would hardly be necessary if the acts of all employees could be attributed to the company.

An illustration of the point arising from interpretation of an insurance contract is *KR v Royal & Sun Alliance plc.*[105] The relevant insurance policy contained an exclusion clause covering 'injury or damage which results from a deliberate act or omission of the insured'.[106] Here, the Court of Appeal held that acts of abuse by the controller of a company operating children's care homes were to be attributed to the company

[104] [2006] EWCA Civ 18; [2006] Lloyd's Rep IR 307.
[105] [2006] EWCA Civ 1454; [2007] Lloyd's Rep IR 368.
[106] In 1981, so for part of the period to which liability attached, this was altered by the addition of 'his partners directors or managerial employees'.

itself,[107] so that the insurers could rely upon the exclusion clause so far as his acts of abuse were concerned. Given the wording of the exclusion, this was the result even though the tort liability which had been established was liability in negligence, for systemic failures.[108] However, other acts of abuse were carried out not by the controller, but by lower level employees. Notwithstanding the decision in *KR v Bryn Alyn Community (Holdings) Ltd*[109] that individual acts of abuse had been the result of the systems in place in the homes, these were not the acts of the company, and in these instances, the insurance contracts were bound to respond. This was a claim brought directly against the insurance company under the Third Parties (Rights against Insurers) Act 1930, the company being insolvent, so that the answer to the insurance contract question directly determined whether funds for compensation were available: the claimants, not the insured company, were seeking the benefit of the indemnity, and in this sense risk-spreading was their only hope. This all illustrates that, while it is extremely important to know which tort is being used as the basis of vicarious liability, as this will determine what the claimant needs to prove in order to support the claim, it is also significant to know whether relevant insurance policies are likely to respond. 'Attributing' abuse to a company or other entity, as the master's tort theory requires, is awkward in any event, but it may also end up removing the source of compensation. On the question of principle, the Court of Appeal expressed itself extremely clearly:

> The court is concerned here with attribution, a principle that is quite distinct from the doctrine of vicarious liability. There is a clear distinction between policy rules governing vicarious liability and the rule of attribution whereby as a matter of law an act or intention of an individual is to be treated as the act or intention of a company.[110]

Not only is vicarious liability wider than the rules of attribution; it is also to be defined in opposition to those rules where some insurance policies are concerned. Nor was the Court of Appeal providing a new answer to a new question. The Court analysed a stream of cases beginning with *Lennard's Carrying Co Ltd v Asiatic Petroleum Co Ltd*,[111] relating to the meaning of 'any loss or damage happening without [the ship owner's] actual fault or privity',[112] and quoted the well-known words of Viscount Haldane LC which again make very clear the distinction between vicarious liability (*respondeat superior*), and attribution:

> It must be . . . that the fault or privity is the fault or privity of somebody who is not merely a servant or agent for whom the company is liable on the footing *respondeat*

[107] *KR v Bryn Alyn Community (Holdings) Ltd* [2003] EWCA Civ 783; [2003] QB 1441.

[108] At this time, if the court had found that the company was vicariously liable in trespass, the action would have been time-barred. The House of Lords (*A v Hoare and other appeals* [2008] UKHL 6, [2008] 2 WLR 311) has now removed the distinction between trespass and negligence for the purpose of determining limitation periods, and courts should therefore not need to have recourse to findings of systemic negligence. Generally this should in turn ease the burden of proving the tort from the claimant's point of view, since the actions of one person are easier to evidence than the default of many people, particularly where a criminal prosecution has succeeded.

[109] n 107. [110] *KR v Royal Sun Alliance*, n 105, [51].

[111] [1915] AC 705; [1914–15] All ER 280. [112] Merchant Shipping Act 1894, s 502.

superior, but somebody for whom the company is liable because his action is the very action of the company itself.

There could not be a clearer statement of the difference between liability for the acts of servants or agents on the basis of *respondeat superior*, and liability on the basis that the acts *are* those of the company. This destroys any recourse to 'symmetry' in the law as a basis for a general attribution theory of vicarious liability. There is no room in that theory for a difference between *actual* acts of the company, and acts *attributed to* the company, because acts 'of the company' are in all cases admitted to be fictional. In the case of vicarious liability, it is the liability, not the act, that is attached to the superior.

10.4.2 Insurance responses to vicarious liability: contractual limits of loss-spreading

Ex turpi causa is not the only boundary to loss-spreading. As we have seen in earlier chapters, contracting is a strategic exercise and may succeed in displacing the law's—or other parties'—preferred allocation of risk.[113] Faced with vicarious liability claims, insurers—other than those covering statutory compulsory risks—have developed a number of defensive mechanisms in their policy terms. Although the insurance of an employer for injury to his employees must cover both personal and vicarious liability, a policy taken out by the employer against other liabilities, including injury to non-employees and property damage, can impose limits on liability. Therefore, once again, we can see that insurance is not always available to spread losses.

In this respect, the most important mechanisms are these. First, the use of deductible[114] clauses may serve to protect the insurer against a multiplicity of claims from an assured who has numerous employees or agents, some or all of whom have committed acts which impose vicarious liability. The clause will typically require each default by an individual within the organization to be treated as a separate claim under the policy, so that if the amount of the claim does not exceed the deductible figure the insurer will not be liable. Some policies do allow all 'related' claims to be aggregated into a single claim, in which case only one deductible is borne for the aggregate of all such related claims; while others define the deductible in terms of an 'originating cause' so that all claims of a similar type and with a common origin (for example, failure to train or to maintain appropriate controls) can be treated as one cause. Second, the policy may require the assured to monitor the conduct of its workforce, so that vicarious liability imposed upon the assured by the misdeeds of an employee will not be covered by the policy if the employee has not been adequately supervised.[115] Third, some policies expressly exclude the insurers' liability for criminal or fraudulent acts irrespective of the identity of the perpetrator.[116] Finally, professional indemnity and directors' and officers' liability covers are 'composite' in nature, so that every person identified as an assured

[113] In particular, Chapters 5 and 7.
[114] Chapter 3 discusses aggregation.
[115] *Summers v Congreve Horner, The Times*, 24 August 1992.
[116] *Warrender v Swain* [1960] 2 Lloyd's Rep 111.

has separate cover. Although the acts of one assured may well give rise to vicarious liability[117] those acts will not be imputed to an innocent co-assured who has not authorized or condoned the wrongdoing. Again we should note that attribution of *acts* between partners (rather than attribution of liability) would deprive them of this opportunity. The result is that the innocent co-insured is not precluded from recovering an indemnity. However, the policy itself may provide that the insurer does not face liability if the conduct of the tortfeasor has been condoned by the assured. In many situations that adds nothing to the common law, which treats a condoning employer, principal, or partner as himself party to the wrongdoing, but *Goldsmith Williams v Travelers Insurance Co Ltd*[118] went further than this general principle, holding that where one of the two partners in a firm of solicitors was aware that her partner had been guilty of fraud on a specific occasion, but had taken no steps to do anything about it, she had condoned later frauds even though she was unaware of them and as a result lost the benefit of her professional indemnity policy.

It is suggested that more attention should be paid to the important principles reviewed in this section, which indicate that risk allocation is not always a precursor to risk-spreading. The limits of risk-spreading are to some degree secured through the operation of a notion of fault, but fault is distinctly not synonymous with negligence.[119] Despite the reputation of insurance concerns as policy driven and 'unjuridical', this operates in the law of insurance contracts, not of tort. The implication is that there are degrees of fault and of acceptable risk which are not captured, as might be assumed, through the idea of the standard of care. On the other hand, fault does not occupy this territory alone. For example, insurers may also succeed in confining the spreading of liability risks through contractual terms.[120]

10.5 Vicarious Liability and Contractual Structure

10.5.1 Ousting vicarious liability by contractual arrangements

The previous section has illustrated that issues of corporate personality, attribution, contribution, and indemnity are all core features of risk allocation and loss-spreading as it is achieved—imperfectly—through vicarious liability and insurance. There is nothing new in this, but these features of the legal system have changed radically since the nineteenth century. Here we consider the allocation of risks within complex contractual arrangements. Oddly, the available literature on such structures, though identifying contract ('the market'), and organization ('the firm') as rival risk-allocation frameworks, says little about insurance, even though, as we have argued in Chapter 7, insurance is fundamental to commercial risk-allocation practices.

[117] Or, in partnership cases, joint and several liability.

[118] [2010] EWHC 26 (QB); [2010] Lloyd's Rep IR 309, applying *Zurich Professional Ltd v Karim* [2006] EWHC 3355 (QB); [2006] All ER (D) 238 (Dec).

[119] For extended discussion, and the relationship with principles of *ex turpi causa* in the law of obligations, see Chapter 11.

[120] See also our review of subrogation and the influence of the parties' allocation of risk, in Chapters 5 and 7.

Construction projects are the most obvious example. The operator of the site will hire a number of contractors and, indirectly, subcontractors, to perform different functions on the site, and every organization involved will have employees working for them. There is a constant risk that one employee will either inflict injury on, or suffer injury at the hands of, another. The victim may have a choice of tort claims, including against the operator for failing to maintain a safe system of work, and against the contractor who is the employer of the actual tortfeasor (which may of course be the victim's own employer). The victim cannot be forced to sue one potential defendant rather than another, and indeed he or she will probably join each of them to the proceedings. This will, if left unregulated, trigger disputes between the public liability and employers' liability insurers of the various parties. It is therefore standard practice for the joint venturers to agree between themselves, by way of indemnities and hold harmless clauses, which of them is ultimately liable to pay any damages awarded to the victim, and to adjust insurance accordingly. We have seen in Chapter 7 that the usual arrangement is that if an employee of the contractor is injured and brings proceedings against the operator, the contractor agrees to provide an indemnity to the operator[121] on the basis that each organization on site is to be responsible for injury to its own employees. That means that the operator's vicarious liability is displaced in practice, and that the contractor's own liability is extended to cover injury claims which are not its responsibility in law.

10.5.2 The incidence of employment

A question central to vicarious liability has been identification of the tortfeasor's employer. The point arises in acute form where employer A either loans its employee to employer B, or at least A's employee performs tasks in the course of a joint venture between A and B. Prior to the most recent developments explored in 9.2, the English courts had handed down a series of fact-based decisions, based on the 'control' test, to respond to this problem. Whichever approach is taken, although identifying the employer will fix the incidence of vicarious liability, it will not necessarily determine who bears ultimate responsibility for paying any claims: that depends upon the contractual and insurance arrangements between A and B, a point which is rarely apparent from the decisions themselves. This may be illustrated by the *locus classicus*, *Mersey Docks & Harbours Board v Coggins & Griffiths*,[122] which on further reflection is

[121] Other than in cases of deliberate conduct or gross negligence on the part of the operator or its employees. Cf *E E Caledonia Ltd v Orbit Valve Co plc* [1994] 1 WLR 1515. As noted above, such clauses do not constitute exclusion clauses for the purposes of the Unfair Contract Terms Act 1977: *Thompson v Lohan (Plant Hire) Ltd* [1987] 1 WLR 649. There is no necessary basis in law for this limitation on the indemnity because, as we have seen, if A's liability is merely vicarious then the nature of the wrongdoing which gives rise to that vicarious liability does not preclude an indemnity. Nevertheless, the restriction is understandable even though in complex cases costly litigation is all but inevitable, as evidenced by *Caledonia North Sea v British Telecommunications plc* [2002] UKHL 4; [2002] 1 Lloyd's Rep 553, where the question of whether the operator's negligence was gross so as to negative the indemnity occupied the Court of Session for many months.

[122] [1947] AC 1.

a most curious case.[123] The Board hired a crane, along with its operator, Mr Newall, to stevedores on terms set out in local regulations, the effect of reg 6 being that Mr Newall became the deemed servant of the stevedores. Mr Newall, while operating the crane, ran down Mr McFarlane, a checker employed by a third party, and he obtained a judgment against the Board. The application before the House of Lords was for an order setting aside the judgment and its replacement with a judgment against the stevedores, an odd means of proceeding given that Mr McFarlane was not a party to the appeal, and it was allowed to go ahead only with his consent.[124] Their Lordships held that Mr Newall remained the employee of the Board, in that control as to how the crane was to be operated remained with them, and that control as to the use to which the crane was to be put did not suffice to transfer employment. In so deciding the House of Lords disregarded the deeming terms of reg 6, which could not affect Mr McFarlane's right to recover from the Board if the Board was the true employer. It would be logical to assume from this reasoning that the Board bore the loss. But that might not have been the case. The following passage appears in Lord Porter's judgment:

> Even if there were an agreement between the appellant board and the respondent company that in the event of the appellant board being held liable for negligent driving of the crane while it is under hire to the latter, the latter will indemnify the appellant board, this would not in the least affect the right of the plaintiff to recover damages from the appellant board as long as the appellant board is properly to be regarded as the crane driver's employer.[125]

Where did Lord Porter get the idea that the stevedores might have been contractually liable to indemnify the Board in the event that the Board faced liability? The answer is to be found in reg 6 itself which, in addition to stating that any loaned employee became the employee of the stevedores, also provided that the stevedores 'must also take all risks in connection with the matter'. The meaning of this provision was not at stake, as the only issue was whether Mr McFarlane was entitled to judgment against the Board. There is no record of subsequent proceedings between the Board and the stevedores, but it is unlikely that, in the light of the indemnity clause, the judgment resolved that separate dispute.[126] The point, therefore, is that where an employee is loaned there will almost certainly be supplementary risk-allocation provisions, although they will not be relevant to the claim

[123] The narrow approach in *Mersey Docks* itself has now been superseded, as was made clear in *Various Claimants*, n 10 and in the following paragraphs; our discussion here relates to the contractual background to vicarious liability claims of this type.

[124] It did not matter to him whether the Board or the stevedores were the employers of Mr Newall because Mr McFarlane was not himself employed by either of them. Had Mr McFarlane himself been employed by the stevedores, a finding that Mr Newall's employment had been transferred to them would have entitled the stevedores to invoke the doctrine of common employment so as to bar any action against them by Mr McFarlane.

[125] n 122, 10.

[126] In the Court of Appeal, (1945) 78 Ll LR 383, 387 Morton LJ noted that 'the Regulation may be intended to place the liability for any tort of the crane driver, as between these parties, upon [the stevedore].' If that was right, the stevedores were either vicariously liable for Mr Newall or, if not, liable under reg 6 to indemnify the Board for the claim against it. That would matter only if, for example, the stevedores were insured against public liability but not against any liability under contractual indemnities. Indeed, but for that possibility the purpose of the proceedings is far from obvious.

made by the victim of the transferred employee's negligence. Subsequent disputes between the parties themselves will turn upon the proper construction of those provisions, as may be seen by the complex litigation following the Buncefield explosion, *Shell UK Ltd v Total UK Ltd*,[127] where the key points were whether the network of overlapping joint venture and operating agreements applicable to the site effected a valid transfer of employment (and thus vicarious liability) from the site operator to a contractor and, if not, whether the contractor was nevertheless required to hold the operator harmless. Both questions were answered in the negative.

The pivotal case of *Viasystems v Thermal Transfer Ltd*[128] again shows that what is nominally before the court is not necessarily the issue at stake. As we have seen in 10.2.1, subsequent courts have recognized as game-changing the broader significance of the case in relation to the priority of function over form.[129] Our point here is that it is characteristic of the new game that it exposes more clearly the risk-allocation function of principles of vicarious liability, and enhances the opportunities for liable parties to engage in partial risk-shifting after the event. Dual employment, and thus shared vicarious liability, is now a possibility. In *Viasystems* itself, V engaged TT to install air conditioning, and the ducting work was subcontracted to SPD. SPD obtained metalworkers from CAT on a labour-only basis. Due to the negligence of one of CAT's workers, Mr Strang, V's premises were flooded. The claim before the Court of Appeal was by V against each of TT, SPD, and CAT. TT faced contractual liability to V, but V nevertheless pressed claims against each of SPD and CAT. The question ultimately became which of SPD and CAT was vicariously liable for the negligence of Mr Strang. The trial judge imposed liability on CAT alone. The Court of Appeal adopted an approach at that time novel to English tort law, that of joint control,[130] and held that SPD and CAT were, by virtue of their respective vicarious liability, jointly and severally liable to V and that contribution between them should be assessed at 50 per cent. There is nothing in the judgments referring to any risk-allocation or insurance arrangements between the various parties, but it is notable that the only parties to the hearing were SPD and CAT so it may be surmised that V received its contractual indemnity from TT, that TT was itself indemnified by CAT, and that the proceedings were all about CAT seeking indemnification from SPD, a venture in which it was only half-successful. Doubtless, insurers were involved at every step. As we have seen, the major doctrinal issue raised by this ruling was the possibility of dual employment, and its assessment for the specific purpose of determining vicarious liability in relation to particular risks.[131] But leaving that aside, the eventual outcome was almost certainly

[127] [2010] EWCA Civ 180; [2010] 3 WLR 1192.

[128] [2005] EWCA Civ 1151; [2006] 2 WLR 428. Note also *Hawley v Luminar Leisure Ltd* [2006] EWCA Civ 18; [2006] Lloyd's Rep IR 307.

[129] Ward LJ, n10.

[130] A ruling which has generated a good deal of debate, eg D Brodie, 'The Enterprise and the Borrowed Worker' (2006) ILJ 87–92 (arguing that the decision was unduly narrowly framed and conservative); R Stevens, 'A Servant of Two Masters', n 48 (suggesting the decision was logical given current understandings of vicarious liability). Though the decision was novel in relation to tort principles, it has been pointed out that adoption of dual employment to resolve puzzles of 'triangular' or multilateral situations is a familiar feature of statutory solutions: Deakin, n 27, 81–2.

[131] The effect of the 'synthesis' of the first and second limbs of the test for vicarious liability (n 36) is that the question 'is X vicariously liable for Y's torts?' no longer yields a single answer: answers may differ in relation to distinct risks.

one that the parties had not contemplated when the agreements were entered into, and it is uncertain how the judgment fitted in with what had actually been agreed and the liabilities insured against. Nevertheless, the point for our purposes is that ultimate responsibility for vicarious liability claims was one of the matters which formed a part of the overall contractual arrangements and the loss was plainly not destined to lie where the common law dictated it should fall.

The influence of legal principles is not, however, easily confinable. The insight in *Viasystems* that employment is not an all-purpose state but dependent on the context in which its relevance falls to be assessed has found equal application outside the domain of commercial contracting. A similar issue arose in Chapter 8, where we explored the possible impact of risk-allocation issues beyond the reach of recognized 'contractual matrix' cases, and pointed to the application of reasoning based on risk allocation far beyond the commercial context. The differences between *Various Claimants* and *Viasystems* are evident. *Viasystems* was a claim in negligence litigated between commercial parties linked by a contractual chain and in respect of damage to commercial property. *Various Claimants* was a claim brought by victims of deliberate sexual abuse who were not linked by a contractual relationship with the potentially liable parties but, rather, were vulnerable children in care at the time of the tortious acts. Nevertheless, there are some structural similarities between the former case, and the case before the Supreme Court in *Various Claimants*. In particular, it is notable that the tort claimants themselves played no part in the appeal to the Supreme Court. Though the ruling may no doubt assist future claimants, these claimants were content with the judgment of liability secured in the Court of Appeal against the appellants, who were in a relationship of formal employment with the tortfeasors. The appeal was aimed at securing contribution from the respondents. It is most likely that one or both of the parties to the appeal was insured, and indeed an expectation that respondents in these circumstances would be likely to carry such insurance is implicit in the discussion of the Supreme Court. Clearly, it is not inevitable that liability insurance policies will be drafted so as to cover such liabilities; but we have emphasized elsewhere that when courts take note of insurance, they do not necessarily assume that cover will be available. However, we have highlighted in this chapter that where liability is purely vicarious and intentional wrongdoing is not that of the assured, insurance policies are at least capable of responding.

Seen in this light, the development in *Various Claimants* illustrates many features of the law to which we have already drawn attention. In particular, it illustrates that multi-party arrangements and relationships are frequently involved in tort, as well as contract claims; that parties will seek to shift and to spread the effects of tort liabilities as well as other losses; and that the courts are well aware that this is the context of their decisions. These features may exist, and be recognized by the courts, well beyond the context of commercial contracting. In conclusion, the widespread presence of vicarious liability, operating largely unnoticed in the majority of cases, underlines the ubiquitous influence of loss-spreading, of loss-shifting, and, inevitably, of insurance.

10.6 Insurance and Vicarious Liability: Conclusions

Through attention to insurance claims, we can turn the 'symmetry' or coherence argument for the 'master's tort' theory on its head. The servant's tort theory, through which liability rather than act is attributed to the employer, is not just the conventional understanding of tort lawyers, but also the basis of a considerable number of legal principles outside the narrower concerns of whether A is liable in tort towards B. Many of these are illustrated by the features of insurance litigation explored above. In this instance, insurance law helps to illustrate that vicarious liability in its very nature involves departure from a two-party model of disputes. This is a widespread phenomenon and no mere detail in the law.

Glanville Williams, who has been described as a supporter of the 'master's tort' theory,[132] recognized certain problems of the sort canvassed here, though in relation to criminal responsibility rather than the boundaries of loss-spreading. In fact, the difficulty forced him to restate the master's tort theory so that it was far more complex, and admittedly much less compelling, than it initially appears: the servant's act, he suggested, 'is the act of the master, but only for some purposes, and not when the law distinguishes between a personal and a vicarious act'.[133] In other words, we suggest, not 'when it most matters'.[134] Because Williams did not relate this to loss-spreading, he did not note quite how wide the 'exception' was. For the same reasons, principles of attribution serving an entirely different purpose cannot be used as the *basis* for vicarious liability.

The more general message of this chapter, however, is about the implications of this widespread secondary liability, and is in tune with the dissenting remarks of Lord Radcliffe in *Lister v Romford Ice and Cold Storage*,[135] a case discussed in Chapter 5. Lord Radcliffe suggested that agreements between employers and employees had to be looked at again 'in a society which has been almost revolutionised by the growth of all kinds of insurance'. His point is too easily understood as a simplistic suggestion that where there is insurance, there should be liability. The loss-spreading effects of insurance are not straightforward, and nor are the combined effects of legal and contractual mechanisms for allocating liability risks necessarily admirable in all their details. The point is, however, that this is the context in which principles of the law of obligations are to be interpreted. The fact that this is a multi-party context spills over into interpretation of the parties' rights and obligations. Loss distribution builds upon the allocation of risks performed by parties and by the law. Not only do parties adopt risk-allocation and loss-spreading goals in their voluntary arrangements, but the capacity to spread losses will certainly influence the terms of their transactions. The law necessarily responds. We have seen numerous instances of this in the course of this book; vicarious liability offers a further illustration.

132 Stevens, 'Vicarious Liability or Vicarious Action?', n 4.

133 n 4, 547.

134 Note also Wedderburn, n 50, 154, referring to employers' personal and vicarious liabilities: 'in situations where the boundaries of vicarious and personal liability have been clearly marked, it is difficult to find profit in their confusion'.

135 [1957] AC 555.

11

Insurance and Illegal Conduct

11.1 Introduction

In Chapter 2, we saw that it has proved tempting to see the relationship between the law of obligations and insurance in terms of a tension, or even a conflict; and that this is often related to the 'actuarial' model of insurance outlined there. We have tested this assumption throughout, focusing on issues of risk transfer, risk allocation, and loss distribution, within the law of obligations itself. Review of the principles relating to illegal conduct, the subject of the present chapter, offers an opportunity to explore a very different facet of the relationship between insurance and the law of obligations. Where, in the broader picture of the law of obligations (expanded to include the operation of insurance), will principles of personal responsibility and of fault be found to operate? In our view, the broadened picture illustrates once again the mutual influence of liability, and of insurance. But it also shows the persistent influence of moral judgments in relation to insurance rather than liability,[1] while illustrating the complex mix of goals and influences which play upon the liabilities themselves.

An important preliminary issue is identification of the various categories of conduct in play. Throughout this chapter, we use the ostensibly simple term 'illegality' interchangeably with the potentially obscure expression, '*ex turpi causa non oritur actio*'. We do this partly because the relationship between civil and criminal law is a significant theme of any such discussion. But the expression is not perfect. In the early stages of an extended review of the area, the Law Commission observed that in no modern case has moral turpitude in the absence of illegality been sufficient basis for the policy bar to operate.[2] More recent cases suggest, at the very least, softer boundaries to the relevant 'turpitude' which might suffice. Even so, courts in these instances have continued to refer to 'illegality' as providing the core of their reasoning, even if by close analogy.[3] Three clarifications are however required.

First, and contrary perhaps to appearances, 'illegality' itself is far from being a straightforward category, and we would argue that the expression should be seen as imprecise. This in itself is one reason, among others, why it may prove difficult to

[1] We noted the long history of engagement between insurance and moral questions in Chapter 2. Also pertinent is Mary Coate McNeely's article, 'Illegality as a Factor in Insurance' (1941) *Columbia Law Review* 26, which begins: 'Throughout its history the insurance device has been alternately hailed as a promoter of communal welfare and damned as a generator of evil'.

[2] *The Illegality Defence in Tort* (Consultation Paper No 160, 2001) (LCCP 160), para 1.16.

[3] In particular, courts have debated whether breaches of statutory prohibition leading to a penalty akin to a fine have a sufficient element of illegality (with the answer yes: *Safeway Stores v Twigger* [2010] EWCA Civ 1472; [2011] 1 Lloyd's Rep 462). The point was not argued before the Court of Appeal, but noted by Longmore LJ at 15, who referred to the acts as 'quasi-criminal'; similarly in the same case, Pill LJ referred to a 'quasi-conviction' on the part of the claimants; and both used the language of 'illegality'. Another question raised is whether evidence of a 'civil law bribe' was sufficient to trigger the bar (again, with the answer yes: *Nayyar v Denton Wilde Sapte* [2009] EWHC 3218 (QB); [2009] All ER (D) 178 (Dec)).

sustain an argument that special weight is always to be attached to a category of conduct which is criminal in nature.[4] It is best to acknowledge that there is no single such category. This, however, will have implications for what is now the most clearly articulated subset of cases in which illegality will bar a claim in tort, namely those where the claimant seeks indemnity for the burden of a legal penalty.[5] If illegality is a disparate, or even fuzzy category, then it is harder to explain why tort should be made consistent with it, irrespective of the substantive fairness of doing so.

Second, in the context of insurance contracts in particular, illegal conduct overlaps with a separate question about the insurability of risks which are brought about intentionally by the assured. The starting position is that insurance policies by their very nature respond only to events which are, as far as the assured is concerned, fortuitous or accidental.[6] Many insurance policies expressly exclude loss caused intentionally or as the result of wilful misconduct, but such clauses add little, other than clarity, to the common law. By contrast, mere carelessness, or even the deliberate creation by the assured of a situation which makes a loss more likely, does not preclude recovery,[7] and 'reasonable care' clauses are construed not at their face value, but as excluding only reckless conduct.[8] While many insurance policies will restrict cover to damage that is 'accidentally' caused by the assured, the policy of the law adds an illegality bar, and that is our core focus here.

Third, categories of 'intention'—such as those employed by the law of tort—do not map neatly onto the criminal law. It is true, and significant, that torts which require an element of intention are more likely to amount also to criminal wrongdoing, in contrast to wholly non-deliberate acts of negligence. However, it is important to be clear that not all breaches of negligence duties are non-deliberate; that torts categorized as 'intentional' are nevertheless often very strict in some of their elements;[9] and (most fundamentally perhaps) that criminal liability itself by no means always requires intention. Intention and illegality are overlapping, but not identical, categories. Insurance

[4] Other reasons relate to the wide variety of forms of criminal liability, including strict liabilities aimed at protection of a class to which the claimant belongs (eg health and safety legislation), or in respect of which the defendant was under an obligation to advise the claimant (eg duties to insure).

[5] The House of Lords accepted this rationale in *Gray v Thames Trains* [2009] UKHL 33; [2009] 1 AC 1339. See our discussion in 11.3.

[6] Loss from the intended consequences of a deliberate act is for this reason uninsurable, although the market has developed an exception as regards suicide, reversing the ruling in *Beresford v Royal Exchange Assurance Co* [1938] AC 586.

[7] *Clothing Management Technology Ltd v Beazley Solutions Ltd* [2012] EWHC 727 (QB); [2012] 1 Lloyd's Rep 571.

[8] *Sofi v Prudential Assurance* [1993] 2 Lloyd's Rep 559.

[9] Note, for example, that libel is generally approached as an 'intentional' tort in the US, because it requires intention to publish; but a strict liability tort in English law, since it requires no intention to defame. Similar issues may be said to arise in relation to trespass torts: they could easily be seen either as strict, or as dependent on intent (volition). Deceit, by contrast, requires a much stronger element of intention in relation both to wrongdoing and to harm caused. See generally, in the US context, C French, 'Debunking the Myth that Insurance Coverage is Not Available or Allowed for Intentional Torts or Damage' (2012) 8 Hastings Bus Law J 65. Many of the 'intentional' torts listed by French as susceptible of insurance cover would not be seen as intentional in the UK. But not all: malicious prosecution clearly has a strong mental element requirement, even if not always on all fours with 'intention'. The general point is that classification of torts is tricky and is not an adequate guide to intention or not.

cover may be lost either because the harm was intended (a prerequisite of some 'intentional' torts, but not others), or because it is caught by the policy bar.

Following this introduction, 11.2 briefly outlines the nature of the law's response to illegal conduct in relation to liability, with a particular focus on the law of tort. In the sections that follow, these principles remain in play as we introduce the role of illegality in relation to insurance. 11.3 reviews the operation of illegality in relation to claims against assured parties. 11.4 explores the operation of illegality in relation to claims against insurers whether on the part of assured parties or on the part of those who have suffered harm through the wrongdoing of an assured. In each of these sections, we explore how the separation of liability and insurance is tested (or their connection defined) by such cases. Where it operates, the impact of the illegality bar is to set limits to the distribution of risks and losses. There is some evidence that in the operation of these limits, courts interpret the principles relating to insurance of liabilities as more susceptible to notions of culpability than the principles of liability themselves. The question inevitably arises of whether this is a satisfactory state of affairs; and that in turn raises the relative nature of the two apparently distinct phenomena—insurance and the law of obligations—with which we started.

11.2 Principles Governing Illegality

The common law rules on public policy, often expressed in the maxim *ex turpi causa non oritur actio*, operate in a range of circumstances to preclude an action by a claimant guilty of some form of 'illegality' sufficiently linked to the claim. Although the rules are often deployed as a pleaded defence, in principle the court may take cognizance of the claimant's illegal actions and bar the claim of its own volition;[10] and it is long established that the aim of the bar is not to protect the defendant, who may benefit while remaining equally undeserving.[11] The policy bar has given rise to much judicial consideration and academic debate. Between 1999 and 2010, the Law Commission undertook an extended review of the operation of public policy in tort and contract claims, as well as unjust enrichment and proprietary claims. Its initial view was that reform was needed to bring some measure of order into the chaos generated by an absence of clear objectives and a series of apparently irreconcilable decisions,[12] which in the Law Commission's view was exacerbated by the adoption of 'rigid rules' with potentially arbitrary effects. Primary among these was the rule, originating in the law of trusts but thought at the time of the review to have more

[10] This allows the court to go behind the claimant's pleaded case and to examine its reality, and reflects the 'public policy' nature of the rule: it is not primarily designed to operate in the interests of defendants. The same principle applies to claims by policyholders against their insurers: 11.4.

[11] There is frequent reference to the comments of Lord Mansfield in *Holman v Johnson* (1775) 1 Cowp 341, 343; 98 ER 1120, 1121: 'The objection, that a contract is immoral or illegal as between plaintiff and defendant, sounds at all times very ill in the mouth of the defendant. It is not for his sake, however, that the objection is ever allowed; but it is founded in general principles of policy, which the defendant has the advantage of, contrary to the real justice, as between him and the plaintiff'.

[12] *Illegal Transactions: The Effect of Illegality on Contract and Trusts* (Consultation Paper 154, 1999) (LCCP 154); LCCP 160, n 2.

general application, that illegality bars a claim where (and only where) the claimant must rely upon its own illegality in framing the claim.[13] In particular, this was thought to have ousted a previously existing 'public conscience' test, which was more adaptable to the kinds of policy reason which the Law Commission thought most fruitful.[14]

The law of tort was not initially a part of the Commission's investigations, but the review was inevitably extended to tort: it was thought that consistency would demand its inclusion if legislation should be the chosen path. Equally, the threatened extension of the 'reliance principle' into tort cases will have played a role in drawing tort claims into the consultation.[15] The Law Commission's initial view was that a structured approach based on clearly stated statutory policy criteria should be adopted. It argued that on the whole, courts had not reached unjust decisions in relation to illegality in tort and contract, but that express appeal to the underlying objectives of the policy bar on a case-by-case basis would improve the clarity and transparency of the law. We suggest that a fuller picture, incorporating the insurance position, is all the more pertinent if attention to policies, results, and the actual impact of illegality rules is indeed considered important, and we hope to show how that fuller picture raises some additional questions.

By 2009 the Law Commission took the view that a series of intervening decisions had to some extent clarified the law, adopting a more open appeal to the policies behind the illegality defence along the lines it preferred, and not rigidly adopting the 'reliance' principle. The Law Commission chose to see the direction of case law as more or less compatible with the structured approach it had put forward, so that there was nothing to be gained by statutory intervention across the majority of areas. In their details, these intervening decisions do not, in fact, appear wholly compatible with the Law Commission's proposals.[16] However, judicial flexibility had largely been maintained, and this was perhaps the crucial factor. Legislation was proposed only in relation to the law of trusts, where *Tinsley v Milligan*[17] was a barrier to judicial development.[18] The government has now expressed itself unlikely to make time for legislation.[19] Perhaps Parliamentary instinct in relation to wrongdoing by parties to litigation is currently inclined to be more moralistic than those reflected in the Law Commission's search for balanced and proportionate responses to claimant wrongdoing, premised on clear

[13] Dubbed the 'reliance principle', and derived from the decision of the House of Lords in *Tinsley v Milligan* [1994] 1 AC 340; [1993] 3 WLR 126.

[14] The House of Lords in *Tinsley v Milligan* disapproved of the 'public conscience' test in quite general terms. The Law Commission's preference for the policy underlying 'public conscience' is stated in *The Illegality Defence: A Consultative Report* (Consultation Paper No 189, 2009) (LCCP 189), 3.105.

[15] Any threat from the reliance principle in tort has in any case been broken by the House of Lords: *Gray v Thames Trains*, n 5; *Moore Stephens v Stone & Rolls* [2009] UKHL 39; [2009] 3 WLR 455, Lord Phillips.

[16] We explore *Gray v Thames Trains* (n 5) in 11.3. The House of Lords' decision arguably takes a less structured approach than the Law Commission proposed in cases where the loss takes the form of a legal sanction, but it does reject the reliance principle, and leaves future courts with the capacity for flexible interpretation of the law.

[17] n 13.

[18] LCCP 189, n 14; *The Illegality Defence* (Report No 320, 2010) (LC No 320).

[19] Ministry of Justice, *Report on the Implementation of Law Commission Proposals*, March 2012, [51]–[52]. This is the second such Report to be presented to Parliament following the Law Commission Act 2009 s 1.

policy reasons.[20] Such questions, though speculative, are significant for our analysis, given that the underlying issues in relation to the policy bar bring into play the very objectives of both liability and (on our account) insurance of liabilities.

As already indicated, our concern in this chapter is with some of the fundamental issues left untouched by the Law Commission's exploration. It is noteworthy that the Law Commission documents—and indeed most of the decisions of the courts—contain little or no discussion of the effect of public policy upon insurance arrangements. Whatever the general theoretical reasons offered for the exclusion of insurance considerations from discussion, this would appear to be an extreme case since the bar is itself expressly based on policy considerations.

The effect of public policy on insurance arrangements, which is felt both for claims against assureds and claims by assureds for indemnity, is profound. First, a claimant guilty of wrongdoing may lose a claim against the assured, and here we consider why it should be the case that the victim of a tort is denied compensation. The question is particularly pertinent where the state had deemed that insurance against the wrongful act in question is compulsory. In principle the decision to require insurance does not in itself change the nature of liability,[21] and in tort theory, the two are insulated from one another.

Second, even where the victim is a paragon of virtue, illegal conduct on the part of the defendant which has given rise to a claim by the victim may strip the defendant of a claim against his or her liability insurers and thereby deprive the claimant of any fund to pay their claim. The irony here is that the more reprehensible the assured's wrongdoing, the less chance there is of recovering an indemnity under the policy. In short, in those instances where compensation is dependent on the defendant's liability insurance, a claimant's chance of full compensation is far better if he or she is the victim of negligence rather than the victim of fraud or deliberate assault. This raises a need to question the priorities of tort law.

There is a correlation between the exclusion of insurance recovery where the assured has acted illegally, and the very shape of the development of the law of tort. In practice, tort law has come to respond habitually—even routinely—to a range of negligence-based and indeed strict liabilities, rather than to liabilities turning on intention. Yet if we were to think in terms of a hierarchy of civil wrongs it seems likely that deliberate harm would be considered most deserving of a remedial response. The practical difficulty of obtaining compensation operates as an unseen factor in this aspect of the shape and reach of the law of tort. The effect—an increased emphasis on negligence

[20] This is an area where the 'echo chamber' of journalism has been particularly highlighted: see particularly the comments of Sedley LJ (employing this term) in *Vellino v Chief Constable of Greater Manchester* [2001] EWCA Civ 1249; [2002] 1 WLR 218 and the earlier case of *Revill v Newbery* [1996] QB 567. Recent government statements about clarifying the rights of householders using force against intruders underline the inclinations of the present coalition in this respect. Underlining the political dimensions of the defence, note also the enthusiastic legislative extension of illegality defences in Australia following the insurance crisis. This is charted by J Goudkamp, 'A Revival of the Doctrine of Attainder?' (2007) 29 *Sydney Law Review* 445; and J Goudkamp, 'Statutes and Tort Defences', in TT Arvind and J Steele (eds), *Tort Law and the Legislature: Common Law, Statute, and the Dynamics of Legal Change* (Oxford: Hart Publishing, 2013).

[21] Chapter 9 explored the emergence of compulsory insurance in the two distinct fields of motor accidents and employer liability. In the latter case, legislation effectively required what was already common practice, with relatively few accompanying changes in the nature of the liabilities, and of insurance, in place.

rather than intentional harm—has been termed 'underlitigation'.[22] This we suggest is evidenced in two distinct ways. First, it goes some distance to explaining the almost complete absence of some serious wrongs from the field of tort despite the availability of legal principles which would attach liability for those wrongs.[23] Second, it would explain the presentation of events which involve intentional wrongdoing as really turning on carelessness or even breach of strict duties. In this second form, 'underlitigation' (not capturing the real nature of the wrongdoing) may also lead the claimant to seek a different defendant, whose insurance policy is more likely to respond (or who may have sufficiently deep pockets). Underlitigation in this second sense is accompanied by the stretching of the law of negligence, as merely negligent parties with a causal link to deliberately cause harm are drawn into the frame.[24] In many instances, these will be professionals, or public authorities, who ought to have protected the claimant and avoided the harm. In some jurisdictions, the limits to insurability of deliberate harms have been instrumental in the development of proportionate forms of liability, designed to protect negligent parties from taking the full burden of liabilities for harm where the most blameworthy perpetrator is not worth pursuing.[25] The general point is that in any tort case the conduct of both parties will determine whether the claimant actually recovers compensation for his or her loss. It is our suggestion in this chapter that consideration of the insurance issues, and therefore of the actual implications of public policy defences, brings these defences and questions about their purpose and limits into much sharper focus.

In considering recoverability for a tort claim or under a liability policy, it is necessary to draw on the distinction between primary and vicarious/secondary liability which was outlined in Chapter 10. The result of this distinction is that a person who faces vicarious liability for the acts of another cannot be barred from making a claim for indemnity against a tortfeasor or its insurers simply because of the nature of the tortfeasor's conduct. As we saw, an organization which faces liability for the acts of an employee or agent may seek indemnification from a tortfeasor or insurers unless the

[22] Ellen Pryor, 'The Stories we Tell: Intentional Harm and the Quest for Insurance Funding' (1996–1997) 75 *Texas Law Review* 1721; Tom Baker, 'Liability Insurance at the Tort-Crime Boundary', in D Engel and M McCann, *Fault Lines: Tort Law as Cultural Practice* (Stanford CA: Stanford University Press, 2009).

[23] Graphically illustrated by Pryor, n 22. Tom Baker, n 22, 66–7, draws on J Wriggins, 'Domestic Violence Torts' (2001) 75 *South Carolina Law Review* 121, to comment on the role of insurance (and exclusion of illegal acts) in the rarity of tort claims involving 'domestic violence, molestation, and other assaults', despite the prevalence of such crimes. Baker argues that this is linked to a greater *de facto* separation between tort and criminal liability than would be expected given the *de jure* overlap between them. Rarity of the event is clearly not the reason. The insurance position and its impact on tort recovery have begun to attract greater attention from scholars: eg D Réaume, 'Insurance and Intentional Torts: The Case of "Sexual Battery"' (2004) 12 *Torts Law Journal* 76 (commenting on the Canadian case of *Non-Marine Underwriters, Lloyd's of London v Scalera* [2000] 1 SCR 551, and particularly the impact on compensation of presuming intent on the part of those committing sexual assault). Vicarious liabilities, as explained in Chapter 10, are different.

[24] The causal link may become very tenuous (or on some accounts, absent): see R Rabin, 'Enabling Torts' (2007) 49 *DePaul Law Review* 435, discussing claims against firearms manufacturers by victims of shootings.

[25] In a number of Australian states, the push toward proportionate liability has come primarily from the insurers of professional defendants such as auditors: note for example the accounts by J Swanton and B McDonald, 'Reforms to the Law of Joint and Several Liability—Introduction of Proportionate Liability' (1997) 5 *Torts Law Journal* 1; and JJ Spigelman, 'Negligence and Insurance Premiums: Recent Changes in Australian Law' (2003) 11 *Torts Law Journal* 3.

employee/agent is the alter ego of the organization,[26] or the organization has condoned or participated in the conduct of the employee/agent. For these reasons there is nothing surprising in the idea that a public liability policy provides coverage for vicarious liability for damages awarded against an employee/agent who has deliberately or recklessly inflicted personal injury on a third party,[27] a principle which has been applied in English law even if those damages are exemplary or punitive in nature.[28]

11.2.1 Why is there a public policy defence?

The public policy rules for tort claims and for insurance indemnity claims[29] are derived from the same sources, though as we will see, the impact of illegality is acknowledged to be highly dependent on circumstance. The law as it applies to contracts has been developing since the eighteenth century, but the extension of *ex turpi causa* from contract to tort is a much more recent and controversial development.[30] As late as 1954, in *NCB v England*,[31] Lord Porter doubted whether the defence had any application to tort at all. These doubts were expressed in a case where the claimant (as well as one of his fellow workers) had breached statutory safety duties backed by criminal sanctions. The duties were designed for the protection of the class (workers) to which the claimant belonged.[32] One reason for this conclusion was that breaches of statutory duty of this sort were clearly included within the definition of 'fault' on the part of claimants to which the Law Reform (Contributory Negligence) Act 1945 applied, so that damages must, under the statute, only be reduced. Further, applying the views of Lord Cohen in *Cakebread v Hopping Brothers*,[33] *ex turpi causa* is based on public policy, and public policy in such a case—far from requiring that damages be refused—requires that the courts should entertain the claim for compensation. And indeed, the effect of applying the bar automatically to breaches designated criminal will be that as Parliament acts to create more criminal sanctions with a view to enhancing protection and deterrence, the reach of compensatory responses is correspondingly—and unintentionally—reduced. This is plainly a perverse result. It is thus positively clear

[26] *KR v Royal & Sun Alliance plc* [2006] EWCA Civ 1454; [2007] Lloyd's Rep IR 368; *Moore Stephens v Stone & Rolls*, n 15; *Twigger*, n 3.

[27] *Hawley v Luminar Leisure Ltd* [2006] EWCA Civ 18 [2006]; Lloyd's Rep IR 307; *S & Y Investments (No 2) Pty Ltd v Commercial Union Assurance Co of Australia Ltd* (1986) 44 NTR 14.

[28] *Lancashire County Council v Municipal Mutual Insurance* [1997] QB 897. French, n 9, argues that most US courts have allowed insurance recovery even for personally incurred punitive damages; and that insurance of punitive damages incurred vicariously is the general rule.

[29] We are here concerned only with illegal acts committed by the assured. Other illegality issues may be relevant to insurance contracts, as where the policy is effected by an insurer who is not authorized under the FSMA 2000 or where it offends trading sanctions, for example, the insurance of Iranian vessels contrary to EU embargoes. Those and related matters affect the legality of the contract as formed, not the consequences of illegality in performance.

[30] LCCP 189, n 14, para 7.3.

[31] *National Coal Board v England* [1954] AC 403, 419.

[32] The House did not conclude on the question of whether there could be vicarious liability where the statutory duty was placed upon the employee and the employer had not been in breach, because it was held that the fellow employee (a shot firer) had also breached his common law duty to take care, in respect of which vicarious liability was unproblematic.

[33] [1947] KB 641, 644.

from *NCB v England*, leaving aside Lord Porter's doubts about whether an illegality defence would ever apply to a claim in tort, that not *all* illegality causally linked to a tort will be caught by the policy bar. Breaches of statutory duty aimed at securing the safety of individuals such as the claimant will not, and this is the preserve of contributory negligence or, in an extreme case, *volenti* or assumption of risk.

We have expressed this conclusion relatively narrowly, by reference to the kind of criminal liability involved in the case.[34] But this attempt to confine the reasoning in *NCB v England* within manageable bounds has its own implications. Particularly, it implies that as a consequence of the authority of this case, it is not possible to maintain that civil courts will never scrutinize Parliament's intentions in creating a criminal liability, or the nature of that liability, when determining a civil claim; though it has been authoritatively stated that this will be the case within the preserve of the 'narrow rule'.[35]

More recently, it has been said that the rules underlying the illegality defence in tort, as elsewhere, are based upon a combination of factors, including deterrence, punishment, removing the proceeds of wrongdoing, and the maintenance of the dignity of the courts.[36] The Law Commission supported the existence of an illegality rule in tort, but its support was balanced and generally not based on a punitive attitude. The Law Commission accepted that public policy might be explained on the basis of the need to maintain consistency in the law, but seems not to have confined its remarks to the precise, indeed rather formal, meaning of 'consistency' adopted by the Supreme Court of Canada and endorsed by Lord Hoffmann in the formulation of a 'narrow rule' in *Gray v Thames Trains*.[37] Nor did it consider 'consistency' to be the sole successful rationale. When looked at in the context of insurance—which is to say, with a fuller range of policy implications in range—our view is that qualifications and objections to the suggested rationales become even more compelling.

Deterrence arguably has its place where two parties knowingly enter into an illegal contract, but it seems of limited significance where it is applied to conduct which may be, and, where tort and insurance claims are concerned often is, isolated, unpremeditated, and motivated by particular unique circumstances.[38] The Law Commission further suggested that '[i]t is difficult to suggest that a person who is not deterred from these activities by the threat of criminal sanction will be deterred by the possibility

[34] For a broader argument, compare J Goudkamp, 'A Revival of the Doctrine of Attainder? The Statutory Illegality Defences to Liability in Tort' [2007] *Sydney Law Review* 445, 484–5, raising the question of whether the 1945 legislation can be taken to preclude the availability of the illegality defence in any claim to which it applies, and correctly noting that *NCB v England* (n 31) has received surprisingly little emphasis.

[35] *Gray v Thames Trains*, n 5, and critical discussion in 11.3. Our point may be compared with that of E Weinrib, 'Illegality as a Tort Defence' (1976) 28 UTLJ 28. Weinrib discerned that strict liability offences were treated differently from other criminal offences in the application of *ex turpi causa* in the courts, but suggested that this reflected the fact that the courts were to some extent uncomfortable with strict liability criminal offences (at 54). We argue, slightly differently, that courts may be justifiably eager not to undermine the objectives of strict criminal offences by removing tort liability.

[36] LCCP 160, n 2, para 4.5; LCCP 189, n 14, para 2.34.

[37] LCCP 160, n 2, para 4.81; *Hall v Hebert* [1993] 2 SCR 159. The Canadian approach is to confine the operation of the illegality bar to cases raising the consistency issue, which is to say where the tort claimant seeks compensation for the penalties attached to a criminal offence.

[38] Cf LCCP 160, n 2, paras 4.31–4.35.

that he or she may not receive compensation for any loss suffered in the course of, or as a result of, committing the offence'.[39] Perhaps counter-intuitively, this is not necessarily sound reasoning. Indeed, one of the few leading English cases where a policyholder sought a benefit from his own crime—though necessarily for his estate rather than for himself—was a case of suicide.[40] *Beresford v Royal Exchange Assurance*[41] is a case of contract rather than tort. Here the terms of a life insurance policy did not exclude recovery following an act of suicide other than in the first year of the policy, but the rule of public policy was deployed to prevent recovery against the insurers. Deeply indebted thanks to a failed business venture, the assured shot himself three minutes before the expiry of a negotiated extension to the renewal date of the policy, evidently with the express intention of securing the insurance for his dependants. The House of Lords held that he (in the guise of his estate) should not be permitted, as a matter of public policy, to benefit from what was then a criminal act. Indeed, even where the malefactor survives, it should not automatically be assumed that criminal sanctions outweigh the civil 'sanction' of being deprived of financial benefit.[42]

The punishment rationale has little to commend it, and was rightly omitted by the Law Commission from its proposed structured discretion. As already pointed out, the civil consequences of depriving a victim of a tort claim or an assured of an insurance claim may be wholly disproportionate to the wrongdoing, there is a risk of double punishment, and the outcome can be a windfall for the defendant.[43]

Another proposed rationale—preventing the claimant from benefiting from his or her own wrongdoing—may have its place where the parties set out on an agreed profit-making illegal enterprise, but that is not the paradigm case. The victim of a tort does not seek to make a profit, but rather to recover compensation for a loss, so the question becomes whether it is appropriate to remove that compensation.[44] The question poses particular difficulties where the defendant is required by law to insure against that very form of loss, as we see below. Equally, in the case of a claim under a liability policy, if indemnity is refused, the impact on the assured personally is likely to be limited unless the assured has the resources to pay the claim from his or her own pocket. In most cases the assured will not be able to pay the claim, and if the insurers do not meet the liabilities the claimant, who has done nothing wrong but simply become a victim, will

[39] LCCP 189, n 14, para 7.9.

[40] Not allowing a claimant to benefit from his crime was treated by the Law Commission as a separate justification from deterrence. However, it will necessarily blend into deterrence, and the example suggests that there may be something to deter.

[41] [1938] AC 586; [1938] 2 All ER 602.

[42] *In the Estate of Hall* [1914] P. 1, referred to in *Gray v Barr* [1971] 2 QB 554, where a woman sentenced to three years' imprisonment for manslaughter having shot her lover was not permitted to recover under his will. The decision of the Court of Appeal in *Gray v Barr* incorporates a note relating to her conviction (*R v Baxter*, otherwise unreported). It seems the shooting was not entirely accidental ('he dared me to do it'). The point here is that in these circumstances the possibility of inheritance is capable of outweighing a prison term, given the effects of impecuniosity (the brief note begins, frankly, 'A man named Julian Hall kept a woman named Jeannie Baxter and had made wills in her favour'). See also Weinrib, n 35, who makes the point that the criminal law in principle fixes penalties with regard to the degree and significance of wrongdoing. The impact of being denied civil compensation is quite capable of being disproportionate.

[43] LCCP 160, n 2, paras 4.10–4.21; n 42; Weinrib, n 35, at 45—tort here would create 'a type of disutility by blurring the gradations in sanction which supposedly channel criminal activity'.

[44] LCCP 189, n 14, para 7.5; *Revill v Newbery*, n 20, per Evans LJ.

go uncompensated unless he or she invokes the full force of insolvency law against the assured, potentially bringing the assured's business to an end or leaving a private assured bankrupt and without means of support. Clear proportionality issues are raised here.

Some care is also needed in any discussion of the need to preserve the dignity of the courts and the reputation of the legal system. This justification may be no more than an articulation of 'an unreasoned, 'gut-feeling' basis . . . which is potentially disproportionate and wrong',[45] and the Law Commission has stated that, at least for tort claims, the circumstances 'in which the court would feel compelled to protect its dignity are likely to be very extreme, and therefore rare'.[46] However, the House of Lords, in *Gray v Thames Trains* formally approved a related but narrower idea that the illegality defence is necessary in order to protect *consistency* in the law: the law could not consistently find the claimant criminally liable for manslaughter, thus personally responsible, and at the same time hold the *defendant* responsible for the claimant's act.[47] In this particular context, the consistency principle appears to protect the law's claim to attach sanctions on the basis of personal responsibility. Whatever may be said about *Gray v Thames Trains* itself,[48] we will later question the ambit of this principle.

The Law Commission nevertheless thought that the illegality bar should be retained in some form, for two particular reasons, and for a more generic reason which may rest on a number of policy considerations. The two limited reasons were to prevent the claimant from suing in tort where the action would otherwise be one to enforce an illegal contract; and to remove the possibility that the claimant might recover indemnity for a fine or other sanction imposed by the criminal law.[49] Those are limited situations: the former is most unlikely to apply to a tort claim and probably never to an insurance claim; and the latter—which the courts have, since the Law Commission's deliberations, adopted as the 'narrow rule' for denying a cause of action—may, as we point out below, have undesirable consequences. The Law Commission added a third ground, where neither of these two was applicable, namely a 'general residual principle' that the court 'should not assist a claimant who has been guilty of illegal conduct of which the courts should take notice'.[50] This, clearly, is more amorphous. However, the Commission proposed a list of accepted policy rationales on the basis of which the illegality defence or policy bar should be 'allowed'; and urged that the *result* of the illegality defence (its impact on the wrongdoer) should remain 'proportionate' to the illegality involved[51]—a signal that whatever the strength of arguments for clear

[45] LCCP 160, n 2, para 1.21. This point was made with particular force in *Hall v Hebert* (n 37). Compare *Parkingeye Ltd v Somerfield Stores Ltd* [2012] EWCA Civ 1338; [2012] 2 Lloyd's Rep 679, where the Court of Appeal rejected the idea that there was an unfettered discretion, and instead the search was for a proportionate response.

[46] LCCP 160, n 2, para 4.25.

[47] [2009] UKHL 33; [2009] 3 WLR 167.

[48] The sanction for manslaughter here was a hospital order accompanied by an indefinite detention order, because of the claimant's mental state—itself the result of the defendant's admitted negligence: the law's reflection of personal responsibility here is real but qualified, through recognition of his lack of capacity to control his own actions.

[49] LCCP 160, n 2, paras 5.4–5.6; LC No 320, n 18, para 7.59.

[50] LCCP 160, n 2, para 2.11.

[51] For example, LCCP 189, n 14, para 2.34.

rules, the court should not flinch from assessing the nature and significance of the rule of law infringed by the claimant, and the quality of the conduct. In ensuring a proportionate response however, can courts avoid consideration of the nature and purpose of liabilities and other surrounding legal rules, in which insurance may be a key consideration? Lord Hoffmann, in *Gray v Thames Trains*, took the view that a court deciding a civil claim should not add to its burden by considering the nature and purpose of aspects of the criminal law and making distinctions between them, or 'having to play the criminal law's conscience'.[52] Lord Phillips' opinion was in marked contrast with that of Lord Hoffmann on this point. He took the view that if the hospital order against the claimant had not been accompanied by an indefinite restriction order,[53] this would not have been a case where *ex turpi causa* should bar the claim. Thus he took the course of interpreting the 'meaning' of the criminal sentence. In the following section, such questions emerge as central to our analysis of the relationship between liability and insurance, for they invite consideration of the multiple potential purposes of the former.

11.3 Claims Against Policyholders

11.3.1 Legal principles

Our key concern in this section is with the law of tort, and particularly with its use against insured defendants. Although the authorities in this area are not fully reconcilable,[54] the most authoritative formulation is that of Lord Hoffmann in *Gray v Thames Trains Ltd*.[55] Lord Hoffmann recognized that *ex turpi causa* may be based on a range of policy reasons which will vary with different contexts.[56] In the context of that case, it consisted of a narrow and a wide rule. The narrow rule is that a claimant cannot recover an indemnity for a fine or other penalty imposed upon him for the commission of a criminal offence. As expressed in *Gray v Thames Trains*, this is an absolute principle, but, as we see in the paragraphs to follow, it has been doubted—with good reason—whether it can apply to strict liability crimes where the assured's infringement was beyond his control, or was the fault of another.

The wide rule is that there can be no claim where criminality can properly be said to be the cause of the loss and is of a nature which would cause a court to refuse to lend its assistance. The wide rule allows the court considerable leeway in determining whether it is appropriate to impose a civil sanction for criminal conduct: as discussed below in

[52] n 5, para 41, citing EK Banakas, 'Tort Damages and the Decline of Fault Liability: Plato Overruled, but Full Marks to Aristotle!' [1985] CLJ 195, 197. Contrast our discussion of *Gray v Barr* (n 42) in the following text.

[53] n 48.

[54] LCCP 189, n 14, para 7.69. Lord Sumption discusses the difficulties posed by the most recent cases in 'Reflections on the Law of Illegality' (2012) 20 *Restitution Law Review* 1.

[55] n 5.

[56] At [30]–[32]. So, for example, he argued that '[o]ne cannot simply extrapolate rules applicable to a different kind of situation' ([31]); and approached the issues in terms of the 'particular rule for which the appellants contend' ([32]). Note also the approach of Ward LJ in *Delaney v Pickett* [2011] EWCA Civ 1532; [2012] 1 WLR 2149, derived from *Gray v Thames Trains*, dissenting but not on the operation of *ex turpi* in common law.

the context of claims by policyholders, this is of particular significance in respect of claims under liability policies, where denial of a claim impacts primarily on the injured victim. Nevertheless the rule, as Lord Hoffmann expressed it, leans heavily on principles of legal causation (whether it can 'properly be said' that the loss was caused by the criminal conduct), which he acknowledged are not straightforward. The notion of 'legal cause' being advanced here is likely to be imbued with notions of responsibility. Interestingly, as Lord Hoffmann presented it, the wide rule in this context depends not on ideas of consistency, incentives, or whether there might be injustice between claimant and defendant, but on the idea that 'public notions of the fair distribution of resources' would be offended by compensating the claimant for the consequences of his own criminal conduct.[57] There has been criticism of the latter argument on the basis that the aim of the law of tort is not in any event to achieve a fair distribution of resources and, indeed, that tort law is unconcerned with achieving such a distribution.[58] We would argue that Lord Hoffmann's point is not that tort can be interpreted as aiming at a fair distribution of resources. Rather, he was pointing out (not for the first time) that the potentially undesirable distributive impact of tort liabilities can legitimately be considered when determining how far those liabilities should extend.[59] Lord Hoffmann may particularly have had in mind the special status of tort victims as enjoying compensation premised on making good losses, rather than the more partial *support* achieved by the majority of those suffering misfortunes, given that the tort claimant in this case had attacked and killed another individual. The issues here are complex, and deserve a little more explanation, but there is a limit to what can be gleaned.

In the particular context of *Gray v Thames Trains*, the most pressing contrast is between potential tort recovery on the part of the claimant, and the position of the relatives of the deceased victim of the claimant's crime. As it happens, the treatment of compensation for the victims of 'crimes of violence' is to a large extent still modelled (somewhat controversially) on tort. The Criminal Injuries Compensation Scheme, on its introduction, had the ambition of replicating tort damages, with the state in effect standing in as 'proxy' for the tortfeasor who was also guilty of crime.[60] That ambition—to reflect the awards that would be made through the law of tort—has proved hard to maintain and the principle has been eroded through adoption of a tariff for particular types of case.[61] The Criminal Injuries Compensation Scheme of course pursues a public purpose, and utilizes public (in this instance, state) funds in order to do so. It is therefore noteworthy that a trace of criminality on the part of the applicant will in most circumstances place them outside the reach of the scheme, which is expressly

[57] Lord Hoffmann, *Gray v Thames Trains*, n 5, at [51].

[58] J Goudkamp, 'The Defence of Illegality: *Gray v Thames Trains Ltd*' (2009) 17 *Torts Law Journal* 1, 8.

[59] Discussed in Chapter 8, particularly with reference to *Stovin v Wise* [1996] AC 923; [1996] 3 WLR 388. See also Lord Hoffmann, 'The COMBAR Lecture: Separation of Powers' [2002] *Juridical Review* 137.

[60] D Miers, *State Compensation for Criminal Injuries* (Oxford: Blackstone Press, 1997) reviews the creation of the Scheme in 1964, and the revisions which placed the Scheme on a statutory footing and also introduced a tariff, through the Criminal Injuries Compensation Act 1995.

[61] One important goal of the new tariff-based approach was to enable governments to exercise some control over the rising cost of criminal compensation modelled on tort awards. Tort awards for personal injury are generally met from insurance (Chapter 9).

aimed at benefiting the 'blameless' victims of crime. Even an unspent criminal conviction which is not causally related to the injury may operate to bar a claim.[62] This distributive scheme, unusual in that its benefits are nevertheless essentially modelled on tort remedies, is closed to those who are not in this sense 'blameless'. In a sense, Lord Hoffmann's remarks in *Gray* present tort liability as comparable to a distributive scheme, which might therefore be subject to legitimate limits. In particular, he pointed to the compensation of tort victims at 'public expense', but for reasons which were not further elaborated. It is of course a common observation that all of us are contributors to insurance funds, and this is so whether the fund in question is a private fund, such as motor insurance, or a public one.[63] We return to this point in the particular context of road traffic, in relation to the MIB, in 11.3.3.[64]

11.3.2 Applying the narrow rule

The narrow rule of *ex turpi causa* precludes an action against a tortfeasor where the claim is one for an indemnity for a fine or penalty for a criminal act. This is now the best-defined and clearest instance of the illegality bar in relation to tort; but even so it is not without difficulty. The application of the narrow rule must by definition be confined to acts which attract a criminal sanction,[65] and it turns on consistency rather than degrees of culpability. This is the effect of *Gray v Thames Trains*.[66] We suggest that it is capable of conflicting with the principle that the illegality rule should be employed in order to further the policy of the rule infringed, and the question arises of which of these is the more significant.

In order to assess the logic of the narrow rule it is necessary to consider in what circumstances it is likely to have any impact. The most likely situation—and it is not easy to think of others—is where the tortfeasor's own conduct has caused the victim to commit a criminal offence.[67] This was, as we have seen, the case with *Gray v Thames Trains* itself. But it also occurred, in a very different context, in the leading case of *Safeway Stores Ltd v Twigger*.[68] Here a company was found to be in breach of a

[62] *Criminal Injuries Compensation Scheme 2012* (Ministry of Justice, 2012) sets out the eligibility criteria. Compensation may be refused on the basis that the 'conduct of the applicant before, during or after the incident' makes it inappropriate to make an award, or a full award (para 25). Unspent convictions unrelated to the incident may also affect the claim, and the principles are set out in Annex D. Relevant unspent convictions are not limited to those giving rise to a custodial sentence, community order, or equivalent. Other convictions will also operate to justify withholding or reducing a claim unless there are 'exceptional reasons' not to withhold or reduce it (Annex D, para 4).

[63] The point is more explicitly made in the COMBAR lecture (n 59), and *Stovin v Wise*, n 59.

[64] The related expression 'public funds' was fleshed out by Tomlinson LJ in relation to the MIB in particular in *Delaney v Pickett and another* [2011] EWCA Civ 1532; [2012] 1 WLR 2149, where he connected it to a fund to which all motorists contribute via premiums. See further 11.3.

[65] Note however the possibility of penumbral cases such as *Nayyar* (n 3) and *Twigger* (n 3), which may fall within the narrow rule.

[66] Prior to this, the English courts had not adopted the consistency argument.

[67] For these purposes, we include failures to prevent amounting to negligent omission, for example *Reeves v Chief Constable* (prisoner ought to have been protected from suicide) [2000] 1 AC 360; and, although the claim was barred for illegality, *Clunis v Camden and Islington Health Authority* [1998] QB 978 (claimant ought to have been securely detained to avoid his fatal attack on another).

[68] n 3.

prohibition in the Competition Act 1998 by entering into price-fixing agreements with competitors, and faced a penalty from the Office of Fair Trading (OFT). In advance of the amount being determined, the company sought a declaration that it was entitled to an indemnity from its directors who had carried out the infringing negotiations. The Court of Appeal held that the narrow rule precluded indemnity: liability under the legislation was personal to the claimant. Only the 'undertaking' could be liable, and there was thus no question of vicarious liability.[69] At the same time, the statute did not impose a strict liability, but was predicated on intention or negligence. This caused some difficulty, but was found to be no reason to enter into questions of 'attribution' of intention or negligence to the company, because the 'offence' was plainly that of the undertaking itself. It is suggested that the reasoning of Longmore LJ thus leans heavily on the consistency argument. The bare fact that the penalty was imposed personally on the undertaking was sufficient to establish—at least where it was not a strict liability offence—that the undertaking itself was barred by its own illegality from seeking recourse against those who, it wished to argue, were actually at fault. There was no need to determine what would be the case had the penalty been one of strict liability. Lloyd LJ agreed with the analysis of Longmore LJ.

The separate and contrasting judgment of Pill LJ, concurring in the result, is instructive for our purposes. Pill LJ sought to explain the application of the illegality bar in terms of the policy of the particular provision breached, and of the particular penalty. The statutory provision, he argued, was clearly aimed at penalizing undertakings themselves, and the objective was to deter breaches and thus protect the public. Support for this can be found in the nature of the substantial penalties imposed: it was clearly not intended that these be passed to others.[70] This difference in approach raises once again the important question of whether the courts will indeed go behind the bald 'consistency' argument, and consider the nature of a *particular* liability.

Extended beyond its particular context, the approach in *Safeway Stores v Twigger* raises the possibility that the narrow rule may have effects which are scarcely reconcilable with notions of personal responsibility. The point may be illustrated by *Osman v J Ralph Moss Ltd*,[71] in which an insurance broker failed to obtain motor vehicle insurance for the claimant, leaving the claimant uninsured and thus guilty of an offence under the RTA 1988. The claimant's action in negligence against the brokers was successful, but doubt is inevitably cast upon that outcome by the narrow rule articulated in *Gray v Thames Trains*, and by some of the reasoning in *Twigger*. Indeed, in

[69] This is reflected in the nature of the penalty itself (in the region of £16 million). This is unlikely to be aimed at individuals.

[70] The 'others' in *Twigger*, the directors, would almost certainly have had their own D&O liability insurance, although such cover would—in line with principle—not respond to deliberate acts. It is a fair bet that the D&O insurers had funded the defence of the directors in the *Twigger* proceedings. However, D&O policies are structured on the basis that once fraud is established against or admitted by a director, there is no substantive coverage, further defence costs cease to be payable, and any defence costs incurred by the insurers become recoverable from the directors (a recoupment process which is generally fruitless and thus ignored). For the significance of insurer funding of D&O defence costs in configuring the tort-crime boundary, see Baker, n 22.

[71] [1970] 1 Lloyd's Rep 313.

Twigger both Longmore and Lloyd LJJ impliedly left open the question of its correctness, noting that the application of the narrow rule to strict liability offences had not been determined,[72] and it was left to Pill LJ to confirm the correctness of *Osman*.[73] In doing so, Pill LJ suggested that there was not necessarily an intention in *Gray v Thames Trains* to overrule cases such as *Osman*. This however, like Pill LJ's emphasis on the policy of the particular statutory provision, reads into the narrow rule a flexibility which is at the very least not apparent from the way Lord Hoffmann expressed it. The question, we suggest, is whether a finding of criminal responsibility, and relevant penalty, must necessarily be seen as requiring a civil court to accept the judgment of responsibility for its own purposes. We argue that this is not the case. For example in a case such as *NCB v England*,[74] dealing with health and safety duties, the consequences of such an approach would undermine the purpose of the combined civil and criminal law liabilities.

The notion that claimants may lose their indemnity claim simply because the defendant's negligence has caused them to commit a strict liability criminal offence rather than suffer any other form of loss is, we submit, unsupportable. But an exception for strict liability offences of this sort goes to the root of the 'consistency' argument itself, and brings into account more complex questions about the extent to which such offences do or do not embody a principle of personal responsibility, and if so in what circumstances. The law needs to speak consistently, but can the courts articulate what the many forms of liability are saying? If not, then the distinction between cases such as *Twigger* and *Gray*, and cases such as *Osman*, will remain elusive. Yet *Osman*, it seems to us, is more easily defensible than *Gray* itself. The contrast between *Osman* and *Twigger* illustrates that the consistency argument in relation to the narrow rule works on one level only, and may come into conflict with other forms of consistency to be seen, for example, in the need to further the purpose of a rule. Take the facts of *Osman*: the claimant was under a strict liability obligation imposed by the criminal law to obtain insurance. He reasonably relied on his broker to secure insurance but the broker failed. A duty on brokers to adhere to their instructions and to ensure that insurance is in place may be more effective in securing that insurance than allowing that duty to be defeated by the claimant's strict criminal responsibility. A parallel outside the confines of the narrow rule may also be found in Lord Mance's argument that it would be positively helpful, in defeating fraud by untrustworthy individuals, to strengthen the duties on auditors of 'one-man companies', rather than to see their negligence liability as defeated by the fraud they failed to prevent.[75]

[72] As we have seen, the relevant offences in *Twigger* (n 3) were not strict liability offences.

[73] Note also *United Project Consultants Pte Ltd v Leong Kwok Omn* [2005] 4 SLR 214; [2005] SGCA 38, and the discussion of an example based upon that case by J Goudkamp, n 58, at 5.

[74] n 31.

[75] *Moore Stephens v Stone & Rolls*, n 15 (in dissent). Recall also the differentiation between our argument on this point, and Weinrib's reasons for doubting the application of the consistency principle to strict liability offences, n 35. Our approach does not suppose any unease with strict liability 'regulatory' offences, but does (like Weinrib's) bring into play questions about the underlying notions of personal responsibility.

11.3.3 Applying the wide rule

The wide rule is altogether more flexible, and allows the court to juggle questions of both proximity and seriousness in determining whether a claimant should be allowed to proceed. One question which might be posed is whether there is any evidence that the courts are prepared to be more generous in relation to the claimant's illegal conduct in cases where the defendant is known to carry liability insurance. Relevant cases have, for the most part, arisen in the context of compulsory insurance under the RTA 1988, and it cannot be said with certainty that the courts have taken into account that a finding of conduct contrary to public policy on the part of the victim operates to deprive him of a required, and virtually guaranteed, statutory source of compensation.[76] What can be said is that the wide principle has been interpreted restrictively and has defeated claims in very few motor cases. A passenger has been deprived of compensation where he was injured in a getaway car being driven at speed,[77] where he encouraged an intoxicated driver to exceed the speed limit,[78] and when he fell from the back of a van used to steal extending ladders.[79] In each of these cases the passenger's own conduct was integral to his injury and, indeed, to the commission of the tort. By contrast, criminal offending has not precluded recovery from a negligent defendant by a passenger injured by negligent driving while carrying a quantity of cannabis to a customer[80] nor by a pedestrian run over by a driver following a fight between them.[81] Given the difficult distinctions here, the Law Commission expressed unhappiness about applying *ex turpi causa* principles to a personal injury victim who had at the time of the accident been engaged in an unlawful 'joint enterprise' with the defendant,[82] and suggested that the cases could be explained on the alternative grounds of the absence of a duty of care or voluntary assumption of risk. It now appears from *Joyce v O'Brien* that neither is correct and that the true basis is that of causal link between the criminality and the injury.[83]

In this connection, one modification to the wide rule should be noted. Where it applies, the exception can have a very significant effect on the prospects of recovery of a claimant not barred by *ex turpi causa* from a claim in tort because his illegal act is not sufficiently causally linked with the tort which caused the injury. *Delaney v Pickett*[84] was a case of this kind, and it illustrates that a victim of personal injury who is tainted

[76] As discussed in Chapter 9, the 1988 Act removes the driver's defence of voluntary assumption of risk, but leaves both the contributory negligence and public policy defences untouched.

[77] *Ashton v Turner* [1981] 1 QB 137; [1980] 3 WLR 736. Cf *Smith v Jenkins* (1970) 119 CLR 397; [2003] All ER (D) 159 (Jun) (stolen vehicle).

[78] *Pitts v Hunt* [1991] 2 QB 24; [1990] 3 WLR 542.

[79] *Joyce v O'Brien* [2013] EWCA Civ 546.

[80] *Delaney v Pickett* [2011] EWCA Civ 1532; [2012] 1 WLR 2149—but note the devastating impact on his claim of illegality in relation to insurance, discussed in 11.4.1.

[81] *Clarke v Motor Insurers Bureau* March 2012, unreported, QBD. Compare *Revill v Newbery* (n 20), where a burglar was allowed to recover damages against the householder who shot him. But contrast *Cross v Kirby* [2000] EWCA Civ 426, where a hunt saboteur who hit a huntsman with a baseball bat, and himself suffered injury at the hands of the huntsmen, was barred from recovery. These cases are not easily reconciled.

[82] Referring to *Ashton v Turner* [1981] 1 QB 137 and *Pitts v Hunt* [1991] 2 QB 24.

[83] LCCP 160, n 2, paras 4.82–4.96; *Joyce v O'Brien*, n 79.

[84] [2011] EWCA Civ 1532; [2012] 1 WLR 2149.

by illegality may be more harshly judged in the context of an insurance claim than in the law of tort. This in turn raises the question of the purpose of the compulsory insurance regime and the MIB safety net. Does the requirement for compulsory insurance, at least, suggest that it is understood to be primarily a source of compensation for those suffering losses at the hands of insured parties, rather than a personal indemnity?[85] If so, how should this affect interpretation of insurance cover?

The victim of an uninsured driver has a default claim against the MIB under the MIB Uninsured Drivers' Agreement 1999, but art 6 of the Agreement removes that right from a passenger who knew or ought to have known that: (i) the vehicle had been stolen or unlawfully taken;[86] (ii) the vehicle was being used uninsured; (iii) the vehicle was being used in the course or furtherance of a crime; or (iv) the vehicle was being used as a means of escape from, or avoidance of, lawful apprehension. Situations (i) and (iv) would probably preclude an action by the claimant at common law in any event, although possibly not situation (ii). The most contentious is situation (iii). In *Delaney v Pickett* a majority of the Court of Appeal held that situation (iii) did not merely replicate the common law. Here, an injured motor vehicle passenger who was at the time of the accident carrying cannabis for supply to a customer was outside the wide *ex turpi causa* rule, in that there was no causal link between his offence and his injuries, but was caught by exclusion (iii) in the MIB Agreement.[87] This seems both curious and harsh, given the limited role that criminality has in civil claims arising out of motor accidents. Admittedly, construing exclusion (iii) as replicating the common law, as Ward LJ preferred, would have rendered it superfluous, although that is not a fundamental objection because much the same can be said of exclusion (iv) and possibly exclusion (ii). More fundamentally, there is nothing in the EU Consolidated Motor Insurance Directive 2009[88] which justifies such an exclusion, and it is unfortunate that the arguments in *Delaney* were not directed to the need to construe exclusion (iii) so as to comply with EU law and so that it did no more than to replicate ordinary tort liability rules which are for the most part[89] untouched by EU law.[90]

In the majority, Tomlinson LJ took the least compromising path. His approach raises the distributive issues which we explored in relation to Lord Hoffmann's brief comments in *Gray v Thames Trains* in the previous section. Unlike Ward LJ, Tomlinson LJ was content to accept that the MIB Agreement would exclude more claimants from compensation than would the principles of the law of tort. This he justified in part by reference to

[85] See E Knutsen, 'Auto Insurance as Social Contract: Solving Automobile Insurance Coverage Disputes Through a Public Regulatory Framework' (2010–2011) 48 Alta L Rev 715, and the discussion in Chapter 9.

[86] Even if the driver is insured, a passenger in a stolen vehicle will not be able to enforce any judgment against the negligent driver's insurers: RTA 1988, s 151(3).

[87] n 85. The first defendant, the negligent driver, had been insured, but the policy was avoided in response to his confessed habitual use of drugs. This would require the insurance company to return the premium, and left the claimant dependent on the MIB.

[88] 2009/103/EC.

[89] But not entirely: Chapter 9.

[90] The dissenting judge, Ward LJ, took up this point. Ward LJ also considered that the judge had insufficient basis on which to conclude that the amount of cannabis with which the claimant was found suggested that the cannabis was intended for supply rather than personal consumption. The difference was germane to the question of whether the vehicle was being used for an illegal purpose; but even if it was, this would be insufficient to establish the common law defence.

the use of what he called 'public funds' in order to meet claims against the MIB. This appears to suggest that the MIB is resourced by 'public funds' to a greater extent than the law of tort in general. The MIB receives no state funding, but operates through a levy on motor insurers carrying on business in the UK. In this sense, the funds are 'public' in that each policyholder helps to cover the cost of others' torts. That is of course generally true of liabilities backed by insurance. The presumed difference is that those others, here, are not contributors to the fund. The funds are also 'public' in the additional sense the levy is plainly imposed for a public purpose—to cover gaps in insurance cover—but again, the same may be said for motor insurance generally, in that it is mandated. These issues are pertinent because Tomlinson LJ seems to have considered that an agreement which extends the use of such 'public funds' to cases where drivers are uninsured can fairly be read restrictively, even though the absence of insurance on the part of the driver evidently does not itself reflect on the claimant. Unlike Richards LJ, the other judge in the majority, Tomlinson LJ did not accept that a *de minimis* provision should be read into the exclusion for those who know that the vehicle is being used in the course or furtherance of a crime. Rather, the inapplicability of the provision even to cases where the offence is trivial was a matter of legitimate agreement on the part of insurers, who were (as above) distributing 'public funds'. Tomlinson LJ put the point bluntly: culpability is not the touchstone of non-recovery in relation to the MIB Agreement; constructive knowledge of an illegal purpose is expressly sufficient. While the courts have developed the policy bar in relation to tort so that a genuine nexus between illegality and injury is required for the bar to take effect, here the possession of cannabis (which could not 'fairly be said to have caused' the injuries)[91] nevertheless had the effect that once the defendant's motor insurance policy had been avoided to reflect non-disclosure of his cannabis use, the MIB would not respond to provide the required fund to cover the defendant's liability.

What happened to the seriously injured claimant in this case was that principles of illegality did not defeat his tort claim, but they did defeat the satisfaction of that claim. He was, in effect, outside the 'social contract' represented by compulsory third-party motor insurance, and the MIB safety net. The purpose of the MIB Agreement, as we explored in Chapter 9, is clearly compensatory and in tune with the objective of the compulsory liability insurance regime itself: it might be suggested that it ought to be interpreted in light of its compensatory social purpose.[92] And yet, while a burglar is not an 'outlaw' for the purposes of the law of tort, even where his injuries are related to his criminal purpose,[93] a claimant whose transgression was not causative of the accident is outside the net of compensation provided via the agreement. This is an unfortunate result. Although the very existence of the MIB Agreement reflects the desire to ensure compensation is available for tort claimants, the MIB safety net contains much larger

[91] A reference to Lord Hoffmann's articulation of the 'wide rule'—n 57 and text.

[92] For related discussion with reference to insurance contracts and their purposes, refer to J Stempel, 'The Insurance Policy as a Social Instrument and Social Institution' (2010) 51 *William & Mary Law Rev* 1489. Stempel suggests that insurance contracts are designed to perform particular risk management, deterrence, and compensation functions that are essential to economic and social ordering, and that this should affect their interpretation.

[93] *Revill v Newbery*, n 20.

holes than the common law. It was considered legitimate for insurers, who are not tortfeasors but indemnifiers, to treat illegality which at common law would be considered merely 'incidental' as grounds for withholding the fund required to support a tort judgment. Despite the purpose and genesis of the MIB, Tomlinson LJ emphasized its status as resting upon *agreement*. But this was not a purely formalistic preference. The approach was supported by reference to a 'distributive' view of the MIB Agreements, akin to that expressed by Lord Hoffmann in relation to tort in *Gray*. In the result, turpitude in this instance has a much greater impact via insurance than through the principles of tort itself. The question is how far this fits with the policy of the law, exemplified in the very existence of the MIB Agreements. But it also illustrates that distributive schemes are not unbounded. One way of summarizing the result is to say that the law therefore differentiates in this particular context between the impact of illegality on the claimant's part in actions against tortfeasors, and in actions against insurance funds—even though it is plain that the source of funds is, in both cases, insurance.

11.4 Claims Against Insurers

11.4.1 The role of *ex turpi causa*

The use of the *ex turpi causa* defence to claims for breach of contract can be traced back at least to the eighteenth century, and in particular to a series of cases involving wagering agreements whose subject matter led them to be regarded as harmful to the public interest.[94] There is now much authority on the law governing contracts illegal in their formation, and contracts lawful at the outset but performed illegally.[95] Non-marine insurance contracts fit into the traditional pattern. The law may prohibit the making of an insurance contract, for example, because it is made by a person not authorized to carry on insurance business, or because it involves infringement of trading sanctions, in which case it is void. Alternatively, a policy lawful in its formation but performed illegally by the assured—typically by the commission of a criminal act giving rise to a claim—remains valid but the claim itself will be lost if the familiar causation criteria embodied in the narrow and wide tests are satisfied. Nice questions under first-party policies may thus arise where the assured ignores traffic rules and takes a prohibited route leading to his vehicle become lodged under a low bridge,[96] or where the assured suffers a loss of goods which he had previously smuggled.[97] It would seem that unless the assured is seeking indemnification from his insurers for a fine or other penalty (the narrow rule), the relevant factors (under the wide rule) will be

[94] Many of those cases indeed involved wagers dressed up as marine or life policies.

[95] The leading authority is *St John Shipping Corp v Joseph Rank Ltd* [1957] 1 QB 267; [1956] 3 WLR 870. For discussion this area in general, see RA Buckley, *Illegality and Public Policy* (London: Sweet & Maxwell, 2nd edn, 2009); N Enonchong, *Illegal Transactions* (London: LLP, 1998).

[96] *Fire & All Risks Insurance Co Ltd v Powell* [1966] VR 513 (recovery).

[97] *Euro-Diam Ltd v Bathurst* [1990] 1 QB 1; [1988] 2 WLR 517 (recovery), approving *Geismar v Sun Alliance and London Assurance Ltd* [1978] 1 QB 383; [1978] 2 WLR 38, in which a contrary result was reached, although it is doubtful whether *Geismar* can survive the reasoning in *Euro-Diam*.

causation and the degree of criminality.[98] Marine insurance has taken a stricter view, a complex series of authorities starting at the end of the seventeenth century[99] establishing that there is a warranty that the adventure is lawful and a further warranty that the adventure is to be carried out in a lawful fashion so far as the assured can control the matter. These rules, which are now codified in the Marine Insurance Act 1906, s 41, do not rest upon causation or affront to the public conscience, and illegality which is any more than purely incidental will bring the risk to an end.

Our key concern however is with third-party policies. In the context of liability insurance, the refusal of the courts to provide an indemnity is likely to leave the assured's victim without the ability to enforce any judgment against the assured. Elaborate and careful reasoning which imposes liability upon a tortfeasor may be undermined by a subsequent refusal to allow the tortfeasor recovery under his liability policy in respect of the claim against him (in much the same way that, in *Delaney*, the limits of the tort defence were overridden by the impact of contractual terms and interpretation of the MIB Agreement). Our task is to consider whether the courts take into account the fact that an *ex turpi causa* defence successfully taken by a liability insurer has its primary impact on the innocent victim of the assured. Our conclusion is that this is clearly the case for motor insurance, but less obviously so for other forms of liability cover.[100] Contemplating possible reasons for this conclusion leads to some profound questions not only about the purpose of insurance, but about the purpose of the liabilities themselves. Switching attention to the use of *ex turpi causa* in relation to claims against insurers is therefore an important part of understanding civil liability.

The notion that *ex turpi causa* and the exclusion of intentional harm preclude an insurance claim has profound effects on the manner in which a claimant against an assured will frame the cause of action. A claimant, by successfully proving that the assured was guilty of deliberate wrongdoing, whether or not this result also takes the action into the realm of criminality, may thereby negative any insurance coverage that the assured might have in place and confine himself to enforcement against any assets that the defendant happens to possess.[101] Should the assured prove to be insolvent, so that the third party acquires a direct action against the assured's liability insurers under the Third Parties (Rights against Insurers) Acts 1930 or 2010, it remains

[98] This principle is codified by the Forfeiture Act 1982, which prevents a person from obtaining any benefit—including insurance benefits—from murder, although the court has a discretion to allow recovery in manslaughter cases.

[99] *Sands v Child* (1692) 4 Mod 176.

[100] This deepens the oddity of *Delaney v Pickett*, discussed in 11.3.3, where the claimant's own illegality in a road traffic case had disproportionate effects by comparison with the common law.

[101] We should not discount the rare cases where this is indeed an objective of the claimant, or not at odds with that objective: it can be assumed that no insurance would respond to the claims in the sexual enslavement case of *AG v Dulghieru* [2009] EWHC 225 (QB); [2009] All ER (D) 194 (Feb), for example, and particularly not the exemplary element of damages. But the claimants may well have sought what has been termed 'blood money': to know that some of the defendant's own funds have been secured to compensate the wrong (in this instance, a particularly heinous one). The notion of 'blood money' is discussed by T Baker, 'Blood Money, New Money and the Moral Economy of Tort Law in Action' (2001) 35 *Law and Society Review* 275. Much more commonly, of course, the assured may not be the tortfeasor and, in cases of vicarious liability for intentional acts, there is scope for insurance cover to be effective, depending on the terms of the policies.

uncertain whether the third party is estopped by the judgment obtained against the assured from arguing against the insurers that the assured's liability was not the result of deliberate wrongdoing.[102] But even if there is no estoppel, the standard of proof required to obtain the judgment against the assured for deliberate wrongdoing will make it all but impossible for the claimant to argue that the judge's findings at trial can be overturned in the later insurance action.[103] Of course in some cases the claimant can only establish any cause of action if he or she can prove deliberate wrongdoing, as with actions for knowing assistance with breach of fiduciary duty or inducing breach of contract. But in others, there is no point in the claimant asserting (uninsured) deceit when he can get by with an action in (insured) negligent misrepresentation. The fact that the claim is framed in negligence rather than deliberate misconduct will not guarantee an insurance recovery, because it is always open to the insurers to assert that the allegations made by the claimant establish fraud,[104] but it is less likely that insurers will take that point if they are not directed to it by the claim itself. But for the same reason, an action against additional parties who clearly were merely negligent,[105] especially if indemnity insurance is sure to be in place, offers additional attractions. Thus, as we have pointed out, illegality in relation to insurance may have helped to feed the rise of negligence and its expansion to additional parties.

11.4.2 Policy terms and *ex turpi causa*

It is important to define the role of public policy in claims against liability insurers. There is no need to consider principles of illegality where the act for which damages or indemnity is sought is designed to bring about the harm inflicted on the third party or is carried out in reckless disregard of the possibility of such harm: both the general principle that insurance is against fortuity rather than deliberate acts,[106] and usually the policy wording itself, will preclude recovery. Public policy can of course operate in such cases, but it has no independent effect.

Public liability, employers' liability, motor policies, and other insurances which respond to liability for personal injury or damage to property normally confine cover to 'accidents' or 'accidental' damage or injury. It is settled that whether or not a loss is accidental has to be looked at from the point of view of the assured,[107] so that injury deliberately and intentionally inflicted by the assured will not be covered by insurance

[102] *Omega Proteins v Aspen Insurance* [2010] EWHC 2280 (Comm). There is related discussion of 'underlitigation' in the text to n 22.

[103] *Persimmon Homes Ltd v Great Lakes Reinsurance (UK) Plc* [2010] EWHC 1705 (Comm); [2011] Lloyd's Rep IR 101.

[104] *MDIS v Swinbank* [1999] Lloyd's Rep IR 516.

[105] Such as the auditors in *Moore Stephens v Stone and Rolls*, n 15.

[106] E Knutsen explores this element of the insurance contract in relation to illegality, 'Fortuity Clauses in Liability Insurance: Solving Coverage Dilemmas for Intentional and Criminal Conduct' (2011) 37 Queen's LJ 73, making the important point however that some criminal action is itself 'fortuitous' and not inherently outside the realms of insurability; note also French, n 9; K Abraham, 'Peril and Fortuity in Property and Liability Insurance' (2000) 36 *Tort and Insurance Law Journal* 777.

[107] *Hawley v Luminar Leisure plc* [2006] EWCA Civ 30; [2006] Lloyd's Rep IR 307 (where the tortfeasor was not the assured and the injury was from this point of view 'accidental').

irrespective of the rules of public policy.[108] In each of the cases on deliberately inflicted injury or damage the discussion nevertheless concerns both the meaning of 'accident' and the ambit of the *ex turpi causa* defence. The latter is truly significant only where the policy does not refer to accidents (as is the case with professional indemnity cover) or where the assured's conduct is accidental in the sense that he does not intend to bring about the damage which has occurred but has nevertheless committed an offence in the course of conduct leading to the loss. That, therefore, is the territory exclusively governed by the principles of *ex turpi causa* in claims against insurers.

Other policy terms may control recoverability for torts flowing from particular forms of conduct by the assured. The *ex turpi causa* defence arises in the context of criminal behaviour, but the policy may exclude liability to provide an indemnity where the assured suffers a non-criminal regulatory sanction which imposes an administrative penalty[109] or an obligation to carry out corrective work.[110] The causation rules may also be adjusted so that any claim directly or indirectly arising out of criminal conduct is to be excluded even though it would be permitted at common law.[111]

11.4.3 Claims against motor insurers

By a series of cases and legislative interventions, the law has reached the point where a victim of a driver whose tortious conduct has caused injury is entitled to receive compensation from an insurance fund even though the driver has intentionally set out to cause harm to the victim. *Ex turpi causa* on the part of the assured has thus been all but eliminated. Questions still arise however about the boundaries of this, and discussion of these boundaries illuminates the purpose not only of motor insurance, but also of the liabilities to which it responds.

The origins of this general elimination of *ex turpi causa* are to be found in two cases which predated the introduction of compulsory motor vehicle insurance by the RTA 1930 and which, despite being overtaken by motor insurance legislation, have remained both influential and controversial in other contexts. In the earliest case in which public policy was discussed in a liability insurance claim, *Tinline v White Cross Insurance Assoc Ltd*[112] the assured was convicted of manslaughter by reason of driving his vehicle at an excessive speed. *Tinline* could be approached as a case determining the acceptability of liability insurance in general in policy terms,[113] but it is clear that the particular issue of public policy concerned was related to insurance not of ordinary negligence, but of gross negligence sufficing, in this instance, for a manslaughter conviction. It therefore concerned the limits of liability insurance in relation to

[108] Subject to modification in the case of motor insurance, discussed in 11.4.3.

[109] For example, professional indemnity and D&O liability policies frequently exclude fines for infringement of the FSMA 2000.

[110] Under environmental legislation. Clean-up costs are generally excluded from public liability policies although specific cover may be obtained under EIL policies.

[111] *Marcel Beller Ltd v Hayden* [1978] QB 694.

[112] [1921] 3 KB 327.

[113] AWB Welford, *The Law Relating to Accident Insurance* (London: Butterworths, 2nd edn, 1932), states that the legality of liability insurance was not definitely raised in a court until *Tinline*; but also notes (p 405) that 'by common consent', such insurance was already legitimate.

non-deliberate harm resulting from criminal activity, before the advent of compulsory motor insurance. Bailhache J held that the driver was entitled to an indemnity against a claim for damages, on the basis that what had occurred was an 'accident' within the meaning of the policy in that the outcome had not been intended, and that public policy had no role to play: the policy covered negligence and the degree of that negligence was irrelevant. This amounts to a robust rejection of the role of public policy in liability insurance claims, and although there is no specific mention of the interests of the victim, consideration of those interests clearly motivated the court. Roche J followed *Tinline* in *James v British General Insurance Co Ltd*,[114] the only factual distinction between the cases being that in *James* the driver was drunk at the time of the incident. Roche J, in rejecting the argument that an engagement to indemnify a policyholder against the consequences of a criminal act was invalid, noted that it would have far-reaching consequences not just for motor insurance but also for workmen's compensation insurances where workmen were injured by inadvertent conduct which nevertheless infringed the criminal law as laid down by the Factories Acts.[115] Indeed, a narrow and inflexible exclusion where the defendant's tortious act is also criminal would ensure that by enhancing duties and adding criminal liabilities, Parliament would incidentally undermine the compensation objective developed in partnership with the courts over many years.[116] The contrast with a reading of liability insurance as benefiting the assured, so that it could be invalidated where the assured had acted criminally, is underlined by the Canadian courts' decision a few years later that public policy operated to bar a drunk driver from relying on his liability insurance policy (though the purpose of the claim was to benefit the injured victim).[117] *Tinline* and *James* thus affirmed that negligence, gross or otherwise, which also constituted a criminal offence, did not defeat a claim for indemnity under a liability policy. The policy would cease to apply only where the vehicle was intentionally used as a weapon.

The position at the implementation of the RTA 1930 was, therefore, that only deliberately inflicted injury would bring the rules of public policy into play and defeat a claim for indemnity under a liability policy. The 1930 Act, now codified and extended by the RTA 1988, removed even that limitation. The Court of Appeal in *Hardy v Motor Insurers' Bureau*,[118] a ruling confirmed by the House of Lords in *Gardner v Moore*,[119] held that the legislation required a driver to be insured against any liability caused by or arising out of his use of a motor vehicle, irrespective of the nature of his conduct, so that liability for deliberately inflicted injuries must be covered by a policy. These rulings raised the further question of whether insurers are required to make payment where the assured acted deliberately: legal policy clearly binds the assured for the benefit of potential victims, but does it have an impact on the insurer? The question relates to the characterization of third-party insurance: is it primarily to be seen as a policy of indemnity between two

[114] [1927] 2 KB 311; [1927] All ER Rep 442.

[115] The House of Lords directly considered issues of this sort in *NCB v England*, n 31. *James* shows an earlier realization of these issues.

[116] Chapter 9 traces the evolution of workmen's compensation and employers' liability.

[117] *Home Insurance Co v Lindal* [1934] SCR 33. The case is no longer of significance in Canada, as Knutsen, n 106, explains.

[118] [1964] 2 QB 745.

[119] [1984] AC 548.

parties, or as a source of compensation required (in this instance) and intended to complete the law's policy where liabilities are imposed? The majority of the Court of Appeal in *Charlton v Fisher*[120] was of the view, *obiter*,[121] that the duty of the insurers under the RTA 1988, s 151 to satisfy a judgment obtained by a victim against the assured overrode the public policy restriction on recoverability by the assured himself and indeed any policy terms limiting coverage to 'accidents': whatever that term might mean in the general law, in motor insurance it is arguably to be construed as referring to 'any incident involving the insured's car'[122] or to 'a set of facts where the insured's liability arises from his own deliberate criminal act'.[123] The majority opinion in *Charlton* was regarded as correct and applied by Tugendhat J in *Bristol Alliance Ltd Partnership v Williams*,[124] a case of property damage pursued by a subrogated first-party property insurer. The assured had caused property damage while attempting to commit suicide by driving his car into a wall. Tugendhat J's decision was reversed on appeal,[125] but only on the grounds that the policy excluded deliberate acts and there was nothing in the 1988 Act which precluded the use of exclusions of that type: no issue of turpitude arose on that reasoning.

Further reference should also be made to the position of the victims of uninsured drivers. As discussed in Chapter 9, the MIB has since 1946 provided compensation to the victim of a driver who did not possess insurance for a liability required to be covered by insurance under the road traffic legislation. In both *Hardy* and *Gardner* the driver committed an act designed to cause harm but was uninsured, and in *Hardy*, confirmed by *Gardner*, it was held that successive MIB Uninsured Drivers Agreements required the MIB to provide compensation on the grounds that the liability incurred was one which was to be insured under the road traffic legislation. The victims of uninsured drivers are thus able to recover from the MIB even though the driver himself would not, had he been insured, have been able to claim.

What is paramount, therefore, is the interest of the injured party, which has trumped the law on *ex turpi causa* on the part of tortfeasors and on the definition of 'accident'. Formally this provides guilty parties with an indemnity, but in reality it does not benefit these parties as the money is destined to the tort victim. The cost is borne by policyholders generally. In a third-party liability regime, better risks in principle share a smaller share of this cost (though those who drive without insurance of course bear none). As Laws LJ said in *Charlton v Fisher*:[126]

> It will be obvious that there are two public policies involved here. The first is the broad principle of the common law that no man may rely on his own wrong to gain advantage or benefit against another. That is behind the first proposition. The second

[120] [2001] EWCA Civ 112; [2002] QB 578, Kennedy and Laws LJJ and Rix LJ expressing doubts but not disagreeing.

[121] The incident occurred on private land, so the 1988 Act was inapplicable, and the case turned on the meaning of the policy itself.

[122] Kennedy LJ at [23].

[123] Laws LJ at [35]. Even Rix LJ, who disagreed with his brethren that policy terms were overridden by s 151, felt that 'a broad definition of non-accidental loss or injury in terms of reckless conduct . . . cannot be too readily applied in the context of motor insurance' (at [60]).

[124] [2011] EWHC 1657 (QB); [2012] Lloyd's Rep IR 285.

[125] *EUI Ltd v Bristol Alliance Partnership Ltd* [2012] EWCA Civ 1267; [2012] All ER (D) 120 (Oct).

[126] [2001] EWCA Civ 112; [2002] QB 578, [33].

is the principle of statute, that innocent third parties should be protected so far as money can do it from the harm—sometimes fatal—that may be inflicted by careless, dangerous and criminal drivers on the public roads: a protection not sufficiently given by the private law of insurance. That is behind the second proposition. The tension between the two arising where the driver's conduct is criminal is resolved by the rule (derived from *Hardy v MIB*, confirmed in *Gardner's* case) that a policy whose words on their face cover liability for death, personal injury or damage to property occasioned by the use of a vehicle on a road is treated—so as to give effect to the second proposition—as still doing so even where the liability arises on the facts from the driver's own criminal act; although in that case—so as to give effect to the first proposition—the insured driver himself cannot take advantage of the policy.

These comments deserve to be emphasized. They show that in the context of compulsory motor insurance, the role of insurance has made an important transition. It exists, at the expense of all drivers, to protect potential claimants, rather than solely to protect assured parties. Indeed in a range of instances where the tortfeasor does not deserve indemnity, or has not secured insurance despite an obligation to do so, the insurance fund will still respond.

This, however, is not the end of the story. One remaining question concerns the limits of the triumph of the social goal of compensation over contractual terms and principles of responsibility within motor insurance itself. A second is how far motor insurance is exceptional, and how far elements of this approach to insurance may exist more generally. If motor cases are truly exceptional, this has lessons for the general approach to the law of tort, for the simple reason that motor cases have provided some tort lawyers with their paradigm of the tort of negligence, as explored in Chapter 9. But more generally, motor cases continue to suggest questions of more general application surrounding the link between insurance and liabilities.

In relation to the first question, two themes already debated—the *de facto* exclusion of many serious intentional wrongs from tort through lack of insurance cover, and the dominance of a compensatory goal in relation to road traffic liabilities and their insurance—are brought together by the recent (perhaps continuing) case of *AXN v Worboys and Inceptum Insurance Co Ltd*.[127] Here, victims of serious sexual assaults perpetrated by a taxi driver, who was convicted of offences relating to the attacks, sought damages from his motor insurers. The assured's convictions indicate the commission of torts including false imprisonment and battery. The claim against insurers raised the question of how wide the purpose of compulsory insurance in this context should be taken to be. While the previously discussed cases related to harm done by the assured's driving of a vehicle, even when using it to inflict deliberate harm, this case did not. On a trial of preliminary issues, the claims failed on a number of grounds. Particularly important among these, for present purposes, were that, first, the harm suffered did not 'arise out of the use of [the] vehicle on a road or other public place'. This was approached as an essentially causal question, with the assistance of a number of Commonwealth cases showing that deliberate action would not necessarily

[127] [2012] EWHC 1730 (QB).

break the chain of causation, but with the conclusion that the purposes of the assured did have that effect here. Second, the RTA 1988, s 145(3)(a), did not require insurance in relation to these acts to be covered by a policy of insurance. Silber J distinguished between the policy of the law as described in *Charlton v Fisher*—to protect innocent third parties from the consequences of harm inflicted by 'careless, dangerous and criminal drivers on the public roads'—and the deliberate acts of poisoning and sexual assault perpetrated in this case. Also significant are concessions on the part of claimants and insurers respectively, that while claims for false imprisonment do not amount to claims for 'personal injury' (so that they lie outside the reach of the legislation), claims for poisoning and sexual assault do fall within this definition.[128]

The effect of the decision is to identify limits to the purposes for which the law seeks to ensure that insurance funds are available. These limits are not defined in terms of the seriousness of harm or the need for compensation, nor even according to the degree of culpability of the assured. Rather, the limits of the 'social contract' represented by compulsory third-party motor insurance are connected with the particular risks of harm arising from driving, whether that driving is negligent or intentional. This is the obverse of the more widely noted point, that *only* tortious harms are included within the distributive net: here, we see that not all tortious harms are within that net. At the same time, the case underlines that the law's goal in this context is distributive. Here we can observe a divergence between the reparative and the risk-spreading accounts of liability. Tort and insurance together operate to cover a wide, but not infinite, set of risks in this context. Some of the most heinous wrongs will escape reparation precisely because they are not within the risks that are spread by the law of tort and insurance. Due to statutory amendment of the rules of public policy, the risks that are spread will include criminal and intentional acts by drivers. If it were otherwise then criminal penalties designed to secure safety, and compensation for victims, would be in tension, and the increasing use of criminal penalties would reduce the availability of compensation to the injured.[129] The aim of the compulsory insurance regime, supported by the MIB scheme, is demonstrably not however to secure reparation for the most serious wrongs, as some of these are outside its distributive reach.

Still further questions for tort law arise when it is considered that modest compensation was awarded to the claimants as part of the criminal process. On this occasion, this was made possible because forfeiture orders had been made in relation to the taxi itself and of a sum of money, which Worboys had used to persuade his victims that he had a casino win to celebrate, and which was therefore part of the commission of the offences.[130] This resulted in the perpetrator's own assets being transferred to his

[128] n 127. The independent claim for poisoning may have been framed with the 'personal injury' criterion in mind.

[129] This is indeed the point made in *NCB v England*, n 31, long before the days of compulsory employers' liability insurance.

[130] The power to seize property and assets used to facilitate commission of an offence will have been exercised under the Powers of Criminal Courts (Sentencing) Act 2000, s 143. The same statute (ss 130–2) makes powers for compensation orders to victims—to come from the defendant's own pocket, even if that defendant is in receipt of state benefits, but dependent on the defendant's means. It appears however to be relatively unusual for seizure of assets and compensation to be linked in this way. Silbey J did not explore this issue at length in his judgment.

victims. The question for tort lawyers is whether one of the ostensible functions of tort liability—to ensure defendants make good the harms resulting from their wrongs—is here more literally pursued, though with no pretence at detailed assessment of full compensation, by the criminal courts, particularly in those circumstances where the defendant's actions were too culpable to be thought appropriately subject to distribution through insurance.[131]

11.4.4 Other liability insurance claims

Our second remaining question concerns the applicability of the compensatory objective outside the RTAs. We have already suggested that it is dangerous to see the road traffic context as typical in any sense. The divergence between the treatment of motor claims and claims under other forms of liability insurance is marked, but the issues cannot realistically be said to be entirely separate.[132] In the first decision on the operation of public policy in a non-motor liability policy, *Haseldine v Hosken* in 1933,[133] the assured solicitor sought indemnity from his liability insurers for a settlement. The Court of Appeal, dismissing the claim, held that the assured's loss had arisen out of a contract illegal by reason of champerty and maintenance, and that the assured had knowingly committed the alleged offences; as a solicitor it was not open to him to assert that he was unaware that the conduct was illegal. The case was thus one which amounted to the wilful or intentional conduct (though not, in this contractual context, harm) recognized in *Tinline*[134] and *James*[135] as justifying a refusal of indemnity on public policy grounds. Scrutton LJ chose not to comment on the correctness of *Tinline* and *James*, noting only that the law of motor insurance was of some complexity. Greer LJ felt that *Haseldine*[136] was indistinguishable from the earlier cases, but conceded that it might be desirable to draw a distinction between the present case and one of compulsory insurance of an unintentional breach of the law (criminality without intent) which led to an accident. Slesser LJ dismissed the claim on the different grounds that there was no 'neglect, error or omission' within the terms of the policy. It may be that third-party considerations were not to the fore in this case: the Court of Appeal was concerned to stamp out champertous agreements, and it would appear that the third-party claimant had been paid by the assured.

The distinction which emerges from the cases is, therefore, between deliberate criminal acts which give rise to unintended losses and deliberate criminal acts which are designed to, or inevitably will, cause those losses or—in a contractual context—where the

[131] Notably this is the very opposite of the improved compensation scheme for criminal injuries proposed by John Fleming. This would represent a more socialized response to the distribution of a common threat, namely harm from the criminal acts of others, than could realistically be achieved through liability insurance: J Fleming, 'Insurance for the Criminal' (1971) 34 Mod L Rev 176. The contrast is consistent with a more punitive inclination. Also M Dyson, 'Connecting Tort and Crime: Comparative Legal History in England and Spain since 1850' [2009] *Cambridge Yearbook of European Legal Studies*, 247.

[132] For example M Clarke, 'The Proximate Cause in English Law' (1981) 40 CLJ 284, 305, arguing that the recognized policy of the RTAs should not be seen as the *only* 'countervailing public policy' standing against the indemnity of an assured who has acted with intent.

[133] [1933] 1 KB 822; [1933] All ER Rep 1. [134] n 112. [135] n 114. [136] n 133.

illegality is intended. It will be appreciated that the test reflects the meaning of the word 'accident' as it is used in insurance policies. However, exactly when loss is the inevitable consequence of a criminal act is a complex question, as exemplified by the much-analysed decision of the Court of Appeal in *Gray v Barr*.[137] The defendant, whose wife had been involved in an affair with the claimant's husband, went to the claimant's house armed with a shotgun, convinced that his wife was there.[138] On his account, he fired a shot to frighten the claimant's husband, and a struggle ensued in which the claimant's husband was killed when the defendant's shotgun went off again. The defendant was prosecuted, and was acquitted of both murder and manslaughter. The jury's decision, encouraged by a very sympathetic judge's direction, was described by Lord Denning MR, it would seem quite fairly, as 'merciful'. This forms the background to the discussion in the civil claim since, importantly for our purposes, the civil court was less willing to be forgiving, and in this instance did not accept that the acquittal by the criminal court was justified as a matter of law.[139]

Judgment was given against the defendant in the tort of negligence, but his liability insurers who were joined to the proceedings asserted that they were entitled to rely upon the parallel defences of *ex turpi causa* and the absence of an 'accident' within the meaning of the policy. At first instance[140] Geoffrey Lane J held that the death was an 'accident' in the sense that it had not been intended, but that an accident of that type was not intended to be covered by the policy. Further, the claim was barred by public policy. In his view the death was the outcome of an unlawful assault involving a threat of violence, a threat which the defendant must have realized was likely to result in injury. Denying recovery only where there was an intent to kill, was thought by the judge to be too narrow, and the troublesome cases of *Tinline* and *James* were held to turn on the grounds 'that the act to be indemnified . . . was one intended by the law that people should insure against'.[141] The Court of Appeal affirmed the judgment of Geoffrey Lane J, although reasoning in different ways. Lord Denning MR focused on causation, and held that the proximate cause of death was not the accidental firing of the shotgun but the deliberate act of the defendant in going to the deceased's house carrying a loaded shotgun in order to frighten the deceased—a deliberate act of assault. Once the cause of death was found to be a deliberate act, it inevitably followed that the claim would be defeated both because there was no accident and because of *ex turpi causa*. The motor manslaughter cases were distinguished by Lord Denning on the grounds that the deaths of the victims were not 'wilful and culpable'. Phillimore LJ delivered a judgment to the same effect. Salmon LJ agreed with Geoffrey Lane J that an unintended death was an accident, but of a type not intended to be covered by the policy, in that the term 'accident' was subject to an implied exception to the effect 'that the policy does not apply to injuries caused by an accident occurring in the course of

[137] [1971] 2 Lloyd's Rep 70.

[138] In fact, she was not. Having spent the evening with her husband and promised to break off her affair with Mr Gray, she had taken an overdose and was unconscious in a field.

[139] This is, in a sense, the reverse of the narrow rule: it appears the civil law is not afraid of inconsistency with the verdict of a criminal court which has been overly lenient.

[140] [1971] 2 QB 554.

[141] Note though that both cases predate the advent of compulsory insurance in 1930.

threatening unlawful violence with a loaded gun.' Salmon LJ found in the alternative that 'public policy undoubtedly requires that no one who threatens unlawful violence with a loaded gun should be allowed to enforce a claim for indemnity against any liability he may incur as a result of having so acted', and that the motor cases involved accidents and were '*sui generis*' in terms of public policy.

It is far from obvious just what the Court of Appeal in *Gray v Barr* was trying to achieve by this tortuous reasoning which hardly stands scrutiny.[142] Despite the analysis of Lord Denning and Phillimore LJ, it is difficult to see how the cause of death could have been anything but the fatal shot: what went before could not constitute a proximate cause, because by itself it could not give rise to loss but could only set the scene. In insurance law, for an anterior event to be the proximate cause, it must of itself be sufficient to have given rise to a claim, allowing any later event to be disregarded unless it changed the nature of the loss by breaking the chain of causation. A true example is the recent decision in *Sealion Shipping Ltd v Valiant Insurance Company*,[143] where a vessel suffered a mechanical breakdown, followed by two more such breakdowns. It was held there was only one cause of loss, the first breakdown, and that the others simply followed on from the first event. Had the assured in *Gray* fired a shot with an intent to wound, leading to a struggle in which the fatal shot was fired, the reasoning in *Gray* would perhaps have made sense. But, looked at in ordinary causation terms, *Gray* is indistinguishable from the motor manslaughter decisions, in that in each of them the assured deliberately committed a criminal offence which of itself did not give rise to a cause of action at the outset but subsequently had the unintended consequence of causing the death of another. If that is right, then there has been a policy decision that motor cases are to be distinguished from others. In *Gray* itself the defendant had been acquitted and faced no punishment from the criminal law. By second-guessing the criminal trial and asserting that the defendant had in fact been guilty of an offence,[144] the Court of Appeal thought that it was sending a message to those who walked round with loaded shotguns that they would have no source of indemnification. But of course, except to the extent that the defendant had resources of his own, the only loser would have been the claimant, who had been deprived of her husband and then, at the hands of the Court of Appeal, deprived of a compensation fund in the form of the defendant's liability insurance.[145] Yet the claimant here was very far from the 'moral monsters' whose liability insurance policies Tom Baker has discussed in relation to the tort-crime boundary as a potential way of securing both compensation and, through the insurer's potential right of indemnity, a much greater chance that a proportion of the sums required will come from the wrongdoer

[142] Fleming, n 131; J Shand, 'Unblinkering the Unruly Horse' [1972] CLJ 144.

[143] [2012] EWCA Civ 1625. See also *McCarthy v St Paul International Insurance Co Ltd* (2007) 14 ANZ Ins Cas 61–725.

[144] In *DPP v Newbury* [1977] AC 500 the House of Lords disapproved only of a potential implication from Lord Denning's words, that a state of mind falling short of that of the claimant in this case would never suffice for an offence of manslaughter.

[145] There may of course have been life insurance in existence, but that could not have been a legitimate inquiry for the court both because no private risk-allocation arrangements between the parties could have been involved in a case such as this, and also because subrogation rights do not apply to life policies so that recoveries may be accumulated.

personally.[146] Does civil law here embody a form of punitiveness in relation to the insurance contract, irrespective of its consequences, which generally has no place in the law of liability itself?[147]

Gray v Barr was nevertheless followed by a majority of the Supreme Court of Canada in *Co-operative Fire & Casualty Co v Saindon*,[148] where the weapon was a lawn mower, raised to threaten the victim but after a struggle causing her serious injury. The Court applied the same causation test, and concluded that raising the lawn mower was an intentional act and it sufficed that the subsequent injury was a foreseeable consequence of that act.[149] Shortly beforehand, the same Court had decided in *Canadian Indemnity Co v Walkem Machinery & Equipment Ltd*[150] that the delivery of a barge and crane in a dangerous state of disrepair, leading to the collapse of the crane, was an 'accident' because there had been no intention to bring about the loss. This ruling is consistent with the motor manslaughter cases,[151] but it seems strange that the Supreme Court of Canada should allow a deep-pocketed major corporation to recover under its liability policy but immediately afterwards, on more or less indistinguishable facts, deny indemnity to a householder and thus, in all probability, to the householder's victim.

11.4.5 The assured as malefactor: concluding thoughts

It is common ground in all of the cases that an assured who deliberately and intentionally inflicts loss upon a third party has no claim against his liability insurers, either because there is no accident or because he is denied recovery on public policy grounds. That position has—with a helping hand from the courts in cases such as *Charlton v Fisher*—been reversed by the RTA 1988 insofar as the loss falls within the compulsory insurance regime, so that there is recovery in virtually all circumstances.[152]

The more difficult policy question is whether claims under liability policies should be denied where the assured has acted in a criminal fashion and thereby brought about the harm, given that the ultimate financial loser is the victim and not the assured. The courts have plainly taken a view on this. The early motor manslaughter cases

[146] Baker, n 22, unflinchingly debates the possibility that murderers' insurance policies might respond to claims by their victims, with a right on the part of the insurer to recover from the assured (to the extent possible), as a means of furthering the policy of the law in both these respects. Note the element of payment from the perpetrator's own assets in *AXN v Worboys*, n 127.

[147] Fleming, n 131, quotes the words of Starke J in *Jenkins v Smith* [1969] VR 267, 276: 'moral indignation must not be mistaken for public policy'.

[148] [1976] 1 SCR 735. *Gray v Barr* (n 42) was also followed at first instance in Australia's Northern Territory in *S & Y Investments (No 2) Pty Ltd v Commercial Union Assurance Co of Australia Ltd* (1986) 82 FLR 130, but the decision was reversed on appeal, (1986) 44 NTR 14, on the grounds that the act of waving a gun by an employee had not been authorized by the employer assured. Thus, from the employer's point of view there was an accident and the rules of public policy did not debar a claim.

[149] Note also the discussion by Knutsen, n 106, in terms of an 'objective' approach to the assured's state of mind in this case, in contrast to various more subjective possibilities.

[150] [1976] 1 SCR 309.

[151] *Mutual of Omaha v Stats* [1978] 2 SCR 1153, in which the Supreme Court of Canada by a majority followed the English approach in holding that motor manslaughter by an intoxicated driver was an 'accident'.

[152] The exception being property damage which is paid for by a first-party insurer, who is then precluded by the MIB Uninsured Drivers Agreement from pursuing subrogation proceedings against the MIB: *EUI Ltd v Bristol Alliance Partnership Ltd*, n 125.

demanded payment, and the subsequent development of the compulsory insurance regime has confirmed that this is the case within the limits of that regime. The claimants in *AXN v Worboys*[153] tested the limits of this regime, and thereby illustrated the dependence of reparation in tort on the availability of an insurance response. By contrast, in all other cases, there is to be no indemnity, apparently because, where the assured has committed a criminal offence leading to foreseeable injury, the proximate cause of the injury is the preparatory offence and not the unintended injury itself. This reasoning, we submit, is a distortion of the law of causation, but that does not remove the question of whether public policy should intervene. Salmon LJ in *Gray v Barr* felt that the use of firearms in a threatening fashion was more antisocial than reckless driving, although this is a purely subjective view which does not necessarily make good sense: each act is liable to cause injury, and in practice the latter is far more significant in terms of death and personal injury than the former.[154] Arguments based on deterrence are also weak: the assured in *Gray v Barr*, just like the assured in *Co-operative Fire & Casualty Co v Saindon*, acted on the spur of the moment and in a state of intense anger, and potential refusal of indemnity under liability cover would not have been to the forefront of their minds. Indeed, certain cases where indemnity has been ordered might be thought better instances for the operation of deterrence (particularly *Canadian Indemnity Co v Walkem Machinery & Equipment Ltd*).

While the impact on the assured is capable of being disproportionate, the real loser in these cases is the innocent victim. The anomaly from the victim's point of view, as we commented earlier, is that the more heinous the assured's act, the less likelihood there is of receiving compensation for it.[155] However, from the insurers' point of view, such claims are outside the scope of cover and (other than in the case of motor insurance where insurers are required to pay for uninsured losses) the premium has been assessed on that basis. The question is whether the law wishes to utilize liability insurance to ensure that the victim is compensated and whether the market is adapted to this. One compromise suggestion is that the insurers should be required to pay despite an *ex turpi causa* defence, but that the insurers should have a right of indemnity from the assured,[156] a solution adopted under the RTA 1988 where insurers are required to pay a claim for which they are not liable under the terms of the policy. The effect is to cast the risk of the assured's insolvency on to the insurers rather than the victim.[157] Other possible approaches would be to operate the principle of the insurers' strict liability in the case of any compulsory policy, or possibly in personal injury cases only, or possibly only where the victim does not have first-party insurance, although such a move would further weaken the argument that personal injury insurance is not to be seen as an indemnity.

[153] n 127.

[154] Fleming, n 131, noting the relative statistics, argues however that death by misuse of firearms is common enough to merit a distributive response.

[155] S Gilles, 'The Judgment Proof Society' (2006) 63 *Wm & Mary Law Rev* 603, provides a general discussion.

[156] Fleming, n 131, 178–9; Baker, n 22.

[157] A similar move to cast the risk of insolvency on to insurers is to be seen at work in *Fairchild v Glenhaven* [2002] UKHL 22; [2002] 3 All ER 305, though here the risk is of insurer insolvency as much as of insolvency of assureds (Chapter 12).

One straw in the wind is the judgment of Mance J in *Total Graphics Ltd v AGF Insurance Ltd*,[158] which involved a successful claim by TGL against insurance brokers, Buntingford, for failing to place cover, followed by an attempt by TGL to recover the damages awarded from Buntingford's professional indemnity insurers under the Third Parties (Rights against Insurers) Act 1930 in the light of Buntingford's insolvency. The claim was rejected because the liability policy did not cover the loss which had occurred, but Mance J commented on the insurers' alternative public policy defence:

> The effect of the 1930 Act is to entitle an innocent third party, TGL, to indemnity in respect of Buntingford's liability to it so far as such liability falls within the scope of Buntingford's professional indemnity insurance. Public policy creates a personal disability to recover. There is no reason why TGL should be affected by any defence of public policy, if any, that would have affected Buntingford.

This goes to the root of the question, by reiterating the public policy basis of *ex turpi causa*. If it is right, then *ex turpi causa* alone would no longer avail liability insurers when the claim against them is made by the victim. However, the point has not been picked up in any more recent case, and it might be thought to be inconsistent with the principle of the 1930 Act that there is a straightforward transfer of rights from assured to third party, with the latter being in no better position than the former. Working against this, and in favour of the approach of Mance J, is a sense that a liability insurance policy exists for the protection of claimants independently of the protection of an assured, and that the rule of public policy known as *ex turpi causa* is a personal disability of the malefactor, not designed to operate for the benefit of defendants. The question arises again: how far should the contract of liability insurance be read as 'personal'; how far is it to be read in the light of the legal policy behind the liabilities that it covers?

11.5 Conclusions

Study of the operation and limits of *ex turpi causa* in relation to liability insurance raises questions both about the purposes of the particular forms of liability involved, and about the purpose of applicable insurance arrangements. We have drawn a number of conclusions to such questions here, but have also highlighted a series of neglected issues and connections for future consideration.

First, we have argued that refusal to look behind criminal liability in a blanket application of the 'narrow rule' is of dubious value and may even undermine the law's purposes in imposing liability. Second, and beyond this, we have illustrated the way in which moral judgments about illegal activity by claimants or assured parties have been subject to proportionality and restraint in the law of tort and contract generally but, perhaps surprisingly, are on occasion given more unbridled effect in relation to insurance cover. Lack of consistency between insurance and the liabilities to which it responds can have unfortunate effects but recognition of this is sometimes resisted, perhaps on the basis that insurance is merely a matter of agreement. Fault-based

[158] [1997] 1 Lloyd's Rep 599.

constraints or punitive thinking appear in sometimes unexpected contexts. Third, we have argued that these issues have inevitable, and little-noticed, effects on the entire shape of tort law itself.

Ultimately, therefore, the questions in this chapter offer distinct reasons for focusing on the purpose and the implications of insurance, and most particularly of liability insurance. As we have seen, there is some broad theoretical significance to the question whether, and to what extent, liability insurance can be defined as a personal matter between defendant and insurer. We visited some dimensions of this question in Chapters 5, 7, and 8, but here the question is raised afresh in a different context. In road traffic cases above all, the law has jumped a gap, and insurance is plainly designed, regulated, and supplemented in order to provide a fund from which tort claimants may be compensated. The purpose of insurance is social and distributive, despite the private law forms employed. Limits to this distributive purpose do exist, but, if anything, these serve to underline the transformation that has been achieved in these allegedly 'paradigm' or 'conventional' cases. Refusal of cover in the most heinous cases of wrongdoing establishes the limits of the distributive response, but also thereby sets limits to tort recovery itself. It is the contrast between these rare cases, which may be rare partly because of the influence of insurance on patterns of litigation, and the usual run of claims, which deserves our attention. Beyond these road traffic claims however, it appears that courts have struggled to define the nature of liability insurance in terms of either a personal or a compensatory purpose.

In short, therefore, a tension between reparative and compensatory goals continues, but their separation into distinct boxes is not possible. Insurance issues are suffused with responsibility judgments, sometimes less balanced than those to be found in the law of obligations. Such issues also deeply affect the reparative function of private law. These tensions will be found hidden away from the usual doctrinal bright lights, partly because only rare cases test the boundaries and reveal the nature of the underlying legal response. In particular, the triumph of compensatory and distributive goals in road traffic cases, and the boundaries that are drawn to the operation of these goals, suggest that the proposed separation of tort and insurance should not go untested given the complexity of the interaction, in practice, between them.

12

The Asbestos Litigation

12.1 The Issues

12.1.1 Our focus: insurance and liabilities

The decision of the Supreme Court in *Durham v BAI (Run off) Ltd* (the *Trigger Litigation*, referred to here as *Trigger*)[1] was centrally concerned with liability insurance policies and their construction. But much more than this, the majority decision decisively interpreted the nature of the liability principles applied in relation to the disease of mesothelioma,[2] and in the process shed considerable light on the relationship between tort liabilities and insurance with which we have been concerned in a number of chapters of this book. The decision should, in principle, allow the conclusion—so far as tort liability is concerned—of an episode in which the courts first created an exceptional approach to causation (*Fairchild v Glenhaven Funeral Services Ltd*[3]) in order to assist claimants who would otherwise founder on a 'rock of uncertainty' (the *Fairchild* exception); then appeared to undermine that exception by interpreting it in a fashion which would redefine the very nature of the liabilities concerned (*Barker v Corus*[4]). This was done in the name of coherence and fairness, but its effect was incoherence and, we suggest, unfairness.[5] These problems of incoherence and unfairness are brought into sharp focus once the distributive consequences, relating to insurance, are taken into account. Only when the Supreme Court had to decide, in *Trigger*, whether employers' liability insurance policies would respond to the liabilities incurred did it become completely obvious what adverse impacts would flow from acceptance of a 'principled' interpretation of *Barker*.

Lord Phillips brought the point to the surface, but we suggest that he drew the wrong conclusions from it. Dissenting, Lord Phillips suggested that the law as set out in *Barker*

[1] [2012] UKSC 14; [2012] 1 WLR 867.

[2] The reasons for special treatment are explained in subsequent paragraphs.

[3] [2002] UKHL 22; [2003] 1 AC 32 (*Fairchild*), a case involving multiple employers all in breach of duty. Lord Bingham referred to the 'rock of uncertainty' in this case, at [7]. Claims would founder on the rock if the court did not adopt an exceptional approach. In later cases, the 'rock of uncertainty' has become the solid foundation for *Fairchild* claims, as without it there is no justification for the exceptional approach to causation: this is most evident in the 'single-employer' case of *Sienkiewicz v Greif (UK) Ltd* [2011] UKSC 10; [2011] 2 AC 229 (*Sienkiewicz*), in which some members of the Supreme Court expressed strong reservations about the position arrived at in *Fairchild*.

[4] [2006] UKHL 20; [2006] 2 AC 572 (*Barker*), sometimes referred to as a 'new tort' theory, since negligence is based on damage and the liability in *Barker* would rest not on damage but on risk. Competing interpretations are discussed in 12.2 and 12.3.

[5] 12.3 deals with the incoherence caused by redefinition of the liabilities as liabilities for risk not injury (where injury is the nature of the claim); 12.3 and 12.4 deal with the unfairness caused when distributive gaps are shifted from the insurance market to claimants. The Compensation Act 2006, s 3, reversed the effect of *Barker* in order to deal with fairness issues; but the interpretive impact of the decision continued until *Trigger*.

should not be redefined (as he saw it) 'with the object of enabling claims to be brought under the employers' liability policies'.[6] The goal of *Fairchild* and *Barker*, in his view, had been to 'ensure that those who had breached the duties that they owed to their employees did not escape liability because of scientific uncertainty'.[7] Our argument is that this would have been a vacuous goal for a special rule if it simultaneously negated the existing insurance cover, not least where (as in *Fairchild*) the defendants were plainly insurers. We therefore do not agree that the liability question and the compensation question are separable justifications for *Fairchild*. It follows that we also do not agree with Lord Phillips that defining the rule as set out in *Barker* to enable insurers to be liable would be to act for 'reasons of policy', and should be a matter for 'Parliament not the courts'.[8] Leaving aside the question of how Parliament could conceivably bring about the required interpretive change,[9] we seek to show in this chapter that the concerns expressed by Lord Phillips are, with great respect, misplaced.

We explain our reasons for these views in the course of the chapter. But it will be apparent that the issues go to the heart of several of the themes of this book. Most notably, *Trigger* underlines that while insurance does not uniquely influence the content of legal principles, neither is it safe to treat insurance factors as irrelevant, most particularly when considering questions of 'fairness'. Further, as the majority judgments of Lords Mance and Clarke made clear, the purpose of liability insurance is to respond to liabilities: insurance is matched to risks. It is inappropriate for the common law to redefine liabilities so that they are not susceptible to being insured by policies already in place, and then to call the result principled. Nor, we suggest, is there any compelling reason why courts should choose to redefine the liabilities in the first place, if this is the result.

12.1.2 Mesothelioma: the special issues

The cases discussed here all concern the dreadful disease of mesothelioma. Here we briefly address those features of mesothelioma which have created a challenge for the law.

Much is still to be learned about the aetiology of the disease. However, the typical pattern for the development of mesothelioma is as follows. Exposure to asbestos leads to asbestos fibres being lodged in the lungs; some thirty-five years after exposure, the fibres take hold, producing a tumour with its own blood supply which causes damage to the lungs; some five years after that, there is manifestation of the disease; and within a matter of months, inevitable fatality. Fortunately, only about 3 per cent of persons exposed will develop the disease. It remains unclear whether a single exposure can cause the disease or whether the disease develops as the result of cumulative exposures,

[6] n 1, [134]. [7] n 1, [135]. [8] n 1, [137].

[9] Parliament had done all it could to ensure compensation of claimants through the Compensation Act 2006, s 3, explained in the following paragraphs. The idea of legislating for an 'interpretation' is problematic. Note that Lord Phillips was influenced by Jonathan Morgan's analysis, 'Causation, Politics and the Law: The English—and Scottish—Asbestos Saga', in R Goldberg (ed), *Perspectives on Causation* (Oxford: Hart Publishing, 2011), which he took to mean that the effect of *Barker* was 'irrevocable' despite legislation (Morgan, for his part, appears to have argued that it was 'too late to go back' on *Fairchild* (at 90), rather than on the interpretation of *Fairchild* arrived at in *Barker*).

although it is obvious that the more exposures there are, the greater the risk of disease becomes. There are very few cases of mesothelioma which are not related to asbestos exposure. It is crucial to an understanding of the legal issues to appreciate that mere exposure is not of itself injury, and the thickening of the pleural membrane which may or may not be a precursor of disease similarly is not injury.[10]

In the next section, we begin our discussion with the approach of the courts to tort principles, and we follow with the insurance litigation which gave practical effect to those principles. But our analysis does not stop there. The reversal of *Barker v Corus*[11] by the Compensation Act 2006 means that each employer faces joint and several liability for any damages claim, thereby removing the complexities of apportionment by employees in their tort claims, and thus the need for tort scholars to speculate upon how allocation would have been effected but for legislative intervention. However, those complexities have not been eliminated, merely shifted to a second-tier range of disputes between the insurers of employers, and onwards to a third tier of disputes between those insurers and their reinsurers. This chapter concludes with a discussion of the complexities of those 'hidden' disputes.

12.2 Establishing Liability in Tort

The decisions in *Fairchild*, *Barker*, and *Sienkiewicz* have been widely analysed.[12] Our core focus, as already explained, is on the implications of *Trigger*; but we must set out the essential features of the preceding tort litigation. In *Fairchild*, the House of Lords responded to a typical scenario in which a person has been exposed to asbestos over a period of years by successive employers. Assuming that each exposure is a breach of the duty of care,[13] and that damage is a given, attention focuses purely on causation. The common law rule of causation, the 'but for' test, requires the conduct of a tortfeasor to be looked at in isolation, the question being: what would the claimant's position have been but for the conduct of the tortfeasor? Where there is a sole tortfeasor and no relevant external cause of injury, the process is relatively straightforward, and an assessment may be made of the tortfeasor's intervention. However, the addition of further tortfeasors, or potential external causes, creates complexity in that it may be that it is impossible to determine the impact of any one breach of duty, or it may be that each breach of duty has made no difference to the claimant because of the existence of the other torts or causes. It would be curious for the law to say that each tortfeasor may

[10] *Rothwell v Chemical & Insulating Co Ltd* [2007] UKHL 39; [2007] 4 All ER 1047, although that position has been reversed by legislation in Scotland and Ireland. The Supreme Court in *AXA General Insurance Ltd v HM Advocate* [2011] UKSC 46; [2011] 3 WLR 871 rejected a challenge by insurers to the validity of the damages (Asbestos-related Conditions) (Scotland) Act 2009.

[11] [2006] UKHL 20; [2006] 2 WLR 1027.

[12] For example T Weir, 'Making it More Likely v Making it Happen' [2002] CLJ 519; S Steel, 'Causation in English Law: Still Wrong After All These Years' (2012) 31 UQLJ 243.

[13] It follows from our emphasis on real breaches of duty that we accept the principle in *Williams v University of Birmingham* [2011] EWCA Civ 1242; [2011] All ER (D) 25 (Nov), namely that no distinctive approach to proof of duty applies to *Fairchild* liability.

rely upon the acts of the other to escape liability,[14] a solution which the law has rejected in other contexts.[15] That possibility was removed in *Fairchild*, albeit only in the context of mesothelioma. Although their Lordships expressed themselves in different ways, sometimes within the same judgment, the outcome of *Fairchild* was that proof of 'but for' causation was to be set aside in the specific case of mesothelioma, because scientific knowledge was not able to pinpoint the triggering exposure. 'But for' was replaced by the principle that each exposure must amount to a material contribution to the risk of injury, and that was enough to impose liability on every person whose breach of duty had resulted in exposure—or perhaps, sufficient exposure.

Fairchild was generally assumed to have produced a joint and several liability principle, with the consequence that a victim could sue any one of the tortfeasors for the full amount of his loss. That is the basis on which insurers made their arrangements for contribution.[16] That assumption was successfully challenged however in *Barker*, where the House of Lords by a majority concluded that liability was several and not joint. Every tortfeasor was thus responsible to the extent to which its own conduct materially contributed to the risk of injury. The *Barker* ruling created a number of immediate problems: the means of allocation was not resolved, potentially giving rise to disputes about whether proportionate liability should follow time on risk or whether it should be varied to take account of periods of particularly intense exposure or the conditions in which exposure occurred; and a victim might have had a period during which he or she was not exposed to asbestos, or in which the exposure was due to his own activities, so that compensation would be reduced by whatever proportion of the loss was to be attributed to those periods.[17] Much more significantly however, the substantial risk of employer or insurer insolvency, or of untraced employers and insurers, and of proof of the relevant proportion of exposure to be allocated to any given defendant once identified, was shifted to claimants. We explore further in 12.4 the distributive impact of joint and several liability, by attention to contribution arrangements.

The unfairness of the outcome in *Barker* in this last respect was identified immediately. As a result, Parliament intervened to impose the joint and several liability principle which had, prior to *Barker*, been thought (rightly, it can now be said)[18] to exist. The Compensation Act 2006, s 3(1), provides that any 'responsible' person who has exposed the victim to asbestos faces liability for the whole loss despite the existence of other wrongdoers or periods in which there was no exposure. Four conditions, set out in s 3(2), have to be satisfied: (a) the responsible person 'has negligently or in

[14] HLA Hart and T Honoré, *Causation in the Law* (Oxford: Clarendon Press, 2nd edn, 1985), 123, give the example of two people who simultaneously shoot the victim.

[15] Chapter 6 discusses 'other insurance' clauses, where concurrent insurers each seek to cast the risk of loss on to others.

[16] R Merkin, 'Insurance Claims and Fairchild' (2004) 120 LQR 233.

[17] In *International Energy Group Ltd v Zurich Insurance Plc UK* [2013] EWCA Civ 39, a case decided under the law of Guernsey which retains *Barker* principles unmodified by the Compensation Act 2006, the insurers agreed that in the circumstances of that case time on risk was the appropriate measure of allocation.

[18] Lords Mance and Clarke, n 1, have now authoritatively explained why this is the better interpretation. One of the present authors argued for the same interpretation of *Fairchild* in J Steele, 'Breach of Duty Causing Harm? Recent Encounters between Negligence and Risk' (2007) 60 CLP 296.

breach of statutory duty caused or permitted' the victim to be exposed to asbestos; (b) 'the victim has contracted mesothelioma as a result of exposure to asbestos'; (c) 'because of the nature of mesothelioma and the state of medical science, it is not possible to determine with certainty' which exposure caused the victim to become ill; and (d) the responsible person is liable in tort, 'whether by reason of having materially increased a risk or for any other reason'. Subsequently, in *Sienkiewicz*, a case involving a single responsible person and also atmospheric asbestos which itself materially increased the risk of injury, the Supreme Court ruled that s 3 did not create liability where none previously existed, and that it merely imposed full liability on any one tortfeasor found to face liability. In *Sienkiewicz* itself, the responsible person carried the full burden: the employer had acted negligently, mesothelioma had been contracted as a result of exposure to asbestos, medical science could not determine which exposure had led to the disease, and the responsible person was liable in tort under the *Fairchild* test because the exposures materially contributed to the risk of injury.

The judgments in *Fairchild* and *Barker* evidently raised the question of the nature of the liability imposed in those cases. From one point of view, their Lordships had simply tinkered with the rules on causation, adjusting them to fit a novel situation and deeming there to be a causal link between each exposure and subsequent injury. This employs an admitted fiction, but it does so in a contained manner, for a particular purpose in particular circumstances. This is the interpretation now authoritatively adopted by the majority of the Supreme Court in the *Trigger* litigation. An alternative analysis was that *Fairchild* had created a new form of liability, perhaps even a new tort of materially increasing the risk of injury.[19] The resolution of that debate does not now affect the joint and several liability of each responsible person towards the victim. There is a need under the 2006 Act, s 3(2)(d), to show liability in tort. Such liability attaches either because the breach of duty of every responsible person is deemed to be the cause of the injury, thereby perfecting the tort arising from negligent exposure and damage, or because the mere act of exposure is a tort in its own right as long as damage follows. In either view the employee does not have to pinpoint a causal exposure, but needs to point only to exposure and subsequent disease. But *Trigger* reignited the debate, because its resolution determines whether or not the responsible person may rely upon liability insurance in order to fund any successful damages claim by or on behalf of the victim. We would underline once again that in *Fairchild* itself, it was abundantly clear that the compensation secured would be payable by insurers, and that insurers were indeed conducting the case as defendants. Every step in the asbestos litigation has been shaped by insurers.

12.3 Insurance Coverage

12.3.1 Insuring liability for personal injuries

It will be seen from the above account that the courts and Parliament have been enthusiastic and inventive in their attempts to ensure that wrongful exposure leads

[19] There are at least two variations here: that there is a new form of liability operating within existing torts; or that a new tort exists. Neither is to be regarded as correct after *Trigger*.

to legal liability in cases of mesothelioma. But of course that is only half of the story. In this context, where claimants are suffering from a dreadful disease and where no responsible individuals, and few if any employing organizations, are likely to bear the brunt of liability, the point of liability is that it is followed by actual payment. We here consider the response of insurance principles. The courts have ultimately ensured that insurance coverage matches legal liability. The 'remarkable' consequence of the alternative view exemplifies the perils of fashioning what appears to be a principled solution without regard to the operation of insurance.

We have already seen that liability insurance can respond in one of three main ways:[20] to an event occurring within the currency of the policy (causation basis); to injury or damage taking place within the currency of the policy (injury basis); and to a claim made against the assured (or, by extension, a circumstance notified to the insurers by the assured) during the currency of the policy (claims made basis). Personal injuries are covered either by employers' liability (EL) policies or by public liability (PL) policies, the latter extending to injuries inflicted upon persons other than the assured's own employees, most importantly, visitors, independent contractors, and members of the public in general. Personal injury liabilities of both types are generally insured under either causation or injury policies: there was a short period in the 1990s when claims made policies were used for EL insurance, but that has since been discontinued.

In the vast majority of cases it matters little whether the insurance is causation or injury based, because there is generally no temporal gap between an act of negligence and the injuries which flow from it, and a policy of either type will respond. The distinction becomes significant where the negligent act occurs in one policy period and the injury occurs in another, a situation which is more or less confined to injuries resulting from a negligent exposure to a harmful substance, and mesothelioma caused by exposure to asbestos is perhaps the most complex example because of the lengthy gap, measured in decades, between exposure and injury. The date of the trigger is important for a number of reasons, which may be illustrated by a simple example. D exposes C to asbestos in 1980, and in 2010 C suffers injury to his lungs. The relevant insurance years are thus 1980 and 2010.

If D has a causation policy in 1980, those insurers are liable, but if he has an injury policy in 1980 then the insurers are not liable because there is no injury in 1980.

If D has a causation policy in 2010, those insurers are not liable because the negligent act of exposure did not occur in 2010, but if D happens to have injury insurance in place in 2010 then—subject to one important consideration—those insurers will face liability. That important consideration rests upon the status of C. If the 2010 policy is PL, it will respond to injuries inflicted on third parties in 2010. However, if the 2010 policy is EL, it is likely to apply only if C is in D's employ in 2010; that is because EL policies cover only injuries to existing employees and not ex-employees. Further, such a policy is likely to exclude claims for injuries arising from earlier exposures.

[20] Chapter 3. There are possible refinements. Burton J in *Employers' Liability Insurance 'Trigger' Litigation: BAI (Run Off) Ltd v Durham* [2008] EWHC 2692 (QB); [2009] Lloyd's Rep IR 295 identified seven triggers, but these are simply variants on the three main types.

It is immediately apparent, therefore, that an injury-based policy is, in the vast majority of employment cases, of little value for a disease such as mesothelioma. If the policy is in 1980 it will not respond at all, and if the policy is in 2010 then it will respond only if C was employed by D in the year of exposure (the negligent act) and remains employed in 2010 (the year of injury), and if there is no exclusion for historic exposures.

A number of factors complicate the position. The first is that assureds regularly change insurers and the wordings used by the insurers may be different. Thus it is perfectly possible that D had taken out an injury policy in 1980 but switched to a causation policy in 2010, in which case neither insurer will be liable because the former responds to injury (which does not occur for a further thirty years) but the latter responds to exposure (which took place thirty years previously). Second, and linked to the first point, it is a fact that many of the EL insurers writing business in 1980 had ceased to do so by 2010, and that many employers in business in 1980 had been dissolved by 2010. Third, even where the same insurer is on risk in both 1980 and 2010, and each of the policies is the same in nature, it is inevitable that one or other of those policies will be applicable, but that does not mean that the problem is solved. It will still be necessary to determine which of the policies covers the loss: D's insurers will almost certainly have had different reinsurance arrangements in 1980 and 2010, and reinsurers will insist that the claim is allocated to the correct policy year; and even if reinsurance is left out of account it is possible that the cover in either of the years may have been exhausted by other claims, so that in practice a claim may only be made in the other year.

This, then, sets the scene both for the insurance litigation which followed the asbestos liability litigation fought so vigorously in the highest court, and for the intervention of Parliament. The problem, stated simply, was that the wordings of both PL and EL policies have long been ambiguous, in that they refer to '*injury sustained*' or '*disease contracted*', or both. In addition, in the EL market, some policies stated that they insured the risks required by the Employers' Liability (Compulsory Insurance) Act 1969. Others did not, but were otherwise no different in their terms. The primary question for the courts in the sequel litigation was the meaning of the italicized phrases, and also what form of policy was required by the 1969 Act.

12.3.2 The prequel: *Bolton v MMI*

The scene for the battle over the meaning of EL policies was set[21] by the decision in *Bolton Metropolitan Borough Council v Municipal Mutual Insurance*.[22] The assured local authority, Bolton, held successive PL policies. The first batch, for the period 1960 to 1965 and issued by Commercial Union's predecessor in title, covered accidental bodily injury to or illness of any person occurring during the currency of the policy. The second batch, for the period 1979 to 1991 and issued by Municipal Mutual

[21] It was alleged in argument in *Trigger* that *Bolton* had been devised as a test case to establish that the wordings were injury and not causation based.

[22] [2006] EWCA Civ 50; [2006] 1 WLR 1492.

Insurance (MMI), applied to liability for 'accidental bodily injury or illness (fatal or otherwise) to any person which occurs during the currency of the policy and arises out of the exercise of the functions of a Local Authority'. Various subcontractors had been employed by Bolton over a number of years before 1979. One of the employees developed a malignancy in 1980, and he died of mesothelioma in 1991. The issue was, which of the batches of liability policies responded to Bolton's claim for indemnification for its settlement with the deceased's representatives? The Court of Appeal held that the loss had to be borne by MMI. Bodily injury occurred when malignancy developed and not when exposure or inhalation took place, and it followed that the insuring words 'bodily injury' referred to the onset of disease in 1980, a time when MMI were on risk. The Court of Appeal further held that the use of the word 'accidental' did not preclude application to an injury which was inevitable once the earlier exposure had caused fibres to lodge in the deceased's lungs. It further ruled that the phrase 'occurs during the currency of the policy and arises out of the exercise of the functions of a Local Authority' did not lay down two concurrent conditions, so that it was not necessary for the injury to arise out of Bolton's activities during the currency of the policy.

The *Bolton* case was confined to PL cover, a point that Longmore LJ emphasized in his judgment. Accordingly it says nothing about EL policies. However, *Bolton* established the idea that an 'injury' occurs when the disease takes hold and not when the exposure to the harmful substance takes place. One notable feature of the decision is that PL policies were held to provide retrospective cover, picking up liability for negligent acts occurring before the inception of cover but resulting in injury in the period of cover. That would appear to be contrary to the intention of such policies, which are designed to give current or prospective cover, not retroactive cover: the latter is the province of claims made policies, which respond to earlier negligent acts. That is of particular significance for PL. As construed by the Court of Appeal, the wording covers injuries to any person arising from earlier exposures, whereas an EL policy is more limited and applies only to persons who are employed and suffer injury during the currency of the policy, so the liability under EL insurance is much more limited than under PL insurance. To confirm the point, PL policies issued since *Bolton* exclude liability for exposures in earlier years which give rise to injury during the currency of the policy.

12.3.3 The *EL Trigger* cases: wordings

Given the ruling in *Bolton*, it became possible for EL insurers to assert that their wordings, insofar as they referred to 'injury sustained', were not causation based but rather were injury based, and that the same interpretation should be given to the phrase 'disease contracted'. Those arguments gave rise to *Employers' Liability Insurance 'Trigger' Litigation: BAI (Run Off) Ltd v Durham*,[23] a series of test cases on twelve different wordings and affecting some 6,000 mesothelioma victims. The ultimate ruling

[23] *Trigger*, n 1.

by the Supreme Court was against the insurers, although of the nine judges who heard the case a variety of quite different approaches was adopted, ranging from a strong determination that *Fairchild* and the Compensation Act 2006 should not be undermined to a formalist approach to contract construction.

At first instance[24] Burton J held that although there was no universal usage in the insurance industry whereby claims were paid on an exposure basis,[25] the terms 'injury sustained' and 'disease contracted' were nevertheless to be construed as attaching to exposure rather than to injury. He reached that conclusion on a number of grounds. First, the wordings were ambiguous and should be construed *contra proferentem*. That approach did minimal violence to the wordings, and it simply meant that the words 'sustained' and 'contracted' should be read as 'caused'. Second, the wordings could be traced back to the Workmen's Compensation Acts 1897 to 1925, and that legislation dealt with disease by imposing liability on the last employer in the chain to expose the employee to the harmful substance. It followed that the factual matrix of the policies was that they were in origin designed to cover exposure. Third, construing the policies on an injury basis would create a black hole, in that the policies covered only current employees and the strong likelihood was that the victims of mesothelioma would have ceased to be employed at the time of injury. Finally, the construction made commercial sense, and was consistent with the requirement in the 1969 Act that liability insurance be taken out and maintained for both bodily injury and disease. Burton J, somewhat bravely, distinguished *Bolton* on the grounds that it was concerned with PL only.

In the Court of Appeal, Smith LJ approved what Burton J had said, and focused on the factual matrix. The majority, Rix and Stanley Burnton LJJ, reversed Burton J on 'injury sustained', which was held to relate to injury, but upheld him on 'disease contracted' which was held to be a causation wording. Rix LJ, despite a lengthy historical analysis of both contract and tort, held that the ultimate question was one of contractual construction. In his view, the settled principles of construction required a court to apply the ordinary meaning of words unless something had plainly gone wrong with the drafting.[26] Given the fact that policies in the same form had been entered into for many years, it was difficult to conclude that something had gone wrong. Thus, while recognizing the commercial purpose of the policies, and in particular the black hole identified by Burton J, Rix LJ felt constrained to give the phrase 'injury sustained' its natural meaning, which was injury and not exposure. However, Rix LJ agreed with Burton J that the phrase 'disease contracted' was ambiguous, and was to be construed in accordance with the commercial purpose of the policies, particularly in the light of the 1969 Act. It is apparent that Rix LJ was uncomfortable with his conclusion that a distinction was to be drawn between 'injury sustained' and 'disease contracted', not the least because the ability of an employer to recover from its

24 [2008] EWHC 2692 (QB); [2009] Lloyd's Rep IR 295.

25 The argument for usage was rejected in the Court of Appeal and was not resurrected in the Supreme Court.

26 This seems to misstate the accepted approach to construction of commercial contracts, as explained in the paragraphs to follow.

liability insurers depended upon the fortuity of which wording had been adopted. He viewed the problem as the ruling in *Bolton*—which was binding on him—that inhalation of asbestos was not of itself an injury. By way of contrast to the more purposive judgments of Burton J and Rix and Smith LJJ, Stanley Burnton LJ approached the matter on the basis that the commercial purpose of the policies was to delimit the cover provided by the insurers, so that there was no basis for construing 'injury sustained' in any way other than according to its terms—an approach which seems to deprive the idea of 'commercial purpose' in contract construction of all content.[27] However, he agreed with Rix and Smith LJJ on the causation meaning to be given to 'disease contracted'.

The Supreme Court by a majority reinstated the judgment of Burton J and ruled that all of the policies were triggered by exposure rather than injury or the onset of disease. A disease was contracted, and an injury was sustained, on exposure.[28] A key development between the Court of Appeal decision and the hearings in the Supreme Court was the Supreme Court's own ruling in *Rainy Sky SA v Kookmin Bank*,[29] where Lord Clarke, speaking for the entire court, commented[30] that: 'The language used by the parties will often have more than one potential meaning . . . If there are two possible constructions, the court is entitled to prefer the construction which is consistent with business common sense and to reject the other.' This is at least an extension of, and arguably a departure from, the orthodox factual matrix text, and *Rainy Sky* has proved to be particularly influential.[31] It played a key role in the arguments in *Trigger*, and was an important plank in the reasoning. Lord Mance, whose judgment on this point was approved by the rest of the Supreme Court, pointed to the following factors to support the causation interpretation: the wording as a whole pointed to employment being contemporaneous with injury and to a close link between the premium and employment in the period of insurance; in the absence of causation wording there would be a black hole for ex-employees; the requirements of the 1969 Act—which the Supreme Court held demanded causation cover—were a powerful indication that policies were intended to comply; and a failure to renew, or an avoidance of a later policy, would remove cover in post-exposure years. Lord Mance dismissed the argument by insurers, that 99 per cent of claims did not straddle policy years so that cover was not undermined by rejecting causation as a trigger. He relied on *Rainy Sky* for the proposition that the argument gave 'too little weight to the implications of the rival interpretations' and that '[t]he 1 per cent of cases in which there might be no cover could not be regarded as insignificant'.[32] Lord Clarke agreed with the reasoning and made clear that any conclusion that the policies did not respond would be 'remarkable'.[33]

[27] R Merkin and J Steele, 'Compensating Mesothelioma Victims' (2011) 127 LQR 329.

[28] There was some authority under the Workmen's Compensation Act 1906 for the proposition that contribution to the onset of risk amounted to the disease being contracted: judgments of Scrutton LJ in *Ellerbeck Collieries Ltd v Cornhill Insurance Co* [1932] 1 KB 401 and *Smith & Son v Eagle Star & British Dominions Insurance Co* (1934) 47 Ll L Rep 88.

[29] [2011] UKSC 50; [2011] 1 WLR 2900.

[30] n 29, [21].

[31] Taken to its natural limits, it could signal the end of *contra proferentem*.

[32] n 29, [26].

[33] n 1, [89].

In the absence of detailed evidence on the operation of PL policies, *Bolton* was neither approved nor disapproved, but distinguished on the basis that EL and PL policies had different natures and purposes. The outcome is that the words 'injury sustained' apparently bear different meanings in EL and PL policies. We have already argued that there is every reason to assimilate the two forms of cover, and it is unlikely that *Bolton* would withstand detailed scrutiny in the Supreme Court. To add to that point, it is noteworthy that the cases discussed in this chapter have involved both employers and occupiers: the latter are insured, if at all, under PL policies which may not respond to the claims if *Bolton* is correct, with the same 'remarkable' outcome rejected by the majority.

12.3.4 The nature of *Fairchild* liability

The comparative brevity of the reasoning in some aspects of its decision, and the reliance on *Rainy Sky*, are clear indications that the majority in the Supreme Court thought it entirely natural to match the insurance trigger with the tort liability created by *Fairchild* and the Compensation Act 2006. Much more powerful evidence is to be found in the issue which emerged on the fourth day of the hearing in the Supreme Court, and which ultimately divided Lord Phillips from the majority, namely, the true basis of *Fairchild* liability. We set out the significance of the issue at the start of the chapter, and here we explain it more fully. As already indicated, the divisive issue was whether *Fairchild* had created a new liability (potentially, a new tort) of materially increasing the risk of mesothelioma, or had simply modified the 'but for' causation test to suit a situation in which proof of actual causation was beyond scientific determination so that causation was 'deemed' to follow from negligent exposure without the need for proof of the year in which exposure occurred.

The significance of the point for insurance may be demonstrated by a simple example. Assume the following. Employee C was employed by employer D1 for the period 1971 to 1975, and by employer D2 for the period 1976 to 1980. Both D1 and D2 exposed C to asbestos, and in 2012 C was diagnosed with mesothelioma. The effect of *Fairchild*, however it is viewed, allows C to sue either (or both) D1 or D2 for compensation. It is no part of C's case that the actual causal exposure was on any one occasion, or indeed in any one year. Assume, therefore, that C sues D1. Plainly D1 faces liability. However, for the purposes of a claim against liability insurers, the question then becomes whether D1 is required to identify one of the policy years from 1971 to 1975 in which to place his claim. This matters to D1 for two reasons. First, D1 may have had different insurers in different years, and each might seek to argue that liability arose in another insurer's year of coverage. Second, even if D1 had the same insurers for the period 1971 to 1975, it does not necessarily follow that the coverage was the same in each year. Each year of coverage will have aggregate limits of indemnity, and it may be that D1 has made claims in the years 1971 to 1974 which have exhausted the coverage, so that only the 1975 policy can respond. Alternatively, the exposures may have been careless in 1971 but deliberate in later years, which means that there is no coverage after the first year, or there may have been different policy terms (for example, exclusions of liability for asbestos exposure). There is a further consideration which affects the insurers themselves, which is that they will have reinsurance for each of the relevant years, and reinsurers may insist—for the same reasons just expressed—that coverage is pinned to one or other of those years.

This is the point at which the correct analysis of *Fairchild* becomes relevant. If the 'deemed' causation approach is adopted, D1 faces liability for every incident of exposure in 1971 to 1975, and accordingly D1 can in principle[34] present his claim in any year and for the full amount of his liability. If, by contrast, the 'new tort' approach is adopted, every exposure by D1 has thereby made a material contribution to the risk of injury, but it remains for D1 to show that any particular exposure has actually caused the injury. By definition it is unable to do that, with the consequence that it is impossible to present an insurance claim within any of the years of cover. C will obtain a judgment but, unless D1 is solvent, it will not be satisfied. The second interpretation renders the liabilities uninsured, despite the shared understanding that liability cover was in place—and in many instances, despite a statutory obligation to ensure that it was.

Lord Mance in his judgment in *Trigger* closely analysed the language used in *Fairchild* and *Barker*. In *Fairchild* itself, Lords Hutton and Rodger plainly analysed the matter in terms of deemed causation, whereas the language of Lord Hoffmann suggests a new form of liability imposed free of any fiction of deeming. Lord Hoffmann in *Barker* regarded the judgments of Lords Bingham and Nicholls as supporting his analysis,[35] although Lord Rodger in *Barker* took the opposite view of them. In reaching the conclusion in *Barker* that an employer should be liable only for his own contribution to the risk of injury, Lords Hoffmann, Scott, and Walker rejected the deemed causation approach[36] whereas Lord Rodger, dissenting, confirmed his earlier view. Lady Hale preferred Lord Rodger's analysis but agreed with the majority on the outcome. Similar ambiguity surrounds *Sienkiewicz*,[37] but this time Lords Brown, Mance, and Kerr spoke of modifications to the law of causation, Lord Dyson was non-committal, and Lord Rodger accepted that he had been outvoted on the deemed causation principle by the majority in *Barker* so that the true principle was that liability was imposed for materially increasing the risk. It mattered in *Trigger*, and the Supreme Court, by a majority, not only stated reasoned arguments in favour of the 'deemed' causation analysis, but also exposed the inconsistencies in the alternative, 'new form of liability' interpretation. The Supreme Court thereby removed the final obstacle to recoverability under the policies. They also resolved the basis of *Fairchild*.

The majority in *Trigger*, represented by the reasoned judgments of Lords Mance and Clarke, concluded that the earlier cases—whatever the precise terminology used by the various judges—had done no more than to adapt causation principles to a novel situation. There was evidence not only in *Fairchild* but also in *Barker* itself that the basis of the claim was not increase of risk, and it had always been the case that actionable injury had to be shown before any action could be brought.[38] Lord Mance

[34] Discussed in subsequent paragraphs. [35] n 4. Contrast Lord Mance in *Trigger*, n 1, [59].

[36] A view repeated by Lord Hoffmann, 'Causation', in Goldberg (ed), n 9, 8. [37] n 3.

[38] A further incoherence not referred to in *Trigger* is that one of the claims in *Fairchild* was an action under the Fatal Accidents Act 1976. This could not have succeeded if the claim was for anything other than death: it would not permit an action for an increase in the risk of death, for example.

suggested that Lord Hoffmann's own judicial statements continued to speak in these terms when closely analysed, and that Lord Hoffmann had (extra-judicially) treated the matter as now settled by the Compensation Act 2006, s 3.[39]

Other features of the reasoning are of equal significance for our purposes. Lord Mance emphasized that it was necessary to match insurance coverage with the *Fairchild* liability[40] and the fact that *Fairchild* had extended previously understood liability was no defence to the insurers.[41] He added that '[I]t would . . . have been anomalous and unjust if the law by "deeming" there to have been causation of the disease could have created policy liability . . . but the law by insisting that the liability in respect of mesothelioma was for the risk of causation achieved a quite different result.'[42] Lord Clarke added that:

> It appears to me that, once it is held that, on these facts, the employers are liable to the employees, it would be remarkable if the insurers were not liable under the policies. Rather as in *AXA*, the whole purpose of the policies was to insure the employers against liability to their employees. That purpose would be frustrated if the insurers' submissions on this point were accepted.[43]

Lord Phillips, dissenting, concluded that the judgments in *Barker* had rejected the deemed causation theory. Crucially, he refused to 'adapt' (in his view) the insurance coverage to *Fairchild*:

> It does not seem likely that the majority [in *Barker*] gave consideration to the implications for the responsibility of EL insurers of the manner in which this object was achieved. Should this Court now redefine the *special rule* with the object of enabling claims to be brought under the EL policies? . . . The object of the special approach in *Fairchild* and *Barker* was at least to ensure that those who had breached the duties that they owed to their employees did not escape liability because of scientific uncertainty. It would be judicial law-making of a different dimension to create a legal fiction as to the policy years in which cases of mesothelioma were initiated in order to render liable insurers who could not otherwise be shown to be liable.[44]

The ruling in *Trigger* is of broad significance. The majority in *Trigger* was not prepared to countenance the possibility that the judicial gyrations which led to the imposition of liability (a 'special rule') could be defeated by the absence of insurance to match it. The entire exercise, from *Fairchild* through to *Trigger*, is best seen as a transparent illustration of holistic law making, identifying an injustice in the application of the rules in causation and then allowing the matching of insurance with the modified rules. While dislike of fictions and special rules may be understandable, it is suggested that far greater harm—including the negation of the entire purpose of *Fairchild*—was threatened by the adoption of what appeared to be a principled version of its result in *Barker*. In 12.4 we explain in a little more detail the distributive picture that lies behind the legislative idea of fairness behind the Compensation Act 2006 s 3. Although

[39] Lord Mance referred to Lord Hoffmann, n 36.

[40] *Trigger*, n 1, [69].

[41] *Trigger*, n 1, [70], enshrining the settled insurance principle that even a change in the law does not discharge insurers from the extended liability, as they run the risk of such changes.

[42] *Trigger*, n 1, [73].

[43] *Trigger*, n 1, [88].

[44] *Trigger*, n 1, [134]–[135].

Fairchild and *Trigger* have dispensed with 'but for' only in the context of mesothelioma, this need not be an isolated example. Lord Bingham in *Fairchild* said that 'I do not . . . consider that the House is acting contrary to principle in reviewing the applicability of the conventional test of causation to cases such as the present. Indeed, it would seem to me contrary to principle to insist on application of a rule which appeared, if it did, to yield unfair results.'[45] There is room for the 'but for' test to be abandoned in other scenarios;[46] but comments on the part of some members of the Supreme Court in *Sienkiewicz* suggest that this is not a path that would be followed with enthusiasm.[47]

12.4 Claims Against[48] and Between Insurers

This section moves beyond tort principles and construction of liability policies, to explore broader questions of distribution. We suggest that arguments of fairness should not be ventured without considering the likely distributive picture. This, then, is a further aspect of the critique of *Barker*.

The outcome of *Trigger* is to allow D1 to assert that its liability arises on any incident of exposure. It follows that every insurer on risk when any exposure took place faces full liability to indemnify the employer. In some cases it may not matter to D1[49] how the claim against insurers is presented: that will be the position where the same insurers have been on risk in each year, the unexhausted cover in each year is adequate to cover the claim and the policy terms are standard. But it will matter if there are different insurers in different years or where the amount recoverable varies from year to year by reason of exhaustion through other claims or policy terms. Accordingly, D1 will focus on the policy year or years in which its recovery is maximized or, if there are different insurers involved, it may—in the interests of a continuing commercial relationship—choose to bring proceedings against an insurer other than its current insurer. That the *Trigger* reasoning confers that very right is implicit from the approach in *Phillips v Syndicate 992 Gunner*,[50] a case decided after *Fairchild* but before *Barker*. Here, the employer had coverage from a number of insurers over the period during which employees had been exposed to asbestos, but the employer claimed against one insurer

[45] *Fairchild*, n 3, [13].

[46] Causation rules apply equally to insurance contracts. In *Orient-Express Hotels Ltd v Assicurazioni Generali SpA* [2010] EWHC 1186 (Comm) an unsuccessful attempt was made to persuade Hamblen J to abandon 'but for'. The effect of applying that test in the case itself was that the assured under a business interruption policy was unable to recover in circumstances where its hotel in New Orleans was damaged by Hurricane Katrina. But for the damage to the hotel the assured would still have suffered loss, because the town had been closed by the state authorities. This would appear to be the very type of case in which 'but for' should be abandoned, but the case came before Hamblen J as an appeal from an arbitration award, and the arbitrators' decision not to disapply 'but for' in the circumstances was one of fact and not law, and thus not capable of challenge on appeal. See also *Aioi Nissay Dowa Insurance Company Ltd v Heraldglen Ltd* [2013] EWHC 154 (Comm).

[47] n 3. Notably critical of the state of the law after *Fairchild* was Lord Brown ([186]).

[48] The following analysis assumes that all insurers are traced. That may not be the case: we addressed in Chapter 9 the voluntary agreements which deal with the problem of tracing.

[49] It will matter to D1's insurers.

[50] [2003] EWHC 1706 (Comm); [2004] Lloyd's Rep IR 418.

only. The insurer did not deny liability, but asserted instead that the claim should be made against all insurers on risk and that accordingly its liability should be limited to its proportion—however that might be calculated, but arguably 'time on risk'—of the losses. Eady J ruled that the insurer was fully liable. There was no implied term in the policy that the assured was limited to a rateable proportion of the total loss, and accordingly the insurer was liable for 100 per cent of the loss. Lord Mance referred to *Phillips* without criticism in *Trigger*, and the reasoning correctly anticipates *Trigger*. Applying *Trigger*, the insurer pinpointed in *Phillips* faced 100 per cent liability to the employer, and the existence of other insurers could not affect that liability. As noted above, the insurer did not suggest that it faced no liability at all, for example, on the basis that the employer should have sued a different insurer, so the case proceeded on the assumption that the employer had a free hand. The point was confirmed post-*Trigger* in *International Energy Group Ltd v Zurich Insurance Plc UK*.[51] Here the employee was exposed to asbestos by one employer only, for a period of twenty-seven years, and in six of those years the employer was insured by the defendant insurers. Those insurers sought to confine their liability to the six-year period, arguing that they had received premiums only for that period and should not be required to face liability for any lengthier period. The Court of Appeal held—applying *Trigger*—that the employer was liable for the entirety of the loss, and that the liability was imposed in any one of the twenty-seven years of exposure. That meant that an insurer on risk in any one year bore the entirety of the loss, so that there was no apportionment. It may be noted that the facts occurred in Guernsey, which has no equivalent of the UK Compensation Act 2006, so that *Barker v Corus* remains good law in that jurisdiction. Nevertheless, the effect of *Trigger* was to impose 100 per cent liability on the employer for any one exposure, which in turn meant that a claim could (subject to policy limits) be brought against any insurer on risk at the time of any exposure for the full amount of the liability for that exposure. It is difficult to see, after this interpretation, what—if anything—remains of *Barker*, even without the assistance of the Compensation Act 2006.

The fact that D1 can choose its insurer does not mean that the loss will ultimately reside with that insurer. To illustrate how liability may be shifted, it is necessary to modify the above illustration by assuming that in the years 1971 to 1974 Insurer I1 was on risk and in 1975 insurer I2 was on risk, and that D1 had chosen to sue I2 for coverage under the 1975 policy year.[52] If it is right that I2 cannot deny liability, what rights does I2 have to seek some sort of recompense? Two possibilities arise, each involving the very causation issue which *Trigger* and the Compensation Act 2006 have removed as a concern for the victim.

First, I2 may, exercising subrogation rights, seek to recover part of its payment from D2 (or, more likely, D2's liability insurers). If in our example D1 and D2 face joint and several liability to C, and D1 has paid, D1 potentially has a claim against D2 under the

[51] n 17.

[52] In this section we are assuming that all insurers remain solvent. It may be of course that one or more of the insurers is insolvent or has ceased to trade. In that situation the claim is to be pressed against the FSCS, described in Chapter 4. To avoid ever further complexity, we are assuming that every insurer has remained in business and is capable of being sued.

Civil Liability (Contribution) Act 1978. That is the case if D1 and D2 are liable for the 'same damage' within the meaning of the 1978 Act, s 1(1), a provision which is purportedly extended to the present situation by the Compensation Act 2006, s 3(3), which states that joint and several liability 'does not prevent... one responsible person from claiming a contribution from another'.[53] The amount of contribution recoverable is, under the 1978 Act, s 2(1), 'such as may be found by the court to be just and equitable having regard to the extent of that person's responsibility for the damage in question', and specific guidance is given by the Compensation Act 2006, s 3(4): 'In determining the extent of contributions of different responsible persons in accordance with subsection (3)(a), a court shall have regard to the relative lengths of the periods of exposure for which each was responsible.' The test is flexible and does permit the court to take account of other considerations, including the intensity and nature of any exposure. Although time on risk is a rough and ready calculation, it is one likely to be adopted by agreement between insurers as a matter of convenience.[54] All of this is in any event a consequence of *Trigger* independently of the 2006 Act.

The second possibility is that I2 has a contribution claim against I1. I2 may justifiably feel aggrieved that it has been asked to carry the entire loss even though only being on risk for 20 per cent of the period of D1's liability. As discussed in Chapter 6, there is double insurance where two insurers face liability for the same loss. The difficulty here is that the insurers are on risk in different policy years, and there is an argument that double insurance applies only to concurrent policies and not to consecutive policies. Eady J took this view in *Phillips v Syndicate 992 Gunner*.[55] The point there arose in an acute form, because the policy issued by the insurer called upon to pay contained a rateable proportion clause, limiting its liability to its rateable share of the total loss. If that clause was effective, it would have followed that the insurer would have been liable only for its proportion of the loss. However, Eady J preferred the view that double insurance could not operate across policy years. Each insurer was liable for its own year and not for all other years, so that there was no double insurance. In the absence of double insurance, there was no other liability upon which the rateable proportion clause could bite. This, we would suggest, cannot be right. There is only one claim against the employer, and not a series of separate claims. The essence of *Trigger* is that C need not identify any one exposure because there is a single liability from all exposures. Just because D1 has placed its claim in 1975 does not mean that the loss occurred in 1975—it occurred also in the years 1971 to 1974. In short, there is a single indivisible loss in every year rather than separate losses in each year, and accordingly it can be said that the same loss is covered by all of the policies. That would indicate a right of contribution, entitling I2 to recover the relevant proportion of its liability from I1: other things being equal, and using a time on risk analysis, that would mean that I2 can recover 80 per cent of its outlay from I1.

[53] This provision is purely negative, and does not in terms deem the 1978 Act to be applicable. Accordingly, whether there can be contribution depends upon whether the damage is the 'same'.

[54] *International Energy Group Ltd v Zurich Insurance Plc UK*, n 17.

[55] n 50.

12.4.1 Summary

Thus far we have focused on the allocation of liability as between years of exposure. We have tried to show that if there are two or more employers, contribution rights under the Civil Liability (Contribution) Act 1978, probably exercised by the paying insurer by way of subrogation, will operate to allocate the total liability between employers on—in the absence of other factors—a time on risk basis. Each employer will thus pay its share. The idea implicit in *Barker v Corus* is replicated in the ultimate outcome, with the differences that the allocation is not a concern of the victim but takes place between insurers once there has been payment to the victim; and that the victim will not lose any proportion of his compensation for any year in which he was not employed. We have further shown that, when the position of any one employer is considered, that employer is free to place its claim against liability insurers in any year during which it exposed the employee to asbestos, and that it is uncertain—in the light of *Phillips*—whether different insurers on risk in that period have contribution rights against each other.

12.4.2 Reinsurance claims

One final matter remains to be considered, and that is the reinsurance position of an insurer which has insured an employer for a period of years during which the employer has exposed the victim to asbestos. This underlines that the further losses progress into the reinsurance chain, the less credible the suggestion of fixed risk pools becomes. Reinsurance, therefore, is an essential component of the distributive picture. Reinsurance treaties entered into by an insurer will cover not just asbestos liabilities, but possibly all employers' liability claims (many of which will almost certainly not be from asbestos) and indeed the insurer's entire portfolio of loss on all of its underwriting accounts. So mesothelioma claims will be lumped in with others from different sources and the reinsurers will be concerned only with aggregate losses from all sources. The origin of the claims will, therefore, be lost unless some issue arises about the reinsurers' liability for a particular class of claims.

Let us assume a five-year period during which an employer is insured by a single insurer. We know from what has gone before that the employer can bring its claim in any one of the years in question, as best suits its prospects of recovery. What, then of the insurer's reinsurance recoveries? The insurer may have different reinsurers in each of the five years of cover, and indeed that is a strong possibility given that reinsurance treaties are typically subscribed to by different reinsurers each taking a proportion of the risk, and the participants and the proportions may change from year to year. Those considerations aside, the insurer may wish to put as many losses as possible into one year so as to take advantage of an aggregate deductible, or it may wish to spread the losses amongst the years of reinsurance because it has exhausted cover in some years and has high aggregate limits in others. Two questions arise: if the insurer adheres to a basis of allocation on which the claims were paid to the employer, can it be challenged by the reinsurers; and, equally, if the insurer chooses to allocate amongst the insurers on a different basis to that on which the insurance claims were paid, is that open to challenge by the reinsurers?

The English cases on allocation indicate that it is not open to the insurer to maximize its recovery from reinsurers by manipulating allocation, and that wherever possible losses must be placed in the year in which they occurred. If that is not possible, then there is a presumption of linear and regular occurrence so that losses are spread equally. Authority for the former proposition is the decision of the Court of Appeal in *Teal Assurance Company Ltd v W R Berkley Insurance (Europe) Ltd.*[56] The claimant, the captive insurer of the BV group provided, in the form of a 'Professional Indemnity Tower', liability insurance in a series of layers above BV's deductible. The primary layers were for US$50 million and covered worldwide but the excess layer of US$10 million excluded North American claims. The reinsurance was placed on the same basis. Four claims were made against BV, two from outside the US and two from inside the US, and the claimant, despite the objections of the reinsurers, sought to treat the US claims as first in time so that the Tower would not be eroded by non-US claims leaving no excess layer coverage for the US claims. The Court of Appeal found for the reinsurers on the construction of the various policies, but it is apparent from the judgments that the Court of Appeal viewed with disfavour the proposition that the claimant could allocate the claims as it thought fit. Tomlinson LJ indeed commented that such an approach would lead to anarchy. So the case decides that, in the absence of clear wording to the contrary, losses must be taken in the order in which they occur and it is not open to the insurer to alter the order simply to maximize recovery.[57] *Teal*, therefore, is a case in which the dates of the claims against the insurer, and thus the chronology, could be determined, so that allocation had to follow the chronology.

Authority for the second proposition is *Municipal Mutual Insurance Ltd v Sea Insurance Ltd.*[58] The assured, a port authority, was insured in three consecutive years against liability for loss of property in its custody. A number of acts of vandalism occurred over an eighteen-month period, and the assured was found liable for them. The dates of the losses within that period were unknown, although the start date for the losses was the last quarter of the first policy and the end date was the first quarter of the third policy. The full amount of the loss was covered by any one of the three policies and so in making a claim there was no need for the assured to identify the policy year into which the losses fell. However, it mattered to the insurers, because the assured had different reinsurers for each of the three years. The Court of Appeal held that, on the balance of probabilities, the losses occurred in a regular fashion, so that they were to be allocated to the three policies in the proportions one-sixth, two-thirds, and one-sixth.

[56] [2011] EWCA Civ 1570; [2012] Lloyd's Rep IR 315.

[57] Note, however, that a claim under a liability policy arises when the assured's liability is established and quantified, so that it would have been open to Teal to settle North American actions first, thereby ensuring that they were allocated to the PI Tower first. Tomlinson LJ recognized the possibility of that form of limited manipulation, although he did not comment on whether there might have been some form of constraint upon Teal and, if so, from what source. Had these been property policies, the issue would not have arisen: a claim under a property policy arises as soon as the insured peril occurs, so the chronology is beyond the control of the reinsured.

[58] [1996] 3 All ER 517; [1996] 1 WLR 1026.

How do these cases relate to mesothelioma claims? Two possible answers may be put forward. The most obvious is that the insurer is bound by the choice of year by the employer. There is only one reinsured loss, in the form of the claim by the employer, and that has occurred in the policy year opted for by the employer. The outwards reinsurance claim must, therefore, be presented in the same way, by analogy with *Teal*. The alternative approach is that the insurer has suffered a series of losses across the insured and reinsured period, and it just happens that the loss was treated as having occurred within a particular policy year for the purposes of the employer. The ability of an insurer to present an allocation of claims to policy years other than those which responded to the claim by the assured has been much discussed in the US, and the cases are inconclusive.[59] As far as English law is concerned, the former approach is almost certainly correct. That was the assumption underlying *IRB Brasil Resseguros SA v CX Reinsurance Company Ltd*,[60] in which the reinsured allocated 70 per cent of US asbestos liability claims to an excess of loss treaty which was in force for 64 per cent of the period of exposure. Burton J, dismissing an appeal by excess of loss reinsurers against an arbitral award, held that the reinsured had proved its loss. The US courts operated the 'continuous trigger' theory under which the insurer faced 100 per cent liability if it was on risk for any part of the period running from exposure to manifestation of injury. Accordingly the reinsured could properly have presented 100 per cent of the loss to the reinsurers, so its decision to present only 70 per cent of that loss was not capable of challenge.

Exactly how reinsurance will apply to mesothelioma cases is as yet unknown, because much will depend upon the types of reinsurance employed and the wordings of individual contracts. Indeed, it may never be known, because reinsurance disputes are typically either settled on a collective 'commutation' basis where individual claims are not identified or resolved behind the arbitration curtain of confidentiality. We have nevertheless set out the general picture by way of demonstrating that any serious assessment of the distributive effects of tort liabilities cannot be achieved by a priori reasoning.

12.5 Conclusions

The asbestos litigation illustrates many of the themes of earlier chapters, and brings them together in a way which underlines the mutual influence of liability and insurance. The saga raises afresh, and in a new context, the question of whether insurance should be recognized as driving and shaping compensation,[61] or whether it is best left out of the picture. *Trigger* demonstrates that insurance should not be artificially ignored. The majority did not manipulate insurance principles on policy grounds. But neither did it accept an apparently 'principled' interpretation of the special rule in *Fairchild* which would have had 'remarkable' adverse effects on insurance coverage. The members of the majority had a clear grasp of the general picture of which *Fairchild* and *Barker* formed part. That picture is inevitably in part a distributive one, the more

[59] O Gurses, *Reinsuring Clauses* (London: Informa, 2010).

[60] [2010] EWHC 974 (Comm).

[61] R Lewis, 'Insurance and the Tort System' (2005) 25 LS 85, and discussed also in Chapter 9.

so as time between breach and liability is prolonged. We have ended the chapter by looking beyond the artificial barrier set by the tort claims, to the impact of decisions such as *Fairchild*, *Barker*, and *Trigger* on insurance disputes and, therefore, on the ultimate location of losses.

Finally, we should emphasize the existence of public interest in distributive questions and in the meeting of liabilities through insurance, exemplified not only by statutory intervention after *Barker*, but also by the intervention of the government in the *Trigger* litigation.[62] Lord Phillips met this issue with a suggestion that successful claims against insurers in *Trigger* would be at the expense of others with 'claims against the same insurers founded on facts and not legal fictions'.[63] This is, we suggest, a little misleading. The claims were based on real injury following real breaches of duty. The fiction of proof of a causal link provided the means for the liabilities to operate as normal liabilities do, namely, to be fed into the insurance market. The rest was achieved not by manipulation, but by application of the ordinary principles of insurance law. The application of these principles is contentious and adversarial. But that is all the more reason for saying that tort claims properly deal with injury; and that the operation of the insurance market is the appropriate place for injury liabilities to be considered in terms of the division and transfer of risks.

[62] The government argued that if liabilities were not met by insurance, they would become a drain on public resources.

[63] *Trigger*, n 1, [136].

13

Insurance in Litigation

13.1 Insurance and the Shaping of Litigation

13.1.1 Outline

We have tried to demonstrate throughout this book the pervasive nature of insurance both in commercial life and in the development of the substantive law of obligations. In this chapter we turn to the effects of insurance on litigation and the enforcement of rights. Although the issues here might be thought to be exclusively procedural, they are far from that; inevitably, procedure spills over into substance and affects the way in which claims are framed and how they are defended.[1] Here, insurance has the capacity to influence the development of private law across a very broad spectrum. Our goal is to use an examination of legal provisions and reforms which govern, enable, and respond to the role of insurers in litigation, to indicate quite how deep and wide the influence of insurance is in shaping the process of claiming both in detail, and in general terms.

We begin by analysing the role played by insurance in assisting the claimant in financing a claim, through the mechanisms of Before the Event (BTE) and After the Event (ATE) insurance. Insurance will feature at the earliest stage in the consultation between claimant and solicitor: the Solicitors Regulation Authority Code of Conduct 2011, General Principle IB1.1.6, demands that a solicitor discusses 'how the client will pay, including... whether the client has insurance that might cover the fees'. BTE insurance is long-standing, and provides cover against the risk that the assured will become engaged in litigation during the currency of the policy and incur costs in doing so. ATE insurance developed comparatively recently, and provides cover for the costs of bringing (and, less commonly, defending) a specific claim. ATE insurance was given a significant boost when it was included in the scheme for the private market replacement for the removal of legal aid from the majority of cases under the Access to Justice Act 1999. Under the 1999 Act ATE insurance worked in tandem with the modification of the laws of champerty, by allowing lawyers to take cases on a 'no win, no fee' conditional fee basis and allowing them to uplift fees in the event of success (conditional fee agreements, or CFAs). The new structure fed existing fears that a 'Compensation Culture' was developing fuelled by lawyers paid by results and by insurance companies funding actions ranging from strong to hopeless, leading to a dramatic increase in both litigation and its cost. Jackson LJ addressed the question of legal costs in his *Review of Civil Litigation Costs* published in December 2009,[2] as subsequently

[1] In relation to tort, see T Baker, 'Liability Insurance as Tort Regulation: Six Ways that Liability Insurance Shapes Tort Law in Action' (2005) 12 *Connecticut Insurance Law Journal* 1.

[2] <http://www.judiciary.gov.uk/NR/rdonlyres/8EB9F3F3-9C4A-4139-8A93-56F09672EB6A/0/jackson-finalreport140110.pdf>, accessed 6 May 2013. A Preliminary Report, containing much of the detail upon which the recommendations in the Final Report were based, was published in May 2009.

implemented in part by the Legal Aid, Sentencing, and Punishment of Offenders Act 2012 to remove the worst excesses. Since the implementation of the Jackson recommendations, certain objectionable aspects of BTE insurance are removed and the use of ATE will inevitably diminish significantly.[3]

We then turn to the impact of the defendant's liability insurance upon the manner in which the claim is made and its defence. This involves some explanation of the role of insurers in defending or funding the defence of claims brought against the assured.

Finally, we explain the operation of the Third Parties (Rights against Insurers) Act 1930, which converts liability insurance into a mechanism for the enforcement of judgments and which plays a vital role in the enforcement of judgments by transferring claims under the policy to the victim in the event of the assured's insolvency.

The inevitable point from all of this is that insurance can be seen to have a profound influence not just on the nature and limits of the defendant's liability, but also on the way in which that liability is established and, ultimately, satisfied.

13.1.2 Impact of insurance on litigation planning

Any decision to initiate judicial or other proceedings against a defendant rests upon two variables: is there a cause of action against the defendant; and is the defendant good for any damages that may be awarded? The second question may to some extent be discounted where the defendant is either of substantial means or is required to insure, but outside those situations the defendant's insurance position is frequently the starting point of the inquiry. There is, after all, no point in undertaking expensive inquiries into the circumstances giving rise to a loss if a fruitless outcome is inevitable. Obtaining insurance information from a potential defendant is not, however, a possibility recognized by English procedural law. CPR 31.17 permits a party to litigation to seek disclosure from a third party, but only where such disclosure 'is necessary in order to dispose fairly of the claim or to save costs'. In a preliminary skirmish to the Buncefield litigation, *West London Pipeline and Storage Ltd v Total UK Ltd*,[4] David Steel J held that this formulation did not extend to obtaining insurance information to determine whether or not a claim should be brought. An earlier decision to the contrary, *Harcourt*

[3] There is a non-insurance alternative, in the form of litigation funding, explained in Chapter 15 of the Jackson Preliminary Report. At the moment this appears to operate only for very large claims. In outline, a funder operates on a 'no win, no fee' basis, receiving nothing if the claim fails (and, following *Arkin v Borchard Lines Ltd* [2005] EWCA Civ 655; [2005] 1 WLR 3055, facing personal liability for costs representing the proportion of funding) but taking a substantial percentage of any damages (figures of 40 per cent were cited by Jackson) if the claim succeeds. This activity is close to the borderline of illegality by reason of champerty and maintenance: AJ Sebok, 'Betting on Tort Suits After the Event: From Champerty to Insurance' (2010–11) 60 DePaul L Rev 453, but has been cleared by the English courts in *London & Regional (St George's Court) Ltd v Ministry of Defence* [2008] EWHC 526 (TCC). Chapter 11 of the Jackson Final Report recognized that the industry is still 'nascent' and that it should be regulated by a draft voluntary code rather than, at least for the moment, statutory intervention; in particular, funders should be able to demonstrate sufficient financial capacity, and should not be permitted to withdraw funding simply because the claim was proving not to be viable. The Code was published in November 2011 and is available online at: <http://www.judiciary.gov.uk/JCO%2fDocuments%2fCJC%2fPublications%2fCJC+papers%2fCode+of+Conduct+for+Litigation+Funders+(November+2011).pdf>, accessed 6 May 2013.

[4] [2008] EWHC 1296 (Comm); [2008] Lloyd's Rep IR 688.

v FEF Griffin,[5] was disapproved, and it is now generally assumed that the restrictive interpretation of CPR 31.17 is the correct one. Insurance information is available only once the wrongdoer has become insolvent and a claim can be made against the insurers under the 1930 Act, which is typically after proceedings have been commenced against the wrongdoer.

Awareness that the wrongdoer does possess insurance is only of partial assistance to the victim. A number of other considerations are relevant here.

First, the insurers may have one or more defences under the policy, any of which may deprive the assured of an indemnity and thus the victim of a source of funds, a possibility which may not become apparent until the victim has incurred a good deal of expenditure in pressing the claim. Even if the wrongdoer has become insolvent, the victim has no basis for a claim against the insurers under the 1930 Act.

Second, the wrongdoer's liability policy will make provision not just for the payment of damages but also for the payment of the costs incurred by the wrongdoer in conducting his defence of the proceedings, and if there is a single combined aggregate limit of indemnity rather than separate sub-limits for each head, the victim may find that the policy has been exhausted by legal costs by the time that a judgment is obtained.

Third, the victim must take care to frame the cause of action in terms which are covered by the class of policy that the wrongdoer is likely to possess. There is conflicting authority on the question whether a victim, who has obtained judgment against an assured by pleading a cause of action which ultimately proves to be excluded from the assured's cover, is estopped in a claim against the insurers under the 1930 Act from putting forward an alternative—and insured—cause of action on which judgment could have been given had it been raised at the outset.[6] Particular danger arises where the victim satisfies a court of illegal conduct or fraud on the part of the wrongdoer, as that will be fatal to indemnity under the policy,[7] and it will not be open to the victim to assert in subsequent proceedings against the insurers under the 1930 Act that judgment could have been obtained against the wrongdoer on other grounds and that the finding of fraud was erroneous.[8] So arguing fraud against a defendant whose only real asset is liability insurance is a self-defeating exercise.[9]

[5] [2007] EWHC 1500 (QB); [2008] Lloyd's Rep IR 386.

[6] *London Borough of Redbridge v Municipal Mutual Insurance* [2001] Lloyd's Rep IR 545 (judgment conclusive); *Omega Proteins Ltd v Aspen Insurance UK Ltd* [2010] EWHC 2280 (Comm); [2011] 1 All ER (Comm) 313 (judgment not conclusive so the victim can change tack).

[7] Chapter 12.

[8] *Persimmon Homes Ltd v Great Lakes Reinsurance (UK) Plc* [2010] EWHC 1705 (Comm); [2011] Lloyd's Rep IR 101. The suggestion by Mance J in *Total Graphics Ltd v AGF Insurance Ltd* [1997] 1 Lloyd's Rep 599, that an *ex turpi causa* defence open to the insurers operates as a personal bar affecting the assured alone and does not affect third-party claims, has not surfaced in later cases.

[9] Although even if the victim is meticulous in alleging nothing more than negligence it remains open to the insurers to go behind the claim as formulated and to ascertain for themselves whether fraud or illegality is involved: *MDIS v Swinbank* [1999] Lloyd's Rep IR 516. Some pleadings refer to 'matters of concern' without actually raising a direct allegation of fraud, a practice condemned by Davis LJ in *Hussain v Amin* [2012] EWCA Civ 1456.

13.2 Funding Litigation

13.2.1 Legal expenses (BTE) insurance

Before the Event (BTE) insurance (also referred to as LEI) provides cover against the costs which may be incurred in bringing legal proceedings.[10] Those costs may be substantial. A successful claimant will generally be granted an order requiring the defendant to bear its own costs and to pay those of the claimant, but it is almost inevitable that the claimant will still be out of pocket to some extent where, as is almost always the case, standard rather than indemnity costs are awarded.[11] An unsuccessful claimant will be required to bear his or her own costs and those of the defendant, a possibility which is a clear deterrent to engaging in litigation. Jackson LJ undertook detailed research into BTE insurance, and his May 2009 Preliminary Report and December 2009 Final Report contain invaluable information on its scope, practicalities, and potential defects.[12]

Unlike After the Event (ATE) insurance, BTE insurance does not relate to known existing disputes, but rather applies to claims which may arise in the future. This type of cover is available to businesses as a stand-alone product where it may be wide ranging or confined to particular matters (for example, tax and employment), although the take-up rate, particularly by small businesses, is low. That contrasts dramatically with the domestic market. BTE insurance is generally included as an add-on to domestic householder and motor policies, increasingly is offered as one of the packaged benefits attached to bank accounts, and is a traditional benefit of trade union membership. Post-Jackson research by Consumer Focus[13] has shown that some 36 million BTE policies were written in 2008, with a premium value of £447 million, and that 25 million households were insured, 15 million by way of add-on to household cover. Some 18 million people also had BTE cover under their motor policies. This plethora of different sources, and particularly packaging with other products, makes value comparisons somewhat difficult. BTE insurance is however relatively cheap, and a premium of around £25 can purchase cover of up to £100,000, although there may be lower limits for particular classes of claim. BTE typically supports actions against motorists, employers, suppliers, medical practitioners, and neighbours, although matrimonial and mental health disputes are normally excluded.

BTE insurance appears to be underutilized, and the research by Consumer Focus has shown that many domestic holders are unaware of its existence. However, the importance of BTE insurance where it is utilized is undoubted. Some 53 per cent of successful claimants studied indicated that, but for BTE, they would not have proceeded at all. BTE insurance facilitates claims that would not otherwise be possible. Looking forward,

[10] See the discussion by Willem H van Boom, *Juxtaposing BTE and ATE: The Role of the European Insurance Industry in Funding Civil Litigation*, OUCLF, 26 March 2010; available at <http://ouclf.iuscomp.org/articles/vanboom.shtml>, accessed 7 May 2013.

[11] CPR Part 44.

[12] Ministry of Justice, *The Market for BTE Legal Expenses Insurance*, July 2007.

[13] Consumer Focus, *In Case of Emergency*, available at <http://www.consumerfocus.org.uk/files/2011/08/In-case-of-emergency.pdf>, accessed 7 May 2013.

it has been argued that it could offer the key to access to justice for many potential litigants.[14] This underlines that in the shift from public to private funding of litigation, insurers hold the key.

Coverage disputes under BTE policies are comparatively rare. Typical wording triggers liability where the claim by the assured has 'reasonable prospects of success', and in case of doubt there is generally a mechanism for a definitive opinion to be obtained from counsel. The real problem with BTE insurance is the inherent conflict of interest where the insurer is both the BTE provider for the claimant and the liability insurer of the defendant. To overcome this problem, the EU's Legal Expenses Directive 1987,[15] implemented in the UK by the Insurance Companies (Legal Expenses) Regulations 1990,[16] requires a BTE insurer to allow the assured to appoint his or her own lawyer[17] whenever a conflict of interest arises and in any event as soon as proceedings have been commenced. BTE insurers generally have their own panel of solicitors, charging fees negotiated with the insurers, but the assured cannot be forced to appoint a member of the panel and has an absolute entitlement to go elsewhere. The overriding nature of that right was emphasized by the CJEU in *Eschig v UNIQA Sachversicherung AG*,[18] where the assured was one of several thousand policyholders who wished to initiate proceedings against the same defendants for losses arising from investments, and was held to be entitled to appoint his own lawyers even though insurers had unsurprisingly insisted upon the consolidation of legal representation.

A distinction is nevertheless to be drawn between restriction on free choice of lawyer and limitations on the amount payable under the policy if the assured opted for a non-panel lawyer. As to the former, in *Brown-Quinn v Equity Syndicate Management Ltd*[19] the Court of Appeal struck down, as inconsistent with the Regulations, policy terms which: (a) reserved the right of the insurers to refuse (albeit only in exceptional circumstances) the assured's initial choice of solicitor; and (b) automatically terminated cover if the assured, having initially appointed a panel solicitor, chose to transfer the case to another solicitor. The insurers were indeed condemned for using terms which were plainly at odds with the Regulations. The Court of Appeal did, however, accept that insurers were entitled to cap their liability for legal fees at the hourly rates charged by panel solicitors, unless the assured could produce evidence that the rates were inadequate to the extent that it rendered the right of free choice of solicitor meaningless.

[14] R Lewis, 'Litigation Costs and Before-the-Event Insurance: the Key to Access to Justice?' (2011) 74 MLR 272.

[15] Council Directive 87/344/EEC, prospectively repealed and re-enacted in the Solvency 2 Directive, European Parliament and Council Directive 2009/138/EC.

[16] SI 1990/1159, accompanied by the Insurance Companies (Legal Expenses Insurance) (Application for Authorisation) Regulations 1990, SI 1990/1160.

[17] This can be a direct access barrister rather than a solicitor if the case can appropriately be managed without instructing a solicitor: *Pine v Das Legal Expenses Insurance Company Ltd* [2011] EWHC 658 (QB); [2012] Lloyd's Rep IR 346. *Stark v DAS Oesterreiche Algemeine Rechtsschutzversicherung AG* Case C-293/10, [2011] EUECJ, upheld the right of the assured to appoint a lawyer from a different region.

[18] [2009] ECR I-08295, [2010] 1 All ER (Comm) 576.

[19] [2012] EWCA Civ 1633.

The Jackson Preliminary Report of May 2009 identified two forms of BTE cover: the most common form, BTE_1, where the insurers pay solicitors to act for the assured when a claim arises; and BTE_2, where insurers will 'sell' to solicitors any claims which arise, the solicitors paying referral fees and handling the claim on some form of CFA. The conclusion in Chapter 8 of the Jackson Final Report was that BTE insurance was on balance beneficial, given its ability to promote access to justice at a comparatively low cost to the assured, and that costs tended to be lower than in claims supported by ATE and CFAs. Accordingly, positive efforts should be made to encourage the take-up of BTE insurance as an add-on to householder's policies and also by small and medium-sized enterprises. Jackson did not recommend any restriction on BTE_2 itself, but effectively sounded its death knell by recommending a prohibition on the payment of referral fees by insurers and rendering success fees charged by solicitors as part of CFAs irrecoverable by way of costs. Those recommendations were implemented by the Legal Aid, Sentencing and Punishing of Offenders Act 2012, ss 56–60 (as regards referral fees for death and personal injury claims) and s 44 (as regards success fees).

13.2.2 After the event (ATE) insurance

13.2.2.1 Rise and fall

ATE insurance provides *ad hoc* funding for individual claims as and when they arise. It is most commonly used in personal injury cases, but in principle it is available for any case in which damages may be awarded to the claimant: that qualification is essential, because ATE insurance is ultimately funded by defendants by way of costs. In essence, payment of the ATE premium is deferred until the outcome of the proceedings. The policy will meet a costs order against the assured if the claim is lost, and if the claim is won then the premium for the ATE policy is paid by the defendant by way of costs. So ATE has the advantage for the assured that it is costless. When it is coupled with a CFA between the assured and his or her solicitors, under which they agree to act on a 'no win, no fee' basis but with an uplift in the form of a success fee which will ultimately be payable by the defendant if the assured is successful, then the assured has no concerns about having to meet even his or her own costs.

An ATE insurer will enter into an agreement with a solicitor, generally in terms of a floating facility, under which the solicitor may apply for ATE insurance cover in respect of any claim referred by a client. There will typically be two criteria for the provision of assistance: that damages of a specified minimum amount are awardable; and that there is a better than evens chance that the claim will succeed. If the solicitor confirms that these criteria are satisfied,[20] the assured will enter into an ATE contract with the insurers. Credit is granted for the premium. At the same time the assured will, almost inevitably, enter into a CFA with the solicitors. Those solicitors may well have their

[20] A duty of care, if not express, is almost certainly owed to the insurers. *Axa Insurance Ltd v Akther & Darby Solicitors* [2009] EWCA Civ 1166; [2010] 1 WLR 1662 concerns this relationship. Similarly, the assured owes a duty of disclosure to the insurers: *Persimmon Homes Ltd v Great Lakes Reinsurance (UK) Plc* [2010] EWHC 1705 (Comm); [2011] Lloyd's Rep IR 101, where the assured's claim was shown to be based on forged documents and fraudulent evidence.

own insurance covering lost fees in the event that the claim is defeated. The solicitors may also provide the assured with a guarantee that he or she will not face any liability for costs, covering the possibilities that the ATE insurers may withdraw cover, deny liability, or avoid the policy. If the guarantee is called in and the insurers' actions are found to have been unjustified then the solicitors will have a restitutionary claim against the insurers on the basis that they have under legal obligation satisfied the debt owed by the insurers.[21] Once the policy has been issued, the insurers are not concerned with the day-to-day running of the case, although there are generally policy provisions which require them to be informed of any significant developments in the case.[22]

The key to ATE is the recoverability of the premium by way of costs. The Access to Justice Act 1999, s 29, conferred statutory authority for judicial discretion to include in any costs order 'an amount in respect of the premium'[23] of a policy taken out in 'those proceedings'.[24] In every case the test for recovery is whether the premium was reasonably incurred, which requires the court to consider: whether the case was one appropriate for ATE funding;[25] whether the claimant had cheaper BTE insurance available to him;[26] whether the policy was taken out at an appropriate time in the course of the proceedings;[27] and whether the amount of the premium was reasonable in the sense that it was individually calculated by reference to the risk faced by the insurers.[28] If the reasonableness criteria are satisfied, there is no automatic bar to recovery simply because the ATE premium is large in comparison to the amount sought.[29]

Unsurprisingly, much of the Jackson Report is devoted to the combined effect of ATE insurance and CFAs. There was conflicting evidence on the impact of ATE insurance on unmeritorious claims: some suggested that they were promoted, others argued that ATE insurance acted as a filter. Jackson LJ accepted that there were instances of tactical use of ATE as a means of pressurizing the defendant to settle,[30]

[21] *Greene Wood McLean LLP v Templeton Insurance Ltd (No 2)* [2010] EWHC 2679 (Comm); [2011] Lloyd's Rep IR 557.

[22] *Quantum Claims Compensation Specialists Ltd v Wren Insurance Services* [2012] ScotSC CSIH 8.

[23] CPR r 43.2 defines 'premium', as construed by *Re Claims Direct Test Cases* [2003] EWCA Civ 136; [2003] Lloyd's Rep IR 677, holding that commissions paid for ancillary services were not premium for the purposes of a costs order.

[24] In *Ord Trustees Jersey Ltd v Stella Global UK Ltd* [2012] EWCA Civ 987; [2012] 1 WLR 3581 the Court of Appeal held that it had no power to award the costs of the trial where a successful appeal was funded by ATE insurance, because the trial was not a part of the proceedings funded by the ATE premium.

[25] *Callery v Gray* [2002] UKHL 28; [2002] 1 WLR 2000; *Motto v Trafigura Ltd* [2011] EWCA Civ 1150; [2012] 1 WLR 657.

[26] *Sarwar v Alam* [2001] 4 All ER 541.

[27] *Ashworth v Peterborough United Football Club* [2002] EWHC 9004 (Costs).

[28] *Callery v Gray (No 2)* [2001] EWCA Civ 1246; [2001] 1 WLR 2142, casting doubt on the practice of block-rating; *RSA Pursuit Test Cases* [2005] EWHC 90003 (Costs).

[29] *Rogers v Merthyr Tydfil CBC* [2006] EWCA Civ 1134; [2007] 1 WLR 808, a case much criticized in the course of the Jackson inquiry given that it made the level of premium for the purposes of costs assessment very difficult to challenge.

[30] However, this can be double edged where details of the policy are made available to the defendant, who may take the view that financial and other limitations on cover justify a refusal to settle. Claimants may thus want the existence of ATE, but not its detail, to be made known. It was held in *Barr v Biffa Waste Services Ltd* [2009] EWHC 1033 (TCC); [2010] Lloyd's Rep IR 428 that if the existence of ATE is mentioned, the entire policy must be disclosed under CPR 31.14.

although he found others where the amount of the ATE premium paid by the claimant inhibited a settlement.[31] Evidence was also given of cases where the ATE premium was close to the amount of the claim itself, and, given that the premium typically ranged between 30 per cent and 50 per cent of the level of costs insured, a high ATE premium can lead to costs becoming far higher than the claim. The Report concluded that costs had become disproportionate and excessive, and that both ATE premiums and CFA success fees should no longer be recoverable from defendants by way of costs. The clinching factor was expressed as follows:[32]

> The flaw in the present regime is that it is not targeted upon those who merit such protection. Any person who finds a willing insurer can take out ATE insurance, whether that person is rich or poor, human or corporate, deserving or undeserving. Furthermore, the protection which a claimant derives from ATE insurance is total. The claimant is not required to make a modest contribution towards adverse costs... even if he can afford to do so.

The Jackson Report's preferred approach to protecting claimants against adverse costs orders was the adoption of 'one-way costs shifting', under which an unsuccessful claimant would generally not be ordered to pay the costs of the defendant, although the system would be qualified in a number of respects: (a) a costs order could be enforced if the claimant proved to be the wealthier party; (b) costs might be awarded against a claimant who refused to accept an offer of settlement[33] and failed to beat it in the proceedings; (c) the principle would not extend to commercial, construction, and similar litigation, given that the parties would generally be in a contractual relationship the symmetry of which should not be upset; (d) professional negligence and householder claims should be excluded, as claimants can protect themselves against adverse costs orders by way of BTE insurance. Qualified one-way costs shifting (QOCS) would thus be confined to personal injury cases and to other situations in which there was some asymmetry in the parties' relationship, such as 'claimants in housing disrepair cases, claimants in actions against the police, claimants seeking judicial review and individuals making claims for defamation or breach of privacy against the media'.[34]

13.2.2.2 ATE insurance post-Jackson

The government accepted the Jackson proposals. Reform came into effect on 1 April 2013. The Legal Aid, Sentencing and Punishment of Offenders Act 2012, s 46, modifies the Access to Justice Act 1999, s 29, by removing the reference to ATE premiums, so that they are rendered irrecoverable other than in two exceptional cases. The first is where the proceedings are for clinical negligence and the claim is for more than £1,000, the insurance covers the risk of liability to pay for an expert medical report, and the premium does not exceed that part of the premium which relates to the risk of

[31] Many settlements are on a 'drop hands' basis, where each party agrees to bear its own costs. Plainly a large ATE premium is an inhibiting factor.

[32] Jackson Report, Chapter 9, para 4.4.

[33] Under CPR Part 36.

[34] Jackson Report, Chapter 9, para 5.11.

incurring liability to pay for an expert.[35] Second, under the 2012 Act, s 48, ATE insurance is permitted in respect of mesothelioma claims, although this exclusion is short term only, and is subject to review by the Lord Chancellor. ATE will thus continue in those exceptional cases, and it will still be available to a claimant who is prepared to risk having to pay the premium as well as the defendant's costs in the event that his or her action is dismissed. ATE will inevitably diminish in importance as a result of these changes. It cannot be said that the ATE experiment was a resounding success, in that the number of insurers who wrote the business was never large[36] and some withdrew from the market after suffering substantial losses.

As proposed by the Jackson Report, the removal from claimants of the right to recover ATE premiums (and also CFA uplift fees) by way of costs is to be replaced by QOCS. Although at the time of writing the detail of the CPR changes has yet to be published, it is anticipated that the regime will apply, at least in the first instance, only to personal injury cases, although all claims will be covered without means-testing of claimants. Costs may be awarded against an unsuccessful claim only if the defendant pleads and substantiates fraud in pursuing the claim, if the claim is struck out for abuse of process, or if the claimant fails to better an offer of settlement under CPR Part 36. It will be appreciated that the vast majority of personal injury claims relate to cases where insurance is compulsory or widespread, so the real effect of QOCS is to require compulsory (and other) insurers to bear defence costs irrespective of the outcome rather than to carry the risk of having to pay large ATE premiums by way of costs where claims succeed. Experience alone will tell whether the new regime will prove to be cheaper for the compulsory insurance market.

13.2.3 'Compensation culture' and the 'insurance crisis'

The phrase 'compensation culture' has passed into popular use as a description of English civil litigation, and in particular personal injury litigation (offering the national equivalent of other jurisdictions' 'insurance crises'). The phrase encompasses three quite separate concepts however.[37] The first is the proliferation and cost of civil litigation. The second is the notion that anyone suffering injury is entitled to compensation, so that organizations at risk of claims have been forced to adopt defensive procedures, and the press abounds with stories of all manner of activities being discontinued for 'insurance' reasons, or fear of litigation.[38] The third is that health and safety rules backed by criminal and regulatory sanctions are suffocating business activity. To some extent, all of this has become a self-fulfilling prophecy. Lord Young's 2010 Report to the Prime Minister, 'Common Sense, Common Safety',[39] which has a

[35] See the Recovery of Costs Insurance Premiums in Clinical Negligence Proceedings (No 2) Regulations 2013, SI 2013/739.

[36] Jackson's estimate was no more than twenty.

[37] Detailed exploration of the politics of 'compensation culture' as it has affected the main political parties can be found in A Morris, 'The "Compensation Culture" and the Politics of Tort', in TT Arvind and J Steele, *Tort Law and the Legislature* (Oxford: Hart Publishing, 2013).

[38] K Williams, 'State of fear: Britain's "compensation culture" reviewed' (2005) 25 *Legal Studies* 499.

[39] <https://www.gov.uk/government/uploads/system/uploads/attachment_data/file/60905/402906_CommonSense_acc.pdf>, accessed 7 May 2013.

'Compensation Culture' chapter, was in essence an attack on health and safety rules, with a few sideswipes at the operation of personal injury litigation, but contains the important admission out of line with much of the rest of the Report that 'The problem of the compensation culture prevalent in society today is, however, one of perception rather than reality'.[40]

In terms of the civil law, however, the relevant point for our purposes is that each of the substantive law of tort and litigation procedure plays a part in the perception of a 'Compensation Culture'. The former focuses on the apparent ease of formulating a cause of action. The latter focuses on the funding arrangements which facilitate litigation, allowing unjustified claims to be pressed and ultimately settled because they are too small to be worth fighting or through fear of establishing a judicial precedent. As we have seen in the preceding paragraphs, the UK's approach to the problem has generally been to restrict insurance funding by cutting away the basis of ATE insurance, although recent changes to employers' liabilities, explored in earlier chapters, mark a significant exception. The Australian approach has been to restrict the substantive law itself. The Ipp Report, *Review of the Law of Negligence*, 2002, was commissioned and completed hurriedly in the light of fears that the level of tort claims had made liability insurance at best expensive and at worst unobtainable, and that to overcome the 'insurance crisis' it was necessary for individuals to take greater responsibility for their own welfare rather than to blame others. Legislation, which has often gone much further than the Ipp recommendations, has been put in place to different extents in each of the Australian states and territories, but in general has led to stricter rules on duty of care and causation, an enhanced role for contributory negligence, tighter limitation periods, and restrictions on the level of damages. Australian literature on whether the reforms were justified at all,[41] and whether they have achieved anything worthwhile, proliferates.[42]

A third approach has been adopted by the US insurance industry. The courts of various US states, faced with claims by the victims of exposure to asbestos, developed the 'continuous' or 'triple trigger' theory of liability, under which liability attached in full to any year in which there had been exposure, actual injury, or manifestation of injury.[43] That level of exposure had a dramatic effect on the availability and affordability of employers' liability and public liability insurance. The problem was tackled by moving insurance litigation away from the US. Leading US insurers, brokers, and banks provided the capital to establish two insurance companies in Bermuda, Ace and

[40] Chapter 8, 8.6, discusses the more influential Löftstedt Review (R Löftstedt, 'Reclaiming Health and Safety for All' November 2011, Cm 8219), which has been used as the basis for the Enterprise and Regulatory Reform Act 2013, s 69.

[41] The hardening of the liability insurance market is equally explicable by the demise of HIH in 1999 for reasons entirely unconnected with tort claims (namely, fraud in the organization and an attempt to increase market share by offering uneconomically low premiums), and the lack of reinsurance capacity.

[42] For example P Cane, 'Reforming Tort Law in Australia: A Personal Perspective' (2003) 27 *Melbourne University Law Review*, 649; B McDonald, 'The Impact of the Civil Liability Legislation on Fundamental Policies and Principles of the Common Law of Negligence' (2006) 14 *Torts Law Journal* 443; JJ Spigelman, 'Tort Law Reform: An Overview' (2006) 14 *Tort Law Review* 443.

[43] *Keene Corp v Insurance Co of North America* 667 F 2d 1034 (DC Cir 1981).

XL, to offer high-level excess-layer insurance under the 'Bermuda Form',[44] with coverage commencing when aggregate losses arising from one or more events reach US$25 million (XL) and US$100 million (Ace). The policies are governed by New York law, but disputes are resolved by arbitration in London. This mechanism keeps disputes away from US juries and prevents any appeal against the award to the New York courts,[45] and an appeal can reach the English courts only where it is asserted that the arbitrators did not possess jurisdiction or had been guilty of serious procedural irregularity in the conduct of the arbitration:[46] issues of substance cannot be appealed.[47] Insurers, in this instance, have succeeded in putting interpretation of insurance contracts beyond the reach of a problematic jurisdiction.

13.3 Defending Litigation by Liability Insurance[48]

Liability policies of all types make provision not just for indemnifying the assured against any judgment, arbitral award, or settlement, but also for protecting the assured against liability for the costs of defending the proceedings brought against the assured. Indemnification for liability and the conduct of the defence are separate obligations undertaken by the insurers and very often there are independent financial limits of liability for each obligation. However, other policies set out a combined aggregate limit of indemnity covering both aspects.

Insurers generally have, under the terms of the policy, the option to defend the proceedings on behalf of the assured. In that situation the assured is required to step aside and to leave negotiations and settlements in the hands of the insurers, who will appoint their own lawyers. In many cases the assured may have no interest in defending the claim itself, as where the assured is no longer trading, and the insurers will have little choice but to defend the proceedings for the assured in their own interests or face a default judgment.[49] The insurer may in the alternative take the view that they do not face liability under the policy, and either may refuse to defend at all,[50] or may do so under a reservation of rights which allows them to refuse indemnity if the claim against the assured is successful.

[44] R Jacobs, P Masters, and LS Stanley, *Liability Insurance in International Arbitration: The Bermuda Form* (Oxford: Hart Publishing, 2nd edn, 2011); D Scorey, R Geddes, and C Harris, *The Bermuda Form: Interpretation and Dispute Resolution of Excess Liability Insurance* (New York: Oxford University Press, 2011).

[45] *C v D* [2007] EWCA Civ 1282; [2008] 1 Lloyd's Rep 239.

[46] Under, respectively, the Arbitration Act 1996, s 67 and s 68.

[47] An appeal is possible under the 1996 Act, s 69, only where the substantive agreement is governed by English law.

[48] Litigation may also be defended by 'litigation buy-out insurance', under which the assured insures against the risk that it may face liability for a claim against it. This type of insurance is useful where the assured wishes to value its liabilities for the purposes of a share or asset sale, so that the prospective purchaser can be satisfied that the risk of a finding of liability against the assured can be left out of account.

[49] If they do, and the action succeeds, the insurers will almost inevitably find themselves facing a third-party costs order under the Senior Courts Act 1981, s 51. The line of authority started with *TGA Chapman Ltd v Christopher* [1998] 1 WLR 12, and runs through to the most recent decision, *Palmer v Palmer* [2008] EWCA Civ 46; [2008] Lloyd's Rep IR 535.

[50] The assured will typically be told to act as a 'prudent uninsured' and to defend the claim itself, so that policy coverage issues can be resolved at a later date. The assured is not relieved from cooperation duties

Most assureds are perfectly happy to leave settlement negotiations in the hands of the insurers. The insurers will be in a better position than the assured to achieve a commercial settlement with the claimant, and the vast majority of settlements are confidential and also effected without admission of liability, so that there is no harm to the assured's continuing reputation or business. Very often, the amount of the settlement is fixed at the limit of indemnity under the policy, which means that the assured is immune from personal liability other than for the amount of the deductible. There is nevertheless a potential risk that the insurers will take the view that the case is one which should be fought. If the insurers choose to reject the settlement offer and fight the case but lose it, the amount of judgment may well exceed the limits of the policy, leaving the assured with an excess uninsured liability. Professional indemnity policies confer some protection in the form of 'QC' clauses, under which, in the event of dispute between the assured and the insurers the decision to defend will turn upon the adjudication of a QC. Independently, there is now a body of case law which indicates that the insurers owe a duty to take into account the interests of the assured as well as their own in making a decision on settlement, and that exposing the assured to personal liability above policy limits by refusal to settle is a breach of that duty which sounds in damages.[51]

Alternatively, the insurers may choose not to conduct the defence themselves, but rather to fund the defence by providing an indemnity for defence costs. Such costs include legal costs, but also investigation costs and—in business cases—public relations costs as well as a variety of other forms of expenditure which may be incurred as a result of the allegations by the third party. If the insurers choose not to conduct the defence, the assured must itself do so, subject to reporting obligations under the policy and subject also to any provisions requiring the assured to obtain the consent of the insurers to incur particular costs[52] and to enter into any settlement agreement.[53] There are many different forms of wording applicable to defence costs, but that most commonly encountered provides that insurers will fund the defence of the assured, under some wordings even though the claim may not fall within the terms of the

under the policy even though the insurers have denied liability: *Lexington Insurance Co v Multinacional de Seguros SA* [2008] EWHC 1170 (Comm); [2009] Lloyd's Rep IR 1, but contrast the Australian approach in *CGU Insurance Ltd v AMP Financial Planning Pty Ltd* [2007] HCA 36.

[51] The basis of the duty is unclear. It has been classified by the Canadian (*Plaza Fibreglass Manufacturing Ltd v Cardinal Insurance Co* 68 DLR (4th) 586 (1990); *Fredrickson v Insurance Corporation of British Columbia* 69 DLR (4th) 399 (1990)) and Hong Kong (*Ace Insurance Ltd v Metropolitan Electrical Appliance Manufacturing Co Ltd* [2009] HKCFI 1132) courts as fiduciary, although the English view is that the matter rests upon an implied term flowing from the duty of the insurers to act with the utmost good faith (*Groom v Crocker* [1938] 1 KB 194; [1938] 2 All ER 394; *Beacon Insurance Co Ltd v Langdale* [1939] 4 All ER 204). Compare *Herde v Oxford Aviation Academy (Australia) Pty Ltd* [2011] NSWCA 385; *Auckland District Law Society v DA Constable Syndicate 386* (2010) 16 *ANZ Insurance Cases* 61.

[52] There is an implied term that consent will not be unreasonably withheld: *Poole Harbour Yacht Club Marina Ltd v Excess Insurance Co* [1990] 2 All ER 1024; *Thornton Springer v NEM Insurance Co Ltd* [2000] 2 All ER 489.

[53] *Gan Insurance Co Ltd v Tai Ping Insurance Co Ltd* [2002] EWCA Civ 248; [2001] Lloyd's Rep IR 667; *Eagle Star v Cresswell* [2004] Lloyd's Rep IR 537; [2004] EWCA Civ 602. These cases adopt a rather narrower 'rationality' test based upon that for judicial review of administrative action, rather than reasonableness, in order to remove any argument that the court is substituting its own commercial views for those of the insurers.

substantive coverage under the policy but arguably does so,[54] although if the assured at any point is found guilty of, or admits to, fraud, the funding ceases automatically and the insurers may seek to recover their costs payments from the assured.[55]

13.4 Liability Insurance as a Means of Enforcing Judgments

13.4.1 The need for an enforcement mechanism

The discussion of compulsory insurance in Chapter 9 pointed out that there are various mechanisms by which a person suffering loss can be compensated. English law has adopted an approach towards the minimal end of the scale, for the most part leaving liabilities to be allocated by common law principles and paid for by private insurance. But liability insurance is compulsory under statute for the vast majority of personal injury claims, widespread in nearly all others, and frequently a requirement of commercial relationships, so there is a general assumption that reliance on the insurance market will guarantee that compensation is delivered. In this regard, the common law is unhelpful, in that the victim can only await the outcome of negotiations or proceedings between the wrongdoer and the insurers to see whether sums become available. There is no contractual or indeed any other relationship between the wrongdoer's liability insurers and the assured's victim, and any policy term which authorizes a third party to sue the insurers directly is almost certainly of no effect.[56] So, any claim can be brought by the victim only against the assured and not against the insurers.[57] If the victim obtains a judgment against the assured which is not satisfied, the enforcement mechanism open to the victim—initiating an insolvency procedure and seeking to prove in the insolvency for debt—is unlikely to be of much use, given that the victim is yet another competing unsecured creditor.[58]

It seems odd that a person whose claim has generated the insolvency procedure cannot derive the full benefits from it. That oddity is compounded where insurance is compulsory. The problem was appreciated by those responsible for the workmen's compensation legislation. The practice of employers taking out liability insurance against claims made possible by the Employers' Liability Act 1880 rapidly became widespread, so much so that the first Workmen's Compensation Act in 1897 correctly anticipated that many employers would procure liability insurance to cover the new liabilities even though there was no legal compulsion on them to do so.[59] The 1897 Act,

[54] *Thornton Springer v NEM Insurance Co Ltd Ltd* [2000] 2 All ER 489. Contrast *AstraZeneca Insurance Co Ltd v XL Insurance (Bermuda) Ltd* [2013] EWHC 349 (Comm) where defence costs were tied to coverage under the policy.

[55] In practice any attempt to obtain repayment is rarely other than fruitless.

[56] The Contracts (Rights of Third Parties) Act 1999 in principle allows the enforcement of a policy term which states that potential victims can sue the insurers directly, but there are few—if any—examples of such clauses and the identification requirement for enforcement under the 1999 Act would require victims to be identified by name or class. That may be fine in a narrow commercial relationship between wrongdoer and victim, but not where the wrongdoer's potential victims constitute the public at large.

[57] It has thus been held that a broker who is instructed by a client to obtain liability insurance, and who fails to do so, owes no duty of care to victims of the client who find that the client is uninsured: *Federation General Insurance Co v Knott Becker Scott* [1990] 1 Lloyd's Rep 98.

[58] *Hood's Trustees v Southern Union General Insurance Co of Australasia* [1928] Ch 793; *Re Harrington Motor Co* [1928] Ch 105.

[59] Policies issued after the 1897 Act typically covered all potential claims against employers from whatever source. They also covered defence costs.

s 5, sought, in the case of the employer's insolvency, to give the injured employee priority over the insurance moneys which his claim had generated, as against other unsecured creditors. It provided that where an employer became liable to pay compensation in respect of any accident and, having become entitled to indemnification from insurers, went into liquidation, became bankrupt, or entered into a composition with creditors, the injured employee had 'a first charge' upon the policy moneys for the amount due to him. The section had an obvious drawback in that the insurer's liability to the employer had to be established before the relevant act of insolvency, so that the victim of an employer who became insolvent before obtaining a judgment against the insurers had no charge. Again, if the employer was in breach of policy terms, there was no fund to which the charge could attach.[60]

To address these problems, and by way of highlighting the reliance of the entire structure on the insurance market, the Workmen's Compensation Act 1906, s 5, set out an improved version of the transfer. There were two main changes. First, the need for the employer to establish the liability of the insurers before insolvency was dropped, and instead the rights of the employer—including the right of suit—were transferred to the injured employee.[61] Second, the notion of a charge on the insurance moneys was abandoned[62] in favour of a deemed vesting in the employee of the right to sue the insurers. The right was not unlimited. The employee had no better rights than the employer, so any defences open to the insurers—including the submission of disputes to arbitration as a condition precedent of payment[63]—were binding on the employee. There were also decisions to the effect that if an employer was insured and became insolvent, the employee could not prove in the employer's liquidation for the insured amount but was confined to an action against the insurers, which was of little comfort if the insurers themselves were insolvent.[64] An important restriction on the operation of the 1906 Act, s 5, became apparent in *Pailin v Northern Employers' Mutual Indemnity Co Ltd*,[65] the facts of which show that death ('extraordinary') cases were treated by the articles of mutual associations as true insurance,[66] whereas lesser ('ordinary') events leading only to injury were subject to a provision whereby non-fatal injury payments made by the insurers had to be repaid by the employer or, because the employee had no better rights than the employer, by the employee him- or herself in the event of the employer's insolvency.[67] The Court of Appeal indeed classified the ordinary events cover as protection rather than insurance and thus outside the 1906 Act, s 5.

[60] *Leech v Life and Health Assurance Association* [1901] 1 QB 707.

[61] But there was no transfer if the insurers themselves became insolvent: *Liquidator of Thrashbush Coal Company Ltd v M'Inally* 1915 1 SLT 430.

[62] But it is still found in other jurisdictions, including New Zealand—as the Law Reform Act 1936, s 9—and also a number of Australian states.

[63] *King v Phoenix Assurance Co* [1910] 2 KB 666.

[64] *Re Pethick, Dix & Co, Burrows' Claim* [1915] 1 Ch 26; and *Re Renishaw Iron Co Ltd* [1917] 1 Ch 199.

[65] [1925] 2 KB 73.

[66] Referred to as 'extraordinary': *Daff v Midland Colliery Owners' Mutual Indemnity Co* (1913) 82 LJKB 1340.

[67] The same provisions had been given equivalent effect under the 1897 Act, s 5, in that there could be no charge if there were no insurance proceeds: *Morris v Northern Employers' Mutual Indemnity Co* (1902) 18 TLR 635; *Northern Employers' Mutual Indemnity Co v Kniveton* (1902) 18 TLR 504.

Although the 1906 Act, s 5, had its weaknesses, and in particular the effect of subjecting any transfer of rights to all defences available to the insurers under the policy, it was the model for the Third Parties (Rights against Insurers) Act 1930. In its first report, dealing with road traffic, the Royal Commission on Transport acknowledged the influence of that provision.[68] The 1930 Act was passed in conjunction with the Road Traffic Act 1930, and its primary purpose was to provide to the victims of road traffic accidents the same means of recovering compensation under the new compulsory motor cover. The 1930 Act was not needed to secure compensation claims brought under the 1906 Act, and its impact was further restricted by the Road Traffic Act 1934 which built upon the compulsory insurance mechanism by providing an alternative means whereby the victims of road traffic accidents could recover compensation, namely, by obtaining a judgment against the assured and then enforcing it against the insurers, a procedure which remains the law under the Road Traffic Act 1988, s 151. That meant that by 1934 both road traffic and statutory (although not common law) workmen's compensation claims could be brought independently of the 1930 Act. Thereafter its significance was in respect of other forms of liability claims, including marine, public liability, and professional indemnity.

The 1930 Act is a significant piece of legislation for scholars of the law of obligations; without it as an enforcement mechanism, tort and other liabilities carefully crafted by the law would frequently be meaningless; and the existence and refinement of such a measure illustrates the recognized interest in enforcement of liabilities, which has survived the transition from workmen's compensation claims to common law. Yet its significance is not always appreciated: some major tort texts omit any mention of it. Here we demonstrate its significance through exploration of its provisions and the nature of the disputes to which it gives rise.

The Act is in essence an insolvency measure, which seeks to protect a claimant who has obtained a judgment against a defendant without the means to satisfy it, by providing the claimant with a prior claim over other unsecured creditors. The Act has been amended from time to time to take account of the introduction of new insolvency procedures and business structures, but for many years the weaknesses which became apparent from decided cases were left untouched other than on an *ad hoc* basis.[69] Attention focused on the measure in the 1990s when the Law Commission commenced its work on privity of contract, its consultation throwing up a number of adverse comments on the operation of the 1930 Act, including an important contribution by Lord Mance writing in an extra-judicial capacity.[70] Those comments were sufficiently numerous, and the importance of the Act thought to be sufficiently great,[71] to lead the Law Commission to initiate a separate inquiry into the 1930 Act.

[68] *First Report. The Control of Traffic on Roads*, July 1929, (1929–30, Cmd 3365), 27–8.

[69] For example *Bradley v Eagle Star Insurance Co* [1989] AC 957, discussed in 13.4.3.

[70] Sir Jonathan Mance 'Insolvency at Sea' [1995] LMCLQ 34. See also Jonathan Goodliffe 'What is left of the Third Parties (Rights against Insurers) Act 1930?' [1993] JBL 590.

[71] Consultation showed that some 30 per cent of employment claims are brought against insolvent employers and are thus possible only by use of the legislation.

A Consultation Paper published in 1998[72] was followed by a Report and draft bill in 2001.[73] The proposed measure was designed to remedy many of the perceived defects in the 1930 Act although, somewhat surprisingly given its non-contentious nature, the bill lay dormant for eight years until it was—with little warning—incorporated into the government's legislative programme at the end of 2009 and became law in March 2010,[74] in the form proposed by the Law Commission with minor variations only. The Third Parties (Rights against Insurers) Act 2010 was scheduled to become law by March 2011, but a minor defect in its references to insolvency procedures was discovered and, at the time of writing (mid-2013) that defect has yet to be corrected so the Act remains unimplemented, and it may be that changes to the Civil Procedure Rules will also have to be made. It remains unclear exactly when parliamentary time will be found to put these matters right, so for the time being attention must be focused on the 1930 Act, with brief mention of the enacted but unimplemented changes in the 2010 Act. Somewhat ironically, the courts have taken their lead from the Law Commission's 2001 Report and, in a series of important decisions, themselves put right a number of the more glaring defects in the 1930 Act.[75] Most importantly, the courts have ruled that where an assured becomes insolvent, the third party obtains contingent rights against the insurers which crystallize once the assured's liability to the third party has been established and quantified,[76] so that in the period between insolvency and judgment the third party is to some extent protected against loss of rights. However, as we will show below, certain key matters remain unreformed and await the implementation of the 2010 Act.

13.4.2 Obtaining insurance information

The starting point is ascertaining whether the defendant is insured and, if so, whether the policy is enforceable. The draftsman of the 1930 Act recognized that a third party might initiate lengthy and expensive proceedings against a tortfeasor, only to be left with a worthless judgment. For that reason, s 2(1) permits a third party to obtain 'such information as may reasonably be required... for the purpose of enforcing [rights under the 1930 Act]'. The third party may seek from the trustee in bankruptcy or the liquidator of the assured details of insurance contracts, premium receipts, and other relevant documents. Under s 2(2) the third party may then, if having 'reasonable ground for supposing that rights had been transferred to him', seek the same information from the insurers themselves. These provisions were initially construed narrowly as meaning that there was no right to information until rights had been transferred, which occurred only after the assured had become insolvent and the assured's liability had been established and quantified, reasoning which effectively deprives the section of its utility.[77]

[72] *Third Parties (Rights against Insurers) Act 1930*, LC No 152.

[73] *Third Parties (Rights against Insurers) Act 1930* LC Report 272, 2001.

[74] The bill was passed in a few weeks and without amendment, using an expedited and experimental parliamentary procedure for non-contentious Law Commission measures.

[75] The courts' response to the Law Commission's review of illegality arguably follows a similar pattern, though here the Law Commission concluded that legislation was unnecessary: Chapter 11.

[76] *Re OT Computers* [2004] EWCA Civ 653; [2004] 3 WLR 886.

[77] *Nigel Upchurch Associates v Aldridge Estates Investment Co Ltd* [1993] 1 Lloyd's Rep 535; *Woolwich Building Society v Taylor* [1995] 1 BCLC 132.

Matters were put right in *Re OT Computers*,[78] where the Court of Appeal applied the principle that the third party obtained contingent rights on the assured's insolvency, and that s 2 was to be construed as allowing the assured to obtain insurance information relating to those contingent rights.[79] But it will be appreciated that this is a partial answer, because it applies only where the assured has become insolvent before judgment has been obtained. If the tortfeasor is solvent but plainly will be unable to meet any judgment, there is no mechanism for the third party to obtain information about the tortfeasor's insurance position. It is generally in the interest of liability insurers to keep their existence hidden from view in the hope that the third party either will not sue or will agree to a low settlement.

Once the 2010 Act is implemented, the third party's right will be improved to some extent. The legislation has not opted for 'cards on the table', so that it will remain the case that a third party cannot obtain insurance information from a potential defendant who is solvent. However, the 2010 Act, in s 11 and Sch 1, lays down elaborate procedures under which a defendant who is reasonably believed by the claimant both to have incurred liability and to have become insolvent, is required to inform the claimant of the existence of and details about any liability policy which might reasonably be regarded as covering the claim. The claimant can then seek further information from the insurers themselves and from any others who may possess that information, including brokers. The effect of these provisions is to set out a procedure for the application of the principle laid down by the Court of Appeal in *Re OT Computers*.[80]

13.4.3 Transfer of rights

Without the benefit of the 1930 Act, a claimant would be deprived of compensation from the wrongdoer assured if the assured is insolvent at the time of the proceedings so that it is known from the outset that the assured is not good for the damages, or if the assured is solvent up until the time of a judgment and is unable to meet it in full. The 1930 Act provides greater protection than the ordinary law of insolvency in both situations by vesting in the third party the rights of the assured against the insurers.[81]

We may dispose relatively quickly of the second situation, where the assured is solvent up to the time of the judgment. The 1930 Act can be used as a pure judgment enforcement mechanism in respect of an assured who has not become subject to an insolvency procedure during the course of the proceedings, but who has failed to satisfy the judgment in favour of the claimant. Here, the claimant can initiate an insolvency procedure against the assured, by presenting a bankruptcy or winding-up petition, as

[78] [2004] EWCA Civ 653; [2004] 3 WLR 886.

[79] The 2010 Act contains an elaborate procedure for this purpose.

[80] n 78.

[81] It is unresolved whether the 1930 Act is to be construed in the same way as the Workmen's Compensation Act 1906, s 5, as removing from the third party the right to sue the assured unless and until the third party's rights against the insurers have been exhausted: conflicting views are expressed in *Centre Reinsurance International Co v Freakley* [2006] UKHL 45; [2006] 1 WLR 2863.

the case may be, and can then claim the sums due under the policy in priority to other unsecured creditors.[82] That is unaffected by the 2010 Act.

The matter is somewhat more complex in the case of an assured who has become insolvent at an earlier stage. Where an assured protected by a liability policy[83] has become subject to a statutory insolvency procedure[84] prior to any judgment, the assured's right to indemnification from the insurers is transferred to the third party. However, there can be recovery from the insurers only if the liability of the assured has been established and quantified in proceedings against the assured itself. The effect is that if the assured becomes insolvent, the third party must continue the proceedings until judgment, and only then can a claim be made against the insurers for the policy moneys. It is not possible under the 1930 Act for the victim of an insolvent assured to transfer attention to the assured's insurers as soon as the assured has become insolvent: that was established in *Post Office v Norwich Union Fire Insurance Society*,[85] where the Court of Appeal held that an action against insurers before the assured's liability had been established and quantified was premature. In practice of course the actions will rarely be sequential, in that the insurers will be defending the proceedings on behalf of the assured or may be joined by one or other of the parties. That means that if there is a dispute about the liability of the assured, and also a dispute about the liability of the insurers under the policy, those issues can be resolved in a single set of proceedings. Commonly, the policy dispute is one of law which can be disposed of fairly quickly and thus an order may be given that it be tried as a preliminary issue in order to avoid a lengthy hearing on tortious liability if there are no policy moneys forthcoming at the end of it.[86] Even if the insurers are not party to the proceedings, it is open to the third party to seek a declaration about the insurers' liability on the policy in order to avoid embarking on a potentially expensive but inevitably fruitless tort claim.[87]

The need to establish and quantify the assured's liability has proved to be somewhat problematic in the case of a long-tail injury, in particular one resulting after a period of years from exposure to asbestos or some other harmful substance. It remains incumbent on the third party to establish and quantify the assured's liability. One of the many problems faced by the third party in doing so is that the assured may be a company that

[82] The courts have allowed this procedure to be used against foreign companies: *Re Allobrogia Steamship Corporation* [1979] 1 Lloyd's Rep 190; *Irish Shipping Ltd v Commercial Union Assurance Co Plc, the Irish Rowan* [1991] 2 QB 206; [1990] 2 WLR 117. The 2010 Act, s 18, clarifies the territorial scope of the 2010 Act by confining its application to cases where there is an insolvency procedure against the assured in the UK.

[83] Including a legal expenses policy: *Re OT Computers* [2004] EWCA Civ 653; [2004] 3 WLR 886, a decision codified by the 2010 Act, ss 1 and 16. Section 1(5), however, excludes reinsurance, so that the policyholders of an insolvent insurer have no direct claims against reinsurers. That remains the case under the 2010 Act, s 15.

[84] The procedures are listed in s 1(1). The 2010 Act contains an expanded list to reflect changes in insolvency law.

[85] [1967] 2 QB 363; [1967] 2 WLR 709.

[86] It was suggested in *Wood v Perfection Travel Ltd* [1996] LRLR 233, although the point was not resolved, that if insurers defended liability proceedings in the assured's name, and only afterwards sought to rely upon a policy defence, they might be estopped from doing so on the basis that they had allowed the victim to waste time and money in pursuing a tort claim which the insurers had no intention of satisfying if it was established.

[87] This follows from the contingent rights reasoning in *Re OT Computers* [2004] EWCA Civ 653; [2004] 3 WLR 886.

has been dissolved by removal from the register of companies and has thus ceased to exist. That situation arose in *Bradley v Eagle Star Insurance Co*[88] where the House of Lords by a majority ruled that a dissolved company could not be sued following the expiry of a statutory two-year period of grace—then set out in the Companies Act 1984, s 651—running from dissolution, during which time a company may be restored to the register purely for the purpose of being sued. Parliament responded speedily and commendably to remove this technical defence to proceedings, by amending the provision[89] to extend the revival period for dissolved companies indefinitely for personal injury claims and to six years for property damage claims. The relevant provisions are now enshrined in the Companies Act 2006, s 1030.

A more elegant approach will be adopted when the 2010 Act comes into force. The two-step (and in the case of a dissolved company, three-step) process demanded by the 1930 Act will be replaced by a single step. If the assured becomes insolvent in the course of the proceedings, the action may proceed against the insurers although the assured may be joined so that the assured, if able, can make good any shortfall. However, the third party must proceed against the insurers if there are available insurance moneys and the assured's liability is excess only (s 14). The main advantage of a single set of proceedings is that it is possible for the court to order the trial of a preliminary issue for a declaration about coverage (s 2), in order to avoid a pointless liability action where no coverage exists. This makes perfectly plain that recoverability may well be the priority issue.

13.4.4 Effect of transfer on the insurers' defences

The transfer of rights under the 1930 Act is subject to any defences open to the insurers to a claim under the policy. In the memorable words of Harman LJ in *Post Office v Norwich Union Fire Insurance Society*, the third party cannot 'pick out the plums and leave the duff behind'.[90] That means that the third party is in no better position than the assured as regards: coverage, including the sum insured[91] and restrictions on recovery if other insurance is in place;[92] and defences such as non-disclosure, misrepresentation, breach of warranty,[93] breach of a condition relating to the conduct of the assured's operations,[94] late notification of a claim,[95] failure to cooperate with the insurers after a claim has been notified,[96] reaching a settlement without the consent

[88] *Bradley v Eagle Star Insurance Co* [1989] AC 957; [1989] 2 WLR 568.

[89] By the Companies Act 1989, s 141.

[90] [1967] 2 QB 363; [1967] 1 All ER 577 at 581.

[91] *Avandero (UK) Ltd v National Transit Insurance Co Ltd* [1984] 2 Lloyd's Rep 613.

[92] *Phillips v Syndicate 992 Gunner* [2003] EWHC 1706 (Comm); [2004] Lloyd's Rep IR 418.

[93] *McCormick v National Motor & Accident Insurance Union Ltd* (1934) 40 Com Cas 76; *Cleland v London General Insurance Co* (1935) 51 Ll LR 156.

[94] *George Hunt Cranes Ltd v Scottish Boiler and General Insurance Co Ltd* [2001] EWCA Civ 1964; [2002] Lloyd's Rep IR 178.

[95] *Hassett v Legal and General Assurance Society Ltd* (1939) 63 Ll LR 278; *Farrell v Federated Employers Insurance Association Ltd* [1970] 1 WLR 1400; *Monksfield v Vehicle and General Insurance* [1971] 1 Lloyd's Rep 139; *Pioneer Concrete (UK) Ltd v National Employers Mutual General Insurance Association Ltd* [1985] 1 Lloyd's Rep 274; *Cox v Bankside Members Agency Ltd* [1986] QB 211; *Total Graphics Ltd v AGF Insurance Ltd* [1997] 1 Lloyd's Rep 599; *Alfred McAlpine v BAI (Run-off) Ltd* [2000] 1 Lloyd's Rep 437.

[96] *K/S Merc-Skandia v Certain Lloyd's Underwriters* [2001] EWCA Civ 1275, [2001] 2 Lloyd's Rep 563.

of the insurers where such consent is required,[97] admitting liability to the third party,[98] and submitting all disputes to arbitration.[99] The statutory limitation period for the assured's claim against the insurers also applies to any claim by the third party.[100] If the assured has not paid the premium, then the insurers have a right of set-off against any policy moneys.[101]

In the absence of a clear statutory policy of the type to be found in the Road Traffic Act 1988, there can be little justification for requiring the insurers of an insolvent assured to make payment to the assured's victim even though there was no coverage under the policy: that would be to change the nature of liability insurance to some form of guarantee fund. More difficulty is occasioned by breach of policy terms by the assured, particularly where those terms relate to claims. If the assured is facing insolvency and has no reputation to preserve, he may be indifferent as to whether or not to claim against his liability insurers, although if he fails to do so then breach of any claims term expressed to be a condition precedent will defeat the third party's own claim under the 1930 Act. Accordingly, the failure to comply with claims conditions may be a side-effect of the very insolvency whose effects the 1930 Act seeks to overcome. Outside the contexts of motor insurance and employers' liability insurance, where the conduct of the assured after the loss cannot defeat the right to claim, the courts have been confined to their traditional weapons of denying notice provisions the status of conditions precedent, and of narrow construction of the obligations imposed, to protect third-party claimants.[102] Inevitably there are textual limits to what can be done. Even where a clause is found not to be a condition precedent but there is nevertheless breach, the third party may be adversely affected by an award of damages representing loss of opportunity on the part of the insurers to defend the claim.[103]

Partial relief will be conferred on the implementation of the 2010 Act. Section 9 restricts the right of insurers to rely upon breach of claims provisions, bringing the general law into line with motor and employers' liability claims. Any clause which requires the assured to notify personally is treated as satisfied if the third party notifies (s 9(2)). Further, if there is an obligation to provide information to, or to cooperate

[97] *Horwood v Land of Leather Ltd* [2010] EWHC 546 (Comm); [2010] Lloyd's Rep IR 453.

[98] *Post Office v Norwich Union Fire Insurance Society* [1967] 2 QB 363; [1967] 2 WLR 709; *Total Graphics v AGF Insurance* [1997] 1 Lloyd's Rep 599. But note that an employee claiming under the 1930 Act has the benefit of the principle in the Employers' Liability (Compulsory Insurance) Act 1969 which prevents the insurer from pleading post-loss breaches of condition.

[99] *The Jordan Nicolov* [1990] 2 Lloyd's Rep 11. This case, one of assignment rather than statutory transfer, also decides that if the arbitration proceedings are ongoing at the time of the transfer then the assignee simply takes over the proceedings, although the point is not straightforward: contrast *The Felicie* [1987] 2 Lloyd's Rep 299, to the effect that fresh proceedings have to be commenced.

[100] *Lefevre v White* [1990] 1 Lloyd's Rep 569. The limitation period for the assured's claim is six years from which the liability of the assured has been established and quantified. However, if the assured becomes insolvent after it has commenced proceedings and the limitation period has expired at the date of its insolvency, the victim is required to commence fresh proceedings and will be time barred, as shown by *Lefevre* itself. The problem can be overcome by the third party seeking permission to be substituted as a party in place of the assured under CPR Part 19.

[101] *Cox v Bankside Members Agency Ltd* [1995] 2 Lloyd's Rep 437, rejecting the contrary view in *Murray v Legal and General Assurance Society Ltd* [1970] 2 QB 495; [1970] 2 WLR 465.

[102] Chapter 3.

[103] *Milton Keynes BC v Nulty* [2011] EWHC 2847 (TCC) where the court assessed damages as 15 per cent of the claim, a measure which was admittedly unscientific and arbitrary. That issue was not raised on appeal. [2013] EWCA Civ 13.

with, the insurers, it is to be disregarded if the assured is a dissolved company or a deceased individual (s 9(3)) and even if the assured remains in existence (s 9(4)). The section is not a model of clarity, and it would appear not to apply to a failure to notify claims made insurers of circumstances which may give rise to a claim, but it seems to operate perfectly well for policies that respond to exposure or injury. It would seem that conditions precedent are to be disregarded, and breach of other conditions will not lead to a deduction from damages. There is also a minor change in the law as regards sums owing by the assured to the insurers: the 2010 Act, s 10, retains the position under the 1930 Act that the amount of premium due under the policy can be set off against the sums payable, but set-off is not permitted in respect of any sums due by the assured to the insurers from other dealings between them.

13.4.5 Protecting the third party against loss of rights

Two steps are taken by the 1930 Act, replicated in the 2010 Act, to protect the third party against agreements which might undermine the operation of the legislation. The first, s 1(3), negatives any term which 'purports, whether directly or indirectly, to avoid the contract or to alter the rights of the parties... upon the happening to the insured of [any insolvency event]'. The purpose is to prevent a policy from stating that cover is withdrawn in the event of the assured's insolvency, a provision which at one time featured in the rules of P&I Clubs. The second, s 3,[104] prevents any post-insolvency settlement between the assured and the insurers under which the assured settles a pre-existing claim by a third party for a sum which may be insufficient to meet that claim. The section is an illustration of the concept that, once the assured has become insolvent, the third party has a contingent claim against the insurers which crystallizes on the establishment and quantification of the assured's liability to the third party. Section 3 does not deal with the situation in which an assured, facing liability to the assured but at that stage in an insolvency procedure, agrees a settlement with the insurers for a figure significantly less than the ultimate claim:[105] that type of arrangement may well prejudice a third party, and it has been argued—albeit unsuccessfully on the facts—that if the agreement is designed to remove the insurance fund from the third party then the parties to it are guilty of conspiracy.[106] Again, although primarily of significance to the assured rather than to the third party, s 3 has no application to settlements negotiated between the insurers and the third party.[107]

13.4.6 Pay to be paid clauses

One particular problem which has proved to be incapable of satisfactory resolution under the 1930 Act is the operation of the 'pay to be paid' provision commonly found in the rules of P&I Clubs in respect of shipowners' liabilities. Under the clause, a shipowner facing liability must make payment in order to receive indemnification, a

[104] 2010 Act s 17. [105] *Normid Housing Association Ltd v Ralphs* [1989] 1 Lloyd's Rep 265.
[106] *Rowe v Kenway & United Friendly Insurance Co* (1921) 8 Ll LR 225.
[107] *Re T&N Ltd (No 4)* [2006] EWHC 1447 (Ch); [2006] Lloyd's Rep IR 817.

requirement which is impossible for an insolvent shipowner to fulfil. The House of Lords in a joined appeal, *The Fanti and The Padre Island (No 2)*,[108] concluded that the words 'shall become liable to pay and shall in fact have paid' rendered the Club's liability conditional on payment by the shipowner, and if that payment could not be made then the Club could not be required to provide an indemnity. Their Lordships further held that a pay to be paid clause was not nullified by the s 1(3) prohibition on varying the assured's rights on insolvency, because the pay to be paid clause applied whether or not the assured was solvent and simply imposed a pre-payment requirement in all cases. In so deciding, their Lordships drew a distinction between a legal variation of rights after insolvency and a practical variation of rights after insolvency, the former but not the latter falling within s 1(3). It is apparent that a pay to be paid clause does not vary the legal requirement for indemnity, but it plainly varies the latter.

The solution to the problem has been the practice of Clubs not to rely upon pay to be paid clauses in personal injury cases but to confine their operation to cargo and other property damage claims faced by the shipowner from third parties. That practice will be given legal effect on the implementation of the 2010 Act. Pay to be paid clauses are rendered ineffective in personal injury cases although they are otherwise permitted (s 9(5)–9(6)).

13.4.7 Allocation of policy moneys

The policy moneys payable may be insufficient to meet the claims against the assured. Two questions here arise: if there are competing claims to the limited fund, what rules of priority apply; and what is the personal liability of the assured?

The legislation is silent on competing claims. The point can arise where different claims result from entirely distinct acts of negligence against different people, or where the assured has committed a mass tort which affects a large number of people in the same class, for example employees or purchasers of dangerous products. The ordinary rule as regards insurance claims is that they are to be treated in the order in which they occur. Under a property policy the assured's claim accrues as soon as the insured peril occurs, and it would be logical to assume that the policy moneys are to be allocated chronologically. As far as a liability policy is concerned, the trigger for indemnity is the establishment and quantification of the assured's liability by means of a judgment award or settlement, and we have already seen that the policy responds on a chronological basis so that the assured cannot seek to order claims so as to maximize insurance recoveries.[109] But is there any reason to apply the same analysis to third-party claims? One approach might be to ascertain the sum of all claims against the assured and to allocate policy moneys pro rata between them, an approach which has the greatest appeal in a mass tort case, in that each of the third parties is in more or less the same position and their rights should not rest on the delays and other vagaries of litigation and in particular the competence of their lawyers. However, pro rata

[108] [1991] 2 AC 1; [1990] 3 WLR 78.

[109] *Teal Assurance Company Ltd v W R Berkley Insurance (Europe) Ltd* [2011] EWCA Civ 1570; [2012] Lloyd's Rep IR 315, discussed in Chapter 12.

allocation has the distinct disadvantage that it may be impossible to identify all of the potential claimants so that aggregate losses cannot be ascertained. That is particularly true where a policy responds to acts of negligence occurring within its currency: if the negligence consists of exposure to a harmful substance, the effects of that substance may not be known for many years and some individuals will be affected before others. Delaying payment until there is no further possibility of new claims is unfair on those who have established and quantified their injuries, and the best that could be achieved is some form of interim payment procedure. This argument is of more or less equivalent strength where the policy responds to injuries suffered within the policy period, because such injuries may take many years to manifest. The argument against apportionment is perhaps at its weakest where the policy is written on a claims made basis, because it will be obvious in any one policy year what claims there are going to be. But even under that form of recovery there remains uncertainty, because claims made policies also allow for the notification of circumstances which may give rise to a claim and deem any later claim to be made in the year of notification. So once again there are potential delays.

Phillips J discussed the point in *Cox v Bankside Members Agency Ltd*,[110] one of the key decisions in the Lloyd's litigation which produced Reconstruction and Renewal in 1996. A substantial number of individuals who were Names at Lloyd's commenced proceedings for negligence against their Members Agents' advice on the spread of investments in Lloyd's syndicates. The litigation was conducted under a management plan although judgments were obtained by different individuals at different times. Phillips J opted for a 'first-past-the-post' principle for the allocation of the policy moneys, relying upon the general law applicable to liability insurance and the potential for open-ended delay before all claims could be resolved. The 2010 Act leaves the first-past-the-post principle untouched.

13.5 Concluding Thoughts

This chapter has focused on the practicalities of litigation and the role that insurance plays in it. We have not attempted to give a comprehensive picture, but we have drawn attention to the points at which insurance can have a decisive influence on whether a claim is brought, how it is defended, how it is settled, and whether it is actually paid. In our view the neglect by scholars of some aspects of this topic, which is the daily fare of practising lawyers, may give a distorted view of how the law of obligations works. There has of course been much academic study of the operation of the civil justice system, and in particular of the manner in which personal injury claims are settled in the light of the fact that the vast majority are defended by insurers rather than the wrongdoer.[111] Nevertheless, scholarly texts on the law of obligations for the most part fail to

[110] [1995] 2 Lloyd's Rep 437.

[111] Examples include H Genn, *Hard Bargaining: Out of Court Settlement in Personal Injury Actions* (Oxford: Clarendon Press, 1987); D Harris et al., *Compensation and Support for Illness and Injury* (Oxford: Clarendon Press, 1984); T Ison, *The Forensic Lottery* (London: Staples Press, 1967); D Elliott and H Street, *Road Accidents* (Harmondsworth: Penguin, 1968).

emphasize the pervasive nature of insurance at the dispute-resolution stage for all classes of disputes. In particular, while there is some recognition of the fact that most tort judgments are defended by liability insurers, there is less understanding that most tort judgments are in fact paid by liability insurers under legislation which does not necessarily guarantee that the liabilities will be satisfied. It is in our view important for students of the subject to understand why, for example, motor claims are nearly always paid, whereas other negligence claims have to be framed with care to establish a cause of action which is likely to be covered by insurance, and run the risk of not being paid even if liability is established. Further, attention is not always drawn to the fact that insurers will regularly be the real claimants in a dispute where they are exercising subrogation rights, or they will be standing behind the claimant because they are funding the proceedings. That has profound effects on settlements in all classes of case, not just personal injury actions.

Index

The manufacturer's authorised representative in the EU for product safety is Oxford University Press España S.A. of El Parque Empresarial San Fernando de Henares, Avenida de Castilla, 2 - 28830 Madrid (www.oup.es/en or product.safety@oup.com). OUP España S.A. also acts as importer into Spain of products made by the manufacturer.
Printed and bound by CPI Group (UK) Ltd, Croydon, CR0 4YY
14/09/2026
02216306-0019